INTRODUCTION TO QUANTITATIVE EEG AND NEUROFEEDBACK

INTRODUCTION TO

QUANTITATIVE EEG

AND

NEUROFEEDBACK

Edited by

JAMES R. EVANS
Department of Psychology
University of South Carolina
Columbia, South Carolina

ANDREW ABARBANEL
Aptos, California

ACADEMIC PRESS
San Diego   London   Boston   New York   Sydney   Tokyo   Toronto

Front cover images courtesy Dr. James Evans, University of South
Carolina, Columbia, and Dr. Paul Burke, Brain Dynamics Research
Laboratory, Melbourne, Australia.

This book is printed on acid-free paper. ∞

Academic Press
A Harcourt Science and Technology Company
525 B Street, Suite 1900, San Diego, California 92101-4495, USA
http://www.apnet.com

Academic Press
Harcourt Place, 32 Jamestown Road, London NW1 7BY, UK
http://www.hbuk.co.uk/ap/

Library of Congress Catalog Card Number: 98-89312

International Standard Book Number: 0-12-243790-X

PRINTED IN THE UNITED STATES OF AMERICA
00   01   02   03   04   EB   9   8   7   6   5   4   3   2

*To Barbara B. Brown, Ph.D., and Joe Kamiya, Ph.D.—
pioneers from a generation where creative genius laid the
foundation of neurofeedback.* J. R. E.

and

*To David Abarbanel, my son, whose generation may be the first
to reap fully the many benefits neurofeedback has to offer.* A. A.

CONTENTS

PART I

GENERAL PRINCIPLES AND HISTORY

1

AN OVERVIEW OF QUANTITATIVE EEG AND ITS APPLICATIONS TO NEUROFEEDBACK

DAVID S. CANTOR

2

EEG DATABASE-GUIDED NEUROTHERAPY

ROBERT W. THATCHER

3

FROM EEG TO NEUROFEEDBACK

THOMAS H. BUDZYNSKI

PART II

CLINICAL APPLICATIONS

4

MEDICAL APPLICATIONS OF NEUROBIOFEEDBACK

RIMA LAIBOW

5

NEUROFEEDBACK ASSESSMENT AND TREATMENT FOR ATTENTION DEFICIT/HYPERACTIVITY DISORDERS

JOEL F. LUBAR AND JUDITH O. LUBAR

6

NEUROTHERAPY IN THE TREATMENT OF DISSOCIATION

THOMAS BROWNBACK AND LINDA MASON

7

NEUROFEEDBACK IN THE TREATMENT OF ADDICTIVE DISORDERS

EUGENE G. PENISTON AND PAUL J. KULKOSKY

8

CLINICAL USE OF AN ALPHA ASYMMETRY NEUROFEEDBACK PROTOCOL IN THE TREATMENT OF MOOD DISORDERS

ELSA BAEHR, J. PETER ROSENFELD, RUFUS BAEHR, AND CAROLYN EARNEST

9

ASSESSING AND TREATING OPEN HEAD TRAUMA, COMA, AND STROKE USING REAL-TIME DIGITAL EEG NEUROFEEDBACK

MARGARET E. AYERS

10

PERFORMANCE ENHANCEMENT TRAINING THROUGH NEUROFEEDBACK

S. LOUISE NORRIS AND MICHAEL CURRIERI

PART III

MODELS FOR NEUROFEEDBACK EFFICACY

11

EEG BIOFEEDBACK: AN EMERGING MODEL FOR ITS GLOBAL EFFICACY

SIEGFRIED OTHMER, SUSAN F. OTHMER, AND DAVID A. KAISER

12

THE NEURAL UNDERPINNINGS OF NEUROFEEDBACK TRAINING

ANDREW ABARBANEL

13

THEORIES OF THE EFFECTIVENESS OF ALPHA–THETA TRAINING FOR MULTIPLE DISORDERS

NANCY E. WHITE

PART IV

LEGAL AND ETHICAL ISSUES

14

ETHICAL, LEGAL, AND PROFESSIONAL PITFALLS ASSOCIATED WITH NEUROFEEDBACK SERVICES

SEBASTIAN STRIEFEL

CONTRIBUTORS

*Numbers in parentheses indicate the pages on which the authors'
contributions begin.*

Andrew Abarbanel (311) Aptos, California 95003

Margaret E. Ayers (203) Neuropathways EEG Imaging, Beverly Hills, California 90210

Elsa Baehr (181) Department of Psychiatry and Behavioral Sciences, Northwestern University, and Private Practice, Evanston, Illinois 60201

Rufus Baehr (181) Department of Psychiatry and Behavioral Sciences, Northwestern University, and Private Practice, Evanston, Illinois 60201

Thomas Brownback (145) Brownback, Mason and Associates, Allentown, Pennsylvania 18104

Thomas H. Budzynski (65) Department of Psychosocial and Community Health, University of Washington, Seattle, Washington 98105

David S. Cantor (3) Psychological Sciences Institute, Alpharetta, Georgia 30022

Michael Currieri (223) Mid-Hudson Medical Psychotherapy Center, Warwick, New York 10990

Carolyn Earnest (181) University of New Mexico, Albuquerque, New Mexico 87131

David A. Kaiser (243) EEG Spectrum, Encino, California 91436

Paul J. Kulkosky (157) Department of Psychology, University of Southern Colorado, Pueblo, Colorado 81001

Rima Laibow (83) Alexandria Institute, Croton on Hudson, New York 10520

Joel F. Lubar (103) University of Tennessee, Knoxville, Tennessee 37996

Judith O. Lubar (103) Southeastern Biofeedback and Neurobehavioral Institute, Knoxville, Tennessee 37996

Linda Mason (145) Brownback, Mason and Associates, Allentown, Pennsylvania 18104

S. Louise Norris (223) Mid-Hudson Medical Psychotherapy Center, Warwick, New York 10990

Siegfried Othmer (243) EEG Spectrum, Encino, California 91436

Susan F. Othmer (243) EEG Spectrum, Encino, California 91463

Eugene G. Peniston (157) Mental Health Service, North Texas Health Care System, Memorial Veterans Center, Bonham, Texas 75418

J. Peter Rosenfeld (181) Department of Psychology, Northwestern University, Evanston, Illinois 60201

Sebastian Striefel (371) Psychology Department, Utah State University, Logan, Utah 84341

Robert W. Thatcher (29) Medical Research Service, Bay Pines Veterans Administration Medical Center, Bay Pines, Florida, and Departments of Neurology and Radiology, University of South Florida College of Medicine, Tampa, Florida 33708

Nance E. White (341) The Neurotherapy Center, Houston, Texas 77027

PREFACE

Before managed care, political correctness, large federal research grants, and the demand for theory-driven research, a creative psychologist at the University of Chicago made a very important discovery. It was the early 1960s, and Dr. Joe Kamiya discovered that some of his research subjects could learn to control the amplitude and frequency characteristics of their own electroencephalogram (EEG) if provided feedback about those characteristics. Many psychologists and medical practitioners soon sensed the possibilities such operant control of central nervous system electrical activity might have for clinical treatment. Within a few years, the term *biofeedback* was applied to these methods (and to similar procedures involving other physiological processes), a biofeedback society was formed, related research was completed at several laboratories, and increasing numbers of clinicians began applying EEG biofeedback in the treatment of anxiety and other psychiatric disorders. Also within a few years, however, what appeared to be an extremely promising treatment modality quite suddenly fell into disrepute. Some say this was because EEG biofeedback became associated with ideas regarding expansion of consciousness, instant Zen, and the like. Others believe it was due to the publication in prestigious journals of two or three articles reporting research results that did not support the efficacy of this type of biofeedback. Still others feel it was because EEG biofeedback was perceived by many as being too closely akin to mind control.

Whatever the reasons, the field of EEG biofeedback was kept barely alive by a few of the original pioneers until its quite dramatic revival in the 1980s. Undoubtedly, the availability of reasonably priced and highly efficient computerized EEG diagnostic and feedback instruments contributed greatly to this revival, as did the publication of controlled research demonstrating remarkably positive effects with alcoholism and attention deficit/hyperactivity disorder in children. The designation by former President Bush of the 1990s as "the decade of the brain" and the scientific respectability gained by the field of behavioral medicine also may be important factors in renewed interest in this field. In any event, EEG biofeedback (now commonly referred to as neurofeedback or neurotherapy) is used as a treatment modality in more than 700 clinical settings in the United States. A journal devoted to research and opinion on this type of biofeedback and closely related topics (*Journal of Neurotherapy*), a special EEG section of the Association for Applied Psychophysiology and Biofeedback, and a professional association (Society for the Study of Neuronal Regulation or SSNR) have all been established for the dissemination of research and clinical findings concerning neurofeedback-related topics. Neurofeedback certification is provided to properly trained applicants through the Biofeedback Certification Institute of America.

A great many, if not most, neurotherapists consider it necessary to have objective data regarding a client's EEG characteristics prior to attempting to modify them through feedback. To accomplish this, computerized EEG analysis techniques that provide measures of a large number of EEG characteristics are used. These techniques are referred to as quantified EEG or quantitative EEG (QEEG). When used in conjunction with a normative database, they are capable of providing useful information for deciding what EEG parameters to modify and for determining the degree to which such parameters have been modified successfully. As with the field of EEG biofeedback, the development of QEEG techniques has been rather recent. Consequently, there is considerable controversy about specific procedures to be used, the range of disorders to which they are applicable, dangers inherent in their use, and qualifications for using QEEG and neurofeedback technology. There is a strong need for research addressing these issues.

To date, no comprehensive source of information has been available to anyone wishing to explore the nature of neurofeedback (and its association with QEEG). Relevant information had to be gathered piecemeal from scattered journal articles, book chapters, proceedings of professional conferences, or the Internet. This book was conceived as a means of remedying this situation by providing an overview of the basics of QEEG and neurofeedback in one source. Embedded in the chapters are descriptions of the nature of QEEG and neurofeedback, brief histories of the development of each, reports of successful applications of neurofeedback to several different clinical conditions (as well as to improving normal performance), speculation on the dynamics of neurofeedback, and discussion of ethical issues in the use of QEEG and neurofeedback. The majority of the chapters are written by "pioneers" in the field (i.e., persons who were active in

QEEG and/or neurotherapy prior to 1980). Some are relative newcomers, especially those who write on the newer applications of neurofeedback.

We hope this text will fill an empty niche in the foundation of this exciting and rapidly developing field. With a proper foundation for this field, there can be high expectations that neurofeedback will remain alive and well and grow into its original promise of becoming one of the major treatment modalities for a wide range of disorders.

ACKNOWLEDGMENTS

As the senior editor, I acknowledge persons who contributed significantly to the development and publication of this book. I am indebted to Dr. John Gilbert of Merino, Colorado, for his encouragement to explore publication of a book on these topics and his suggestions for potential contributors, and to Dr. Fred Medway, former director of the School Psychology Training Program at the University of South Carolina, for his support of my pursuit of the topic of neurofeedback. I also thank Ms. Peggy Tindal and Ms. Suzanne Claycomb, graduate students at the University of South Carolina, for inspiration and for editing of details. The efforts and patience of Ms. Nikki Levy, Executive Editor, and Ms. Barbara Makinster, Editorial Coordinator, at Academic Press are very much appreciated. I am grateful for the creative talent of Ms. Chris Owens of Academic Press, who designed the cover. And, I thank my wife, Martha Young-Evans, for her encouragement and patience during the several months when work on the book detracted from our time together.

As co-editor, I acknowledge the people who introduced me to the field of neurotherapy and those who sustained (and tolerated) my interest in it. Colin Wright, Ph.D., of San Jose, California, introduced me to the field and demonstrated its efficacy, especially for the patients for whom other treatment modalities had failed. It was Colin who first urged me to investigate the neurophysiology underlying neurofeedback. Colin's wife Betty's clinical expertise and empathic approach to treatment did much to increase my early interest. Likewise, Mark Steinberg, Ph.D., of San Jose, helped teach me a good deal about the field and how effective it can be for a range of disorders. Joel Lubar, Ph.D., Seigfried Othmer, Ph.D., and Margaret Ayers, M.A., have been exceedingly gracious in welcoming me into the field. Barry Sterman, Ph.D., was especially generous, overlooking a four-decade difference in our neurophysiological experiences to accept me as something of a colleague. Most important, I thank my children, Katie, David, Daniel, and Rachel, who had to trade too much real time with their father for the too-intangible assertion that my work will someday make their world a better place. I also thank Patricia Smith for enduring the same over-modest proposition, and much else.

James R. Evans
Andrew Abarbanel

GENERAL PRINCIPLES AND HISTORY

1

AN OVERVIEW OF QUANTITATIVE EEG AND ITS APPLICATIONS TO NEUROFEEDBACK

DAVID S. CANTOR

Psychological Sciences Institute, Alpharetta, Georgia

I. HISTORICAL OVERVIEW

... it seems surprising that I was so slow to realize that these electrophysiological phenomena were potentially of great practical clinical utility for the evaluation of people with cognitive disorders. They could be used as tools to probe such brain mechanisms as those concerned with focus and maintenance of attention, the memory of recent events and their use to generate expectations about the future, and the identification of meaningful information within the sensory barrage from the environment.

(John, 1977a)

The field of computerized neurophysiology (now commonly known as quantified or quantitative EEG [QEEG]), like other fields intertwined with the emergence of computer science in the middle of the century, has grown exponentially in recent years. Observation of electrical signals from the nervous system goes back as early as 1848 when researchers such as Duboi-Reymond reported the presence of electrical signals as a marker of a peripheral nerve impulse. These early studies revealed that peripheral nerve conduction involved electricity and led Caton in 1875 to propose a similar finding for brain wave activity as noted in animal studies on monkeys and rabbits.

The notion that features of measurable electrical activity can describe brain functions remained relatively obscure for nearly 50 years until Hans Berger published an article in 1929 describing a pattern of oscillating electrical activity recorded from the human scalp. Adrian Matthews replicated Berger's work in 1934 and Berger continued to publish numerous other articles chronicling this work in both pathological and normal cases. Berger's notion was that if the electroencephalogram (EEG), as his technique came to be called, could be used to measure and define biological markers corresponding to human behaviors more precisely, such a technique could prove to be useful diagnostically and therapeutically by measuring the impact of interventions.

In the 1930s and 1940s the EEG became the object of much interest in the realm of psychiatric and neurological sciences by researchers such as Gibbs, Holwell, Davis, Donald Linsey, Grey Walters, and Herver Jasper. These studies suggested a relatively greater preponderance of certain EEG features in clinical populations compared to normal individuals. However, it became increasingly apparent that the EEG was, at best, a tool that could be used for confirmation of clinical disorders such as epilepsy and brain trauma. The EEG, without a more precise way in which to study its complex and idiopathic nature, revealed little about the neuro-anatomic-neurophysiologic continuum and even less about the subtleties in human behavior and function.

As digital computer technology developed in the 1960s and 1970s, it became feasible to assess and quantify precisely many more EEG parameters than is possible through human visual inspection of raw EEG waveforms. With these developments the field of QEEG came into existence.

II. BASIC CONCEPTS OF EEG

A. GENESIS

There are two prominent classes of cells in the central nervous system, *neurons* and their support cells, called *glia*. The neuron's basic parts are the cell body (soma), axon, and dendrites (Fig. 1.1). The cell body contains the organelles of the cell including the nucleus, Golgi apparatus (metabolic center), and the endoplasmic reticulum. A neuronal membrane covers the cell body protecting it from extracellular fluid. The dendrites are finger-like projections that extend out from the cell body. The dendrites serve as receptor sites and receive signals from other cells. The axon typically has a long trunk, which can extend as far as 1 m into the peripheral system. The end of the axon divides into many branches to form synaptic terminals. Most neurons are multipolar; that is, there is one axon with many dendrites. Multiple dendrites enable the cell to make contact with many other cells and thereby receive multiple input. Neurons communicate with each other

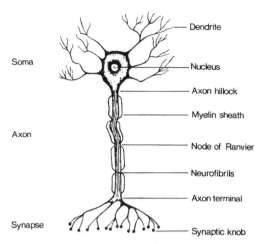

FIGURE 1.1   Diagram of a neuron showing the major structural features. [From Duffy, F., Iver, V., & Surwillo, W. (1983). "Clinical Electroencephalography and Topographic Brain Mapping." p. 69. Springer-Verlag, New York, with permission.]

by sending electrochemical signals from the synaptic terminal of one cell to the dendritic process of other cells (Fig. 1.2).

The chemicals emitted from the synaptic junctions can either excite (depolarize) or inhibit (hyperpolarize) the neural membrane. Excitation of the neural membrane changes its permeability to ions in the extracellular fluid. Typically, a cell at rest is highly permeable to potassium ions and relatively impermeable to sodium ions. The concentration of potassium ions inside the cell is 35 times greater than the concentration of potassium ions outside the cell. This concentration gradient tends to drive the potassium ions out of the cell. The resulting outward diffusion of potassium ions, which are positively charged, leads to an excess of negatively charged ions inside the cell. The resulting imbalance of charge across the cell membrane prevents further escape of more potassium ions. Sodium ions line up on the outside of the cell membrane, but the membrane is not sufficiently permeable to neutralize the negative internal charge resulting from the potassium flux.

As the membrane continues to separate charges on each of its sides, it becomes polarized. Excitatory neurotransmitters, such as acetylcholine, bind to a dendritic receptor site in the postsynaptic membrane, resulting in an increase in the cell membrane's permeability to sodium ions. The resulting influx of positive charge establishes an excitatory postsynaptic potential (EPSP). EPSPs are small, usually 5 mV, and are not sufficient to trigger an action potential, that is, the change in membrane potential needed to send a signal along an axon to the synaptic terminal causing the release of neurotransmitters into the postsynaptic gap. As mentioned earlier, however, most neurons are multipolar, and thus have many dendrites whose

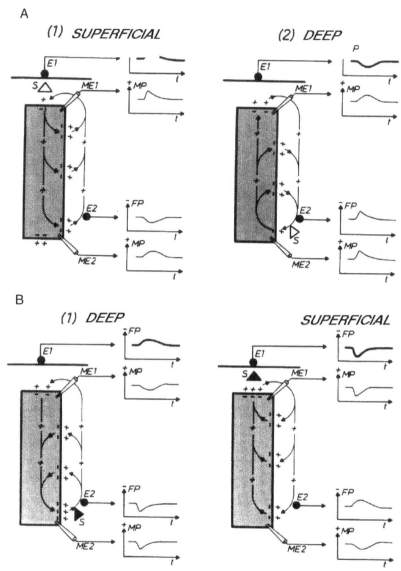

FIGURE 1.2 Membrane potential (MP) changes and field potentials (FP) elicited by the activation of excitatory and inhibitory synapses in the central nervous system. The elementary processes are explained by means of a neuronal element (*hatched area*), the one end of which contacts the surface of the structure in the central nervous system. The MP of the neuronal element is recorded at both ends by the microelectrodes ME_1 and ME_2. The extracellular field is picked up at the surface of the neuronal structure by the electrode E_1, as well as in the vicinity of ME_2 by the electrode E_2. Active excitatory and inhibitory synapses are marked by open and black triangles (S), respectively, *A1*, the inward current at S generates an EPSP that appears in the region of ME_1, as well as in that of ME_2. Because S is located superficially, the FP generated is, due to the direction of the extracellular current flow (*arrows*), of negative

inputs create a summation of EPSPs sufficient to trigger an action potential (about 20–30 mV). Summations can occur be either spatial or temporal. Spatial summation is the summation of several EPSPs that are produced simultaneously at different sites. Temporal summation is the summation that occurs as a result of successive potential changes at a single site such that several EPSPs are superimposed on each other.

Inhibitory neurotransmitters such as gamma amino butyric acid (GABA), work by increasing membrane permeability to negatively charged chloride ions, leading to intracellular negativity. In this way the cell becomes inhibited from firing; that is, an inhibitory postsynaptic potential (IPSP) is created. IPSPs, like EPSPs, utilize spatial and temporal summation processes.

Action potentials are very rapid (about 1 ms); the EEG recorded at the scalp is made up of summations of billions of individual action potentials (from the summation of IPSP and EPSP field potentials from large groups of cortical neurons; see Fig. 1.3). The rhythmic cycles observed in scalp-recorded EEGs are generally agreed to be the result of neural activity between the thalamus and the cortex. The thalamus is a central subcortical structure, which relays signals to the cortical level and relays signals between ascending and descending pathways into multiple other brain areas. Rhythmicity is produced by action of complex feedback in the thalamus. It is generally believed that cortical rhythmicity results from a complex interplay between thalamo-cortical circuitry and both local and global cortico-cortical circuitry (Thatcher, Krause, & Hrybyk, 1986).

B. RECORDING

Thus far we have discussed how a scalp-recorded EEG is generated by the pooled activity of billions of cortical neurons influenced by shared activity between cortical and subcortical regions. It is important to note that the brain is a gelatinous mass suspended in cerebrospinal fluid. This fluid, along with brain tissue, serves as a volume conductor and therefore renders the signals recorded at the scalp very complex. Furthermore, each

polarity at the surface (E_1) and of positive polarity in the deeper recording (E_2). *A2,* the activation of a deep excitatory synapse elicits a current flow with inverse direction as compared with A1. Therefore, the extracellular FP consists in a positive deflection at the surface and in a negative one at the depth. *B1,* the outward current at S generates an IPSP in the region of ME_2, as well as in that of ME_1. Due to the direction of the extracellular current flow, the FP generated consists in a positive fluctuation in the depth (E2) and in a negative one in the surface recording (E1). *B2,* the current flow during the activation of a superficial inhibitory synapse is inverse as compared with B1. Therefore, the FP recorded from the surface consists in a positive fluctuation. Differences in the time course of the various potentials are caused by the electrical properties of the tissue. [From Niedermyer (1987). "Electroencephalography," 4th ed. pp. 4–5. Lippincott, Williams & Wilkins, Baltimore, with permission.]

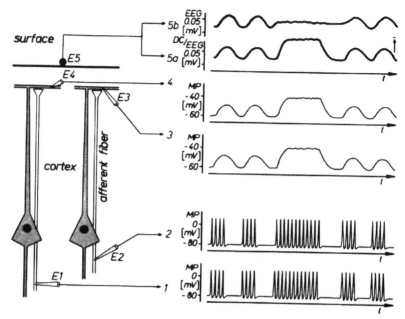

FIGURE 1.3 Principles of wave generation. The excitatory synapses of two afferent fibers contact the superficial dendritic arborization of two longitudinal neuronal elements. The afferent fiber activity is recorded by means of the intracellular electrodes E_1 and E_2 and the electrodes E_3 and E_4 record the membrane potentials (MP) of the dendritic elements. The electrode E_5 leads the field potential at the surface of the neuronal structure (cortex). Synchronized groups of action potentials in the afferent fibers (E_1, E_2) generate wave-like EPSPs in the dendritic areas (E_3, E_4) and corresponding field potentials in the EEG and DC/EEG recording (E_5). Tonic activity in the afferent fibers results in long lasting EPSP with small fluctuations. During this period, the EEG (5b) shows only a reduction in amplitude, whereas the DC/EEG recording (5a) reflects the depolarization of the neuronal elements as well. [From Niedermyer (1987). "Electroencephalography," 4th ed. pp. 4–5. Lippincott, Williams & Wilkins, Baltimore, with permission.]

EEG electrode site records rhythmic activity from multiple generators of EEG activity. To understand this complex system more fully, a standard for the placement of electrodes was established. Jasper (1958) suggested a placement of electrodes that is known as the 10-20 International System of Electrode Placement. An illustration of this system is shown in Fig. 1.4. The letters F, C, T, P, and O refer to the frontal, central, temporal, parietal, and occipital cortical regions, respectively. Odd numbers refer to left hemisphere sites and even numbers refer to right hemisphere sites. Thus, "T3" refers to the left temporal region. The term "10-20" refers to the placement of electrodes placed 10% or 20% of the total distance between specified skull locations. Use of a percentage-based system allows for differences in skull size. Studies have shown that these placements correlate with the corresponding cerebral cortical regions. Of the 21 electrodes used, 19 are

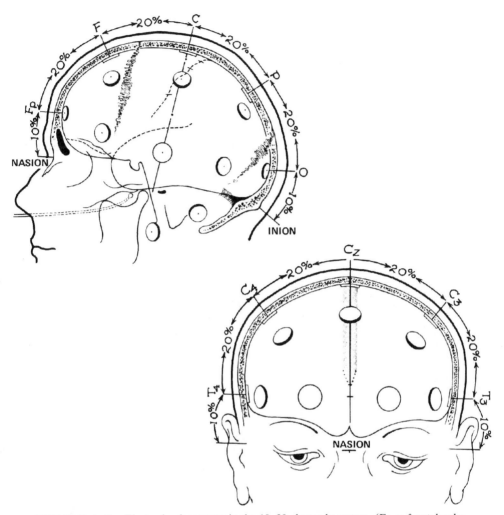

FIGURE 1.4   Electrode placements in the 10–20 electrode system. (Fp = frontal pole; C = central; P = parietal; O = occipital). *Top:* lateral view showing measurements in the midsagittal plane. C is placed at 50% of the nasion-inion distance; F, P, Fp, and O are placed at 20% intervals. *Bottom:* frontal view showing measurements in the central coronal plane, with electrodes at 20% intervals of distance between the left and right preauricular points. (Reproduced from EEG Clin Neurophysiol 10:372, 1958, with permission of Elsevier Science.)

used for scalp sites recording cortical areas, and 2 electrodes are typically placed on the earlobes as reference electrodes.

Two basic types of EEG montages are used, referential (or monopolar) and bipolar (Fig. 1.5). The referential montages involve collecting information at the active site and comparing this activity with a common reference

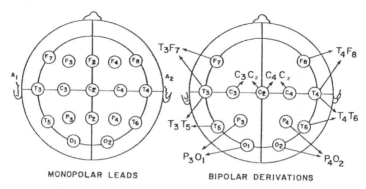

MONOPOLAR LEADS   BIPOLAR DERIVATIONS

FIGURE 1.5   Electrode sites and derivations. The left head diagram shows the monopolar electrode sites used for the monopolar derivations. The right head diagram shows the monopolar pairs used for the bipolar derivations.

electrode. The common reference electrodes, such as earlobes, should be unaffected by cerebral activity. The main advantage of referential montages is that the common reference allows valid comparisons of activity in many different derivations (electrode pairings). A major disadvantage of the monopolar or referential montage is that no reference site is ideal. For example, the earlobe sites may pick up some EEG activity from the temporal lobes. Another disadvantage is that electromyographic (EMG) or heartbeat (EKG) artifacts may occur. The specific sources of various artifacts in relation to the montages and references used are discussed in more detail in Table 1.1. Analysis and interpretation of EEGs must be adjusted depending on artifacts. Other reference sites that have been used include the angle

TABLE 1.1   Sources of Artifact That May Be Found in the EEG Record Which Contaminate Information in the QEEG Analysis

Frequency band most affected	Source of artifact
Delta	Drowsiness
	Drugs/medications
	Electrode popping/poor connection
	Body/facial/eye movement
	Sharp waves
Theta	Drowsiness
	Drugs/medications
	Normal variant in younger patients
	Heartbeat artifact (EKG)
Beta	Drugs/medications
	Electrical noise (e.g., 60 cycle)
	Muscle tension (EMG)

of the jaw, the tip of the nose, and the neck. However, these noncephalic reference points are subject to EMG artifact from muscle activity.

Bipolar montages compare activity between two active scalp sites. Any activity in common with these sites is subtracted such that only the difference in activity is shown. Information, therefore, is lost with this technique. A major advantage of bipolar montages, however, is that localization of electrophysiological events is easier. By examining a sequence of bipolar derivations, the occurrence of a specific spike of the EEG (or other notable event) can be found when searching for a phase reversal of the electrical signal as one moves spatially from anterior to posterior or from left to right across bipolar derivations.

C. REVIEWING AND INTERPRETING QEEGS

Computerized analyses of EEG signals involve a number of factors: (1) frequency distribution, (2) voltage (as amplitude of the electrical signals), (3) locus of the phenomena, (4) waveform or wave shape morphology, (5) interhemispheric symmetries (symmetry of voltage, frequency, wave shapes for homologous sites), (6) character of waveform occurrence (random, serial, continuous), (7) regulation of voltage and frequency, and (8) reactivity (changes in an EEG parameter with changes in state). These factors are described briefly as follows. The procedure for selecting segments for EEG analysis is discussed elsewhere (Möcks & Gasser, 1984).

1. Frequency

Frequency refers to the rate at which a waveform repeats its cycle within 1 sec (also referred to as hertz or Hz). Frequency analysis, that is, analyzing the EEG signal in terms of the range of its frequencies, has been traditionally of two basic types: spectral analysis by narrowband filters (often dividing the signal into 1-Hz segments or bins) or by wideband electronic filters (Kaiser, Petersen, Sellden, & Kagawa, 1964; Kozhevnikov, 1958). Spectral analysis is concerned with the exploration of cyclical patterns of data. The purpose of the analysis is to decompose a complex time series with cyclical components into a few underlying sinusoidal (sine and cosine) functions of particular wavelengths. Probably the most common method of analyzing the frequency of the spectrum of EEG is to use the fast Fourier transform (FFT) for spectral analysis (see, for example, Walter, 1963). Other methods include recursive filtering techniques, which are described elsewhere (for a review, see Cantor, 1983). The results of spectral analysis of a complex waveform such as EEG are measures of the amount of energy distributed in frequency bands of the waveform. In most EEG work, the range of frequencies is divided into four bands: delta (less than 4 Hz), theta (4–7.5 Hz), alpha (7.5–12.5 Hz), and beta (greater than 12 Hz). Activity that falls into the delta or theta bands is referred to as *slow-wave activity* and activity falling into the alpha or beta bands is referred to as *fast-wave activity.* The term *monorhythmic* is used when a particular portion of activity shows a rhythmic component in a singular frequency. The term *polyrythmic* activity refers to portions of the EEG in which multiple frequencies all demonstrate very rhythmic activity.

2. Amplitude

The amplitude of the EEG is defined as the voltage in microvolts (1/1,000,000 volt), measured from the peak of a wave to the trough of a wave. This is illustrated in Fig. 1.3. The amplitude of the EEG generally falls into the range of 20–50 mV. However, there is a great deal of variability, with amplitudes varying from less than 10 mV to more than 100 mV. The amplitude of the EEG tends to be attenuated in response to stimulation. For example, fast activity is attenuated in an eyes-open situation compared to an eyes-closed recording condition. The term *suppression* is used when little or no rhythmic activity within a frequency band is discernible. Paroxysmal activity is a term referring to high amplitude activity (compared to background) if of sudden onset and offset.

3. Morphology

A combination of frequency and amplitude of the EEG signal affect the "shape" or "morphology" of the EEG, and certain features may be filtered by the recording apparatus, thus permitting their detection. Waveforms continuously fluctuate in response to stimuli and depend on the state of the patient (alert, drowsy, etc.). A *transient* is an isolated form or feature that stands out from the background EEG activity. If it has a peak duration of less than 70 msec it is called a *spike,* but if the duration is between 70 and 200 msec, it is known as a *sharp wave.* The term *complex* is used when two or more waves occur together and repeat at consistent intervals. A *monomorphic complex* is one in which the subsequent waveforms are similar, whereas a *polymorphic complex* is one in which they are dissimilar. A waveform also may include a number of positive or negative swings in voltage. Thus, a wave may be *nonphasic* (positive or negative), *diphasic* (positive and negative), *triphasic,* or *polyphasic.*

4. Symmetry

Most electroencephalographers consider the degree of bilateral symmetry of the waveform amplitude between homologous electrode sites to be an important factor of the EEG and one that is sensitive to neuropathology. The amplitude of the waveforms within a specific time period to be compared are measured as discussed in the previous section on amplitude. Matousek and Petersen (1973) computerized measures of bilateral symmetry between different frequency bands of the EEG from various homologous derivations (electrode pairings). This work revealed that the symmetry values of amplitude for different frequency bands were usually comparable and corresponded well to the symmetry of the overall EEG activity. John's (1977a) neurometric analytic approach to QEEGs typically defined amplitude asymmetry of transformed measures at specific electrode sites by the ratio:

$$(left - right)/(left + right)$$

or

$$(anterior - posterior)/(anterior + posterior).$$

EEG symmetry also includes the extent to which corresponding peaks and troughs of two waveforms within frequency bands are in phase with one another. One of the early methods for measuring phase symmetry in the complex EEG signal used the polarity coincidence correlation (PCC) (John, 1977a). The correlation is calculated from a large number of comparisons of the polarity (positivity or negativity) of two simultaneous electrical signals (e.g., from two homologous interhemispheric sites in a monopolar montage). The PCC is calculated as

$$PCC = A - B$$

$$\frac{A - B}{M}.$$

Here, A is the number of instances in which the two signals were of the same sign, B is the number of instances in which they were of the opposite sign, and M is the total number of measurements.

When every pair of signals is in phase (i.e., both positive or both negative), $A = M$, and $B = 0$, and PCC $= (M-0)/M = 1$. When every pair of signals is identical but 180 degrees out phase, then $A = 0$, $B = M$, and PCC $= -1$. If the relation between the signals is random, then the average is

$$A = B = \frac{M}{2}$$

or

$$PCC = 0.$$

John (1977a) has argued that this method of quantifying symmetry is superior to other methods because of the physiological significance of the polarity of the EEG signal. When EEG signals are sampled at a high rate (e.g., 10 kHz), the frequency response (or resolution) of the correlation exceeds the bandwidth of the EEG signals. However, a digital delay circuit permits one signal to be delayed with respect to the other by a specified quantity. Measures of phase provide estimates of lead or lag times between spatially separate but connected systems of generators. Quantification of phase shifts or *lags* using pairings from within lateralized hemispheres as well as between hemispheres can provide information regarding neural pathway propagation (Thatcher *et al.*, 1986).

Previously, we defined spectral analysis as the exploration of cyclical patterns of data. When we are comparing these patterns across two inputs we are discussing the cross spectra, that is, cross-spectral analysis delineates the correlation between two series at different frequencies. The symmetry of frequency patterns between two time series is also described as *coherence*. Coherence is analogous to a cross correlation in the frequency domain and reflects the number and strengths of connections of spatially distant generators. Mathematically, the theory of coherence[1] expresses the relationships of two time series in the following way: Let $x(t), y(t)$ be two EEG time series—t(time). Then let $X(w)Y(w)$ be the Fourier transforms of the EEGs with complex values and w = frequency. Then we define the filters that are wideband filters as follows: Let the transfer function for the filter of the band, say, S, be the $Hg(w)$. Then the following definitions hold:

$$Eg(x) = \mid Hg(w) \mid^2 \mid X(w)^2 dw,$$

$$Eg(y) = \mid Hg(w) \mid^2 \mid Y(w)^2 dw.$$

where the real coherence is defined as

$$X(w)Y(w)\sqrt{|X(w)|^2 \, |Y(w)|^2} \, .$$

Thus, the general coherence for any frequency (w) is

$$Rgxy = \frac{\int H(w)X(w)H(w)Y(w)dw}{\sqrt{(EgzEgy)}},$$

where $E(w)Y(w)$ is a complex conjugate and $Rgxy$ is a complex number.

A more detailed discussion regarding coherence is given elsewhere (e.g., Glaser & Ruchkin, 1976). Thus, symmetry can be broken into amplitude symmetry within a frequency band as well as phase and coherence functions within respective frequency bands.

D. DISPLAYS OF QUANTITATIVE EEG FINDINGS AND CLINICAL UTILIZATION

In an effort to visualize better the distribution of specified frequency band powers and amplitudes and symmetries of these measures, computerized display programs have been developed. These methods used techniques called *compressed spectral arrays* (CSAs) or, later, density spectral arrays (DSAs) to examine visually frequency-analyzed EEGs over time. Bickford and his colleagues were among the earliest to introduce the compressed spectral array (Bickford, Fleming, & Billinger, 1971; Bickford, Brimm,

---

[1] Taken from Dan Brown in a laboratory communication. See Cantor, 1983.

Berger, & Aung, 1973). The compressed spectral array divides the EEG record into successive time segments and subjects each segment (epoch) to a power spectral analysis using an FFT. Then successive spectra are displayed one above the other using the technique of *hidden line suppression,* which ensures that no subsequent line spectrum crosses a previous plotted spectrum, thereby providing a three-dimensional display. The final step in the CSA is to arrange the CSA from single EEG channels into an array corresponding to the position from which they were sampled on the scalp. An example is shown in Fig. 1.6.

The dynamic display is useful to illustrate noteworthy disproportionate frequency distributions that might be caused by a structural anomaly. Although the CSAs increased visualization of spectral analysis, they did little to provide a quantified evaluation regarding deviation from normal. To minimize this drawback, Gotman, Skuce, Thompson, Gloor, Ives, and Ray (1973) used a ratio method for each channel of the EEG that applied a weighting coefficient for each frequency band for all but the frontal electrodes (different values were used for the frontal leads because these were more susceptible to artifact). Once this channel feature was calcu-

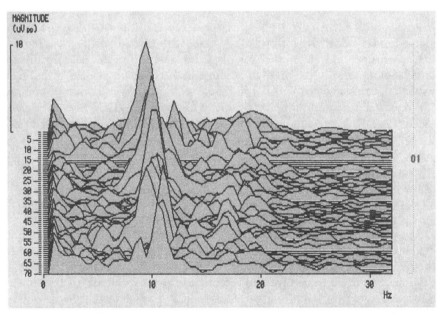

FIGURE 1.6   CSA from a left occipital electrode site of a normally functioning person, showing the usual concentration of power around 10 Hz during an eyes closed, resting condition.

lated, it was multiplied by a symmetry coefficient. Finally all channel features were summed to yield a type of global index or estimate of pathology.

Duffy and his associates were among the first to develop techniques to extract meaningful information from the volumes of data generated by quantitative EEG techniques (Duffy, Bartels, & Burchfiel, 1981). Prior to the use of computerized quantification procedures there are two major elements of EEG analysis. The first is to identify obvious discontinuities in brain electrical activity such as epileptic spikes or sharp waves, or obvious features likely due to artifact. The second element pertains to evaluation of the background continuous activity in which the subjective interpretation by one's visual examination is confounded by one's experience, attention to detail, and qualification of subtle deviations. The latter is where quantification of EEGs is put to the best use. When breaking the EEG into its spectral components, numerical values for the various components are obtained. By then referencing these values to normal values, a probability of normalcy can be established. Once a scaled value is established for a spectral component (e.g., relative power in the alpha band) at each electrode site, a method for interpolating theses values spatially between sites is used to display a map of the values using a grayscale or color scale to reflect changes of the values over the scalp. Numerous approaches to interpolation have been used depending on the clinical system employed, and there is no established agreement as to the best method. For example, a three-point interpolation method creates values for unknown locations (the spaces between electrodes) using data from the three nearest electrode sites. A test of reliability on an interpolation algorithm is to compare interpolated values with real values. Depending on the algorithms and electrode sites used, both two-dimensional and three-dimensional perspective maps can be created to illustrate QEEG findings over the scalp surface. This is the basis of statistical probability mapping (SPM) created from brain electrical activity mapping (BEAM) developed by Duffy and his colleagues and for "Neurometric" Z-score maps developed by John and his colleagues (Fig. 1.7).

To increase the clinical value of the QEEG, a normative database is needed. Implicit to the concept of comparing an individual to a normative population is an understanding of how the normative database is constructed and the statistical methods used to quantify the degree to which an individual varies from normal. It is important to note that different QEEG techniques do not all share the same algorithms for determining deviations from normal. For example, John et al. (1977a) have emphasized the need to first normalize quantitative data by using transformation functions such as a log transform and then to adjust these values for the subtle effects of aging by fitting these values to age-dependent regression equations. Additionally, John et al. (1977a) recognized the need to correct (mathematically) for the influence of electrical activity in one area of the brain on another area. Thus, we need to derive, statistically, the influence

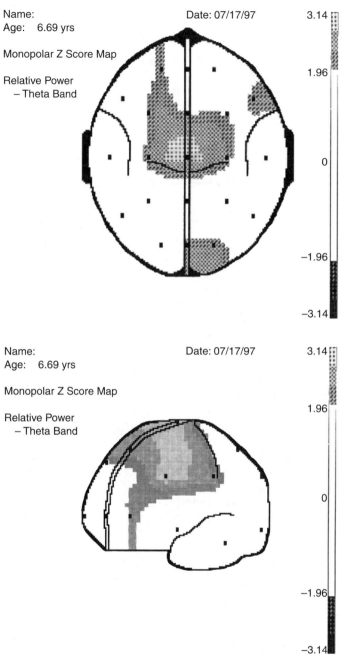

FIGURE 1.7 Neurometric Z score maps using a 4-point linear interpolation mapping method of the deviations from age regressed norms. The maps reflect a gray scale shading showing abnormalities in the range of −3.14 to 3.14 Z-scores for a 6.9-year-old child identified with ADD. Shown on top is a 2-dimensional perspective of the deviations from normal while the figure on bottom illustrates the same child's brain map in an angled 3-dimensional perspective.

of activity in multidimensional space and determine how this activity has a correlative effect on other measures in that same multidimensional space.

One method for assessing this effect is through measurement of the *Mahalanobis distance.* The Mahalanobis distance is the distance of a case from the centroid in multidimensional space of correlated independent variables (if variables are uncorrelated then they can be discussed using simple Euclidean distances). Thus, the use of Mahalanobis distance equations provides us with an indication of whether or not an observation is an outlier with respect to the independent variable values. By using Mahalanobis distance multivariate equations, deviation activity in the left hemisphere can be corrected for deviations in the right hemisphere and vice versa. Similarly, activity in the anterior regions can be calculated from activity in the posterior regions. These calculations are conducted for both the monopolar and bipolar derivations, because, as we previously outlined, each type of montage contributes different and potentially useful information. Further, multivariate *discriminant* analysis can be used to calculate the probability of fitting an individual neurometric QEEG profile to profiles established for certain clinical groups. Also, because age correction regression methods can be used, the ability to "fit" an individual's data can be tested to fit the regression curves at earlier ages, thereby assessing for maturational lag of cortical development (John *et al.,* 1977a).

Numerous problems have prevented the widespread acceptance and use of QEEG methods for clinical purposes. One problem is that not all QEEG methods apply the same filter cutoffs to define their frequency bands relative to their normative databases; for example, excessive delta by one method may be reflected as excessive theta by another method. A more detailed discussion regarding the use of databases in QEEG is provided in Chapter 2 of this volume. Furthermore, acceptance of QEEG and its clinical applications has been hampered by failures of replication and the difficulties interpreting data analysis from one system and applying it to another on the same patient. In an effort to curb potential abuse from the lack of standardization, conservative reports regarding clinical utility of QEEG methods have been issued by both the American Academy of Neurology and the American Psychiatric Association (e.g., Nuwer, 1997). In general, these reports recommend that the clinician using the method have appropriate training and experience, use QEEG only as an adjunct to standardized EEG data collection and review procedures, and refrain from making diagnostic conclusions based on QEEG findings alone.

III. CLINICAL APPLICATIONS OF QEEG

A. DIAGNOSTIC CONDITION CLASSIFICATION

Earlier studies illustrated the use of neurometric QEEG techniques to define an individual's brain function deviation from normal (Gotman *et al.,* 1973). Since then, many other studies have been conducted to describe specific univariate and multivariate feature sets that appear to form specific

TABLE 1.2   Representative Studies Contributing QEEG Information to Normative and Selected Clinical Populations

Populations studies	Studies documenting QEEG measures
Normals	Matousek & Petersen, 1973; John *et al.*, 1977a; Ahn *et al.*, 1980; John *et al.*, 1980; Gasser *et al.*, 1982, 1983, 1985; Thatcher *et al.*, 1986; Gasser *et al.*, 1988; Gimeno *et al.*, 1990; Marciani *et al.*, 1990; Hudspeth & Pribram, 1992
Affective disorder	Perris, 1980; Prichep, 1983, 1987; John *et al.*, 1988b; Roemer *et al.*, 1992
Schizophrenia/thought disorders	Flor-Henry *et al.*, 1983, 1984; Cantor *et al.*, 1986b; Grebb *et al.*, 1986; Garber *et al.*, 1989; Prichep & John, 1992
Attention deficits/learning disorders	John *et al.*, 1977b, 1981; Thatcher *et al.*, 1982; Fein *et al.*, 1983; John *et al.*, 1995, 1988a; Prichep & John, 1990
Dementia	Prichep, 1983; Brenner *et al.*, 1986, 1988; Giannitrapani & Collins, 1988; Fisch & Pedley, 1989; Oken & Kaye, 1992
Closed head injury/neurologic conditions	Duffy *et al.*, 1979; Burchfiel & Duffy, 1982; Cantor *et al.*, 1986a, 1986b; Gotman, 1986; Senf, 1988; Thatcher *et al.*, 1989; Matousek & Bader, 1990; Thatcher *et al.*, 1991

clusters and define abnormal brain function in various clinical populations. The extent of the studies and their findings are too extensive to review here, but some of the populations studied are listed in Table 1.2 along with references to the studies conducted.

While neurometric QEEG studies often have shown impressive statistical correlation with clinical classifications, the application of QEEG in this context is limited. After all, it can be argued that the findings of the QEEG only confirm what other techniques have indicated. More recently, however, QEEG has begun to demonstrate an ability to improve the determination of prognoses of such processes as closed head injuries (Thatcher, Cantor, McAlaster, Geisler, & Krause, 1991) and dementia (Prichep, Gomez-Mont, John, & Ferris, 1983). The value of applying these techniques for these purposes requires more work and replication.

B. NEUROMETRIC QEEG–TREATMENT APPLICATIONS

1. Pharmacotherapeutic Management

While providing for confirming diagnoses, QEEG has been of some utility, but the greatest promise of neurometric QEEG techniques may be that of guiding treatment toward improved outcome over other techniques. Itil and colleagues (Itil, Cora, Akpinar, Herrmann, & Patterson, 1974; Itil & Simeon, 1974; Itil, Marasa, Saletu, Davis, & Mucciardi, 1975; Itil, Patterson, Polvan, Bigelow, & Bergey, 1975; Itil, Shapiro, Schneider, and Francis, 1981; Itil, Mucci, & Eralp, 1991) were among the earliest researchers to argue that QEEG methods could be used to specify psychopharmacology. The basic premise is that since the QEEG measures activity reflecting neurophysiological function, distinctive feature sets may be used to predict physiological responsiveness to pharmacological interventions. These studies demonstrated responsiveness of various clinical populations to specific pharmacotherapy based on predominant QEEG features sets. Using multivariate analytic methods, Prichep and John (1990) demonstrated specific responsiveness to methylphenidate within a population of children with an attention deficit and hyperactivity. More recently, Suffin and Emory (1995) demonstrated that specific QEEG features sets correlated to optimal clinical response to different classes of medication independent of specific psychiatric diagnostic labels. QEEG methods have been reported anecdotally to be used in clinics to monitor changes in neurophysiological status with medication trials and, in this context, the results from such tests have been argued to provide objective evidence of treatment efficacy.

2. Neurofeedback Treatment and Brain Wave Conditioning

QEEG results have continued to support Berger's original notion that abnormal activity in the EEG reflects psychopathology. This relates to the concept in psychopharmacology that by altering neurophysiological functioning (as reflected in the QEEG) by chemical means, we can alter certain behaviors. However, learning theory and methods of operant and classical conditioning have also been employed to propose that functions of autonomic and central nervous system functioning in humans can be retrained for better adaptive functioning (Cantor *et al.*, 1983). Indeed, operant methods in the form of what is now commonly referred to as EEG biofeedback, or neurofeedback, have been developed and demonstrated to promote improved functioning in populations having attention deficit disorders (Lubar, Smartwood, Smartwood, & O'Donnell, 1995; Lubar, 1997; Tan & Schneider, 1997), alcoholism (Saxby & Peniston, 1995), strokes (Rozelle & Budzynski, 1995), chronic fatigue syndrome (James & Folen, 1996), and asthmatic conditions (Nahmias, Tansey, & Karetzky, 1994). These methods utilize certain features of the EEG, such as digitized amplitudes, in a computerized game-like form in which the patient attempts to use feedback concerning these features to achieve a specified goal of EEG change consistently by maintaining a certain "correct mental state." These "correct states" are those that have been shown by QEEG measurements to correlate with a "normal" state of brain functioning. Thus, for example, if QEEG findings reveal a disproportionate ratio of theta to beta amplitudes in a given brain region (compared to the normal), a computer game in which one needs to keep a "Pac-Man" moving solely by developing a more normal theta/beta amplitude ratio is conducted during a therapeutic session. Over a series of sessions, the ease of maintaining this correct ratio by the patient usually increases and, upon psychometric testing of attention abilities, a corresponding improvement in scores is commonly seen. The number of sessions required to achieve a stabilized effect appears to vary from patient to patient, but anecdotal reports indicate positive effects are considered stable over years.

Several considerations regarding the use of QEEG test results in the context of neurotherapy appear to date not to have been comprehensively addressed in neurotherapy paradigms in a comprehensive and standardized manner. Some of the considerations are as follows:

1. Not all paradigms properly monitor and correct for artifact during calculation of the ongoing QEEG measure being conditioned. For example, eye movement (which was described earlier as a potent contaminant of QEEG measures), if left unchecked, can produce false readouts of beta voltages and percent values, particularly in the frontal regions. These false measures may prevent or at least hamper the biofeedback process in trying to maintain certain conditions employing beta measures. The problem is further compounded if other types of artifact are also left unchecked or uncorrected during the feedback process.

2. Few paradigms utilize age-corrected or normalized data. As reported earlier, in determining whether or not QEEG measures are deviant, parametric or proper nonparametric statistics need to be employed, and then properly referenced. For example, in attempting to achieve a "target" range in which to keep the theta amplitude, one needs to know what is the normal for the age of the patient in order to determine the degree of abnormality in the EEG measurements. This information is also important in reassessing when the patient has attained a "normal" level for his/her age, thus indicating successful completion of the therapeutic process.

More recently, the premise that classical conditioning methods can alter cyclic neural patterns has lead to models for training and altering brain wave parameters with resulting changes in behavior (Cantor, Pavlovich, & Brown-Lewis, 1994). This is different from the operant conditioning methods employed in classic biofeedback paradigms.[2] The model used is as follows:

---

[2] UCS = unconditioned stimulus; UCR = unconditioned response; CS = conditioned stimulus; CR = conditioned response.

UCS (Sensory Environment)   —————————→   UCR (Predominant background EEG)

CS (Specific frequency modulated stimulation) → CR (Modified background EEG)

In this model, multimodal sensory stimuli in the environment (UCS) contribute to the predominant background EEG (UCR). A device is used to provide multimodal rate-modulated stimulation (CS) to drive the background EEG to a modified rate (CR) over repeated training sessions in which the random sensory stimuli in the environment are coincident with the rate-modulated stimuli. Eventually any sensory stimuli may trigger and maintain a conditioned background EEG.

Thus, if the predominant background frequency in a defective system is 5.7 Hz in the theta band for an awake and alert state and we know this from quantitative normative data, we may use such a conditioning paradigm to increase the mean background frequency to, say, 8.0 Hz. In theory, the changes in background EEG activity should produce systemic effects yielding functional changes. Validation for the effectiveness of such paradigms needs to be provided by two means: (1) documented changes in the background EEG by quantitative EEG analysis and (2) measured changes in functional performance by empirically based psychological instruments. Several factors should be considered in the use of such paradigms:

1. As in the traditional biofeedback paradigm, it is useful to use a validated normative database that employs age-corrected methods.
2. One should identify the modality of frequency-modulated stimulus conditioning depending on which cortical regions are most affected. For example, if we are conditioning the temporal regions, these may be ideally conditional by auditory stimulation rather than visual.
3. Some conditions may be optimally responsive to multimodal stimulation, but it is important to know if the nature of the dysfunction is focal or cortically diffuse.
4. It is important to know if the baseline EEG frequency being conditioned is stable over diurnal cycles versus conditions that are periodic, reflecting possible metabolic conditions (e.g., hypoglycemia or reactive hypoglycemia, cf. Hudspeth, Peterson, Soli, & Trimble, 1981).

The paradigms that arise when using this classical conditioning approach are still relatively new, and not enough is understood about the effectiveness or safety of such an approach with different mental conditions at different ages, and in interaction with other features such as coherence.

IV. SUMMARY

EEG as a methodology for understanding neural processes as they relate to human behavior has come a long way since the early days of Berger's work with observations of alpha activity in awake humans. Computer methods to measure EEG activity in humans (QEEG) have permitted us to detect subtle univariate and multivariate profiles which have unique patterns associated with different psychiatric and neurologic conditions. Clinicians can use both age-adjusted normative databases and clinical databases to develop specific treatment protocols employing chemical agents to alter underlying neurophysiology and/or adjusting EEG parameters through operant or classical conditioning models of EEG biofeedback. Like all procedures used to measure human function and behavior, the methods employed in QEEG normative databases are critical. Similarly, the methods employed to train changes in EEG require careful consideration of factors that can influence the recording, monitoring, and defining of outcome effects on the EEG. It is critically important that future EEG clinicians using QEEG diagnostic and treatment techniques consider the findings from decades of research about how to properly interpret QEEG data and to develop appropriate neurofeedback and/or neural conditioning protocols for each individual patient.

REFERENCES

Ahn, H., Prichep, L., John, E. R., Baird, H. Trepetin, M., & Kaye, H. (1980). Developmental equations reflect brain dysfunctions. *Science,* **210,** 1259–1262.

Bickford, R. G., Fleming, N. I., & Billinger, T. W. (1971). Compression of EEG data by isometric power spectral plots. *EEG Clin. Neurophysiol.,* **31,** 632.

Bickford, R. G., Brimm, J., Berger, L., & Aung, M. (1973). Application of compressed spectral array in clinical EEG. *In* "Automation of Clinical Electroencephalography" (P. Kellaway & I. Petersen, eds.), pp. 55–64. Raven Press, New York.

Brenner, R. P., Ulrich, R. F., Spiker, D. G., Sclabassi, R. J., Reynolds III, C. F., Marin, R. S., & Boller, F. (1986). Computerized EEG spectral analysis in elderly normal, demented and depressed subjects. *EEG & Clin. Neurophysiol.,* **64,** 482–492.

Brenner, R. P., Reynolds III, C. F., & Ulrich, R. F. (1988). Diagnostic efficacy of computerized spectral versus visual EEG analysis in elderly normal, demented and depressed subjects. *EEG Clin. Neurophysiol.,* **69,** 110–117.

Burchfiel, J. L., & Duffy, F. H. (1982). Organophosphate neurotoxicity: Chronic effects of sarin on the electroencephalogram of monkey and man. *Neurobehav. Toxicol. Teratol.* **4,** 767–778.

Cantor, D. S. (1983). Neurometric indices of autism: EEG analyses. *Dissertation Abstracts International.*

Cantor, D. S., Fischel, J., & Kaye, H. (1983). Neonatal conditionability: A new paradigm for exploring the use of interoceptive cues. *Infant Behav. Devel.* **6,** 404–413.

Cantor, D. S., Wolff, A., Thatcher, R. W., Gardner, J., & Kammerer, B. (1986a). Neurophysiological differences between deaf and hearing children. *J. Clin. Exper. Neuropsychol.* **8,** 2.

Cantor, D. S., Thatcher, R. W., Kaye, H., & Hrybyk, M. (1986b). Computerized EEG analyses of autistic children. *J. Autism Devel. Disorders* **16,** 169–187.

Cantor, D. S., Pavlovich, M., & Brown-Lewis, R. (1994). Electrical stimulation and classical conditioning of brain wave activity in a comatose TBI patient. Presented at annual conference of the National Academy of Neuropsychology, 1994.

Duffy, F. H., Burchfiel J. L, Bartels P. H., Gaon, M., & Sim, V. M. (1979). Long-term effects of an organophosphate upon the human electroencephalogram. *Toxicol. Appl. Pharmacol.,* **47**(1), 161–176.

Duffy, F. H., Bartels, P. H., & Burchfiel, J. L. (1981). Significance probability mapping: An aid in the topographic analysis of brain electrical activity. *EEG Clin. Neurophysiol.,* **51,** 455–462.

Fein, G., Galin, D., & Johnstone, J. (1983). EEG power spectra in normal and dyslexic children. I. Reliability during passive conditions. *EEG Clin. Neurophysiol.,* **55,** 399–405.

Fisch, B. J., & Pedley, T. A. (1989). The role of quantitative topographic mapping or 'neurometrics' in the diagnosis of psychiatric and neurological disorders: The cons. *EEG Clin. Neurophysiol.,* **73,** 5–9.

Flor-Henry, P., & Koles, Z. (1984). Statistical quantitative EEG studies of depression, mania, schizophrenia and normals. *Biol. Psychol.,* **19,** 3–4, 257–279.

Flor-Henry, P., Koles, Z. J., & Sussman, P. S. (1983). Multivariate EEG analysis of the endogenous psychoses. *Adv. Biol. Psychiat.* **13,** 196–210.

Garber, H., Weilburg, J., Duffy, F., & Manschreck, T. (1989). Clinical use of topographic brain electrical activity mapping in psychiatry. *J. Clin. Psychiatry* **50**(6), 205–211.

Gasser, T., Bächer, P., & Möcks, J. (1982). Transformations towards the normal distribution of broad band spectral parameters of the EEG. *EEG Clin. Neurophysiol.,* **53,** 119–124.

Gasser, T., Von Lucadou-Müller, I., Verleger, R., & Bächer, P. (1983). Correlating EEG and IQ: A new look at an old problem using computerized EEG parameters. *EEG Clin. Neurophysiol.,* **55**(5), 493–504.

Gasser, T., Bächer, P., & Steinberg, H. (1985). Test–retest reliability of spectral parameters of the EEG. *EEG Clin. Neurophysiol.,* **60**(4), 312–319.

Gasser, T., Verleger, R., Bächer, P., & Sroka, L. (1988). Development of the EEG of school-age children and adolescents. I. Analysis of band power. *EEG Clin. Neurophysiol.,* **69**(2), 91–99.

Giannitrapani, D., & Collins, J. (1988). EEG differentiation between Alzheimer's and non-Alzheimer's dementias. *In* "The EEG of Mental Activities" (D. Giannitrapani & L. Murri, eds.), pp. 26–41. Karger, New York.

Gimeno, V., Sagales, T., & Calzada, M. D. (1990). Brain mapping of the electroencephalogram envelope: normal patterns. Presented at the XIIth International Congress of Electroencephalography and Clinical Neurophysiology, Rio de Janeiro, Brazil, January 14–19, 1990.

Glaser, E. M., & Ruchkin, D. S. (1976). "Principles of Neurological Signal Analysis." Academic Press, New York.

Gotman, J. (1986). Computer analysis of EEG in epilepsy. *In* "Clinical Applications of Computer Analysis of EEG and Other Neurophysiological Signals. Handbook of Electroencephalography and Clinical Neurophysiology" (F. H. Lopes da Silva, W. Storm van Leeuwen, & A. Remond, eds.), pp. 171–204. Elsevier, Amsterdam.

Gotman, J., Skuce, D. R., Thompson, C. S., Gloor, P., Ives, J. R., & Ray, W. F. (1973). Clinical applications of spectral analysis and extraction of features from electroencephalograms with slow waves in adult patients. *EEG Clin. Neurophysiol.,* **35,** 225–235.

Grebb, J. A., Weinberger, D. R., & Morihisa, J. M. (1986). Encephalogram and evoked potential studies of schizophrenia. *In* "Handbook of Schizophrenia. The Neurology of Schizophrenia" (H. A. Nasrallah & D. R. Weinberger, eds.), pp. 121–140. Elsevier, Amsterdam.

Hudspeth, W., & Pribram, K. (1992). Psychophysiological indices of cerebral maturation. *Int. J. Psychophysiol.* **12**(1), 19–29.

Hudspeth, W. J., Peterson, L. W., Soli, D. E., & Trimble, B. A. (1981). Neurobiology of the hypoglycemia syndrome. *J. Holistic Med.,* **3,** 60–71.

Itil, T., & Simeon, J. (1974). Proceedings: Computerized EEG in the prediction of outcome of drug treatment in hyperactive childhood behavior disorders. *Psychopharmacol. Bull.* **10**(4), 36.

Itil, T., Cora, R., Akpinar, S., Herrmann, W., & Patterson, C. (1974). "Psychotropic" action of sex hormones: Computerized EEG in establishing the immediate CNS effects of steroid hormones. *Curr. Ther. Res. Clin. Exper.* **16**(11), 1147–1170.

Itil, T., Patterson, C., Polvan, N., Bigelow, A., & Bergey, B. (1975). Clinical and CNS effects of oral and IV thyrotropin-releasing hormone in depressed patients. *Dis. Nerv. Syst.* **36**(9), 529–536.

Itil, T., Marasa, J., Saletu, B., Davis, S., & Mucciardi, A. (1975). Computerized EEG: predictor of outcome in schizophrenia. *J. Nerv. Ment. Dis.* **160**(3), 118–120.

Itil, T., Shapiro, D., Schneider, S., & Francis I. (1981). Computerized EEG as a predictor of drug response in treatment resistant schizophrenics. *J. Nerv. Ment. Dis.* **169**(10), 629–637.

Itil, T., Mucci, A., & Eralp, E. (1991). Dynamic brain mapping methodology and application. *Int. J. Psychophysiol.* **10**(3), 281–291.

James, L., & Folen R. (1996). EEG biofeedback as a treatment for chronic fatigue syndrome: A controlled case report. *Behav. Med.* **22**(2), 77–81.

Jasper, H. (1958). The ten-twenty electrode system of the International Federation. *EEG Clin. Neurophysiol.,* **10**, 371–375.

John, E. R. (1977a). "Functional Neuroscience," Vol. 2, "Neurometrics: Clinical Applications of Quantitative Electrophysiology." Lawrence Erlbaum Associates, New Jersey.

John, E. R. (1977b). Early detection and diagnosis of cognitive dysfunction. *Proceedings of RANN2 Symposium.*

John, E. R., Karmel, B. Z., Corning, W. C., Easton, P., Brown, D., Ahn, H., John, M., Harmony, T., Prichep, L., Toro, A., Gerson, I., Bartlett, F., Thatcher, R., Kaye, H., Valdes, P., & Schwartz, E. (1977a). Neurometrics: Numerical taxonomy identifies different profiles of brain functions within groups of behaviorally similar people. *Science,* **196,** 1383–1410.

John, E. R., Karmel, B. Z., Prichep, L. S., Ahn, H., & John M. (1977b). Neurometrics applied to the quantitative electrophysiological measurement of organic brain dysfunction in children. *In* "Psychopathology and Brain Dysfunction" (C. Shagass, ed.), pp. 291–337. Raven Press, New York.

John, E. R., Ahn, H., Prichep, L., Trepetin, M., Brown, D., & Kaye, H. (1980). Developmental EEG equations for the electroencephalogram. *Science,* **210,** 1255–1258.

John, E. R., Ahn, H., Prichep, L., Kaye, H., Trepetin, M., & Fridman, J. (1981). Neurometric evaluation of EEG in normal, learning disabled and neurologically "at-risk" children. *In* "Recent Advances in EEG and EMG Data Processing" (N. Yamaguchi & K. Fujisawa, eds.), pp. 163–177. Elsevier, Amsterdam.

John, E. R., Prichep, L., Fridman, J., Ahn, H., Kaye, H., & Baird, H. (1985). Neurometric evaluation of brain electrical activity in children with learning disabilities. *In* "Dyslexia: A Neuroscientific Approach to Clinical Evaluation" (F. Duffy & N. Geschwind, eds.), pp. 157–185. Little, Brown, Boston.

John, E. R., Prichep, L. S., Ahn, H., Kaye, H., Brown, D., Easton, P., Karmel, B. Z., Toro, A., & Thatcher, R. (1988a). "Neurometric Evaluation of Brain Function in Normal and Learning Disabled Children." University of Michigan Press, Ann Arbor.

John, E. R., Prichep, L. S., Friedman, J., & Easton, P. (1988b). Neurometrics: Computer-assisted differential diagnosis of brain dysfunctions. *Science* **293,** 162–169.

Kaiser, E., Petersen, I., Sellden, U., & Kagawa, N. (1964). EEG data representation, in broad-band frequency analysis. *EEG Clin. Neurophysiol.,* **17,** 76–80.

Kozhevnikov, V. A. (1958). Some methods of automatic measurement of the electroencephalogram. *EEG Clin. Neurophysiol.,* **10,** 269–278.

Lubar, J., Smartwood, M., Smartwood, J., & O'Donnell, P. (1995). Evaluation of the effectiveness of EEG neurofeedback training for ADHD in a clinical setting as measured by changes in T. O. V. A. scores, behavioral ratings and WISC-R performance. *Biofeedback Self Regulation* **20**(1), 83–99.

Lubar, J. F. (1997). Neocortical dynamics: Implications for understanding the role of neurofeedback and related techniques for the enhancement of attention. *Appl. Psychophysiol. Biofeedback* **22**(2), 111–126.

Marciani, M. G., Stefani, N., Stefanini, F., Sabbadini, C., Baggio, C., Palin, E., & Bolcioni, G. (1990). EEG topographic mapping and high resolution mosaic imaging in normal subjects: Different cortical activation patterns. Presented at the XIIth International Congress of Electroencephalography and Clinical Neurophysiology, Rio de Janeiro, Brazil, January 14–19, 1990.

Matousek, M., & Bader, G. (1990). EEG brain mapping in focal brain lesions: Normality ratio versus Z score. Presented at the XIIth International Congress of Electroencephalography and Clinical Neurophysiology, Rio de Janeiro, Brazil, January 14–19, 1990.

Matousek, M., & Petersen, I. (1973). Frequency analysis of the EEG in normal children and adolescents. *In* "Automation of Clinical Electroencephalography" (P. Kellaway & I. Petersen, eds.), pp. 75–102. Raven Press, New York.

Möcks, J., & Gasser, T. (1984). How to select epochs of the EEG at rest for quantitative analysis. *EEG Clin. Neurophysiol.* **58**(1), 89–92.

Nahmias, J., Tansey, M., & Karetzky, M. S. (1994). Asthmatic extrathoracic upper airway obstruction: Laryngeal dyskinesis. *N. J. Med.* **91**(9), 616–620.

Nuwer, M. (1997). Assessment of digital EEG, quantitative EEG, and EEG brain mapping: Report of the American Academy of Neurology and the American Clinical Neurophysiology Society. *Neurology,* **49**(1), 277–292.

Oken, B., & Kaye, J. (1992). Electrophysiologic function in the healthy, extremely old. *Neurology* **42**(No. 3, Part 1), 519–526.

Perris, C. (1980). Central measures of depression. *In* "Handbook of Biological Psychiatry" (H. Van Praag, ed.), pp. 183–225.

Prichep, L. S. (1983). Electrophysiological subtyping of depressive disorder. *Proceedings of the American Psychiatric Association Session on Subtyping of Depressive Disorders,* pp. 22–27. Educational Symposia, Inc.

Prichep, L. S. (1987). Neurometric quantitative EEG features of depressive disorders. *In* "Cerebral Dynamics, Laterality and Psychopathology" ("Developments in Psychiatry," Vol. 2) (R. Takahashi, P. Flor-Henry, J. Gruzelier, & S. Niwa, eds.), pp. 55–69. Elsevier, Amsterdam.

Prichep, L. S., & John, E. R. (1990). Neurometric studies of methylphendiate responders and non-responders. *In* "Dyslexia: A Neuropsychological and Learning Perspective" (G. Pavlidis, ed.). John Wiley and Sons, New York.

Prichep L., & John, E. R. (1992). QEEG profiles of psychiatric disorders. *Brain Topog.* **4**(4), 249–257.

Prichep, L. S., Gomez-Mont, F., John, E. R., & Ferris, S. (1983). Neurometric electroencephalogram characteristics of dementia. *In* "Alzheimer's Disease: The Standard Reference" (B. Reisberg, ed.), pp. 252–257. The Free Press, New York.

Roemer, R., Shagass, C., Dubin, W., Jaffe, R., & Siegal, L. (1992). Quantitative EEG in elderly depressives. *Brain Topog.* **4**(4), 285–290.

Rozelle, G. R., & Budzynski, T. H. (1995). Neurotherapy for stroke rehabilitation: A single case study. *Biofeedback Self Regulation* **20**(3), 211–228.

Saxby, E., & Peniston, E. (1995). Alpha-theta brainwave neurofeedback training: An effective treatment for male and female alcoholics with depressive symptoms. *J. Clin. Psychol.,* **51**(5), 685–693.

Senf, G. M. (1988). Neurometric brain mapping in the diagnosis and rehabilitation of cognitive dysfunction. *Cognitive Rehabilitation,* November–December, 20–37.

Suffin, S., & Emory, H. (1995). Neurometric subgroups in attentional and affective disorders and their association with pharmacotherapeutic outcome. *Clin. Electroencephalography,* **26**(2), 76–83.

Tan, G., & Schneider, S. C. (1997). Attention-deficit hyperactivity disorder: Pharmacotherapy and beyond. *Postgrad. Med.* **101**(5), 201–204, 213–214, 216.

Thatcher, R. W., McAlaster, R., Lester, M., Horst, R., & Cantor, D. S. (1982). Hemispheric EEG asymmetries related to cognitive functioning in children. *In* "Cognitive Processing in the Right Hemisphere" (E. Percerner, ed.). Academic Press, New York.

Thatcher, R. W., Krause, P. J., & Hrybyk, M. (1986). Cortico-cortical associations and EEG coherence: A two-compartmental model. *EEG Clin. Neurophysiol.,* **64,** 123–143.

Thatcher, R. W., Walker, R. A., Gerson, I., & Geisler, F. H. (1989). EEG discriminant analyses of mild head trauma. *EEG Clin. Neurophysiol.,* **73,** 94–106.

Thatcher, R. W., Cantor, D. S., McAlaster, R., Geisler, G., & Krause, P. (1991). Comprehensive predictions of outcome in closed head-injured patients: The development of prognostic equations. In: "Windows on the Brain: Neuropsychology's Technological Frontiers" (R. A. Zapulla, F. F. LeFever, J. Jaeger, & R. Bilder, eds.), *Ann. N.Y. Acad. Sci.* **620,** 82–101.

Walter, W. G. (1963). Specific and non-specific responses and autonomic mechanisms in human subjects during conditioning. *Prog. Brain Res.* **1,** 395–401.

2

EEG DATABASE-GUIDED NEUROTHERAPY

ROBERT W. THATCHER

Medical Research Service, Bay Pines Veterans Administration Medical Center, Bay Pines, Florida, and Departments of Neurology and Radiology, University of South Florida College of Medicine, Tampa, Florida

I. INTRODUCTION

This chapter is a slightly modified version of a recent journal article (Thatcher, 1998) that addresses many of the issues raised in the present book. The modifications involve a brief integration of biofeedback of the electroencephalogram (EEG) with the field of neuroimaging as well as a brief introduction of non-Gaussian distributed statistics in the form of modern nonparametric statistics. Because the ideas expressed in the Thatcher (1998) paper are extensive and cover a broad range of EEG database issues, the decision was made to present these ideas in the present chapter in only a slightly modified form.

A. MODERN NEUROIMAGING ADVANCES

There has been a veritable explosion in new discoveries in the field of neuroscience during the last 10 years. For example, since about 1990 the multimodal registration of electroencephalography (EEG), positron emission tomography (PET), magnetic resonance imaging (MRI), functional magnetic resonance imaging (fMRI), and single positron emission computerized tomography (SPECT) has resulted in the rapid growth of a new discipline called *functional neuroimaging,* which embodies the ability to measure four-dimensional biophysical brain processes related to many aspects of normal and pathological brain function, including perception and cognition (Thatcher *et al.,* 1994, 1996; Frackowiak *et al.,* 1997). The evidence of this growth is the now commonly reported high spatial and temporal resolution of EEG that yields 3-D current sources capable of being coregistered with PET (or fMRI) using spherical and/or realistic head models as determined by conventional MRI (Thatcher, 1995; Pascual-Marqui, 1995). Such publications have only been available during the last few years. Only in the very recent past have the biophysical aspects of MRI been directly correlated with disease and cognitive dysfunction. In these studies the conventional MRI machine was used to conduct nuclear magnetic resonance by measuring the relaxation of water protons (^{1}H), tensor diffusion weighted imaging and carbon, phosphorous and hydrogen spectroscopy (Gillies, 1994; Minshew & Pettegrew, 1996). The MRI-based relaxation of water protons (^{1}H) and tensor diffusion weighted imaging measure biophysical processes related to the movement of water protons within the cytoplasm, myelin, and extracellular space of the brain (Szafer *et al.,* 1995; Kroeker & Henkelman, 1986; Does & Snyder, 1995). The MRI-based spectroscopic methods measure biophysical processes related to the concentrations of organic and nonorganic compounds found in the bioenergetics of cells (e.g., ^{31}P measures of phosphomonesters and diesters, ATP-related high-energy phosphates) and the membrane contents of cells (e.g., creatine, choline, and *N*-acetyl aspartate). The rapidity of scientific discovery in the neurosciences is further emphasized by the fact that only since 1997 have direct biophysical integrations of the MRI and EEG been reported (Thatcher *et al.,* 1997, 1998a, 1998b).

A biophysically based MRI integration to EEG is a welcome arrival because it harkens a measurable linkage between membrane and molecular biology and the electrogenesis of the EEG. The implications of a molecular and biophysical linkage between MRI and EEG biofeedback have not yet been explored. Solid scientific and mathematical exploration is needed to guide us as we test and reject hypotheses about one's ability to modify the biophysical and electrophysiological operations of the brain through EEG biofeedback. Note that clinical electrophysiologists, such as those using EEG biofeedback or neurotherapy, are involved in the process of evaluating the clinical efficacy and sensitivity of EEG biofeedback during the recent exponential increase in knowledge about the brain referred to earlier. As an aid in this endeavor, the present chapter is designed to discuss the use of a "reference" normative EEG database[1] in conjunction with clinical

---

[1] The term *normative* when used alone tends to obscure or mask the fundamental fact that only a "sample" of subjects drawn from a much larger population are contained in any database. The practical utility of all clinical databases exists only to the extent that the database constitutes a representative sample of the general population of neurologically and clinically normal individuals.

EEG biofeedback and neurotherapy as we enter the next century. One goal of this chapter is to discuss the clinical use of the electroencephalogram by discussing some of the criteria for the use of a reference normative EEG database.

B. LIFE SPAN REFERENCE EEG DATABASES AND NEUROTHERAPY

EEG biofeedback is an operant conditioning procedure whereby an individual modifies the amplitude, frequency, or coherency of the electrophysiological dynamics of his/her own brain (Cohen, 1975; Blanchard & Epstein, 1978; Rosenfeld, 1990). The exact physiological foundations of this process are not well understood; however, the practical ability of humans and animals to modify directly their EEG through feedback is well established (Fox and Rudell, 1968; Rosenfeld et al., 1969; Hetzler et al., 1977; Sterman, 1996). The ease with which direct modifications of EEG can be accomplished is partly responsible for the rapid, almost explosive rise in the use of EEG biofeedback for the purposes of therapeutic amelioration of a wide range of psychological and neurological disorders (see reviews by Cohen, 1975; Rosenfeld, 1990; Lubar, 1997). The therapeutic application of EEG biofeedback is often referred to as *neurotherapy* and, most importantly, the therapeutic efficacy and success of neurotherapy is a force that is driving the development and clinical application of EEG biofeedback (Lubar, 1997).

As pointed out by several studies (Johnson, 1997; Lubar, 1997; Striefel, 1995; Schwartz, 1995), EEG biofeedback is not a "kid's toy" because in the hands of a professional it is a strong and effective methodology and must be treated with great respect and competence. The reader must be reminded that modifications of one's own EEG is a very serious undertaking because it involves direct manipulations of neuronal excitabilities and neural connections in the brain. Although no ill effects of EEG biofeedback have been noted to date, nonetheless caution, professionalism, and knowledge are the prerequisite requirements for the application of this technique. It is in this spirit that the present chapter reviews electrophysiological analyses as they pertain to EEG biofeedback and discusses the use of a *normative EEG database* (NDB) to aid professional neurotherapists in evaluating the neurological status of their patients prior to therapy, to evaluate the course of their therapy, and to provide a guide for the development of therapeutic strategies using EEG biofeedback. It is assumed that knowledge about the electrophysiology and anatomy of the brain, which are being modified by the patient under the guide of the neurotherapist, is important and that deeper knowledge can only benefit the patient, the therapist, and the field of neurotherapy.

It is likely that in the future *life span normative EEG databases* (LNDBs) will be commonly used for purposes of EEG biofeedback and will play an increasingly important role in the clinical evaluation and treatment of patients. It is important to contrast a LNDB to the more age-limited databases that may be currently available or may become available in the future. A life span EEG database covers the entire or at least the major portions of the human life span from birth to senescence, whereas an age-limited database contains only a small sample of individuals from a restricted age range. The advantage of a LNDB is that it is applicable to infants, early childhood, middle childhood, adolescence, early adulthood, middle adulthood, and late adulthood. As discussed in more detail in Section V, a LNDB has three primary uses: (1) to assess the extent to which there is a neurological basis for the patient's complaints (i.e., the issue of *organicity*), (2) to identify possible strengths and weaknesses in the organization and electrophysiological status of the patient's brain in order to aid in the efficient and optimal design of neurotherapy (i.e., the issue of *therapy design*), and (3) to increase efficiency and to evaluate objectively the efficacy of treatment by comparing the patient's EEG before, during, and after treatment (i.e., the issue of *treatment evaluation*). Currently, only a small number of EEG normative reference databases seem adequate to meet the minimal standards necessary for responsible and ethical uses of a NDB in the field of EEG biofeedback.

C. ACTIVE TASKS VERSUS EYES-CLOSED AND EYES-OPEN QEEG DATABASES

An active task refers to the recording of EEG and/or evoked potentials (EPs) while a subject performs some kind of perceptual or cognitive task. Many EEG and EP studies have reported reproducible changes in brain dynamics that are task dependent. Such studies are important for understanding normal and pathological brain processes responsible for perceptual and cognitive function. In contrast, an eyes-closed or eyes-open EEG state involves an alert subject simply sitting quietly and not moving. The eyes-closed and/or eyes-open conditions are commonly used as reference normative EEG databases because of the simplicity and relative uniformity of EEG recording conditions. Such databases can be compared across laboratories and populations with relatively high reliability. Active tasks, on the other hand, are dependent on the intensity of stimuli, the background noise of the room, the distance between the subject and the stimuli, the subject's understanding of the task instructions, the subject's motivation, etc. These conditions are very difficult to control across experimenters or across clinics for the purposes of constructing a "reference" normative EEG database. It is for this reason that there are few if any active task reference normative EEG databases, whereas there are at least three eyes-closed life span EEG normative databases [e.g., E. Roy John (John, 1977; John *et al.*, 1988); Frank Duffy (Duffy *et al.*, 1994), and Robert Thatcher (Thatcher, 1987)].

These databases are unique in that they cover most if not the entire human life span from birth to senescence.[2]

Keep in mind that the alert eyes-closed EEG state is very much an active state; for example, there is still about 20% glucose metabolism of the whole body occurring in the brain of an eyes-closed subject (Herscovitch, 1994). During the eyes-closed state, there is dynamic circulation of neural activity in connected cortical, reticular, and thalamocortical loops (Thatcher & John, 1977; Nunez, 1981). The allocation of neural resource is simply different from when the subject is directing his/her attention to an experimentally controlled situation. Active tasks are very important because they reflect the switching and dynamic allocation of neural resource and they do have clinical importance. However, in the present chapter only the alert and resting EEG have been used for the purposes of a reference EEG normative and, therefore, this chapter is only concerned with the EEG recorded during these conditions. This emphasis occurs only from a practical point of view, and comparisons between resting EEG conditions and active EEG conditions should be encouraged. A good and stable resting EEG normative database can enhance and facilitate the understanding of the underlying neural dynamics and clinical condition of a patient during an active task.

Therefore, one purpose of the present chapter is to discuss the minimal standards for the creation and use of a resting EEG normative database. Our discussion emphasizes the Thatcher *life span normative EEG database,* which was first introduced in 1987 (Thatcher, 1987) and has been in use throughout much of the EEG biofeedback community since 1992. This database is referred to as a life span normative EEG database or LNDB because it spans the full human life span from birth to 82 years of age. Savitsky and Golay (1964) smoothing of the LNDB was first conducted in 1988. This procedure allowed for the creation of derivatives of the LNDB as well as a more statistically stable version of the means and standard deviations. The reader should note, however, that databases other than the Thatcher LNDB are available for clinical and research purposes and each of these databases contains its own strengths and weaknesses. It is not the goal of this chapter to examine and compare each currently available EEG database. Although some comments will be made regarding some of the databases, these comments are made only in the discussion of a given topic and do not provide in-depth analysis of any given database.

II. CRITERIA FOR THE DEVELOPMENT AND USE OF EEG DATABASES

In contrast to a "conventional" visual reading of an EEG printout or display, I will refer to the exact quantification of the electroencephalogram

---

[2] The Matousek and Petersen (1973) EEG database is not considered a complete life span normative EEG database because it only covered the period from 1 year to 21 years of age and used a very limited number of channels, that is, four bipolar channels.

as QEEG. The essential criteria for a clinically useful quantitative EEG (i.e., QEEG) database are the same as for all clinical normative databases: (1) full disclosure of the demographics, sampling procedures, and technical details of the database; (2) representative demographic sampling and certainty that only "normal" or nonclinically compromised subjects are included; (3) large enough sample sizes at different ages to measure properly any nonlinearities in development; (4) nonartifact or "clean" EEG samples with proper amplifier and digital sampling procedures; and (5) correct statistical properties of the database samples to ensure interpretable parametric statistical analyses.

A. FULL DISCLOSURE OF THE CONTENT OF EEG NORMATIVE DATABASES

Currently, several normative EEG databases are available that may have relevance for clinical diagnoses and evaluation of therapy. However, the extent to which these databases are useful is largely determined by the degree of open disclosure of the contents of the databases themselves. This refers specifically to open disclosure of the number of subjects per age group, gender, the demographics of the sample, the geographic location of the samples, quality control measures, acquisition, and technical procedures (e.g., artifact rejection, filter and gain settings, digitization rates, spectral procedures, etc.). Users of these databases must demand full disclosure of the makeup of a database so the relative merits and applicability of the database for their particular needs can be assessed. Especially important is the establishment of the relative sensitivity and specificity of the normative database, which depends on knowledge of the population and statistical details of the database.

In the following pages clinical and statistical criteria for "normative" and/or "reference" EEG databases are presented. The goal is to understand the concepts and value of parametric statistics for the determination of diagnostic sensitivity and specificity. Next some of the most crucial EEG analyses are reviewed in an attempt to highlight the clinical and physiological bases of each one. Finally, a practical discussion of the diagnostic and therapeutic applications of EEG databases is presented. Special emphasis is placed on the uses of "reference" normative EEG databases to determine the "organic" basis of a patient's complaints, and then to design and evaluate neurotherapy.

B. DEMOGRAPHICS AND GENDER CRITERIA FOR NORMALITY AND SUBJECT SELECTION

In the remainder of this chapter the term *normative database* will be used only in the sense of a *reference normative database*. The term *normative* when used alone tends to obscure or mask the fundamental fact that only a "sample" of subjects drawn from a much larger population is contained in any database. Mathematically, the practical utility of a database is measured only to the extent that the database constitutes a representative sample of the general population of neurologically and clinically normal individuals. Therefore, the concepts of normalcy and demographic representation are crucial to the creation of a "reference" EEG database of normal individuals. The "reference normative" population must be drawn from a representative sample of people whose ethnic and cultural backgrounds are as diverse as the clinical populations that will be studied. Many demographic populations analyses of the United States are broken down by individual states. In general, the U.S. ethnic population is comprised of approximately 18% African-American, 3% Oriental, 12% Hispanic, and 63% Caucasian. Socioeconomic status and handedness are also important factors when evaluating a normative reference database. Figures 2.1 and 2.2 show the distribution of socioeconomic status (SES) and handedness, respectively, in the Thatcher (1987) database.

Stringent normalcy criteria for membership in a normative QEEG database must also be followed. One of the first reference normative QEEG databases was created in 1973 by Matousek and Petersen (1973). An independent replication of specific ages in the Matousek and Petersen NDB established the reliability and clinical value of quantitative methods in EEG (John *et al.,* 1977). The clinical criteria for normalcy used by Matousek and Petersen set a standard that has been followed in the development of subsequent quantitative EEG databases. Table 2.1 shows the listing of clinical criteria for inclusion into the Matousek and Petersen QEEG database. These clinical criteria should be considered as a minimum standard for the screening and elimination of individuals with histories of neurological problems. These same clinical criteria were used in the creation of the early E. R. John (John, 1977; John *et al.,* 1977) reference database and in the later Thatcher (1987) reference EEG database.

In addition to these nominal clinical criteria for exclusion, additional objective criteria should also be applied if available. For example, measures of intelligence, neuropsychological functioning, school achievement, successful life work, etc., should also be considered when individuals are selected for inclusion in a "reference normative" database.

C. STATISTICAL STANDARDS OF QEEG DATABASES

A fundamental rule of parametric statistics is the rule of *independent Gaussian distributions* in which each measurement is independent of all other measures and each one exhibits a histogram shape referred to as a *bell-shaped* curve. Mathematically the bell-shaped curve or *Gaussian distribution* is defined as:

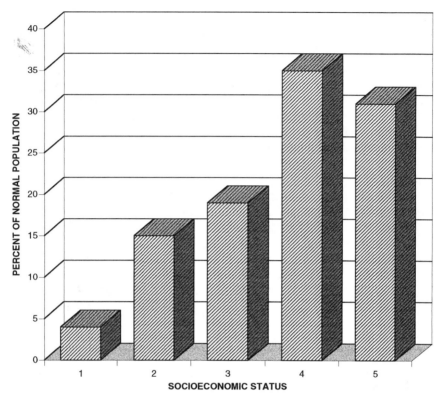

FIGURE 2.1   The distribution of socioeconomic status in the Thatcher (1987) EEG reference normative database as measured by the Hollingshead four-factor criteria (Hollingshead, 1975).

$$Y = \frac{N}{\sigma \sqrt{2\pi}}\, \bar{e}^{(x-v)^2/2\sigma^2}$$

where Y = height of the curve for particular values of X, π = 3.1416, e = 2.7183, and N = number of cases, which means that the total area under the curve is N, and N and σ = mean and standard deviation of the distribution, respectively. This equation can be simplified by writing it in standard-score form with a mean of 0 and a standard deviation of 1. When we substitute 0 and 1 for the mean and standard deviation, respectively, then we can write:

$$Y = \frac{1}{\sqrt{2\pi}}\, e^{-z^2/2}$$

Here Z is a standard score on X and is equal to $(x - v)/\sigma$. The score Z is a deviation in standard deviation units measured along the baseline of the curve from a mean of 0, deviations to the right of the mean being positive and those to the left negative. By substituting different values of

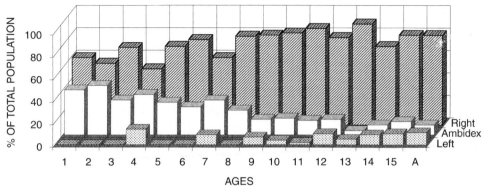

FIGURE 2.2   The distribution of handedness as a function of age in the Thatcher (1987) EEG reference normative database as measured by an eight-item "laterality" test consisting of three tasks to determine eye dominance, two tasks to determine foot dominance, and three tasks to determine hand dominance. Scores ranged from –8 (representing strong sinistral or left-hand preference) to +8 (representing strong dextral or right-hand preference). Ambidextrous subjects were defined by a laterality score between plus and minus 2.

Z in the preceding formula, different values of Y can be calculated. For example, when $Z = 0$, $Y = 0.3989$ or, in other words, the height of the curve at the mean of the normal distribution in standard-score form is given by the number 0.3989. For $Z = +1$, $Y = 0.2420$, and for $Z = +2$, $Y = .0540$. For purposes of assessing deviation from a NDB, the values of Z above and below the mean, which include a proportion 0.95 of the area of the Gaussian, is commonly used as a level of confidence (i.e., to minimize Type I and Type II errors, or the probability of saying something is present when in fact it is not, or saying something is not present when in fact it is,

TABLE 2.1   Neurological Normalcy Criteria

A neurological questionnaire and interview with the subjects and/or, parents and guardians were conducted. Entry into the normative data base required:

1. An uneventful prenatal, perinatal and postnatal period.
2. No disorders of consciousness.
3. No head injury with cerebral symptoms.
4. No history of central nervous diseases.
5. No convulsions of emotional, febrile, or other nature.
6. No abnormal deviation with regard to mental and physical development.

respectively). As shown in Fig. 2.3, the proportion 0.95 or 95% of the area of the Gaussian curve falls within the limits $Z = 1.96$ with the proportion of 0.05 or 5% falling outside of these limits. Similarly, 99% of the area of the curve falls within, and 1 % outside, the limits $Z = 2.58$.

The Gaussian or normal distribution, especially when used in a multivariate statistical test, provides methods to ensure independence of measures or zero correlation between different measures as they relate to statistical inferences. However, note that the Gaussian distribution is a hypothetical distribution that, in sampling procedures, is never actually achieved. That is, the ideal of the Gaussian equation can only be obtained mathematically but, in real life sampling procedures, one can never exactly reproduce a Gaussian distribution. Therefore, in the real world of sampling statistics, efforts must be taken to minimize departures from a Gaussian distribution. The most serious type of deviation from normality is *skewness* or an unsymmetrical distribution about the mean (e.g., a tail to the left or right of the mean), while the second form of deviation from normality, *kurtosis,* is the amount of peakedness in the distribution, which is not as serious a problem because the variance is symmetrical about the mean (mean = median). However, it is preferable to attempt to achieve normality as best as one

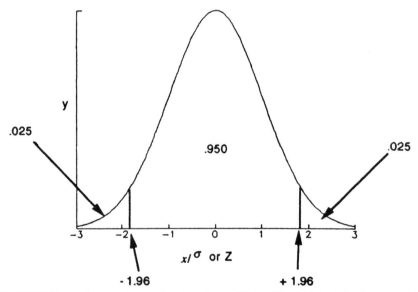

FIGURE 2.3   A normal curve showing values of Z (±1.96), which includes the proportion that is o.95 of the total area. The left and right tails of the distribution show probability values of 0.025 (one-tailed). The clinical evaluation of EEG measures relies on such a normal distribution by estimating the probability of finding an observed EEG value in a given range of a normal population.

can to ensure unbiased estimates of error. The primary reason to achieve *normality* is that many different frequency distributions can be reduced to one common distribution and that for this distribution "there is an exact and known relationship between z-score and percentile rank" (Ferguson, 1976). In this way comparisons between "apples and oranges" such as evoked potentials and EEG or relative power and coherence, etc., can be made with accuracy (see Fig. 2.3).

It is important to note that automatic and blindly applied transformations of EEG measures do not ensure improved normality of the sampling distribution. For example, John *et al.* (1988) state that specific logarithmic and ratio transforms must be applied to all EEG power, EEG coherence, EEG phase, and EEG amplitude asymmetries in order to best approximate a normal distribution. However, it is simple to demonstrate that while some transformations may improve the normality of distributions, these same transforms can also degrade the normality of the distributions. For example, Table 2.2 shows the effects of transforms on the distributions of the adult EEG variables in the Thatcher (1987) reference normative database. Note that, with the exception of absolute phase (which tends to be chi-square distributed because of the absolute transform), the EEG variables were relatively well behaved and normally distributed without using any trans-

TABLE 2.2   Gaussian Distributions (<3.0) of Normative EEG Measures from the Thatcher NDB (1987)

	Untransformed (<3)		Transformed[a] (<3)	
	Skewness (%)	Kurtosis (%)	Skewness (%)	Kurtosis (%)
Rel. power (64)[b]	100	100	100	100
Tot. power (16)	100	69	100	94
Amp. asymmetry				
Int (32)	100	94	99	85
Left (112)	100	98	100	91
Right (112)	100	99	100	70
Coherence				
Inter (32)	97	91	91	82
Left (112)	98	93	100	93
Right (112)	99	87	100	94
Phase				
Inter (32)	77	56	100	91
Left (112	87	57	99	94
Right (112)	79	58	93	88

[a] Mathematical details of the transformations are given in Thatcher *et al.* (1983, 1986).
[b] Number of variables for each QEEG category are given in parentheses.

forms. Actually one would expect, based on the central limits theorem, that EEG variables would approximate a normal distribution as the sample size increases, assuming no artifact or experimenter bias.

D. STATISTICAL INFERENCES AND RELIABILITY

Two crucial and interacting concepts to determine valid statistical inference are (1) multiple statistical comparisons and (2) reliability. Because a large number of statistical comparisons are typically conducted in QEEG analyses, one must be careful not to bias judgments that unduly favor Type I or Type II statistical errors. A general rule to determine the number of expected statistically significant differences is to multiply the total number of statistical tests by the probability value or alpha value, for example, if there were 100 statistical tests then $100 \times 0.05 = 5$ or one would expect five statistically significant effects by chance alone. A second method is to use a "multiple comparison" adjustment procedure such as the Schafe, Bonferroni, or Tukey adjustments. The latter adjustments for multiple comparisons tend to bias the statistical tests toward reduced Type I errors and increased Type II errors (Hays, 1973; Ferguson, 1976) and thus must be used with caution. Another method to minimize inferential errors is to compute a multivariate analysis of variance (MANOVA) test, which provides a measure of the overall F value of statistical significance after adjusting for the intercorrelations among all of the variables. When comparisons to a NDB are being made, the null hypothesis for the MANOVA is that $Z = 0$ and that there are equal numbers of negative and positive Z values with the overall mean $Z = 0$. If a statistically significant overall F (e.g., $P < 0.05$) is present, then adjustments for multiple comparisons are not necessary (Hays, 1973).

The second statistical concept to minimize inferential errors is the concept of reliability.

Reliability can be measured using the reliability coefficient defined as:

$$r_{xx} = \frac{S_1^2}{S_2^2}$$

where S_1^2 is the sample estimate of variance of the QEEG test at time one and is the estimate of the sample variance of the QEEG from the same patient at test time two. The reliability coefficient is the proportion of obtained variance that is true (i.e., reliable) and thus it represents the reproducible aspects of the QEEG test. For example, if $S_2^2 = 400$ and $S_1^2 = 360$, then the reliability coefficient = 0.90. This means that 90% of the variation in the QEEG measurement is attributable to variation in true score, the remaining 10% being attributable to error. Two practical methods of estimating QEEG reliability are the *test–retest method* and the *split-half method*. In the former method, a beginning of session sample of EEG is compared to an end of session sample of EEG; in the latter, a testing session is randomly divided into two samples of EEG (assuming the size of each sample is of adequate length, e.g., >60 sec). Reliability measures are important because they minimize both Type I and Type II errors and eliminate the need for multiple comparisons because "by definition chance findings do not replicate" (Duffy *et al.*, 1994, p. XI).

E. UNIFORM DATA ACQUISITION PROCEDURES AND QUALITY CONTROL

Quality control is essential for the creation of a useful reference QEEG database. That is, the EEG amplifiers must be carefully calibrated with daily checks to ensure their stability, and precisely the same acquisition parameters and procedures must be employed on all individuals included in the database. In addition, all artifact must be eliminated prior to subsequent spectral analyses. Furthermore, comparisons of an individual to a given NDB must be made using the exact same procedures and settings that were used for the creation of the NDB.

F. ARTIFACT REJECTION

An especially important aspect of quality control is the elimination of EEG artifact due to eye movements, blinking, scalp sweating, movement, EKG, and other nonbrain sources of electrical activity. The importance of this aspect of EEG data acquisition cannot be overstated. In the Thatcher normative QEEG database, the artifact rejection procedures were contained within two general categories of EEG artifact rejection: (1) on-line artifact rejection and (2) off-line artifact rejection. The on-line method used representative samples of artifact-free EEG as templates to reject subsequent EEG samples that significantly deviated from the template. The on-line method also used diagonal eye electrodes to detect eye movement as well as eye blinks. EEG technicians were trained to minimize artifact during the acquisition procedure by monitoring the subject's EEG and helping maintain the subject's comfort and alertness. In the off-line category of artifact rejection, considerable and diligent efforts must be made to edit out any evidence of artifact after the EEG has been digitized. Care must be taken to ensure that "real" electrophysiological events are not deleted or misinterpreted as artifact, such as high-amplitude alpha or beta bursts or mu rhythms. Properly trained individuals are necessary for this phase of quality control. As mentioned previously, in the Thatcher reference QEEG database, both on-line and off-line procedures were followed, and trained Ph.D.s visually edited the data from each and every subject who was included in the database. Only when there was agreement between two independent QEEG readers were the final sections of EEG passed on for the purposes of power spectral analysis.

In addition to nonbrain types of artifact (e.g., eye movements, blinking, sweating, EMG, EKG), brain state types of artifacts such as drowsiness or medication effects must also be either removed or controlled for. Drowsiness is a physiological state that produces slowing of the alpha rhythm and diffuse delta (and associated eye movements). Fortunately, the effects of drowsiness and sleep on the EEG have been extensively studied and such states are easily recognized by a competent EEG technician or clinician. In the case of medication effects, whenever possible patients should be taken off of medication at least 48 hr prior to testing. When this is not possible, then the clinician must take into consideration the published effects of a given medication or class of medications on the EEG when comparing a patient to a NDB.

G. QEEG REFERENCE DATABASE
AGE DISTRIBUTION

It is important that a reference normative database contain an adequate sample size per age group, and that it span the age range from birth to adulthood. Of course, the adequacy of the sample size will vary depending on the age under investigation. For example, development is most rapid in young children and, consequently, the sample size should be large enough to resolve EEG changes related to brain development (see Section IV,A and Fig. 2.4). The importance of spanning the period from birth to adulthood stems from the fact that growth spurts and rapid sequences of change in brain development must be understood in the context of the entire human life span (Thatcher, 1991, 1992, 1994a; Thatcher et al., 1996).

Figure 2.4 shows the number of subjects per year in the Thatcher reference normative database, which spans the human developmental period from 2 months to 82 years of age. The largest number of subjects are in the younger ages (e.g., 1–6 years) when the EEG is changing most rapidly. Figure 2.5 shows the distribution of WRAT (Wide Range Achievement Test) reading, spelling, and arithmetic scores as well as full-scale IQ, verbal IQ, and performance IQ in the Thatcher reference normative database. Figure 2.5 shows that the average IQ is consistently greater than 100 and that there is consistency in mean values on the three subcategories of the IQ test as well as the WRAT.

H. TIME OF DAY AND OTHER
MISCELLANEOUS FACTORS

Many uncontrollable factors influence the frequency spectrum of the EEG. For example, time between EEG acquisition and food intake (Fishbein et al., 1990), the content of food intake (Cantor et al., 1986; Fishbein et al., 1990), the amount of previous night's sleep, the time of

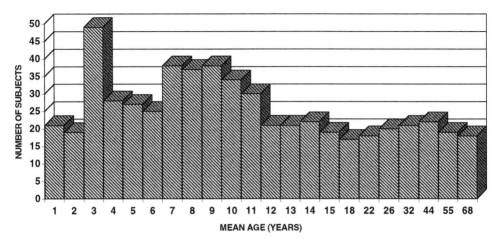

FIGURE 2.4 The number of subjects per year in the Thatcher EEG reference normative database. The database is a life span database with 2 months of age being the youngest subject and 82.3 years of age being the oldest subject. This figure shows the number of subjects constituting mean values, which range from a mean of 0.5 to 68 years of age and constituting a total number of subjects = 564.

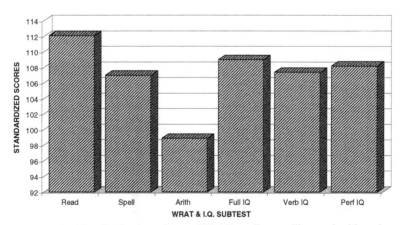

FIGURE 2.5 The distribution of mean WRAT reading, spelling, and arithmetic scores as well as the mean full-scale IQ, verbal IQ, and performance IQ in the Thatcher 1987 EEG reference normative database (NDB).

day on a circadian basis, and motivational interest and involvement of the subject, etc. In general, these factors are all confounded, and it would require an enormously expensive and large sample size to control each factor individually. Even if one could control each factor, such experimental control would preclude the practical use of a NDB since each patient's EEG would have to be acquired in a precisely matching manner. Statistical randomization is one of the best methods to deal with these uncontrollable and miscellaneous factors. Statistical randomization of a NDB involves randomly varying time of day of EEG acquisition, time between food intake and EEG acquisition, food content and EEG acquisition, etc., across ages, gender, and demographics. Because these factors are confounded with each other, randomization with a sufficient sample size will result in increased variance, but, nonetheless, convergence toward a Gaussian distribution. Such convergence, even in the face of increased variance, still allows quantitative comparisons to be made and false-positive and false-negative error rates (i.e., sensitivity and specificity) to be calculated. The method of statistical randomization of miscellaneous factors was used in the Matousek and Petersen, Thatcher, John, and Duffy EEG normative databases, and the sensitivity and specificity of these databases range from approximately 80 to 97% (John et al., 1988; Thatcher et al., 1989; Duffy et al., 1994).[3]

III. POWER SPECTRAL MEASURES OF A QEEG DATABASE

Because of the inherent complexity of EEG, some form of time series analysis must be employed in order to derive quantifiable measures. The spectral analysis is an efficient method for transforming a time series into frequency (i.e., hertz or cycles per second) (Blackman & Tukey, 1958). The power spectral analysis is only one, albeit a very powerful, method of time series quantification. In general, all spectral analyses decompose a complex wave form into a linear sum of more elemental wavelike components; in other words, they transform a time series into the frequency domain. In the case of Fourier analyses, the elemental waves are sine waves; in the

---

[3] Recently Kaiser and Sterman (1994) have stated that they have observed circadium periods in the EEG spectrum in a cross-sectional study. However, because they conducted a cross-sectional study and not a repeated measures study their conclusions are not supportable. For example, the Kaiser and Sterman study was confounded with time between food intake and EEG acquisition, food content and EEG acquisition, and amount of sleep deprivation experienced the night before EEG acquisition. These and other factors can only be controlled in a counterbalanced or randomized repeated measures design.

case of wavelet analyses the elemental components are wavelets,[4] etc. The elemental wavelike components of spectral analyses are often referred to as *basis functions* with the important mathematical property of *orthonormality*. The property of orthonormality allows for efficient and linear analyses to be performed in which the independence of the basis functions can be established, and simple translations from the time domain to the frequency domain can occur.

Many time series methods are available for obtaining a frequency spectrum (Otnes & Enochson, 1972). These methods have been mathematically derived and thoroughly tested and no further discussion of the mathematical details of these methods will be provided. One need only state that given the specific spectral method used to derive a specific reference QEEG database, then one must also use, as close as possible, that exact same method to compare individuals to that database.

Most important for the present discussion is determining which derived EEG measures are most critical for the clinical evaluation of a patient, and then ensuring that these measures are included in a reference normative QEEG database. The clinical usefulness of derived QEEG measures is the result of work presented in the scientific literature that has evolved during the past 25 years. Much of this literature has been reviewed in various publications and the reader is encouraged to consult these reviews and this literature (John *et al.,* 1988; John, 1997; Duffy *et al.,* 1994; Harmony, 1983; Thatcher *et al.,* 1983, 1989; Nunez, 1981, 1995; Lopes da Silva, 1991). Approximately 98% of the energy of the human EEG lies between 0 and 30 Hz; thus some form of spectral analysis within the delta (e.g., 0.5–3.5 Hz), theta (e.g., 3.5–7 Hz), alpha (e.g., 7–13 Hz), and beta (e.g., 13–25 Hz) frequency bands is crucial. The finer the frequency resolution the better (e.g., alpha 1 and 2 or beta 1, 2, 3); however, there are operational or practical limits. This is because for every single increase in the number of frequency bands, there is a squared increase in the number of statistical comparisons (i.e., for every element in a matrix there are at least two indices). Thus, given the practical limits of data analysis the authors of all current NDBs decided to emphasize only a selected subset of EEG frequencies. The Duffy, John, and Thatcher databases share in coverage of the broad spectrum of EEG from 0.5 to 30 Hz, albeit in slightly different ways and with different emphases. Within the frequency range from approximately 0.5 to 30 Hz, there are in general three categories of EEG spectral variables that are of critical clinical value: (1) power and/or amplitude,

---

[4] A wavelet is a symmetrical and smoothly increasing and decreasing oscillation that forms a "basis" function for orthonormal mathematical formulations. What makes wavelet bases especially interesting is their property of *self-similarity,* that is, every function in a wavelet basis is a dilated and translated version of one (or possibly a few) *mother function.* Once one knows about the mother function, one knows everything about the basis functions.

(2) coherence and/or phase, and (3) derived ratios of amplitude and/or coherence and/or phase.

A. POWER AND/OR AMPLITUDE
EEG SPECTRAL MEASURES

Power is defined as uv^2/cycle/sec, whereas amplitude is simply the square root of power or uv/cycle/sec. Power and amplitude are related by the square and square root operation and transformations can be easily performed to ensure Gaussian normality and, at the same time, to fit one's preference.[5] For the purposes of this chapter, I will refer to EEG amplitude with the understanding that a simple squaring or square root operation equates amplitude and power. The crucial issues are these: (1) To what extent is amplitude sensitive to nonbrain electrical activity (i.e., various non-EEG artifacts such as EKG, EMG, eye movements)? (2) Is EEG amplitude Gaussian distributed? It is important to note that both power and amplitude are considered as "absolute amplitude" measures in that they do not only reflect the amplitude of brain-generated EEG, but also nonbrain factors such as scalp resistance, skull thickness, and various anisotropic conductance properties of the skull (i.e., different regions of the skull have different conductances), dura, and scalp (Nunez, 1981, 1995). A typical method often used to control for differences in scalp resistance and skull thickness, etc., is to calculate *relative power* and/or *relative amplitude*. Relative amplitude is a percentage measure and is defined as amplitude in a frequency band divided by total amplitude (i.e., total amplitude is the sum of amplitude in all frequencies). In other words, relative amplitude is a measure of the proportion of total amplitude within a given frequency band and is thus independent of skull thickness, skin resistance, and other, but not all, nonbrain sources of electrical activity (e.g., eye movement artifact, EKG artifact, etc., are not controlled for).

The clinical relevance of EEG amplitude is related to the fact that the output of a population of EEG generators is a function of the number of generators, the synchrony of the generators, and the geometry of the generators (Thatcher & John, 1977; Nunez, 1981, 1995). Synchrony is especially important because mathematical calculations show a highly disproportionate (e.g., >8:1) contribution to surface EEG amplitude by small groups of synchronous generators (e.g., Lopes da Silva, 1991; Cooper *et al.*, 1965;

---

[5] The term *power* was historically used by engineer's during the early applications of spectral analysis. As explained by Blackman and Tukey (1958) power is defined as the square of the autocovariance function in which the time measure was voltage across (or current through) a pure resistance of one ohm, and the time average power dissipated in the resistance is strictly proportional to the variance of the voltage or current. This important special case is the origin of the adjective "power" and readers should be aware that a pure one ohm resistance is not commonly present in EEG recordings.

Nunez, 1981, 1995). It is known that the relative and absolute amplitude of the EEG varies as a function of age and scalp location and with the extent of clinical pathology. For example, at birth approximately 40% of the amplitude of the EEG is in the delta frequency band and only approximately 10% of EEG amplitude is in the alpha frequency band. In a normal adult, the percent of amplitude in the delta frequency band is typically less than 5%, whereas the percent amplitude in the alpha band is approximately 70% in occipital areas. In normal subjects delta activity arises from the slow, modulated depolarization of large masses of geometrically aligned cortical pyramidal cells, such as that which occurs during states of expectancy and sustained attention (Walter *et al.,* 1965; Karahashi & Goldring, 1966; Tecce & Cattanach, 1995; Toro *et al.,* 1994; Polich, 1997). Such low-amplitude (e.g., 1–20 uv) slow fluctuations in EEG occur within the DC (1- to 5-sec time constant) to the 3.5-Hz delta frequency range. Thus, EEG amplitude in the delta frequency range is not necessarily a sign of pathology or abnormal thalamic hyperpolarization, rather it may be a normal part of the EEG spectrum.

The studies of delta activity in normal subjects illustrate why it is critical that the full frequency spectrum from, at least, 0.5 to 30 Hz be measured and spectrally analyzed (less than 0.5 Hz, e.g., 0.1 or 0.01 Hz, is even better). It is a serious error not to measure this full range of EEG frequencies because of the developmental importance of EEG frequency changes and the clinical interpretation that can be derived from the EEG. Caution should be exercised when using a database with restrictive high-pass filter settings (e.g., 3 dB down at 2.0 Hz), thus limiting the delta frequency band. Other limitations of restrictive filtered databases are their nonapplicability to infants, children, adolescents, or geriatric populations and their lack of coherence and phase EEG measures. Most importantly, however, the filter limitation of delta EEG frequencies generally reduces the usefulness of such databases. For example, meaningful comparisons of relative power to other existing databases (e.g., Matousek & Petersen, 1973, and the Duffy, John, and Thatcher databases) are difficult if not impossible with restrictive filtered databases.

B. BIOPHYSICAL LINKAGE BETWEEN MRI AND EEG AMPLITUDE

The EEG arises from the rapid movement of ions (e.g., Na, K, Cl) across large areas of neural membrane surface, thus it is not surprising that strong correlations between magnetic resonance imaging biophysical measures of the brain and the EEG have been reported (Thatcher *et al.,* 1998a, 1998b). The biophysics of the MRI arises from the spin–lattice (called longitudinal or T1) and spin–spin (transverse or T2) relaxation properties of water protons. The rate at which water protons relax in a magnetic field is dependent on the extent to which the water protons are "free" (e.g., CSF) or bound by protein and/or lipid molecules (e.g., gray and white matter) (Szafer *et al.,* 1995; Kroeker & Henkelman, 1986; Does & Snyder, 1995). Recent MRI and EEG correlation analyses have demonstrated different relationships between the cerebral white matter and gray matter and the EEG in closed head injured patients. For example, a commonly reported clinical EEG correlate of white matter damage is increased delta EEG amplitude (Jasper & van Buren, 1953; Gloor *et al.,* 1968, 1977). In contrast, decreased EEG amplitude and not increased delta amplitude is a common clinical correlate of gray matter damage (Gloor *et al.,* 1968, 1977; Golden-sohn, 1979a, 1979b). Independent confirmation of this relationship between EEG amplitude and white versus gray matter damage was provided in biophysical MRI correlations to the EEG in traumatic brain-injured patients (Thatcher *et al.,* 1998a). The results of this study indicate that the integrity of the protein–lipid membranes of the brain as measured by T2 relaxation time is correlated with cognitive performance and the amplitude of the scalp recorded EEG. This further emphasizes the importance of not arbitrarily restricting the frequency spectrum of the EEG when compiling EEG normative databases or comparing individuals to EEG normative databases. Concordance between QEEG and MRI and multimodal integration of QEEG with other imaging methods is likely to enhance the value of QEEG normative databases and discriminant analyses in the future.

C. EEG COHERENCE MEASURES

Coherence is mathematically analogous to a cross-correlation coefficient in the frequency domain. For example, coherence that varies between 0 and 1 is a measure of the linear association between two variables in the same manner as the square of a correlation coefficient. Mathematically, the correlation coefficient is defined as:

$$r = \frac{\Sigma xy}{\sqrt{\Sigma x^2 \, \Sigma y^2}}$$

where x and y are deviations from the means $\bar{x}$ and $\bar{y}$, respectively. The correlation coefficient is a very important mathematical concept because it represents the linear association between two measures, independent of their relative or absolute amplitudes. Amplitude normalization occurs because the numerator of the equation (i.e., cross-products or covariance) is divided by the standard deviation in the denominator. EEG coherence is similarly defined as:

$$Coh_{xy} = |R_{xy}(f)|^2 = \frac{|S_{xy}(f)|^2}{S_{xx}(f) \, S_{yy}(f)}$$

where $|S_{xy}(f)|^2$ is the square of the cross-power spectral density at a given

TABLE 2.3   Relationships between Normalized and Unnormalized Measures[a]

	Time-domain transient EPs	Frequency-domain EEG, steady-state EPs
Unnormalized	Covariance	Cross-spectral density
Normalized	Correlation function and coefficient	Coherence and coherency

[a] From Nunez et al. (1997).

frequency (f), and $S_{xx}(f)$ and $S_{yy}(f)$ are the respective autopower spectral densities at that same frequency (f) (Otnes Enochson, 1972; Bendat Piersol, 1980). Similar to the correlation coefficient, coherence is the ratio of covariance divided by the cross products of variance and, thus, coherence is normalized with respect to amplitude. This is important in EEG analysis because it means that coherence evaluates the linear association or correlation between the EEG waveforms recorded from two different scalp locations, independent of the EEG amplitude at either location. Recently, Nunez et al, (1997) thoroughly evaluated the electrophysiological bases of coherence, including issues about reference electrodes and Laplacian derivations, etc. The reader is encouraged to consult this important review. Table 2.3 from Nunez et al. (1997) illustrates the relationships between normalized and unnormalized EEG measures.[6]

EEG coherence has considerable clinical utility and can directly reflect neural network connectivity and neural network dynamics. Nunez (1981) first pointed out that EEG coherence does not simply decrease as a function of interelectrode distance, but rather can increase with increased electrode separation. Thatcher et al. (1986) systematically investigated this feature of human EEG coherence and experimentally elaborated Nunez's suggestion that EEG coherence reflects the action of corticocortical connections and specific corticocortical fasiculi by developing a *two-compartmental* model of EEG coherence. The two-compartmental model of EEG coherence is based on Braitenberg's (1978) two-compartment analysis of cortical axonal fiber systems in which compartment A is composed of the basal dendrites that receive input primarily from the axon collaterals from neighboring or "short-distance" pyramidal cells, whereas compartment B is composed of the apical dendrites of cortical pyramidal cells that receive input primarily from "long-distance" intracortical connections. The short-

[6] There may be confusion about the terms 'coherency' versus 'coherence'. Coherency is defined as the complex number representation where the real or x-axis is magnitude and the imaginary or y-axis is phase (Bendat and Piersol, 1980). Coherence is defined as the absolute length of the resultant vector or hypotenuse in the complex plane (i.e., the coherency complex number representation). Thus, mathematically, coherence is defined as where x and y are the coherency measures of magnitude and phase.

distance A system primarily involves local interactions on the order of millimeters to a few centimeters, whereas the long-distance B system involves long-range interactions on the order of several centimeters, which represent the majority of white matter fibers. These two systems exhibit two different network properties. System B, due to reciprocal connections and invariant apical dendrite terminations, is involved in long-distance feedback or loop systems. In contrast, system A, due to the variable depths of the basal dendrites, is not involved in reciprocal loop processes but rather in a diffusion type of transmission process (Thatcher *et al.*, 1986; Pascual-Marqui *et al.*, 1988; Braitenberg, 1978; Braitenberg & Schuz, 1991).

The developmental changes in EEG coherence in a large group of subjects reflects changes in the mean coupling constants between connected neuronal networks (Thatcher *et al.*, 1987, 1998b; Thatcher, 1992, 1994b). For example, if we assume that volume conduction has been controlled, then we can postulate a relationship between EEG coherence and two primary factors: (1) the number of corticocortical connections between neural assembles and (2) the synaptic strength of connections between neural assemblies (the terms *corticocortical connections* and *intracortical connections* are considered synonymous). This relationship is mathematically described as

$$\text{coherence} = (N_{ij} \times S_{ij}),$$

where N_{ij} is a connection matrix of the number of connections between neural systems i and j, and S_{ij} is the synaptic strength of those connections. This equation provides a logical means by which developmental changes in EEG coherence can be interpreted in terms of changes in the number and strength of connections between assemblies of neurons (Thatcher *et al.*, 1986, 1987; Pascual-Marqui *et al.*, 1988; Thatcher, 1992, 1994b). For example, increased coherence is due to either an increase in the number and/or strength of connections and, conversely, decreased coherence is due to a decreased number and/or reduced strength of connections. The neurophysiological mechanisms responsible for the changes in the numbers or strengths of connections include axonal sprouting, synaptogenesis, myelenation, expansion of existing synaptic terminals, pruning of synaptic connections, presynaptic changes in the amount of neurotransmitter, and changes in the postsynaptic response to a given neurotransmitter (see discussions by Purves, 1988; Huttenlocher, 1984, 1990). Currently, measures of EEG coherence cannot discern among these various possibilities.

The two-compartmental model of EEG coherence was subsequently confirmed and extended by Pasqual-Marquie *et al.* (1988) and many others (Wright, 1997; Nunez, 1981, 1995). Strong support for the existence of a genetically determined short- versus long-distance two-compartmental model of EEG coherence was also provided (van Baal, 1997; van Baal *et al.*, 1998). For example, in the van Baal (1997) paper an extensive EEG study of 209 identical and nonidentical twin pairs was conducted in which the heritability of short-distance EEG coherence was approximately 48% and the heritability of long-distance EEG coherence was approximately 70%. As van Baal concluded ". . . the heritability estimates provide support for a two compartmental model [of human EEG coherence]" (p. 110) and that "The fact that heritability was sensitive to the direction of cortico-cortical connectivity supports Thatcher's claim that individual differences in coherence reflect axonal connectivity of the brain" (p. 111).

As mentioned previously, EEG coherence has been shown to exhibit clear and important clinical utility. For example, EEG coherence is often one of the strongest and most sensitive of all QEEG measures in studies of schizophrenia (Ford et al., 1986; Nagase et al., 1992; Shaw et al., 1979), obsessive compulsive disorders (Prichep et al., 1993), depression (Prichep et al., 1990), mild traumatic brain injury (Thatcher et al., 1989), prediction of outcome following head injury (Thatcher et al., 1991), Alzheimer's disease and infarct dementia (Leuchter et al., 1987, 1992) and ADHD (John et al., 1988; Marosi et al., 1992). In addition, a growing number of studies have also demonstrated relationships involving EEG coherence during normal cognitive function (Petch, 1996; Thatcher et al., 1983, 1987; Thatcher, 1992; Lubar, 1997). Given the anatomical and physiological relevance of EEG coherence plus its clinical utility, it would be remiss for any normative reference EEG database to omit either intrahemispheric or interhemispheric EEG coherence.

D. BIOPHYSICAL LINKAGE BETWEEN MRI AND EEG COHERENCE

As mentioned previously (Section III,B) the EEG arises from the rapid movement of ions (e.g., Na, K, Cl) across the neural membrane surfaces of large numbers of neurons, and correlations between MRI biophysical measures of the brain and the EEG amplitude have been reported (Thatcher et al., 1998a). Biophysical correlations between MRI measures of T2 relaxation time and EEG coherence have also been reported (Thatcher et al., 1998b). The biophysical analyses showed that in closed head injured patients lengthened T2 relaxation times of the cortical gray and white matter were related to (1) decreased EEG coherence between short interelectrode distances (e.g., 7 cm), (2) increased EEG coherence between long interelectrode distances (e.g., 28 cm), and (3) differences in EEG frequency in which T2 relaxation time was most strongly related to the gray matter in the delta and theta frequencies. The results were interpreted in terms of reduced integrity of protein–lipid neural membranes and the efficiency and effectiveness of short- and long-distance EEG coherence compartments following traumatic brain injury.

E. EEG PHASE MEASURES

EEG phase is usually computed at the same time as is EEG coherence. EEG phase is operationally defined by the amount of time shift of one time series with respect to another in the computation of coherence. The phase of the coherence function is the phase angle or time delay in milliseconds for S_{xy} where x and y are the EEG times series recorded from channel x and channel y. The EEG phase delay between two channels is measured whenever EEG coherence is measured because they are intrinsically related. Studies by Thatcher et al. (1986) have shown that EEG phase delays increase as a function of interelectrode distances and can be used to estimate axonal conduction velocities (Nunez, 1981, 1995). EEG phase has also been shown to be related to the underlying corticocortical connectivity of the human brain and has also been demonstrated to carry considerable clinical utility (Thatcher et al., 1989, 1991). Unlike EEG coherence, however, EEG phase is more variable and less stable and must be evaluated with even more caution than EEG coherence. The instability of EEG phase results from the fact that complex numbers exhibit a fundamental discontinuity in their computation of phase angle. That is, 0^0 and 360^0 are adjacent to each other, thus resulting in large variability. To minimize this inherent variability, Thatcher et al. (1986, 1987) computed absolute phase (i.e., no negative numbers). However, even with this transformation and additional logarithmic transformations EEG phase is more variable and less stable than EEG coherence. Nonetheless, EEG phase is an important measure because it can be related to the intrinsic integrity of the gray and white matter as well as the conduction velocities of the corticocortical white matter (Nunez, 1981, 1995; Thatcher et al., 1986). Also, whenever EEG phase is significantly greater than 0 msec (e.g., >5 msec) then EEG coherence, by definition, does not reflect volume conduction.

In the studies of mild to severe traumatic brain injury by Thatcher et al. (1989, 1991), EEG phase was among the most predictive and sensitive of all of the EEG measures. Again, given the anatomical and physiological relevance of EEG phase plus its clinical utility it would be remiss for any normative reference EEG database to omit EEG phase. However, the reader must be cautioned in the use of EEG phase and urged to rely on EEG experts who have experience in the clinical interpretations and use of EEG phase before making clinical judgments based exclusively on EEG phase.

F. EEG AMPLITUDE DIFFERENCES AND RATIOS

Differences in the absolute amplitude between EEG recorded at different electrode sites has also been shown to be of clinical utility (John et al., 1977; John, 1977). In normal subjects the greater the amplitude differences, the higher the mean IQ (Thatcher *et al.,* 1983). These amplitude differences appear to be within a "normal range" and reflect the amount of functional differentiation in the brain. When pathology is present or neurologically suboptimal conditions persist, then there may be significantly increased or decreased amplitude differences. For example, a focal lesion may result in increased delta activity or reduced beta activity, which may manifest itself through a change in amplitude differences between two or more electrode sites. A problem with amplitude differences is that they, by themselves, do not reveal the source of the differences. For example, increased F3–C3 amplitude difference may be due to reduced amplitude at F3 or C3 or increased amplitude at F3 or C3 (i.e., one electrode relative to the other). Examination of the z-score referenced amplitudes may reveal which electrode location is increasing or decreasing and thus contributing most to the amplitude differences.

Other ratios such as theta/beta ratios, or alpha/beta ratios, or theta/alpha ratios also have been shown to be of clinical use (Matousek & Petersen, 1973; Lubar, 1997). Again, however, in order to understand more about the source of these ratio differences examination of the EEG frequencies from individual leads is necessary.

IV. UNIVARIATE STATISTICS VERSUS MULTIVARIATE STATISTICS

Most QEEG databases use both parametric univariate statistics and parametric multivariate statistics to compare an individual to a NDB. The z score or t score is commonly used in statistics to express the deviation from the normative reference EEG values in standard deviations. While univariate and multivariate z scores or Wilk's lambda scores are useful statistics, the reader must use caution in order to understand the Type I (saying something is true when it is actually false) and Type II (saying something is false when it is actually true) statistical errors that are inherent in any inferential statistical procedure. In addition to adherence to univariate and multivariate normal distributions, inferential "inflation" through the use of too many z or t tests can occur (i.e., increased Type I errors due to multiple comparisons). Various statistical adjustments are available to minimize the problem of multiple comparisons. As a rule of thumb, all one has to do is count the total number of statistical tests within a specific EEG category (e.g., power, coherence, phase) and then multiply by 0.05 to determine the number of expected statistically significant comparisons at the probability of $P < 0.05$, which will occur by chance alone. For example, if 112 univariate EEG coherence z tests were performed then, one would expect 5.6 significant (i.e., $P < 0.05$) comparisons to occur by chance alone. Bonferroni or Scheffe or Tukey statistical adjustments for multiple comparisons assume sampling distribution independence and are often overly conservative (i.e., increase Type II errors). As described in Section II,C one can simply eliminate the need for multiple comparisons by calculating reliability in a test–retest or split-half sampling procedure (Duffy et al., 1994; Ferguson, 1976).

Important virtues of univariate statistical analyses are their simplicity and both frequency and anatomical localization strengths. For example, a four-standard-deviation z score in excess delta activity from the left parietal region (P3) points the clinician toward a possible focal abnormality that is located near to the left parietal area of the brain. With univariate statistics as a guide then, biofeedback or neurotherapy can be focused on a particular region(s) and/or EEG frequency with some confidence as to the location of the deviation from expected values. A similar argument pertains to EEG coherence in which both short- and long-distance EEG coherence z-score deviations from the NDB may carry specific clinical meaning and help target neurotherapy. In contrast, multivariate statistics are complicated and reduce the ability to localize the possible regions of the brain that are deviating from normal frequency and/or amplitude. Multivariate statistics involve the summation and correlation correction among a set of variables. This necessarily results in a type of anatomical and frequency smearing in which large collections of variables are averaged. As a consequence multivariate statistics may or may not improve the sensitivity and specificity of QEEG and certainly reduce one's ability to devise neurotherapy strategies. For example, if one obtains a multivariate discriminant score of -1.85 involving 20 or more EEG measures, how does this help one plan neurotherapy sessions in order to address this multivariate deviation from normal? In the case of univariate statistics, the answer is to identify the most deviant and clinically significant EEG feature and/or location and then use neurotherapy to move this deviant area toward the normal distribution. In the case of multivariate statistics, EEG measures in combination may be giving rise to the multivariate Wilk's lambda or discriminant values, and individual univariate statistics may actually be normal (Cohen & Cohen, 1983).

In general, it is best to restrict the use of multivariate statistics by making specific hypotheses and posing specific clinical questions. A good use of multivariate statistics is in the development of discriminant functions when a large number of variables are combined into a single equation designed to classify members of two or more populations, followed by independent validation of the discriminant function (John et al., 1977, 1988; Thatcher et al., 1989). However, the univariate examination of the individual variables that are entered into the discriminant function is important in understanding the physiological and clinical meaning of the analyses. It is for this reason that publications of discriminant functions should contain a list of the variables that are used in the discriminant function (Thatcher et al., 1989). Factor analyses are useful to reduce redundancy and the size of measure sets; however, the ability of factor analyses to predict outcome or provide inferential statistics is limited (Cohen & Cohen, 1983). Multivariate analyses of variance (MANOVA) are useful in determining group differences after adjusting for intercorrelations; however, MANOVA is limited in its predictive and clinical application. A similar argument holds for other multivariate statistics such as Mahalanobis distances (Cohen and Cohen, 1983).

A. QEEG DISCRIMINANT FUNCTIONS

The use of QEEG discriminant functions for the purposes of diagnosis is an important and complicated topic. QEEG discriminant functions must only be used in conjunction with other medical or clinical evaluations and diagnoses should never be made simply based on a given QEEG discriminant score (Duffy et al., 1994). A QEEG discriminant function should not be used blindly or without explicit publication of the internal details of the discriminant function in a refereed journal, for example, exact descriptions of the variables that are contained in the discriminant function, exact description of the subjects in the study, the number of false positives, the number of false negatives, the sensitivity and specificity, and one or more independent cross validations. Publication of these details is necessary and required before a discriminant function can be used, especially the independent cross validation(s) of the discriminant function. All of these criteria were met in the Thatcher et al. (1989) mild head injury discriminant function, which has been used in various settings since its publication.

The Thatcher et al. (1989) QEEG discriminant function is sometimes confused with a "normative EEG database" (i.e., NDB). A discriminant function is not a "database," rather it is a set of derived measures that act as a type of "pattern recognition" procedure. A discriminant function examines a limited number of variables to determine whether the multivariate combination or pattern of the variables is sufficient to classify an individual as a member of a clinical group or an age-matched normal control group. The discriminant function merely states that such an EEG pattern is present or absent and provides a statistical estimate of classification accuracy. The clinical merit of a discriminant function is partly measured by the extent that the variables co-vary with the predicted pathology, for example, increased coherence in the frontal lobes or decreased high-frequency amplitude in the case of mild head injury (Thatcher et al., 1989). All of these factors must be considered when one uses a QEEG discriminant function.

Importantly, a discriminant function is a multivariate statistical test and it suffers from all of the problems mentioned in Section IV and later in Section V,B with regard to its use for neurotherapy. Univariate NDB comparisons are the best choice for tailoring neurotherapy, with the evaluation of the EEG discriminant function being used as a diagnostic monitor and not as a variable to be used in the biofeedback procedure itself (at least not until a definitive study is published that shows that this is possible).

B. GROWTH SPURTS IN EEG DEVELOPMENT

Human cerebral development does not occur as a smooth linear function of age; rather it is nonlinear with abrupt changes and oscillations (Thatcher *et al.,* 1987; Thatcher, 1991, 1992, 1994a; van Baal, 1997; van Baal *et al.,* 1998; Chugani, 1996). One advantage of a life span database, extending from birth to adulthood, is that it provides the ability to evaluate the rate and time course of human cerebral development. Two issues of major importance in understanding child development are (1) determining the extent to which the left and right cerebral hemispheres develop at different rates and at different ages and (2) determining whether human cerebral development occurs as a smooth function of age or in discrete steps or stages. If human cerebral development occurs in steps or stages, then it is important to quantify which cortical regions develop at what ages. The clinical relevance of this information concerns (1) the early detection of deviation from normal development in individual children, (2) the use of EEG to evaluate remediation strategies and treatment, and (3) the distinction between a psychological versus an organic basis for a childhood disorder.

The presence of specific cerebral growth spurts at particular ages are clearly revealed in the Thatcher EEG normative reference database (Thatcher *et al.,* 1987; Thatcher, 1994a). Figure 2.6 shows the velocity curves or the first derivatives (i.e., rate of change of EEG coherence) of the developmental trajectories of mean EEG coherence from the subgroupings of electrode pairs that had the highest factor loadings (e.g., >0.80) (Thatcher, 1991). Growth spurts were defined by a positive peak in the first derivative (i.e., a postnatal time of maximum growth) in multiple interelectrode combinations. These data provide evidence of differential cerebral development and stages of corticocortical connectivity. The data also emphasize the nonlinearity of cerebral development and, thus, the need for large sample sizes especially during the early childhood and adolescent periods of development.

The nonlinearity of EEG development was also demonstrated in analyses of Matousek and Petersen's (1973) NDB using relative power (Thatcher, 1980; Epstein, 1986). Thus, caution should be exercised when using NDBs that are based on a linear analysis of EEG development or NDBs that use linear regression equations to adjust for age (John *et al.,* 1980). For example, in the John *et al.* (1988) studies, linear regression analyses of the Matousek and Petersen (1973) NDB as well as the NYU Medical Center NDB were conducted. Examination of the figures shows that a relatively small amount of variance was explained by the linear regression equations (e.g., <70%, personal analyses); thus considerable error is inherently present when such

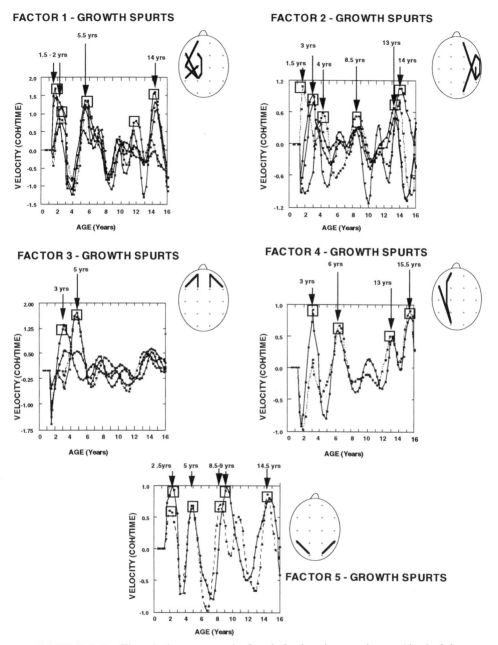

FIGURE 2.6 The velocity curves or the first derivatives (mean coherence/time) of the developmental trajectories of mean EEG coherence from the subgroupings of electrode pairs that had the highest factor loadings (e.g., >0.80) (Thatcher, 1991). Growth spurts were defined by a positive peak in the first derivative (i.e., a postnatal time of maximum growth) in multiple interelectrode combinations. [From Thatcher, R. W. (1994b). Cyclic cortical reorganization: Origins of cognitive development. *In* "Human Behavior and the Developing Brain" (G. Dawson & K. Fischer, eds.). Guilford Publications, New York.]

linear analyses are used for normative EEG database comparisons. Because of the inherent nonlinearity in human life span EEG development, the Thatcher NDB does not use age regression and, instead, uses sliding averages with approximately a 3-month age resolution (see Fig. 2.6 and Thatcher, 1992, 1994a, 1994b).

V. INDIVIDUALIZATION OF NEUROFEEDBACK BASED ON REFERENCE QEEG EVALUATION

To my knowledge, the first use of a life span NDB for the purpose of neurotherapy was devised by Thatcher and Lexicor, Inc., in 1992. Prior to 1992, neurotherapy protocols were widely different, with differing rationalizations and were essentially arbitrary protocols. A typical pre-1992 example is where a given neurotherapist discovered by practice that a certain protocol, for example, increased alpha power at C3, seemed to help his or her patients. Over time, this protocol became favored and was sometimes promoted as an "effective" protocol for neurotherapy. Also, prior to 1992, the objective assessment of the strengths and weakness of the neural organization in a given patient was not used. Also, the ability to use EEG to determine whether there was an "organic" basis for a patient's complaints was not used, and neurotherapy protocols were not individualized based on the EEG features and anatomy most deviant from normal. It was the recognition of this "gap" in clinical assessment that inspired the first applications of a NDB to the field of neurotherapy.

As mentioned in the introduction, there are at least three primary reasons to use a NDB for the purposes of neurotherapy: (1) to assess the neurological status of the patient and to determine to what extent there is a neurological basis of the patient's complaints (i.e., the issue of *organicity*), (2) to identify possible strengths and weaknesses in the organization and electrophysiological status of the patient's brain so as to aid in the efficient and optimal design or choice of neurotherapy (i.e., the issue of *therapy design*), and (3) to evaluate objectively the efficacy of treatment by comparing the patient's EEG before and after treatment (i.e., the issue of *treatment evaluation*). A fourth and long-term reason is that the use of a standardized and objective EEG test may help promote scientific publications in refereed journals to evaluate the efficacy of neurotherapy as it applies to different patient populations.

A. THE ISSUE OF ORGANICITY

As a clinical practitioner one is often faced with the problem of determining whether or to what extent purely psychological factors such as divorce, emotional trauma or malingering, etc., are contributing to the symptoms presented by the patient. Conversely, the clinical practitioner needs to understand whether and to what extent there is a neurological or organic basis for the patient's complaints. Quite different therapeutic strategies follow depending on the extent to which neurological and/or psychological factors are contributing to the patient's problems. The use of QEEG evaluations using a NDB may aid in this basic clinical assessment by disclosing a *normal* EEG or an *abnormal* EEG. For example, the presence of large-amplitude *spikes and waves* may indicate the presence of epilepsy for which a conventional neurological evaluation and treatment may be recommended. The presence of large-amplitude delta activity may indicate an infarct or other lesion for which an MRI and other neurological evaluations would be recommended. Less dramatic and more subtle neurological problems may also be present such as significant deviation from normal in short- and/or long-distance EEG coherence or in the scalp distribution of EEG power. In the latter case, neurotherapy may be highly recommended. At this point it is important to reemphasize, however, that the clinical practitioner must always be aware of the statistical issues involved in the use of a NDB (see Sections II–IV) and, thus, must ultimately rely on his or her clinical judgment. Such reliance is not unique to QEEG since any clinical diagnostic test provides only partial information that is taken into consideration in the context of the total patient evaluation when rendering a clinical judgment.

B. THE ISSUE OF THERAPY DESIGN

The use of a NDB allows for individualization of EEG biofeedback or neurotherapy based on the EEG features and anatomical locations that are most deviant from normal. Individualization of neurotherapy should be contrasted to the standard pre-1992 methods whereby a relatively rigid and arbitrary set of predesigned protocols was administered without awareness of an individual's EEG profile. NDB analysis allows for more standardization of neurotherapy across patients and clinics, as well as for potentially more efficient neurotherapy by focusing on the most statistically deviant EEG features and anatomy. It is important to recognize that neurotherapy is a young and growing discipline, and NDB should not be considered the only diagnostic method or be used to the exclusion of biofeedback protocols that a given clinician has found useful. However, NDB-based neurotherapy can help facilitate the optimal or most efficient biofeedback approach and help quantify the efficacy of any given protocol, in comparison to other protocols. Finally, univariate and not multivariate analyses are the most straightforward and interpretable QEEG measures to be used for therapy design. Caution should be exercised in the design of neurotherapy based solely on multivariate analyses, including discriminant analyses and Mahalanobis statistics.

C. THE ISSUE OF TREATMENT EVALUATION

There are at least two categories of treatment evaluation where NDBs play a role: (1) improved efficiency or optimization of treatment protocols and (2) evaluation of the outcome of treatment. Both of these categories benefit from a quantitative and objective evaluation of methods used for treatment as well as the efficacy of treatment. For example, the extent to which brain EEG measures *normalize*, that is, exhibit reduced z scores following treatment can be assessed using a NDB (Hoffman *et al.,* 1996a, 1996b). The test–retest reliability and the sensitivity and specificity of treatment can also be evaluated using an EEG NDB. The number of sessions may be minimized by evaluating the progress of "normalization" of the EEG with respect to an NDB. Through this means, reduced time and cost to patients and third-party insurers plus improved therapeutic outcome may be derived.

The use of a NDB for the purposes of neurotherapy is relatively recent and the full benefits of such an approach have yet to be realized. However, it is believed that increasing knowledge about anatomy and the genesis of EEG coupled with the objective evaluation of a patient's EEG with respect to a normative database will facilitate the application of neurotherapy and eventually improve its efficacy as well as its scientific foundations.

REFERENCES

Barlow, J. S. (1993). "The Electroencephalogram: Its Patterns and Origins." MIT Press, Cambridge, MA.

Bendat, J. S., & Piersol, A. G. (1980). "Engineering Applications of Correlation and Spectral Analysis" John Wiley & Sons, New York.

Blackman, R. B., & Tukey, J. W. (1958). "The Measurement of Power Spectra." Dover, New York.

Blanchard, E. B., & Epstein, L. H. (1978). "A Biofeedback Primer." Addision-Wesley, Reading, MA.

Braitenberg, V. (1978). Cortical architectonics: General and areal. *In* "Architectectonics of the Cerebral Cortex" (M. A. B. Brazier and H. Petsche eds.). Academic Press, New York.

Braitenberg, V., & Schuz, A. (1991). "Anatomy of the Cortex: Statistics and Geometry." Springer Verlag, Berlin.

Cantor, D. S., Thatcher, R. W., & Ozand, P. (1986). Choline supplementation in Downs Syndrome: A case study. *Psychol. Reports* **58,** 207–217.

Chugani, H. T. (1996). Neuroimaging of developmental nonlinearity and developmental pathologies. *In* "Developmental Neuroimaging: Mapping the Development of Brain and Behavior" (R. W. Thatcher, G. R. Lyon, J. Rumsey, & N. Krasnegor, eds.). Academic Press, San Diego.

Cohen, J., & Cohen, P. (1983). "Applied Multiple Regression/Correlation Analysis for the Behavioral Sciences." L. Erlbaum Associates, Hillsdale, New Jersey.

Cohen, M. J. (1975). Recent developments in biofeedback training. *In* "Eighth Annual Winter Conference on Brain Research," pp. 1–10, January 18–25, 1975, Colorado Springs, CO. Brain Information Service/BRI Publications Office.

Cooper, R., Winter, A. L., Chow, H. J., & Walter, W. G. (1965). Comparison of subcortical, cortical and scalp activity using chronically indwelling electrodes in man. *EEG Clin. Neurophysiol.* **18,** 217–228.

Does, M. D., & Snyder, R. E. 1995. T2 relaxation of peripheral nerve measured in vivo. *Mag. Res. Imag.* **13,** 575–580.

Duffy, F., Hughes, J. R., Miranda, F., Bernad, P., & Cook, P. (1994). Status of quantitative EEG (QEEG) in clinical practice, 1994. *Clin. EEG* **25**(4), VI–XXII.

Epstein, H. T. (1986). Atages in human brain development. *Develop. Brain Res.* **30,** 114–119.

Ferguson, G. A. (1976). "Statistical Analysis in Psychology and Education," 4th Ed., McGraw-Hill, New York.

Fishbein, D., Thatcher, R. W., & Cantor, D. S. (1990). Ingestion of carbohydrates varying in complexity produce differential brain responses. *Clin. EEG* **43,** 21–36.

Ford, M. R., Goethe, J. W., & Dekker, D. K. (1986). EEG coherence and power in the discrimination of psychiatric disorders and medication effects. *Biol. Psychiat.* **21,** 1175–1188.

Fox, S. S., & Rudell, A. P. (1968). Operant controlled neural event: Formal and systematic approach to electrical codifing of behavior in brain. *Science* **162,** 1299–1302.

Frackowiak, R. S. J., Friston, K. J., Frith, C. D., Dolan, R. J., & Mazziotta, J. C. (1997). "Human Brain Function." Academic Press, San Diego.

Gillies, R. J. (1994). "NMR in Physiology and Biomedicine." Academic Press, San Diego.

Gloor, P., Kalabay, O., & Giard, N. (1968). The electroencephalogram in diffuse encephalopathies: Electroencephalographic correlates of gray and white matter lesions. *Brain* **91,** 779–802.

Gloor, P., Ball, G., & Schaul, N. (1977). Brain lesions that produce delta waves in the EEG. *Neurology* **27,** 326–333.

Goldensohn, E. S. (1979a). Use of the EEG for evaluation of focal intracranial lesions. *In* "Current Practice of Clinical Electroencephalography" (D. Klass & D. Daly, eds.). Raven Press, New York.

Goldensohn, E. S. (1979b). Neurophysiologic substrates of EEG activity. *In* "Current Practice of Clinical Electroencephalography" (D. Klass & D. Daly, eds.). Raven Press, New York.

Harmony, T. (1983). "Functional Neuroscience," (E. R. John & R. W. Thatcher, eds.), Vol. III. L. Erlbaum Associates, Hillsdale, New Jersey.

Hays, W. L. (1973). "Statistics for the Social Sciences," 2nd Ed. Holt, Rhinehart and Winston, New York.

Herscovitch, P. (1994). Radiotracer techniques for functional neuroimaging with positron emission tomography. *In* "Functional Neuroimaging: Technical Foundations" (R. W. Thatcher, M. Halletr, T. Zeffro, E. R. John, & M. Huerta, eds.). Academic Press, San Diego.

Hetzler, B. E., Rosenfeld, J. P., Birkel, P. A., & Antoinetti, D. N. (1977). Characteristics of operant control of central evoked potentials in rats. *Physiol. Behav.* **19,** 527–534.

Hollingshead, B. (1975). "Four Factor Index of Social Status." Yale Station Press, New Haven, CT.

Hoffman, D. A., Stockdale, S., Van Egeren, L., Franklin, D., Schwaninger, J., Bermea, A., & Graap, K. (1996a). EEG neurofeedback in the treatment of mild traumatic brain injury. *Clin. EEG* **27**(2), 6.

Hoffman, D. A., Stockdale, S., Van Egeren, L., Franklin, D., Schwaninger, J., Bermea, A., & Graap, K. (1996b). Symptom change in the treatment of mild traumatic brain injury using EEG neurofeedback. *Clin. EEG* Suppl. No. 1, p. 7.

Huttenlocher, P. R. (1984). Synapse elimination and plasticity in developing human cerebral cortex. *Am. J. Mental Deficiencies* **88,** 488–496.

Huttenlocher, P. R. (1990). Morphometric study of human cerebral cortex development. *Neuropsychologia* **28,** 517–527.

Jasper, H., & van Buren, J. (1953). Interrelationship between cortex and subcortical structures: Clinical electroencephalographic studies. *EEG Clin. Neurophysiol.* **4**(Suppl), 168–188.

John, E. R. (1977). "Functional Neuroscience" (E. R. John & R. W. Thatcher, eds.), Vol. II. L. Erlbaum Associates, Hillsdale, New Jersey.

John, E. R. Karmel, B., Corning, W. Easton, P., Brown, D., Ahn, H., John, M., Harmony, T., Prichep, L., Toro, A., Gerson, I., Bartlett, F., Thatcher, R., Kaye, H., Valdes, P., & Schwartz, E. (1977). Neurometrics: Numerical taxonomy identifies different profiles of brain functions within groups of behaviorally similar people. *Science* **196**, 1393–1410.

John, E. R., Ahn, H., Prichep, L., Trepetin, M., Brown, D., & Kaye, H. (1980). Developmental equations for the electroencephalogram. *Science* **210**, 1255–1258.

John, E. R., Prichep, L. S., Fridman, J., & Easton, P. (1988). Neurometrics: Computer assisted differential diagnosis of brain dysfunctions. *Science* **293**, 162–169.

Johnson, F. 1997. Editorial Comment. J. Neurotherapy, 2(3), i.

Kaiser, D. A., & Sterman, M. B. (1994). Periodicity of standardized EEG spectral measures across the waking day. Paper presented at Seventh Annual Summer Sleep Workshop Multisite Training Program for Basic Sleep Research, September 16–21, Lake Arrowhead, CA.

Karahashi, Y., & Goldring, S. (1966). Intracellular potentials from "idle" cells in cerebral cortex of cat. *EEG Clin. Neurophysiol.* **20**, 600–607.

Kroeker, R. M., & Henkelman, R. M. (1986). Analysis of biological NMR relaxation data with continuous distributions of relaxation times. *J. Magn. Reson.* **69**, 218–235.

Leuchter, A. F., Spar, J. E., Walter, D. O., & Weiner, H. (1987). Electroencephalographic spectra and coherence in the diagnosis of Alzheimer's-type and multi-infarct dementia. *Arch. Gen. Psychiat.* **44**, 993–998.

Leuchter, A. F., Newton, T. F., Cook, I. A., Walter, D. O., Rosenberg-Thompson, S., & Lachenbruch, P. A., (1992). Changes in brain functional connectivity in Alzheimer's disease. *Arch. Neurol.* **51**, 280–284.

Lopes da Silva, F. H. (1991). Neural mechanisms underlying brainwaves: From neural membranes to networks. *EEG Clin. Neurophysiol.* **79**, 81–93.

Lubar, J. F. (1997). Neocortical dynamics: Implications for understanding the role of neurofeedback and related techniques for the enhancement of attention. *Appl. Psychophysiol. Biofeedback* **22**, 111–126.

Marosi, E., Harmony, T., Sanchez, L., Becker, J., Bernal, J., Reyes, A., de Leon, A. D., Rodriguezd, M., & Fernandez, T. (1992). Maturation of the coherence of EEG activity in normal and learning-disabled children. *EEG Clin. Neurophysiol.* **83**, 350–357.

Matousek, M., & Petersen, I. (1973). Frequency analysis of the EEG in normal children and adolescents. *In* "Automation of Clinical Electroencephalography" (P. Kellaway & I. Petersen, eds.), pp. 75–102. Raven Press, New York.

Minshew, N. J., & Pettegrew, J. W. (1996). Nuclear magnetic resonance spectroscopic studies of cortical development. *In* "Developmental Neuroimaging: Mapping the Development of Brain and Behavior" (R. W. Thatcher, G. R. Lyon, J. Rumsey and N. Krasnegor, eds.). Academic Press, San Diego.

Nagase, Y., Okubo, Y., Matsuura, M., Kojima, T., & Toru, M. (1992). EEG coherence in unmedicated schizophrenic patients: Topographical study. *Biol. Psychiat.* **32**, 1028–1034.

Nunez, P. (1981). "Electrical Fields of the Brain." Oxford University Press, Cambridge.

Nunez, P. (1995). "Neocortical Dynamics and Human EEG Rhythms." Oxford University Press, New York.

Nunez, P. L., Srinivasan, R., Westdorp, A. F., Wijesinghe, R. S., Tucker, D. M., Silberstein, R. B., & Cadusch, P. J. (1997). EEG coherency I: Statistics, reference electrode, volume conduction, Laplacians, cortical imaging and interpretation at multiple scales. *EEG & Clin. Neurophysiol.* **103**, 499–515.

Otnes, R. K., & Enochson, L. (1972). "Digital Time Series Analysis." John Wiley & Sons, New York.

Pascual-Marqui, R. D. (1995). Reply to comments by Hamalainen, Ilmoniemi and Nunez. *In* "Source Localization: Continuing Discussion of the Inverse Problem" (W. Skrandies, ed.), pp. 16–28. ISBET Newsletter No. 6 (ISSN 0947-5133).

Pascual-Marqui, R. D., S. L., Valdes-Sosa, P. A., & Alvarez-Amador, A. (1988). A parametric model for multichannel EE spectra. *Int. J. Neurosci.* **40**, 89–99.

Petsche, H. (1996). Approaches to verbal, visual and musical creativity by EEG coherence analysis. *Int. J. Psychophysiol.* **24**, 145–159.

Polich, J. (1997). On the relationship between EEG and P300: Individual differences, aging and ultradian rhythms. *Int. J. Psychophysiol.* **26**(1), 299–317.

Prichep, L. S., John, E. R., Essig-Peppard, T., & Alper, K. R. (1990). Neurometric subtyping of depressive disorders. *In* "Plasticity and Morphology of the CNS" (C. L. Cazzullo, G. Invernizzi, E. Sacchetti, & A. Vita, eds.). M. T. P. Press, London.

Prichep, L. S., Mas, F., Hollander, E., Liebowitz, M., John, E. R., Almas, M., DeCaria, C. M., & Levine, R. H. (1993). Quantitative electroencephalographic (QEEG) subtyping of obsessive compulsive disorder. *Psychiat. Res.* **50**(1), 25–32.

Purves, D. (1988). "Brain and Body: A Trophic Theory of Neural Connections." Harvard University Press, Cambridge, MA.

Rosenfeld, J. P. (1990). Applied psychophysiology and biofeedback of event-related potentials (brain waves): Historical perspective, review, future directions. *Biofeedback Self-Regul.* **15**(2), 99–119.

Rosenfeld, J. P., Rudell, A. P., & Fox, S. S. (1969). Operant control of neural events in humans. *Science* **165**, 821–823.

Savitzky, A., & Golay, M. J. E. (1964). Smoothing and differentiation of data by simplified least squares procedures. *Analyt. Chem.* **36**, 1627–1639.

Schwartz, M. S. (1995). "Biofeedback: A Practitioner's Guide," 2nd ed. Guilford Press, New York.

Shaw, J. C., Brooks, S., Colter, N., & O'Connor, K. P. (1979). A comparison of schizophrenic and neurotic patients using EEG power and coherence spectra. *In* "Hemisphere Asymmetries of Function in Psychopathology" (J. Gruzelier, & P. Flor-Henry, eds.). Elsevier, Amsterdam.

Sterman, M. B. (1996). Physiological origins and functional correlates of EEG rhythmic activities: Implications for self-regulation. *Biofeedback Self-Regul.* **21**(1), 3–33.

Striefel, S. (1995). The odyssey of ethics and application standards. *Biofeedback* **23**(4), 8–9.

Szafer, A., Zhong, J., & Gore, J. C. (1995). Theoretical model for water diffusion in tissues. *Magn. Reson. Med.* **33**, 687–712.

Tecce, J. J., & Cattanach, L. (1995). Contingent negative variation (CNV). *In* "Electroencephalography: Basic Principles, Clinical Applications and Related Fields," (E. Niedermeyer & F. Lopes da Silva, eds.), 3rd Ed. Williams & Wilkins, Baltimore, MD.

Thatcher, R. W. (1980). Neurolinguistics: Theoretical and evolutionary perspectives. *Brain Language* **11**, 235–260.

Thatcher, R. W. (1987). Federal Copyright (TXu-347-139) of the "Life span EEG Normative Database" and all of its derivatives, transformations, and revisions.

Thatcher, R. W. (1991). Maturation of the human frontal lobes: Physiological evidence for staging. *Develop. Neuropsychol.* **7**(3), 370–394.

Thatcher, R. W. (1992). Cyclic cortical reorganization during early childhood. *Brain Cognition* **20**, 24–50.

Thatcher, R. W. (1994a). Psychopathology of early frontal lobe damage: Dependence on cycles of postnatal development. Develop. *Pathol.* **6**, 565–596.

Thatcher, R. W. (1994b). Cyclic cortical re-organization: Origins of human cognitive development. *In* "Human Behavior and the Developing Brain" (G. Dawson & K. Fischer, eds.). Guilford Press, New York.

Thatcher, R. W. (1995). Tomographic electroencephalography/magnetoencephalography: Dynamics of human neural network switching. *J. Neuroimag.* **5**, 35–45.

Thatcher, R. W. (1998). Normative EEG databases and EEG biofeedback. *J. Neurother.* **2**(4), 8–39.

Thatcher, R. W., & John, E. R. (eds.). (1977). "Functional Neuroscience, Vol. 1: Foundations of Cognitive Processes." L. Erlbaum Associates, Hillsdale, New Jersey.

Thatcher, R. W., McAlaster, R., Lester, M. L., Horst, R. L., & Cantor, D. S. (1983). Hemispheric EEG asymmetries related to cognitive functioning in children. In "Cognitive Processing in the Right Hemisphere" (A. Perecuman, ed.). Academic Press, New York.

Thatcher, R. W., Krause, P., & Hrybyk, M. (1986). Corticocortical association fibers and EEG coherence: A two compartmental model. EEG Clin. Neurophysiol. 64, 123–143.

Thatcher, R. W., Walker, R. A., & Guidice, S. (1987). Human cerebral hemispheres develop at different rates and ages. Science 236, 1110–1113.

Thatcher, R. W., Walker, R. A., Gerson, I., & Geisler, F. (1989). EEG discriminant analyses of mild head trauma. EEG Clin. Neurophysiol. 73, 93–106.

Thatcher, R. W., Cantor, D. S., McAlaster, R., Geisler, F., & Krause, P. (1991). Comprehensive predictions of outcome in closed head injury: The development of prognostic equations. Ann. N Acad Sci. 620, 82–104.

Thatcher, R. W., Hallet, M., Zeffiro, T., John, E. R., & Huerta, M., (1994). "Functional Neuroimaging: Technical Foundations." Academic Press, San Diego

Thatcher, R. W., Lyon, G. R., Rumsey, J., & Krasnegor, N. (1996). Developmental Neuroimaging: Mapping the Development of Brain and Behavior." Academic Press, San Diego.

Thatcher, R. W., Camacho, M., Salazar, A., Linden, C., Biver, C., & Clarke, L. (1997). Quantitative MRI of the gray-white matter distribution in traumatic brain injury. J. Neurotrauma 14, 1–14.

Thatcher, R. W., Biver, C., Camacho, M., McAlaster, R, & Salazar, A. M. (1998a). Biophysical linkage between MRI and EEG amplitude in traumatic brain injury. NeuroImage 7(4), 1–16.

Thatcher, R. W., Biver, C., McAlaster, R., & Salazar, A. M. (1998b). Biophysical linkage between MRI and EEG coherence in traumatic brain injury. NeuroImage 8, 307–326.

Toro, C., Deuschl, G., Thatcher, R. W., Sato, S., Kufts, C., & Hallett, M. (1994). Event related desynchronization with voluntary movements in humans: Subdural scalp recordings and their relation to movement-related cortical potentials. EEG Clin. Neurophysiol. 93(5), 380–389.

Walter, W. G., Cooper, R., McCallum, C., & Cohen, J. (1965). The origin and significance of the contingent negative variation or "expectancy" wave. EEG Clin. Neurophysiol. 18, 720–731.

Wright, J. J. (1997). EEG simulation: Variation of spectral envelope, pulse synchrony and 40 Hz oscillation. Biol. Cybernet. 76, 181–194.

van Baal, C. (1997). A genetic perspective on the developing brain. Dissertation, Vrije University, The Netherlands, Organization for Scientific Research (NWO), ISBN: 90-9010363-5.

van Baal, G.C., de Geus, E.J., & Boomsma, D.I. (1998). Genetic influences on EEG coherence in 5-year-old twins. Behav. Genet. 28(1), 9–19.

3

FROM EEG TO

NEUROFEEDBACK

THOMAS H. BUDZYNSKI

Department of Psychosocial and Community Health,
University of Washington,
Seattle, Washington

In this chapter I provide a brief history of the field of neurofeedback. It is from my perspective and I apologize for any significant omissions. It is being told as I know and remember it.

The roots of modern neurofeedback and the related field of quantified EEG or QEEG can be traced back to Berger (1929), who recorded the first human EEG [although Caton (1875), years earlier, had noted that it was possible to record "feeble currents" from electrodes on the surface of the skull]. Berger and others such as Adrian and Matthews later examined the use of the electroencephalogram or EEG as a diagnostic procedure in clinical populations. In an early 1930s paper, Adrian and Matthews (1934) also described what we now know as entrainment of the "Berger rhythm" (10 Hz) induced by a flicker. They found that this phenomenon could occur with flicker frequencies as high as 25 Hz. Of interest to today's neurofeedback specialists, some of whom also use audiovisual stimulation to augment the feedback, was the finding by Adrian and Matthews that the EEG would also reflect harmonics and subharmonics of the stimulating frequency. Moreover, when the flicker was slightly lower or faster than the subject's Berger rhythm, there were often periods of complete irregularity. [Recently Rosenfeld, Reinhart, and Srivastava (1997) found exactly this response in their study of photic stimulation.] Frederick Gibbs and his colleagues Davis and Lennox, in a 1934 paper (Gibbs *et al.*, 1934) described the 3-Hz spike/wave complexes associated with *petit mal* absence seizures (first discovered by Berger). W. Grey Walter named both the "delta" rhythm (Walter,1937) and later the "theta" wave (Walter,1953). Donald Lindsley, Herbert Jasper, and Mary Brazier in the United States were also early pioneers. [See Brazier (1980) for an excellent review of the history of EEG research.]

However, five paths of EEG interest that appeared in the 1960s and 1970s later coalesced about 1990 with a sixth path of addictions application into the area now known as *neurofeedback, neurotherapy,* or *EEG biofeedback.* These are the six paths:

1. The alpha feedback, twilight learning, and alpha/theta protocols
2. The SMR studies
3. The development of QEEG systems
4. EEG database generation
5. Development of the QEEG feedback system
6. The Peniston–Kulkosky protocol

I. THE ALPHA CONNECTION

Quite probably the era of what has come to be called EEG biofeedback or neurofeedback began, in large measure, with the research breakthrough of Dr. Joe Kamiya at the University of Chicago about 1962. Kamiya (1962) discovered that when subjects were told whenever alpha bursts appeared in their EEG they could eventually learn to be aware of subtle cues and control alpha consciously. Later, Kamiya had an electronic unit built that would sound a tone whenever alpha was present. The present author, a graduate student at the University of Colorado in 1965, read of Dr. Kamiya's work in an assigned reading on sleep by a new professor, Dr. Johann Stoyva, who had just completed a postdoctoral position with Kamiya. Later that year, I carried out a case study of thanatophobia using a systematic desensitization paradigm that incorporated alpha EEG feedback training to counter anxiety between visualizations of the fear hierarchy scenes. Because the research findings of Kamiya indicated that the "alpha state" felt peaceful and relaxing, it was reasonable to assume that this state could counter anxiety. With this early form of neurofeedback, the client learned to increase his percent alpha from 10 to 70. Later, in the desensitization sessions, he attempted to produce a high alpha percentage, and when he attained approximately 60% or more, the feedback tone was turned off and a hierarchy scene was presented for his visualization. He signaled when he felt any anxiety, at which time the alpha tone was made available again. Banishing the anxious scene by concentration on the alpha tone allowed a quick, thorough desensitization. Understandably, the more anxiety the scene gen-erated, the longer it took to regain the high alpha percentage (Budzynski & Stoyva, 1972).

This alpha desensitization protocol was very successful (follow-up of 32 years) and resulted in a permanent cure of a long-term phobia in just four sessions. Note that during the desensitization the client suddenly recalled an event from childhood that he had forgotten many years before. That event involved the client and his brother being forced to kiss the face of their dead grandmother as she lay in her open coffin. The client was 4 years old at the time.

The significance of this successful case is not only that it represents one of the first applications of this early neurofeedback technique to a clinical problem, but that it allowed a breakthrough into consciousness of the initial traumatic event just as the alpha/theta protocol does today.

II. THE DAWNING OF BIOFEEDBACK

In the mid- to late 1960s, inspired initially by the operant control of alpha work of Kamiya, which was featured in an article in *Psychology Today* in 1968 (Kamiya, 1968) and by Neal Miller's operant conditioning of autonomic responses in animals (abstracts of his presentations at a collo-quium in Moscow, USSR, became available to me in 1966 when a professor in the office next to mine returned from the colloquium with these papers), a small number of researchers began exchanging phone calls and mimeo-graphed copies of papers about the exciting, new technique of feeding back electrophysiological signals with the goal of teaching people to develop some degree of conscious control over these responses. The group included Joe Kamiya, Joe Hart, Barbara Brown, Thomas Mulholland, Erik Peper, Elmer and Alyce Green, Dale Walters, Ken Gaarder, Johann Stoyva, and myself. During the next 2 years this EEG feedback information exchange group grew rapidly until 1968 when it had become extremely labor intensive to send copies of papers to everyone. Consequently, Barbara Brown orga-nized the first meeting of the by now more than 100 individuals interested in these procedures. It was held in Santa Monica, California, in 1969, and a name for the process was chosen. The new name was *biofeedback,* and at that time it consisted primarily of EEG, with some electromyogram (EMG) and temperature work. All presenters at this first meeting were given 10 minutes. We had 4 years of experimentation to report in this very short period of time. Barbara Brown later published a number of books on biofeedback including the very useful *Alpha Syllabus of Human EEG Alpha Activity* (Brown & Klug, 1974) and *The Biofeedback Syllabus: A Handbook for the Psychophysiologic Study of Biofeedback* (Brown, 1975).

III. A BRIEF LOOK AT OTHER EARLY WORK

Joe Hart is credited with presenting one of the earliest papers on "The Autocontrol of EEG Alpha" at the Society for Psychophysiological Research in San Diego in October 1967 (Hart, 1967). Brown studied the subjective correlates of EEG states as produced with feedback (Brown, 1970). Dewan (1971), working with Mulholland, showed how one could learn to communicate in Morse code by turning alpha on and off. Engstrom, London, and Hart used alpha feedback to enhance hypnotic susceptibility and published the study in 1970. Erik Peper (1972) was one of the first biofeedback researchers to attempt to shape differential alpha characteristics over the two cerebral hemispheres. Subjects received a high tone when alpha appeared in one hemisphere and a low tone when alpha occurred in the other. In two sessions, however, only one of eight subjects was able to switch alpha (and therefore cortical activation) back and forth. Later, Ray, Frediana, and Harman (1977) used a computer-generated visual feedback of hemispheric asymmetry. Subjects were more successful in this study and the investigators concluded that most individuals could selectively control the EEG output of one hemisphere in comparison to the other.

Korein, Maccario, Carmona, Randt, and Miller (1971) reported the use of alpha biofeedback in 23 patients with "psychogenic" disorders. Supposedly, the patients learned the technique in 2 weeks and gained control over their symptomatology. There was, unfortunately, no follow-up report. Another early report was that of Mills and Solyom (1974) who applied alpha biofeedback to ruminating obsessives and had encouraging results. The 5 patients received from 7 to 20 training sessions. The ruminating thought patterns could be blocked during the alpha biofeedback sessions, but this inhibition did not appear to persist after the treatment period. Weber and Fehmi (1975) reported at the annual meeting of the Biofeedback Research Society on the successful use of alpha biofeedback in patients who had psychosomatic or character problems or were severely neurotic. The alpha EEG activity from five different sites was used either simultaneously or sequentially. Patients received 2 sessions per week for a total of 20 sessions. When they learned control of alpha activity they were switched to theta feedback.

Under a grant from the Department of Defense (DOD) during the latter years of the Vietnam War, Stoyva and Budzynski endeavored to develop an EMG/EEG training protocol that could be used to train officers to sleep better under extremely stressful combat conditions. We were able to demonstrate a workable two- or three-stage (depending on level of frontal EMG) training sequence that involved frontal EMG training if this level was high, followed by alpha feedback training, and finally theta training until subjects could take themselves into stage 2 sleep twice in 20 minutes (Sittenfeld *et al.*, 1976).

IV. PERFORMANCE UNDER STRESS

A number of these DOD grants were given to biofeedback researchers to improve performance under stress. Thus was born the idea of peak performance training. To satisfy a second requirement of the grant, to demonstrate it was possible to teach officers to keep their physiological arousal at moderate levels under stress, we developed the PSP or Psychophysiological Stress Profile (Budzynski & Stoyva, 1984). A sequence of relaxation, stress, and recovery was used during which a number of physiological responses were measured. Subjects were asked to perform a cognitive test while being presented with loud, sharp, annoying sounds. Initially we tested the stressor paradigm with volunteers from our department of psychiatry. The performance of the psychiatric department volunteers fell off dramatically under the stressor conditions and we were very encouraged; however, later participants recruited from newspaper advertisements did not deteriorate under our "stressful" condition. Nevertheless, even these individuals showed lower physiological arousal levels during the stressors after biofeedback training than did an untrained control group. Fortunately, the war ended soon thereafter–unfortunately, so did the grant funding.

V. TWILIGHT STATES

If the alpha state was pleasant and relaxing, the theta state was mysterious and unknown, although a good deal of research hinted at its ability to facilitate creative ideas or even recover forgotten memories. Green, Green, and Walters (1971) at the Menninger Foundation had examined the subjective reports of numerous subjects taught to produce alpha and theta waves. The reports included several themes that repeated, such as archetypal images, images of a wise old man, professor, or teacher who would appear to offer advice. Other images were of tunnels, staircases, caves, and pyramids. More importantly, forgotten memories from childhood were reported. Elmer Green once referred to this process as *subliminal dredging.* Perhaps the most telling result was that subjects felt fatigued, sluggish, or nervous the first week or two of training, but these effects were only temporary. Later, there were many reports of calmer, more peaceful, more relaxed feelings, greater energy, clearer thinking, and better concentration. These researchers noted that this extended alpha–theta training produced integrative experiences.

The present author, with assistance from John Picchiottino, began development of a device about 1970 that monitored the EEG from the left hemisphere and would turn on tape-recorded affirmations whenever the EEG showed a theta pattern (Budzynski, 1972, 1976, 1986, 1993, in press). It was believed the positive statements had a higher probability of acceptance than if they were presented in a fully conscious state since the critical screening present in the conscious state would be weakened in the primarily theta state. The therapist also could opt to watch the alpha–theta meter and deliver positive statements to the client with a mike as the client sequenced into a predominantly theta "state." The *twilight learner,* as this was called, also could turn on a second tape player with other messages when the client showed alpha rhythms. The unit featured a background pink noise, which facilitated the appearance of theta rhythms. A "bump" circuit adjusted the tape volume level according to theta amplitude and frequency; that is, the higher the amplitude and the lower the frequency, the louder the volume. The bump circuit served two purposes: It would awaken the user if he began to fall into deeper sleep, and the process of increasing cortical arousal after suggestions were delivered in an unconscious state was believed to act as a "print" command to ensure the longevity of these affirmations in memory.

Several attempts were made to generate grant funding for this device, but the climate of the times fostered the impression that twilight learning was simply brainwashing. However, it has been used in clinical practice with selected cases over a 15-year period (Budzynski, in press).

In 1970 the Menninger group invited a host of clinicians and researchers to the second Council Grove Conference. A wonderful assortment of people were there to demonstrate various methods of obtaining an altered state. Hypnotists put people in trances. The Esalen gurus used their interpersonal techniques with the whole group. Zen and Yoga masters lectured and demonstrated their approaches. We (Budzynski and Stoyva) spoke to people about twilight state learning, but this technique seemed mild compared to the LSD-assisted psychotherapy that many of the conferees were using at that time. Elmer Green (with Dale Walters as the subject) demonstrated an EEG feedback system that reflected energy in select frequency bands with different harmonic tones. The conference was an exciting environment and discussions went on late into the night. Breakfast was served at 8:00 A.M., so the lack of sleep began to add to the aura of "altered-statetism" that pervaded the conference.

As the Greens and Dale Walters at Menninger's and Budzynski and Stoyva at the University of Colorado Medical School pursued theta state applications in the late 1960s and early 1970s, Fehmi (1978) was studying the effect of shaping a global alpha state by using multiple EEG electrodes. Wickramasekera (1976) found that twilight learning increased hypnotic susceptibility. Hardt had joined Kamiya who now was at Langley-Porter Neuropsychiatric Institute and they began to investigate the application of alpha states to a variety of clinical problems (Hardt & Kamiya, 1978).

Finley (1984) at one lab and Fox, Dowman, Rudell, Heinricher, and Rosenfeld at another pioneered the study of operant conditioning of the cortically evoked response (Dowman & Rosenfeld, 1985; Fox & Rudell,

1968; Rosenfeld *et al.,* 1969). Rosenfeld (1990) has documented the history of the operant conditioning of the cortically evoked response research, which eventually led to an application to chronic pain. Tansey (1990) was the first to use feedback of a single frequency (14-Hz) band from the Cz scalp site. His clinical work has included applications to asthma, migraine, ADHD, and chronic fatigue syndrome.

In Germany in the late 1970s and early 1980s Birbaumer and his colleagues began to study the feedback of the slow cortical potential brain response (Birbaumer *et al.,* 1981). Subjects were able to control this brain electrical response and the technique has since been applied to epilepsy (Kotchoubey *et al.,* 1997) and schizophrenia (Mattes *et al.,* 1995).

The writer first met Dr. Birbaumer in Munich in 1973 after returning from presenting a paper on biofeedback called "Biofeedback in the West" at the Seventh International Conference on Psychiatry in Erfurt, East Germany. Dr. Birbaumer had arranged for me to give a lecture at the University of Munich on the same topic. The year before, Dr. Birbaumer had included one our first papers on biofeedback in a text he edited and which was published in 1972 (Budzynski & Stoyva, 1972). We initially had shopped this paper around to several American journals but the paradigm was too novel for them.

The European trip just mentioned was topped off with an invited lecture at Oxford University for the Department of Psychiatry. They wanted to know of this new technique, especially of our work with tension headache and anxiety. Later, at the buffet luncheon with faculty, all they wanted to hear about was the Watergate scandal!

VI. THE FALLING FROM GRACE OF THE ALPHA STATE

Because alpha biofeedback had never managed to allow persons to realize the "Nirvana state" promise indicated by numerous early reports, and because of a few publications such as one by Lynch, Paskewitz, and Orne (1974), which reported that EEG biofeedback subjects seated in a dimly lit room with their eyes open were unable to learn to increase their alpha levels above their baselines recorded in a darkened room with eyes closed, scientists began to lose interest in the phenomenon. In fact, Echenhofer and Coombs (1987) noted that this single negative finding may have had more to do with the decrease in scientific interest in EEG alpha biofeedback than any other single factor. However, Echenhofer and Coombs also referred to the article by Ancoli and Kamiya (1978) which suggested that studies that failed to demonstrate enhancement of alpha activity had one or more methodological flaws. They suggested that the negative findings could be explained by (1) too few training sessions, (2) the use of dichotomous feedback rather than continuous, and (3) training sessions of too short a duration. However, as Echenhofer and Coombs stated, "By the time of the Ancoli and Kamiya publication, most scientific investigators had written off the area of EEG biofeedback training" (p. 162). Many of the EEG researchers turned to other physiological response systems for study in a feedback paradigm. The present author and Stoyva (Budzynski & Stoyva, 1969) had published an article which described an early surface EMG feedback system with a proportional audio tone and a tri-light display. Research funding from NIMH in the mid- to late 1970s was now directed primarily to such EMG biofeedback applications. At our laboratory some work continued on EEG applications; however, it was done surreptitiously.

VII. THE SENSORY MOTOR RHYTHM PATH

In the mid- to late 1960s, Sterman and associates began a series of experiments with cats in order to determine dose levels to convulsion using a type of rocket fuel. Some of the cats used in the rocket fuel study had previously received training in operant conditioning of an EEG rhythm in the band of 12–15 Hz named SMR (sensory motor rhythm) for the cortical region where the rhythm was obtained. As the cats learned to increase SMR they appeared to do so by becoming motorically quiet. The SMR cats also showed a significantly higher convulsion threshold than untrained cats. Sterman hypothesized that humans also could be trained to produce this rhythm and that individuals prone to epileptic seizures might benefit from a higher convulsive threshold. The forthcoming landmark human research, begun by Sterman and associates (Wyricka & Sterman, 1968; Sterman, 1977), did establish that SMR training resulted in decreased seizure activity in humans.

Seifert and Lubar (1975) carried out an early study of SMR and epilepsy in which they introduced the contingency of suppressing theta frequency EEG as well as enhancing SMR. Later, building on the finding of the quieting of the motor system response with SMR training, Lubar and associates hypothesized that this sort of brainwave training might be useful in treatment of attention deficit hyperactivity disorder (ADHD) since these individuals suffered from an overactivation of the motor system in addition to deficits in learning.

Subsequent studies by Lubar and associates (Lubar & Shouse, 1976; Lubar & Bahler, 1976) determined that the EEG protocol that involves increasing activity in the SMR band (12–15 Hz) while suppressing activity in the theta (4–7 Hz) band, significantly improved the ability of ADHD children to focus and concentrate while quieting their hyperactivity. The result was better learning and improved social behavior. The research of Lubar and Lubar and associates (1984) has spawned a number of research studies as well as a large amount of clinical application in the area of ADHD and attention deficit disorder.

VIII. QEEG: THE QUANTIFIED EEG

Computer development, including the fast Fourier analysis chip, allowed raw EEG signals to be quantified in a variety of ways. The computer could not only store the raw signals indefinitely, but could quantify or convert the raw voltage into spectral averages, that is, averages of the voltages in specified frequency bands. Later developments by Duffy (1982) resulted in a topological mapping capability called BEAM (brain electrical activity mapping) that produced a colorful map of various aspects of the QEEG. (An even earlier topological variation had been created by Remond in France using the old PDP8 computers. These maps looked much like the topological charts used by geologists, surveyors, and hikers.) Duffy's maps were generated by the computer from signals obtained by 19 or so surface electrodes located on the scalp according to the International 10/20 EEG placement system. The computer interpolated between these electrode sites and voltage or power levels at these sites and their interpolated values were assigned colors to allow discrimination. The "topo," as it is called, provides a color-coded scan of a momentary EEG pattern, or that of a pattern averaged over some longer time period. Along with the topo came the compressed spectral array. A single spectral array shows the EEG magnitude or power as a function of frequency. Successive spectral arrays differing by a few seconds and layered one behind the other produce what is known as a compressed spectral array or CSA. The CSA graph thus shows how the EEG magnitude or power varies as a function of frequency over time. A listing of the magnitude or power in selected bands is often displayed to the right of the CSA.

IX. EEG DATABASE DEVELOPMENT

A third path contributing to contemporary neurofeedback was the development of large normative and discriminative EEG databases by Duffy (1982), John (1977), who coined the name *neurometrics,* and Thatcher (Thatcher *et al.,* 1989). Data from the full 19-electrode EEG pattern of a given client could now be compared with normative figures in the database. Comparisons are usually made with z-score conversions. These databases, in contrast to qualitative visually read raw EEGs, can provide precise comparisons of not only power and magnitude, but coherence and phase relationships and wave amplitude asymmetrics between various paired sites. Phase and coherence especially cannot be determined accurately by the qualitative method. Note, however, that the spiking or ictal activity often seen in the raw EEG of seizure-prone individuals usually cannot be detected with these averaging techniques.

The QEEG provides information about the EEG that supplements and complements the standard visual interpretation. The normative databases allow the particular client information to be compared with the normative z scores as long as artifacts have been accurately deleted and the database is appropriate for the client in terms of age, sex, and condition. Typically, client data are taken in a resting, eyes-closed state. After artifacting, the data are subjected to fast Fourier transformation. Absolute and relative power, mean frequency, phase and coherence relationships, and wave amplitude asymmetries can be generated for any bandpass or series of bandpasses including the standard delta, theta, alpha, and beta bands. The output of the database operation typically is a printout of z scores referenced to a database for each of the standard frequency bands at each electrode site or pair of sites. Moreover, diagrams for each standard band show any value that deviates from the norm by one, two, or three standard deviations for relative power, phase, coherence, and asymmetry.

Some of the database systems can produce a topographic map of statistical differences between the client and the database norms, or between groups of same-diagnosed clients and the norms. Certain of the systems can also show a topographic mapping of evoked responses. Discriminant databases such as the Mild Head Injury Database by Thatcher *et al.* (1989) permit a head injury case (Glasgow Coma Score between 13 and 15 with no loss of consciousness or a period of unconsciousness of 20 minutes or less) to be compared with a database of mild head injured persons.

X. THE QEEG FEEDBACK SYSTEMS

Until the mid-1980s all EEG feedback systems were standalone devices used by clinicians, or lab systems employed by researchers. However, in this time period (mid-1980s) Edgar Wilson and David Joffe in Boulder, Colorado, had combined ideas and programming skills to develop software to allow a 24-channel QEEG that could be used both for diagnostic purposes and to provide feedback of selected EEG parameters through a multimedia computer display. The system was called the *Neurosearch* and a private company was formed to produce and market it. It might be claimed that the Lexicor Corporation's Neurosearch with its Biolex feedback software and excellent quantification capability became the mainstay instrument of the modern neurofeedback area.

Margaret Ayers (1987), a clinician, was instrumental in the design of an EEG polygraph system that also allowed auditory and visual feedback of the raw EEG as well as filtered traces of the EEG. She has applied it primarily to a large number of head injury cases with reported success. Siegfried Othmer designed a similar system that also included elements of the Ayers device and added some graphic displays, for example, a game driven by several EEG variables. Dr. Othmer and his wife have since been at the forefront of private clinic development featuring their neurofeedback approach to a number of disorders especially ADHD.

Charles Stroebel had also maintained an enduring interest in EEG applications and began development of an EEG feedback system called *CAPSCAN,* which could feed back patterns of EEG including coherence in a colorful topographical-like real-time display. In his 1978 presidential address before the Biofeedback Society of America, Stroebel described the EEG synchrony Capscan system:

> Navigating the ultimate spaces of biofeedback is finally possible with CAPSCAN. It realistically combines Central Nervous System EEG neurofeedback sensitive to brain lateralization (multiple channel power, phase angle, coherence and synchrony) with bilateral peripheral measures of skeletal muscle (EMG), smooth muscle (thermal), and hormonal-immune-neurotransmitter systems (EDR, plethysmography and variants) in a single display to address all four QR (Quieting Reflex) Compass Points of Stress as predicted in the James-Lange Theory of Emotions. . . . As a navigational and clinical tool CAPSCAN possesses unusual emergent and evolutionary power to revolutionize our concepts of central and peripheral integration in Mind/Body Cartography.

Adam Crane later helped Stroebel develop CAPSCAN into an affordable research and clinical instrument.

XI. THE MODERN ERA OF NEUROFEEDBACK

In 1989 Peniston and Kulkosky published their first paper on the use of an alpha–theta protocol. Their treatment combined some preliminary relaxation and hand temperature training with later neurofeedback-induced theta-state or twilight state goal imagery to reduce alcohol addiction. The surprising results with 20 male alcoholics randomly assigned to either the neurofeedback/imagery group plus conventional therapy, or conventional therapy only, and 10 nonalcoholic controls, astounded the biofeedback community, and the study report initially was met with a great deal of skepticism. The MCMI (Millon Multiaxial Inventory) results (Peniston & Kulkosky, 1990) showed the treatment clients improving significantly on 13 scales as opposed to only two significant improvements and a significant increase in compulsivity for the alcoholic controls. The treatment group also showed significant improvement on the Beck Depression Inventory and improvement on seven of the 16PF (16 Personality Factor) scores, whereas the conventional treatment alcoholic group showed a decline on almost all of the 16 categories. The nonalcoholic controls produced normal scores and showed no significant changes on pre- and post-tests. Later, a 36-month follow-up showed that all but 2 of the neurofeedback-trained group were still abstinent, yet all 10 alcoholic controls were rehospitalized by 15 months post-treatment.

One could suggest that these remarkable results were attributable in good measure to the in-patient condition, and the regularity and duration of training (5 alpha–theta biofeedback sessions per week for a total of 30, plus a preliminary relaxation training period of six sessions during which autogenic phrases were combined with hand temperature biofeedback and an imagery procedure). This protocol, designed to use goal-oriented communication with the unconscious, while maintaining a relatively unguarded EEG theta state, is quite similar to Budzynski's twilight learning and Green and Green's (1986) programming of the unconscious. However, the genius of the Peniston–Kulkosky protocol may be in its frequent and numerous sessions.

About the time that Peniston and Kulkosky (1989) published their landmark paper, Lexicor came out with their QEEG diagnostic and feedback system as designed and tested by Wilson and Joffe. These two events, happening almost simultaneously, appear to have ushered in the modern era of neurofeedback with its heavy use of QEEG systems that permit precise quantification of a number of EEG parameters, plus multimedia feedback of researcher/therapist selected EEG responses.

At the Fifth International Conference of the Psychology of Health, Immunity and Disease in Hilton Head, South Carolina, in 1993 the writer was privileged to present a paper entitled "Neurotechnology: The New Frontier." I felt excited on that occasion to be able to apprise that audience of this area of research and application–and I still am.

REFERENCES

Adrian, E. D., & Matthews, B. H. C. (1934). The Berger rhythm: Potential changes from the occipital lobes of man. *Brain,* **57,** 355–385.

Ancoli, S., & Kamiya, J. (1978). Methodological issues in alpha biofeedback training. *Biofeedback Self-Regul.,* **3,** 159–151.

Ayers, M. (1987). Electroencephalographic neurofeedback and closed head injury of 250 individuals. *In* "National and Head Injury Syllabus. Head Injury Frontiers," p. 380.

Berger, H. (1929). Uber das elektrephalogramm des menschen. *Arch. Psychiatr. Nervenkr.* **87,** 527–570.

Birbaumer, N., Elbert, T., Rockstroh, B., Lutzenberger, W., & Schwartz, J. (1981). EEG and slow cortical potentials in anticipation of mental tasks with different hemispheric involvement. *Biol. Psychol.* **13,** 251–260.

Brazier, M. A. B. (1980). The early developments of quantitative EEG analysis: The roots of modern methods. *In* "Psychophysiology 1980" (R. Sinz & M. Rosenzweig, eds.). Elsevier, Amsterdam.

Brown, B. B. (1970). Recognition of aspects of consciousness through association with EEG alpha activity represented by a light signal. *Psychophysiology*, **6**, 442–452.

Brown, B. B. (Ed.). (1975). "The Biofeedback Syllabus: A Handbook for the Psychophysiologic Study of Biofeedback." Charles C. Thomas, Springfield, IL.

Brown, B. B., & Klug, J. W. (1974). "A Handbook: The Alpha Syllabus of Human EEG Alpha Activity." Charles C. Thomas, Springfield, IL.

Budzynski, T. H. (1972). Some applications of biofeedback-produced twilight states. *In* "Biofeedback & Self-Control" (D. Shapiro, T. X. Barber, L. V. DiCara, J. Kamiya, N. E. Miller, & J. Stoyva, eds.). Aldine-Atherton, Chicago.

Budzynski, T. H. (1976). Biofeedback and the twilight states of consciousness. *In* "Consciousness and Self-Regulation: Advances in Research" (G. E. Schwartz & D. Shapiro, eds.), Vol. 1, pp. 361–385. Plenum Press, New York.

Budzynski, T. H. (1986). Clinical applications of non-drug-induced states. *In* "Handbook of States of Consciousness" (B. B. Wolman & M. Ullman, eds.). Van Nostrand Reinhold, New York.

Budzynski, T. H. (1993). Neurotechnology: The new frontier. Paper presented at the Fifth International Conference of The Psychology of Health, Immunity and Disease, Hilton Head, NC.

Budzynski, T. H. (in press). Twilight learning revisited. *In* "Applied Neurophysiology and Brainwave Biofeedback" (R. Kall, J. Kamiya, & G. E. Schwartz, eds.). Futurehealth, Bensalem, PA.

Budzynski, T. H., & Stoyva, J. M. (1969). An instrument for producing deep muscle relaxation by means of analog information feedback. *J. Appl. Behav. Anal.* **2**, 231–237.

Budzynski, T. H., & Stoyva, J. M. (1972). Biofeedback techniques in behavior therapy. *In* "Neuropsychologie der Angst. Reihe Fortschritte der Klinischen Psychologie, Bd. 3" (N. Birbaumer, ed.), pp. 248–270. Verlag Urban & Schwarzenberg, Berlin. [Republished in "Biofeedback and Self-Control: 1972" (D. Shapiro, T. X. Barber, L. V. DiCara, J. Kamiya, N. E. Miller, & J. Stoyva, eds.), Aldine, Chicago.]

Budzynski, T. H., & Stoyva, J. M. (1984). Biofeedback methods in the treatment of anxiety and stress. *In* "Principles and Practice of Stress Management" (R. L. Woolfolk & P. M. Lehrer, eds.). Guilford Press, New York.

Caton, R. (1875). The electrical currents of the brain. *Br. Med. J.* **2**, 278.

Dewan, E. (1971). Occipital alpha rhythm eye position and lens accommodation. *In* "Biofeedback and Self-Control" (T. Barber, L. Dicara, J. Kamiya, N. Miller, D. Shapiro & J. Stoyva, eds.). Aldine-Atherton, New York.

Dowman, R., & Rosenfeld, J. P. (1985). Operant conditioning of somatosensory evoked potential (SEP) in rats. I. Specific changes in SEP amplitude and a naloxone-reversible, somatotopically specific change in facial nocioception. *Brain Res.* **333**, 201–212.

Duffy, F. (1982). Topographic display of evoked potentials: Clinical applications of brain electrical mapping (BEAM). *Ann. NY Acad. Sci.* **388**, 183–196.

Echenhofer, F. G., & Coombs, M. M. (1987). A brief review of the research literature and controversies in EEG biofeedback and EEG meditation. *Res. J. Transpersonal Psychol.* **19**, 161–171.

Engstrom, D. R., London, P., & Hart, J. T. (1970). Hypnotic susceptibility increased by EEG alpha training. *Nature* **227**, 1261–1262.

Fehmi, L. G. (1978). EEG biofeedback, multichannel synchrony training, and attention. *In* "Expanding Dimensions of Consciousness" (A. Sugerman, ed.). Springer Verlag, New York.

Finley, W. W. (1984). Biofeedback of very early potentials from the brainstem. *In* "Self-Regulation of the Brain and Behavior" (B. Rockstroh, T. Elbert, W. Lutzenberger, & N. Birbaumer, eds.). Springer Verlag, Berlin.

Fox, S. S., & Rudell, A. P. (1968). Operant-controlled neural event: Formal and systematic approach to electrical coding of behavior in brain. *Science* **162**, 1299–1302.

Green, E. E., & Green, A. M. (1986). Biofeedback and states of consciousness. *In* "Handbook of States of Consciousness" (B. B. Wolman & M. Ullman, eds.). Van Nostrand Reinhold, New York.

Green, E., Green, A., & Walters, D. (1971). Psychophysiological training for creativity. Paper presented at the 1971 meeting of the American Psychological Association, Washington, DC.

Gibbs, F. A., Davis, H., & Lennox, W. G. (1934). The electroencephalogram in epilepsy and conditions of impaired consciousness. *Arch. Neuro. Psychiat.* **34**, 1133–1148.

Hardt, J. V., & Kamiya, J. (1978). Anxiety change through electroencephalographic alpha feedback seen only in high alpha subjects. *Science* **201**, 79–81.

Hart, J. T. (1967). Autocontrol of EEG alpha. Paper presented at the meeting of the Society for Psychophysiological Research, San Diego, CA. Abstract in *Psychophysiology*, **4**, 506.

John, E. R. (1977). "Functional Neuroscience: Vol. 2. Neurometrics: Clinical Applications of Quantitative Electroencephalography," p. 21. L. Erlbaum Associates, Hillsdale, NJ.

Kamiya, J. (1962). Conditioned discrimination of the EEG alpha rhythm in humans. Paper presented at the Western Psychological Association, San Francisco, CA.

Kamiya, J. (1968). Conscious control of brain waves. *Psychol. Today*, **1**, 56–60.

Korein, J., Maccario, M., Carmona, A., Randt, C. T., & Miller, N. (1971). Operant conditioning techniques in normal and abnormal EEG states. *Neurology* **21**, 395 (abstract).

Kotchoubey, B., Schneider, D., Uhlmann, C., Schleichert, H., & Birbaumer, N. (1977). Beyond habituation: Long-term repetition effects on visual event-related potentials in epileptic patients. *EEG Clin. Neurophysiol.* **103**, 450–456.

Lubar, J. F., & Bahler, W. W. (1976). Behavioral management of epileptic seizures following EEG biofeedback training of the sensorimotor rhythm. *Biofeedback Self-Regul.*, **1**, 77–104.

Lubar, J. F., & Shouse, M. N. (1976). EEG and behavioral changes in a hyperkinetic child concurrent with training of the sensorimotor rhythm (SMR): A preliminary report. *Biofeedback Self-Regul.* **3**, 293–306.

Lubar, J. O., & Lubar, J. F. (1984). Electroencephalographic biofeedback of SMR and beta for treatment of attention deficit disorders in a clinical setting. *Biofeedback Self-Regul.* **2**, 1–23.

Lynch, J. L., Paskewitz, D., & Orne, M. T. (1974). Some factors in the feedback control of the human alpha rhythm. *Psychosomatic Med.* **36**, 399–410.

Mattes, R., Schneider, F., Heiman, H., & Birbaumer, N. (1995). Reduced emotional response of schizophrenic patients in remission during social isolation. *Schizophrenia Res.* **17**(3), 249–255.

Mills, G. K., & Solyom, L. (1974). Biofeedback of EEG alpha in the treatment of obsessive ruminations: An exploration. *J. Behav. Ther. Exp. Psychiat.* **5**, 37–41.

Peniston, E. G., & Kulkosky, P. J. (1989). Alpha–theta brainwave training and B-endorphin levels in alcoholics. *Alcohol. Clin. Exp. Res.* **13**, 271–279.

Peniston, E. G., & Kulkosky, P. J. (1990). Alcoholic personality and alpha–theta brainwave training. *Medical Psychother.* **3**, 37–55.

Peper, E. (1972). Localized EEG alpha feedback training: A possible technique for mapping subjective, conscious, and behavioral experiences. *In* "Biofeedback and Self-Control: 1972" (D. Shapiro, T. X. Barber, L. V. DiCara, J. Kamiya, N. E. Miller, & J. Stoyva, eds.). Aldine, Chicago.

Ray, W. S., Frediani, A. W., & Harman, D. (1977). Self-regulation of hemispheric asymmetry. *Biofeedback Self-Regul.* **2**, 195–199.

Rosenfeld, J. P. (1990). Applied psychophysiology and biofeedback of event-related potentials (brain waves): Historical perspective, review, future directions. *Biofeedback Self-Regul.*, **15**, 99–119.

Rosenfeld, J. P., Rudell, A. P., & Fox, S. S. (1969). Operant control of neural events in humans. *Science* **165**, 821–823.

Rosenfeld, J. P., Reinhart, A. M., & Srivastava, S. (1997). The effects of alpha (10-Hz) and beta (22-Hz) "entrainment" stimulation on the alpha and beta bands: individual differences are critical to prediction of effects. *Appl. Psychophysiol. Biofeedback* **22,** 3–20.

Seifert, A. R., & Lubar, J. F. (1975). Reduction of epileptic seizures through EEG biofeedback training. *Biol. Psychol.* **3,** 157–184.

Sittenfeld, P., Budzynski, T., & Stoyva, J. (1976). Differential shaping of EEG theta rhythms. *Biofeedback Self-Regul.* **1,** 31–46.

Sterman, M. B. (1977). Sensorimotor EEG operant conditioning: experimental and clinical effects. *Pavlovian J. Biol. Sci.* **12,** 63–92.

Tansey, M. A. (1990). Righting the rhythms of reason: EEG biofeedback training as a therapeutic modality in a clinical office setting. *Medical Psychother.* **3,** 57–68.

Thatcher, R. W., Walker, R. A., Gerson, I., & Geisler, F. H. (1989). EEG discriminant analyses of mild head trauma. *EEG Clin. Neurophysiol.* **73,** 94–106.

Walter, W. (1937) Electroencephalogram in cases of cerebral tumour. *Proc. R. Soc. Med.* **30,** 579–598. Walter, W. G. (1953). "The Living Brain." Norton, New York.

Weber, E. S., & Fehmi, L. G. (1975). The therapeutic use of EEG biofeedback. Paper presented at the Biofeedback Research Society Meeting, Monterey, CA.

Wickramasekera, I. (1976). "Biofeedback, Behavior Therapy and Hypnosis: Potentiating the Verbal Control of Behavior for Clinicians." Nelson-Hall, Chicago.

Wyricka, W., & Sterman, M. B. (1968). Instrumental conditioning of sensorimotor cortex EEG spindles in the waking cat. *Physiol. Behav.* **3,** 703–707.

PART

II

CLINICAL APPLICATIONS

4

MEDICAL APPLICATIONS OF
NEUROBIOFEEDBACK

RIMA LAIBOW

Alexandria Institute, Croton on Hudson, New York

I. INTRODUCTION

The term *NeuroBioFeedback* (NBF), as used in this chapter, is a medical discipline based in neurophysiology, drawing heavily on EEG, neuroanatomy, pathophysiology, and the multicentric discipline of behavioral medicine (BM).

BM arose out the search for effective and efficient ways to decrease pathological automatic responses (and, conversely, increase voluntary, salutary ones) in those conditions impacted by psychoemotional processes (Luthe, 1969; Schwartz, 1979). The primary impetus for this way of looking at disease and self-regulation for healthy functioning came out of the emerging psychophysiology research of the 1960s. Although its popularity has waxed and waned since that time, BM attracted significant attention and has continued to produce results in the clinical and research arenas that are often beyond expectation. By 1988 Wickramasekera (1988) was able to state "Biofeedback, behavior therapy, and hypnosis, because of their technological emphasis, circumscribed and quantifiable goals, and origins in the experimental laboratory, provide the primitive but promising cutting edge of useful tools for clinical behavioral medicine. These technologies provide the roots of a systematic approach to the behavioral investigation, assessment and management of chronic stress-related physical disorders that are replacing acute infectious diseases as the major cause of death and disability today." He was referring, of course to biofeedback as distinct from NBF.

Early work in NBF and BM goes back to the 1930s (Adrian, 1934; Dietsch, 1932), when pioneering EEG studies led to the detection of alpha rhythms in humans and, surprisingly, in cockroaches by the German investigator, Berger. At that time, because of the lack of computing power and sensitive electronic signal detection equipment, EEG was difficult to monitor and could not be analyzed and responded to in real or near real time. Although theoretical interest in voluntary and selective regulation of EEG states was strong, the technology of the time did not permit productive exploitation of EEG-related modulation. BM, therefore, focused largely on physiological processes more readily observed, modified, and quantified than the EEG. These included heart rate, blood pressure, galvanic skin response, and finger tip temperature. BM practitioners, researchers, and physiologists developed a vast scientific literature and body of clinical practice in the application of voluntary self-regulation of these processes. These techniques are now known collectively as *biofeedback* and often subsumed under the term *behavioral medicine*. But NBF (or EEG biofeedback) had to wait for the development of electronic and mathematical techniques that allow for the monitoring of real (or near-real) time response to the EEG on a clinical basis. The early impetus in the development and implementation of biofeedback and other non-EEG related areas of BM led to an active resurgence of research and practice effort in this area during the 1960s and 1970s (Shapiro, 1979).

Although interest continued in the area of biofeedback (so that by 1985 about 3000 books, articles, and doctoral dissertations on biofeedback-related topics had been produced) (Hatch, 1985), emerging pharmacological tools and their socioeconomic impact resulted in the relegation of biofeedback and other self-regulation techniques to a secondary niche in most medical, educational, and clinical environments.

Three simultaneously emerging trends have served to make BM, including both biofeedback and NBF, much more significant contenders for attention as primary clinical options for treatment of a wide array of medical and psychophysiologically mediated diseases and conditions. The first of these trends is the emergence of technology and algorithms that allow the near simultaneous recording, analysis, and response to neuronal depolarization/repolarization (that is, EEG). The development of near-real-time fast Fourier transforms (FFTs), which can be applied to the raw EEG of the patient, and the computing power that allows nearly immediate return of information via sensory feedback on degree of change in specific desirable EEG characteristics has added EEG to the long and impressive list of physiological functions available for self-regulatory treatment (Laibow & Bounias, in press). Pursuant to this increasing technical capability, a number of manufacturers have developed easily available and modestly priced treatment devices that are suitable for clinical application.

The second converging trend that has brought NBF to clinical maturity is the increased caution and skepticism with which pharmacological treatments (e.g., "drugs") are now regarded within and, even more adamantly, outside of the medical profession. The frequent and sometimes disastrous problems associated with pharmacological solutions to diseases and conditions that can often be treated with less toxicity though nonpharmacological means are best illustrated by the overuse of antibiotics and their subsequently dangerously diminished efficacy. Overdosing, polypharmacologies, and the treatment of medication side effects with further side-effect-producing medications are now perceived as serious (and usually avoidable) problems. It is becoming clear that good medical practice involves options other than drugs. In many situations nontoxic, safe, and effective remedies are being sought by the clinical and consumer communities alike. NBF is an exemplary tool in that search for nontoxic, noninvasive treatment modalities. Recently, Mulholland (1995) stated: "The fact that EEG biofeedback is noninvasive with no deleterious side effects and that substantial benefits have been reported for some cases whose symptoms have been severe, even life-limiting, whose levels of medications are unacceptably high or with severe side effects, or which have been refractory to other treatments has made this an option chosen by some clinicians, patients and their families" (pp. 263–279). Gratifyingly, NBF represents a startling breakthrough in the application of self-regulation techniques to conventional medical practice. The clinician gives up none of the sophistication, precision, and sensitivity to clinical issues and processes in which he or she has been trained.

The third trend that supports the emergence of NBF as a powerful force in the treatment of a wide variety of medical conditions is the development of a strong popular interest and a commitment to safe, nontoxic, noninvasive, and self-regulatory ways of dealing with symptoms and the achievement of well-being which transcends the achievement of a symptom-free state (i.e., so called "alternative," "complementary," "[w]holistic," "functional," or "integrative" approaches).

Progressive or alternative medical practices are of great interest both to the medical profession and to the population at large. Phytochemicals (herbs), self-regulation techniques such as meditation and yoga, stress management, nutritional medicine, "body work," and certain "energy techniques" are no longer considered "fringe." It has been reported that the American public is voting with its wallet by spending more money in nonreimbursable expenses for alternative treatment modalities than for reimbursable medical treatments–often while keeping their conventional practitioners ignorant of the treatment choices they are making for themselves (Eisenberg, 1993, 1998).

The intolerably high cost of high-tech, pharmaceutical-based medical treatment, along with an emerging poor record of success with cancer, degenerative diseases, environmental sensitivity, allergy, and disorders of energy metabolism, as well as with all of the disorders related to chronic stress response, has been coupled with a growing recognition that allopathic medicine deals primarily with the suppression of symptoms and not their resolution. In sharp and significant contrast, BM's self-regulatory techniques, led first and foremost by NBF, deal with the re-regulation of the entire organism, resulting in the resolution, not the suppression, of symptoms. This resolution is often accompanied by not only an expected clinical improvement in the symptom picture that brought the patient to treatment in the first place, but also by a more pervasive resolution of the causal factors that led to the development of the symptom picture itself.

An emerging level of sophistication on the part of the health consumer, also known as the "patient," demands that treatment assist in accomplishing a transition from having symptoms (being "sick" in the medical paradigm) through having no symptoms (known as "being healthy" in the medical paradigm) to being well, that is, having a fully integrated and healthy mental, emotional, physical, and, for some, spiritual, life. Because of its locus of activity, NBF is a powerful tool in literally teaching patients how to be well.

Biofeedback or self-regulatory techniques may be divided into somatic (or peripheral) and central (or EEG-related) techniques. Somatic biofeedback has been used extensively for so-called psychophysiological disorders such as neuromuscular problems, cardiac arrhythmia, hypertension, vascular migraine (Shapiro, 1979), visual and ophthalmological disorders (Rotberg & Surwit, 1981), fecal incontinence and enuresis, gait training, bruxism and TMJ, Raynaud's disease (Schwartz, 1987), and a host of other mechanically mediated disorders referable to excess sympathetic tone. Treatment thus consists largely of teaching patients strategies for lowering arousal and maintaining a healthful sympathetic/parasympathetic tone that can be transferred to nontreatment periods in their lives. NBF is similar to somatic biofeedback in that it teaches skills through the rewarding experience of inducing changes in a readily perceivable, simple signal that the patient interprets as "I just did the right thing!" Light (in the form of a display on a computer monitor) or sound (in the form of tones from headphones or speakers), vibratory sensation, or other direct "reward" are supplied to the patient when the EEG amplitude and/or other characteristics are successfully modified according to criteria previously set for this patient. Autonomic tone may or may not be part of the treatment focus, whereas neural processing activities are modified directly in order to achieve a desired end result.

In somatic biofeedback treatment it is possible to segment results so that a patient with Raynaud's disease learns finger warming techniques but has no change in, say, his or her allergic status. NBF reduces the possibility of segmentation of results because of the locus of regulation and treatment. NBF is directed and applied to that organ whose function is the complex integration of all functions carried out by the organism: the brain. When one function is changed in a positive direction, it has been our experience that a cascade of results and positive integration takes place since no aspect of brain function (or, for that matter, of body function) actually exists remote from or isolated from any of the others. It has been our Cartesian custom to act, think, talk, and treat patients as if humans are comprised of discrete sets of functions; but NBF, perhaps more than any other medical discipline, makes it clear that this is illusory at best, misguided for certain, and destructive at worst when patients are treated as if such functional segmentation is reality rather than a sparse and inaccurate map of reality. Because it is neither possible nor desirable to segregate clinical results when changing the nature and direction of the brain's integration and activity through selective operant conditioning, and because the organism seeks under all circumstances to right itself in the most adaptive ways available to it, the net result of properly applied NBF far exceeds the simple reduction or suppression of symptoms seen with most conventional treatments. Instead, the successfully treated patient experiences and manifests increasing levels of mastery and well-being in interlocking spheres of his or her life, finally culminating in true wellness. Unlike health, true wellness contains within itself the possibility of transcendence of, as well as a lack of, pathology or distress. Not surprisingly, such profound systemic changes require more active support and medical supervision than treatment narrowly focused on simple symptom reduction. In this process it thus becomes imperative to offer the integrating and meaning-making, emotional part of the system opportunity for taking in the newly emerging wellness and relinquishing old patterns of belief and behavior (biological as well as conscious behavior) associated with the symptoms themselves.

Because there may well be strong experiential up-welling of emotionally charged material during or after a NBF treatment session, it is essential to have skilled support built into the treatment program from the beginning lest this component be neglected and only the more physiological foci attended to with a resultant loss of clinical effect and durability of results. Therefore, as part of the treatment program any patient (regardless of diagnosis or previous psychotherapy history) receiving NBF treatment must also be engaged in a process of biobehavioral integration with a psychotherapist. This psychotherapist must be specially trained to interpret and work with the physiological changes occurring in the patient and with the impact of emotions, thoughts, feelings, and belief systems on physiology and pathophysiology. Properly applied in this way, NBF is a tool for evolving not only health, but wellness, by eliciting the profound capacity for repair in human beings.

The strong relationship between emotion, perception, and neurological system-wide functioning should not be surprising in light of recent knowledge concerning the ubiquitous nature and patterns of the mechanisms and organizing functions of neurotransmitters and neuromodulator systems throughout the body. However, in addition to the strong new research emerging in this area, the power of this connection is shown through examination from another direction: actuarial statistics on utilization of medical services and resource consumption. This mind–body connection is clearly underscored and its financial ramifications sharply apparent in studies that show a significant drop in medical care cost when psychotherapy services are available to patients. For example, outpatient psychological services reduce both the incidence of service utilization and the length of hospital stays (Cummins, 1977; Mumford et al., 1984). When Mumford et al. (1984) reviewed 58 controlled studies of medical utilization patterns, 85% of them clearly documented a decrease in medical utilization following psychotherapy, and the major areas in which costs were offset were in the treatment of older people and in-patient medical care. These are the very areas of care that consume the vast majority of our health care costs in this country. Noting that "the[se] findings are a powerful challenge to the mind-body dichotomy that dominates healthcare. . . . The philosophical doctrine of the mind-body dichotomy that underlies the biomedical model is one of the major obstacles to a cost-effective health care system" (p. 48). Wickramasekera (1988) gives a clear framework to the importance of NBF treatment as a whole person, all-systems treatment—the portal to which is neuronal integration and the results of which are system-wide. Without appropriate attention to the psychological and emotional integration requirement of this treatment modality, the treatment will fail either during or shortly after it is concluded (Laibow & Bounias, in press).

Research as early as 1981 has shown that not only is the central nervous system (CNS) the integrative and regulatory organ of the patient, it also is highly responsive to psychosocial and emotional stressors (Sklar & Anisman, 1981; Jemmot & Locke, 1984), and that the immune system and other portions of the CNS, are subject to classical or Pavlovian conditioning (Ader, 1981). In the intervening time, an explosion of data has confirmed and expanded on that information. On the other hand, the fact that there is an intimate mind–body connection does not mean that the assessment of EEG and the treatment of psychophysiologically responsive systems should be regarded purely as a psychological endeavor. For example, all stress-related symptoms and diseases initially, or over the course of disease, involve the autonomic nervous systems (ANS). Many nonmedical NBF clinicians appear to believe they can safely treat any of the signs or symptoms of dysregulation of the ANS without medical consultation and involvement. This is a serious error. Dysautonomia, as described in a recent neurophysiology text, provides an important and relevant illustration (Fogel et *al.,* 1996). The authors caution "The clinical features of Dysautonomia vary in different patients and depend in part upon the nature of the underlying disorder, as does the existence and nature of any somatic neurological manifestations. For example, Dysautonomia occurring in diabetics may be associated with symptoms and signs suggestive of peripheral neuropathy whereas parkinsonism, cerebellar dysfunction, pyramidal disturbance or other combinations of these abnormalities occur in patients with central disorders of autonomic function" (p. 107). In addition, the same authors note that "Autonomic disturbances also occur in patients with the neuropathy of chronic renal failure (Naik *et al.,* 1981), leprosy (Kyriakidis *et al.,* 1983), vitamin B12 deficiency (McCombe & McLeod, 1984), Chagas' disease (Iosa *et al.,* 1989), involvement of the heart and gastrointestinal systems, sporadic systemic myeloid neuropathy or familial amyloidosis (Kyle & Greipp, 1983; Kyle *et al.,* 1966; Fogel *et al.,* 1996)." A condition obviously should not be regarded as simple Dysautonomia without further diagnostic discrimination and treatment. In other words, although NBF might be the treatment of choice, the treating clinician must have the training and capacity to recognize those conditions, signs, and symptoms which should be medically treated before (or concurrently with) NBF or other self-regulatory strategies are introduced.

To illustrate this point further, Fogel *et al.* (1996) note that loss of libido and ejaculatory difficulties or failure, blood pressure dysregulation, thermoregulatory disturbances (which might include excessive sweating or cold hands or feet), fainting or dizziness, disturbances of bladder or bowel regulation, visual blurring, dry eyes, irregular breathing, and sleep disturbances are all potentially associated with serious and, in some cases, life-threatening abnormalities of ANS function. There is no symptom, in fact, which can be assured to be unrelated to potential medically relevant causes. Therefore, it is urgently important that both medical and nonmedical practitioners keep this in mind when evaluating patients and choosing treatment options for them.

Because the CNS functions as the central regulatory agent of the organism, any attempt to bring about changes in its functioning must take into account the complex (and only partly understood) nature of the brain's activities in that regulation. Cortical EEG, it must be remembered, is not a complete picture of brain-wide functioning, but a summated electrical portrait of complex and interrelated functions taking place throughout the brain mass, which results in a final cortical signal. Under ordinary conditions, the complex multitract potentials that result in the EEG signal are available for measurement only at the cortex or scalp. Similarly, inputting signals and rewards for functions measured at the scalp (NBF) is a process in which we are feeding information into a highly multivariant and complex brain state and functional system. Good NBF treatment and practice absolutely require a widening of the practitioner's scope of attention to far more information than local EEG and putative diagnosis alone. For either diagnostic or treatment purposes, NBF should never be attempted in the absence of a full qualitative EEG (at least 19 recording sites) recorded, artifacted, and interpreted in accord with the highest standards of practice accompanied by a careful medical history and, if appropriate, examination and laboratory investigations, before treatment is commenced.

II. DIAGNOSIS CONSIDERATIONS

A detailed pretreatment intake interview should include mental status, prior and current illness, history of malignancies and any treatment received for them, surgeries, pre- and perinatal medication, birth, head injury, and seizure (febrile and nonfebrile) histories, a complete review of systems, family history, psychiatric and psychosocial history, educational level, legal land illicit drug use (including alcohol and tobacco), medication, supplement and nutrient intake, acute and chronic illness history, assessment of stresses (chronic and acute), pain (chronic and acute), major lifestyle choices and activities, risk factors and habits, hobbies, relationship patterns, exposure to toxins that may have powerful neurotoxic effects (Bounuias et al., 1997) and other CNS poisons and stressors. If a significant possibility of clinical irregularities or illness is suspected, a mechanism should be readily available that will allow blood, urine, hair, and other laboratory tests to be carried out. Review of medical records and dialogue with the physicians currently or recently treating the patient is essential to excellent patient care.

During assessment it often is useful to use tests that measure other characteristics of the patient's functional state such as continuous performance tests and neuropsychological assessments in addition to the EEG/QEEG. In my practice we use several computer and noncomputer assessment tools designed to develop a profile of symptomatic behavior, psychological and psychosocial status, pain or symptom severity, malingering, etc. Not only are these tests useful in establishing the functional state of the patient, they provide an excellent post-treatment battery when treatment is completed and documentation of improvement is desired. This is often of consequence when the existence of initial deficit or injury is disputed in cases such as worker's compensation or other lawsuits. Despite the fact that third-party payers sometimes balk at payment for such tests, they are valuable aids in diagnosis, documentation, treatment planning, and treatment outcome assessment. In situations in which legal ramifications to assessment and treatment results are expected, it is wise to discuss frankly with patients and with their attorneys the reasons for these assessments and offer them the option of paying for them even if the third-party does not wish to do so.

In recording the EEG, impedance should always be kept below 5 milliohms at each scalp electrode site, and carefully recorded for each site as part of the permanent clinical record. Any special characteristics in the recording should be well documented; that is, the patient and EEG should be simultaneously videotaped using a single camera creating a split-screen effect so that unexpected or unusual events can be accurately and easily compared with patient state and status using the video data. Eyes-open and eyes-closed EEGs should be recorded during the same session. This ensures that pretreatment data are available in both eyes-open and eyes-closed conditions. This information will be used to assist in clinical decision making and in post-treatment assessment.

The data from each recording [i.e., eyes open (EO) and eyes closed (EC)] should be analyzed in five stages: (1) careful examination of the raw data; (2) detailed examination of the compressed spectral array (CSA) of individual sites and comparison of relative characteristics of site-derived CASs for amplitude, wave characteristics, anterior-posterior, lateral and quadrant symmetry, etc.; (3) examination of the topographic map characteristics using fine subdivisions of the frequency range being addressed (0.5–32 Hz in my practice); (4) detailed examination of epoch-by-epoch characteristics of CSA, dominant frequency characteristics, power and magnitude characteristics; and (5) comparison of EO and EC records.

After removing artifacts from the data examination of the power spectra for six basic frequency bands should be made. These bands are:

1. Delta (0.5–4 Hz)
2. Theta (4–8 Hz)
3. Alpha (8–13 Hz)
4. SMR Beta (12–16 Hz)
5. Beta 1 (16–20 Hz)
6. Beta 2 (20–32 Hz)

Clinical conclusions must also take into account age and clinical state.

The described procedure is not a simple one and it should not be attempted without extensive clinical training followed by ongoing supervision by an experienced clinician or electroencephalographer skilled in QEEG. It cannot be too strongly stated that since the organizing and regulating organ of the patient (his or her brain) is about to be regulated on the basis of this information, considerable effort, time, and care are warranted in the artifacting, interpreting, and clinical use of the EEG and QEEG.

Much has been written and discussed in clinical EEG circles about eliminating artifact (Lopes da Silva, 1993; Thornton, 1996; Barlow, 1986). It is strongly recommended that the person artifacting these data be certified by an organization dealing specifically with this crucial clinical activity (such as the Association of Quantitative EEG Technologists). Likewise, it is imperative that the QEEG data be interpreted by persons with extensive training and clinical experience in EEG/QEEG. Any suggestion of brain wave abnormality or maldistribution should be promptly investigated by the clinician and, if indicated, referral made to a neurologist, internist, pediatrician, or other appropriate medical specialist for clinical collaboration and development of a team treatment approach. This collaboration in no way should be understood as necessarily contraindicating NBF. Quite the contrary; if the clinician feels that NBF is indicated it may then be carried out in close collaboration with the team physician. Furthermore, it is important that no clinician, regardless of professional training or discipline, assume that because the patient presents with a "ready-made" diagnosis (e.g., "My son has ADHD" or "My fingers are cold: I have Raynaud's syndrome") the treatment is obvious or that the nature of the dysfunction has been identified or accurately assessed.

Among the areas of expertise needed for the development of an accurate assessment of diagnostic data and the development of a treatment plan are EEG age-and gender-normal characteristics; the impact of hormones, medications, and various diseases and developmental states on EEG (and QEEG); and menstrual effects such as the cycle status of the patient (if appropriate). It also is important to know whether the patient meditates and, if so, how advanced he or she is and in what type of meditative practice. Also of relevance are the number of so-called normative databases available to the NBF clinician. Many of these are quite expensive. Debate rages over their usefulness. Several of these databases offer detailed mathematical analysis of such factors as coherence and synchrony, in terms of deviation from expected norms and statistical analyses of such deviation. While they are easy to use in terms of generating lengthy reports and data output, the definitive word on their clinical usefulness is not yet in. Some clinicians strive to increase or decrease synchrony and coherence between EEG signals at various sites as a general treatment modality based on the statistically significant deviations from "normal" generated in a printout from a database program. In my estimation, it is not clear whether the commercially available databases are "normative" at all, since the actual clinical significance of synchrony, coherence, phase, and other EEG wave characteristics is a highly complex and unsettled area. The clinician should approach the intentional manipulation of these characteristics with serious trepidation and caution. In these clinically uncertain waters, more is absolutely *not* better in all of these states. For example, certain psychotic states such as schizophrenia are sometimes characterized by more (increased) intrahemispheric synchrony and coherence. As in most clinical situations, treating a lab result or a database finding with no further rationale is unwise and unwarranted. Treating a deviation from a putative "normative" based upon database findings strikes me as very poor clinical practice. I do not know of a database that has been constructed on the basis of data generated by a very large, unimpaired, multiage population where data were recorded under closely matched conditions and in which the subjects were free of all toxic and deleterious substances, drugs, and influences. I believe that in order to be meaningful in terms of coherence, synchrony, etc., these same subjects would have to be measured in a wide variety of states and tasks such as deep creativity, sincere appreciation, rage, deep concentration, bliss, etc., in which these characteristics are believed to change. For example, it has been found that 5 min of sincere appreciation can enhance immune function for as much as 6 h as indicated by an elevation of IgA. We also know that 5 min of rage can depress the immune system by an amount approximately equal to the elevation caused by sincere appreciation or love for an approximately equal time. During both rage and sincere appreciation, we may assume that not only brain wave frequency, but also phase and other relational characteristics such as synchrony and coherence are affected. Thus, training such complex characteristics without understanding them well is, in effect, playing with the immune system and with inter- and intrasystemic regulatory components in the absence of sufficient clinical information and experience to warrant such treatment (except in special circumstances such as a well-controlled experimental studies).

III. TREATMENT

After the initial assessment (which, with an extensive medical and psychosocial history, QEEG, other tests, and patient information may take as long as 4–5 h) and a careful evaluation of all relevant clinical and historical data, the clinician, in collaboration with other health professionals involved in the patient's care, can develop a treatment plan that reflects the individual requirements of the patient's neurological, physiological, emotional, and developmental state as well as consideration of the chief complaint or primary diagnosis that brought the patient to treatment. To apply NBF technology to the patient's underlying requirements, and not just to the diagnosis or chief complaint at the forefront of the patient's awareness at his or her initial presentation, it is essential to keep sharply in focus the concept of "the final common pathway." Many pathological or physiological disorders may result in common expression of symptoms, disease, or disorder. This common expression of multiple origins of dysfunction is called the *final common pathway* in biochemistry and pathology. If the symptom picture or presenting complaint alone is treated, there is little likelihood of treating the problem at deeper levels. If, on the other hand, the symptom picture is recognized as the result of many possible pathological dysfunctions and enough investigation is carried out to elucidate these underlying dysfunctions, the underlying pathology can be treated.

The treatment plan has several components. Chief among them is a willing patient. This may not even require that the patient be conscious, but an active unwillingness is a strong contraindication mitigating heavily against the treatment. If a patient is unwilling to participate in treatment, but a family member or other person is eager for treatment it is crucial that the clinician assess the real likelihood of cooperation by the patient, *not* by the interested other. By its very nature, NBF is voluntary, noncoercive, and self-regulatory. Clinical skill and the development of a strong rapport and subsequent alliance can sometimes turn a reluctant "victim" into a willing participant. But for those potential patients who are not interested in this mode of treatment (as sometimes happens, for example, when a patient has a legal case pending which they perceive would be weakened by a significant improvement in their pain or suffering before the case goes to trial or is settled), or for those situations in which the particular psychodynamics make NBF inappropriate, treatment should not be initiated. Instead, alternative means of treatment should be offered with the hope that other types of intervention might change the situation enough to revisit the topic of NBF at another point at which time there might be greater likelihood of success.

Because of the unique nature of NBF, it is not always necessary to have a conscious patient to carry out successful treatment. Comatose patients and those in persistent vegetative states have been successfully treated by skillful and dedicated personnel. These patients, however, were not combative, oppositional, or restless and cooperated well with the demands of treatment. In fact, as treatment progressed they were increasingly participatory. Age is no barrier to NBF treatment although very young patients require special modifications such as sitting an infant on the parent's lap, using alternative reward strategies (e.g., animating a teddy bear or favorite toy, enthusiastic smiling or other emotionally rewarding behaviors closely following desired state changes). Somewhat older children often require very brief initial sessions, but tolerance for longer sessions usually increases rapidly since the act of self-regulation and the externally signaled rewards are both satisfying to the child. Significant warm, appropriate praise is highly motivating to both children and adults, and should be actively dispensed by clinicians and technicians since self-esteem is heavily invested in "my brain." However, insincere or excessive praise is at emotional, neuronal, and cognitive dissonance with the actual work of the treatment and hence reduces the credibility of the clinician or technician. Competitiveness with other patients' progress or results can impede progress. Irrational and unrealistic demands or expectations should be neutralized by the clinical staff and the patient should be taught to avoid them as well. It is important to foster hope and positive expectations while not feeding unrealistic or "magical" expectations. The line is a thin and fine one since magical-seeming results often occur. Many patients call on belief systems that strengthen and motivate them. This often works very positively. Adults who are significantly impaired physically or mentally need creative modification as well.

Once a clinician has determined that a patient is a good candidate for NBF, and there is a reasonable support system or treatment situation, a protocol can be developed as part of the treatment plan. This protocol must include electrode site, frequency bands to be modified, desired direction of modification, type of equipment to be used, ancillary procedures to be carried out, special precautions, and other detailed and individualized specifics of treatment. Every treatment plan, regardless of the nature of the problem being treated, should include some regular (at least weekly) opportunity for BioBehavioral integration, and the practice of skills acquired in conjunction with the NBF treatment segment of the program in the form of homework. BioBehavioral integration can take place in groups or in individual sessions, or by phone. If group integration sessions are used, an opportunity for individual sessions should exist as well in the event that abreaction or other emotionally significant material emerges (i.e., dream material, flashback-like episodes, etc.) and needs to be processed. Abreaction episodes often signal critical turning points in the treatment. Personnel at all levels should be trained to deal appropriately with abreaction episodes so that technicians and administrative staff direct this material to the appropriate clinician, and supervising personnel are kept appropriately informed of their emergence and content. Regular clinical meetings during which clinical personnel are kept apprised of significant issues in the treatment of each patient and continuing clinical education takes place are essential components of treatment settings so that treatment does not become fragmented. This helps ensure that transference and countertransference, splitting, etc., do not interfere with the patient's progress, especially in the presence of comorbid or primary psychopathology. In our clinic no NBF treatment is conducted that does not also include nutrition concerns, lifestyle considerations, and treatment in the following ancillary modalities: autogenic training including relaxation techniques, finger tip temperature (FTT) training, quieting response training, an excess muscle contraction (EMG) component, and deep diaphragmatic breathing training (DDB) (typically employing a disposable inspirometer that is used by the patient either at home or at our facility), psychoneuroimmune programming consisting of goal setting, multisensory visualization training, anchoring [a neurolinguistic programming (NLP) technique], blood pressure regulation, and "freeze frame" techniques and stress management skills specific to the needs of the individual. Typically, each NBF session involves DDB, visualization and goal setting, FTT, blood pressure biofeedback, relaxation practice, presession coaching, EEG biofeedback (30 min), postsession result interpretation, and debriefing of internal events, perceptions, and mastery events. The elapsed time of a session of NBF treatment is between 45 and 60 min.

We regard it as a strict rule that all contact time with the patient is used for clinically focused and appropriate treatment-enhancing activity. Even casual interactions are always patient centered and staff members are educated in the many ways to make that a continuing and consistent reality. No personal or outside fraternization between staff and patients is permitted.

In some practices, there is much less clinical interaction, and patients may be instructed to conduct their own electrode hookups, and, in some cases, their own postsession processing. Although patient empowerment and autonomy are excellent goals, prematurely abandoning the patient to his or her own devices during treatment time is unwise and unwarranted. Indeed, the practice of providing NBF-type services without providing significant therapeutic contact and inputs is in direct contravention of the position taken in the Biofeedback Society of America's guidelines for practitioners. These guidelines make it clear that it is considered to be unethical to provide little or no presence and guidance to the patient in the context of each clinical interaction (Schwartz & Fehmi, 1982). An apparent exception appears to exist in the case of NBF services rendered using telemedicine protocols and portable equipment since, in this condition, the patient is at a significant distance from the treating professional. In these telemedicine treatment cases, however, every attempt must be made to initiate and maintain close contact via electronic or telephonic means since regular communication is essential for positive outcome. This is another reason why the initial assessment, treatment, and training phases of treatment must be carried out in an intense and involved way which necessitates a great deal of clinician input, time, contact, and training. The patient (and patient's caregiver) must not leave the clinic setting feeling that they have entered and left a "mill," with which there is a weak tie (or none at all) once they are at home, perhaps thousands of miles away from the facility. To incorporate changes in NBF treatment at a distance, tolerate uncertainties, and develop compliance with treatment regimens, strong and skillful contact, support, and direction must be intact and be meaningful for the patient before he or she leaves the clinic. Otherwise, once the patient gets home and gets busy with other activities, session frequency will dwindle, nonsession practice of newly acquired self-regulatory skills will not occur, and treatment success will be very poor.

The other exception to this close support paradigm is in "peak performance" training, which is not properly considered a medical protocol. Portable peak performance training units make home training feasible. Peak performance training using NBF technology should not be initiated when there is a medical problem that takes precedence (such as evidence of head trauma). Following a peak performance evaluation (which should include a quantitative EEG and medical screening), only those persons who display no significant EEG, medical, or emotional abnormalities should be offered peak performance training. Others should be offered the opportunity to correct their medical problem using the appropriate means (which typically includes NBF) with the peak performance option following the correction of their EEG abnormalities using a medical paradigm. The distinction between NBF as a tool in the treatment of a significant number of medical conditions and neural regulation techniques in the achievement of high levels of voluntary performance enhancement skills must be maintained carefully, and scrupulous adherence to this distinction must be retained so that the most ethical practice standards are maintained. NBF practice should, of course, rest solely on patient condition and needs, not practitioner preference or financial interest.

Immediately after a NBF treatment session has been carried out, results are viewed for the session just elapsed, and the intrasession track is examined so the patient can learn to associate states, precepts, and experiences with high or low mastery. All experiences are positively framed so that mastery is enhanced and resistance minimized. The patient is strongly encouraged to generalize treatment-framed mastery to nontreatment segments of life, and he or she is enthusiastically rewarded when reports of successful generalization are presented to the clinician or technical staff.

In the construction of neural treatment goals and protocols, the clinician must choose a treatment site or sites (scalp electrode placements) based on diagnostic data and history. Most training is monopolar. This means that a reference electrode is placed on the earlobe after it has been properly prepared (and skin impedance lowered) and an active electrode is placed at the desired spot on the scalp (after similar preparation) to detect (and hence enable responding to) signals in that region of cortex. The other earlobe is used for the placement of a ground electrode.

Sometimes the clinician will choose a so-called "bipolar hookup" in which two electrodes are placed on the scalp and the ground electrode attached to the earlobe. Some may believe that this gives two active recording sites, but it does not; one of the scalp electrodes becomes the reference electrode. A few specialized devices depart from this pattern but, in general, placing two electrodes on the scalp merely changes the location of the reference electrode. This may, however, be desirable if the clinician feels that the difference between two scalp sites (either on the same hemisphere or on different ones) is of clinical significance and wishes to have the patient train up, or down, the difference between particular frequencies or amplitudes between these two sites.

Most currently available NBF treatment equipment makes it possible for the clinician to choose which frequency bands should be rewarded or inhibited and, distinct from those choices, whether other bands and relationships are to be monitored even though not being actively inhibited or rewarded. The monitoring of frequencies which are not being actively modified is a powerful extension of the treatment option itself. It allows a greater level of observation and precision, which is of great importance both for the treatment of the patient and the ongoing education of the clinician because patterns of response can be observed within individuals and within classes of patients. For example, while rewarding alpha frequencies and inhibiting beta 2 and theta bands, we might also be tracking delta and beta 1 as well.

In our practice we feel that not only the absolute amplitudes of signals within a frequency band but also the ongoing relationships between them are of great importance. This is because absolute amplitudes can vary along many continua and parameters including skull thickness, skin impedance, hydration, etc. Ratios between absolute amplitudes, however, are more stable. We, therefore, constantly monitor a series of ratios in every patient's treatment such as slow wave/SMR, theta/alpha, etc. In other words, we construct a series of ratios that allows us to see intra- and intersession patterns of relative neuron modulation and also allows the patient to grasp at experiential, proprioceptive, kinesthetic, and, finally, cognitive levels, exactly what these modulating behaviors feel like, relate to, control, and change. These ratios allow us and the patient, to learn more about the complex nature of brain wave regulation and to develop a common language for dialogue. The absolute values do not readily lend themselves to this dialogue. These ratios are useful training tools to document and detail specific treatment results as they evolve. Almost every patient rapidly learns to correlate both absolute and ratio changes with proprioceptive, cognitive, affective, and/or pain level changes. High data loads of this type often paradoxically speed the process, even in massively dysfunctional patients (Bounias *et al.,* 1997). Frequency of treatment is an important consideration. For neurological training to occur, neural connections must be established and neuronal patterns of behavior brought from explicit and intentional to implicit and automatic. A great deal of practice is required to accomplish skillful and automatic integration of learned self-regulatory neuronal skills and thus achieve the desired endpoint of treatment. Therefore, in the treatment of medical conditions it consistently has been my experience that treatment frequencies of less than three times per week are ineffective. In my practice, a patient who cannot, or will not, engage at least three times per week in full half-hour treatment sessions and in a BioBehavioral session for another 45 min per week is not a candidate for treatment.

Duration of treatment at each treatment site (scalp location) is also a significant issue. Some clinicians use a strategy of brief and rapidly alternating treatment at a great many sites per session or per treatment course. Typically these clinicians do not use single electrodes attached to scalp and earlobes, but use an electrode cap with sensors attached to the inside. This allows the clinician to switch from site to site with ease. Because a durable training affect is established through the creation of new neuronal pathways supported by rewarding newly efficient functioning and since cortical electrical potential represents only a small portion of the actual electrical activity involved both in training and function, it seems counterproductive to switch "therapeutic horses" often. I strongly advise against treating patients in this fashion.

Frequency domains (bands) for training must be chosen carefully. The following paragraphs provide brief summaries of the clinical significance associated with dominant frequency domains (relative to scalp site CZ, in the eyes-closed patient over 14 year of age).

Delta (approximately 0.5–4 Hz), often referred to as "slow wave," ordinarily is associated with restorative processes of repair, especially during deep sleep. It is pathologically increased in a variety of serious disorders including head injury, coma, profound metabolic injury (including anoxia), congenital injury such as fetal alcohol syndrome, disorder of the immune system, severe substance abuse, severe anxiety, and major vegetative depression. While delta predominates in children up to the age of 4, after that age if it predominates in the waking state, (especially in the eyes-open condition). It is a particularly strongly pathological finding. Excessive slow wave activity is a sine qua non of attentional problems, and as such it should be screened for carefully when this is being considered as a diagnosis. Its presence, however, does not rule out the search for underlying causes of the final common pathway presenting as an attention deficit disorder nor does the presence of excessive levels of slow wave activity necessarily warrant an attention disorder as a diagnosis.

Increased levels of theta (commonly defined as 4–8 Hz) often are seen in psychotic states, delusion, and other states associated with poor reality testing and with seizure disorders. Theta may also be excessive in head injury and trauma. During healthy function, however, theta is associated with deep creativity, the "Ah ha!" experience and complex, sustained inspiration.

Alpha (8–12 Hz), which is predominantly associated with a relaxed, alert, unfocused state (often characterized by creativity and dreamy thoughtfulness), may be pathologically increased at the lower end of the frequency band in head injury and metabolic impairment. It may be pathologically decreased in mood disorders, chronic pain, and all stress-related disorders (whatever the organ or organs of final expression). Fear, whether chronic or acute, anxiety, and attention deficit disorders also are often associated with this alpha depression.

SMR (sensory motor rhythm) (usually considered as 12–14 Hz) normally is associated with a quiet body and active mind, an external focus of attention, paying attention, sequencing, and information storage and retrieval. It is often depressed in attention deficit disorders, mood disorders, anxiety, panic, obsessive compulsive disorder, fear, chronic pain, and the entire gamut of stress-related disorders. It is also deficient in migraine headache.

Beta 1 (commonly 12–16 Hz), normally associated with higher cognitive processes and rational analytical, problem-solving thinking and with focused concentration, usually is deficient in attention deficit disorders, stress-related disorders, chronic pain, depression and other mood disorders, psychotic states, substance abuse, panic, anxiety, and fear.

Beta 2 (commonly 16–24 Hz), normally associated with states of physiological arousal and response to threat, is elevated in all stress-related disorders, some mood disorders, panic, anxiety, fear, and chronic pain. In addition, some substance abusing and behaviorally abusive persons show high levels of beta 2.

All of these frequency deviations from normal or desirable are subject to "sculpting" via therapeutic training and therefore to remediation in the course of appropriately applied NBF treatment accompanied by ancillary and supportive modalities (Bounias *et al.,* 1997).

In addition to the schema mentioned, it is important to note that absolute EEG amplitude deviations from normal (and related ratios among frequencies) are only one consideration among many others that must be addressed (for example, location of deviations and relative symmetry or asymmetry, etc.).

An abbreviated list of medical conditions that may be appropriately treated with carefully applied NBF and related modalities include stroke (Chmielowska & Pons, 1995; Lubar & Deering, 1981; Laibow *et al.,* 1996), and other brain injury (surgical and otherwise) (Bounais *et al.,* 1997), hypertension (Byers, 1995; Ikemi, 1988), immune and autoimmune disorder, seizure disorders, whether postsurgical, post-traumatic, or idiopathic (Andrew & Schonfeld, 1992), substance abuse, and psychiatric illnesses such as OCD, anxiety and depressive disorder, and bipolar as well as a large number of other serious medical conditions (Byers, 1995). It is easy to see from this list that large numbers of patients benefit from the use of this nontoxic, noninvasive, and highly empowering treatment. In my opinion, NBF's clinical power and lack of contraindications, when properly applied, position it (along with nutritional medicine) as the central feature of the next great wave of medical advances.

The single most powerful block to professional collaboration in NBF is territorial parochialism. Once clinicians of all disciplines accept the fact that no one discipline, and no one practitioner in any discipline, can know enough or function in a wide enough scope of practice to serve the full needs of any patient by "going it alone" and begin seeking other like-minded, collaborative clinicians to form loose consortia and teams, this conceptual barrier will have been overcome and patient care will improve dramatically. Indeed, patient outcomes improve, and word-of-mouth and professional recognition surges. In our litigious times, it is important to note also that the collaborative model strongly recommended here may assist in protecting medical and nonmedical practitioners alike from medical legal problems.

The factors that lead to health and disease, function and dysfunction are deeply intertwined and refuse to be neatly separated into compartments. Physical, mental, and emotional aspects are invariably associated with a presenting diagnosis regardless of the organ system(s) involved in the chief complaint. If these vital cross-connections are ignored, both patient and practitioner will find themselves dealing with the unexpected and undesirable consequences of ignorance or inattention to the interactive potential of these aspects once treatment has been initiated. If properly attended to, however, these same cross-linkages are accelerators for health and healing at both the superficial and deepest levels of well being.

REFERENCES

Ader, R. (1981). "Psychoneuroimmunology." Academic Press, New York.

Adrian, E. D., & Matthews, B. H. (1934). The Berger rhythm: Potential changes from the occipital lobes in man. *Brain* **57,** 355–385.

Andrew, D. J., & Schonfeld, W. H. (1992). Predictive factors for controlling seizures using a behavioral approach. *Seizure* **1,** 111–116.

Barlow, J. S. (1986). Artifact processing (rejection and minimization) in EEG data processing. *In* "Handbook of Electroencephalography and Clinical Neurophysiology" (F. Lopes da Silva, W. Storm van Leeuwen, & A. Remond, eds.), pp. 15–62. Elsevier, Amsterdam.

Bounias, M., Laibow, R. E., Stubblebine, A. N., Sandground, H., & Bonaly, A. (1997). Changes in EEG parameters following QEEG NeuroBioFeedback rehabilitation of brain injured adults. (Unpublished manuscript).

Byers, A. P. (1995). "The Byers Neurotherapy Reference Library," p. 393. The Association for Applied Psychophysiology and Biofeedback. Association for Psychophysiological Education, Pueblo, Colorado.

Chmielowska, J., & Pons, T. P. (1995). Patterns of thalamocortical degeneration after ablation of somatosensory cortex in monkeys. *J. Comp. Neurol.* **36,** 377–392.

Cummins, N. A. (1977). The anatomy of psychotherapy under national health insurance. *Am. Psychol.* **32,** 771–718.

Dietsch, G. (1932). Fourier-Analyse von Elekrenkephalogrammen des Menschen. *Pflugers Arch.* **230,** 106–112.

Eisenberg, D. M., Davis, R. B., Ettner, S. L., Appel, S., Wilkey, S., Van Rompay, M., & Kessler, R. C. (1998). Trends in alternative medicine use in the United States, 1990–1997: Results of a follow-up national survey. *JAMA* **280**(18), 1569–1575.

Eisenberg, D. M., Kessler, R. C., Foster, C., Norlock, F. E., Calkins, D. R., & Delbanco, T. L. (1993). Unconventional medicine in the United States. Prevalence, costs, and patterns of use. *N. Engl. J. Med.* **328**(4), 246–252.

Fogel, B. S., Schiffer, R. B., & Rao, S. M. (1996). "Neuropsychiatry," p. 107. Williams and Wilkins, Baltimore, MD.

Hatch, J. P. (1985). Controlled group designs in biofeedback research: Ask, "what does the control group control for?" *Biofeedback Self-Regul.* **7**(3), 377–401.

Ikemi, A. (1988). Psychophysiological effects of self-regulation methods: EEG frequency analysis and continent negative variations. *Psychother. Psychosom.* **49,** 230–239.

Iosa, D., DeQuattro, V., Lee, D., Elkayam, U., & Palmero, H. (1989). Plasma norepinephrine I Chagas' cardioneuromyopathy: A marker of progressive dysautonomia. *Am. Heart J.* **117,** 882–887.

Jemmot, J. B., & Locke, S. E. (1984). Psychosocial factors, immunologic mediation, and human susceptibility to infectious diseases: How much do we know? *Psychol. Bull.* **95**, 52–77.

Kyle, R. A., & Greipp, P. R. (1983). Amyloidosis: Clinical and laboratory features in 229 cases. *Mayo Clin. Proc.* **58**, 665–683.

Kyle, R. A., Kotke, B. A., & Schirger, A. (1966). Orthostatic hypotension as a clue to primary systemic amyloidosis. *Circulation* **34**, 883–888.

Kyriakidis, M. K., Noutsis, C. G., & Robinson-Kyriakidis, C. A. (1983). Autonomic neuropathy in leprosy. *Int. J. Leprosy* **51**, 331–335.

Laibow, R. E., & Bounias, M. (in press). NeuroBioFeedback. In "The Textbook of Complementary and Alternative Medicine" (W. B. Jonas & J. S. Levin, eds.). Williams & Wilkins, Baltimore, MD.

Laibow, R. E., Bounias, M., Stubblebine, A. N., & Sandground, H. (1996). Rehabilitation of brain injured adults and adolescents through neural therapy (voluntary regulation of EEG activity). *In* "Effective Strategies for Assessment and Intervention, Proc. 20th Annual Postgraduate Course on Rehabilitation of the Brain Injured Adult and Child," pp. 153–155. Office of Continuing Medical Education, Virginia Commonwealth University, Medical College, Williamsburg, VA, June 6–9, 1996.

Lopes da Silva, F. (1993). Computer-assisted EEG diagnosis: Pattern recognition and brain mapping. *In* "Electroencephalography. Basic Principles, Clinical Applications and Related Fields" (E. Niedermeyer & F. Lopes da Silva, eds.), 3rd Ed. Williams & Wilkins, Baltimore, MD.

Lubar, J. F., & Deering, W. M. (1981). "Behavioral Approaches to Neurology." Academic Press, New York.

Luthe, W. (1969). "Autogenic Therapy," Vol. 4. Grune and Stratton, New York.

McCombe, P. A., & McLeod, J. G. (1984). The peripheral neuropathy of vitamin B12 deficiency. *J. Neurol. Sci.* **66**, 117–126.

Mulholland. T. (1995). Human EEG, behavioral stillness and biofeedback. *Int. J. Psychophysiol.* **19**, 263–279.

Mumford, E., Schlesinger, H. J., Glass, G. V., Patrick, C., & Cuerdon, T. A. (1984). A new look at evidence about reduced cost of medical utilization following mental health treatment. *Am. J. Psychiatry* **141**(10), 1145–1158.

Naik, R. B., Mathia, C. J., Wilson, C. A., Reid, J. L., & Warren, D. J. (1981). Cardiovascular and autonomic reflexes in haemodialysis patients. *Clin. Sci.* **60**, 165–170.

Rotberg, M. H., & Surwit, R. S. (1981). Biofeedback techniques in the treatment of visual and ophthalologic disorders: a review of the literature. *Biofeedback Self-Regul.* **6**, 375–388.

Schwartz, G. (1979). Disregulation and systems theory: A behavioral framework for biofeedback and behavioral medicine. *In* "Biofeedback and Self-Regulation" (N. Birbaumer & H. D. Kimmel, eds.), pp. 19–48. Lawrence Erlbaum Associates, Hillsdale, NJ.

Schwartz, M. S. (1987). "Biofeedback: A Practitioner's Guide." Guilford Press, New York.

Schwartz, M. S., & Fehmi, L. (1982). "Applications Standards and Guidelines for Providers of Biofeedback Services." Biofeedback Society of America, Wheatridge, CO.

Shapiro, D. (1979). Biofeedback and behavioral medicine: An overview. *Psychother. Psychos.*, **31**(1–4), 24–32.

Sklar, L. S., & Anisman, H. (1981). Stress and cancer. *Psychol. Bull.* **89**, 369–406.

Thornton, K. E. (1996). On the nature of artifacting the QEEG. *J. Neurother.* Winter, 32–39.

Wickramasekera, I. E. (1988). "Clinical Behavioral Medicine: Some Concepts and Procedures," p. 48. Plenum Press, New York.

5

NEUROFEEDBACK ASSESSMENT AND TREATMENT FOR ATTENTION DEFICIT/HYPERACTIVITY DISORDERS

JOEL F. LUBAR* AND JUDITH O. LUBAR†

*University of Tennessee, Knoxville, Tennessee, and †Southeastern Biofeedback and Neurobehavioral Institute, Knoxville, Tennessee

I. BACKGROUND

Attention deficit disorder (ADD) and attention deficit hyperactivity disorder (ADHD) is a lifelong disorder that affects perhaps as high as 10% of the population depending on which review article one reads and how it is classified and characterized (Whalen & Henker, 1991). ADD/ADHD overlaps with other disorders and presents in three main forms: inattentive, hyperactive-impulsive, and combined, according to the DSM-IV [American Psychiatric Association (APA), 1994]. An older term, hyperkinesis, is still used at times to represent attention deficit with hyperactivity. The overlap of both ADD/ADHD and specific learning disabilities (LDs) is as high as 70% (Hynd *et al.,* 1991). There are reported to be more than 250 different kinds of LDs (Hooper & Willis, 1989); and in some cases, ADD/ADHD and LD overlap with conduct problems (Barkley, 1990). The attention deficit disorder without hyperactivity is sometimes referred to as ADD–, according to Barkley's (1990) classification. This subtype tends to overlap more with anxiety disorders and learning disabilities. The attention deficit

Introduction to Quantitative EEG and Neurofeedback

disorder with hyperactivity, ADD+, also overlaps with learning disabilities, but is more concurrent with oppositional defiant disorder (ODD) and conduct disorder (CD).

ODD is diagnosed behaviorally when the individual, often a child, purposely does not follow rules, does not see the significance of them, and therefore does not believe they are important. If this is not corrected or treated, it can evolve into a conduct disorder. Conduct disorder is more severe and tends to involve more premeditative or purposefully destructive behaviors than ODD. If the conduct disorder is not brought under control, especially in late adolescence and early adulthood, it can evolve into a much more serious disorder known as antisocial personality disorder. Many individuals who have antisocial personality disorder spend part of their lives in prison, as do some with conduct disorder. When only oppositional defiant disorder is present, they usually do not reach the point in the legal system at which they are jailed.

A great deal of overlap of this whole constellation is seen with some other disorders such as depression. Some children with ADD/ADHD have movement disorders or tic disorders ranging from benign tic disorders to the more severe Tourette's syndrome. Occasionally they may have seizure disorders, and there is a higher incidence of substance abuse in the ADD and ADHD population than in the non-ADD/ADHD population.

New evidence from Kenneth Blum and colleagues (Miller & Blum, 1995; Noble *et al.,* 1991) suggests there is a strong genetic component in a whole constellation of problems located on chromosome 11. They have identified the series of alleles that are associated with ADD/ADHD that lie close to another set associated with alcoholism, other addictions, and Tourette's syndrome. They refer to the whole constellation of problems as the "reward deficiency syndrome." Perhaps this is one of the reasons why these disorders often occur together as comorbidities. We find in our evaluation of children with ADD/ADHD that it is very common to be able to follow its manifestations back one to three generations in the family. In doing an intake evaluation, one of the questions we ask is to what extent the disorder is seen in other family members, particularly in males, because it is between four and six times more common in males than in females (Lubar *et al.,* 1991).

Some considerations of the criteria for ADD/ADHD listed in DSM-IV (APA, 1994) require elaboration. A main behavioral deficit includes difficulty in task completion, particularly if the task is perceived by the child, adolescent, or even adult as irrelevant. For example, if a teacher tells the child, "I want you to go home and do the fifty math problems on page one hundred," the child will probably not get the work done. A common excuse offered to the parents is "There is no homework tonight" or "I lost the assignment on the way home," or, if the assignment is brought home, there will be a pitched battle between the child and parents over each math problem. The child will plead "I want to go out and play" or "I want to watch TV." The parent may say, "If you do the next problem, I'll give you a nickel; if you don't do the next one, I'll send you to your room." This kind of behavior goes on and on and the assignment may get done, very sloppily, and then the next day, it does not get turned in, is destroyed, or is lost.

Consider another scenario: The mother is called into the principal's office because the child is not getting the assignments done and the principal says, "Your child has attention deficit disorder" and the parent says, "That's not possible. My child will come home and sit in front of a TV set for four hours, play computer games, or play in the arcade with his friends for hours without stopping. He also likes to build models all the time, beautiful models, and does it very meticulously; how can you say my child has an attention deficit disorder?" The answer is that attention deficit disorder is extremely selective, it is not global. These children are not necessarily distractible; they are mainly distractible when doing tasks that they do not see the point of doing. This is only one aspect of ADD/ADHD behavior; another is that with regard to the child's life space, he or she is living "in the moment," everything important is happening right this minute. These problems relate to the child's inability to perceive rewards. If you say to the child, "Now look, you've got to get this homework done, you have an exam this week. If you don't get these problems done, you're going to have difficulty getting through the exam," the typical response is "Oh, that exam isn't until Friday, so why do I have to do it today on Monday? I'll do it Thursday night." The child does not *process* the consequences of his or her behavior. These are some of the aspects of ADD/ADHD that are not well covered in the current DSM manual.

The selection of treatments typically used includes stimulant medications, especially for children who have the hyperactive form of ADD/ADHD. Amphetamine sulfate (Benzedrine) was first prescribed by Bradley (1937). The other common treatment is behavior therapy (Barkley, 1990). Regardless of which treatment is employed, whether it is neurofeedback, behavior therapy, drug therapy, and all the possible combinations with and without family and individual psychotherapy, there is one sad reality: ADD/ADHD is not *curable* at this point in time; it can merely be managed. Diabetes is also not curable, but one can become asymptomatic with proper management, live a normal long life, and not suffer any significant consequences if it is not too severe. There are many other medical-psychological disorders that can be treated to the level of becoming asymptomatic. The hope for individuals with ADD/ADHD is that they, too, can experience long asymptomatic periods (except perhaps under extreme conditions of demand or stress). But for the present, it appears that ADD/ADHD is a pervasive, lifelong neurologically based disorder.

Although ADD/ADHD is expressed in terms of poor educational achievements, inappropriate emotional behavior, and all of the problems seen in terms of compliance, academics, etc., the problem is not a primary emotional disorder, an educational disorder, or a behavioral disorder; it is neurological. This means that ADD/ADHD is reflected in the way the child, adolescent, or adult processes information, which is, in turn, affecting how the individual perceives the world and therefore responds to it. The point of view in working with this disorder using neurofeedback is that if we can change the underlying neurology, perhaps we can effect a more long-term change in this disorder. This relates to the reason why behavior therapy has not been particularly successful. It works very well while it is being done. You can set up complex schedules of time-outs and reinforcements for behaviors. You can say to the child, "Okay, you have twenty-five math problems to do. If you get them done, we're going to go out to your favorite restaurant for dinner." Half an hour later, they are done perfectly. The next night, however, the child says, "I'm not going to do the homework." What is the parent going to do now? There is very little carryover of the seemingly potent reward. The hope is that if you continue to do the behavior therapy, from age 6 to somewhere around age 16, the message will finally get through and the child will develop insight as an adolescent and will be able to self-integrate the task-appropriate behaviors without continuous reinforcement or punishment. But very often, that is not the case.

The stimulant medications are powerful for many children with hyperactivity, and 60–70% of children on medication show a very marked improvement of the hyperkinetic component of the syndrome and may perform better educationally. However, as soon as medication is out of the body, the ADD/ADHD behaviors return. If one is using a very short-term medication such as methylphenidate or Ritalin, inattentive, impulsive, or hyperactive behaviors will reappear within 3–6 hr after the last dose is given. Then you have to administer the drug in the morning, again at noon, and maybe another small dose in the afternoon just to get through the homework. If you do not give the medication during weekends or on vacation, ADD/ADHD behaviors return. Parents often despair of taking their hyperactive children on vacation because they say they are unmanageable. Some experts in the field such as Wender *et al.* (1985) say that it does not matter if they are 8 or 80 years old–keep them on medication all the time, even during vacations. Because the disorder is not curable, the theory of medication is to alter the distribution of neurotransmitters, especially dopamine and norepinephrine in the brain, and thus maintain the appropriate behaviors pharmacologically. Unfortunately, pharmacologic treatments do not seem to have a long-term carryover. If a child has been on Ritalin for 10 years, and an attempt is made to phase him off the drug, you are likely to find that the improved behaviors continue to be maintained for approximately 3 months but then are lost, at which point it may be necessary to return to the medication regimen (Whalen & Henker, 1991).

Another fallacy from the older literature is if the child has hyperkinesis or is hyperactive, and you do not do anything, it will go away (Swanson &

Kinsbourne, 1979). What eventually will happen in many cases is that the hyperactivity does decrease, but the attention deficit becomes worse, and you have an adolescent or young adult who has ADD− characteristics. They start failing courses in high school or they get expelled from school. They cannot go to college, or, during college, they cannot succeed academically and have to leave. If they get a job, they very often get fired because they do not meet the employment demands, or they get in power struggles with peers or superiors. We have treated adults who come in to talk about their marital situation and say, "I've been married several times." Then we ask, "Do you have an idea of what some of the problems may have been that caused this to happen?" They may say, "Yes, I got bored with the relationship, it wasn't interesting anymore. I found somebody else." Their ability to stay in any particular setting is very difficult. They often will go from job to job, from location to location, sometimes from marriage to marriage, thus exemplifying some other aspects of this pervasive disorder. Sometimes children with ADD/ADHD will perform well up to about grade 3 or 4, if they are very bright, and then perform more poorly, until eventually they just cannot make it as the demands of school become greater.

II. SUBTYPES OF INDIVIDUALS WITH ATTENTION DEFICIT HYPERACTIVITY DISORDER

As noted earlier, children and adults with ADD/ADHD often experience comorbid difficulties including oppositional defiant disorder (ODD), conduct disorder (CD)a, anxiety disorder (AD), substance abuse, depression, and in some cases, tic or movement disorders. To complicate matters further, between 50 and 70% of children with ADD/ADHD also experience learning disabilities. Barkley (1990) has already pointed out that children with ADD+ may experience primary difficulties in terms of attention, impulse control, or impulsiveness or hyperactivity. He also has pointed out that it usually can be diagnosed before the age of 7 and generally is associated with distractibility, poor planning, poor rule-following behavior, and inability to engage in sustained activities for any significant period of time. Although some individuals are described as hyperactive, others are described as hypoactive or lethargic, easily bored, uninterested in most play activities, and extremely uninterested in school-related activities. The latter are classified as ADD of the inattentive type. Children who have coexisting specific LDs may be classified additionally in terms of specific areas of disability, such as subtypes of reading disability. For example, Flynn and Deering (1989) and Flynn et al. (1992) have described two subtypes of dyslexics, diseidetic and disphonetic.

The question arises as to whether these different subtypes of ADD/ADHD, for example, with or without specific learning disabilities, CD,

ODD, or depression, can also be characterized as neurologically distinct. If they are neurologically distinct, it is important to tailor neurofeedback treatment for the neurology that is presented by these different subtypes. Recently Amen *et al.* (1993) and Amen (1997) have been evaluating ADD/ADHD using brain SPECT (single proton emission cerebral tomography) imaging. SPECT imaging is a technique similar to PET (positron emission tomography). SPECT measures cerebral blood flow and indirectly brain metabolism, and has the advantages that it involves less radiation than PET, is less expensive, and allows for a longer data collection period while the tracer is being distributed through the nervous system. Furthermore, SPECT employs intravenous administration of the tracer, whereas PET uses an intra-arterial line. There appears to be a high correspondence between the findings reported by our group using quantitative EEG and topographic brain mapping and the SPECT scan findings. Both the quantitative EEG and the SPECT scan findings indicate that for the most part ADD/ADHD is a disorder that involves hypoactivation of the prefrontal lobes and medial central cortex, particularly during an intellectual or academic stress task. The more ADD/ADHD children try to concentrate, the poorer they perform on academic tasks and the more they show slowing or decreased cortical metabolism, particularly in frontal and central areas. One of the advantages of SPECT and PET scan over EEG is that they allow examination of what is happening in subcortical structures as well as changes in the cortical surface in terms of blood flow and cortical activity. The Amen *et al.* study involved 54 children who met the DSM-III-R criteria for ADD/ADHD and who were compared with 18 controls. Their work identified the following subtypes:

1. One subtype is frontal lobe deactivation without other findings. This is the more classic ADD+ type individual who often responds well to stimulant medication if pharmacotherapy is the treatment chosen. These individuals show markedly decreased frontal lobe metabolism, particularly during academic tasks as compared with a resting, eyes-open baseline.

2. A second subtype is represented by temporal lobe dysfunction. These individuals will often have deep temporal lobe dysrhythmias or epileptiform activity, and experience an attention deficit disorder that seems to respond best to anticonvulsants, sometimes combined with Ritalin, if pharmacotherapy is chosen.

3. A third subtype is ADHD with homogeneous cortical suppression. These individuals tend to respond to antidepressants in combination with Ritalin. The main difference between this subtype and the first subtype is that individuals with this type of disorder have more widespread cortical deactivation than the stimulant responders alone. Very often these individuals will respond well to tricyclics such as Desipramine or Norpramine.

4. A fourth subtype includes individuals who actually have *increased*

activity in the anterior medial aspects of the frontal lobes. This refers to an anatomical region known as the gyrus rectus or the region that lies in front of the septal region. These individuals are also hyperactive, distractible, and restless. This pattern is also associated with obsessive–compulsive disorder and overfocusing to the point of being unable to complete a variety of tasks. Hence, these individuals experience a type of attention deficit which includes an inability to shift attention and excessive overattending to often irrelevant details. Some individuals with medial orbital-frontal hyperactivation express emotional volatility, explosiveness, and aggression. These individuals often respond to alpha-adrenergic blockers such as clonidine. The anterior cingulate gyrus, which projects to the orbital-frontal cortex, has been found to be hypermetabolic in many of these individuals.

5. A fifth subtype is characterized as ADHD with hypofrontality at rest, but normal frontal activity with the challenge of intellectual stress. These individuals are also distractible, impulsive, and restless, but there often are also extremes of oppositional-defiant behavior in comparison with some of the other subtypes. They also tend to respond well to methylphenidate (Ritalin).

Overall, the Amen et al. (1993) study found that in 87% of the cases, prefrontal lobe deactivation occurs with intellectual stress (65%) or decreased activity in the prefrontal lobe at rest (22%). In our own work with quantitative EEG, some preliminary evidence suggests that individuals who show more slowing in the right prefrontal lobes experience difficulties with impulse control and often act inappropriately in social situations, but show good organizational skills. Children with left prefrontal lobe slowing tend to have poor organizational skills, but are more appropriate in social settings; children with right posterior parietal slowing tend to be in the lethargic, hypoactive category and often complain that everything is "boring."

In an often referenced study by Henriques and Davidson (1991), it has been shown that individuals experiencing reactive or monopolar depression have more left frontal alpha than right frontal alpha activity, whereas nondepressed individuals tend to have more right frontal alpha activity than left frontal alpha activity. The overlap of hypofrontality, in terms of theta activity and perhaps excessive left frontal alpha activity, might represent a type of individual who experiences both ADHD and depression. To make matters more complicated, it is known from the research of Peniston and Kulkosky (1989) that many individuals experiencing alcohol addiction and certain other types of chemical dependency (which often co-occur with ADD/ADHD) experience increased beta activity and decreased alpha and theta activity. This pattern was originally shown by the work of John and colleagues (1988).

One final point regarding the neurology of ADHD and associated disorders is that many of the "executive functions," including planning, judgment, and appropriateness of behavior in social settings, are mediated not only by the prefrontal cortex but by the frontal pole and the area underneath the frontal pole known as the orbital-frontal cortex. Furthermore, according to Posner and Raichle (1994) the arterior cingulate gyrus, which projects to the orbital-frontal cortex, is important for initiating action or "executive attention." The orbital-frontal cortex has extensive projections to the amygdaloid complex and other structures within the limbic system that have been shown for nearly a century to mediate strongly emotion and motivational states. The orbital-frontal cortex thus is one of the cortical organizing areas for the control of emotional behavior through the limbic system and ultimately through the output systems of the autonomic and skeletal motor pathways. It is most unfortunate that we cannot reach this area of the brain in terms of neurofeedback strategies. Although the orbital-frontal cortex is for all practical purposes relatively inaccessible for EEG assessment, it is a region of the brain that is very sensitive to medication effects. Thus, individuals for whom SPECT and PET scans show abnormalities in this region, pharmacotherapy rather than a neurofeedback approach remains the first course of intervention. In contrast, patients who show excessive EEG slowing in the superior frontal cortex or the midline central cortex are candidates for neurofeedback interventions.

A question raised by this literature is whether we should encourage an extensive neurological assessment of a patient candidate before engaging in neurofeedback. Is the use of EEG sufficient or should we probe further with neuroimaging techniques that may involve radioactive tracers? In our own work, we have usually placed our electrode sensors bilaterally, halfway between CZ and FZ (FCZ), or halfway between CZ and PZ (CPZ) for feedback training. The reasons for using these particular placements are that, based on 19-channel QEEG and topographic brain mapping, these locations represent the areas where the highest ratios of theta to beta activity are seen, and it is assumed that this is the most relevant neurological (EEG) correlate of ADD/ADHD. The treatment success rate with this particular set of placements has been found to be very high by our group and many others who are using this protocol for training, especially for children and young adolescents.

We wish to encourage both clinicians and researchers to consider other sites based on the individual neurology that is presented, and to do the training either with bipolar or referential electrode placements over those sites where EEG assessments indicate that abnormal activity is more focal (particularly if it is not along the midline). If the greatest amount of dysfunction is in the orbital frontal cortex, the logical locations for recording this activity would be FP1 and FP2; however, eye roll, blink, and frontal EMG artifacts make these sites virtually impossible to use. If one were treating depression, perhaps placing electrodes at either F3 and F4 or C3 and C4 or some intermediate point between F3 and C3, and F4 and C4, would be acceptable in terms of changing alpha ratios between left and right hemispheres. This has been demonstrated by Rosenfeld *et al.* (1995). These same locations, utilizing a combination of feedback to change alpha distribution and to decrease the amount of theta activity and increase the amount of beta activity, might be ideal for working with ADD/ADHD individuals who are also depressed. This protocol might be the neurofeedback analog for individuals who are placed on a combination of stimulants and tricyclic antidepressants. Individuals who show the slow lethargic pattern sometimes characterized by slowing in the right posterior parietal region around P4 might be trained in that location, or with electrodes perhaps at C4–P4, a bipolar placement, or trained to change the ratio of theta–beta activity in the right parietal region with respect to the left parietal region in order to equalize distribution of this activity between the two hemispheres.

One final point that is of relevance with regard to electrode placement is the question of generalization. We have seen in more than a dozen cases, in which training was carried out along the central cortex with electrode placements either at FZ, CZ, PZ, or at FCZ–CPZ, prepost training changes in the theta–beta ratios in all 19 standard electrode locations. Although the changes are greatest in the central cortex, they can be seen even in occipital and temporal regions where small improvements are noted. This indicates that even with a central location, the effects of the neurofeedback are experienced in widespread cortical areas. The issue of whether there is generalization from locations lateral to the midline to all other locations is unknown at the present time and represents a researchable question. Lubar (1997) refers to the theories and mechanism of neocortical dynamics to explain how this generalization might occur in terms of resonant intercortical and thalamocortical loops. At the present time, we do not recommend electrode placements that employ summation of activity from multiple sites. The algebraic sum of EEG activity from multiple sites bears no resemblance to the activity seen at each site individually and may result in feedback that is either irrelevant or perhaps even injurious.

The question also arises as to which bandpasses are appropriate for neurofeedback training. In working with children, typically we reinforce increasing beta activity between 16 and 20 Hz and decreasing theta activity between 4 and 8 Hz. This has worked for the majority of patients. However, above the age of 14, we find that there are many individuals who show excessive alpha activity and lack of alpha blocking. With these individuals we often train to decrease activity between 6 and 10 Hz, high theta low alpha (thalpha), and increase beta activity between 16 and 22 Hz, 16 and 24 Hz, or even 18 and 24 to 26 Hz. These decisions are based on QEEG spectral analyses to determine whether there are areas in which there is decreased beta activity or increased alpha and/or theta activity during task specific conditions. It is difficult to train activity above 28 Hz with conventional feedback systems because of overlap with the electromyogram

(EMG) spectrum and the possibility of training individuals to increase certain types of muscular activity in order to achieve reinforcement for these higher frequencies.

III. ADDITIONAL NEUROFEEDBACK CONSIDERATIONS FOR ADD/ADHD

Neurofeedback, a form of EEG biofeedback, has developed very rapidly. We were the first to develop this methodology for treatment of hyperactivity, learning, and attention problems in the mid-1970s, but in the last 10 years, there has been a burgeoning of interest in this area. Now there are more than 800 groups we know of that are using neurofeedback to treat this complex of disorders. They are reporting very impressive results with their patients. Some clinics claim success rates from 70 to 90%. That seems extremely high because medications are effective for only about 60–70%, or sometimes 75% with multiple medications. Behavior therapy seems to be effective for about 40–50% of the children. With neurofeedback, if you choose the children, adolescents, or adults properly, there is long-term carryover. After they are phased out of treatment, some patients may need occasional "booster" sessions. We have followed 52 individuals for up to a 10-year period and find that the behavioral changes assessed by the Connor's Parent Scale have been maintained long after the treatment was over (Lubar, 1995). These data were gleaned from a retrospective study by independent survey. Many of our former patients have made statements such as "If I hadn't had that experience five or eight or ten years ago, I would've never made it. It was the biofeedback that made a difference in my life." Some of them were even able to eliminate stimulant medication. Neurofeedback, especially as part of a multimodal treatment, holds the promise of long-term carryover.

Patient selection is extremely important. Our position statement regarding who is appropriate for neurofeedback treatment for ADD/ADHD is a living document (Lubar, 1995) and was developed empirically. If practitioners follow these guidelines carefully, they will derive maximally positive results from a majority of the patients they treat. If one treats individuals who fall outside the guidelines, the treatment is experimental, and the patient should be told this and it should be stated in writing in a consent-to-treat form. Probably the most dramatic example of an exception to that set of guidelines was a boy we worked with in our summer program 8 years ago. This child was very hyperkinetic, was on Ritalin, and was having considerable difficulties in school. Based on our current guidelines, we probably would not have worked with this child. His parents were very insistent and stated that they knew it was a risk and may not work, but wanted to try it. The child responded incredibly well–so well that he went off all of his medication, never went back on it, and was an honor student in junior high school.

The efficacy of patient selection is further enhanced if one considers any mood disorders and addictive disorders in the patient and in the family. The dysfunctional family pattern such as the family projection process (Bowen, 1978) may exacerbate the behavior of the child with ADD/ADHD and make them the target of family anger. Parental anger at some member of the previous generation (parents or same generation siblings) may be projected and focused (Friedman, 1985) on the individual with ADD/ADHD. Because of the amount of emotional turmoil in the family which surrounds ADD/ADHD behaviors, the child with ADD/ADHD is a perfect target for such anger to be projected. In addictive families children with ADD/ADHD can become the scapegoat for the family dysfunction. The dysfunction due to the addiction is then denied and treatment is sought for the child instead of the addicted parent.

Because of factors such as those just mentioned, and because we have empirically found that our ADD/ADHD neurofeedback protocol is not successful with primarily depressed patients, it becomes extremely important to do a thorough family evaluation and a genogram. A decision next can be made as to whether (1) the patient could benefit from neurofeedback with a minimal amount of parent education, (2) the patient is acceptable in neurofeedback if the parents agree to go into therapy over issues of emotional abuse and the neurofeedback is done concurrently, (3) the family issues of physical and sometimes sexual abuse and/or parental addiction have to be dealt with first before any neurofeedback is considered, and (4) the patient is unacceptable on other criteria such as low intelligence, too young for treatment, personal abuse of drugs, or primary depression, in which case treatment should not be initiated. Both depression and bipolar disorder can accompany ADD/ADHD. The depression may be reactive to the patient's school or job failure, or secondary to the patient's inability to pay attention to what he or she considers unimportant or boring. The depression could also be endogenous and exacerbated by inappropriate social skills secondary to a neurological condition, in which case the family dysfunction plays a minimal role in the patient's depression. Neurofeedback with or without medication still may be the treatment of choice when accompanied by some parent education. This education may take the form of appropriate limit setting, a good understanding of appropriate reactions to oppositional behavior, and an understanding on the part of the parent of which behaviors are actually oppositional and which are nonvolitional and neurologically based. However, some patients come for treatment with an intergenerational history of depression and bipolar disorder. A great majority of the latter have a history of addictive behaviors in their families. They may experience ADD/ADHD, but they also have a primary depression due to genetic factors and/or emotional, physical, and sometimes sexual abuse. It is our empirical experience that if one tries to do neurofeedback with this group of patients without any other interventions, one may obtain some success in the treatment within the clinical setting, but the overall treatment is unsuccessful, especially with regard to long-term results.

Figure 5.1 shows a more typical pattern of neurofeedback treatment illustrated by increased percentage of beta over sessions which occurred with reactive depression in a patient who came from a family with a history of primary depression. This patient's family history showed several generations of depressed relatives some of whom had been hospitalized at times for "nervous breakdowns." Neither parent ever had a psychotic depressive episode, but both parents were dysthymic and on antidepressants. The family was a dysfunctional family in which the father was not at all involved with the children, and the mother and the children formed a "triangle" (Friedman, 1985), both emotionally and in terms of their activities. This patient was accepted for neurofeedback because at his initial appointment he did not exhibit any signs of depression except for a reactive depression to the school setting, and the family had agreed to come into family therapy over their issues. They had several family therapy sessions before the onset of neurofeedback.

The patient's graph shows averaging of all within-session conditions for each session. That is, the percent beta averages for a baseline segment, neurofeedback segment, reading segment, and listening segment have been

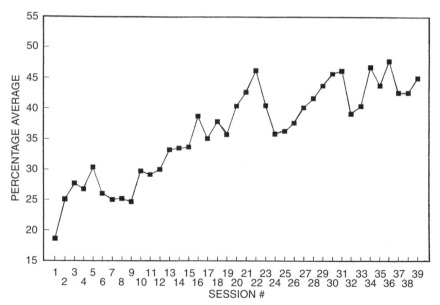

FIGURE 5.1   Grief over imagined illness in parents. The figure represents average percent of beta over initial baseline and four training sessions.

averaged into one value for this patient at each of 39 sessions. Note that the patient shows a very even steplike mode of learning in which he incrementally increases the percentage of beta over 23 sessions from about 18% to approximately 47%. At that point however, the patient lost almost 25% of his gain in two sessions. Both he and his parents denied any problems. It was suggested to them that the boy and his therapist go fishing as a way of encouraging him to talk more freely in a congenial environment. The patient and therapist went to a nearby lake to fish and simply talk and relax. While fishing he was able to focus on the ducks and ducklings swimming across the pond and asked what the therapist thought would happen to the ducklings if their mother died. When the therapist asked him what he thought would happen, he said that he was too young to bring up his brother. It turned out that he had overhead a conversation, unknown to both his parents, in which his mother had told a good friend of hers that she had a lump in her breast and was going in for a biopsy. Because he was not supposed to know about the biopsy, nobody told him when the test came out negative. As a result, he had become extremely depressed during that period of time, believing he would be motherless and would have to bring up his brother alone when his mother died. After this crisis was resolved and the mother was able to tell him that she did not have cancer, and the father agreed to become more involved with the children and spend some more time with them, the patient was able to recover all of his losses in EEG beta over the next eight sessions. He had only one small loss again at session 31 and then continued to do well. We have seen many graphs which show a loss of previously appropriate EEG changes during a depressed or grieving episode.

A child who has a family history of depression and the genetics for depression, or one who becomes overwhelmed with grief, most likely will not maintain gains obtained in neurofeedback for ADD/ADHD. In fact, if a major depression is present and diagnosed at the very beginning, and treatment nevertheless is provided, the patient's graph often "flatlines." It is our suggestion that if one is working with a patient with a primary depression, one needs to take care of the depression through therapy and/ or medication first and then, when the depression is stabilized, proceed further. Sometimes a patient starts neurofeedback and events in his or her life result in depression and grief. If this occurs it is important to either stop treatment and begin other therapy or continue such therapy concurrently with neurofeedback. Usually it has worked best for us to have separate therapy sessions. However, if qualified, one may add some therapy during the feedback session. Figure 5.2 shows a change in the percentage of beta in a patient whose grandmother had died at session 16. He was dealing with his grief during the next 2 weeks. One can see that the microvolts of beta diminish for a period of time and then increase again, resuming

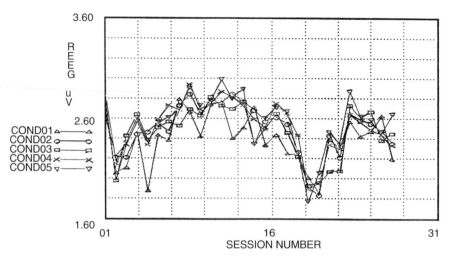

FIGURE 5.2   Change in beta microvolt levels in a male patient during grieving over the death of a grandmother.

the gains acquired in the first part of treatment as the grieving begins to be somewhat resolved.

For some patients, positive EEG changes during the first few sessions show a regression toward beginning readings after sessions 7–11. This probably indicates that boredom has occurred, and the true hard work in neurofeedback has just begun. For most patients, gains after this period of regression represent the true learning that has occurred. If a depressive episode occurs at the beginning of treatment or during the first 11 sessions, it becomes much harder to ascribe the change in EEG to depression. The therapist has to depend on clinical knowledge, which includes the fact that childhood depression often expresses itself in either lethargy or overactivity. The graph shown in Fig. 5.3 represents microvolt changes in a child who suffered reactive depression due to a family event. As can be seen in this figure, microvolts of theta increased for a 10-year-old child with ADD/ADHD during an episode of maternal drinking. Microvolts of theta then decreased when the episode terminated.

In this case the child had been accepted into treatment because the mother had been in Alcoholics Anonymous for several years, and her sponsor had assured us that she had had a long period of sobriety. However, when an episode of drinking did occur, the microvolts of theta actually increased starting with session 7. At this point, had we not become aware of the child's mood change, we could not have been certain that the theta microvolts were not simply going up as a reaction to the fact that a novelty or placebo effect had ended. A therapist intervention with the mother and child during sessions 7–21 helped the mother to seek treatment and deal

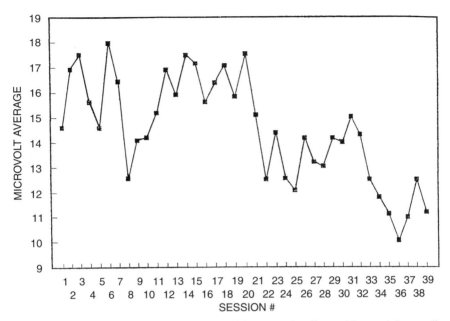

FIGURE 5.3   Change in microvolt levels of theta over baseline and four training conditions in a 10-year-old whose mother started drinking.

with the remaining family pain. Thus, for the therapist, it becomes extremely important to obtain a long-term family history and be able to focus immediately on EEG changes in a patient who previously had been successful, but now is regressing early in treatment. The therapist needs to ask appropriate questions to determine whether there is an ongoing event that is resulting in depression. If there is a reactive depression to some family incident, therapy is required.

By contrast, if the patient starts treatment while some family issues (such as parental anger) are still being worked on in therapy, the patient may not show any changes in terms of his or her EEG until some of the family issues are resolved. In another patient (Fig. 5.4), EEG theta level has remained the same for approximately 22 sessions. The child was emotionally and verbally abused by his mother, and it was not until resolution of the issues with his mother came about as a result of her therapy that a change in the microvolts of theta occurred. In summary, if you engage in therapy with a patient who is presently being abused or is the focus of family dysfunction, a depressive episode will prevent a successful neurofeedback experience until problems in the family are resolved, either before the start of the therapy or during the early portion of the therapy.

A group of patients who typically suffer from depression are children who live in alcoholic families. They are targets of or witnesses to a great

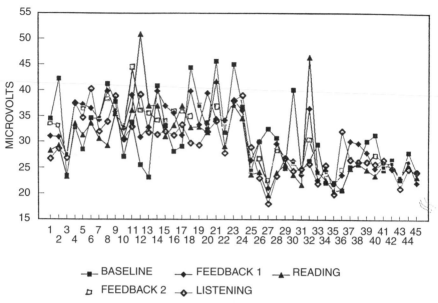

FIGURE 5.4 Change in theta microvolt levels in a 13-year-old male whose family had reached a significant resolution of important issues around session 21.

deal of emotional and sometimes physical and sexual abuse. They may carry genetic tendencies to addiction, and they may show abnormal P300 evoked potentials (Lubar *et al.,* 1995). If the family is actively using alcohol or drugs, it is important not to take the child into neurotherapy until the family problems are resolved. If one takes into neurotherapy a child from a family in which alcohol or drugs are presently the primary problem, the patient may be depressed and may even do very well in therapy sessions, but still fall asleep in class. He may not be able to remember or pay attention in the same way that severely depressed adults cannot focus and remember. The same mechanisms that disturb both attention and memory in adult depressed individuals also affect memory and attentional mechanisms in children. Their response to a treatment that primarily teaches them directed volitional attentional behavior cannot be successful as a result. Further, allowing the child into neurofeedback therapy not only creates a failure for him, but can reinforce a family sense that the patient is the primary problem and if they did not have this child with ADD/ADHD they would function quite well. Focusing on the child prevents the other family members from seeking further help for the family issues and for the issue of addiction. Thus, if a genogram indicates a primary problem of addiction, we simply tell the family that they have a larger problem at this point than the one they focused on when they came to us. We suggest that this family problem needs to be taken care of first. When the addiction is resolved and abstinence has occurred for a year or more, preferably with some Alanon and AA experience, then and only then is it appropriate for the child to come into treatment.

Sometimes other scenarios occur. A child can come from an addictive family in which the parents may not presently be using drugs or alcohol. They may have abused in the past and have gone through a period of sobriety and recovery. Sometimes the parents have never abused substances, but carry the genetic predisposition for alcohol or drug addiction. In such cases, a patient may start treatment without using any drugs, but during treatment he or she will suddenly start using them. For example, we worked with a patient with ADD/ADHD who had never used drugs and was heading for college. He had started his treatment while he was still in high school and was very successful. Then half way through the treatment he had a session in which the percentage and microvolts of activity to be inhibited (6–10 Hz) far exceeded his baseline. He eventually admitted that this was a time when he had used cannabis quite extensively. Why should a patient suddenly have such a change in his percentage of inhibit and microvolts of inhibit? Our inhibit frequency band for patients who are adults and for older teenagers is not set strictly for theta, but for some theta and some alpha between 6–10 Hz. Therefore, what the EEG was really reflecting was the increase in alpha, which occurs in patients when they smoke cannabis or use it in any other form. This patient originally denied that he had used cannabis and insisted that he had been ill and using very large amounts of antihistamine. Certain antihistamines also could have produced increased slow activity, although we had never seen an increase quite that dramatic. However, when this increase in inhibit microvolts and percentage of 6–10 Hz activity occurred several times, he was confronted and he admitted that he had discovered the use of this substance in college. He was quite unwilling to give it up since he equated it with extremely successful sexual experiences. His treatment was terminated at that point.

A similar issue can be observed for the use of cocaine. The literature has shown that cocaine users have similar psychomotor activity, overfocused episodes, and/or euphoria and rapid thoughts as people with ADD/ADHD and bipolar disorder (Cocores et al., 1987). If a patient starts using cocaine, he begins to look more and more hyperactive and his thought processes are more and more disturbed. It would be inappropriate to treat somebody who is using cocaine with the ADD/ADHD protocol. We feel that for successful treatment a patient has to be completely free of any inappropriate drug intake during the time of treatment.

Finally, we offer one last note of caution when dealing with bipolar disorders. The latter, as stated earlier, often have some symptoms similar to individuals with attention deficit disorder. Much misdiagnosis has occurred over the years in both directions: Patients with ADD/ADHD have been diagnosed as having bipolar disorder, and patients with bipolar disorder have been diagnosed as having attention deficit disorder. This is not an easy distinction to make in some adults, especially at certain points within the bipolar cycle; therefore, it is important to first ask the patient whether what they are now feeling has been cyclical or permanent, as far as they or their parents can remember, and seek consultation for greater certainty in terms of testing and psychiatric evaluation.

One can say that if the patient is a child or adolescent who is either living in a family that is using drugs or alcohol or is using drug and alcohol himself or herself, he or she is unacceptable as a candidate for neurofeedback for the beta–theta protocol. If the patient starts using drugs in the middle of treatment, then treatment needs to be terminated because it cannot be brought to a successful conclusion during the time of use.

In the remainder of this chapter, we explore issues relevant for the treatment of individuals with ADD/ADHD. We will not review the work that we and others have done in the development of this technique, since it has been reviewed in detail elsewhere (Lubar, 1991, 1995). The issues that will be considered are instrumentation considerations, how to differentiate different subtypes of individuals with ADD/ADHD, and the integration of neurofeedback with other therapies. There are also practical considerations such as informed consent, working with adults with ADD/ADHD, the relationship between ADD/ADHD and addictions, the design of neurofeedback treatments for individuals with both disorders, and needs to be addressed in future research.

IV. RECORDING EEG AND ARTIFACT CONSIDERATIONS

Recording quality EEG through the human scalp is not an easy task. Electrodes are placed on the scalp, and so they are also recording activity from the skin, such as skin potential electrodermal activity, and from underneath the skin, where there are several layers of muscle producing electromyographic activity (EMG). Furthermore, because one has to record through bone, there is further attenuation of the EEG, especially the higher frequency components. As a result, we are struggling with primarily non-EEG artifacts. There is EMG artifact, which is part of the signal, starting from as low as 12 Hz and ranging to greater than 300 Hz (although most of the EMG spectrum is between about 30 and 150 Hz). This is why a lot of EMG feedback machines for both EMG recording and EMG biofeedback will have a frequency range of 50–150 Hz. We are also concerned about EKG, electrocardiogram, since this is a very powerful artifact that is often seen in the EEG. EKG artifacts are occurring from the electrodes that are picking up activity from underlying pulsating blood vessels in the scalp. The EKG artifact is more prevalent in the recording as one gets older because, with aging, the EEG amplitude becomes smaller. This is because the skull becomes thicker, as do the meninges, the connective tissues between the skull and the scalp, and the skin layers. Furthermore, the amplitude of neurological activity decreases.

Trying to get a perfect multichannel recording from 19 or up to 32 channels becomes very challenging in adults. One might think children are going to be very difficult to gather EEG data from, but we have obtained some of the most ideal recordings from children because their EEG is so large that artifacts are less of a problem. If you are recording from frontal locations, you also pick up ocular artifacts, blinks, and electroretinal activity. If you examine the EEG, you sometimes see these large excursions, which look like slow-wave activity; however, these often are simply eye rolls. Eye movement and blink artifacts occur in the delta range 0–4 Hz, and sometimes up to 6 Hz, and occur over the anterior half of the scalp. If recording from any leads from the lateral surface, temporal, lateral frontal, parietal, or posterior (specifically sites F3, T3, P3, F4, T4, P4), we invariably pick up a lot of EMG activity from the masseter and temporalis muscles and with every swallow. Every time that happens, even to a small degree, we get a burst of very fast activity in the EEG that can create problems in terms of signal processing, sometimes leading to feedback for non-EEG activity. When recording from the posterior half of the scalp, one may pick up EMG activity from the occipitalis, trapezius, and supraspinal muscles. How does one obtain "clean" EEG signals from an individual? We spend a lot of time, especially if we are going to do quantitative topographic brainmapping, trying to clean up all of these signal problems; this can be done with relaxation or through positioning of the head. Sometimes you have to hold the head of the individual or use pillows to stabilize the head, so that you can minimize these artifacts. If you record from central locations along the midline, such as FZ, FCZ, CZ, CPZ, or PZ, you can get a relatively pure EEG signal.

One other important issue relative to feedback is an unresolved issue. This has to do with the difference between what is called *referential* recording and *bipolar* recording. When you employ referential recording, you are asking what the EEG activity is at a particular point on the head as compared with some reference point or points that are electrically neutral. The way we usually do this is to place a reference electrode on each earlobe. Essentially we are examining the relationship between activity at CZ or some other scalp point while making the assumption that the ears are neutral or act as a ground so any activity seen in that EEG recording represents the activity at that one point. This approach is good in terms of knowing what is happening at each point and differentiating the activity at each point from any other point. However, the energy field is maximal right under the electrode, and it decreases with the square root of the distance from the electrode so that, for example, the activity surrounding CZ, the central location, falls rapidly as we move away from CZ. If we have a montage where we have only one electrode with ear references that we use for feedback, we have to realize that what is really going to be influencing the feedback signal is a limited area around the electrode, and activity occurring more than a centimeter from that electrode probably will have relatively little effect. However, because of the resonant loops within the cortex, training at any one location can also change activity at many others.

Because referential recording for feedback purposes is very prone to artifacts, another alternative is bipolar recording. Bipolar recording depends on the algebraic subtraction of activity between two scalp sites. From an electrophysiological point of view or neurological point of view, we do not know exactly what that means, yet, nevertheless, training that type of activity seems to work very well for many different disorders. Bipolar recording has two advantages. One is that we are directly influencing activity over a larger area and that, of course, seems to be advantageous. Perhaps it affects the spread of EEG activity because if we are looking at the activity of apical dendrites in layer 1 of the cortex and that activity is linked to many cortical areas, it is going to have more influence on other regions of the brain.

Another advantage of bipolar recording is that anything (including artifacts) occurring in both channels at exactly the same time, at the same amplitude, and completely in phase is subtracted. This is called *common mode rejection*. If you clench your jaw, there will be a burst of activity in temporal electrodes, and if it occurs at the same time and in phase at both bipolar electrode locations, much of this EMG artifact will be subtracted. Certainly EKG is a problem when electrodes are placed over blood vessels in different scalp areas, and EKG artifacts are usually rejected or decreased as common mode activity. Eye roll and eye blink artifacts may also be reduced. However, if one is interested, for example, in pure alpha conditioning, and if electrodes are at 01 and 02, the alpha that is in phase and coherent between these locations will be subtracted. Such situations favor the use of a referential montage.

Because a considerable amount of neurofeedback concerns either increasing beta and/or decreasing theta activity for ADD/ADHD, or teaching individuals to increase alpha and theta activity and decrease beta for treatment of addictive behaviors (Peniston & Kulkosky, 1989), it is important to determine whether bipolar or referential recording and training is more appropriate. One of us has illustrated differences among referential and bipolar measurements recorded on the same individuals in a recent publication (Lubar, 1998). Another important consideration, however, deals with coherence and/or phase training. This can *only* be done with a bipolar configuration. Coherence is a correlational measurement of the degree to which two loci have a constant phase relationship for a designated frequency (Shaw, 1984). Coherence training has been used to help individuals with mild closed head injury reestablish more normative coherence measures (Stockdale & Hoffman, 1997).

V. EEG SIGNAL PROCESSING

How is the EEG signal processed in order to produce feedback? There are actually several techniques. One involves use of an active bandpass filter to isolate the particular frequencies of interest. If, for example, we are trying to train activity between 16 and 20 Hz, and the EEG signal is mixed with other EEG frequencies, one can design a filter that oscillates so that activity in the center frequency, which is 18 Hz, will maximally drive the filter to output. The highest output amplitude of this filter will be for activity between 16 and 20 Hz, and this then will be the frequency range that can trigger a feedback signal. Outside of that range, the filter will be less active, and it will not significantly respond to EEG one octave above or below the center frequency. Next we set an amplitude threshold so that as long as the activity of the filter is above that threshold, we will sample the signal at a certain rate, for example, 128 times a second. Finally, we can set a criterion, such that as long as the filter output is above a certain threshold (e.g., 7 microvolts), and we accumulate X samples in a Y-second period (e.g., 50 samples in 0.5 sec), feedback will be triggered.

Another technique is to apply Fourier analysis to the EEG signal to obtain the output needed to trigger the desired feedback. This is based on a theorem that was developed by Joseph Fourier in 1822 which states that you can take any complex waveform or *any* periodic waveform in the frequency spectrum from zero to many megahertz and decompose it into a series of sine and cosine waves. If we calculate the period of all the sine and cosine waves and take the inverse of their periods, we can calculate the frequency and the relative amplitudes of all the components in the complex waveform. Having thus isolated the components with the frequencies of interest (e.g., 16–20 Hz), these can be used to trigger the feedback signal. This technique has been utilized by the music industry, where it is called additive synthesis. One type of music synthesizer employs a large number of sine wave and cosine wave oscillators at different frequencies and combines them into a very complex waveform which simulates a flute, a clarinet, or a human voice. One disadvantage of Fourier analysis is that it takes time to make the initial calculation, so that the shortest length of time or *epoch* that one can use reliably to calculate a Fourier transform is about 2 sec. If less than 2 sec, there is loss of some of the lower frequencies. The way to get around this problem partially is to use a shifting time window, but there is still an initial delay. This procedure calculates the output during that first 2-sec period and updates it every 0.1 sec. This provides a moving average that follows the EEG even though there is a lag initially.

The faster the computer, the better it works, so that if one is going to use a biofeedback machine that involves this type of analysis, a recommendation is to employ as a minimum a 486-66-MHz computer with math coprocessors. If anything below that is used, there will be a significant feedback lag. Feedback lag with some Fourier analysis procedures can easily be observed. For example, when a client closes his or her eyes, some alpha activity appears on the monitor, and only after a delay of greater than 0.5 sec does the feedback occur. According to classical conditioning theory, the period between the conditioned and the unconditioned stimulus should be less than half a second. In contrast, if using an active bandpass filter, the delay between the raw signal and the filter response can be as little as 0.1 sec, especially for higher frequencies. There is no perfect signal processing device for feedback at the present time. The ideal system would probably be based on a pattern analysis. That would be ideal because it could be programmed to "see" a specific configuration in the EEG, and then give feedback only for that configuration or for a specified close approximation.

Regardless of the method of signal detection and processing used, make sure electrode leads are as short as possible, and that your electrodes are as stationary as possible. The impedance between electrodes and the skin surface should be less than 5 kohms. One also must be very careful about offset voltages in the electrodes, which can create amplifier problems. If you have gold or silver electrodes, they eventually become electroplated and will act like a little battery between the electrode and the scalp. That can happen if you take the electrodes off and keep them in water a few hours and then try to clean them. If you have a feedback system that depends on an EEG signal that is symmetrical around a zero voltage reference, and an electrode that acts like a battery, an offset voltage is imposed on the EEG. This distorts the signal and the signal processing circuits in the instrument might be processing only a portion of a signal, which also may be truncated with square wave components. Fourier analysis of a square wave has odd harmonics and, hence, the system might reinforce events that do not exist in the EEG. With a bandpass filter, the sharp cutoffs on square waves will cause the filter to "ring" or oscillate, which will also result in false feedback. Thus, what you may end up with is feedback that has very little if any relationship to the original waveform because of the offset voltage. If the waveform is offset enough that it is totally out of the amplifier range, the amplifier may respond by producing random noise. You can have excellent impedances and get poor recordings because the offset is too great, or you can have perfect offset and high impedance and get poor recordings so both criteria have to be met. When a session is done, take the electrode off the scalp, wipe it off with a Q-tip very carefully or wipe it off with a piece of cloth; or if you put it in water, hold the electrode so water cannot get up under the electrode collar. Use a toothbrush just to get the excess paste off, and then wipe the electrode dry as soon as you can after you use it. We have used the same electrodes daily for up to 5 years by taking good care of them.

VI. DATABASES

The determination of whether an individual is appropriate for a particular treatment employing neurofeedback is based on many factors, one of which is whether they present neurological evidence of functioning outside of the normal range. To determine this, databases need to be established for different disorders for which neurofeedback is currently being used. An excellent normative database has been developed by Thatcher *et al.* (1987) for normal controls of all ages from near birth to through senescence. The purpose of that database was to determine whether an individual with a closed head injury differs significantly from matched normal controls. However, the Thatcher database may have other applications besides closed head injury, one of which may be assessment of ADD/ADHD. When individuals with a particular disorder are compared with a normative database, the questions that might be asked are whether they differ in terms of the percentage of power in different frequency bands at different scalp locations. Also, one could question whether there are abnormalities in terms of coherence (a measure of the degree of phase correlation between two signals from different scalp locations), and whether there are abnormalities in terms of phase relationships in different regions. The Thatcher database is designed to answer these and other more complex questions. We believe that databases are particularly important if one wants to determine whether an individual is appropriate for neurofeedback treatment.

If a database is to have any significant validity, it must contain information from a large number of subjects. Recently we completed a multicenter study (Monastra *et al.,* 1999) involving eight neurofeedback organizations. Information was gathered only at location CZ, and only for the percent power ratio of theta to beta (defined as 4–8 Hz divided by 13–21 Hz), and calculated under four different conditions: an eyes-open baseline, reading, listening, and drawing. The study involved more than 615 individuals, including subjects with the inattentive form of ADD, the combined-hyperactive form of ADD/ADHD, and non-ADD/ADHD controls. The ages of the subjects ranged from 6 to 60 with most individuals in the database being below age 30. Very large statistically significant differences were obtained between the ADD/ADHD groups and controls for all ages up to approximately 50. Above 50, the number of subjects was much smaller, and it appears that finally, with age, the individuals with attention deficit disorder obtained similar ratios to the controls. We have also presented power ratios for a group of 27 controls with an average full-scale WISC-R IQ of 107, and a group of matched individuals with pure attention deficit disorder without hyperactivity with a mean full-scale WISC-R score of 102.5 (Mann *et al.,* 1992; Lubar, 1995). These children were between the ages of 9 and 12 with a mean age of 10.55. Measures were taken under three conditions: a baseline eyes-open condition, during reading material that was grade and comprehension level appropriate, and during reproduction of figures from the Bender Visual- Motor Gestalt Test. The data were normalized by log transform and power ratios were computed for the ratio of theta (4–8 Hz) to beta (13–21 Hz) and the ratio of alpha (8–12 Hz) to beta (13–21 Hz). Individuals with attention deficit disorder without hyperactivity experienced higher theta–beta and alpha–beta ratios for all conditions combined. More detailed analysis also showed greater differences during the drawing task than during the reading task, and relatively minor differences occurred during the eyes-open baseline task. These task-related differences were highly significant and have been reported in a previous paper (Lubar, 1991).

The database mentioned in the preceding paragraph was gathered on a particular instrument with a particular software program (Stellate Systems, Westmount, Canada), and the actual ratios obtained are matched for the Stellate brainmapping system. Data were also collected on another group of more than 60 individuals ranging in age from 7 to 11, and two older groups, 12- to 14-year-olds, and 15- to 55-year-olds. The total number of individuals in the entire group is greater than 100. These data were analyzed using the Lexicor Neurolex 24-channel system and are presented in another publication (Lubar, 1995). The basic finding that theta and alpha activity is increased with respect to beta appears to hold for individuals who have an attention deficit disorder *without* hyperactivity. Because the actual ratios obtained may differ somewhat depending on the instrument used and the way in which power is calculated, it will eventually be necessary to develop conversion factors that can be used to translate from one quantitative EEG mapping system to another. Eventually it should be possible to obtain ratio data as well as absolute power data that can be compared across a variety of different EEG systems.

Regardless of the results from QEEG, the first criterion for treatment consideration should involve behavior and history. Does the individual experience significant academic, organizational, and social adjustment difficulties? Has the individual been independently evaluated as having attention deficit disorder with or without hyperactivity, oppositional disorder, conduct disorder, or other comorbidities by a variety of measures including psychometrics, behavior rating scales, and academic performance? Note that reaction to medication is not included as a criterion since stimulant medications will improve cognitive functioning on a short-term basis for most individuals, regardless of whether or not they have an attention deficit disorder. If an individual experiences increased theta or alpha activity with respect to beta which is two or more standard deviations from a control group, they may also have a neurological marker for the disorder and might be a good candidate for neurofeedback interventions. However, there may be individuals whose ratios are within the normal range, but still may be good candidates for neurofeedback if it can be shown within 10–15 sessions that they are experiencing significant improvements in the areas that most typically demarcate their disorder.

If neurofeedback treatment is to be undertaken, it must be emphasized that the average number of sessions is 35–50, and comprehensive treatment requires, if not demands, the integration of neurofeedback with a variety of other treatment protocols, which often also include medication. In addition, a long-term follow-up is required. Patients must be weaned from the treatment gradually and followed for several years on an occasional basis to ensure that the gains attained are not lost. Patients should not be given false hope that a small number of sessions is going to remediate drastically their disorder. Additionally, we should emphasize that at the present time there is no definitive cure for attention deficit disorder (with its comorbidities) regardless of the treatment protocol! The purpose of neurofeedback is to help the clients function more like individuals without ADD/ADHD, which may or may not result in the reduction of medication, but hopefully will result in better academic, cognitive, and social functioning. At the present time there are no comprehensive replicated studies indicating that small numbers of sessions (less than 25) lead to long-term success. Until this is established, claims regarding this possibility should be undertaken with extreme caution; otherwise they border on a gross misrepresentation of what can be accomplished with neurofeedback regardless of the frequencies and locations trained, or whether the training was done with referential or bipolar montages or with a particular manufacturer's feedback system. The fact remains that ADD/ADHD is one of the most complex disorders that is treated with EEG or other forms of biofeedback and requires an enormous amount of effort, both on the part of the patient and the therapist.

One further question that is often raised in conjunction with neurofeedback treatment for attention deficit disorder is whether there is any relationship between success in training and degree of change in the EEG. Published data from our laboratory and clinic indicate that there is a strong relationship between these measures (Lubar *et al.*, 1995). We have obtained data on 17 children and young adults who had undergone neurofeedback training where we were able to do a complete 19-location quantitative EEG on the same individuals before and after training. Six of these individuals were not able to learn the task and 11 of them were able to learn the task very well. The 11 individuals who were able to learn were able to decrease their theta–beta ratios by at least 30% particularly in those locations that have been found most related to ADD/ADHD, specifically C3, FZ, CZ, PZ, and C4. Those individuals who did not learn showed no changes in their pre- and post-brainmap data.

VII. TERMINATION ISSUES

In employing neurofeedback for individuals with ADD/ADHD, we have found empirically that certain EEG changes seem to be markers of long-term improvement and for continuing to do well on cognitive and scholastic tasks. First, we have seen very quick changes in most patients between sessions 1 and 7 or sometimes sessions 1 and 11. These changes tend to be temporary and to represent the effect of novelty of engaging in an initially stimulating task. Somewhere around sessions 9 to 11 patients begin to be bored, and some regression occurs. If treatment is done appropriately, this boredom simply indicates that the novelty effect has worn off, and the patient is now entering the actual phase of learning how to pay attention to a less interesting stimulus. The regression, unless it is indicative of a depressive episode, may not be of concern for the therapist. However, after the patient has started his or her gains in the second phase of learning, the gains should show distinct learning curves somewhere between the 15th and 20th session of neurofeedback (or sometimes as far as the 25th session). To be successful with treatment, the therapist needs to determine the learning style of the patient and graph the progress in each of the feedback segments. These segments should include a baseline, pure feedback segments, and segments combining neurofeedback and academic tasks. Once the therapist knows the patient's learning style, he or she is able to make some prediction of the outcome of the treatment. For example, a patient whose graphs demonstrate a relatively linear improvement in their training parameters can be safely deemed to have met termination criterion when their learning curves have demonstrated an asymptote for at least 2 weeks for at least one condition, or after a minimum of 25 sessions (usually 40–50 sessions). This can be seen in Fig. 5.5.

However, for those patients who seem to learn incrementally, with or without intermittent plateaus, the best termination criteria are the ability to (1) approximate normative age-based EEG criteria and (2) maintain a level of 50–70% reward and 30–50% inhibit activity with, hopefully, a decrease in the microvolt level of the inhibit activity and increase in the microvolt level of the reward activity. Another very important variable to consider is a trend to decrease both the intrasession and intersession variability of the different measured and graphed parameters. A statistical measure reflecting this is called the *coefficient of variation*.

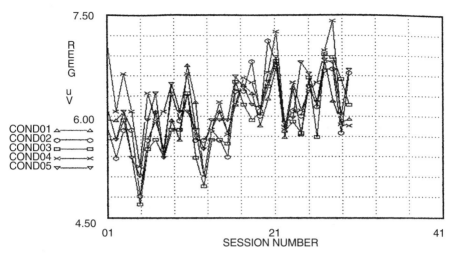

FIGURE 5.5 Examples of change in the beta microvolt level of a 12-year-old male who is *now* ready to start termination of his treatment.

In summary, it is important to first determine the patient's learning style, whether linear or incremental or with intermittent plateaus, and then to see which one of the following measures is changing in the correct direction: (1) the percent of time in beta or theta, (2) the microvolt levels of theta or beta, or (3) the number of rewards obtained and if the ratio of theta to beta is changing. One does not need a change in all of these three items to have successful treatment, but usually successful treatment does show a change in at least one or two of these measures. Similarly, a measure of variability such as the coefficient of variation intra- and intersession becomes very important because it indicates the patient's ability to respond in a stable manner across different tasks which may be either more or less interesting to him. It also indicates his ability to maintain these changes in a reliable way from one session to the next. In some cases we have obtained a successful treatment even if a change in variability is the only change that has occurred. Notice in Fig. 5.5 that the salient feature of this change in microvolts of beta is the reduction of variability over sessions even though the last four sessions are 2 weeks, then 3 weeks, then 1 month apart. To be able to see this possible physiological change one has to leave all of the parameter settings alone and watch the change of the EEG across tasks over many sessions. Some examples show the kind of integration over time that can occur in a patient who plateaus in terms of microvolts of beta with reduced variability in the last 10 sessions (Fig. 5.6), and in one who has reduced and stabilized theta–beta ratios (Fig. 5.7).

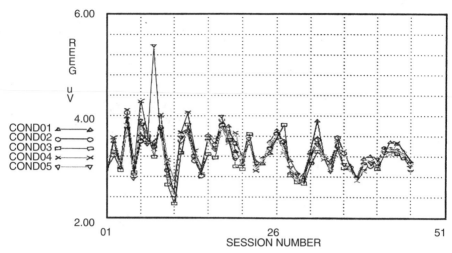

FIGURE 5.6   Change in variability in reward (beta) microvolt levels for a 13-year-old.

VIII. INTEGRATION OF NEUROFEEDBACK WITH OTHER PSYCHOLOGICAL THERAPIES

Attention deficit disorder with or without hyperactivity has been shown to be exceedingly complex and often associated with significant comorbidities as discussed previously in this chapter. It is clear that there is no

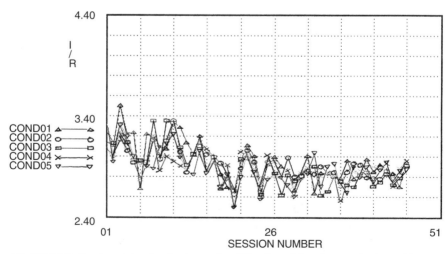

FIGURE 5.7   Example of reduction and stabilization of theta/beta ratios in an 18-year-old male.

monolithic treatment approach that is highly effective for dealing with this disorder. This includes psychotherapy, behavior modification, family therapy, cognitive behavior therapy, attribution therapy, medication, neurotherapy, or any other single approach. Numerous studies have compared various therapeutic procedures. For example, Reid and Borkowski (1987) have looked at the relationship between cognitive behavioral self-control techniques and attribution training for ADD/ADHD children. The rationale is that these children often interpret the cause of their successes or failures to be uncontrollable and external, leading to beliefs of helplessness and poor self-efficacy or self-esteem. In children who perceive themselves as helpless, repeated failures lead to a deterioration in the quality of their performance and their ability to sustain acceptable performance under stressful conditions. However, Reed and Borkowski's research has shown that teaching children who feel helpless to attribute their failures to *controllable* causes of insufficient effort, when combined with successful experiences, leads to increased motivation and improved performance. Those authors examined the influence of both antecedent (general historically based attributions relating to self-concept) and program-specific (domain-specific attributions of success or failure on a task) attribution training in combination with self-control training for the maintenance and generalization of newly acquired strategic behaviors. They found that attribution training which involved helping the child become aware of the role of personal effort in success or failure on a task was much more successful than the use of cognitive behavioral approaches alone. When children learned that they had control over situations that led to failure and that, by changing those strategies, they could change failure to success, they were much better at being able to modify certain aspects of their ADD/ADHD behavior than when simply reinforced for "doing the right thing." The results showed general *short-term* success in strategy-based learning, attributional beliefs, and more reflective self-control. These effects persisted at a 10-month follow-up, although there was a decrease in their size and scope. The two main problems that have plagued cognitive behavioral treatments, maintenance and generalizability, were significantly improved by including attributional training in the approach.

The point of the preceding study is that it represents one of the solely *behavioral approaches* that has shown any degree of success. Other behavioral approaches, such as operant control of behavior through standard behavior modification techniques, have poor carryover, and relapse occurs as the complex schedules or reinforcement are discontinued. As far as medication is concerned, by itself, it is also not sufficient. Studies by Satterfield (1973) showed that individuals who are placed on Ritalin alone had very poor long-term outcome in terms of ADD/ADHD behaviors and oppositional defiant behaviors. Many individuals who had been incarcerated as young adults had a history of ADD/ADHD and had been placed only on medication with no other attendant therapies. As a result of these findings, Satterfield believes that the integration of medication with psychologically based procedures is absolutely essential. We recently published data on 23 hyperaroused hyperactive children which indicated that methylphenidate at optimal dosage resulted in no overall significant changes in QEEG measures (Lubar *et al.,* 1995). The same caution holds for neurofeedback. Although there are 700+ groups now claiming very high rates of success with neurofeedback, we believe that unless the neurofeedback is integrated with educational approaches, assessment of specific learning disabilities, family therapy approaches, behavioral approaches, and (when needed) medication, it is very unlikely that long-term changes will persist.

Family therapy allows children and their parents to change their behaviors by changing the parents' cognitive views of and emotional responses to their children, and by allowing the children to perceive parental involvement as caring. Some family issues, such as the issue of a child with ADD/ADHD becoming the focus of parental projection of the parents' own intergenerational anger, have already been discussed. Another issue is that individuals with ADD/ADHD exhibit behavior that can compound an emotionally fragile parent's self-doubt and own sense of failure. Instead of seeing the child as a person with a neurological disorder who is doing his or her best to survive in a very difficult cognitive and emotional milieu, the parent assumes that the child is purposefully defying them. The parent then punishes the child in order to make them "follow the rules." And, when punishment is not successful, the parents feel even more failure and increase punishment in an effort to alleviate their own self-doubt. This loop of misunderstanding and inappropriate parental behavior results in growing resentment in the child. The child feels helpless in his ability to please the parent, and these feelings result in passive aggressive and defiant behavior on the part of the child and sometimes angry and aggressive behavior or frustration on the part of the parent. Family therapy allows both the patient and the parents to share with each other their frustrations, their sense of inadequacy, and their love. This often breaks the preceding cycle very successfully and allows the child to become free to pursue a change in their neurological symptoms through neurofeedback. The parents become free to parent at their best levels of ability without a sense of personal failure.

In a retrospective study of 52 patients followed for up to 10 years (Lubar, 1995), it was found that the greatest area of maintained success was in the specific categories assessed by the Connor's Behavior Rating Scale dealing with school performance, completion of tasks, and better peer and family relationships. We now believe that the reason for the greatest improvements lying primarily within the categories having to do with academic success was that we built into the program for these children academic training as part of the neurofeedback session. Specifically, we combined neurofeedback with exercises in reading, spelling, mathematics, and other learning skills.

During a typical neurofeedback session with children a baseline is obtained without feedback, and this is compared later with their performances while combining feedback with reading, math, writing, spelling, and other academic skills, as well as feedback when used by itself. By building academic skills training within the neurofeedback session, a student is prepared to use the skills directly in homework and in school settings. If the neurofeedback had been done only in isolation, many children may not have known how to apply the technique in real situations. Because repeated failure in the school setting creates a conditioned anxiety when academic tasks are presented, it becomes imperative for the patient to gain assurance that he or she can combine neurofeedback skills with specific academic tasks. We believe this is best done in a supportive environment (i.e., the therapist's office). Once those skills are perfected in the therapist's office, with a great deal of encouragement they can be transferred to a threatening environment (i.e., the school in which so many previous failures have occurred).

This raises another theoretical point which has been in the biofeedback literature since the late 1960s, that is, whether awareness or direct perception of the actual psychophysiological change is necessary in order for learning to occur. Kamiya (1979) showed that it is possible to obtain autoregulation of the EEG alpha rhythm without necessarily being aware of how learning took place. Furthermore, there is an extensive literature dealing with autonomic control without awareness. However, in our direct experience with more than 500 individuals in neurofeedback settings, I believe that, at least for younger individuals, some degree of awareness of process is necessary. It is important to help the child to develop strategies so that he/she can tell what it "feels like" when they produce increased beta, or inhibit alpha and/or theta and can demonstrate that they can do this on demand without receiving feedback. We believe that individuals who can do this will experience greater carryover of the effects than those who have no idea how they are able to change EEG activity and how it feels to do so. This may be necessary because of the fact that children think more concretely. In contrast, for adults it may not be necessary to be specifically aware of exactly what strategies one uses, although it is helpful to recognize the "feel" of success. Children will often tell us when they concentrate on point scores on displays and imagine the numbers increasing as they receive more feedback. Sometimes, using color displays, they imagine the colors changing, for example, on a color wheel or in a figure moving through a maze, and as they imagine a change is going to take place, it does, apparently because this event has been paired with feedback for producing the appropriate pattern. Once an EEG change has been paired with feedback enough times, eventually it becomes almost reflexive. If I ask a child to raise an arm, he or she can do this successfully without telling the processes required to do it. They just say, "I did it." They cannot describe by specifying muscle and nerve processes exactly how the action was initiated or what stopped it. This is true of all automatic motor learning and is probably true of a great deal of other conditioning, as well. However, it takes a great many repetitions before this occurs to the degree that awareness is no longer a critical factor.

Another reason for integration of neurofeedback with other therapies is that a majority of children who experience ADD/ADHD come from dysfunctional families. Many of these children do not live with both biological parents. In many cases we have worked with, there is a stepparent, and in many cases, the child has been adopted by parents without ADD/ADHD; such parents may blame their child's behavior on poor genetics or on some other kind of biological defect, but yet respond to their inappropriate behaviors through punishment. Children with ADD/ADHD as a group are often physically and emotionally abused more than unaffected children at home, in school, and, as adolescents and adults, in work settings and by peers and colleagues. All of this leads to a desperate feeling of inadequacy that, if not dealt with as part of a treatment, also reduces the overall success of the program. Which type of intervention to use depends to a great extent, of course, on the training of the therapist. Some therapists tend to be more behavioral, and others psychodynamic or family oriented, while some may use more cognitive behavioral or rational emotive techniques. We believe that, ultimately, it is the skill of the therapists and their understanding of the ADD/ADHD syndrome, and their correct assessment and remediation of the patient's comorbidities and the family issues surrounding and exacerbating the patient's symptoms, that lead to a successful long-term outcome.

We believe that there are many children with ADD/ADHD who really need to be on medication at least part of the time. Without medication, their hyperactivity would be so pervasive that they would be unmanageable in any therapeutic situation. There are other individuals for whom comorbidities such as depression, impulsiveness, or obsessive behavior need to be dealt with in a pharmacological manner. For this reason it is totally inappropriate to tell an individual with ADD/ADHD that the *purpose* of treatment is to free them from medication. The purpose of the treatment is to obtain better control of the various aspects of this syndrome and to be able to recognize how it is creating problems for them and how to cope with it. If, in the process of the training, they are able to reduce their medication and maintain the same level of control that they had with a full medication regimen, then medication reduction trials could be considered in conjunction with the referring physician or medical specialist. Sometimes stimulant medication can be reduced partially, and in some cases it can be phased out completely. A number of individuals who have been in neurofeedback training have had the medication dropped entirely. This is ideal if it should occur, but by no means should it be promised to a prospective client or parent of a client.

There are other cases in which a stimulant medication may be reduced or eliminated entirely, but it continues to be essential that the patient remain on a tricyclic antidepressant, alpha blocker, or, in some rare cases, an antipsychotic or anticonvulsive medication. Just as neurofeedback is a powerful adjunctive treatment used in combination with other treatments, it is equally accurate to say that psychotherapy or medication are also powerful adjunctive treatments that need to be used in conjunction with neurofeedback in most cases. A multicomponent model is by far the most successful approach at the present time.

IX. INFORMED CONSENT AND FINANCIAL CONSIDERATIONS

Neurofeedback and its various applications are quite recent in terms of the history of biofeedback as a field. At the present time there are still relatively few published studies that establish neurofeedback as effective based on the criteria that ideally are used in the development of a new treatment. Drug studies require double-blind crossover designs; all new procedures require studies in which there are adequate control groups. These research considerations will be covered in more detail later. At the present time, however, many third-party payers have decided to classify neurofeedback treatment for ADD/ADHD, addictive disorders, and other new applications as *experimental*. This then gives the third-party payer the option of covering the cost of the treatment or not, as they so desire. In fact, at the present time, many third-party payers in many states are covering EEG neurofeedback treatment and such coverage is increasing. The reason is that this approach has been shown to be very effective clinically. However, it is an expensive treatment, often involving between 30 and 50 or more sessions. In addition, patients might require other interventions such as family therapy, behavioral approaches, or integration of the technique with pharmacotherapy.

Because this treatment has been deemed experimental, it is important to develop an informed consent that clearly describes the realistic expectations and limitations of the technique. Practitioners should be urged to follow the guidelines of the position statement that has been described previously (Lubar, 1995). Patients falling outside of these guidelines clearly fall within the realm of experimental treatment. Because of this, questions of appropriateness, ethics, and liability may be raised if the outcome is very poor. An appropriately designed informed consent should state that EEG neurofeedback treatment for any specific disorder cannot be guaranteed to produce a successful outcome, that biofeedback interventions, including neurofeedback, as well as psychotherapeutic interventions or behavioral interventions, are not an exact science but depend on the appropriateness of the clients and their willingness to commit themselves to treatment and its goals, and are dependent on the ability of a client and practitioner to work together in order to achieve these goals.

Informed consent should state the approximate number of sessions that will be involved in the treatment, for example, treatment will involve approximately 40–50 sessions over a period of several months with long-term follow-up. It is also important to state that the practitioner cannot guarantee the treatment will be a success, especially if the patient stops the treatment before it is completed or does not engage in follow-up sessions or consultations when necessary. It is also important to elaborate that EEG neurofeedback is a safe treatment, does not involve any internal sensors, and does not produce any known negative side effects, but it is a powerful adjunctive technique that must be integrated with other approaches to be maximally effective. It would be appropriate in the consent form to state that there are approximately 700 organizations currently using this technique, and that although overall the results are very promising in terms of improved grades, test scores, and better behavioral adjustment, in any individual case these results cannot be guaranteed. The practitioner also has the option in the consent form of stating that the results of the treatment might be utilized in research, but that the individual patients would not be identified, and that the data would be used primarily for statistical purposes. Relevant to this, many journals now require that authors sign a certificate of compliance with American Psychological Association (APA) ethical principles.

Another question that many parents ask is whether the school is responsible for payment if their child is engaged in a psychological intervention, and whether this includes neurofeedback. At the present time, this is not clear. Some schools in some states are paying partially for psychological interventions for children with ADD/ADHD. This is something that needs to be investigated by the practitioner in his or her own locale, because it may be possible to obtain some third-party funding for treatment with neurofeedback. Other questions that may arise regarding this type of treatment is whether the treatment is carried out by the health care practitioner or by individuals supervised by the health care practitioner. At the current time, certification procedures have been developed. The Biofeedback Certification Institute of American (BCIA) has developed guidelines for the certification of practitioners and trainees who employ neurofeedback (EEG biofeedback) treatment for a variety of different disorders. Individuals engaged in neurofeedback are strongly encouraged to become certified. If health care providers can, under their own guidelines, supervise therapists (this might include graduate students who are entering the health care provider professions), then they need to state in the consent form that their supervisees will be carefully monitored throughout the treatment program.

Furthermore, the consent form should include a statement that the results of treatment will be available to the patient and/or parents at any time, and that these results may be made available to third-party payers if payment from another source is desired.

Very often children in treatment will require school consultations. These may consist of meetings with significant teachers of classes (where problems may have arisen in terms of behavior and performance), school psychologists, or the principal. It is important that the practitioner explain at these meetings the purpose of the treatment and how it is integrated with other conventional treatments. This also is an opportunity for the practitioner to inform the school about neurofeedback services and in what ways they may be helpful. Very often school psychologists, counselors, and teachers are good referral sources once they see good results.

X. TREATMENT OF ADD/ADHD IN ADULTS

It is clear that ADD/ADHD is a lifelong disorder. It does not completely go away in adulthood. The main feature that may change is that ADHD may evolve more toward ADD without hyperactivity. At least 70% and perhaps as many as 90% of children with ADD/ADHD continue to experience significant problems as they approach adolescence and adulthood. Because this is a neurologically based disorder, it is unlikely that it ever really is "cured." As mentioned previously, adults with ADD/ADHD may have great difficulty with planning, which is often reflected in poor job performance and impaired interpersonal skills. Sometimes even marital relationships are severely compromised. For the adult, there is more likely to be a reactive depression because of repeated failures and inability to meet sometimes unrealistic standards set by the individual. Affected individuals usually do not like to admit that they have a significant disability. They often will try to compensate for their disability by overwork or impulsive behaviors; in some cases, addictive behaviors become a significant problem.

As far as the neurology of ADD/ADHD is concerned, as we approach adulthood the amount of fast (beta) activity in the EEG normally increases in comparison to slower activity. The dominant occipital rhythm, which is less than 8 Hz for young children, becomes established as the alpha rhythm (8–13 Hz) in adults, and, by ages 12–14, reaches its adult level and remains relatively constant in terms of frequency until advanced age. Beta activity continues to increase, particularly in the frontal regions, until approximately age 20 where it also stabilizes. Some adults show excessive slow activity in the theta frequency band just as children do. More often, however, one should look for increased alpha activity during academic tasks as one of the signs of an attention deficit disorder. Normally alpha activity blocks or decreases when one is engaged in active processing. The greatest amount of alpha activity is seen when individuals are resting with their eyes closed or in an eyes-open situation when they remain in a relatively blank "relaxed mind" state. As soon as they engage in any kind of complex mental activity such as mental arithmetic, reading, writing, or other type of cognitive challenge, alpha activity decreases and more beta activity appears. In an initial assessment of adults suspected of having attention deficit disorder (with or without hyperactivity), we note whether they show alpha blocking and increased beta activation with academic or cognitive challenges. If they do not, it may be necessary during neurofeedback training to extend the inhibit frequency bandpass from the usual 4–8 Hz (theta region) to include some low-frequency alpha activity as well. We often train adults to inhibit 4–10 Hz activity or 6–10 Hz activity, and to increase beta activity between 16 and 22 Hz (or even 18–24 Hz because beta activity in adults is faster than beta activity in children). We have found that inhibiting alpha in adults can be extremely helpful and has very much the same effect as inhibiting theta activity in children.

XI. ADDICTION CONSIDERATIONS

The work described previously by Peniston and his colleagues (1989) indicates that many alcoholics show increased beta activity and decreased alpha and theta activity. Individuals with ADD/ADHD, on the other hand, have almost the opposite pattern. They experience too much theta or alpha activity and decreased beta activity. The question often arises as to whether teaching someone with ADD/ADHD to increase beta activity makes them more prone to alcoholism. At the present time it is not possible to answer this definitively because relatively few children with ADD/ADHD have been followed into adulthood.

In the neurofeedback work with alcoholics, it has been found that it is unwise to allow a client to leave a session after only having been trained to increase slow-wave activity and inhibit beta because this leads to an increase in hypnogogic states and can result in disorientation, particularly when the person has to go out into a world where there is traffic, driving responsibilities, and other activities that require rapid shifts in attention. It was found that the best approach is to train the alcoholic individual toward the end of a session to increase beta activity voluntarily so that he or she is able to be alert in demand settings. In working with both children and adults with ADD/ADHD or ADD (or any other disorders), the important thing is to be able to learn to shift EEG activity voluntarily into any appropriate pattern for the activity in which one is needing to be engage. Hence, ADD individuals need to be able to increase levels of fast activity in demanding academic situations and, if they wish, to increase slow activity for purposes of daydreaming and imagery in situations that are purely relaxation oriented or when they are not required to meet schedule demands, etc.

Alcoholics and individuals with other types of substance abuse for which the Peniston protocol is appropriate need to use alpha–theta training to help them to relax and maintain antiabuse images, but also need to be able to shift into increased beta in demand situations. Even in cases of biofeedback regulation of muscle (EMG) activity, sometimes it may actually be desirable to increase muscle activity in certain muscle groups while decreasing it in others, depending on the setting. Essentially then all forms of neurofeedback as well as other types of feedback have to be learned in terms of their utilization in task appropriate situations.

XII. RESEARCH NEEDS

In closing this chapter, we would like to point out some needs in the research area that must be addressed if neurofeedback for ADD/ADHD is to be accepted as a mainstream treatment. Over and over again we have been told that no matter how well we do clinically and no matter how convincing our clinical results appear to be even with follow-up, there is always the possibility that placebo effects account for success. In many ways we are being held to a much higher standard than certain other treatments have been held in the past. An excellent article by DeGood (1993) explores the question of whether biofeedback produces specific effects and, whether in the case of pain, these effects are site specific. He points out that although biofeedback has been used for the management of pain for many years and particularly for the management of muscle contraction and migraine headaches, and even where the effects of the biofeedback training are as strong as those obtained with medication and where there has been documented improvement in literally thousands of patients with long-term follow-up, ". . . evidence of specific effects in mechanism has been inconsistent." He notes further that "changes in muscle tension are not always correlated with changes in tension headache, nor are skin temperatures reliably related to the level of migraine discomfort" and "to date however it appears that biofeedback for headaches may produce a nonspecific therapeutic effect that is at least as powerful as the specific effects associated with medication."

This exemplifies a very important standard that we are being asked by some to meet. One end of a continuum of demands is stated by Furedy (1987). His published view is that because biofeedback approaches involve physiological feedback, it is *essential* to show that the mechanism of action is a *specific physiological mechanism* and not due to some kind of psychological change or some vague change in arousal mechanisms. In conjunction with the work described in this chapter, Furedy likely would argue that unless we can show that the neurofeedback produces very specific changes in the EEG that can be documented, and that these specific changes are linked to the degree of behavioral change in the individual with ADD/ADHD, then in fact the biofeedback has produced only some kind of vague nonspecific placebo effect. Relevant to this, recent research (Lubar *et al.,* 1995) did demonstrate specificity in that only those children with ADD/ADHD who were able to decrease significantly microvolts of theta over sessions experienced significant improvements on a visual continuous performance test (TOVA).

There are researchers who believe that we must show with controlled outcome studies involving either a double-blind or matched groups design that only those individuals who are successful in neurofeedback training are the ones who show positive changes in behavior ratings, school performance, academic achievement, and other measures of ADD/ADHD. Further, they feel we must demonstrate that individuals who do not change their EEG do not show these changes. For these critics, the fact that thousands of children have benefited from neurofeedback in terms of these various behavioral and academic achievement measures is irrelevant unless attendant neurophysiological and neurological changes have also occurred. Why do we who espouse neurofeedback approaches have to meet higher standards than have been met for the biofeedback treatment of headache or pain mechanisms, for which hundreds of thousands of individuals have achieved success even though the underlying physiological mechanism is not always clearly established and is, in some cases, totally unknown? If one examines the Physicians' Desk Reference (PDR) there are many drugs, including Ritalin (methylphenidate), in which the statement "mechanism of action unknown" is clearly stated yet the drug is used–and used quite successfully. Even the mechanisms of action of many anesthetics is not known; nevertheless they are essential. This controversy has been discussed elsewhere in considerable detail (Lubar, 1992, 1993).

The two most common experimental designs that can be used to separate neurofeedback effects from nonspecific effects and other treatment effects are the matched groups design and the double-blind crossover design. The double-blind crossover design is inappropriate, especially for children, because for part of the treatment individuals are exposed to treatment conditions that could actually make them worse. This could lead to them dropping out of treatment early and feeling that they had only experienced another failure in a long line of failures with which they are already coping. A matched groups design is a much better approach. In this design one suggestion is to have a group that receives only EEG neurofeedback, a group that receives EEG neurofeedback plus a second intervention such as behavior therapy or psychotherapy, a third group that receives a form of behavior therapy or psychotherapy as the only intervention, and perhaps a waiting control group, or a control group that receives only some kind of attention training, such as computer games or cognitive rehabilitation tasks. At present, two large multicenter studies are being started in conjunction with two neurofeedback equipment manufacturers employing the matched groups design. We predict that the results of the neurofeedback will be weaker in this type of design than it would be if integrated into a multicomponent treatment process. We believe that neurofeedback clearly facilitates the use of medications, behavior therapy, and cognitive interventions, and that these other interventions facilitate the use of neurofeedback. Overall, combining them seems to produce a very powerful outcome that affects positively most of the measures that are currently used in terms of academic achievement, behavior ratings, etc. Fortunately at the present time, several small studies have been completed that used multiple outcome designs, and some of these studies are already showing positive effects of neurofeedback training (Scheinbaum *et al.*, 1995; Rossiter & LaVaque, 1995). Hopefully, within the next year or two, the results of all of these studies will appear in the published literature, and much of the controversy surrounding neurofeedback will abate as it becomes a more mainstream treatment for attention deficit hyperactivity disorder.

REFERENCES

Adduci, L. (1991, Sep.). My child couldn't pay attention. *Woman's Day,* pp. 102, 106.

Amen, D. G. (1997). Brain SPECT imaging: Implications for EEG biofeedback. Keynote address presented at 28th annual meeting of the Association for Applied Psychophysiology and Biofeedback, San Diego, CA.

Amen, D. G., Paldi, J. H., & Thisted, R. A. (1993). Evaluating with brain SPECT imaging. Paper presented at the meeting of the American Psychiatric Association.

American Psychiatric Association. (1994). "Diagnostic and Statistical Manual of Mental Disorders," 4th Ed. American Psychiatric Association, Washington, DC.

Barkley, R. (1990). "Attention Deficit Hyperactivity Disorder: A Handbook for Diagnosis and Treatment." Guilford Press, New York.

Bowen, M. (1978). "Family Therapy in Clinical Practice." Aaronson, New York.

Bradley, C. (1937). The behavior of children receiving Benzedrine. *Am. J. Psychiatry* **94,** 577–585.

Cocores, J. A., Patel, M. D., Gold, M. S., & Pottash, A. C. (1987). Cocaine abuse, attention deficit disorder, and bipolar disorder. *J. Nervous Mental Dis.* **175**(7), 431–432.

DeGood, D. E. (1993). What is the role of biofeedback in the treatment of chronic pain patients? *APS Bull.* **3,** 1–6.

Flynn, J. M., & Deering, W. M. (1989). Subtypes of dyslexia: Investigation of Boder's system using quantitative neurophysiology. *Devel. Med. Child Neurol.* **31,** 215–223.

Flynn, J. M., Deering, W. M., Goldstein, M., & Rahbar, M. H. (1992). Electrophysiological correlates of dyslexic subtypes. *J. Learning Disabil.* **25**(2), 133–141.

Friedman, E. (1985). "Generation to Generation." Guilford Press, New York.

Furedy, J. J. (1987). Specific versus placebo effects in biofeedback training: A critical lay perspective. *Biofeedback Self-Regul.* **12,** 169–184.

Henriques, J. B., & Davidson, R. J. (1991). Left frontal hypoactivation in depression. *J. Abnormal Psychol.* **100**(4), 535–545.

Hooper, S. R., & Willis, W. G. (1989). "Learning Disability Subtyping. Neuropsychological Foundations, Conceptual Models, and Issues in Clinical Differentiation." Springer Verlag, New York. Hynd, G. W., Marshall, R., & Gonzales, J. J. (1991). Learning disabilities and presumed central nervous system dysfunction. *Learning Disabil. Quart.* **14,** 283–296.

John, E. R., Prichep, L. S., Fridman, J., & Easton, P. (1988). Neurometrics: Computer-assisted differential diagnosis of brain dysfunctions. *Science* **239,** 162–169.

Kamiya, J. (1979). Autoregulation of the EEG alpha rhythm: A program for the study of consciousness. *In* "Mind/Body Integration: Essential Readings in Biofeedback" (E. Peper, S. Ancoli, & M. Quinn, eds.), pp. 289–297. Plenum Press, New York.

Lubar, J. F. (1991). Discourse on the development of EEG diagnostics and biofeedback treatment for attention-deficit/hyperactivity disorders. *Biofeedback Self-Regul.* **16,** 201–225.

Lubar, J. F. (1992). Point/counterpoint: Is EEG neurofeedback an effective treatment for ADHD? Paper presented at the 4th Annual Meeting of Ch.A.D.D. Conference, Chicago, IL.

Lubar, J. F. (1993, Mar.). Innovation or inquisition: The struggle for ascent in the court of science: Neurofeedback and ADHD. *Biofeedback*, pp. 23–30.

Lubar, J. F. (1995). Neurofeedback for the management of attention deficit disorders. *In* "Biofeedback: A Practitioner's Guide" (M. S. Schwartz, ed.). Guilford Press, New York.

Lubar, J. F. (1997). Neocortical dynamics: Implications for understanding the role of neurofeedback and related techniques for the enhancement of attention. *Appl. Psychophysiol. Biofeedback* **22,** 11–126.

Lubar, J. F. (1998). EEG biofeedback applications for the management of attention deficit hyperactivity disorder. *In* "Foundations of Neurofeedback" (R. Kall, ed.). Futurehealth, Philadelphia, PA.

Lubar, J. F., Gross, D. M., Shively, M. S., & Mann, C. A. (1990). Differences between normal, learning disabled and gifted children based upon an auditory evoked potential task. *J. Psychophysiol.* **4,** 249–260.

Lubar, J. F., Swartwood, J., Swartwood, M., & O'Donnell, P. (1995). Evaluation of the effectiveness of EEG neurofeedback training for ADHD in a clinical setting as measured by changes in T.O.V.A. scores, behavioral ratings, and WISC-R performance. *Biofeedback Self-Regulation.*

Mann, C. A., Lubar, J. F., Zimmerman, A. W., Miller, B. A., & Muenchen, R. A. (1992). Quantitative analysis of EEG in boys with attention deficit/hyperactivity disorder (ADHD). A controlled study with clinical implications. *Pediat. Neurol.* **8,** 30–36.

Miller, D. K., & Blum, K. (1995). "Overload: Attention Deficit Disorder and the Addictive Brain." Andrews and McMeel, Kansas City, MO.

Monastra, V. J., Lubar, J. F., Linden, M., Van Deusen, P., Green, G., Wing, W., Phillips, A., & Fenger, T. V. (1999). Assessing ADHD via quantitative electroencephalography: An initial validation study. *Neuropsychology* (in press).

Noble, E., Blum, K., Ritchie, T., Montgomery, A., & Sheridan, P. (1991). Allelic association of the D2 dopamine receptor gene with receptor-binding characteristics in alcoholism. *Arch. Gen. Psychiat.* **48,** 648–654.

Peniston, E. G., & Kulkosky, P. J. (1989). Alpha–theta brainwave training and beta–endorphin levels in alcoholics. *Alcohol. Clin. Exp. Res.* **13,** 271–279.

Posner, M. I., & Raichle, M. E. (1994). "Images of Mind." Scientific American Library, New York.

Reid, M. K., & Borkowski, J. G. (1987). Causal attributions of hyperactive children: Implications for teaching strategies and self-control. *J. Educ. Psychol.* **79,** 296–307.

Rosenfeld, J. P., Cha, G., Blair, T., & Gotlib, I. H. (1995). Operant (biofeedback) control of left-right frontal alpha power differences: Potential neurotherapy for affective disorders. *Biofeedback Self-Regul.* **20**(3), 241–258.

Rossiter, T. R., & LaVaque, T. J. (1995). A comparison of EEG biofeedback and psychostimulants in treating attention deficit/hyperactivity disorders. *J. Neurother.* **1,** 48–59.

Satterfield, J. H. (1973). EEG aspects in children with minimal brain dysfunction. *Sem. Psychiat.* **5,** 35–46.

Scheinbaum, S., Zecker, S., Newton, C. J., & Rosenfeld, P. (1995). A controlled study of EEG biofeedback as a treatment for attention-deficit disorders. *In* "Proceedings of the 26th Annual Meeting of the Association for Applied Psychophysiology and Biofeedback," pp. 131–134.

Shaw, J. C. (1984). Correlation and coherence analysis of the EEG: A selective tutorial review. *Int. J. Psychophysiol.* **1**(3), 255–266.

Stockdale, S., & Hoffman, D.A. (1997). Status of mild traumatic brain injury. Digital electroencephalography and neurofeedback. *Biofeedback* **25,** 12–13.

Swanson, J. M., & Kinsbourne, M. (1979). The cognitive effects of stimulant drugs on hyperactive children. *In* "Attention and Cognitive Development" (M. Hale & T. Lewis, eds.), pp. 249–274. Plenum Press, New York. Thatcher, R. W., Walker, R. A., & Guidice, S. (1987). Human cerebral hemispheres develop at different rates and ages. *Science* **236,** 110–113.

Wender, P. H., Reimherr, F. W., Wood, D. R., & Ward, M. (1985). A controlled study of methylphenidate in the treatment of attention deficit disorder, residual type, in adults. *Am. J. Psychiat.* **142,** 547–552.

Whalen, C. K., & Henker, B. (1991). Therapies for hyperactive children: Comparisons, combinations, and compromises. *J. Consult. Clin. Psychol.* **59,** 126–137.

6

NEUROTHERAPY IN THE TREATMENT OF DISSOCIATION

THOMAS BROWNBACK AND LINDA MASON

*Brownback, Mason, and Associates, Group Psychological Practice,
Allentown, Pennsylvania*

Because of its psychobiological components, dissociation may be seen as a psychological defense mechanism for which neurotherapy holds much promise as an adjunctive treatment. At its core, dissociation is a process "in which certain information (such as feelings, memories and physical sensations) is kept apart from other information with which it would normally be logically associated" [Executive Council of the International Society for the Study of Dissociation (ECISSD), 1997].

As a maladaptive disruption in integrated functioning, dissociation is described in the fourth edition of the *Diagnostic and Statistical Manual of Mental Disorders* [American Psychiatric Association (APA), 1994] as involved in dissociative amnesia, dissociative fugue, depersonalization disorder, acute stress disorder, post-traumatic stress disorder, somatization disorder, dissociative identity disorder, and dissociative disorder–not otherwise specified. In addition, Carnes (1994) has hypothesized that dissociation is present in addictive behaviors. Because of the central role dissociation plays in the creation and persistence of dissociative identity disorder (DID), the latter may be considered a sort of litmus test for the value of neurotherapy in the treatment of dissociation.

The hallmark of DID is the presence of at least two distinct identities or personality states; hence, its former nomenclature of multiple personality disorder. In addition, these personality states "recurrently take control of behavior. There is an inability to recall important personal information, the extent of which is too great to be explained by ordinary forgetfulness" (ECISSD, 1997). Typically, early and severe childhood trauma can be recognized as the precursor to DID (Braun & Sachs, 1985; Fink, 1991; Fink & Golinkoff, 1990; Putnam, 1985). Kluft (1985) considers overwhelming traumata and its possible repetition as the *raison d'être* of DID. The personality states (alternate personalities or alters) are distinct from each other, each having "its own relatively enduring pattern of perceiving, relating to, and thinking about the environment and self" (APA, 1994). Usually, these alters have different names, ages, and predominant affect. They may be of different gender than the physical body. There can be differences in physiological functioning, including visual acuity, response to pain, allergic reactions and blood glucose response to insulin (ECISSD, 1997).

Alters are believed to be created by the use of dissociation as a part of the psychobiological response to overwhelming psychological trauma (Lowenstein, 1994). As part of this response, memories and affective states relating to the trauma become neurally encoded (Van der Kolk, 1993). This dissociated material often manifests itself in nightmares, reenactments, flashbacks, overwhelming affect, and somatic symptoms (Lowenstein, 1994; Chu, 1994). The number of alters present can vary from a few to several hundred, but the number is not important; rather, "the critical issues are to understand how such a number came to be, and to make sure that no aspects of the mind are neglected or lost in the shuffle in the course of the therapy" (Kluft, 1988a). Some therapists treating DID believe that focusing on the alters as if they actually are separate personalities only increases the strength of the internal dissociative barriers (Chu, 1991). This issue has particular relevance to Manchester's work with DID using neurofeedback, which will be discussed later in this chapter (Manchester *et al.,* 1994).

Prior to the early 1980s, treatment for DID tended to focus on the alters, in part because therapists became absorbed in the strange, flamboyant behavior of the alters of more florid DID clients. The shift to a greater utilization of cognitive behavioral therapy resulted in clinicians being encouraged "to keep a rational, clinical perspective, and not to be distracted by patients' unusual and dramatic clinical presentation" (Chu, 1994). As is discussed later, this cognitive behavioral component is an underpinning of our work with dissociation utilizing neurotherapy.

Presently the conventional treatment for DID is long term and generally intensive, with psychodynamic psychotherapy as the primary modality (Putnam, 1991). While clinicians from all specialty groups ranked hypnotherapy as the second most commonly used modality, the third choice varied by specialty. That is, psychiatrists and social workers ranked psychopharmacology third, while psychologists and other therapists rendered art and group therapies third (Lowenstein, 1994). Because of the complexity of the disorder and its frequent comorbidity with other disorders such as personality disorders, addictions, eating disorders, sexual disorders, mood disorders, and anxiety (Fink, 1991), there is much value in comprehensive treatment planning that includes not only these three primary modalities, but also other adjunctive therapies, such as psychoeducational and bibliotherapy (ECISSD, 1997).

Treatment for this disorder is considered intensive because the minimum recommended frequency of sessions for the average DID patient with a therapist of average skill and experience is said to be twice a week, with the actual number of sessions reflecting the patient's level of function and stability. Treatment is considered long term: Its minimum length is 3–5 years following the diagnosis of DID. Treatment of more complex cases of DID may last 6 years or more (ECISSD, 1997).

The initial goals of treatment are symptom localization, control of dysfunctional behavior, restoration of functioning, and improvement of relationships. For many therapists the ultimate goal of treatment is integration, which is an "ongoing process of undoing all aspects of dissociative dividedness that begins long before there is any reduction in the number or distinctness of the personalities, persists through their fusion, and continues at a deeper level even after the personalities have blended into one" (ECISSD, 1997). However, there is a group of therapists who put the goal of integration secondary to helping DID clients learn to manage their daily lives more effectively. Healthy daily functioning often achieves primacy when circumstances such as financial limitations exist or when the client's primary motivation is for symptom relief. Despite the severity and chronicity of DID, a return to healthy functioning is highly likely. Of 184 DID patients treated by Kluft (1988b), 81% were reported to have achieved "stable fusion" by the criteria of that research project. These criteria included the requirement that all clinical signs of multiplicity and related clinical phenomena be absent for at least 27 months before a fusion could be designated as stabilized. Patients in this study have had regular follow-up for as long as 2–10 years after the conclusion of treatment (Lowenstein, 1994).

I. NEUROTHERAPY TREATMENT

Some of the earliest reporting of the use of psychophysiological procedures with DID was not for treatment, but, rather, for the collection of data on the characteristics of DID. For example, Putnam reported on evoked potential states of clients with DID. Also, significant to our own neurotherapy findings with DID clients is Putnam's finding that the EMG "often mistakenly viewed as an annoying artifact, may be a robust marker for different states of consciousness" (Putnam, 1991).

The first to utilize neurotherapy as a treatment modality for dissociative symptoms were Peniston and Kulkosky (Peniston & Kulkosky, 1991; Peniston et al., 1993). Their work focused on Vietnam War veterans with a history of 12 years or more of chronic combat-related post-traumatic stress disorder (PTSD), including many symptoms of dissociation. On the basis of Everly's (1989) hypothesis that the neuroanatomical structures that mediate the symptomatology of PTSD are in the hippocampal region, they concluded that effective treatment would best include attention to this physiology, and that neurotherapy had the potential to be an appropriate modality for this therapeutic component.

Their original protocol included beginning with eight 30-min sessions of hand temperature biofeedback. This "pretraining" was based on Hall's (1977) work showing how "temperature training stimulates the production of the theta state" (Peniston & Kulkosky, 1991). These sessions were followed by thirty 30-min neurotherapy sessions. The veterans were seen five times per week for 28 days. Electrode placement was at scalp site 01 with reference to the left earlobe, with the right earlobe as ground. There were three active bandpass filters: theta (4–8 Hz), alpha (8–13 Hz), and beta (13–26 Hz). The sessions began with the subject being told to visualize scenes of his nightmares and flashbacks, then images of increased alpha rhythm amplitude, and finally scenes of the normalization of his personality. The subject was then instructed to "sink-down into theta, keeping the mind quiet and alert (but not active), and the body calm." Following these instructions, the subject was left alone in a darkened room while receiving alpha and theta feedback (Peniston & Kulkosky, 1991).

Pre- and post-MMPI testing revealed statistically significant changes, compared to two control groups. By 30 months following treatment, all 14 in the control group had a return of PTSD symptoms, while only 3 of the 15 experimental group subjects relapsed. Peniston and Kulkosky (1991) concluded that "these clinical observations lend some support to the hypotheses that Vietnam theater combat veterans are unable, in most incidences, to identify their combat-related flashbacks/nightmares with specific repressed combat anxiety-evoking traumatic events. BWNT (brainwave neurotherapy) tends to induce the vivid re-experiencing (reliving) of those extremely traumatic combat events that were repressed in Vietnam."

Subsequently, Peniston *et al.* (1993) turned their focus to EEG synchrony, which they defined as "phase and frequency synchrony between the dominant frequency components from two channels in a one-second epoch." The in-phase criterion was that the phase angles of the dominant frequency components lie in the same quadrant. In a study of 20 Vietnam veterans with PTSD and coexisting alcohol abuse, four paired sites were studied: F7, F8; F8, O2; F7, 01; 01, 02. The bands were theta (4–8 Hz), alpha (9–13 Hz), and beta (14–29 Hz). One purpose of this study was to examine effects of four-channel EEG alpha–theta brain wave neurofeedback training on EEG synchronization and waveform abundance and amplitude. The protocol used with these veterans was essentially the same as that in the 1991 Peniston–Kulkosky study, except now at the end of each 30-min training session the therapist conducted a clinical interview during which the subject shared any visual or auditory images that were experienced during training. As in the previous study, the relapse rate for the experimental group was much lower than for those patients receiving traditional therapy. Only 4 of the 20 had experienced PTSD symptoms during the 26 months of follow-up (Peniston et al., 1993).

The Peniston et al. (1993) study of the EEG data recorded during the experiment revealed several findings. First, there were significant amplitude increases in theta and beta, but not in alpha during the abreactive imagery component of each training session. Second, a pattern of statistically reliable interaction was seen as a "crossover" in which theta amplitude increased across trails, while alpha amplitude decreased. Peniston et al. (1993) consider this pattern "to identify a state of consciousness in which the patient is sensitive to hypnogogic imagery which relates symbolically to issues in the patient's own life." Significant to more recent neurotherapy work by Manchester et al. (1994) and by the present authors, these images apparently represent past traumatic material. Thus a goal of their training has been to provoke the surfacing of this repressed material.

Additionally, the training "produced significant increases in the percentages of brain channel pair synchrony in the frontal and parieto-occipital lobes of the cerebral cortex" (1993). Furthermore, increases in hemispheric synchrony occurred during the reverie state of the training session. These changes and the fact that the increased synchrony was maintained after treatment support the researchers' theories that the frontal and parieto-occipital brain regions show decreased synchrony when a person is repressing traumatic material. Moreover, when a person relived a traumatic memory, these brain regions were found to be in greater synchrony.

Carol Manchester at Ohio State University has been one of the first to work intensely with neurotherapy for DID. Details of one of her studies are presented later.

Because PTSD and DID share a number of dissociative features, including amnesia, flashbacks, and feelings of detachment, Manchester's use of neurotherapy with patients with DID may be considered a natural outgrowth of Peniston and Kulkosky's work. Relatedly, Brende (1986) described the severity of PTSD dissociative symptoms as existing on a continuum ranging from intrusive memories to DID. In addition, Branscomb (1991) concluded "(t)he essential difference between the severe PTSD resulting from combat and classic childhood onset MPD (Multiple Personality Disorder) may not live in the extent of switching and the functional dynamics of alter states, but rather in the degree of elaboration of separate alters and their fantasized attributes."

From Peniston and Kulkosky's work, Manchester et al. (1994) (quoting Kissen) hypothesized that "the integration of neurofeedback techniques with internal self-exploration could allow DID patients to utilize their mind's own naturalistic means of self-healing through an experience of reassociation and reorganization of their own experiences to bring about unification. A brain state achieveable through neurofeedback (i.e., a window of opportunity) could enable patients to integrate traumatic memories while in a state of low arousal, thereby minimizing the risk of retraumatization." This goal of maintaining a state of low arousal is evidenced in the alteration of the Peniston–Kulkosky protocol to include therapeutic attention to the theta–beta ratio in the formulation and execution of the neurotherapy programs.

Manchester *et al.* (1994) reported details of their neurotherapy study. The study's population was 11 females with DID, with an average age of 41 and an average level of 16 years of education. Although 10 of these women were working at the time of the study, their quality of life had been severely compromised by the DID, as evidenced by an average GAF (Global Assessment of Functioning) score of 39 out of 100.

Before beginning neurotherapy, the subjects were either able to meet the criterion of maintaining a hand temperature of 95°F for three consecutive 30-min sessions, or they received from 1 to 12 temperature biofeedback training sessions. Then they constructed two positive visualizations: one that incorporated a new behavior they desired to have as part of their lives following integration, and one of a scene in which they resisted performing a self-destructive or addictive behavior. Manchester provided them with a third visualization in which the subject would see herself as an integrated person–one "who knows, feels, senses, and behaves as one."

The 30-min neurotherapy training sessions were conducted with an 01 active lead placement, the earlobes as reference location sites, and the forehead as ground. Frequency bands were delta (0–4 Hz), theta (4–8 Hz), alpha (8–12 Hz), low alpha (8–10 Hz), high alpha (10–12 Hz), SMR (12–15 Hz), beta (16–20 Hz), and EMG (26–32 Hz). A normal theta–beta ratio was considered to be 1.1–1.5, based on Lubar's work (Lubar, 1983). In each session, the subject's shift from high-frequency alpha to low-frequency alpha was monitored, since the mind "free of thoughts," is associated with greater amplitude of low alpha than high alpha (Manchester *et al.*, 1994). The alpha–theta audio feedback was inhibited by delta activity greater than 30 UV or EMG greater than 15 UV. In addition, for patients whose theta–beta ratio was below 1.0, the feedback tones were also inhibited when beta was greater than 12 UV and/or the theta–beta ratio became greater than 2.5. "This 'deepening' protocol allows those who can to tolerate deep theta states yet remain aware of the formerly unconscious processes and phenomena" (Manchester *et al.*, 1994). For patients with an average theta–beta ratio above 3.0, the feedback tone was inhibited whenever the ratio exceeded 3.0, because such subjects tended to fall asleep or decompensate with the alpha–theta training.

Each training session began with the visualizations. The therapist remained in the room during the training, but was silent. A hand signal was arranged if the patient wanted to stop the training because of the intensity of the experience. At the end of each session there was a discussion between the therapist and patient in the manner of Peniston's clinical interviews. In addition to the 30 neurotherapy sessions, there were 10 group sessions in which each participant had 5–10 min to share experiences from their training sessions. Each group began with a verbal affirmation by participants of their ability to reexperience their trauma without dissociating.

At the end of the 30 neurotherapy sessions and 10 group meetings, all 11 reported being integrated and met Kluft's criterion for unification (Kluft, 1988b). As with the Peniston *et al.* (1993) research, this group also had significant positive changes in pre- and post-Millon test scores. In addition, their GAF scores increased to an average of 82 ($p < 0.05$ significance). The patients were given the Dissociative Experiences Scale 13–27 months following the experience and continued to have scores ranging from normal to high normal.

II. THE BROWNBACK–MASON PROTOCOL

The mainstream treatment approach in the field of dissociation was psychodynamic in the late 1970s (Putnam, 1991), and the primary treatment component of the Peniston–Kulkosky protocol and the Manchester protocol was neurotherapy in the late 1980s and early 1990s. By the mid-1990s the present authors began utilizing a fully integrated therapeutic approach that incorporated psychodynamic psychotherapy, cognitive–behavioral therapy, group therapy, and neurotherapy (Brownback, 1996). We hypothesized four brain states in the treatment of dissociation: (1) conscious connecting to the buried traumatic material, (2) emotional self-comforting subsequent to reexperience of the trauma, (3) physiological (primarily somatosensory) self-quieting subsequent to reexperiencing the trauma, and (4) external focusing subsequent to reexperiencing the trauma. We postulated the concept of attentional flexibility in our treatment paradigm: "In order for a dissociative to achieve healing and experience wholeness, he or she must learn how to shift attention to feelings, to comforting, to quieting and to cognitive processing and be able to do so fluidly in response to the demands of daily living" (Brownback, 1997a).

In addition to the four attentional components, we also developed a four-factor framework with 16 subcategories in our dissociative treatment regimen, which we call the *bio-psycho-socio-theological framework* (Brownback, 1984). This framework has been formulated into a cognitive–behavioral checklist for weekly assessment of client present-day healthy functioning. We noted: "Although there are a number of other technologies and therapies which augment dynamic shifting into the four states of consciousness and which increase compliance with the bio-psycho-socio-theological cognitive behavioral framework, nothing has facilitated the overall therapeutic process like neurotherapy" (Brownback, 1997b). Furthermore, "Neurotherapy very powerfully facilitates, at a neurological and in all likelihood biochemical level, the process of attentional shifting into the varied brainstates of feeling, comfort, quieting and externally focused cognitive processing. This enhanced volitional attentional shifting significantly augments one's ability to become connected on a biological, psychological, social and spiritual level" (Brownback, 1997c).

The Brownback–Mason protocol (BMP) is grounded in enhancing client mastery over volitional attentional shifting into and out of a number of brain wave-related states. When we began our work with dissociatives in the late 1970s we utilized and developed many strategies to accomplish this shifting, including hypnosis, guided imagery, breathing techniques, thermal biofeedback, prayer, journaling, and exercise (Brownback, 1983). Our work using neurotherapy with attention deficit disorder clients in the early 1980s, together with the Penniston and Kulkosky findings with PTSD clients in the late 1980s, caused us to evaluate the potential benefits of utilizing neurotherapy in the process of enhancing attentional shifting in dissociatives. With Abbott et al. (1996) reporting enhanced cognitive processing as beta increased, Sterman (1994) reporting somatosensory quieting accompanying SMR frequency increases, Kamiya (1969) reporting decreased anxiety as alpha increased, and Peniston et al. (1993) reporting increased awareness of buried, emotionally charged memories as theta increased, we concluded that training dissociative clients to produce some or all of these different EEG frequencies at a variety of International 10–20 system electrode locations might facilitate attentional flexibility and, hence, promote self-mastery.

Eight EEG bands are used in the neurotherapy component of the BMP. Each band is 4 Hz wide beginning with delta 0–4 Hz (Fig. 6.1).

The first 12–15 sessions of the BMP (stage 1) are used to teach clients how to achieve attentional flexibility and "grounding" (i.e., stabilization of present-day functioning) through enhancement of alpha, beta 1, and beta 2 states of consciousness. Typically the first several sessions are used to train either alpha or beta 1. The client may begin alpha enhancement training at site PZ or F4. This continues for 3–4 sessions. Each session consists of three to four segments approximately 5–7 min in length. In sessions 4–7 whichever frequency band was not trained during the first 3–4 sessions is now added to the training. For example, the client may begin session 4 with two 5–7 min segments of alpha training at PZ or F4 and then go to two 5–7 min segments of beta 1 training at CZ. By session 8, beta 2 training at FZ or F3 typically would be added. For example, the client might begin the eighth session doing one 5–7 min segment of alpha training at PZ or F4, then one 5–7 min segment of beta 1 training at CZ

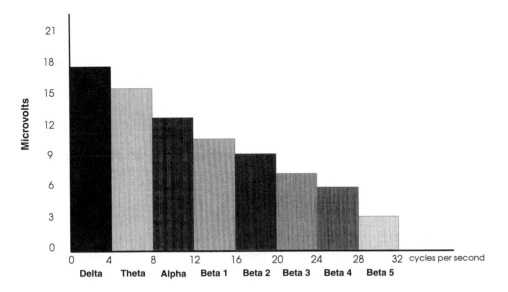

Based on client reports of personal experiences

FIGURE 6.1   Delta: sleep, dissociation (disconnection from body—i.e., out of body experience). Theta: feelings, diffuse focus (hypnogogic state, fuzzy, foggy), creativity, strong sense of being alive. Alpha: peaceful, calm, relaxed, underactivated, slushy. Beta 1: narrow focus (mild). Beta 2: narrow focus (intense). Beta 3: hypervigilant, extreme anxiety, panic. Beta 4: robotic, compulsive, little or no sense of self or others. Beta 5: absence of the sense of existence.

and then two 5–7 min segments of beta 2 training at FZ or F3. This alpha, beta 1, beta 2 training would continue for 12–15 sessions. Clients are encouraged to utilize imagery, breathing techniques or any other methods that help them to enhance the production of these three different brain wave states.

Stage 2 involves facilitating memory retrieval with accompanying stabilization. During stage 2 of the BMP, the goal of training is to enhance conscious awareness of traumatic memories and the accompanying feelings, generally caused by early childhood abuse. Within the same session the client is also taught how to leave this traumatic memory state and become grounded. Memory retrieval is accomplished by doing theta training at any–and eventually all–of the 12 placements from the central, temporal, parietal, and occipital sites included in the International 10–20 system. After 1–7 min of theta training at one of these locations, the client begins alpha training. At this point, alpha training is usually done at F4 or at the same location as the theta training. The alpha training is done for approximately 5 min. Following the alpha training there is approximately

5 min of beta 1 training at CZ, followed by approximately 5 min of beta 2 training at FZ or F3.

Stage 2 is designed to provide the client with an opportunity to get in touch with feelings and memories and then, by utilizing the alpha, beta 1, and beta 2 training, to shift focus away from the traumatic material. This provides for a relatively smooth transition from conscious emotional awareness of traumatic memories (theta) to a state of emotional comforting (alpha) and physiological quieting (beta 1), and then to a more externally focused cognitive processing state (beta 2). It has been our experience that even though the client is now highly focused following the beta 2 training, in most cases he or she is able to go back and talk about what was felt and remembered during the theta training segment of the session.

Stage 3 is designed to foster more in-depth memory retrieval, stabilization, and personality integration. After Stage 2, clients typically feel a security in their ability to shift into and out of the theta state that is the focus of Stage 3. This security, coupled with a growing desire to be able to "feel the feelings" that have been cut off from them for so many years, causes most clients to want to lengthen the time of their theta training in stage 3. Theta training is often done for as long as 20 min per session. This may involve one long segment or two to four shorter segments. This training may be done at the same location or at different scalp locations.

Utilizing the Brownback–Mason protocol (including the neurotherapy component) has facilitated many positive results with 10 clients who had been diagnosed with dissociative identity disorder. During the past 6 years, their need for hospitalization has been completely eliminated. Although the amount of time required to achieve integration is a very individual matter, based on more than 20 years of experience with more than 100 cases of DID, it is the first author's estimation that, on average, the time necessary for integration has been cut in half. Utilizing the increase-theta training paradigm in various forms provides a means whereby most clients are able to "connect," during virtually every session, with "buried" trauma within 5–10 min after the session begins. Two of our most successful theta-increase paradigms involve increase of theta band magnitude using a monopolar montage with a posterior electrode placement, and increase of phase-theta utilizing site FP1 connected to a left posterior placement or FP2 connected to a right posterior placement.

Another benefit of utilizing the Brownback–Mason protocol is the marked increase which all of these clients reported in feeling a sense of mastery over their present-day functioning through enhanced attentional flexibility. For example, in addition to being able to connect to buried trauma far more quickly, clients also were able to disconnect from the trauma far more effectively. This significantly facilitates more effective present-day living as a client goes through the therapeutic process (which often takes several years of uncovering buried traumatic material). Additionally, with the beta 2 training, clients report being more focused in carrying out present-day work, home, and relational responsibilities. Utilizing the Brownback–Mason Protocol with its increased facilitation of attentional flexibility has significantly reduced "wear and tear" on both client and therapist.

III. FUTURE DIRECTIONS

We believe that a very promising future direction for neurotherapy in the treatment of dissociation involves multiple channel training. Peniston and the present authors have reported on using EEG phase, coherence, synchrony, and linear channel combination training. That is, Peniston *et al.* (1993) have used synchrony as a means of measuring treatment success, and we have used phase, coherence, synchrony, and linear channel combination as training feedback modalities. Utilizing two to five scalp placements seems to enhance therapeutic effectiveness.

REFERENCES

Abbot, P. L., Lubar, J. F., McIntyre, A., Rasey, H., & Zuffuto, A. (1996). EEG biofeedback for the enhancement of attentional processing in normal college students. *J. Neurosci.* **1**(3), 15–21.

American Psychiatric Association. (1994). "Diagnostic and Statistical Manual of Mental Disorders," 4th Ed. American Psychiatric Association, Washington, DC.

Branscomb, L. P. (1991). Dissociation in combat-related post traumatic stress disorder. *Dissociation* **4**(1), 13–20.

Braun, B. G., & Sachs, R. G. (1985). The development of multiple personality disorder: predisposing, precipitating and perpetuation factors. *In* "Childhood Antecedents of Multiple Personality" (R. P. Kluft, ed.). American Psychiatric Press, Washington, DC.

Brende, J. O. (1986). Dissociative disorders in Vietnam combat veterans. Presentation at Conference for Multiple Personality Disorder and Dissociative States, Chicago, IL.

Brownback, T. S. (1983). The Brownback–Mason treatment for multiple personality disorder. Presented at the meeting of the Lehigh Valley Psychological Association, Bethlehem, PA.

Brownback, T. S. (1984). The Brownback–Mason cognitive–behavioral framework. Presented at the meeting of the International Society for the Study of Dissociative Disorders, Chicago, IL.

Brownback, T. S. (1996). The Brownback–Mason Protocol. Presented at the meeting of Future Health, Inc., Key West, FL.

Brownback, T. S. (1997a). The Brownback–Mason protocol. Presentation at meeting of the Christian Society for the Healing of Dissociative Disorders, Dallas, TX.

Brownback, T. S. (1997b). The Brownback–Mason protocol. Presented at the meeting of Future Health, Inc., Palm Springs, CA.

Brownback, T. S. (1997c). The Brownback–Mason treatment for multiple personality disorder. Presented at the meeting of Future Health, Inc., Palm Springs, CA.

Carnes, P. J. (1994). Sexual addiction and trauma bonding. Keynote address at the Eastern Regional Conference for the Study of Dissociative Disorders, Washington, DC.

Chu, J. A. (1991). On the misdiagnosis of multiple personality disorder. *Dissociation* **4**(4), 200–204.

Chu, J. A. (1994). The rational treatment of multiple personality disorder. *Psychotherapy* **31**(I), 94–100.

Everly, G. S., Jr. (1989). "A Clinical Guide to the Treatment of the Human Stress Response." Plenum Press, New York.

Executive Council of the International Society for the Study of Dissociation. (1997). "Guidelines for Treating Dissociative Identity Disorder (Multiple Personality Disorder) in Adults." International Society for the Study of Dissociation, Glenview, IL.

Fink, D. (1991). The comorbidity of multiple personality disorder and DSM-III-R axis II disorders. *Psychiat. Clin. North Am.* **14**(3), 547–565.

Fink, D., & Golinkoff, M. (1990). MPD, borderline personality disorder and schizophrenia: A comparative study of clinical features. *Dissociation* **3**, 127–133.

Hall, M. P. (1977). Theta training: imagery and creativity. *In* "Beyond Biofeedback" (E. E. Green & A. M. Green, eds.). Delacorte, San Francisco.

Kamiya, J., (1969). Operant Control of the EEG alpha rhythm and some of its reported effects on consciousness. In C. T. Tart. (Ed.), Altered States of Consciousness. New York: Wiley and Sons.

Kluft, R. P. (1985). Childhood multiple personality disorder: Predictors, clinical findings and treatment results. *In* "Childhood Antecedents of Multiple Personality" (R. P. Kluft, ed.), p. 172. American Psychiatric Press, Washington, DC.

Kluft, R. P. (1988a). The phenomenology and treatment of extremely complex multiple personality disorder. *Dissociation* **1**(4), 47–58..

Kluft, R. P. (1988b). The postreunification treatment of multiple personality disorder: First findings. *Am. J. Psychother.* **42**(2), 212–228.

Lowenstein, R. J. (1994). Diagnosis, epidemiology, clinical course, treatment and cost effectiveness of treatment for dissociative disorders and MPD: Report submitted to the Clinton administration task force on health care financing reform. *Dissociation* **7**(1), 3–9.

Lubar, J. (1983). Electroencephalographic biofeedback and neurological applications. *In* "Biofeedback: Principles and Practice for Clinicians" (J. V. Basmajian, ed.), 2nd Ed. Williams and Williams, Baltimore, MD.

Manchester, C. F., Allen, T., & Tackiki, K. H. (1994), Treatment of dissociative identity disorder with neurotherapy and group self-exploration. Presented at the meeting of the Association for Applied Psychophysiology and Biofeedback, Atlanta, GA.

Peniston, E. G., & Kulkosky, P. J. (1991). Alpha–theta brainwave neurofeedback therapy for Vietnam veterans with combat-related post-traumatic stress disorder. *Medical Psychother.* **4**, 47–60.

Peniston, E. G., Morrinan, D. A., Deming, W. A., & Kulkosky, P. J. (1993). EEG alpha–theta brainwave synchronization in Vietnam theater veterans with combat-related post-traumatic stress disorder and alcohol abuse. *Adv. Medical Psychother.* **6**, 37–50.

Putnam, F. W. (1985). Dissociation as a response to extreme trauma. *In* "Childhood Antecedents of Multiple Personality" (R. P. Kluft, ed.), pp. 66–87. American Psychiatric Press, Washington, DC.

Putnam, F. W. (1991). Recent research on multiple personality disorder. *Psychiat. Clin. North Am.* **14**(3), 493–494.

Sterman, B. (Speaker). (1994). Physiological and functional implications of EEG rhythmic activities. Cassette recording of presentation at SSNR Second Annual Conference, Las Vegas, NV.

Van der Kolk, B. (1993). "Trauma and Memory I: The Dissociative Defense," videotape. Cavalcade Productions, Ukiah, CA.

7

NEUROFEEDBACK IN THE TREATMENT OF ADDICTIVE DISORDERS

EUGENE G. PENISTON* AND PAUL J. KULKOSKY†

*Mental Health Service, North Texas Health Care System,
Memorial Veterans Center, Bonham, Texas, and †Department of Psychology,
University of Southern Colorado, Pueblo, Colorado

I. INTRODUCTION

A. HISTORICAL BACKGROUND

Interest in the use of alpha or theta brain wave biofeedback for treatment of psychopathology began with research in the 1960s and 1970s (Kamiya, 1969; Green *et al.,* 1970; Brown, 1970; Budzynski & Stoyva, 1972). Alpha brain waves (8–12 Hz) were shown to be associated with relaxation and feelings of well-being, theta brain waves (4–7 Hz) were associated with reverie or spontaneous imagery (hypnagogia), beta brain waves (13–20 + Hz) were associated with concentration or anxiety, and delta brain waves (1–3 Hz) were associated with deep sleep.

These early workers hypothesized that anxiety could be reduced, insight could be developed into repressed psychic contents, and self-actualization could be facilitated through EEG biofeedback training to produce higher amplitude, lower frequency (e.g., alpha and theta) brain waves.

These early speculations were met with skepticism, especially after the popularization of inadequate procedures and exaggerated claims of effectiveness in several areas of application to psychopathology (Stroebel &

Glueck, 1973). Research results tended to refute the notion of brain wave biofeedback as a panacea for psychopathology. For example, application of alpha brain wave biofeedback to the treatment of alcoholism and drug abuse produced positive subjective comments from patients, but no sustained prevention of relapse (Beausejour & Lamontagne, 1977; Passini *et al.*, 1977; Watson *et al.*, 1978). The efficacy of relaxation therapy in the treatment of substance abuse remained at best equivocal (Klajner *et al.*, 1984).

Nonetheless, it had long been clear that alcoholism is associated with poor synchrony and deficient alpha EEG activity (Funderburk, 1949; Funkhauser *et al.*, 1953; Gabrielli *et al.*, 1982; Johanesson *et al.*, 1982; Pollock *et al.*, 1983; Porjesz & Begleiter, 1983; Propping *et al.*, 1980; Propping *et al.*, 1981; Vogel *et al.*, 1979; Volavka *et al.*, 1985). Further, alcoholics were shown more likely to increase the amount of alpha activity after consumption of alcohol. Taken together, these findings suggest that those with a predisposition to alcoholism have deficient alpha activity and are especially vulnerable to alcohol's capacity to produce an electroencephalographically measurable reinforcing state of increased slow-wave activity (Peniston & Kulkosky, 1989).

B. ALPHA–THETA NEUROFEEDBACK THERAPY

In an earlier study, we found that the application of a relaxation training technique, EMG biofeedback-assisted reduction of forehead muscle tension, reduced depression scores on the MMPI scale 2 in chronic pain patients (Peniston *et al.*, 1986). A number of previous studies had shown depression is also reliably associated with alcoholism (Dorus *et al.*, 1987; Hengeveld *et al.*, 1987; Steer *et al.*, 1983, 1985). Because depression and poorly synchronized brain waves are both associated with alcoholism, an EEG-based relaxation therapy would target both of these symptoms. Thus, we hypothesized that biofeedback-assisted relaxation training, specifically EEG alpha–theta brain wave training, would provide an efficacious treatment for alcoholism. Chronic alcoholism is notorious for extremely high relapse rates after traditional psychotherapies or medical interventions (Marlatt, 1983; Moos & Finney, 1983; Vaillant, 1983). Therefore, we further hypothesized that only a prolonged application of brain wave therapy would produce sustained prevention of relapse. Previous efforts mentioned above typically employed only brief application of alpha brain wave therapy and found little sustained benefits. To further enhance the likelihood of durable results, our approach combined alpha–theta brain wave training with a battery of other relaxation therapies: systematic desensitization, temperature biofeedback, visualization training, rhythmic breathing, autogenic training, guided imagery, and constructed visualization. These are described in the following section and in the original reports, which also include studies of application

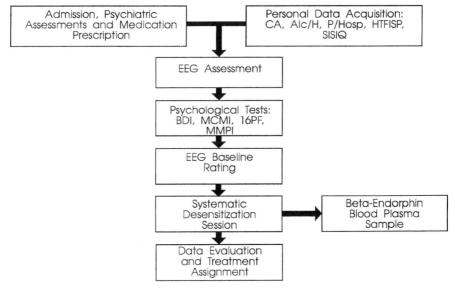

FIGURE 7.1   A schematic of therapeutic procedures of the PKBNT for alcoholism and PTSD. Phase I: initial assessments.

of this therapy to treatment of post-traumatic stress disorder (PTSD) in association with alcoholism and substance abuse (Peniston & Kulkosky, 1989, 1990, 1991a, 1991b; Peniston *et al.,* 1993).

II. METHODOLOGY AND RESULTS

A. NEUROFEEDBACK FOR ADDICTION AND PTSD

Figures 7.1 through 7.5 present a schematic of the therapeutic procedures employed in the Peniston and Kulkosky brain wave neurofeedback therapy (PKBNT) for alcoholism and PTSD.

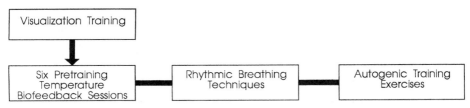

FIGURE 7.2   A schematic of the PKBNT for alcoholism and PTSD. Phase II: temperature and pretraining.

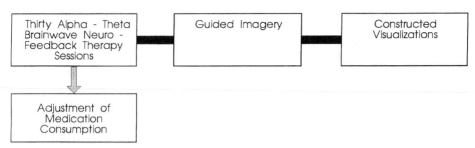

FIGURE 7.3   A schematic of the PKBNT for alcoholism and PTSD. Phase III: alpha–theta brain wave training.

1. Admission and Personal Data Acquisition

The first step before using the Peniston and Kulkosky therapy involves psychiatric assessments and collection of personal data. These data include chronological age (years), alcoholic and/or PTSD history (years), prior

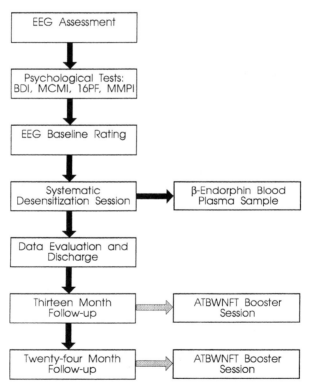

FIGURE 7.4   A schematic of the PKBNT for alcoholism and PTSD. Phase IV: final assessment and follow-up.

Abbreviations:

CA:	Chronological Age
Alc/H:	Alcoholic History
P/Hosp:	Prior Hospitalizations
HTFISP:	Hollingshead's Two-Factor Index of Social Position
SISIQ:	Shipley Institute Scale Intelligence Quotient
EEG:	Electroencephalographic
MMPI:	Minnesota Multiphasic Personality Inventory
BDI:	Beck Depression Inventory
MCMI:	Millon Clinical Multiaxial Inventory
16PF:	Sixteen Personality Factor Test
ATBWNFT:	Alpha-Theta Brainwave Neuro-feedback Therapy

Peniston, E.G. & Kulkosky, P.J. (1989). α-θ brainwave training and ß-endorphin levels in alcoholics. Alcoholism: Clinical and Experimental Research, 13: 271-279.

Peniston, E.G. & Kulkosky, P.J. (1990). Alcoholic personality and alpha-theta brainwave training. Medical Psychotherapy 3:37-55.

Peniston, E.G. & Kulkosky, P.J. (1991). Alpha-theta brainwave neuro-feedback therapy for Vietnam veterans with combat-related post-traumatic stress disorder. Medical Psychotherapy 4: 47-60.

Peniston, E.G., Marrinan, D.A., Deming, W.A. & Kulkosky, P.J. (1993). EEG alpha-theta brainwave synchronization in Vietnam theater veterans with combat-related post-traumatic stress disorder and alcohol abuse. Advances in Medical Psychotherapy 6: 37-50.

FIGURE 7.5   Abbreviations key and reference for schematics of the PKBNT for alcoholism and PTSD.

hospitalizations (number), social position (Hollingshead's two-factor index), and intelligence quotient (Shipley Institute scale).

Criteria for selection of alcoholic patients for the PKBNT include the following: (1) Patients receive alcoholism diagnoses based on DSM-III (American Psychiatric Association, 1987) and clinical records; (2) patients' medical records indicate four or more prior hospitalizations (P/Hosp) for alcoholism treatment at various hospitals; (3) patients' medical records indicate 20 or more years of alcoholic history (Alc/H); (4) patients' Shipley Institute of Living Scale Intelligence Quotients (SISIQ) (Zachary, 1987) are low average, average, or above average; (5) prior to admission, patients are not on psychotropic medications for psychiatric problems; and (6) patients are representative of lower, middle, and upper middle socioeconomic statuses, as measured by Hollingshead's Two-Factor Index of Social Position (HTISP) (Hollingshead, 1957).

2. Electroencephalographic Assessment

Following admission, psychiatric assessments, medication prescription (optional, but usually), and personal data acquisition, an electroencephalographic (EEG) assessment is performed on each candidate for the PKBNT. A Beckman Accurate TM 200 Autoencephalogram Sixteen-Channel Recorder is used to register 60-min EEG recordings both before and after administration of the PKBNT. The EEG assessments are administered to the patients during the same hours of the day. The International 10–20 system for electrode placement is used (Jasper, 1958). The patients' EEG assessments include the bilateral central (C3,C4), parietal (P3,P4), and occipital (O1,O2) scalp derivations referenced against linked ears. All EEG records are visually inspected and rated by an EEG consultant for artifact (EMG, EKG, EOG, etc.) detection and EEG synchrony. The EEG record is rated on the following distinct EEG markers: (1) average alpha wave frequency (in hertz), (2) average amplitude (in microvolts) of alpha rhythm generated in the EEG record, (3) percentage of alpha frequency waves exhibited in the EEG record, and (4) EEG organizational pattern of the record.

3. Psychological Tests

Following EEG assessment, all patients who are candidates for the PK-BNT are administered a battery of psychological tests. Each subject is asked to respond to the Beck Depression Inventory (BDI), a self-report measure designed to assess the severity of a variety of symptoms of depression (Beck *et al.,* 1961). Each of 21 items consists of four sentences and the subject is instructed to choose the one that best describes him- or herself at the present time. Each set of sentences describes symptoms of depression, ranging from normalcy to severe, clinically significant symptoms. Each item is scored from 1 to 4, resulting in a range of total scores from 21 to 84. Limits of severity are based on mean scores: Normal range is considered below 50, mild to minimal depression is 50–59, moderate to marked depression is 60–69, and severe to extreme depression is 70 and over.

Each subject is asked to complete the Millon Clinical Multiaxial Inventory (MCMI), an objective personality test. The MCMI consists of 175 true–false items, takes 15–25 min to administer, and requires an eighth-grade level of reading (Millon, 1983). Base rate (BR) scores are provided for eight basic personality patterns (schizoid, avoidant, dependent, histrionic, narcissistic, antisocial, compulsive, and passive-aggressive), three pathological personality disorders (schizotypal, borderline, and paranoid), and nine clinical syndromes (anxiety, somatoform, hypomania, dysthymia, alcohol abuse, drug abuse, psychotic thinking, psychotic depression, and psychotic delusion). In addition, there are two correction scales which provide identification and adjustment of possible test-taking distortion. Interpretations are based on the presence (BR scores over 75) or prominence (over 84) of specific scale elevations.

All subjects fill out Cattell's 16 PF questionnaire (Cattell *et al.,* 1970) which provides a measure of 16 personality factors that give a picture of a subject's personality, as well as a rough measure of intelligence. High school male norms are used to convert the raw scores to "sten" units ($X = 5.5$).

4. EEG Baseline Rating

Each subject is rated for baseline (untrained) production of beta, alpha, and theta brain wave frequencies prior to initiation of the PKBNT. Monopolar electrode placements are used to provide a stable, high-amplitude signal to the input of the specific instruments that are used subsequently in the PKBNT. Earlobes and the area around the inion (protuberance at the back of skull) are cleaned with alcohol prior to attaching the electrode leads. Omni Prep and Ten20 are used as a conduction medium to fill the electrode cups, and in preparation of the electrode scalp site. An occipital (O1) electrode is attached approximately 1 cm above and 1 cm left of the inion and held in place by a stretching headband. Two ear-clip electrodes are attached and the active electrode is referenced to the left earlobe (A1), with the ground electrode on the right earlobe (A2). Before recording commences, electrode impedance is checked, and electrodes are reapplied if necessary.

EEG output is attached to an EEG feedback monitor (Model E430, RI Company), and beta, alpha, and theta brain wave sensitivity threshold (amplitude) settings are adjusted. Threshold dials of the feedback monitor are adjusted (aided by the use of a MFE Posi-Traci one-strip chart recorder) to a point at which brain waves characteristic of beta, alpha, and theta are registered on the feedback monitor and on a cumulative recording, computer-based timer. Beta rhythm sensitivity threshold is set to encourage 40–50% of beta rhythm presence; alpha rhythm sensitivity threshold is set to encourage approximately 50% of alpha rhythm presence; and theta rhythm threshold is set to encourage 20–30% of theta rhythm presence. If theta brain waves are not produced uniformly during the baseline sessions, theta thresholds are set at points approximately 10 microvolts below the threshold for alpha (because we have found that the theta and alpha thresholds of previous patients who produced theta during baseline tend to differ by that amount). Beta (13–26 Hz), alpha (8–13 Hz), and theta (4–8 Hz) rhythms are defined in terms of the time that the input signals exceed the machine-set thresholds. After a 5-min baseline session, the average alpha rhythm amplitude and percentage of the time of activity in beta, alpha, and theta brain wave bands is retrieved from an EEG computer-based timer (Model ET 330, RI Company), and recorded.

5. Systematic Desensitization and Blood Sample

In the original report of the Peniston and Kulkosky therapy, blood samples were taken from each patient before and after brain wave training, in order to measure serum levels of beta endorphin. Beta endorphin is an endogenous neuropeptide that may be regarded as an index of severity of stress in the environment. The absence of a rise in beta endorphin levels during the course of therapy may be considered a correlate of the success of treatment of alcoholism (Peniston & Kulkosky, 1989). In the practical application of the PKBNT, this procedure may be optional.

To measure beta endorphin levels in blood, two 5.0-mL blood samples are drawn by venipuncture from each patient, one before and one after alpha–theta brain wave training. Each sample is taken after a 14-hr fast, between the hours of 9:00–10:30 A.M., when the circadian rhythm of plasma endorphin is at a moderate level. The first blood sample is collected 1 week after admission of the patient and abstinence from alcohol. For 1 hr prior to each sampling, each patient is given a systematic desensitization session (Boeringa, 1986; Wolpe, 1969). Specifically, 1 hr prior to blood sampling, while the patient remains deeply relaxed, he or she is instructed to imagine various situations or stimuli that normally produce a mild anxiety reaction. The second blood sample is obtained after completion of alpha–theta brain wave training, and, as noted earlier, a systematic desensitization session is again given 1 hr prior to blood sample extraction.

Two 5.0-mL whole-blood samples are collected in 5- or 10-mL Vacutainer glass tubes with EDTA (7.2 mg/5 mL) as an anticoagulant, and spun in a refrigerated centrifuge for 15 min at 750g. The plasma samples are then placed into storage tubes and immediately frozen and stored at $-20°$C. The specimens are then immersed in liquid nitrogen, packed in dry ice, and shipped by air express to an endocrinology laboratory that can perform the radioimmunoassay of beta endorphin. Beta endorphin concentrations are determined from extracted serum samples of blood by radioimmunoassay, with materials such as supplied by the Incstar Kit No. 46065, at an assay sensitivity of 4.7 pmol/liter.

6. Data Evaluation and Treatment Assignment

All data collected on each patient are reviewed to determine the appropriateness of assignment to the PKBNT. Candidates for the PKBNT should meet the criteria for assignment described earlier in Section II,A,1, on admission and personal data acquisition, and should not display evidence of any psychotic disorder, based on psychiatric assessment and psychological testing. Also, patients are excluded from the PKBNT if there is evidence of epilepsy or organic brain disorder from EEG assessment. If all criteria are met, patients are assigned to receive the PKBNT. This involves steps that are described in the following sections.

7. Temperature Pretraining Phase

Autogenic training exercises are used in combination with temperature biofeedback training to achieve relaxation of the body and a quiet, inward-turned state of mind. In addition, a modified version of rhythmic breathing control techniques is taught: increased ventilation to activate the nervous system, followed by other types of breathing to still body functions and concentrate (focus) attention. Each patient is given a total of six or seven 30-min sessions of pretraining in temperature biofeedback-assisted auto-genic training combined with rhythmic breathing control techniques. During these pretraining sessions, a practitioner or psychotherapist attaches a tem-perature thermistor to the tip of the patient's middle finger and/or middle toe of the dominant hand and/or foot with micropore tape, and connects it to an Autogen 2000 Feedback Thermonitor (Autogenic Systems, Inc.). The patient is seated in a comfortable reclining chair in a soundproof room, and is instructed to sit quietly and relax with eyes closed for 5 min, while a base rate recording is obtained. Then, the patient is introduced to autogenic training exercises (Schultz, 1960) and rhythmic breathing techniques to induce relaxation of the body and quieting of the mind. During these sessions, the following specific autogenic training exercises and rhythmic breathing techniques are implemented (from Green & Green, 1977). The patient is instructed to:

Take five slow, full breaths, exhaling and inhaling through both nostrils. . . . Then begin "equalized" breathing:
Exhale and inhale through both nostrils slowly and smoothly, with no pause between the exhalations and inhalations. . . .
Concentrate attention of the flow of breath past the space between the nostrils. . . . If your mind wanders, bring it back to the space between the nostrils. . . . Continue doing this rhythmic breathing for a few minutes. . . .

Now forget the breathing entirely and focus attention on the autogenic exercises for quieting the body (low muscle tension), and quieting the mind (inward-turned attention).
Visualize, imagine, and feel the relaxation of each part of the body as you silently repeat the following autogenic relaxation phrases:

[Heaviness Phrases (To Promote Muscular Relaxation)]

I feel quite quiet. . . .
I am beginning to feel quite relaxed. . . .
The muscles in my toes and feet feel heavy and relaxed. . . .
The muscles in my calves, thighs, hips and waist feel heavy and relaxed. . . .
My abdomen, solar plexus, ribs and chest feel heavy, relaxed and comfortable. . . .
My fingers, hands, arms and shoulders feel heavy and relaxed.
My neck, jaws and lips, eyes, and forehead feel relaxed, comfortable and smooth.
. . .
The muscles in my whole body feel heavy, comfortable, relaxed and quiet. . . .

[Warmth Phrases (To Promote Increased Blood Flow in the Hands and Fingers)]

I am quite relaxed. . . .
My arms and hands feel heavy and warm. . . .
I feel quite quiet. . . .
My whole body is relaxed and my hands are warm, relaxed and warm. . . .

I can feel the warmth flowing down my arms into my hands. . . .
My hands and fingers are warm, pleasantly warm. . . .
Warmth is flowing into my hands, they are warm, very warm. . . .
My hands and fingers are warm, relaxed and warm. . . .

[Warmth Phrases (To Promote Increased Blood Flow in the Feet and Toes)]

I feel quite quiet. . . .
My legs, feet, and toes feel heavy and warm. . . .
I am quite relaxed. . . .
My whole body is relaxed and my feet feel warm and relaxed. . . .
I can feel the warmth flowing down my legs into my feet and toes. . . .
My feet and toes are warm, relaxed and warm. . . .
Warmth is flowing into my feet, they are warm, very warm. . . .
My feet and toes are warm, relaxed and warm. . . .

[Quietness Phrases (To Promote the Calming of the Mind])

My whole body feels relaxed and my mind is quiet. . . .
I release my attention from the outside world and I feel serene and still. . . .
My attention is turned inward and I feel at ease. . . .
Gently, I can visualize, imagine, and experience myself as relaxed and still. . . .
I am aware in an easy, quiet, inward-turned way. . . .
My mind is calm and quiet. . . .
I feel an inward quietness. . . .
I am at peace, I am at peace. . . .

[Reactivation Phrases (To Bring the Individual Back to the World of Activity)]

The relaxation is now concluded and the whole body is reactivated with a deep
  breath and the following phrases:
(a) I feel life and energy flowing through my toes, feet, calves, knees, thighs, hips,
  waist, abdomen, solar plexus, chest, shoulders, arms, hands, fingers, neck, jaws,
  hips, and head. (b) This energy makes me feel light and alive. (c) I open my eyes
  and make contact with the outside world. (d) Maintain this inward quietness for
  about two minutes. Reactivate by taking five slow, full breaths. Stretch and feel
  energy flowing through your body. . . .

During the following five or six sessions, the patient practices tempera-
ture-biofeedback-assisted autogenic training and rhythmic breathing exercises until the hand and foot are warmed to more than 95°F and held there
over one session. It is thought that temperature training stimulates the
production of the "theta state" or "reverie state," and pretrains the patients
for alpha–theta brain wave training.

8. Visualization Training Phase

Each patient is shown his or her EEG record, informed of his or her
exhibited deficient alpha brain wave activity and decreased alpha brain
wave amplitudes, and told that increased latencies (slow starts) in some
subwaves of event-related potentials are suggestive of alcoholism. Each

patient is shown an illustration of the correlation of normal beta, alpha, theta, and delta brain waves with states of consciousness, as depicted in Fig. 7.6.

Each patient is also introduced to a model of the human brain and hypothalamus system, as depicted in Fig. 7.7 (Sperry, 1930). It is explained that the hypothalamus secretes the neuropeptide beta endorphin in response to pain or stress.

The patient is then instructed to close his or her eyes and practice visualizing his or her alpha brain waves increasing in size (amplitude), and his or her hypothalamus system decreasing the amount of beta endorphin secretion in the brain. Next, the patient is encouraged to practice imaging the type of personality that he or she would like to be. Finally, the patient is instructed to visualize him- or herself in a number of everyday life situations, dynamically possessing and acting out the qualities and attitudes of that image. This exercise of imagery is briefly practiced to form the vision and the images of that which the individual can become.

9. Alpha–Theta Brain Wave Training

For alpha–theta brain wave training, the patients are first familiarized with the EEG feedback monitor exactly as described in Section II,A,4. Instructions in guided imagery and constructed visualizations are now combined with alpha–theta brain wave biofeedback. After attachment of electrodes, a 5-min baseline rating of alpha rhythm amplitude and percentage of alpha and theta brain waves is obtained with eyes closed. The patient is then instructed to open his or her eyes and concentrate on an object (a picture, light switch, etc.) in the room for 5 min, while beta rhythm sensitivity (amplitude) threshold is set to encourage 40–50% of beta rhythm presence. Following baseline sensitivity threshold settings (previously described), the patient is instructed to close his or her eyes and construct visualized abstinence and alcohol rejection scenes, imageries of increased alpha rhythm amplitudes, and scenes of the normalization of his or her personality. A practitioner or psychotherapist instructs the patient to "sink down" into the theta (reverie) state, while keeping the mind quiet and alert (but not active), and the body calm. Then, the patient is instructed by the practitioner or psychotherapist to initiate the session with a quiet command "Do it." Prior to the therapist's exit from the room, the beta feedback volume control is turned off; alpha and theta feedback volumes are adjusted to a comfortable listening level for the patient, and the overhead light is turned off. The therapist returns to the room 30 min later, presses the stop button of the computer-based timer, and gently returns the patient to a state of awareness. These aforementioned procedures are employed for a total of thirty 30-min sessions across a duration of 28 days. At the conclusion of each session, the therapist records the average alpha rhythm amplitude and the cumulative percentage of duration of feedback for each brain wave

WHEN A PERSON IS ACTIVE WITH EYES OPEN, THE EEG RECORD FROM
A SCALP ELECTRODE AT THE BACK OF THE HEAD GENERALLY SHOWS
THE PRESENCE OF BETA WAVES, 13 TO 26 *CYCLES* PER SECOND,
OR HIGHER (AS SHOWN IN "A" RECORD ABOVE).

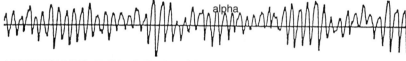

WHEN THE EYES ARE CLOSED AND THE BODY IS RELAXED, ALPHA WAVES
AT 8 TO 13 CPS OFTEN BEGIN TO APPEAR. WHEN ALPHA FIRST APPEARS
IT IS SOMETIMES A BIT RAGGED FROM MIXTURE WITH BETA (SEE B).

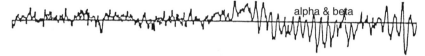

AS TIME PASSES, ALPHA OFTEN BECOMES SMOOTH AND REGULAR IN
FREQUENCY, THOUGH OF FLUCTUATING AMPLITUDE (AS IN C).
WHEN THE BODY IS DEEPLY RELAXED AND A PERSON BECOMES DROWSY,
THETA WAVES AT 4 TO 8 CPS ARE OFTEN SEEN (AS IN D).

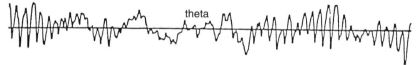

IN MEDITATORS, A SMOOTH THETA PATTERN (RATHER THAN RAGGED,
AS IN D) IS OFTEN ASSOCIATED WITH A QUIET BODY, QUIET EMOTIONS
AND A QUIET MIND, BUT CONSCIOUSNESS DOES NOT DIMINISH.

AT THIS STAGE, WHICH IS HINTED AT IN E, ONE CAN BEGIN TO
"BECOME CONSCIOUS OF THE UNCONSCIOUS." IF THE SUBJECT GOES
TO SLEEP, IRREGULAR DELTA WAVES AT 1 TO 4 CPS BEGIN TO
BE SEEN (AS INDICATED IN F).

FIGURE 7.6 An illustration and explanation of beta, alpha, theta, and delta brain waves.
(Reprinted with permission of Elmer Green.)

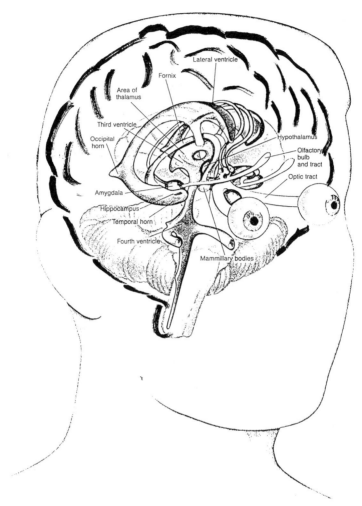

FIGURE 7.7   A diagram of the human brain and hypothalamus system. (Reprinted with permission of Roger Sperry.)

band (beta, alpha, theta), as retrieved from the computer-based timer. Each patient then completes the EEG Feedback Training Questionnaire of the Menninger Clinic, which is reproduced in Fig. 7.8.

10. Prevention of Dissociation and/or Flooding

As mentioned earlier, beta rhythm sensitivity threshold is set to encourage 40–50% of beta rhythm presence, alpha rhythm sensitivity threshold is set to encourage approximately 50% of alpha rhythm presence, and theta rhythm threshold is set to encourage 20–30% of theta rhythm presence.

Your Initials _____ Date _____ Time of Day _____
Thresholds: Beta _____ Alpha _____ Theta _____
Did you hear?
  a. The Alpha tone: Often   Seldom   Not at All
  a. The Theta tone: Often   Seldom   Not at All

How did the training session seem?
Were you able to relax?   YES   NO   If not, what seemed to interfere?
Physical sensations that occurred.
Emotional feelings that occurred.
Thoughts, fantasies, and imaginings.

Did your mind wander at all?   YES   NO   If so,   A LOT   MODERATELY   SLIGHTLY
Did you have any tendency to fall asleep (or get drowsy)?   YES   NO
Did you have any dream-like experiences or mental pictures?   YES   NO
  a. If so, did these experiences occur in
      a particular way?   VISUAL   AUDITORY   SPATIAL
                               TOUCH (PRESSURE)   SMELL   TASTE
  b. If so, were you aware of these experiences all
      of a sudden (very quickly) or in a gradual way?   SUDDEN   GRADUAL

Was there anything that you particularly liked ... did not like about this training session?

Further experiences you would like to share, or remarks you would like to make
(if necessary please use reverse side of this sheet).

Elapsed Time =	SECS.	XXXXXXXXXXX
Beta Time =	SECS.	%
Alpha Time =	SECS.	%
Theta Time =	SECS.	%

FIGURE 7.8   The EEG Feedback Training Questionnaire of the Menninger Clinic. (Reprinted with permission of the Menninger Clinic.)

The consequences associated with higher theta ratio settings are possible side effects that include temporary disorientation immediately following treatment, increased frequencies of abreactions, and dissociations. If these types of episodes occur, the psychotherapist will need to return the patient to a "normal state of consciousness" at the conclusion of the alpha–theta brain wave training session. The training protocol for moving the patient into a "normal state of consciousness" consists of the following procedures:

1. Beta sensitivity threshold setting will be turned on and set at a pleasant listening volume.
2. Alpha sensitivity threshold setting will be turned off completely.
3. Theta sensitivity threshold setting will be elevated approximately 2–3 microvolts higher than the present threshold setting.
4. With these new settings for feedback, the patient is returned to the "reverie state of consciousness" for 25 min.
5. The practitioner or psychotherapist will initiate the aforementioned protocol for the next six training sessions (i.e., 30-min sessions), which are designed to help ensure that the patient will not exhibit any state of confusion or side effects, and will maintain control over his or her emotions during abreactions as they continue to surface. This should prevent dissociation, or flooding, or a state of confusion.

11. Adjustment of Medication Consumption

After 1 week of daily practice of alpha–theta brain wave training, the drug dosage (e.g., antidepressants) of patients may be gradually reduced by the physicians, in accord with the request of the patients. During brain wave training sessions, patients are monitored by attending physicians on the alcoholic treatment unit or outpatient clinic. The physicians are aware of the treatment program, and a weekly record is maintained on each patient's medication reductions. If an attempt by the physician to reduce the patient's initial medication results in intense depression or anxiety, the patient is reintroduced to initial dosage levels.

12. Final Assessments

After 15 sessions of alpha–theta brain wave training are completed, the same assessment procedures described in the initial assessment phase are again performed. That is, patients again receive an EEG assessment, psychological tests (BDI, MCMI, 16PF) are readministered, an EEG baseline rating is obtained again, and a systematic desensitization session and blood sampling are performed again. These procedures are conducted exactly as described in the preceding sections on initial assessments.

13. Data Evaluation and Discharge

All data from each patient are summarized and reviewed. A decision to discharge the patient is made if the following indications are present: (1) Increased alpha rhythm amplitudes and alpha and increased theta rhythm production are detected from a comparison of initial and final assessments of EEG and EEG baseline ratings; (2) no large increase in beta endorphin levels is evident; (3) psychological tests indicate a normalization of the personality, that is, values are closer to, or within the range of, normal controls; and (4) psychiatric assessment is in agreement with psychological test results. If each of these measures is within the acceptable range, the patient is discharged.

14. Follow-Up Phase

If the patient experiences alcoholic (or PTSD) relapse, according to observers or self-report, they may elect to undergo alpha–theta brain wave training "booster sessions." These booster sessions are conducted according to the previously described procedures of the PKBNT. In the absence of specific complaints, patients are contacted at 13 and 24 months after discharge, and invited to participate in booster sessions, if they desire.

B. RESULTS OF BRAIN WAVE THERAPY

The preceding sections presented a detailed description of the methodology of the PKBNT. In this procedure EEG alpha–theta brain wave neurofeedback training is used as an innovative treatment technique for chronic alcoholics and/or post-traumatic stress disorder (PTSD) patients. When conducted according to the preceding methods, this procedure can produce profound increases in alpha and theta brain rhythms as depicted in Figs. 7.9 and 7.10 (Peniston & Kulkosky, 1989), prevent an elevation of serum beta endorphin levels during the course of treatment of alcoholism, and produce decreases in self-assessed depression and other fundamental changes in personality variables. The personality changes reported correspond to being more warmhearted, more intelligent, more emotionally stable, more socially bold, more relaxed, and more satisfied (as depicted in Figs. 7.11 and 7.12) (Peniston & Kulkosky, 1990).

In the original report of the Peniston and Kulkosky therapy (1989), results of a follow-up study showed that most of the patients (8 out of 10) who were treated by alpha–theta brain wave training maintained abstinence and prevented alcoholic relapse during a 2-year period. Of the 2 PKBNT-treated patients who had alcoholic relapse over the 24 month follow-up phase, 1 elected to return to the Medical Center for six EEG alpha–theta brain wave "booster" sessions and the other 1 now (1998) continues to maintain abstinence. These 2 patients' observers (wives, family members, halfway-house superiors) reported that the patients' tolerance for alcohol

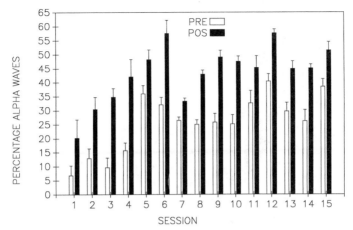

FIGURE 7.9   Mean (+ standard error, SE) percentage of EEG record in alpha rhythm frequency range, for PKBNT-treated alcoholics, before and after 15 daily sessions. [Reprinted from Peniston, E. G., & Kulkosky, P. J. (1989) with permission of Lippincott, Williams and Wilkins.]

was significantly reduced, resulting in a psychophysiological reaction of rejection of ethanol exposure. In addition, most (9) of the original PKBNT-treated patients are steadily employed and 1 is self-employed. In contrast, Medical Center records indicate that all 10 alcoholic-control patients (who received traditional treatment) have been readmitted to Medical Centers for alcohol dependence treatment, in some cases several times during the

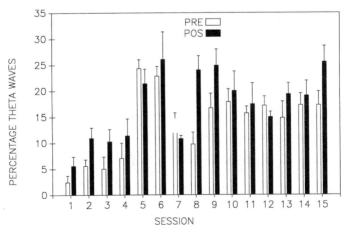

FIGURE 7.10   Mean (+ SE) percentage of EEG record in theta rhythm frequency range, for PKBNT-treated alcoholics, before and after 15 daily sessions. [Reprinted from Peniston, E. G., & Kulkosky, P. J. (1989) with permission of Lippincott, Williams and Wilkins.]

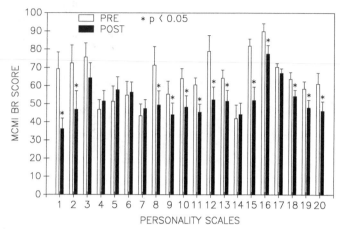

FIGURE 7.11   Mean (+ SE) MCMI BR scores of PKBNT-treated alcoholics on 20 scales, before and after treatment. [Reprinted from Peniston, E. G., & Kulkosky, P. J. (1990) with permission of Hogrefe and Huber Publishers.]

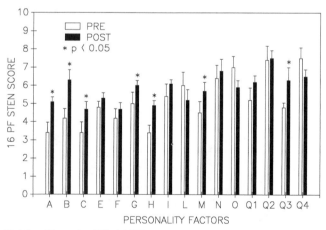

FIGURE 7.12   Mean (+ SE) 16 PF sten scores of PKBNT-treated alcoholics, before and after treatment. [Reprinted from Peniston, E. G., & Kulkosky, P. J. (1990) with permission of Hogrefe and Huber Publishers.]

24-month follow-up period. Thus, the experimental results and follow-up evidence indicate that alpha–theta brain wave neurofeedback therapy for the treatment of chronic alcoholism is an effective alternative to traditional medical treatment of alcoholism (Peniston & Kulkosky, 1989, 1990).

III. SUMMARY AND PROSPECTUS

A. REPLICATIONS

No external, controlled experimental replication of this method has yet been published in a refereed journal. Internally, Saxby and Peniston (1995) in a within-subjects assessment design showed that the PKBNT produced similar changes in personality variables and sustained prevention of alcohol relapse (92%) in 8 male and 6 female outpatients over 21 months. Also, in a repeated measure design, Kelley (1997) employed the PKBNT protocol in a 3-year follow-up analysis of Native American (Navajo) alcoholic inpatients (14 males, 6 females), and reported increased EEG synchrony and alpha–theta amplitudes, the extinguishing of drinking behavior, and less damaging comportment in the majority (81%) of the participants' lives. The general life-skill functioning of these clients has improved significantly. Furthermore, there was a dramatic reduction of the mean Beck Depressive Inventory scores after training. At the 3-year follow-up interview, participants typically voiced that these experiences, and their corresponding insights, had been beneficial both in their ability to cope and in their sobriety. Although they did not conduct direct or systematic replications of the PKBNT, two groups recently reported that biofeedback training enhanced sobriety (Denney et al., 1991) or prevented alcoholic relapse (Taub et al., 1994) in comparison with traditionally treated control alcoholics.

B. CASE STUDIES

Three case studies using alpha–theta neurotherapy have been published in refereed journals. One study employed brainmapping of EEG activity and concluded that neurotherapy produced more relaxed central nervous system functioning under stress and a reduction of craving for alcohol (Fahrion et al., 1992). Another case study described the "normalization" of personality in a male outpatient via alpha–theta neurotherapy, as indicated in a battery of personality tests. This normalization was accompanied by increased alpha and theta wave amplitudes (Byers, 1992). Eating disorders share many common features with alcoholism (Kulkosky, 1998). A study of two adults with bulimia nervosa showed that application of alpha–theta brain wave training resulted in increased alpha and theta amplitudes, decreases in clinically elevated personality measures, and remission of eating problems (Greco, 1994). Many other case studies have been reported in conference proceedings and other forums but not yet in archival journals.

C. COMMENTARY

In sharp contrast to the dearth of external, controlled experimental replications and the few published case studies, there has been an abundance of commentary on the PKBNT. These commentaries, largely very supportive, have appeared in professional journals (e.g., Ochs, 1992; Boeving, 1993; Beckwith, 1993; Fritz, 1992; Peniston, 1994; Erickson, 1989; Peniston *et al.,* 1992; Rosenfeld, 1992; Wuttke, 1992; Sams, 1995), texts (e.g., McNeese & DiNitto, 1994; Hutchison, 1994; Goldberg, 1993), and in other media such as conference proceedings, abstract volumes, workshop summaries, newsletters, magazines, newspapers, and the Internet.

It is clear that large-scale controlled replications of the alpha–theta neurotherapy technique are required for widespread acceptance of this innovative alternative to traditional therapy of alcoholism and PTSD. Such experiments could examine several factors of interest to clinicians, including (1) mechanism of the therapeutic effect (e.g., the role of neuropeptides), (2) essential components and durations of this multistage therapeutic procedure, (3) for which populations the therapeutic effect will prove successful (e.g., inpatients versus outpatients, ages, gender, ethnic groups, types of psychopathology, etc.), and (4) contribution of placebo and Hawthorne effects (subjects' reactivities to demand characteristics of experiments) to the therapeutic outcome. Given the widely expressed interest in this therapy, and its demonstrated potential for solving difficult, costly clinical problems, it is surprising that no external, controlled experimental work has been reported archivally at the time of this summary.

ACKNOWLEDGMENTS

The authors thank Sharon Pruett of the University of Southern Colorado for her assistance in the production of this manuscript. This research was supported in part by Minority Biomedical Research Support Grant No. 5 S06 GM08197-14 from the National Institute of General Medical Sciences of the National Institutes of Health to Paul J. Kulkosky.

REFERENCES

American Psychiatric Association. (1987). "Diagnostic and Statistical Manual of Mental Disorders," 3rd Ed., rev. American Psychiatric Association, Washington, DC.

Beausejour, R., & Lamontagne, Y. (1977). Effect of biofeedback on selected behaviors of psychology students identified as drug users. *Bull. Psychol.* **31,** 95–99. (Abstract)

Beck, A. T., Ward, C. H., Mendelson, M., Mock, J., & Erbaugh, J. (1961). An inventory for measuring depression. *Arch. Gen. Psychiat.* **4**, 561–571.

Beckwith, W. J. (1993). Moving beyond metaphors of the mind: Addiction, transformation and brain wave patterns. *Megabrain Report J. Mind Technol.* **1**(3), 6–8.

Boeringa, J. A. (1986). Rapid treatment of a blood phobia. *VA Practitioner* **3**, 66–71.

Boeving, H. (1993). Watching addictions disappear. *Menninger Perspective* **1**, 9–11.

Brown, B. B. (1970). Recognition of aspects of consciousness through association with EEG alpha activity represented by a light signal. *Psychophysiology* **6**, 442–452.

Budzynski, T. H., & Stoyva, J. M. (1972). Biofeedback techniques in behavior therapy. In D. Shapiro, T. X. Barber, L. V. DiCara, J. Kamiya, N. B. Miller, & J. Stoyva, (Eds.), "Biofeedback and Self Control," pp. 437–459. Aldine, Chicago.

Byers, A. P. (1992). The normalization of a personality through neurofeedback therapy. *Subtle Energies* **3**, 1–17.

Cattell, R. B., Ebner, H. W., & Tatsuoka, M. H. (1970). "Handbook for the Sixteen Personality Factor Questionnaire (16 PF)." Institute for Personality and Ability Testing. Chicago.

Denney, M. R., Baugh, J. L., & Hardt, H. D. (1991). Sobriety outcome after alcoholism treatment with biofeedback participation: A pilot inpatient study. *Int. J. Addictions* **26**, 335–341.

Dorus, W., Kennedy, J., Gibbons, R. D., & Ravi, S. D. (1987). Symptoms and diagnosis of depression in alcoholics. *Alcohol. Clin. Exp. Res.* **11**, 150–154.

Erickson, C. K. (1989). Reviews and comments on alcohol research. *Alcohol* **6**, 525–526.

Fahrion, S. L., Walters, E. D., Coyne, L., & Allen, T. (1992). Alterations in EEG amplitude, personality factors and brain electrical mapping after alpha–theta brain wave training: A controlled case study of an alcoholic in recovery. *Alcohol. Clin. Exp. Res.* **16**, 547–552.

Fritz, G. (1992). Letter to the editor. *Biofeedback* **20**(3), 5; 9.

Funderburk, W. H. (1949). Electroencephalographic studies in chronic alcoholics. *EEG Clin. Neurophysiol.* **1**, 369–370.

Funkhauser, J. B., Nagler, B., & Walker, D. N. (1953). The electroencephalogram of chronic alcoholism. *South. Med. J.* **46**, 423–428.

Gabrielli, W. F., Mednick, S. A., Volavka, J., Pollack, V. . E., Schulsinger, F., & Itil, T. M. (1982). Electroencephalograms in children of alcoholic fathers. *Psychophysiology* **19**, 404– 407.

Goldberg, B. (ed.). (1993). "Alternative Medicine: The Definitive Guide." Future Medicine, Tiburon, CA.

Greco, D. (1994). A case study approach examining the effects of alpha–theta brain wave training upon bulimia nervosa. *Adv. Med. Psychother.* **7**, 163–174.

Green, E. E., & Green, A. (1977). Breathing exercises and autogenic phrases. *In* "Beyond Biofeedback" (E. E. Green & A. Green, eds.), pp. 337–338. Delacorte, San Francisco, CA.

Green, E., Green, A. M., & Walters, E. D. (1970). Voluntary control of internal states: Psychological and physiological. *J. Transpersonal Psychol.* **2**, 1–26.

Hengeveld, M. W., Ancion, F. A., & Rooifmans, H. G. (1987). Prevalence and recognition of depressive disorders in general medical inpatients. *Int. J. Psychiat. Med.* **17**, 341–349.

Hollingshead, B. A. (1957). "Two Factor Index of Social Position." Wiley, New York.

Hutchison, M. (1994). From Prozac nation to the new reformation. *Megabrain Report J. Optimal Performance* **2**(4), 2–3.

Jasper, H. H. (1958). The 10–20 electrode system of the International Federation. *EEG Clin. Neurophysiol.* **10**, 371–375.

Johanesson, G., Berglund, M. J., & Ingvar, D. H. (1982). EEG abnormalities in chronic alcoholism related to age. *Acta Psychiat. Scandinavica* **65**, 148–157.

Kamiya, J. (1969). Operant control of the EEG alpha rhythm and some of its reported effects on consciousness. *In* "Altered States of Consciousness" (C. T. Tart, ed.), pp. 519–529. Wiley, New York.

Kelley, M. J. (1997). Native Americans, neurofeedback, and substance abuse theory. Three year outcome of alpha/theta neurofeedback training in the treatment of problem drinking among Dine' (Navajo) people. *J. Neurother* **2**(3), 24–60.

Klajner, F., Hartman, L. M., & Sobell, M. B. (1984). Treatment of substance abuse by relaxation training: A review of its rationale, efficacy and mechanisms. *Addictive Behav.* **9**, 41–55.

Kulkosky, P. J. (1998) Satiation of alcohol intake. *In* "Satiation: From Gut to Brain" (G. P. Smith, ed.), pp. 263–286. Oxford University Press, New York.

Marlatt, G. A. (1983). The controlled-drinking controversy: A commentary. *Am. Psychol.* **38**, 1097–1110.

McNeece, C. A., & DiNitto, D. M. (1994). "Chemical Dependency: A Systems Approach. Prentice Hall, Englewood Cliffs, NJ.

Millon, T. (1983). "Millon Clinical Multiaxial Inventory" 3rd Ed. National Computer Systems, Minneapolis, MN.

Moos, R. H., & Finney, J. W. (1983). The expanding scope of alcoholism treatment evaluation. *Am. Psychol.* **38**, 1036–1044.

Ochs, L. (1992). EEG treatment of addictions. *Biofeedback* **20**(1), 8–16.

Passini, F. T., Watson, C. B., Dehnel, L. Herder, J., & Watkins, B. (1977). Alpha wave biofeedback training therapy in alcoholics. *J. Clin. Psychol.* **33**, 292–299.

Peniston, E. G. (1994). EEG alpha–theta neurofeedback: Promising clinical approach for future psychotherapy and medicine. *Megabrain Report J. Optimal Performance* **2**(4), 40–43.

Peniston, E. G., & Kulkosky, P. J. (1989). Alpha–theta brain wave training and beta-endorphin levels inn alcoholics. *Alcohol. Clin. Exp. Res.* **13**, 271–279.

Peniston, E. G., & Kulkosky, P. J. (1990). Alcoholic personality and alpha–theta brain wave training. *Med. Psychother.* **3**, 37–55.

Peniston, E. G., & Kulkosky, P. J. (1991a). Alpha–theta brain wave neuro-feedback therapy for Vietnam veterans with combat-related post-traumatic stress disorder. *Med. Psychother.* **4**, 47–60.

Peniston, E. G., & Kulkosky, P. J. (1991b). Alpha–theta EEG biofeedback training in alcoholism & post-traumatic stress disorder. *Newsletter Int. Soc. for the Study of Subtle*, **2**(4), 5–7.

Peniston, E. G., Hughes, R. B., & Kulkosky, P. J. (1986). EMG biofeedback-assisted relaxation training in the treatment of reactive depression in chronic pain patients. *Psychol. Record* **36**, 471–482.

Peniston, E. G., Kulkosky, P. J., Fahrion, S. L., & Walters, E. D. (1992). Letter to the editor. *Biofeedback* **20**(3), 11.

Peniston, E. G., Marrinan, D. A., Deming, W. A., & Kulkosky, P. J. (1993). EEG alpha–theta brain wave synchronization in Vietnam theater veterans with combat-related post-traumatic stress disorder and alcohol abuse. *Med. Psychother.* **6**, 37–50.

Pollock, V. E., Volavka, J., Goodwin, D. W., Mednick, S. A., Gabrielli, W. F., Knop, J., & Schulsinger, F. (1983). The EEG after alcohol in men at risk for alcoholism. *Arch. Gen. Psychiat.* **40**, 857–864.

Porjesz, B., & Begleiter, H. (1983). Brain dysfunction and alcohol. *In* "The Pathogenesis of Alcoholism" (B. Kissin & H. Begleiter, eds.), pp. 415–483. Plenum, New York.

Propping, P., Kruger, J., & Janah, A. (1980). Effect of alcohol on genetically determined variants of the normal electroencephalogram. *Psychiat. Res.* **2**, 85–98.

Propping, P., Kruger, J., & Mark, N. (1981). Genetic disposition to alcoholism: An EEG study in alcoholics and their relatives. *Human Genet.* **59**, 51–59.

Rosenfeld, J. P (1992). "EEG" treatment of addictions: Commentary on Ochs, Peniston, and Kulkosky. *Biofeedback* **20**(2), 12–17.

Sams, M. W. (1995). Mathematically derived frequency correlates in cerebral function: Theoretical and clinical implications for neurofeedback training. *J. Neurother.* **1**, 1–14.

Saxby, E., & Peniston, E. G. (1995). Alpha–theta brain wave neurofeedback training: An effective treatment for male and female alcoholics with depressive symptoms. *J. Clin. Psychol.* **51**, 685–693.

Schultz, J. (1960). The clinical importance of "inward seeing" in autogenic training. *Br. J. Med. Hypnotism* **11**, 26–28.

Sperry, R. (1930). Probing the two minds of man. *In* "The Human Body, the Brain: Mystery of Matter and Mind" (R. B. Pinchot, ed.), p. 33. U.S. News Books, Washington, DC.

Steer, R. A., McElroy, M. G., & Beck, A. T. (1983). Correlates of self-reported and clinically assessed depression in outpatient alcoholics. *J. Clin. Psychol.* **39**, 144–149.

Steer, R. A., Beck, A. T., & Shaw, B. F. (1985). Depressive symptoms differentiating between heroin addicts and alcoholics. *Drug Alcohol Dependence* **15**, 145–150.

Stroebel, C. F., and Glueck, B. C. (1973). Biofeedback treatment in medicine and psychiatry: An ultimate placebo? *Sem. Psychiat.* **5**, 379–393.

Taub, E., Steiner, S. S., Smith, R. B., Weingarten, E. L., & Walton, K. G. (1994). Effectiveness of broad spectrum approaches to relapse prevention in severe alcoholism: A long term, randomized, controlled trial of transcendental meditation, EMG biofeedback and electronic neurotherapy. *Alcohol. Treatment Quart.* **11**, 187–220.

Vaillant, G. E. (1983). "The Natural History of Alcoholism: Cause, Patterns and Paths to Recovery." Harvard University Press, Cambridge, MA.

Vogel, F., Schalt, E., Kruger, J., Propping, P., & Lehnert, K. F. (1979). The electroencephalogram (EEG) as a research tool in human behavior genetics: Psychological examination in healthy males with various inherited EEG variants. I. Rationale of the study; material; methods; heritability of test parameters. *Human Genet.* **47**, 1–45.

Volavka, J., Pollack, V., Gabrielli, W. F., Jr., & Mednick, S. A. (1985). The EEG in persons at risk for alcoholism. *In* "Recent Developments in Alcoholism" (M. Galanter, ed.), Vol. 3, pp. 21–36. Plenum, New York.

Watson, C. G., Herder, J., & Passini, E. T. (1978). Alpha biofeedback therapy in alcoholics: An 18-month follow-up. *J. Clin. Psychol.* **34**, 765–769.

Wolpe, J. (1969). "Psychotherapy by Reciprocal Inhibition." Stanford University Press, Stanford, CA.

Wuttke, M. (1992). Addiction, awakening, and EEG biofeedback. *Biofeedback* **20**(2), 18–22.

Zachary, R. A. (1987). "Shipley Institute of Living Scale" 2nd Ed. Western Psychological Service, Los Angeles.

8

CLINICAL USE OF AN ALPHA ASYMMETRY NEUROFEEDBACK PROTOCOL IN THE TREATMENT OF MOOD DISORDERS

ELSA BAEHR,* J. PETER ROSENFELD,† RUFUS BAEHR,* CAROLYN EARNEST‡

Department of Psychiatry and Behavioral Sciences, Northwestern University, and Private Practice, Evanston, Illinois, †Department of Psychology, Northwestern University, Evanston, Illinois, and ‡University of New Mexico, Albuquerque, New Mexico

I. INTRODUCTION

The relationship between mood disorders and cortical asymmetry was first described by Robinson *et al.* (1984) when they observed that damage to the left frontal lobe results in symptoms of depression. On the other hand, they found that patients who displayed manic symptoms following a lesion were much more likely to have sustained damage to the right frontal area. This led Davidson (1995) and others (cited in his 1995 work) to postulate that brain systems mediating positive or approach behavior are located in the left frontal area (so that lesions here would lead to negative affect), whereas systems mediating negative or withdrawal behavior are located in the right frontal area (so that lesions here would lead to mania). Davidson's group has, for the past decade, largely confirmed this hypothesis of localization of emotion using electrophysiological (EEG) methods (Davidson, 1995). Davidson's group utilized alpha magnitude or power as an inverse index of cortical activation, such that high alpha means low activation; that is, alpha activity may thus be viewed as a kind of lesion. High right frontal alpha, like a right frontal lesion, would correlate with

181

positive affect, whereas high left alpha power is comparable with a left frontal lesion.[1] (Tomarken et al., 1990, 1992).

Davidson's early work (Henriques & Davidson, 1990, 1991; Davidson, 1995) confirmed his hypotheses by recording from scalp sites F4 and F3, both referenced to CZ, and developing an asymmetry measure based on the formula, $A = \log(R) - \log(L)$, where R and L are right (F4) and left (F3) alpha power, respectively. It may be seen that as this A score increases, there is relatively more right than left frontal alpha activity (less right than left cortical activation). His research group has shown that normals have higher A scores than currently depressed persons. In a separate study, they showed that normals have higher A scores than previously depressed (but now remitted) persons. One of us replicated and extended this study by comparing all three groups in one study, finding no differences between currently and previously depressed persons, but a difference between normals and the other two groups (Gotlib et al., in press). The lack of difference between previously (remitted) and currently depressed persons has been interpreted as evidence that the low A score is a trait marker for vulnerability to depression, as well as a correlate of current state, as suggested by Rosenfeld et al. (1996). Davidson's group has provided much confirmatory evidence of the A score as both state and trait marker (Davidson, 1995; Wheeler et al., 1993) using a variety of referencing methods.

This research led us to speculate about the possibility of developing a new EEG biofeedback modality for treatment of depression. The first thing we needed to show was that the A score was modifiable in normals using a simple operant conditioning program that presented reward tones for significant increases in A scores on an epoch-to-epoch basis. This we did in a study (Rosenfeld et al., 1995) in which we reported that 9 of 13 normals learned after 3 days of training to double the number of EEG epochs containing increased A scores. This work was replicated by Allen and Cavendar (1996). It then seemed appropriate to try out this novel neurofeedback protocol in real clinical patients (Baehr et al., 1995; Baehr & Baehr, 1997). This work, still ongoing, is described in the next section of this chapter with a review of five specific cases.

Two technical details need to be clarified: (1) In our work with patients we use a different algorithm, $A = [(R - L)/(R + L)]$, to define the A score, rather than the metric used in the aforementioned studies (Henriques & Davidson, 1990, 1991; Davidson, 1995). In this case R and L are the magnitudes of alpha activity (in microvolts) at F4 (R) and F3 (L). Charan Ranganath and Peter Rosenfeld, in unpublished pilot studies, took data from five

---

[1] Beta activity might be thought of as a preferable direct measure of activation, but since electromyographic activity (EMG) has sizeable harmonics in the Beta range, Beta could confound cortical and muscle activity unless considerable care is taken to remove EMG-contaminated data. It is quite straightforward to use alpha as an inverse index of activation, and virtually no EMG leaks into the alpha band.)

subjects run in the Gotlib *et al.* (in press) study and analyzed *A* scores as defined earlier in both ways. They found correlations of 0.996–0.999 between *A* scores defined in the two ways described earlier. (2) It must be noted that with a dependent variable such as *A*, which is defined and measured as a function of two other variables, *R* and *L*, one cannot attribute any observed change in *A* to either *R* or to *L*. All we can know is that the relationship of *R* and *L* has changed. Thus, when we report an increase in *A* with training, we do not know whether this involves an increase in *R*, a decrease in *L*, or both of these changes simultaneously. Other referencing schemes (of a complex nature for a clinical setting) or imaging methods may be utilized in future work to localize precisely the source(s) of change in *A* score with neurofeedback.[2]

II. CLINICAL USE OF THE ASYMMETRY PROTOCOL

Beginning in spring of 1994, a small group of depressed patients of Drs. Elsa and Rufus Baehr agreed to try an experimental treatment for mood disorders. The rationale for this treatment stems from research mentioned earlier in this chapter in which differences in frontal EEG asymmetry, characterized by apparent left frontal hypoactivity, have been linked with depression (Henriques & Davidson, 1991). Furthermore, such asymmetry was found to be present in infants who were separated from their mothers (Davidson & Fox, 1989), and was found to index a trait identified with depression-vulnerable individuals, even when they were not experiencing depression (Allen *et al.*, 1993; Henriques & Davidson, 1990; Gotlib *et al.*, in press). In addition, resting brain asymmetry was found in adolescent children whose mothers had a history of depression, as compared to a group of children whose mothers had no history of depression (Tomarken *et al.*, 1994).

We reasoned that depressed persons might benefit from training to increase differences in activation in the right and left frontal cortices. Other researchers such as Lubar (1991) and Sterman *et al.* (1972) had demonstrated that EEG biofeedback training can have stable, long-lasting effects on clinical conditions. We hypothesized that if this asymmetry training was successful, then tests designed to assess depression would reflect improvement in affect, and that the asymmetry changes would hold over time.

---

[2] A major new finding (Baehr *et al.*, 1998) demonstrates that the percent of the time of the recording session in which the positive A score is greater than zero, better discriminates depressed vs. control subjects than the A score itself, the latter being the only metric correlated with affective performance in earlier studies. On the basis of preliminary results in only 24 subjects, it may be suggested that PCT <55 suggests the presence of depression; a PCT score of >60 suggests no depression.

In the remainder of this chapter we review briefly the various major symptoms associated with a variety of mood disorders. This information is followed by a discussion of our initial clinical findings in this small sample of patients. We then discuss some of the factors believed to be associated with the successes and failures observed with the use of the asymmetry protocol.

III. THE CLASSIFICATION OF DEPRESSIVE DISORDERS

In the fourth edition of the *Diagnostic and Statistical Manual of Mental Disorders* (DSM-IV; American Psychiatric Association, 1994), diagnostic criteria for mood disorders are presented. This classification is widely used by clinicians to categorize the symptomology presented by depressed patients. The general category of depressive disorders consists of unipolar and bipolar disorders. These are distinguished from mood disorders categorized by specific etiology, such as depression due to generalized medical condition and substance-induced mood disorders.

A. UNIPOLAR DEPRESSIVE DISORDERS

Major Depressive Disorder (296.xx). Characterized by one or more major depressive episodes (at least 2 weeks of depressed mood or loss of pleasure or interest, plus four or more other symptoms of depression).

Dysthymic Disorder (300.4). Characterized by depressed mood for a minimum of 2 years, plus at least four or more symptoms of depression.

Depressive Disorder Not Otherwise Specified (311.0). Characterized by depressive features that do not meet the criteria for the preceding disorders, or an adjustment disorder with depression/and or depression and anxiety.

B. BIPOLAR DISORDERS

Bipolar I Disorder (296.xx). Characterized by one or more manic or mixed episodes. A major depression usually accompanies bipolar I disorders.

Bipolar II Disorder (296.xx). Characterized by at least one hypomanic episode and one or more major depressive episodes.

Cyclothymic Disorder (301.13). Characterized by numerous periods of hypomanic symptoms and numerous periods with depressive symptoms occurring over at least a two year period. These symptoms do not meet the criteria for either a manic episode or a major depressive episode.

Bipolar Disorder Not Otherwise Specified (296.80). Characterized by bipolar features that do not meet the criteria related to a general medical condition.

Substance Induced Mood Disorders (29x.xx). Characterized by mood disturbance caused by a drug of abuse, a medication, exposure to a toxin, or another somatic treatment for depression.

The coding allows for the addition of specifiers that further describe the disorder; that is, mild, moderate, with psychotic features, etc.

During the last several decades depression has emerged as a central mental health issue in our society. Anxiety disorders are no longer viewed consistently as the most prevalent illness. It has been estimated that about 14% of the general population will experience depression at some point in their lives, and that about twice as many women as men will be depressed (Rosenfeld, 1997). It has become evident that the phenomenon of depression requires more understanding as to its nature, as well as the exploration of more effective treatment strategies.

In a new book, edited by Akiskal and Cassano, (1997) entitled *Dysthymia and the Spectrum of Chronic Depressions,* mood disorders are presented as being chronic and occurring on a continuum, rather than as discrete episodes separated by periods of remission. This conceptualization encompasses the unipolar and bipolar disorders, and the subclinical disorders, as well as major melancholia (p. 54). Mood disorders are seen as enduring illnesses with an endogenous etiology. Chronicity, in this view, does not mean that symptoms are ever-present, but that there is an underlying depressive temperament that could emerge as mild temperamental pathology or as a major depressive illness with manic episodes. This concept is consistent with the aforementioned fact that previously depressed individuals have the EEG alpha asymmetry trait, whether they are currently depressed or not (Henriques & Davidson, 1990; Allen *et al.,* 1993; Gotlib *et al.,* in press).

Roth and Mountjoy (1997) argue that there is a spectrum of depressive states that extends from bipolar states at one end, to neurotic depression at the other end, and that nonendogenous disorders should be distinguished from endogenous disorders, not only because of differences in etiology, but because of differences in the course of the illness and the prognosis. They argue that the neurotic depressions have a different clinical profile; they are characterized by "episodic attacks which are separated by relatively clear intermissions broken by no more than mild occasional symptoms." They frequently evolve after some traumatic event, such as loss, demotion, or failure, and lack a history of trauma in childhood or adolescence, whereas dysthymia often occurs without a clear reason for onset, as well as sometimes being triggered by adverse life events. The category "neurotic or reactive depression," found in DSM-III, has been eliminated from DSM-IV. Roth and Mountjoy (1997) argue for its inclusion, based on the fact that both the etiology and the treatment of this disorder are different from the chronic dysthymic disorders. They argue that the neurotic depressions are most amenable to psychological treatments, while the endogenous disorders are not "curable," and are at best treated with long-term psychotropic medications. Arieti and Bemporad (1978), in their study of severe and mild depression, recognize the value of medication, but they claim that a psychotherapeutic approach is basic to the treatment of all types of depression, whether or not there is a hereditary predisposition. All of the depressed subjects who participated in the studies Davidson and his colleagues conducted (as mentioned earlier) were classified as endogenously depressed. Henriques and Davidson (1991) hypothesized that frontal alpha asymmetry is a "state-independent marker of vulnerability to depression." Gotlib et al. (in press), as noted, recognize the inherited nature of the depressive pattern when they cite studies showing that nondepressed children of depressed parents show this asymmetry pattern, but they also refer to studies that demonstrate that the pattern of EEG alpha asymmetry may be found in subjects with nonendogenous backgrounds as well.

The patients we have treated all have family histories of depression, and are thus classified as endogenous. This distinction is crucial, because as we attempt to change a pathological EEG brain wave asymmetry pattern, we are also challenging widely held assumptions regarding the stability of a biochemically maintained trait, whether inherited or acquired. In any event, even if it is possible with neurofeedback to modify the neural circuitry, we feel there is still a need to psychotherapeutically process the emotional factors that accompany mood disorders.

IV. TREATMENT OF DEPRESSION USING THE ASYMMETRY PROTOCOL[3]

A. SUBJECTS

Four depressed female patients and one depressed male patient who participated in the asymmetry training were patients seen by Drs. Elsa and Rufus Baehr in their private practice. They were classified as endogenously depressed. The sixth person was the client of a colleague.[4] She was classified as nonendogenously depressed.

[3] A patented asymmetry protocol was used under license in this study. For information, contact Dr. Peter Rosenfeld, Department of Psychology, Northwestern University, Evanston, Illinois 60208.

[4] The authors wish to thank Carolyn J. Earnest, MSN, RN, CS for the contribution of her client's material.

B. PROCEDURES

The Beck Depression Index (BDI) and the Minnesota Multiphasic Personality Inventory–2 (MMPI-2)[5] were administered to assess emotional functioning before and after a series of EEG asymmetry training sessions designed to increase the difference between right and left alpha magnitude.[6] Adult clinical interpretations of the MMPI-2 were computer generated by the National Computer Center.

Prior to neurofeedback training the patients were trained to use diaphragmatic breathing exercises and autogenic suggestions such as "I feel quite relaxed" and "Warmth is flowing down my arms into my hands and fingers" to promote relaxation and hand warming. Subjects were taught to meet a hand warming criterion of 95°F. This technique serves to reduce EEG artifacts caused by muscle tension. The patients were also encouraged to focus their thoughts on pleasant, unemotional imagery during EEG training sessions. They sat in a reclining chair with their feet elevated, and were encouraged to maintain a relaxed state, closing their eyes and moving as little as possible.

The patients were seen once or twice a week for 1-hr-long sessions which consisted of approximately 50% brain wave biofeedback followed by 50% psychotherapy. During biofeedback, scalp sites F3 and F4, referenced to CZ, were recorded. Impedances were 5 ohms or less, as measured by an EIM electrode impedance meter. The threshold was set at zero so that A scores below zero represented greater left than right alpha magnitude, and A scores above zero represented the reverse asymmetry. Alpha rhythm reflects cortical hypoactivity; therefore, an increase in left frontal activation corresponds to decreased alpha and a positive change in the asymmetry score.[7]

The EEG data for A-score training was recorded on either a four-channel unit or on a Neurosearch 24-channel unit (both by the Lexicor Corp.). Fast Fourier transforms (FFTs) were derived on Blackman-Harris windowed analog signals over 1-sec epochs (Harris, 1978). This device also outputs the mean value over the entire session each day as a mean asymmetry score, which is manifested as a positive or negative asymmetry score and as a mean percentage score, reflecting the percentage of time that the

[5] The MMPI-2 is the most widely used clinical testing instrument in the United States. It was selected for use in this study because it provided an objective way of measuring ten basic personality factors, including depression.

[6] Our protocol utilized the index $[(R - L)/(R + L)] \times 100$ as the asymmetry index or A score, where R and L represent right and left frontal alpha magnitude (microvolts), respectively. The *higher* the value of this index, the *less* depressed the patient is assumed to be (see earlier parts of this chapter and Rosenfeld, 1997).

[7] We cannot know from the data whether changes in alpha asymmetry resulted from a decrease in alpha rhythm in the left frontal lead or an increase in alpha rhythm in the right frontal lead, or both changes simultaneously; see Rosenfeld (1997).

TABLE 8.1   Pre- and Post-Alpha Asymmetry Training Measures of Depression for the MMPI-2 and BDI, and the Percent of Time Asymmetry Is Greater Than Zero

Subjects	MMPI-2 Pre-alpha	MMPI-2 Post-alpha	BDI Pre-alpha	BDI Post-alpha	A% Pre-alpha	A\% Post-alpha
Bob	76	54[a]	21	03	48	84
Celia	74	62[b]	40	04	57	80
Katy	n/a[c]	n/a	07	25	50	69
Ann Rose	64	47[a]	n/a	01	49	69
Catherine	62	36[a]	11	01	59	64
Diedre	n/a	n/a	34	18	36	55

[a] Two SEM $p > 0.0005$
[b] One SEM $p > 0.0025$.
[c] N/A, tests were not administered.

difference between the right and left alpha magnitude is greater than zero (A score >0). A bell tone or a clarinet tone that fluctuates in pitch (the greater the A score, the higher the tone) was used as a reinforcement when the asymmetry score exceeded zero.

V. CASE STUDIES[8]

A. BOB

Bob is a 37-year-old professional man. He sought therapy several months ago when his marriage was breaking up. He was diagnosed as having a Dysthymic Disorder of moderate severity (DSM-IV: 300.4). His mood was depressed and irritable for most of the day, for more days than not. He frequently had problems with insomnia, and his self esteem was poor. His condition was chronic, first appearing in his adolescence. Bob's father also suffered from dysthymia. Neither Bob nor his father ever suffered from a Major Depressive Episode.

Bob started on a course of the antidepressant medication Zoloft, 75 mg, for depression at the time he began neurotherapy in May 1997. He gradually discontinued his medication after his 18th session using the asymmetry protocol. His proportion of A scores >0 during the first quarter of his treatment was 43%. His average proportion of A scores >0 during the fourth quarter of his treatment was 84% (based on 22 sessions). Post-treatment test scores on the BDI and the MMPI-2 indicate significant reduction in his depression (Table 8.1, Fig. 8.1). Subjectively, he now reports

[8] The names and occupations of the clients discussed throughout this section have been changed to ensure their privacy. The authors wish to thank those patients who allowed their data to be used in this chapter.

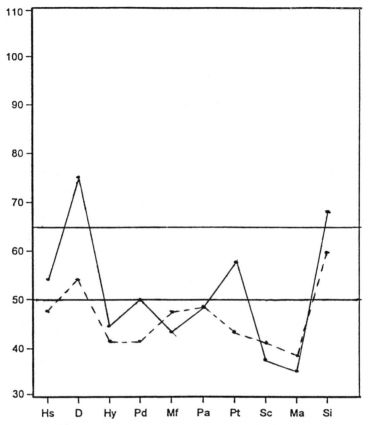

FIGURE 8.1   MMPI-2 basic scale profile pre- and post-asymmetry training for Bob. The clinical scales: Hs, hypochondriasis; D, depression; Hy, conversion hysteria; Pd, psychiatric deviate; Mf, masculinity-femininity; Pa, paranoia; Pt, psychasthenia; Sc, schizophrenia; Ma, hypomania; Si, social interaction. (————, before asymmetry training; --------, after asymmetry training).

feeling good, even though his marital problems are still unresolved. He has become more positively assertive and he is developing a sense of humor.

B. CELIA

Celia is a 34-year-old single teacher. She sought therapy 18 months ago when she was experiencing the onset of a major depressive episode (DSM-IV, 296.21). Her father had symptoms of dysthymia. Her mood was depressed for most of the day, nearly every day. She was experiencing difficulty sleeping, felt a loss of energy, had feelings of worthlessness, and had recurrent suicidal thoughts. She had been taking Prozac, 20 mg daily, for 15 months prior to starting the alpha asymmetry neurofeedback sessions in January 1997. Because she felt less depressed after initiating the neurotherapy sessions, she abruptly stopped taking her medication at the end of February. Her average proportion of A scores >0 during the first quarter of her treatment was 57%. This level decreased to 48% during the second quarter, coincident with the discontinuation of her medication. Her proportion of A scores >0 during the fourth quarter of her treatment was 80% (based on 32 sessions). Post-treatment test scores on the BDI and the MMPI-2 indicate significant reduction in her depression (Table 8.1, Fig. 8.2). Subjectively she has been experiencing a range of feelings, but no depression. During the sessions she has recalled memories, both happy and sad, from her childhood. These associations were processed during her psychotherapy sessions. She feels more confident in her work and her self-esteem has improved.

C. CATHERINE

Catherine is a 40-year-old divorced woman. She has been a registered nurse for 12 years. She initially sought psychotherapy in the spring of 1993 when she was experiencing severe agitation and depression. She was diagnosed as has having a single episode of major depressive disorder (DSM IV, 296.2). Her symptoms included the presence of depression during most of the day every day, psychomotor agitation, insomnia, weight loss, obsessive thinking, and inability to concentrate. Catherine's mother has a history of depression. Catherine began using Paxil, 20 mg, per day at the onset of therapy. In spite of taking antidepressant medication, Catherine had another less serious episode of depression when one of her parents became depressed and a close friend became seriously ill. Her depression then was characterized by chronic, nonsevere depressive symptoms such as feeling sad and having low self-esteem and low energy. She also gained weight because of overeating. She became reclusive and socially isolated. Her diagnosis was changed to dysthymic depressive disorder (DSM-IV, 300.4).

She was offered neurofeedback treatment soon after the onset of this less severe episode. She initially rejected the offer, but because her feelings were unremitting after 2 years on medication, she agreed to try the alpha asymmetry protocol. She began the first of a series of 36 neurofeedback sessions in June 1996. Her proportion of A scores >0 during the first quarter of her treatment was 59%. Her average level of A scores >0 during the fourth quarter, which ended in June 1997, was 64%. Post-treatment test scores on the BDI and the MMPI-2 indicated significant improvement in her depression (Table 8.1, Fig. 8.3). During the last two quarters of

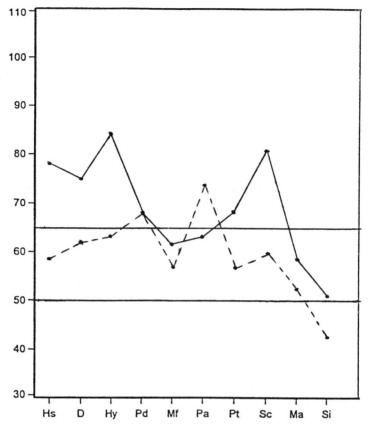

FIGURE 8.2   MMPI-2 basic scale profile pre- and post-asymmetry training for Celia. The clinical scales: Hs, hypochondriasis; D, depression; Hy, conversion hysteria; Pd, psychiatric deviate; Mf, masculinity-femininity; Pa, paranoia; Pt, psychasthenia; Sc, schizophrenia; Ma, hypomania; Si, social interaction. (———, before asymmetry training; --------, after asymmetry training). [Reprinted with permission from "The Clinical Use of an Alpha Asymmetry Protocol in the Neurofeedback Treatment of Depression: Two Case Studies," (1997), Fall/Winter.]

neurofeedback therapy she reported feeling better, and she became interested in increasing her sphere of activities with friends. She joined a dating service and began meeting men. She observed that she felt more flexible and less oppositional. She discontinued treatment when she became engaged and moved to another city. She elected to continue her medication during the transitional period of relocating.

D. ANN ROSE

Ann Rose is a 65-year-old semiretired librarian. She was referred for therapy 12 years ago by a psychiatrist who had been treating her for major

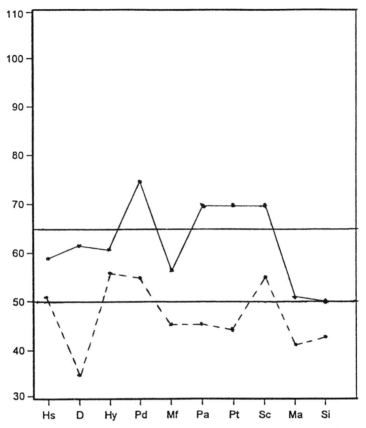

FIGURE 8.3   MMPI-2 basic scale profile pre- and post-asymmetry training for Catherine. The clinical scales: Hs, hypochondriasis; D, depression; Hy, conversion hysteria; Pd, psychiatric deviate; Mf, masculinity-femininity; Pa, paranoia; Pt, psychasthenia; Sc, schizophrenia; Ma, hypomania; Si, social interaction. (————, before asymmetry training; --------, after asymmetry training). [Reprinted with permission from "The Clinical Use of an Alpha Asymmetry Protocol in the Neurofeedback Treatment of Depression: Two Case Studies," (1997), Fall/Winter.]

depressive episodes over a period of 28 years. Her diagnosis at that time was recurrent major depressive disorder of moderate severity (DSM-IV, 296.32). She was seen periodically by Dr. Baehr when she was experiencing a major depressive episode, and she would typically stay in psychotherapy for a short period of time until her symptoms remitted. Her most recent episode occurred in spring of 1993. There was no precipitating event known to have caused this recurrence.

On a daily basis she presented six of the nine criteria for a major depressive episode listed in DSM-IV. Her symptoms included depressed mood during most of the day, a loss of interest and pleasure in activities, significant weight loss, insomnia, fatigue and loss of energy, indecision, and diminished ability to concentrate. Obsessive thinking was a major personality trait. There was a family history of depression. After 6 months in therapy in which she failed to improve significantly, she was offered 32 neurotherapy sessions for the treatment of depression, using an alpha/theta protocol.[9] She reported some improvement in her feelings after this course of therapy, but her depression returned, particularly when she awoke in the morning. In June 1994 she began the first of 34 sessions using the alpha asymmetry protocol. At that time she also began taking 20 mg of Paxil per day.

Her progress was measured by her quarterly average proportion of A scores >0 (Table 8.1), based on a total of 34 sessions.[10] During the third quarter, stress in her life increased when her daughter developed lung cancer, her sister-in-law died, and a close family friend died. Her lowered A score in this period apparently reflected her reaction to life's vicissitudes, but she was not experiencing clinical depression. She could distinguish between the emotions generated by depression and those associated with appropriate worry or sadness evoked by situations in her life. Her fourth quarter A scores >0 of 67% demonstrated her ability to rebound in a healthier direction. While her sessions formally ended in April 1996, follow up visits in June, July, and November of that year indicated that she was maintaining a proportion of A score >0 of 67%. A follow-up visit 1 year later, in June 1997, yielded a proportion of A score >0 of 69%.

Ann Rose can no longer be considered depressed. She commented that at times she feels like she may be going into a depression again, but it does not materialize. She also commented that "her mind seems to be functioning better." She feels energetic and outgoing, and while she still tends to worry when things go wrong, she is not as obsessive in her thinking as she was in the past. Post-treatment scores on the BDI and the MMPI-2 indicated significant reduction in her depression (Table 8.1, Fig. 8.4).

E. KATY

Katy[11] was single and 40 years old when she began therapy in the fall of 1993. She worked as a salesperson in a boutique. She initially sought therapy because she experienced alternating manic and depressive symp-

---

[9] Alpha–theta treatment was selected because previous researchers using the Peniston protocol reported that depression (as measured by the MMPI-2) was alleviated during the course of alpha–theta training (Peniston & Kulkosky, 1990).

[10] The protocol used in this initial use of alpha asymmetry differed from the one used at a later date for the other subjects as it did not produce a score which indicated the percentage of right hemisphere alpha asymmetry. Progress was measured as the mean alpha asymmetry score over the entire session.

[11] Katy was an unusual case and was included in this chapter because of the many complications that occurred during her therapy.

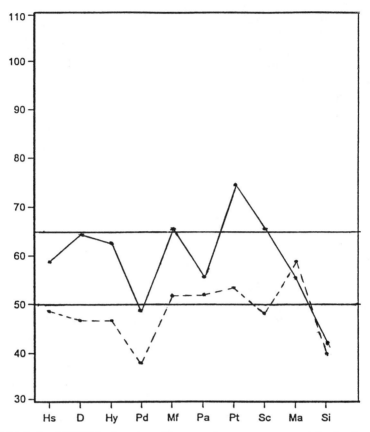

FIGURE 8.4   MMPI-2 basic scale profile pre- and post-asymmetry training for Ann Rose. The clinical scales: Hs, hypochondriasis; D, depression; Hy, conversion hysteria; Pd, psychiatric deviate; Mf, masculinity-femininity; Pa, paranoia; Pt, psychasthenia; Sc, schizophrenia; Ma, hypomania; Si, social interaction. (———, before asymmetry training; --------, after asymmetry training).

toms. She had been taking Prozac for a period of 6 years for depression. She claimed that for several years the medication made her feel "elated and alive," but she was no longer feeling the positive effects. In June 1994 her physician changed her medication to Zoloft. The manic and depressive symptoms emerged again as when she had initially taken Prozac. She was given a diagnosis of bipolar disorder, not otherwise specified (DSM-IV, 296.80) because her symptoms did not meet the minimal duration criteria for a manic episode or a major depressive episode. It was also unclear whether her bipolar symptoms may have been medically induced.

  She began a series of 34 neurofeedback sessions in June 1994 that ended in November 1995. Her progress was measured by dividing the sessions into four periods.[12] Her learning curve was excellent during the first three quarters. She reported feeling good after the sessions in which she had achieved a positive A score. While she was not experiencing depression, she missed the highs she had initially obtained with Prozac.

At the end of June 1995, she changed medication again to Effexor. She reacted badly to the new medication, developing flu-like symptoms and edema. During this period of time, which coincided with the fourth quarter, her average A score >0 declined. She also elected to stop the neurofeedback sessions. In January her medication was changed once more to a combination of lithium and Prozac. She could not tolerate these medications either, and by June 1996 she had totally discontinued all medications. Periodic assessment of her functioning when on the asymmetry protocol indicated that her level of alpha asymmetry in the right frontal cortices was generally 50% or less. Her BDI also reflected her regression. Her depression score of 25 was higher at the end of treatment than her score of 7 in the beginning of her neurotherapy sessions. In June 1997 she again tried medication (Wellbutrin). She again demonstrated that she could not physically tolerate antidepressants because she developed a skin rash and edema. By the end of July she had discontinued all medication. Clearly this was not a successful case. Her bipolar symptoms have disappeared, however, she remains in a chronic dysthymic condition, and is now considering trying another course of neurotherapy.

F. DEIDRE

Deidre is a single, 47-year-old woman. She has been a special education teacher for 20 years, but has been unable to work since May 1995. Her recent depression began insidiously in April 1994 following an acute viral infection in February 1994, complicated by mild hepatitis and post hepatitis C infection. Her current condition was diagnosed by her physician as post polio syndrome with major depressive episodes. She had been taking Nortriptyline, 50 mg daily, for 2 months prior to beginning neurofeedback treatment, and has continued the medication during the alpha asymmetry training . She met all the criteria for mood disorder due to a general medical condition (DSM-IV, 293.83). These criteria require that the disturbance be the direct physiological consequence of a general medical condition, the disturbance cannot be accounted for by another mental disorder, the disturbance does not occur exclusively during the course of a delirium, and the symptoms cause clinically significant distress or impairment in social,

---

[12] Katy's case used an early form of the asymmetry protocol that did not provide a percentage score. Instead, a score based on the mean alpha asymmetry score (ALAY) was used to evaluate progress.

occupational, or other important areas of functioning. She also met the full criteria for mood disorder with major depressive-like episodes: depressed mood most of the day, markedly diminished interest or pleasure in all or almost all activities most of the day, nearly every day, significant weight gain, hypersomnia nearly every day, psychomotor retardation nearly every day, fatigue every day, feelings of worthlessness and inappropriate guilt, and diminished ability to think or concentrate or indecisiveness. There is no previous history of depression for this client, and there is no immediate family history of depression.

Deirdre was initially seen for 24 alpha asymmetry training sessions. Her proportion of A scores >0 during the first quarter of training was 36%; her proportion of A scores >0 during the last quarter of training was 55%. Her BDI scores also showed improvement, decreasing from an initial score of 34 to a post-treatment score of 18 (Table 8.1). While her scores indicate that she was still functioning in the depressed range, she was beginning to feel better. At the completion of the 24 sessions Deirdre stated that she was "now more me than not, although a different me." She still had brief periods of 1–2 hr of feeling sad, but these periods are limited and not long lasting. Her overall energy improved and she believes she is thinking more clearly. Her self-esteem has improved, she is more optimistic about the future, and her guilt has diminished. There was a reemergence of a strong sense of humor. She has recently returned to continue the alpha asymmetry training.

VI. CLINICAL FACTORS ASSOCIATED WITH EEG NEUROFEEDBACK TREATMENT

Five of the six patients in the preceding study were seen in the private psychotherapy practices of Dr. Elsa Baehr and Dr. Rufus Baehr. One patient was the patient of Carolyn Earnest, MSN, RN, CS. Several factors were taken into consideration when EEG neurofeedback was introduced as an adjunct to ongoing psychotherapy. The nature of the relationship between the therapist and patient was, of necessity, altered; that is, a switch was made from a purely talking, "hands-off" therapy, to one where the therapist had to touch the patient to apply electrodes, and where at least 50% of the time, the therapist sat quietly beside the patient who was connected to the EEG machine and was silently responding to a feedback tone. The therapy sessions were conducted in a small lab room rather than in the more spacious therapist's office. Prior to beginning the EEG neurofeedback sessions, the changes in the relationship and the setting were discussed with the patient. The EEG neurofeedback treatment was initiated only after both the therapist and patient felt comfortable with the altered treatment structure.

Some changes likely occurred as a result of the changes in treatment. The more informal atmosphere in the lab, and the physical closeness of the chairs in which the patient and therapist were seated probably created an environment in which the patient felt secure and free to discuss feelings. Also a feeling of alliance likely was created because both patient and therapist were involved in the success of the EEG neurofeedback process. The environment is a nurturing one in which the unconscious dependency needs of the patient can be met in a nonthreatening way. These factors need to be taken into account when evaluating the progress of the patient being trained on the alpha asymmetry protocol. Perhaps the emotional environment reinforces and facilitates the EEG changes in alpha asymmetry as they are occurring. Studies need to be done to determine whether the same degree of improvement in mood would occur in a lab setting that was purely electrophysiological and the person applying the electrodes was an objective technician rather than a therapist.

VII. NEGATIVE FACTORS IN THE CLINICAL SITUATION

The patients who agreed to try the EEG neurofeedback also consented to allow their data to be used for research. This situation became an issue for one patient (not a participant in the present study) who was feeling stressed because of many outside demands on her time. She was attending graduate school part time, and was working as an administrator in a corporation. Her job required her to travel frequently, which interfered with the continuity of the EEG neurofeedback treatment. Although she had initially been successful in responding to the asymmetry protocol, she was unable to maintain positive scores. When it was suggested that she try two sessions in one day to "get back on track" she agreed; however, her scores consistently fell within the negative alpha asymmetry range. In a discussion following the sessions she admitted that she felt resentful in coming to therapy but did so to please the therapist. It was also revealed that she felt the therapist was more interested in collecting data than in her problems.

Two patients who had agreed to try the EEG neurofeedback became impatient after one or two sessions and expressed their need for "talking therapy" before engaging in further EEG treatments. It is of course crucial to the success of any therapy to be sensitive to the needs of the patient. In the EEG neurofeedback treatment this can be accomplished very easily by watching for A-score changes in the negative direction during a therapy session,[13] and then processing the thoughts that have occurred during the

[13] In this study the "trend" display in the Biolex program was useful because it allows the therapist to observe changes in asymmetry as they occur.

treatment. This can be done by interrupting a session when the asymmetry becomes negative, or by doing a briefing after the session.

VIII. MEDICATION AND THE ASYMMETRY PROTOCOL

Most patients were using antidepressant medication at the beginning of the EEG neurotherapy and continued it for varying amounts of time.[14] The effect of the medication on the asymmetry protocol is unknown and needs to be studied. It is apparent that the medication did not prevent the A score from slipping into the negative range when the patient was responding to an emotionally disturbing thought or situation. One patient, Katy, a long-time Prozac user who had achieved a consistently positive asymmetry score, began to develop a severe reaction to her medication. She developed edema and complained of flu-like symptoms. Changes in medication made her situation worse. Her A score was erratic and declined overall in the fourth quarter. She agreed to slowly terminate all medication, and after a month had passed she began to feel better physically, but her mood remained dysphoric.

Another patient, Celia, reported on earlier, had been on Prozac for more than 2 years when she began EEG neurotherapy. She abruptly stopped taking medication. Her asymmetry score, which had been consistently in the positive range, dropped into the negative range, and remained low for several weeks. She rebounded and has maintained positive scores since that time. She is no longer depressed.

Ann Rose, also reported on earlier in this chapter, gradually decreased her medication (Paxil) after 6 months of EEG neurotherapy. After 1 month she was completely off her antidepressant.

Bob, who started a low dose of Zoloft at the beginning of asymmetry treatment, has totally cut out his medication after 22 EEG neurofeedback sessions. While he experienced slight withdrawal feelings, he maintained his level of asymmetry percentage and did not become depressed.

In summary, three of the six patients reported on in this chapter successfully discontinued their medication before the end of the fourth quarter of their treatment. Their proportion of A scores remained stable.

IX. DISCUSSION

In this chapter we have described how theories of emotion and anterior cerebral asymmetry led to an investigation of an alternative way to treat

[14] The authors wish to thank Dr. Miepje DeVryer for her cooperation and assistance.

depression. A striking finding was that differences in frontal brain asymmetry discriminated populations of depressed and nondepressed subjects (Henriques & Davidson, 1990; Gotlib *et al.*, in press). It was also learned that normal subjects could be trained to modify their brain waves by changing their frontal alpha asymmetry (Rosenfeld *et al.*, 1995). In addition, it was demonstrated that there was a relationship between daily changes in frontal alpha asymmetry and changes in mood (Rosenfeld *et al.*, 1996).

The transition was made from the theoretical foundations and experimental studies to the practical applications when we trained depressed persons to change their frontal alpha asymmetry to resemble the asymmetry pattern found in nondepressed persons. Some depressed patients presented earlier in this chapter appeared to benefit from this alpha asymmetry training, as measured not only by their subjective feelings, but also by their post-training scores on the MMPI-2 and the BDI. There appears to have been general improvement in the MMPI-2 personality profiles for four of the subjects on which we had MMPI-2 data (Figs. 8.1–8.4). Clinically we observed that our patients were generally less obsessive and more positive in their thinking. Finally, along with our colleague Carolyn Earnest, we found that they were displaying a sense of humor.

A comparison of the patients' pre- and post-MMPI-2 depression scales indicates a significant change. For three patients the pre- to post-depression score differences exceeded two times the standard error of measurement (SEM), and for one patient, one SEM (Table 8.1).[15] The SEM is based on the standard deviation of the sampling distribution. The standard deviations used in this study were derived from a sample of 1184 white females and a sample of 933 white males (Hathaway & McKinley, 1989, p. 105). Interpretation of change in a patient's profile at the retest should not be made unless the differences exceed the standard error of measurement, and preferably are two times the SEM for conservation personality appraisal (Butcher, 1990, p. 11).

Five of the six subjects scored above 9 on the BDI in the pretest, while four of the six scored below 9 in the post-test. (Scores above 9 on the BDI commonly are considered to be in the depressed range.)

While we may wish to view this asymmetry protocol as a major innovative treatment for mood disorders, it is apparent that it does not work for everyone. For example, in the case of bipolar depression presented earlier, improvement occurred in terms of eliminating mood swings, but the patient remained in a dysphoric state at the end of the treatment. This case also

---

[15] The SEM is based on the standard deviation of the sampling distribution. The standard deviations used in this study were derived from a sample of 1184 while females and a sample of 933 white males. (Hathaway and McKinley, 1989, pg. 105. Interpretation of change in a patient's profile at the retest should not be made unless the differences exceed the standard error of measurement, and preferably are two times the SEM for conservation personality appraisal. (Butcher, 1990, p. 11).

was complicated by reactions to psychotropic medications. Further study is needed to determine the type of mood disorders that are most amenable to treatment. At this time we also view neurofeedback as an adjunct to ongoing psychotherapy, and not as a "stand-alone" treatment. The lab setting where the neurofeedback treatment occurs, and the alliance with the therapist also may be important factors in the treatment situation. Some question is raised as to whether the positive effects we have observed would also occur in a lab setting where a therapist was not present.

Taking these factors into account, we feel that the crucial next step for research is to demonstrate that appropriate control cases do not improve clinically as much as cases given the specific asymmetry protocol. We have preliminary evidence along this line, noting a case in which the asymmetry protocol, but not the alpha–theta protocol was helpful. In another case, not reported in this chapter, a patient of Dr. Elsa Baehr was seen for 50 neurofeedback sessions with a different protocol to improve cognitive functioning after a head injury. Although the treatment was successful, the patient was still depressed at the end of the neurotherapy sessions as measured by the MMPI-2 and the BDI. She has returned for treatment of her depression using the asymmetry protocol and is currently showing progress.

This novel approach to the treatment of depression is in its infancy. We have reported here on the first clinical uses of the alpha asymmetry protocol for treatment of depression. Based on our initial findings we feel that alpha asymmetry neurofeedback is a promising alternative adjunctive treatment for mood disorders.

REFERENCES

Akiskal, H. S., & Cassano, G. B. (eds.). (1997). "Dysthymia and the Spectrum of Chronic Depressions." Guilford Press, New York.

Allen, J., Iacono, W., Depue, R., & Arbisi, P. (1993). Regional electroencephalographic asymmetries in bipolar seasonal affective disorder before and after exposure to bright light. *Biol. Psychiat.* **33,** 642–646.

American Psychiatric Association. (1994). "Diagnostic and Statistical Manual of Mental Disorders," 4th Ed. American Psychiatric Association, Washington, DC.

Arieti, S., & Bemporad, J. (1978). "Severe and Mild Depression." Basic Books, New York.

Butcher, J. N. (1990). "MMPI-2 in Psychological Treatment." Oxford University Press, New York.

Davidson, R. J. (1995). Cerebral asymmetry, emotion and affective style. *In* "Brain Asymmetry" (R. J. Davidson & Hugdahl, eds.), pp. 369–388. The MIT Press, Cambridge, MA.

Davidson, R. J., & Fox, N. A. (1989). Frontal brain asymmetry predicts infant response to maternal separation. *J. Abnormal Psychol.* **98,** 127–131.

Gotlib, I. H., Ranganath, C., & Rosenfeld, J. P. (in press). Frontal EEG alpha asymmetry, depression and cognitive functioning. *Cognition Emotion.*

Harris, F. J. (1978). On the use of windows for harmonic analysis with the discrete Fourier transformation. *Proc. IEEC* **16,** 51–84.

Hathaway, S. R., & McKinley, J. C. (1989). "Manual for Administration and Scoring MMPI-2," p. 105. University of Minnesota Press, St. Paul, MN.

Henriques, J. B., & Davidson, R. J. (1990). Regional brain electrical asymmetries discriminate between previously depressed and healthy control subject. *J. Abnormal Psychol.* **99,** 22–31.

Henriques, J. B., & Davidson, R. J. (1991). Left frontal hypoactivation in depression. *J. Abnormal Psychol.* **100,** 534 –545.

Lubar, J. (1991). Discourse on the development of EEG diagnostics and biofeedback for attention-deficit/hyperactivity disorders. *Biofeedback Self-Regul.* **16**(3).

Peniston, E. G., & Kulkosky, P. J. (1990). Alcoholic personality and alpha–theta brain wave training. *Med. Psychother.* **3,** 37–55.

Robinson, R. G., Kubos, K. L., Starr, L. B. Rao, K., & Price, T. R. (1984). Mood disorders in stroke patients: Importance of location of lesion. *Brain,* **107,** 81–93.

Rosenfeld, J. P. (1997). EEG biofeedback of frontal alpha asymmetry in affective disorders. *Biofeedback* **25**(1), 8–25.

Rosenfeld, J. P., Cha, G., Blair, T., & Gotlib, I. (1995). Operant biofeedback control of left-right frontal alpha power differences. *Biofeedback Self-Regul.* **20,** 241–258.

Rosenfeld, J. P., Baehr. E., Baehr, R. Gotlib, I., & Ranganath, C. (1996). Preliminary evidence that daily changes in frontal alpha asymmetry correlate with changes in affect in therapy sessions. *Int. J. Psychophysiol.* **23,** 241–258.

Roth, R., & Mountjoy, C. Q. (1997). The need for the concept of neurotic depression. *In* "Dysthymia and the Spectrum of Chronic Depressions" (H. S. Akiskal & G. B. Cassano, eds.). Guilford Press, New York.

Sterman, M. B., MacDonald, L. R., & Stone, R. K. (1972). Biofeedback training of the sensorimotor electroencephalographic rhythm in man: Effects on epilepsy. *Epilepsia* **15,** 395–416.

Tomarken, A. J., Simien, C., & Garber, J. (1994). Resting frontal brain asymmetry discriminates adolescent children of depressed mothers from low-risk controls. *Psychophysiology* **31**(Suppl.), S97–S98.

9

ASSESSING AND TREATING OPEN HEAD TRAUMA, COMA, AND STROKE USING REAL-TIME DIGITAL EEG NEUROFEEDBACK

MARGARET E. AYERS

Neuropathways EEG Imaging, Beverly Hills, California

In this chapter, I attempt to summarize more than two decades of clinical work using real-time digital EEG neurofeedback for cases of head trauma, coma, and stroke. I begin with a brief discussion of differences between real-time digital EEG measures and those based on derived and EEG averaging methods. Throughout the chapter my beliefs regarding the advantages of using real-time EEG measures will be stressed. The basic organization of the chapter is around separate sections devoted to the nature, diagnosis, and EEG neurofeedback treatment of head trauma, coma, and stroke.

Historically, the electroencephalograph has evolved from analog recordings, the first one by Hans Berger involving paper and ink pens in 1929 (Berger, 1929). The first digital machines were used for evoked potentials. Quantitative analysis of the digital EEG was done by the fast Fourier transform spectrum, with results expressed as the square root of the spectral power. Samples of EEG are taken, added, and averaged. Other averaged or derived measures of evoked potentials included current source density, such as Horft and Laplacian methods, dipole localization method, and focus method. Individuals such as Duffy (1986), Ebersole (1991), Gevins *et al.* (1994), Wong (1991), Perrin *et al.* (1987), Thatcher *et al.* (1989) and Scherg and Ebersol (1993) have described such averaged or derived measures.

Quantitative analyses of the same EEG using analog and real-time digital versus averaged or derived measures result in different sets of data. Thus, research results based on averaging may not accurately display what occurs in the actual EEG, and neurofeedback using such systems could provide erroneous information to clients. Averaging EEG data eliminates primary raw EEG data. Once the data are averaged into a power spectrum the original primary EEG can no longer be displayed. In addition, frequency values averaged in a power spectrum are real in the mathematical notation, but may not exist in a real EEG. The squared fast Fourier wave is representative of a finite number of sine waves, which cannot be seen in the original EEG. Fast Fourier low frequencies appearing in power spectral analysis have increased power because of the mathematical logarithm. Also, the fast Fourier delta frequency can be artifact or complex waveforms so that delta waves emerge when they do not exist in the raw EEG. In the analog EEG those complex waveforms or spikes appear in the 4–7 Hz range, but often appear as delta in fast Fourier. Only real-time all digital EEG can display complex EEG patterns. They cannot be seen in the analog EEG or in averaged or derived measures. Fast Fourier brain wave maps of open or closed head trauma patients often indicate an abundance of delta, but analog and real-time digital EEG's display large quantities of theta.

I. OPEN HEAD TRAUMA AND OTHER TRAUMATIC BRAIN INJURY

Open head trauma or traumatic brain injury results from any force crushing the skull, or penetration by objects such as bullet, knife, or blunt object. One may not become unconscious. Furthermore, contusion of the brain may occur in the absence of skull penetration or skull fracture. For example, the brain can bruise against the skull when in rapid acceleration-acceleration or coup-countercoup injury, often resulting in brain stem shearing or axonal lesions.

In determining severity of head trauma, Williams and Denny-Brown (1941) first showed initial EEG changes of attenuated cerebral activity followed by slow waves and then return of more normal electrical activity. In more severe head trauma the EEG contains mostly theta and some delta waves. Progressive clinical EEG decline is characterized by low-voltage delta activity. In some clients, epileptiform activity such as sharp waves, spikes, and spike-slow wave discharges are seen according to Courion *et al.* (1971).

Individuals with open head trauma or closed traumatic brain injury have symptomatology of memory loss as documented by Ayers (1983), Levin (1989), and Van Zomeren and Van Denberg (1985). Some individuals may have retrograde amnesia, the inability to remember events before the trauma. Second, individuals with open head trauma often incur intellectual deficits as documented by Mandelberg and Brooks (1975) and Tabaddor *et al.* (1979). Individuals with closed head trauma often show little impairment in general intellectual functioning according to Drudge *et al.* (1989). However, usually the more severe the trauma, the more severe the cognitive deficits.

Third, individuals may have more language problems with open as opposed to closed head trauma. Sarno (1980) found all of 56 cases with such traumatic brain injury had some degree of language impairment, for example, problems with word retrieval or aphasia, paraphasia, alexia, agraphia, lack of spontaneous speech. Loury (1970) found 37.5% of left hemisphere injuries had language deficits that did not improve. But according to Ruff *et al.* (1991), visuospatial abilities (assessed by block design tests) returned to near normal performance at 6 and 12 months after injury.

Individuals sustaining open head trauma often have damage to frontal lobes and therefore present poor social and rational judgment and impaired planning. Damasio *et al.* (1994) and Adams *et al.* (1980) found poor judgment and impaired planning. Bechara *et al.* (1994) found that where an individual had to make a decision based on expected future consequences, frontal lobe damage resulted in difficulty with these decisions. This often prevents individuals from returning to work where normal judgment is required. There also may be major changes in personality due to traumatic brain injury. Personality changes may include depression, agitation, anger, problems with impulsivity, poor judgment, oversensitivity to sound, light, and temperature, effort fatigue, and lack of initiative.

Chronic headaches may occur following open head injury. However, according to Yamaguchi (1992), headaches are more common in closed minor head trauma than in major head trauma. Goddard *et al.* (1994) call it post-traumatic or postconcussive headache. Others have called it post-head trauma syndrome. Positional vertigo or dizziness may also be a consequence of open head trauma. According to Steadman and Graham (1969) dizziness and/or headaches may persist years postinjury.

Unlike closed head trauma, individuals with severe open head trauma have suppression of cellular immunity according to Quattrocchi *et al.* (1992). Also, according to Quattrocchi *et al.* (1991) helper T-cell function and lymphokine-activated killer cell cytotoxicity is impaired following severe head injury.

II. ASSESSMENT

Regardless of the site of injury, my real-time digital EEG assessment of open head trauma or traumatic brain injury always involves recording sensorimotor cortex (sites T4C4, T3C3) along with other International 10–20 system electrode placements. The sensorimotor cortex controls all sensory and motor functions and mediates behavior based on incoming sensory input and past experience. Consistent with neurological findings generally, I have found that injuries on the right side often result in mood swings, personality change, problems with visuospatial organization, temper outbursts, impulsivity, and poor organization. Injuries on the left often involve problems with language, such as lack of spontaneous speech, difficulty retrieving words, aphasia, paraphasia, agraphia or alexia, and/or problems with logic, math, and judgment.

In the real-time digital EEG we can selectively filter out and display any frequency along with the raw EEG. During a 3–5 min baseline, the precise peak-to-peak microvoltage of each frequency, as well as the EEG in a specific area, may be seen. For example, if the theta frequency microvoltage at T4C4 is 4.5 μV and at T3C3 the theta is 2.5 μV, then the higher voltage on T4C4 indicates probability of injury. In the analog EEG one has to hand measure the μV, and in fast Fourier digital one can only measure power, not EEG voltage. Another tremendous advantage of the real-time digital EEG display is the ability to recognize that no two EEG patterns are exactly alike. However, families who are genetically similar, and individuals with closed head trauma, open head trauma, depression, epilepsy, postviral infection, or migraine may have similar EEG patterns. For example, in closed trauma one sees frequent phasic spikes attached to 4–7 Hz activity. In open head trauma one may see two or more spikes together attached to slow 4–7 Hz activity. The spikes appear to act as an interruption or short circuit in the cortical surface dc shift from frontal to occipital cortex. Usually when EEG amplitudes show extreme variation due to phasic spikes, open head trauma symptoms are most pronounced. Diagnostically, even when an individual cannot speak, the EEG pattern indicates what type of problem is involved. When looking at other derived or mathematically averaged quantitative analyses of EEG, one cannot reconstruct the original EEG or see true EEG wave patterns to most accurately diagnose and treat.

III. REAL-TIME DIGITAL NEUROFEEDBACK OF OPEN HEAD TRAUMA

Assessment of the real-time digital EEG gives precise peak-to-peak microvoltages at each site. The higher amplitude often indicates the site of impact. In severe head trauma one may see either extremely elevated microvoltages or overall central nervous system (CNS) depression (with amplitude lowered overall).

The open head trauma pattern of two or more spikes together attached to slow 4–7 Hz activity is often seen immediately in the temporal lobes. Courville (1958) discovered that the temporal lobes often scrape on the bony middle fossa of the skull, causing lesions or brain trauma resulting in psychomotor epilepsy.

Delta activity occurring in intermittent bursts may be seen in some open head trauma, especially when a lesion that can be documented on a CT scan or MRI has occurred. In children under the age of 12, higher microvoltages of both theta and delta waves may be seen in the raw EEG or in digitally filtered delta or theta displays, years after the injury.

As noted earlier, if peak-to-peak real-time digital microvoltage is higher in one area it indicates the probable site of impact. During neurofeedback we always work from the sensorimotor cortex, going from the center of the brain to get sensory and motor control. The International 10–20 system sites T4C4, T3C3 are used. Relevant to this, epilepsy researchers at Johns Hopkins in 1992 found that anatomy texts erred when saying motor cortex was only 1 cm wide. They found it to be as wide as 4 cm.

In open head trauma, theta and beta amplitudes usually are elevated (unless there is CNS depression with overall lowered microvoltage amplitudes). It appears that the beta amplitude is increased in an effort to compensate; that is, it is an attempt by the body to "override" the excessive theta or delta. One of our goals is to reduce theta activity. In reducing theta activity we train to inhibit theta just below the top peak of theta displayed digitally. For example, if the peak-to-peak theta is 5 μV we set our equipment to encourage the client to inhibit theta activity at or about 4.5 μV, and we reward 15–18 Hz activity over 0.40 μV. As the theta progressively decreases in amplitude, theta microvoltage settings will be lowered to 4 μV, then 3.7, and then 3.5. The beta or 15–18 Hz voltage never changes from 0.40 μV. Such progressive real-time digital feedback commonly results in the open head trauma pattern of two or more spikes together with excessive slow-wave activity decreasing in frequency. Phasic spikes often disappear with this theta activity inhibition. Often it is not just inhibition of all slow-wave activity, but inhibition of the abnormally high phasic spike microvoltage that occurs. The raw EEG shows a more consistent amplitude with spike microvolt reduction. As the open head trauma pattern becomes less frequent the client often subjectively notes improvement in energy, concentration, memory, reduced sensitivity to sound and light, fewer headaches, and reduction in positional vertigo.

I never attempt to increase beta amplitude directly in open head trauma because the theta amplitude will also increase. If the client has spasticity, seizure activity, or tics, they can also increase. A paradox of treatment is that as the theta and or delta amplitude is decreased, the beta amplitude automatically increases. I always leave the 15–18 Hz reward threshold set at 0.40 μV and train to progressively decrease the voltage of the slow-wave activity. The choice of 0.40 μV, 15–18 Hz was made for various reasons. For one, the brain of the client apparently can discriminate readily between inhibiting 4–7 Hz and rewarding 15–18 Hz. Also some coma patients, open head trauma patients, and seizure patients produce an excess of 12–15 Hz activity. They generally remain in coma, have increased muscle spasticity, or produce seizure activity in the 12–15 Hz range.

In open head trauma different sites have different microvolt amplitudes, so training more than one site at one time can potentiate, or kindle, seizure activity. I alternate between EEG training on both sensorimotor cortices to get sensory and motor return. Later, one may train frontal or occipitoparietal areas. For example, if seizure activity has occurred from head trauma one may train F8T4 or F7T3 to inhibit frontotemporal epileptic activity discharge, if present. One may also train just the site of impact.

Open head trauma may require from 20–70 treatment sessions. The more widespread the open head trauma pattern, usually the more severe the injury and the more time required to reduce phasic spikes and excessive slow-wave activity. Figures 9.1, 9.2, and 9.3 show pre–post-treatment real-time digital EEG records in a case of open head trauma. This man was hit by a car at age 8 and did not receive real-time digital EEG neurofeedback until age 17. He was wheelchair bound, barely understandable, with slurred speech, extreme spasticity, and shortened arm and leg on the right side from a stroke. Following 50 treatment sessions he is walking without assistance, speaks clearly but slowly, and can function independently. His pretreatment (Figs. 9.1 and 9.2) and post-treatment EEGs (Fig. 9.3) are shown. The top line is the raw EEG, the middle line is 15–18 Hz, and the bottom line is 4–7 Hz digitally filtered out of the raw EEG. Peak-to-peak EEG on T4C4 was 4.57 μV for theta. Beta of 15–18 Hz was 3.08 μV. T3C3 was 4.25 μV

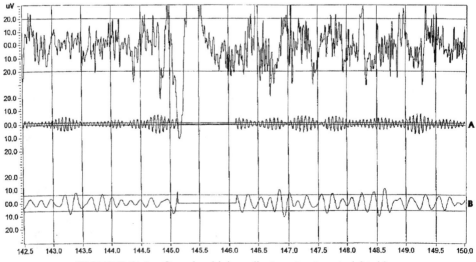

FIGURE 9.1   Open head injury client, pretreatment, right side.

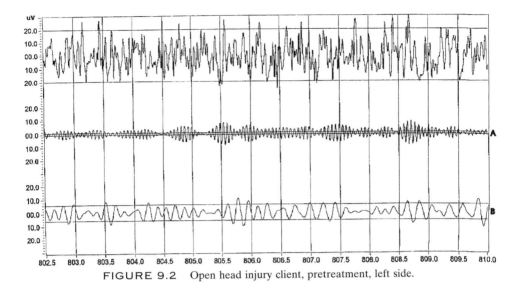

FIGURE 9.2   Open head injury client, pretreatment, left side.

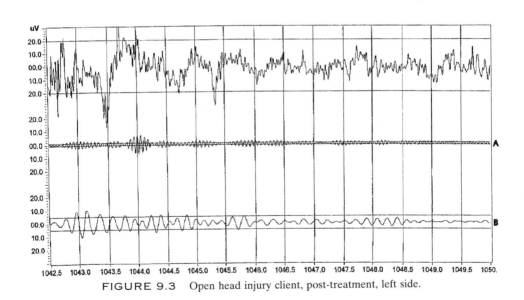

FIGURE 9.3   Open head injury client, post-treatment, left side.

for theta and 3.92 for the 15–18 Hz. Following EEG real-time digital feedback, theta at T3C3 was 2.10 μV and 15–18 Hz was1.03 μV.

IV. COMA

Many labels and definitions of coma exist. Coma is defined as a state of profound unconsciousness caused by disease, injury, or poison. Individuals in a deep coma have no response to external stimuli. Coma and sleep are not the same. Moruzzi (1972) found that sleep was an active physiological process with distinct EEG sleep stages 1–4 and with rapid eye movement (REM) that corresponds with behavior changes. However some patients do not have behavioral changes, and may not have sleep stage changes in an organized pattern.

The EEG of coma patients varies. Principally, there are four types of patterns: alpha coma, theta coma, spindle coma, and attenuated EEG mixed with high-amplitude bursts. The alpha coma is a pattern of diffuse alpha activity that may be reactive or nonreactive to external stimuli according to Westmoreland et al. (1975). The alpha activity is maximum in anterior regions, and delta may be present. Young et al. (1994) found that alpha coma, theta coma, or alpha–theta coma changes to a more definitive pattern 5 days after coma onset. They found that EEG reactivity with subsequent pattern without reactivity is unfavorable.

The theta coma involves intermittent theta activity, maximum in the anterior region and combined with delta activity. Synek and Synek (1984) indicated it may be reactive or unreactive to stimuli. Spindle coma looks like stage 2 sleep spindles and was named by Chatrain et al. (1963). Loeb et al. (1959) described it as fast frequency activity in the 8–15 Hz range. According to D'Aleo et al. (1994), spindle activity appears to be more preserved in traumatic injury patients than in hypoxic patients.

Another pattern described by Stokkard et al. (1975) was an attenuated EEG mixed with high-amplitude bursts. A mixture of alpha, theta, and delta activity was seen more often in ventilator-dependent patients. Rae-Grant et al. (1994) describe burst suppression EEG interspersed with large theta spikes, slow waves, and sharp waves.

Coma is assessed in the United States by the Glasgow Coma Scale described by Teasdale and Jennett (1974) and the Rancho Coma Scale described by Hagen and Malkumo (1979). The Japanese have a PCS scale with a neurological grading system and an electrophysiological classification system described by Tsubokawa et al. (1990). Evoked potentials and visual potentials have been used to classify coma level. Laser Doppler eliminate measures of regional cerebral cortical blood flow sometimes are used to predict coma levels and outcomes of severe head trauma. However, no measure of level of coma has been precise in predicting outcome.

According to Gennarelli *et al.* (1982), 50% of patients survive after coma from severe trauma. Of those survivors, 42% make moderate recovery and 17% are severely disabled or vegetative. According to Sazbon and Groswasser (1991), 96% of all surviving patients have cognitive deficits, 50% have motor deficits, and 58% exhibit behavioral problems.

An invasive procedure was done by Tsubokawa *et al.* (1990) to treat coma. It involved eight patients who remained in "a persistent vegetative state for over six months." In Tsubokawa's study, causes of coma were severe head trauma and anoxia. Deep electrical brain stimulation was used. Two were stimulated in mesencephalic reticular formation and six at non-specific thalamus nucleus for more than 6 months. After 6 months the coma scale rose in four of the eight and three emerged from persistent state. In another treatment approach, Neubauer has utilized hyperbaric oxygen for coma patients with some success (Neubauer, 1985).

The only noninvasive coma treatment procedure reported in the literature is sensory stimulation to enhance alertness in coma patients used in the arousal program at the Institute for the Achievement of Human Potential in Philadelphia. However, many individuals have used sensory stimulation in prolonged coma to try to increase alertness.

V. REAL-TIME DIGITAL EEG NEUROFEEDBACK WITH LEVEL 2 COMA (RANCHO ScALE)

Previous researchers believed that being unconscious with a total lack of responsivity to environmental stimuli (as in level 2 coma) inferred that learning could not occur. I considered that perhaps in coma the sensory cortex was disengaged from motor cortex so that the motor cortex could not engage or "start the engine." The longer one stays in level 2 coma, the greater the sensory deprivation, which I believe further disengages sensory from motor cortex. We know that, according to Iriki *et al.* (1991), thalmocortical input from ventrolateral nucleus of thalamus to the motor cortex is potentiated only when coactivated with corticortical input from somatosensory cortex. The question was how to link sensory and motor again so behavior could occur. As noted earlier, various types of stimulation have been utilized on coma patients. However, it would seem that coma clients might learn based on intrinsic reward rather than simply experiencing sensory or electrical stimulation.

Thirty-two individuals in level 2 coma have been treated with neurofeedback in my clinic. All individuals were in coma longer than 2 months. Most authorities refer to this as persistent vegetative state, but I will use coma. None of the individuals treated was responsive to external stimuli. The process involved utilizing Neuropathways EEG imaging real-time digital EEG neurofeedback, attached computer, two speakers. and a light box with a dark green light. First a baseline EEG was taken, and then all individuals were trained to inhibit 4–7 Hz activity. Beta amplitude was never directly trained. Progressively, theta amplitude was lowered at both T4C4 and T3C3. To accomplish the training, client's eyelids (or one eye) were held open and a dark green light the size of a dilated pupil would become brighter green as the theta amplitude was inhibited. Speakers were on either side of the client's head providing auditory beep whenever the theta was inhibited *and* simultaneously "replaced" with 15–18 Hz activity for half a second. I talked to the clients (as if they were learning) about their former favorite activities, whether fishing, family. or other hobbies. Of the 32 individuals in level 2 coma, 25 came out slowly in one or two sessions. Most exciting was that none of the individuals went through the violent aggressive stage of coming out of coma. Two required more EEG neurofeedback treatments before coming out. Five did not come out after six treatments. No one previously has been able to bring patients noninvasively out of level 2 coma based on the intrinsic reward of EEG feedback. Three different cases of coma are discussed in some detail in the following paragraphs.

Case 1 was Peter, age 30, who had eight brain surgeries to remove an intraventricular tumor the size of a baseball. He remained in level 2 coma for 3 months, eyes closed, and nonresponsive to sound, light, pressure, or verbal commands. In addition, Peter suffered a massive stroke adjacent to the third ventricle on the left side.

He was evaluated and treated utilizing Neuropathways EEG imaging on-line feedback equipment. After 3 months in level 2 coma, evaluation indicated excessive 4–7 Hz activity at both T4C4 and T3C3, with the amplitude of phasic spikes at T3C3 exceeding 20 μV. At the first visit Peter was trained to inhibit 4–7 Hz to under 9 μV on both T3C3 and T4C4, and then to produce 15–18 Hz over 1 μV. While being treated, sensory stimulation was carried out in the form of talking about his reported interests. His interests were computers, God, his wife, family, and photography. Prior to treatment Peter's wife had talked with him about his interests for 3 months, but he had not come out of coma. Peter came out of coma in one treatment, kissed his wife, opened his paralyzed left eye, and 3 days later opened the fingers on his left hand. After four 1-hr treatments spaced 1 month apart, Peter was able to eat, speak, and lift the left side of his body, but he was not able to lift his right leg or open his right hand (see Figs. 9.4 and 9.5).

Peter's peak-to-peak theta amplitude at T3C3 prior to feedback was 8.41 μV and 15–18 Hz was 3.42 μV. Post-EEG neurofeedback at T3C3 the theta peak-to-peak amplitude was 4.28 μV and the 15–18 Hz was 1.21 μV. As alertness improved, theta voltage decreased along with compensatory 15–18 Hz. T3C3 is shown because the most damage, including stroke, occurred on the posterior left side. The post-treatment example (Fig. 9.5) is nine sessions after the evaluation.

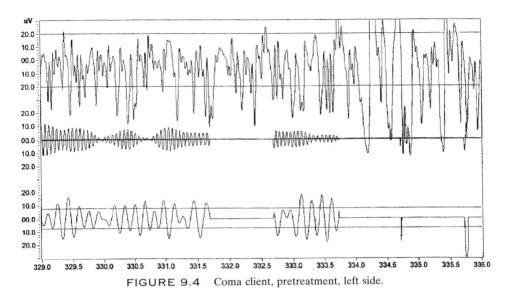

FIGURE 9.4 Coma client, pretreatment, left side.

Case 2 is Collin, age 21, who had been in level 2 coma for 2 years following a motorcycle accident in which he incurred a 2.5-cm hematoma in the left temporal area near the internal capsule with some blood found in the right thalamic area. Collin was nonresponsive to sound, light, pressure, or touch. During the second year of coma, his physician tried to use a variety of drugs to bring him out of coma to no avail.

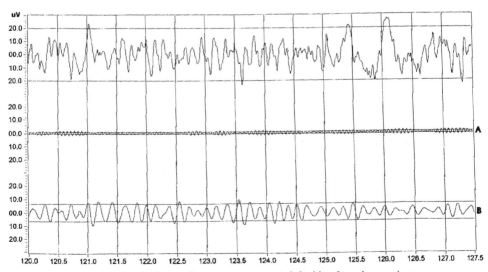

FIGURE 9.5 Coma client, post-treatment, left side after nine sessions.

Collin was producing excessive 4–7 Hz activity at both T4C4 and T3C3, with phasic spikes of higher amplitude (above 20 μV on T3C3). He was trained at T4C4 and T3C3 to inhibit 4–7 Hz to below 10 μV (and indirectly to produce 15–18 Hz activity above 1 μV). Sensory stimulation included talking about his family, motorcycles, sports, and women. Collin came out of coma after two 1-hr treatments. He now stands, communicates by computer, and lifts both hands.

A third example is Raymond, age 80, who was in an alpha–theta coma for 2 months in intensive care, and on a ventilator and respirator due to anoxia. He was trained to inhibit theta. He came out of coma during the first treatment and made a "thumbs up" gesture. The second day he was off the ventilator. The third day he was in a wheelchair. Now he is walking, driving a car, and is back home with his family. Prior to treatment his family was told that perhaps they should let him die.

Often individuals in a coma can only be treated 5–6 min, and then will suddenly show fatigue. The overall EEG and particularly 15–18 Hz may suddenly decrease in amplitude. When this happens I stop treatment and wait perhaps an hour before doing another treatment. I have done up to six EEG neurofeedback treatments in 1 day varying from 4 to 10 min in duration. I believe it is of utmost importance to use only real-time digital feedback with coma clients because any delay in feedback between when the event occurs in the brain and when one receives the information concerning it could reinforce intermittent spikes, sharp waves, and excessive slow-wave activity. With the equipment used there is currently less than one thousandth of a second delay between any actual EEG event and its display.

Implications of this type of feedback are that if it is possible to see the EEG representation with digitally filtered out frequencies on-line, it is possible to bring someone out of level 2 coma. If we think of low-level coma as prolonged sensory deprivation where motor systems are disengaged, then we must try to relink sensory input with motor output. I infer that people hear and understand in level 2 coma by their EEG on-line responses, but they cannot respond (and they forget it when they do come out of coma). Attempts are being made to revise the coma scale for organ transplants. Hopefully, the coma scale revision will take into account that the person may be there and hear and feel, but cannot respond. I believe that direct learning can occur in coma clients by linking sensorimotor cortex input directly to intrinsic EEG patterns during inhibition of theta activity. Such learning apparently occurs in an unconscious state. When provided with sensory input from the real-time digital EEG feedback about sensorimotor brain activity, learning apparently results and eventually enables a conscious state to occur.

VI. STROKE

Most strokes result in lesions in corticospinal tracts. Almost 60% of corticospinal axons originate from the primary motor areas. Corticospinal fibers meet within coronal radiata and pass downward through internal capsule and pons, and cross the cerebri and medulla. In the medulla area most fibers cross the midline to the opposite side of the medulla, resulting in the crossed lateral or pyramidal, uncrossed lateral, and anterior or ventral corticospinal tracts.

The majority of stroke patients have hemiparesis, according to Libman *et al.* (1992), Herman *et al.* (1982), and Ayers (1981). Monoplegia or paraplegia is said to be found (Herman *et al.,* 1982) in about 19% of stroke patients. In hemiparesis most individuals have upper arm and shoulder tonic spasticity with leg extensor spasticity. A few individuals may have arm flaccidity. According to Donnan *et al.* (1993), some individuals following stroke may have transient ischemic attacks that may warn of a subsequent capsular infarct.

Individual stroke patients may also have sensory loss or pain in paralyzed limbs. The thalamus plays a critical role in sensation. The medioventral portion of thalamus or VPM has somatic afferents coming from the tongue, face, and fingers. However, somatic afferents from the trunk and legs go dorsolaterally to lateral ventral thalamus (VPL). Other thalamic areas also receive inputs from ascending sensory pathways and convey information to the cortex. Sensation loss also is often seen in medullary strokes sometimes with homolateral facial analgesia, contralateral thermoanalgesia, and eye movement disorders. In midbrain strokes, pontine strokes, and spinal strokes sensory loss varies. Strokes with only sensory loss have been described by Delu *et al.* (1992) and Kim and Jo (1992), while thalamic-based pain with severe burning has been described by Boivie *et al.* (1989).

Strokes may result in abnormal motor movements such as tremor, dystonia, myoclonus, or ataxia. Ataxia is usually found with cerebellar lesions, but may be found in cortical lesions according to Nighoghossian *et al.* (1993). In some cases, dystonia, or persistent inappropriate posture, can be triggered by sensory stimuli. Migraine headaches can also occur after stroke. They may disappear or may persist long after the stroke. Fisher (1968) reported 43% of poststroke headaches were in the basilar area, and Edmeads (1979) reported headaches in 25% of patients with infarcts in the carotid artery area. Visual disturbances may also occur. There may be nystagmus, conjugate or disconjugate eye movements, visual field deficits such as loss of peripheral vision, visual hallucinations, and loss of depth perception.

Some stroke clients may have vertigo and/or seizures. Dysphagia (problems with swallowing) has been more commonly seen with brain stem lesions. Another autonomic change may be asymmetrical sweating as described by Nakajme (1983). As known since Broca's pioneering work, strokes that occur in certain locations on the left side may result in aphasia where oral and written language expression is impaired, but one can still understand written and spoken words. In such cases difficulty in initiating or maintaining control and coordination of speech output is noted, and apraxia or phonemic substitution of a word or syllable for the desired word may occur.

I have observed the frustration associated with paralysis or inability to perform previous tasks. The lesion may result in dramatic personality changes. Often personality traits existing prior to the stroke become exaggerated following the stroke. Clients and their families may need psychotherapy to deal with changes in personality.

VII. REAL-TIME DIGITAL EEG FEEDBACK WITH STROKE

In 1981 I published a within-group, controlled research design utilizing electromyometry and analog electroencephalographic feedback (Ayers, 1981). Six stroke clients were included. All were at least 3 years poststroke. Three had lesions on the left with aphasia, and three had lesions on the right with no aphasia. None had dominant hand extension over hand flexion. The total study time was 15 months. For 10 months twice a week all six individuals had surface electromyographic (EMG) readings taken from hand extensors versus hand flexors. None obtained dominant hand extension. At the end of 10 months, each individual in the study received an additional 30 min of electroencephalographic feedback from the left sensorimotor cortex (T3C3). Muscle feedback training (EMG) also continued biweekly for 5 months. Each muscle feedback training session occurred just after each EEG training session. The muscle recordings were collected as before. Remember that all six received EEG feedback on the left even though three had strokes on the right. All progressively decreased theta amplitude. There were two hypotheses. First, that the EEG feedback intervention would result in a significant increase in finger muscle performance. The second hypothesis was that the variables of age, side of paresis, number of years poststroke, amount of skilled hand use, and gender of the subject would not affect EMG performance either prior to or during EEG intervention.

Results showed that EEG intervention had a significant effect of increasing muscle performance ($p = 0.025$; $t = 2.4949$). On hypothesis 2, regression analysis showed two significant factors in the equation. One involved left side of paresis ($F = 27.893$, $p = 0.001$). Individuals did not improve in gaining dominance of finger extension over finger flexion during EMG training, but changed almost immediately when EEG feedback was initiated. And, the older the client, the more the gains in finger extension. Since all six gained dominant finger extension with EEG feedback only on left side sites T3C3, this implied ipsilateral connections in stroke recovery of finger extension.

If older individuals made more significant gains, one might wonder about effects with pediatric stroke? In 1995 I published a controlled study of EEG neurofeedback and physical therapy with pediatric stroke when there was no maternal drug use, hypertension, or viral infection. Six individuals age 7 months to 15 years were selected randomly for EEG digital neurofeedback 30 min per week, while 6 control subjects ages 1–14 were in physical or occupational therapy once a week. All 12 were administered baseline range of motion measures, a self-description of mood, and short-term memory tests. The 6 experimental subjects received EEG neurofeedback from bipolar sites T4C4 and T3C3 for 3 months to inhibit 4–7 Hz, lower its voltage, and indirectly but simultaneously produce 15–18 Hz for 0.5 sec at 1 μV. Children receiving EEG neurofeedback had improvement of motion, dorsiflexion of foot, improvement in concentration and short-term memory, and fewer mood swings. The control group had improved range of motion, no dorsiflexion of foot, and no improvement in cognitive or emotional status.

It appears that both children and adults with stroke can significantly improve even after spontaneous recovery appears to be complete. It was interesting that the 7-month-old subject had *no* signs of paresis after treatment. Prior to treatment, he could not crawl, stand, or take steps. After treatment he was able to stand, crawl, and take steps. Perhaps this implies that due to plasticity of the young developing brain, the sooner EEG neurofeedback is administered, the more improvements can be made.

As with open head trauma, in stroke syndrome my EEG neurofeedback treatment *starts* from the sensorimotor cortex and works toward the peripheral area. For example, if the individual has aphasia or apraxia, then one eventually can work on Broca's and Wernicke's area–two speech-related areas. If one has a lesion in the parietal area resulting in inability to identify a body part, one can eventually work on that specific area. If one has extreme flexor spasticity of the arm, one can train on just the arm area of the motor cortex to inhibit tonic spasticity. If one has extensor spasticity of the leg (with the dominant anterior tibialis muscle swinging the leg outward or causing the individual to flap the foot flat on the ground), one can train just the motor cortex leg area to inhibit the spasticity. In such cases increased dorsiflexion and less abduction of the leg have been observed.

If the EEG amplitude is very high at the site of damage, one can train the contralateral motor cortex, apparently transferring learning through the corpus collosum to the damaged side. After treatment on the nondamaged side, one often can go back to the damaged side and find that the voltage has decreased. This then makes it much easier to treat the damaged side.

An example of an adult stroke client follows. This woman had a stroke at age 46, resulting in extreme flexor adduction of the left arm with fist clenched. She also wore a brace on the left leg. She tried all types of therapy prior to EEG neurofeedback. She did not receive EEG neurofeedback until the age of 50. Within two sessions her arm opened and dropped away from her body. Now her hand has opened so that she is able to write with it. Her leg spasticity has decreased and she can walk without a cane. As shown in Figs. 9.6, 9.7, and 9.8, there were major pre- to post-treatment changes. Prior to EEG neurofeedback at T4C4 (where the stroke occurred), theta was 4.13 μV and 15–18 Hz was 2.06 μV. Prior to EEG neurofeedback at T3C3 theta was 1.96 μV and 15–18 Hz was 1.59 μV. Theta amplitude progressively decreased. Notice also that as theta is decreased the EEG began to normalize.

VIII. SUMMARY

This is the first time in the history of EEG that it has been demonstrated that the EEG is malleable in cases of open head injury, coma, and stroke. Real-time digital EEG feedback technological advances now enable permanent changes in the EEG pattern, often with improved neurological function and emotional well-being.

I consider two clinical factors to be of utmost importance in the field of

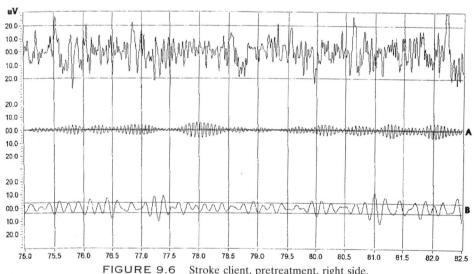

FIGURE 9.6   Stroke client, pretreatment, right side.

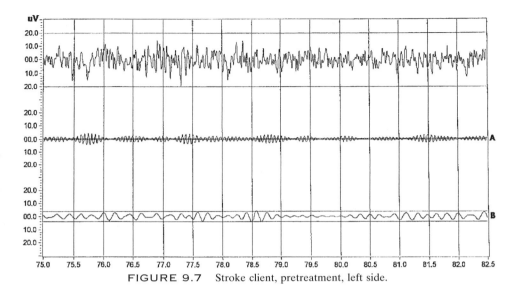

FIGURE 9.7   Stroke client, pretreatment, left side.

neurofeedback. First is that practitioners of EEG neurofeedback need to be familiar with brain anatomy and physiology. Second, they should always observe the raw EEG, whether analog or digital, and constantly view in real time the minute-by-minute voltage changes and the evolving EEG pattern during training.

For further details of the Ayers' research mentioned in this chapter and

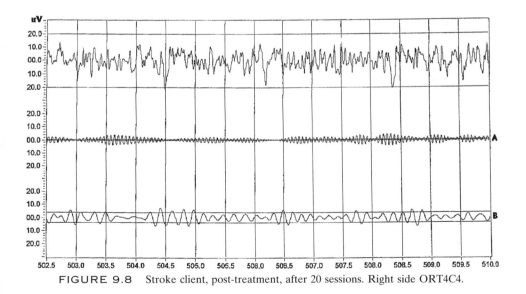

FIGURE 9.8   Stroke client, post-treatment, after 20 sessions. Right side ORT4C4.

the equipment used, the reader is advised to consult the following references: Ayers, 1990, 1995a, 1995b, 1996a 1996b.

REFERENCES

Adams, J. A., Graham, D., & Scott, G. (1980). Brain damage in fatal non-missile head injury. *J. Clin. Pathol.* **33**, 1132–1145.

Ayers, M. (1981). A report on a study of the utilization of electroencephalography for the treatment of cerebral vascular lesion syndromes. *In* "Electromyometric Biofeedback Therapy" (L. Taylor, M. E. Ayers, & C. Tom, eds.), pp. 244–257. Biofeedback and Advanced Therapy Institute, Los Angeles.

Ayers, M. E. (1983). Electroencephalographic feedback and head trauma. *In* "Head and Neck Trauma, The Latest Information and Perspectives on Patients with a Less Than Optimal Recovery" (G. Heuser, ed.), pp. 8–11. Pub. Department of Continuing Education in Health Sciences, UCLA School of Medicine, Los Angeles.

Ayers, M. E. (1990, April 24). Electroencephalographic neurofeedback apparatus and method for bioelectrical frequency inhibition and facilitation. *Official Gazette,* U. S. Patent Office, Patent Number 4,919,143.

Ayers, M. E. (1995a). A controlled study of EEG neurofeedback and physical therapy with pediatric stroke, age seven months to age fifteen, occurring prior to birth. *Biofeedback Self-Regul.* **20**(3), 318.

Ayers, M. E. (1995b). EEG neurofeedback to bring individuals out of level 2 coma. *Biofeedback Self-Regul.* **20**(3), 304–305.

Ayers, M. E. (1996a, June 18). Electroencephalographic neurofeedback apparatus and method for bioelectrical frequency inhibition and facilitation. *Official Gazette,* U. S. Patent Office, Patent Number 5,024,325.

Ayers, M. E. (1996b, November 5). Apparatus and method for changing a sequence of visual images. *Official Gazette,* U. S. Patent Office, Patent Number 5,571,057.

Bechara, A., Damasio, A. R., Damasio, H., & Anderson, G. W. (1994). Insensitivity to future consequences following damage to human prefrontal cortex. *Cognition* **50**, 7–15.

Berger, H. (1929). Uber das electroenzephalogram des menschen. *Arch. Psychiat. Nervenke* **87**, 527–570.

Boivie, J., Leigon, G., & Hohansson, I. (1989). Central post stroke pain–a study of the mechanisms through analyses of the sensory abnormalities. *Pain* **37**, 173–185.

Chatrain, G. E., White, L. E., & Daly, D. (1963). Electroencephalographic patterns resembling those of sleep in certain comatose states after injuries to the head. *EEG Clin. Neurophysiol.* **15**, 272–280.

Courion, J., Naquet, R., & Baubino, C. (1971). Valeur diagnostique et prodiagnostique del EEG dans les suites immediates des trauma tisems craniens. *Rev EEG Neurophysiol. Clin.* **1**, 133–150.

Courville, C. B. (1958). Traumatic lesions of the temporal lobe as the essential cause of psychomotor epilepsy. *In* "Temporal Lobe Epilepsy" (M. Baldwin & P. Bailey, eds.), pp. 220–239. Thomas, Springfield, Ill.

D'Aleo, G. Bramanti, P., Silvestri, R. Saltuari, L., Gerstenbrano, F., & Perrir, D. (1994). Sleep spindles in the initial stages of the vegetative state. *Ital. J. Neurolog. Sci.* **15**, 347–351.

Damasio, H., Grabowski, T., & Frank, R. (1994). The return of Phineas Gage: Clues about the brain from the skull of a famous patient. *Science* **264**, 1102–1109.

Delu, D., DeWaele, J., & Blisseret, T. (1992). Dorsolateral pontine hemorrhage producing pure sensory stroke. *Eur. Neurol.* **321**, 222–224.

Donnan, G. A., O'Malley, H. M, Quang, L., Hurley, S., & Bladin, P. F. (1993). The capsule warning syndrome: Pathogenesis and clinical features. *Neurol.* **43**, 957–962.

Drudge, O. W., Williams, J. M., Kessler, M., & Gomes, F. R. (1989). Recovery from severe head trauma injuries, repeat testing with the Halstead–Reitan Neuropsychological Battery. *J. Clin. Psychol.* **40**, 259–265.

Duffy, F. (1986). "Topographic Mapping of Brain Electrical Activity." Butterworth Publishers.

Ebersole, J. S. (1991). EEG dipole modeling in complex partial epilepsy. *Brain Topog.* **4**, 419–423.

Edmeads, J. (1979). The headaches of ischemic cerebrovascular disease. *Headache* **19**, 345–349.

Fisher, C. M. (1968). Headache in cerebrovascular disease. *In* "Handbook of Clin. Neurology, Vol. V, Headache and Cranial Neuralgias" (P. J. Winken & G. W. Bruyn, eds.), pp. 124–156. New York: Wiley.

Gennarelli, T. A., Speilman, G. M., Langfit, T. W., & Gildenber, P. L. (1982). Influence of the type of intracranial lesion on outcome from severe head injury. *J. Neurosurg.* **56**, 262.

Gevins, A, Martin, N., Brickett, P., Desmond, J., & Reuter, B. (1994). High resolution EEG: 124 channel recording spatial deblurring and MRI integration. *EEG Clin. Neurophysiol.* **90**, 337–358.

Goddard, M. J., Dean, B. Z., & King, J. C. (1994). Pain rehabilitation. 1. Basic science, acute pain and neuropathic pain. *Arch. Phys. Med. Rehabil.* **75**(4) (suppl.), 4–8.

Hagen, C., & Malkmuo, D. (1979). Intervention strategies for language disorders secondary to head trauma. Presented at American Speech–Language–Hearing Association Convention short course.

Herman, B., Ceyten, A. C. M., Van Luuk, J. H., Frenken, C. W. G. M., Op De Coul, A. A. W., & Schulte, B. P. (1982). Epidemiology of stroke in Tilburg, the Netherlands. The Population Based Stroke Incidence Register: 2. Incidence, initial clinical picture and medical care and three week case fatality. *Stroke* **62**(5), 9–34.

Iriki, A., Pavlides, C., Kelter, A., & Asanuma, H. (1991). Long-term potentiation of thalmic input to the motor cortex induced by coactivation of thalmocortical and corticocortical afferents. *J. Neurophysiol.* **63**(6).

Kim, J. S., & Jo, K. D. (1992). Pure lemniscal sensory deficit caused by pontine hemorrhage. *Stroke* **23**, 300.

Levin, H. S. (1989). Memory deficit after closed head injury. *J. Clin. Neurophsychol.* **12**, 129–153.

Libman, R. B., Sacco, R. L., Shi, T., Tatemici, T. K., & Mohe, J. P. (1992). Neurologic improvements in pure motor hemiparesis: Indications for clinical trials. *Neurology* **42.**

Loeb, C., Rosadni, G., & Poggi, O. G. (1959). Electroencephalograph during coma. *Neurology* **9**, 610–618.

Loury, A. R. (1970). "Traumatic Aphasia: Its Syndromes, Psychology and Treatment." Mouton, Paris.

Mandelberg, I. A., & Brooks, D. N. (1975). Cognitive resources after severe head injury, serial testing on the Weschler Adult Intelligence Scale. *J. Neurol. Neurosurg. Psychiat.* **38**, 1121–1126.

Moruzzi, G. (1972). The sleep–wake cycle. *Renal Physiol.* **64**, 1–165.

Nakajme, K. (1983). Clin. pathological study of pontine hemorrhage. *Stroke* **14**, 485–493.

Neubauer, R. (1985). The effect of hyperbaric oxygen in prolonged coma, possible identification of marginal functioning brain zones. *Medicina Subacquea Ed. Iperbarica* **5**(5), 75–79.

Nighoghossian, N., Trouillas, P., Vial, C., & Mauguiere, F. (1993). Monoparesie ataxique du membre superieur et suspension du tonus d'attitude par lesion parietale. *Rev. Neurol.* **149**, 262–266.

Perrin, F., Pernier, J., Bertrano, O., Giard, M. H. & Edallic, J. F. (1987). Mapping of scalp potentials by surface spline interpolation. *EEG Clin. Neurophysiol.* **66**, 75–81.

Quattrocchi, K., Frank, E., Miller, C., Amin, A., Issel, B., & Wagner, F. (1991). Impairment of helper T-cell function and lymphokine-activated killer cytotoxicity following severe head injury. *J. Neurosurg.* **75,** 766–773.

Quattrocchi, K., Miller, C., Wagner, F., DeNardo, S., Ovodov, K., & Franke, F. (1992). Cell mediated immunity in severely head injured patients: The role of suppressor lymphocytes and serum factors. *J. Neurosurg.* **77,** 694–699.

Rae-Grant, Alexander D., & Kim, Y. W. (1994). Type III intermittency: a nonlinear dynamic model of EEG burst suppression. *EEG Clin. Neurophysiol.* **90,** 17–23.

Ruff, R., Young, D., Gautille, T., Marshall, L., Barth, J., Jane, J., Kreutzer, J., Marmarou, A., Gevin, H., Eisenberg, H., & Foulkes, M. (1991). Verbal learning deficit following severe head injury: Heterogeneity in recovery over 1 year. *J. Neurosurg.* **75,** 50–58.

Sarno, M. T. (1980). The nature of verbal impairment after closed head injury. *J. Nervous Mental Dis.* **168,** 68–69.

Sazbon, L., & Groswasser, Z. (1991). Time-related sequelae of ITBI in patients with prolonged post-comatose unawareness (PC-U) state. *Brain Injury* **5**(1), 3–8.

Scherg, M., & Ebersole, J. S. (1993). Models of brain sources. *Brain Topog.* **5**(4), 419–423.

Steadman, J. H., & Graham, J. G. (1969). Rehabilitation of the brain injured. *Proc. Soc. Med.* **63,** 23–28.

Stokkard, J. J., Bickford, R. G., & Aung, M. H. (1975). The electroencephalogram in traumatic brain injury. *In* "Handbook of Neurology, Vol. 23, Injuries of the Brain and Skull, Part 1" (P. J. Vinken & G. W. Bruyn, eds.). Oxford, North Holland.

Synek, V. M., & Synek, B. J. I. (1984). Theta pattern coma, a variant of alpha pattern coma. *Clin. EEG* **15,** 116–121.

Tabaddor, M., Matts, S., & Zazula, T. (1984). Cognitive sequelae and recovery course after moderate and severe head injury. *Neurosurgery* **14,** 701–708.

Teasdale, G., & Jennett, B. (1974). Assessment of coma and impaired consciousness, a practical scale. *Lancet* **2,** 81–84.

Thatcher, R. W., Walker, R. A., & Gerson, I. (1989). EEG discriminant analysis of mild head trauma. *EEG Clin. Neurophysiol.* **73,** 94–106.

Tsubokawa, T., Yamamoto, T., Katayama, V., Hirayama, T., Maejima, D., & Moriya, T. (1990). Deep brain stimulation in a persistent vegetative state: Follow-up results and criteria for selection of candidates. *Brain Injury* **4**(4), 315–327.

Van Zomeren, A. H., & Van Denberg, W. (1985). Residual complaints of patients two years after severe head injury. *J. Neurol. Neurosurg. Psychiat.* **48,** 21–28.

Westmoreland, B. F., Klass, D. W., Sharbrough, F. W., & Regan, T. J. (1975). Alpha coma: Electroencephalographic clinical, pathologic and etiologic correlations. *Arch. Neurol.* **32,** 713–718.

Williams, S. D., & Denny-Brown, D. (1941). Cerebral electrical changes in experimental concussion. *Brain* **64,** 223–238.

Wong, P. K. H. (1991). Source modeling of the Rolandic focus. *Brain Topog.* **4**(2), 105–112.

Yamaguchi, M. (1992). Incidence of headache and severity of head injury. *Headache* **32,** 427–431.

Young, G. B., Blume, W. T., Campbell, J. D., Demelo, L. S., Leung, L. S., McKewin, M. J., McLauchlan, R. S., Ram, D. A., & Schieven, J. R. (1994). Alpha, theta and alpha–theta coma: A clinical outcome study utilizing serial recordings. *Elsevier Sci. Ireland Ltd.* 93–99.

10

PERFORMANCE ENHANCEMENT TRAINING THROUGH NEUROFEEDBACK

S. LOUISE NORRIS AND MICHAEL CURRIERI

Mid-Hudson Medical Psychotherapy Center, Warwick, New York

Cognitive behavioral psychology has demonstrated that action follows thought, and as EEG neurofeedback has shown, thought or cognition can be a function of our brain electrophysiology. Peak performance, as defined in this chapter involves the art and science of altering one's state of mind *at will* in order to most effectively meet any challenges before us. For centuries this type of high-performance mind was laboriously cultivated over a lifetime of experience with various forms of meditation, mystical practice, and martial art. Western society, however, prefers rapid development as opposed to a lifetime of disciplined practice. It is in this milieu that creative minds decided to apply neurofeedback (EEG biofeedback) to the realm of performance enhancement training (PET) as a means of optimizing personal growth. EEG neurofeedback is a form of operant conditioning, where visual stimuli, sounds, or scores are employed to reinforce voluntary control over EEG patterns. In the 1960s, Sterman *et al.* (1969) effectively used a conditional stimulus to teach cats to generate 12–20 cycles/sec rhythm in the sensorimotor cortex. This was an excellent example of operant conditioning altering the EEG; which is essentially what one hopes to accomplish with EEG performance enhancement training.

The crux of neurofeedback is that it permits us to employ the computer screen to deliver reinforcement of desired brain waves. It serves as a mirror reflecting our states of consciousness, thus permitting us to control those states voluntarily. Research has been published that demonstrates the clinical benefits of this technique for improving cognitive functions such as

Introduction to Quantitative EEG and Neurofeedback

attention, concentration, reaction time, accuracy, and decision making with a range of disorders. But neurofeedback for PET did not spring from the clinical realm. It was spawned in laboratories attempting to study the ways in which we control our own minds, and then further developed by watching ordinary people overcome extraordinary odds. As William James once wrote: "Most people live . . . in a very restricted circle of their potential being. . . . Great emergencies and crises show us how much greater our vital resources are than we had supposed." These crises provide us a glimpse of our potential by fostering short-lived peak performances. The goal of PET is to increase the occurrence and duration of peak performances in normal people under normal circumstances. The objective is to help us optimize our human potential.

I. THE ESSENTIALS OF PEAK PERFORMANCE

Attaining peak performance involves certain key components. First, there must be a desire or a commitment to a valued self-chosen goal—whether it is good health, playing the pro golf tour, or improving the effectiveness of your management skills–which provides purpose, motivation, and energy. As Stephen Covey (1989) says: "We must begin with the end in mind, be proactive and put first things first." Second, we know from a wide range of research that stress is a major contributor to psychological, physical, emotional, and social disturbances; and as such is an impediment to personal peak performance. For this reason, being able to rapidly achieve a sustained state of inner calm or peace is an essential component of peak performance training. Charles Garfield, a psychologist, computer scientist, and world-class athlete emphasized a third component: peak performance is an internal focus of control which is intuitive. He reports that peak performers act on intuitive knowledge with confidence and security even when in unfamiliar territory. In other words, their knowledge about what to do, why to do it, and when to do it is so integrated as to be automatic and unconscious. Related to this, Steve Fahrion (1995) reports that in his early work with college students he found that training for self-regulation using thermal biofeedback resulted in a perceived locus of control shift toward internalization on the Rotter I-E scale.

Peak performers also have a creative optimism that permits them to view obstacles as challenges to be overcome. These are individuals who think in win–win terms (Covey, 1989), viewing consequences as natural and logical results of the process. They often employ positive mental preparation and skills such as visualization to foster their own peak performances. This process of visualization permits them to refine the "how to" of the craft they are mastering. Then, at the time when performance is demanded, they are able to maintain persistent concentration, setting their priorities and focusing exclusively on the task at hand. Although there are many components of peak performance, it is in the areas of increasing inner calmness, learning to hear our intuitive inner voice, fostering concentration, developing an internal sense of control, and cultivating a sense of optimism that neurofeedback offers much potential for performance enhancement training.

II. DEFINITIONS OF TERMS

For those readers who are new to neurofeedback, we will define some basic terminology before proceeding to look at the research related to the use of neurofeedback for enhancing the efficiency of the brain of normal individuals. Amplitude, as used in neurofeedback, refers to the power of an electrical impulse generated by the brain. If you conceive of a brain wave as similar to a sound wave, you could think of the amplitude as the volume or intensity of the wave. We measure amplitude in microvolts. Frequency is the number of times the wave repeats within a second. Once again, comparing our brain waves to sound waves, one could conceptualize frequency in terms of how fast music is playing. For convenience sake, we routinely categorize brain waves by their frequency. Delta is the slowest group of waves ranging from 0 to 4 Hz (or repetitions per second). We might compare delta to first gear in a car with a standard shift. When you are predominately in delta you are not going anywhere quickly. Theta commonly ranges from 4 to 8 Hz, and could be likened to second gear. Alpha generally is considered to span from 8 to 13 Hz and represents the neutral or "idle" position for the brain. Beta usually is defined as a broadband of 13 Hz and above; this equates to drive and hyperdrive. Most EEG activity occurs between 0 and 25 Hz, though some interesting research and clinical interventions are now being done in the 40-Hz range (Sams, 1995).

III. EEG MODIFICATION
AND CONSCIOUSNESS

The earth's field low-frequency components, micropulsations, range from less than 1 to about 25 cycles/sec falling in the same range as the bulk of our EEG activity (Becker *et al.,* 1985). This provokes the interesting question of whether our levels of cognitive performance may be influenced by variations in these micropulsations. If so, it becomes even more likely that we could effectively alter states of consciousness and efficacy of processing information by altering these rhythms through neurofeedback. Becker discovered that passing a minute current from the front to the back of the brain can cancel its internal current and induce unconsciousness. This also suggests that there is a considerable potential for altering states of consciousness if we are able to voluntarily manipulate the electrical impulses generated by the brain through neurofeedback. Such self-manipulation or self-regulation of the brain's electrical impulses is precisely the goal of PET. As noted earlier, ability to voluntarily manipulate the electrical impulses generated by the brain has been demonstrated in clinical research. For example, the capacity to control seizure activity by training to increase 11–15 Hz sensory motor rhythm EEG activity over the Rolandic cortex has been repeatedly demonstrated (Sterman *et al.,* 1969; Bowersox & Sterman, 1981). Lubar and others have demonstrated that suppressing 4–8 Hz activity while increasing 16–23 Hz activity improves attention and organization in individuals with attention deficit disorder (ADD) (Lubar & Lubar,1984). PET strives to expand the benefits of EEG neurofeedback from the realm of clinical treatment to the realm of peak performance.

IV. UNDERSTANDING BRAIN WAVE STATES

Each state we experience as we meander through life may be considered to reflect a symphony of brain wave frequencies, but various frequencies dominate when we engage in different types of tasks. For instance, delta waves are generally present primarily during sleep. However, according to Ana Wise (1995), author of *The High Performance Mind,* they also domi-nate when we are in an empathetic state. She conceives of delta waves as reflecting the unconscious mind and believes they are associated with empa-thy because she finds a greater percentage of delta waves in psychothera-pists, counselors, and other healers.

Theta waves have been associated with creativity and intuition. They occur more when we are daydreaming or fantasizing, and when we are in the state between sleep and wakefulness. Ana Wise feels that theta waves also relate to our subconscious. She believes that the subconscious exists and is a repository for memories, emotions, and sensation. She hypothesizes that much repressed material is accessed in "theta" states. In fact, Eugene Peniston's work in the 1980s and 1990s with alpha–theta training (Penis-ton & Kulkosky, 1989, 1990, 1991) of alcoholics would tend to support this characterization because he found that many individuals doing theta training recalled repressed events and emotions. His work also demon-strated that alpha–theta training leads to significant increases in sensations of warmth, abstract thinking, ability, stability, conscientiousness, boldness, imaginativeness, and self-control as assessed by the Cattell Sixteen Person-ality Factor Questionnaire. Many of the latter are hallmarks of peak perfor-mance according to authorities such as Charles Garfield (1986) and Stephen Covey (1989). Theta waves have also been shown to be predominant during internal focus meditation, prayer, and periods of increased spiritual awareness. Sterman (1996) hypothesizes that theta may be therapeutically useful in tapping suppressed content due to suspension of brain stem and thalama-cortical regulatory influences, which leads to a state of relative cortical disinhibition. This a state that EEG neurofeedback may facilitate.

A state of heightened alpha activity has been likened to the state of idle in a car. It is the state from which you can move quickly and efficiently to whatever "gear" you need to accomplish the task at hand. When alpha predominates, most people feel at ease and calm and are passively "mind-ful." Alpha predominates posteriorly when we are passively relaxed and when we are visualizing. It appears that alpha may serve as a "bridge" linking the conscious and subconscious. Most people are able to produce some increases in alpha brain wave activity simply by closing their eyes or breathing deeply.

Finally, increased beta waves are commonly associated with analytical problem solving, judgment, externally focused attention, and decision mak-ing. They are generally produced during the normal waking state and may help us consciously attend to and process information about the world around us.

It is as if our brain is an orchestra playing an incredible array of music with at least four types of instruments. No matter what state of consciousness we are in, all of the brain waves are present. We have the strings, the brass, the percussion, and the woodwind instruments. Each has an important contribution for every melody, but one group may predominate during a particular piece and another group may steal center stage during yet another piece. A goal in peak performance is to cue the right group to take center stage at the right time and right location, and to conduct the orchestra such that the melody is a powerful harmonious meld rather than a discordant cacophony. To achieve this end, we may need both hemispheres of the brain to make their unique contributions by working hand in hand with appropriate symmetry and balance.

V. A MINI REVIEW

To review, when we are concentrating and solving problems, beta waves generally dominate and we are considered to be in an alert state. As our body begins to relax and we slow our breathing and pulse, we begin to experience more passive cognition and progress to a state where alpha waves predominate. As our attention becomes directed to imagined activity and we begin to lose awareness of our surroundings, theta waves dominate and we may be considered to be in a state of moderate trance. With further relaxation we move into a deeper trance where slower theta waves dominate and we see a further reduction in activity and energy output, limpness, a narrowing of attention, increased suggestibility, and heightened creative functions.

Generally, in a mild or deep trance state, one is receptive to suggestions. This is a time when one can give oneself positive motivational statements to help restructure cognitions and focus on the positive. It is in these states that one often can visualize himself/herself as a competent, capable professional consistently performing at peak in various endeavors. It is in such trance states that individuals using hypnosis reportedly have motivated weight loss, eliminated smoking habits, reduced stress and reprogrammed negative behaviors, eliminated irrational fears, reduced symptoms of major illnesses such as colitis, promoted self-esteem, improved study habits, enhanced memory, refined athletic performance, and released blocked creative potential. Hypnotism continues to be a widely used path to enhancing performance. Neurofeedback complements hypnotism with technology, which permits us to monitor objectively our own mind states and guide our future efforts. To comprehend the power of the theta state and these self-statements, imagine telling yourself that you are an incompetent buffoon, repeatedly hearing a voice in your head say "I can't make it," "I'm an impostor," "I don't have the skills," "Most people are better qualified than I," and then entering an employment interview situation. It would be similar to Muhammad Ali having constantly replaced the statements "I'm the greatest" and "I'm the Champ" with "He's gonna wipe the ring with me" and "I know I'm gonna lose."

To enhance our performance and achieve our personal best we need to be able to imagine our goals because we cannot implement a plan of which we are unable to conceive. For example, if we had not conceived the concept of controlling the flow of a river, a dam would have never been built. We also need to screen out nonessential distractions and focus on what is important, otherwise we will flow without direction from one idea to another, and fail to implement any of them. Perhaps most important of all, we need to maintain an inner calm and physical relaxation while mentally "zooming in" on our future accomplishment and imagining its achievement in the present. Otherwise, anxiety alone may function to distract us from the task at hand. Athletes sometimes define this state of heightened mindfulness, visualization, and relaxation as "being in the zone." Sales agents may talk of the same state in terms of being "tuned in" to their clients, while mystics may speak of levels of meditation. Regardless of the descriptors or the field of expertise this state means fewer errors, greater efficiency, improved decision making, more rapid information processing, and better outcomes. For this reason, we call it the peak performance state. It is a state that can be different for each individual and different for various tasks performed by the same individual.

VI. THE CAPACITY TO SHIFT

When we examine individuals who are consistently peak performers we discover that the actual physical circumstances of their lives are not crucial to their performances. Rather, it is their reactions to those events which matter. They invariably describe their constructive reactions as being a function of the ability to voluntarily shift to a desired state of being in order to handle those obstacles and challenges with which they are confronted. Peak performance is not necessarily a function of a particular state of mind per se, but, rather, the capacity to shift states at will. It is not playing Bach which makes the orchestra superb, but rather the ability to play a whole gamut of music spanning from improvisational jazz and rock to opera and ballads which distinguishes a superb performing orchestra. Similarly, a peak performing brain can combine its "instruments" (delta, theta, alpha, and beta) to play any tune demanded by life, shift states as needed and enhance the outcome of any situation.

If it is the capacity to shift into the optimal brain wave pattern for the desired task that is facilitated by neurofeedback, one wonders exactly what areas of the brain are impacted by peak performance training to enable such shifting. James Henry (1992) in *Instincts, Archetypes and Symbols: An Approach to the Physiology of Religious Experience* (quoted in Fahrion, 1995, p. 77) may give some hints when he states:

> It would seem that the basic mechanisms underlying consciousness are closely bound up with the brainstem reticular systems whose activity is, from the subjective viewpoint, that of the most primitive level, which in turn is elaborated upon and informed by the emotions, inborn patterns of behavior and affective drives of the limbic system, and beyond this, by the modern neocortex with its abstract signs and patterns, and its long-term predictions and analysis (p. 77).

The linking of consciousness and peak performance requires that we integrate internal and external experiences, our emotions and our thoughts. According to Steve Fahrion (1995), there are no major connections between the sensorimotor cortex and the limbic cortex; therefore, the sensorimotor cortex, which we often suppose ourselves to be affecting with neurofeedback, cannot logically control the capacity to shift. It is more likely that this capacity lies within the reticular activating system, which affects both the sensorimotor and other parts of the neocortex. This is where the locus coeruleus is located.

In this view, the capacity to shift between symbolic primary processes and active coping processes is considered to be controlled by the locus coeruleus nuclei in the brain stem, which can switch off coping responses by stopping the release of the neurotransmitter norepinephrine. This has the effect of enabling inherent brain programs such as sleep, grooming, and meditation. The locus coeruleus can also release additional norepinephrine and provoke activation of the cerebral cortex, orienting responses and preparation to actively engage in interaction with the world. Thus, one wonders if EEG neurofeedback somehow affects more than the cerebral cortex; perhaps we are unknowingly affecting subcortical structures such as the locus coeruleus and, thereby, improving our capacity to shift.

VII. RESEARCH RELATED TO PEAK PERFORMANCE

I wish to preface this review of the research literature with the warning that when we speak of the changes in personality and thought patterns that accompany peak performance training, we are talking more about possibilities and inference than documentable facts. In part, this is because the human brain is so intricate that it is difficult to connect specific cognitive or emotional behaviors to isolated EEG events, much less to complex patterns or events. Moreover, all EEG data are affected by distortions of field potentials resulting from the tissues and skull surrounding the brain.

The EEG was discovered by Hans Berger in 1929. At that time, he named the most obvious rhythm observed "alpha." Actual attempts at training to increase the percentage of alpha with operant conditioning began in the early 1960s with Joe Kamiya's (1969) work. Kamiya initially asked subjects to tell him at the sound of a tone whether their brain waves were in an alpha state or a non–alpha state, and found some subjects could successfully make this discrimination. Subsequently, he determined that subjects could speed up or slow down their alpha production by providing either higher or lower pitched aural feedback. Experienced mediators were particularly facile at alpha enhancement. Moreover, his subjects preferred alpha enhancement, which they found to be relaxing, over alpha suppression. All this was despite the fact that they were not effective at verbally describing these states.

Most of the early work with EEG biofeedback centered on alpha training. In 1961, Arnand et al. (1960) published findings that yogis experience increased alpha amplitude during Samandhi meditation, which is a state of deep physical relaxation and intense mindfulness. Moreover, this alpha enhancement appeared to be related to unique abilities demonstrated by the yogis such as the capacity to voluntarily tolerate unpleasant physical stimuli such as immersing their hands in ice cold water without reporting discomfort. In reality, as Hardt (1993) speculates, alpha EEG feedback training is probably more similar to Zen meditation (which encourages a balance between inner and outer focus) than it is to yoga (which encourages a completely internal focus). EEG biofeedback requires that one be mindful of both inner state and the feedback from the machine. The critical points of Arnand et al.'s work, however, are that alpha training is related to a shift in arousal and that subjects show generalized increases in alpha as a result of training. These generalized increases apparently enable one to obtain beneficial effects even with a single electrode placed at a solitary site.

By 1970 Joe Kamiya had demonstrated that with minimal training subjects could effectively increase alpha amplitude. In fact, they demonstrated significant change in generation and suppression of alpha even after an initial session, reporting both relaxation and a pleasant experience associated with alpha enhancement. Later in the 1970s Kamiya expanded on this research working with a high- and a low-trait anxiety group. He demonstrated that alpha enhancement lowered state anxiety in the high-trait anxiety group, while alpha suppression increased state anxiety. Kamiya's low-trait anxiety group did not evidence further reduction in state anxiety with alpha enhancement. Hardt and Kamiya (1978), on the other hand, subsequently demonstrated that low-trait anxiety subjects were better at "increase alpha" training than high-trait anxiety subjects. They also showed that enhancing alpha was associated with both improved creativity and workload enhancement. These findings are relevant for individuals who work in competitive situations, and suggest that those who can most efficiently reduce anxiety and produce increased alpha amplitude may be those least likely to experience workload burnout.

Watson (1978) discovered that an experimental group using EEG biofeedback significantly increased alpha and decreased trait anxiety scores relative to a control group. Impressively, at the time of follow-up 18 months later these findings persisted, thereby demonstrating that a relatively short period of increased alpha training could yield long-term benefits. These subjects experienced long-term reductions in anxiety, which should contribute to long-term improvements in functions such as memory, speed of processing, mental tracking, and decision making because all these functions have been shown to be impeded by anxiety.

Hardt and Gale (1993) demonstrated that alpha enhancement resulted in significant improvements on a scale of ideational fluency. In other words, they demonstrated increased capacity to brainstorm solutions to problems—a mental fluidity that should benefit most individuals regardless of their target performance goal(s). More recently, Sterman *et al.* (1994) demonstrated that high workloads produced a sustained attenuation of alpha, which contributed to an external focus, anxiety, and rigidity in problem solving. One could speculate that the converse would also be true. That is, that increased alpha training should improve one's capacity to cope with a high workload during periods of increased production needs. In fact, Sterman and his associates subsequently were able to demonstrate that 9–13 Hz alpha in the centroparietal region is involved in efficient cognitive processing.

Recently, Sterman and Mann (1994) demonstrated that the brain cycles through different phases of alpha when solving problems. Sterman has further revealed that as the brain engages in cognitive processing it selectively lowers its alpha rhythm in certain topographical positions. When the task is completed the PRS (post reinforcement synchronization; which is 8–10 Hz in humans) is engaged apparently to resynchronize or revitalize the brain with alpha. Slow PRS recovery has been associated with poor recognition or recall or cognitive associations. It is speculated that training a stronger, more vital alpha pattern will assist in PRS and, thereby, reduce confusion and inefficiency in processing. Sterman notes that sensory input, cognitive integration, and motor output are key elements in effective information processing. Because these events can be operantly reinforced by neurofeedback, EEG brain wave training should be effective in enhancing our cognitive information processing.

Ray and Cole (1985) demonstrated that "intake" tasks involving internal mental manipulations and an internal focus of attention were associated with more overall alpha production. On the other hand, "rejection" tasks requiring externally oriented attention and environmental input produced lesser amounts of overall amplitude. In short, they demonstrated that alpha levels can reflect a type of internal attentional focus necessary for mental manipulations. Similarly, Pfurtscheller and Klimesh (1991) demonstrated that the higher alpha frequencies are attenuated by sensory encoding and lower frequencies are suppressed by internal attentional processing. These findings raise the possibility that specific types of alpha training might improve attention and concentration. Greater increases in high alpha in the left hemisphere were reported by Crawford et al. (1995) in subjects with high sustained attention than in those with low sustained attention. This high alpha was associated with error reduction and improved decision-making capacities, suggesting that high alpha neurofeedback training can, in fact, enhance cognitive functioning.

O'Hanlon and Kelly (1993) were able to demonstrate the reciprocal of Crawford's findings when they revealed a direct relationship between theta production and increase in driving errors for long-distance truck drivers. In other words, Crawford showed that as the peak alpha range brain wave frequencies became faster, cognitive processing improved, while O'Hanlon and Kelly showed that as brain wave frequencies slowed down, the brain became less efficient and made more errors. Likewise, Beatty et al. (1974) showed that when individuals engage in monotonous work their theta levels tend to increase. Training subjects to decrease theta brain waves decreased errors in well-trained radar operators; and the converse also was true, demonstrating a direct relationship between the theta levels and error rate. More recent work by Rasey et al. (1996) has demonstrated that normal college students can obtain measurable improvements on the Intermediate Visual and Auditory Test (IVA) following training to decrease theta and increase SMR (sensorimotor rhythm is a narrow band of beta generally defined as 14–16 Hz). A major improvement evidenced by their subjects was a reduction in mean reaction time. For athletes, surgeons, pianists–

anyone who works with their hands or their body–training to decrease theta and increase SMR should be extremely beneficial in terms of enhancing work performance by decreasing reaction time. Recent research by Crawford *et al.* (1995) also highlighted the benefit of inhibiting theta in distractible situations. Thus, just as training to increase cerebral activation by training to increase high alpha has beneficial effects on information processing, training down the amplitude of or percentage of total EEG power in slower theta waves has been shown to increase accuracy and speed of processing.

In the area of athletic shooting it has been shown that while mentally preparing to squeeze the trigger there is a significant increase in left temporal and occipital alpha activity while right hemisphere alpha remains essentially constant (Hartfield, 1984). Likewise, Crews (1989) found that expert golfers showed an increase in left hemisphere alpha and right hemisphere beta during swing preparation. Landers *et al.* (1991) found the same pattern of a burst of left hemispheric alpha immediately before archers shot their arrows. This melds nicely with Sterman's work (Sterman *et al.,* 1994) demonstrating that pilots who reduced alpha attenuation during high workloads increased accuracy in flight simulators.

All of the just mentioned peak performance related research employed essentially one EEG channel. In other words, it required feedback from only one electrode at one location on the scalp. The trainer might be training "up alpha" or "down theta" or both, but would not be training a characteristic of EEG that required comparison of electrical activity at two sites on the head. As we move into the area of synchronicity, however, we begin to look at two or more sites simultaneously. *Synchronicity* essentially refers to how similar waves are in terms of *timing*. It measures the degree to which EEG amplitude increases or decreases simultaneously at different locations on the head. We might consider the well-performing brain to be a balanced brain. In other words, each task performed recruits both the left and right hemispheres, and the brain normally evidences some degree of symmetry. Returning to the analogy of the orchestra, imagine the orchestra divided in half. To maintain balance, all four instrumental groups would need to be represented equally on both sides (symmetry) and play at the same time (synchrony). Garoutte and Aird (1958) completed some relevant research. Their work with synchrony revealed that 75% of the homologous alpha wave pairs (homologous pairs refers to mirror image positions on the left and right sides of the brain) fell within 10 msec of perfect synchrony and an equal portion of beta waves fell within 5 msec. This finding led them to hypothesize that there is a central pacemaker in the brain that causes the brain to push toward synchrony. Levine *et al.* (1963) also report a remarkable degree of synchrony in active portions of the cortex for up to a second in duration. This implies that the brain has a natural tendency to flow in and out of synchrony. Therefore, a brain with either excessive dyssynchrony or excessive synchrony may fail to function at its peak level. Thus, training to normalize this function may improve performance.

A relationship between synchrony differences and depression has been discussed by Rosenfeld (1997); and a high degree of synchrony in persons engaging in high levels of meditation has been found (Banquest, 1973; Levine *et al.*, 1975). However, during task engagement such meditators showed greater degrees of lateral asymmetry than controls. For meditators, analytic tasks showed more left-hemisphere involvement and spatial tasks more right-hemisphere involvement than in controls. In short, mediators have high synchrony when meditating but apparently shift to very low synchrony when engaging in certain tasks (Bennet & Trinder, 1977).

If the ability to shift voluntarily between states of high and low synchrony is related to improved mental performance, neurofeedback training to increase and decrease synchrony at will should function somewhat like a program of mental gymnastics to condition the brain for peak performance. Les Fehmi (1974) tested this hypothesis directly and found that training subjects for 20 sessions to increase multisite synchrony resulted in increases in calmness, concentration, self-initiation, detachment, observation, insightfulness, and satisfaction with life. Fehmi describes alpha synchrony as a measure of the brain's intracommunication system, with increases in synchrony being associated with improvements in communication within the brain. Increased synchrony is the central physiological change observed in meditators and is associated with the benefits of resilience to stress, increased creativity, and greater awareness. Thus, it is reasonable to assume that utilizing neurofeedback to train increased alpha range synchrony may function to enhance personal performance in a wide range of areas.

There is evidence that excitability and reaction time are related to alpha phase. Logically, this implies that reduced alpha phase would contribute to slower reaction times and poorer performance on job tasks that rely on rapid reaction times. Conversely, one might argue that increasing alpha phase will enhance performance on such tasks.

On integration of all of this research it appears that performance enhancement training should center around increasing the percentage of alpha or high alpha, increasing alpha phase or synchrony, decreasing alpha attenuation, and/or decreasing theta amplitude. The benefits of increased alpha have been demonstrated to include relaxation and stress reduction, as well as improvements in ideational fluency and complex problem solving. Training to decrease mean percent of theta has been associated with improved ability to sustain accuracy, more effective decision making, and improved mental tracking.

VIII. PEAK PERFORMANCE TRAINING PREPARATION

For beginners in the field of neurofeedback and peak performance training, a cookbook approach to peak performance training may be most appropriate. Yet, when dealing with clinical disorders it may be dangerous to employ standard protocols for remediation of various deficits, because similar symptomatology may result from very different EEG patterns. For this reason, clinical practitioners are urged to obtain a quantitative EEG (QEEG) as a baseline from which to customize neurofeedback protocols for their patients. Ethically, those offering peak performance training also should refer their clients for a pretreatment QEEG so that individuals with abnormal patterns may be identified and referred to a clinician. This is especially important because many individuals certified as peak performance trainers may lack clinical training and experience. Moreover, it might be harmful to use some of the PET protocols on individuals with specific abnormalities. For instance, training to increase alpha in an individual with depression might increase the depression rather than improve cognitive processing. Thus, the first step in peak performance training is to obtain a QEEG on each prospective trainee. If there are no abnormalities, it should be safe to use standard protocols to enhance performance.

In preparing a client for performance enhancement training the trainer must take note of a vital point made by Steve Fahrion (1995) in reference to alpha–theta training. He stated that "alpha–theta training is not, and can never be, a purely mechanical process of following a protocol, but rather is a process that requires, and only emerges successfully during, a caring relationship that is focused on authentic self-discovery, on uncovery of primal sources of behavior and beliefs that have operated unconsciously in the individual's life, but which can be brought to the light of day during treatment, and integrated into ongoing behavior as a part of a maturational process (p. 58)." So, too, those who seek PET are following a road of self-discovery that will foster maturation and will require the guidance of a trainer to help structure the experiences engendered by this process.

IX. PEAK PERFORMANCE TRAINING
GENERAL PRINCIPLES

Based on my years of experience doing clinical neurofeedback and the preceding review of the literature, it appears that improvements in concentration, reaction time, and accuracy can be promoted by training to increase either alpha (8–12 Hz) amplitude or high alpha (11–13 Hz) amplitude. PZ would be a likely scalp electrode location, although others suggest using P4 or O2.

For the goals of reducing anxiety, increasing creativity, and improving the ability to cope with a high workload, training to increase the amplitude of alpha, the percentage of alpha, or both the amplitude and percentage of alpha would appear appropriate. Research has yet to be conducted that would indicate which of these protocols would be most effective. In any case, PZ would again appear to be an appropriate location.

One could reason that decision making and reasoning would be enhanced by increases in high alpha (11–13 Hz). Once again the desired results could probably be achieved by either training to increase the amplitude and/or the percentage of high alpha.

Perseverance, targeting accuracy, reaction time, and recovery from stress are all likely to be improved by synchrony or phase training or by coherence training. By *phase* I refer to the simultaneity of timing between brain waves. In other words, using our earlier analogy, we are referring to how closely the various "instruments in the orchestra" begin and end notes in time with one another. By *coherence* I refer to the similarities between the volume (power) of instruments acting in phase. For instance, if two pianists were simultaneously playing the scales at the same volume and both simultaneously increased volume 10%, the listener would be unable to differentiate the signals. This state of dedifferentiation represents hypercoherence. If one pianist played slightly louder or lower than the other, the listener would be able to perceive both signals and this might be considered optimal coherence. Synchrony or phase would represent both timing and instrument. So flutes and guitars that are off a beat would have extremely low synchrony, while two flutes in concert with each other temporally would have a high degree of synchrony. To improve recovery from stress and perseverance it can be speculated (based on reasoning presented earlier) that one may want to train to increase phase, coherence, and/or synchrony. Once again, there is a dearth of research on which protocols are most helpful for the development of which cerebral functions and cognitive skills. For this reason, it is hoped that this article will spur considerable debate and that the debate will spur research.

X. THE COOKBOOK

Until definitive research is completed, practitioners who want to use this technology to assist others in optimizing performance will need to rely heavily on their own reasoning abilities in selecting which protocols will be most helpful for which client. The following paragraphs, however, represent some crude guidelines that others may wish to follow as a "primer."

To assist bureaucrats in sustaining attention for monotonous work and reducing stress, training to increase alpha amplitude or alpha percentage would appear appropriate. Students wishing to improve their attentional processes, problem solving, creativity, and ability to cope with heavy workloads may find it beneficial to progress from increase alpha amplitude training, to increase alpha percentage training, to increase synchrony training. This type of training regime should improve attention to tasks, task completion, task accuracy, and consistency or productivity. Individuals involved in real estate, insurance, or other sales need to maintain a high level of motivation and creativity and be able to cope effectively with rejection and failure. For these individuals learning to increase their percentage of alpha, alpha coherence, and percentage of high alpha may equip them to deal with the high level of performance pressure they routinely experience. Stock brokers also need confidence, motivation, creativity, drive, and concentration. Training to increase alpha amplitude, coherence, synchrony, and percent of alpha can function to help these individuals improve organizational skills, self-discipline, ability to relate to customers, and, most important of all, the ability to relax when not at work.

To improve performance in endurance sports, one would want to increase determination and concentration and improve self-discipline. Toward this end, training to increase alpha amplitude, percent alpha, and synchrony might be a good starting point. More motivated performers also might want training to increase high alpha amplitude and higher percentage of high alpha. Golf is an individual sport that requires accuracy and the ability to perform consistently under pressure. For this reason, it might be desirable to train golfers to increase alpha amplitude, coherence, synchrony, and alpha percentage, as well as high alpha percentage. Training to increase alpha amplitude, coherence, synchrony, and alpha percentage also might help skiers improve reaction times and increase their mental flexibility so they can master novel or unusual movements. Tennis players may improve their game focus, improve the accuracy of shots, and increase their reaction time by training to increase alpha amplitude, coherence, synchrony, and alpha percentage. Even weight lifters may find that they can improve their attention, concentration, determination, and inspiration through training to increase alpha amplitude, percent alpha, and phase.

Pilots and truck drivers need good concentration and alertness during lengthy monotonous tasks. They also need quick reaction times, a good ability to recover from stress, and the capacity to be at ease during critical periods. For these individuals training to increase alpha amplitude, synchrony, high alpha percentage, and coherence may function to improve concentration and reduce errors. Police officers, firefighters, ambulance squads, and other emergency personnel all need to be able to drive for long periods of time, to tolerate monotony well, and then to have accurate decision-making skills during periods of crisis. Training to increase alpha percentage, alpha amplitude, high alpha amplitude, coherence, and synchrony may function to help these individuals increase concentration during emergencies, increase relaxation, improve recovery from viewing traumatic events, and enhance decision making in dangerous situations.

Remember these are only suggestions. We need much more research to be conducted to determine which protocols would be helpful for the development of particular skills. We recommend that trainers take every opportunity to collect data. If you are not a writer, find someone who is and ask them to publish your research findings. We strongly believe that neurofeedback has exciting possibilities as a tool to promote peak performance, and the more well designed the research studies that demonstrate the particular effects of specific treatment protocols, the more powerful this tool will be.

XI. THE BUSINESS

For those in pursuit of self-empowerment, EEG performance enhancement training (PET) technology provides an objective means of assessing changes in brain wave states. For clinicians, it opens the gate to a world of intervention without the specter of HMOs, PPOs, and insurance precertifications, denials, and collections. It provides the client with a means to promote and track his or her level of personal mental conditioning, and the trainer the opportunity to receive reimbursement at the time of service for being an educator and coach: a textbook win–win situation.

A wide range of activities will help you develop and market a performance enhancement (PET) business. The first step is to become a certified peak performance specialist. For information on training, supervision, the certification process and marketing, feel free to contact the authors.

REFERENCES

Anand, B. K., China, G. S., & Singh, B. (1960). Some aspects of electroencephalographic studies in Yogis. *EEG Clin. Neurophysiol.* **13,** 452–456.

Banquest, J. P. (1973). Spectral analysis of the EEG in meditation. *EEG Clin. Neurophysiol.* **35,** 143–151.

Beatty, J., Greenberg, A., Deibler, W. P., & O'Hanlon, J. F. (1974). Operant control of occipital theta rhythm affects performance in a radar monitoring task. *Science* **133,** 871–873.

Becker, R., & Seldon, G. (1985). "The Body Electric." William Morrow and Company, Inc., New York.

Bennett, J. E., & Trinder, J. (1977). Hemispheric laterality and cognitive style associated with transcendental meditation. *Psychophysiology* **14,** 3.

Bowersox, S. S., & Sterman, M. B. (1981). Changes in sensorimotor sleep spindle activity and seizure susceptibility following somatosensory deafferentation. *Exp. Neurol.* **74,** 814–828.

Bowersox, S. S., & Sterman, M. B. (1982). Effects of somatosensory deafferentation on spectral characteristics of the sensorimotor EEG in the adult cat. *Exp. Neurol.* **77,** 403–418.

Covey, S. (1989). "The Seven Habits of Highly Effective People." Fireside, New York.

Crawford, H. J., Kenebel, T. F., Vendemia, J. M., Kaplan, L., & Ratcliff, B. (1995). EEG activation patterns during tracking and decision-making tasks. Differences between low and high sustained attention adults. Presented at the Eighth International Symposium on Aviation Psychology, Columbus, OH.

Crawford, H. J., & Vasilescu, I. P. (1995). Differential EEG pattern activity of low and high sustained attention adults during decision making tasks. Presented at Annual Scientific Meeting of the Society for Psychological Research, Toronto, Canada.

Crews, D. L. (1989). The influence of attentive states on golf putting as indicated by cardiac and electrocortical activity. Doctoral Dissertation, Arizona State University.

Fahrion, S. L. (1995). Human potental and personal transformation, *Subtle Energies* **6**(1), 55–86.

Fahrion, S. L., Walters, E. D., Coyne, L., & Allen, T. (1992). Alerations in EEG amplitude, personality factors and brain electrical mapping after alpha–theta brainwave training: A controlled case study. *Alcohol. Clin. Exp. Res.* **16**, 547–552.

Fehmi, L. G. (1974). Effects of EEG biofeedback on middle management executives. Presented at the Biofeedback Research Society Annual Meeting, Colorado Springs, CO.

Garfield, C. (1986). "Peak Performers: The New Heroes of American Business." p. 28. Morrow and Company, New York.

Garfield, C. (1984). "Peak Performance: Mental Training Techniques of the World's Greatest Athletes." pp. 158–159. Tarcher, Los Angeles, CA.

Garoutte, B., & Aird, R. B. (1958). Studies on the cortical pacemaker: Synchrony and asyncrohony of bilaterally recorded alpha and beta activity. *EEG Clin. Neurophysiol.* **10**, 259–267.

Hardt, J. V. (1993). Alpha EEG feedback: Closer parallel with Zen than yoga. *Biocybernaut Inst.,* pp. 131–135.

Hardt, J. V., & Gale, R. E. (1993). Creativity increases in scientists through alpha EEG feedback training. *Biocybernaut Insti.* pp. 136–139.

Hardt, J. V., & Kamiya, J. (1978). Anxiety change through electroencephalographic alpha feedback seen only in high anxiety subjects. *Science* **201**, 79–81.

Hartfield, B. D., Landers, D. M., & Ray, W. J. (1984). Cognitive processes during self-paced motor preference: An electroencephalographic profile of skilled marksmen. *J. Sports Psychol.* **6**, 42–59.

Henry, J. P. (1992). "Instincts, Archetypes and Symbols: An Approach to the Physiology of Religious Experience. College Press, Dayton, OH.

Hoovey, Z. B., Heinman, U., & Cruetzfeldt, O. D. (1972). Interhemispheric "synchrony" of alpha waves. *EEG Clin. Neurophysiol.* **32**, 337–347.

Kamiya, J. (1969). Operant control of the EEG alpha rhythm and some of its reported effects on consciousness. *In* "Altered States of Consciousness" (C. T. Tart, ed.). Wiley and Sons, New York.

Landers, D. M., Petruzzello, S. J., Salazar, W., Crews, D. J., Kubitz, K. A., Gannon, T. L., & Han, M. (1991). The influence of electrocortical biofeedback on performance in pre-elite archers. *Med. Sci. Sports Exercise* **23**(1), 123–128.

Levine, P. H., Herbert, J. R., Haynes, C. T., & Strobel, U. (1975). EEG coherence during the transcendental meditation technique. *Electroencephalography and Clinical Neurophysiology,* Scientific Research on the Transcendental Meditation Program: Collected Papers Part I, 187–207.

Levine, R. B., Smith, R. P., & Hawkes, G. R. (1963). On synchrony of the alpha rhythms. *Aerospace Med.* April, 349–352.

Lubar, J. F., & Bahler, W. W. (1976). Behavioral management of epileptic seizures following biofeedback training of the sensorimotor rhythm. *Biofeedback Self-Regul.* **1**, 77–104.

Lubar, J. F., & Shouse, M. N. (1976). EEG and behavioral changes in a hyperkinetic child concurrent with training of the sensorimotor rhythm (SMR): A preliminary report. *Biofeedback Self-Regul.* **3**, 293–306.

Lubar, J. O., & Lubar, J. F. (1984). Electroencephalographic biofeedback of SMR and beta for treatment of attention deficit disorders in a clinical setting. *Biofeedback Self-Regul.* **9**, 1–23.

O'Hanlon, J. F., & Kelly, G. R. (1993). Comparison of performance and physiological changes between drivers who perform well and poorly during prolonged vehicular operation. *Human Fact. Res. Inc.,* pp. 87–109.

Peniston, E. G., & Kulkosky, P. (1989). Alpha–theta brainwave training and beta-endorphin levels in alcoholics. *Alcohol. Clin. Exp. Res.* **13**, 271–279.

Peniston, E. G., & Kulkosky, P. (1990). Alcoholic personality and alpha–theta brainwave training. *Adv. Med. Psychother.* **3**, 37–55.

Peniston, E. G., & Kulkosky, P. (1991). Alcoholic personality and alpha–theta brainwave training. *Adv. Med. Psychother.* **4,** 1–14.

Pfurtscheller, G., & Kimesch, W. (1991). Event-related desynchronization during motor behavior and visual information processing. *In* "Event-Related Brain Research" (C. H. M. Brunia, G. Mulder, & M. N. Verbaten, eds), EEG Supplement, Vol. 42, pp. 58–65.

Rasey, H., Lubar, J. F., Mc Intryre, A., Zuffuto, A., & Abbot, P. L. (1996). EEG biofeedback for the enhancement of attentional processing in normal college students. *J. Neurother.* **1**(3), 15–21.

Ray, W. J., & Cole, H. W. (1985). EEG alpha activity reflects attentional demands, and beta activity reflects emotional and cognitive processes. *Science* **228,** 750–752.

Rosenfeld, J. P. (1997). EEG biofeedback of frontal alpha asymmetry in affective disorders. *Biofeedback* **25**(1), 8–25.

Sams, M. (1995). Mathematically derived frequency correlates in cerebral function: Theoretical and clinical implications for neurofeedback treatment. *J. Neurother.* **1**(2), 1–14.

Sterman, M. B. (1996). Physiological origins and functional correlates of EEG rhythmic activities: Implications for self-regulation. *Biofeedback & Self-Regulation* **21**(1), 3–33.

Sterman, M. B. (1982). EEG biofeedback in the treatment of epilepsy: An overview circa 1980. *In* "Clinical Biofeedback: Efficacy and Mechanism" (L. White & B. Tursky, eds.), pp. 330–331. Guilford, New York.

Sterman, M. B., & Macdonald, L. R. (1978). Effects of centrocortical EEG feedback training on incidence of poorly controlled seizures. *Epilepsia* **19,** 207–222.

Sterman, M. B., Lo Presti, R. W., & Fairchild, M.D. (1969). Electroencephalographic and behavioral studies of monomethylhydrazine toxicity in cats. Technical Report AMRL-RT-69-3, Air Systems Command, Wright-Patterson Air Force Base, OH.

Sterman, M. B., Mann, C. A., & Kaiser, D. A. (1992). Quantitative EEG patterns of differential in-flight workload. *In* "1992 Space Operations Applications and Research Proceedings." Johnson Space Center, TX.

Sterman, M. B., Mann, C. A., Kaiser, D. A., & Suyenobu, B. Y., & Brandall, Y. (1994). Multiband topographic EEG analysis of simulated visuomotor aviation task. *Int. J. Psychophysiol.* **16,** 49–56.

Watson, C. G., Herder, J., & Passini, F. T. (1978). Alpha biofeedback therapy in alcoholics: An 18-month follow-up. *J. Clin. Psychol.* **34,** 765–769.

Wise, A. (1995). "The High Performance Mind. G. P. Putnum & Sons, New York.

MODELS FOR NEUROFEEDBACK EFFICACY

11

EEG BIOFEEDBACK: AN EMERGING MODEL FOR ITS GLOBAL EFFICACY

SIEGFRIED OTHMER, SUSAN F. OTHMER,
AND DAVID A. KAISER

EEG Spectrum, Encino, California

EEG biofeedback has a favorable research history for both epilepsy and attention deficit hyperactivity disorder (ADHD). Recently, interest has expanded as clinical success with ADHD has led to good outcomes for a wide variety of other conditions. These new findings have yet to be subjected to systematic evaluation in controlled research. Nevertheless, the richness of clinical findings to date justifies a review of the field. EEG biofeedback bifurcates into two domains: training with an emphasis on the low beta range of frequencies of 12–19 Hz, and training in the lower frequency regime of 2–12 Hz. The former is directed largely toward normalization of neurophysiological functioning and the latter mainly toward psychological reintegration. The present review is restricted to the higher frequency training.

Much of the difficulty being encountered by clinicians in attempting to gain recognition for the startling results being obtained with EEG biofeedback has to do with the inadequacy of models that could account for their findings. Another reason is that large claims demand good evidence, which is conventionally supplied through well-funded, large-scale, university-based, controlled studies. Whereas much evidence has been accumulated in the clinical sphere, it has not generally been in the form of controlled studies with large subject populations. Thus, the highly promising results variously reported have not yet reached the level of mainstream acceptance. In the following, the attempt is made first to provide a comprehensive model that can account for the findings, and then to consider the evidence that supports the model. To date, the emphasis has been on trying to document efficacy of EEG biofeedback in the context of existing models of psychopathology. Because the existing models are well established and self-reinforcing, the appearance of an occasional clinical report that lies outside of the models is unlikely to gain attention, much less to compel conviction. However, the various existing clinical reports can become mutually supportive, and collectively persuasive, if regarded from the standpoint of a new model.

The new model being proposed is one that treats the brain as a self-regulatory control system, and much of psychopathology will be seen in terms of specific failure modes of such a control system. It will be referred to as the *disregulation model* (Schwartz, 1979, 1989; Grotstein, 1986). It is argued that the regulatory machinery of the brain must be regarded from the bioelectrical as well as the neurochemical perspective, and considered as well in the time, or frequency, domain. Much of the basic regulatory activity of the central nervous system manifests itself in rhythmic EEG activity. EEG biofeedback will then be seen as a means of appeal to that regulatory machinery, by operant conditioning on its rhythmic manifestations. EEG biofeedback is therefore a "regulatory challenge," to which the system responds by becoming more robust as a control system, which means specifically to become more stable, and to be more capable of returning toward homeostatic balance.

What is currently known about segmentation and localization of cortical function implies that EEG biofeedback may have site-specific effects that can serve as a check on the model. Additionally, a dependency of EEG training effects on reinforcement frequency is expected. Clinical findings are brought to bear in support of the models, and both the frequency and spatial specificity of the training in any one individual are powerful arguments against the placebo hypothesis, since they allow any subject to act as his or her own control during the ongoing training. The clinical data support the view that EEG biofeedback is nonspecific with respect to individual disorders, even though the training may be quite specific in terms of the regulatory functions it addresses. In actuality, of course, the clinical data came first, and the models mentioned only gradually emerged, as the comprehensiveness of clinical findings became compelling.

I. STRAINS IN THE PARADIGM

Quite apart from any claims for EEG biofeedback, strains are already appearing in the conventional paradigm of discrete, canonical disorders, as embodied in the *Diagnostic and Statistical Manual of Mental Disorders* 4th edition (DSM-IV). Disorders are less discrete and less differentiable than has been implied. Disorders seem also to have a distinct time course rather than being stable over time. And distinctions at the phenomenological level are not consistently grounded in physiology. As the model under-girding the DSM is increasingly stretched to cover the emerging errant data, and as it progresses toward ever more refined differential diagnosis, an opportunity arises to reframe the discussion in terms of a new paradigm: a return to a "spectrum theory" of mental disorders. As it happens, intimations of this are already discernible within the mainstream literature, and it is remarkable to observe the extent to which the case for the new paradigm can be made from the standard literature itself. This literature is of course being written largely by academic scientists who are entirely unfamiliar with the claims for EEG biofeedback emerging from the clinical realm. The evidentiary support afforded by clinical data will hopefully close the loop and provide needed confirmation for the emerging models.

The prevailing consensus model for mental disorders is reflected in the structure of the DSM-IV, which exists in symbiotic relationship with psycho-pharmacology. The specificity of drug action has been accompanied by increasing specificity in diagnostic categories. This symbiosis was historically initiated by the specific efficacy of lithium for manic-depressive illness, which gained acceptance in the United States in the late 1960s. The development of pharmacologic agents which paralleled the evolution of the DSM also cemented an emerging view of the organic or physiological basis of mental disorders, largely displacing the then-standard psychodynamic models. The latter suffered the handicap of being more difficult to document scientifically, not to mention being difficult to model in terms of underlying physiology.

The scientific thrust toward an understanding of the brain compatible with pharmacology focused the energies of the neurosciences toward the building blocks of the brain: neurotransmitter mechanisms, receptor site properties, the operation of simple neural circuits that could be monitored in brain slices in a petri dish. This thrust took us further away from the larger scale perspective of whole-brain function that was the preoccupation of the neurosciences up to about 30 years ago.

The pharmacological thrust was complemented by developments in the field of genetics, which launched a search for the genetic basis of mental disorders. This search often led to dead ends, but the appearance in the literature of a variety of preliminary successes gave the field an aura of continuing progress in teasing out the genetic basis of abnormal behavior, despite the fact that some of these findings subsequently failed in replication. This aura of progress was in symbiotic relationship with the emerging belief system that mental disorders were largely grounded in immutable, structural flaws traceable in large measure to genetic influences (see Weinberger, 1997, for example).

Recent developments in the neurosciences, as well as in pharmacology, suggest that the intellectual hegemony sustained and regimented by the DSM-IV is coming under challenge. The boundary between what we consider to be immutable structure and malleable function is being moved and also blurred. New findings in what is called neural or brain plasticity suggest that the central nervous system is far more adaptable than once thought (McGaugh *et al.,* 1995; Bennett *et al.,* 1996). The term *neural plasticity,* which refers to changes in reactivity of the nervous system and its components as a result of constant successive activations, is itself a newcomer to the scientific literature, having been in common use in major journals only since 1994. It is being realized that even though some 30% of the human genome is committed to specifying the central nervous system, that is insufficient for more than general instructions for neuronal development and synapse formation. Most mental disorders have not been traceable to gross mal-ordering of synapse or receptor or neurotransmitter function (Roth-schild, 1988).

Developments in pharmacology are also manifesting a need for a different organizing principle and do not align well with the diagnostic specificity of the DSM-IV. For example, the use of antidepressants, anxiolytics, stimu-lants, and anticonvulsants now cuts broadly across diagnostic categories (Suffin & Emory, 1995). This points up a need for a more physiologically based taxonomy of mental disorders (e.g., Harro & Oreland, 1996). And finally, the emergence of imaging technologies such as PET, SPECT, and functional MRI is refocusing the attention of neuroscientists on the realm of brain function rather than structure (e.g., George *et al.,* 1993; El-Hilu *et al.,* 1997; Klemm *et al.,* 1996).

II. AN EMERGING NEW MODEL

The climate of dissonance between the established order and the new findings provides an opening for a reframing of the entire treatment of mental disorders in a manner which takes into account the underlying physiology. This reframing is of necessity a large mental leap, one that at this point has only modest theoretical support. It is being presented here as a possible basis for organizing both clinical findings and recent scientific developments. There is no implication that this model at the present time enjoys broad support either in the scientific or the clinical community.

In its simplest terms, the model recognizes that most "information trans-fer" in the brain occurs via the action potential. The information content of the action potential resides first of all in its existence or nonexistence at a particular instant in time (Ferster & Spruston, 1995). Over a longer period of time, information can be encoded in the repetition rate of the action potential (Judd & Aihara, 1993; Gabbiani & Koch, 1996). Such repetition rate can scale with the magnitude of a particular physiological measure, and this is known as *rate coding* (Connor & Johnson, 1992). Because events of interest can occur on timescales short compared to typical firing rates, it must also be true that information can be encoded more subtly in the specific timing of the neuronal firing, on a timescale short compared to its firing repetition rate (Spitzer & Sejnowski, 1997; Rieke *et al.*, 1996). Timing, however, has no absolute reference point. It can only be meaningful in the context of other firing events.

The nexus between the "information" encoded in a neural firing event and something we may recognize as "information," or experience as a cognitive event at the conscious level, may lie in the collective activity of an ensemble of neurons. That is, brain activity, as we are aware of it, may intrinsically be a group property of large neuronal ensembles, rather than the "atomistic" property of individual neurons (Sakurai, 1996). If this is the case, then the brain has the problem of organizing neuronal ensembles into functional groupings for as long as a particular mental task requires (MacCormac, 1996). Such dynamic ordering of neuronal activity may be marshaled by the brain using rhythmic generator circuits, or they may be the outcome of more purely self-organizing cortical–cortical interactions leading to rhythmic activity (Hardcastle, 1996; Whittington *et al.*, 1995).

It is the relatively recent discovery of rhythmicity as the basis for organization of brain function that makes possible our new departure. It may be helpful here to use the analogy to the conductor of an orchestra who, by the measured gyrations of his baton, synchronizes and organizes activities by "ensembles" of musicians (violins, basses, etc.) under his guidance. Their instruments function at much higher frequencies than those of the conductor's baton. However, his activity "entrains" that of the individual musicians and the ensembles of musicians. To improve the analogy to brain function, we must jettison the conductor and talk strictly of self-organizing, self-sustaining, and self-reinforcing mechanisms underpinning the rhythmicity. (Self-organization used to characterize orchestras as well, since they didn't always have conductors.)

We will return to each of the key points in more detail in the following. However, to complete the argument it is necessary to assert that the EEG reflects the rhythmic activity of these ensembles. The EEG, therefore, is not simply random "brain noise" but rather the manifestation of explicit brain activity through which function is organized (Wright & Liley, 1996). That is, the brain is very dependent on the activity we measure in the EEG, and it manages that activity quite precisely when the brain is under challenge to function well. If we then subject the rhythmic activity of the EEG to operant conditioning at a particular frequency, we might expect to alter the functions that the particular rhythmicity subserves.

The rhythmic activity is undoubtedly managed by the complex interaction of a variety of feedback loops that operate on different spatial scales and timescales (Sillito *et al.*, 1994; Munglani & Jones, 1992; Modell *et al.*, 1989). To this network of interactions we have now added an external feedback loop via biofeedback. This new feedback path is just one additional influence on the degree of rhythmicity then present in the brain at the particular frequency being reinforced. As the brain responds to the challenge by increasing rhythmicity in the moment, through the operation of one or another feedback loop, all the other relevant feedback paths see altered inputs, and respond accordingly, in an attempt to restore equilibrium. Hence, the biofeedback represents an influence that takes the brain away from the then-prevailing equilibrium in rhythmicity to a different state, and this deviation engages restorative forces that move the brain back toward the state it had been maintaining. Thus, any interaction with brain function is deemed to elicit a corresponding response by the brain. There may then be two aspects to the remediation by EEG biofeedback: the facilitation of particular states of brain function, and the challenge to regulatory function as the brain is moved out of its prevailing state.

In this model, EEG biofeedback can be seen as directly impinging on the self-regulatory activity of the brain in the bioelectrical domain. It gently challenges the brain out of equilibrium or homeostasis, to which the brain then attempts to return, in a kind of push–pull or action–reaction fashion reminiscent of a stair-stepper in an exercise gym (that is, the more one pushes on it, the more it pushes back—and yet it moves). We refer to this as the *regulatory challenge* model of EEG biofeedback. A successive, repetitive exercise of the control mechanisms of a self-organizing system can be expected to achieve two objectives (as will be argued in further detail in the following): (1) an improved ability to maintain homeostasis and (2) an improved stability of the regulatory system.

Where does neurochemistry fit into the above model? We know that much of neurochemistry is in the service of the management of the action potential. Scientists can talk about neurochemistry (and have done so) entirely without reference to the ultimate purpose, which is managing information. However, information can equally well be regarded from the perspectives of the electrical and the timing domains, without reference to neurochemistry. In fact, a rather comprehensive description of brain function in the information theory realm, and in the bioelectrical domain, should in principle be possible. Neither treatment would necessarily require us to talk about the neurochemical implementation of those models. We can go further. It must be possible in principle to describe the brain in terms of control and stability requirements of ordinary servosystems, and it must meet those stability criteria just like any other system of feedback loops, irrespective of whether it be electrical, fluid-mechanical, or neurochemical in character.

Seen in this light, we can describe the physiological basis of much psychopathology in terms of the ordinary failure modes of servosystems (Hamilton *et al.,* 1993; Newman & Wallace, 1993). Such systems typically fail either by having insufficient gain to maintain "setpoints" (not unlike thermostat settings) or by not meeting loop stability criteria, in which case they are subject to various instabilities. These may include overshoots in response to a transient stimulus, ringing in the system (successive over- and undershoots that die out only slowly), or oscillations. Relevant examples of setpoint errors in the central nervous system may include dysthymia, a persistent low threshold of pain, and generalized anxiety. Relevant examples of instabilities include seizures as an oscillatory response; hypoglycemia as overshoots and undershoots in glucose regulation; and motor or vocal tics, hot flashes, and episodic vertigo as short-term instabilities. Even such a complex condition as schizophrenia has been described in terms of instabilities (Saugstad, 1994).

This perspective motivates what we call the *disregulation model* of psychopathology, which is to say that the fundamental issue in many mental dysfunctions may be the failure of the brain to operate properly as a control system (Hamilton *et al.,* 1993). This control system can best be described in the bioelectrical domain and in the timing domain (as opposed to the domain of neurochemistry, for example). We resort to the argument that rhythmic activity in the brain is the mediator of brain timing, and the facilitator and organizer of intracortical and subcortical–cortical communication. Hence, mental dysfunction is expected to manifest itself in inappropriate brain rhythmicity, which may, however, be amenable to remediation by explicit operant conditioning of brain rhythms. The converse is likely also to be true, namely, that deviance in brain rhythmicity is likely to have discernible implications for mental dysfunction. However, it is not necessary for complete reciprocity to prevail in order to make the case for our model of EEG biofeedback.

The EEG biofeedback challenge is expected to address the two key failure modes identified for control systems, and thus achieve (1) an improved ability to maintain homeostasis and (2) an improvement in stability when responding to a sudden challenge or insult to the regulatory system. At the subjective level, improvement in homeostatic balance may be perceived as "improved control"; improved stability may be described as heightened "toughness"; and improved transient response may be likened to "improved resiliency."

It remains to be demonstrated that much of psychopathology can be described either as a setpoint or as a stability problem (or both) in the various brain subsystems, which are required to function stably and reliably in a servomechanism sense, and to bring forth evidence that operant conditioning of the EEG can serve to remediate these conditions. The preceding discussion is useful to this end because it allows us to bring to bear any of the clinical evidence for EEG biofeedback in support of these more global propositions respecting operating points and stability criteria. To date, it has been fashionable to require that efficacy for EEG biofeedback be demonstrated individually and separately for each diagnostic category. This can certainly be done in a research setting, given adequate funding. However, confronted as we are with data mainly from clinical settings, this approach segments the data unnecessarily. Such compartmentalization of data is partly due to the explicit constraints imposed by the DSM-IV classification scheme. The claims for EEG biofeedback are placed at a disadvantage because EEG training addresses problems in neurological control mechanisms rather than specific disorders. The varied benefits that derive from such training in fact militate against acceptance of the claims. Whereas the technique may in fact exhibit marked specificity in terms of impacting physiological functioning, its lack of specificity with respect to DSM-IV classifications is a detriment to the cause of documenting efficacy.

It is important to note that in our attempt to provide a reformulation of the physiological basis of psychopathology, we are not being reductionist. In many prior treatments of EEG biofeedback the resort to this modality is defended on the basis that the condition being addressed (such as ADHD) has a physiological basis or, more specifically, is traceable to some physical defect (e.g., Lubar *et al.,* 1995). This presumably distinguishes the problem from one with a more psychogenic basis. In the future, this may increasingly be seen as a false dichotomy. At a minimum, the distinction will become blurred and of diminished practical import. In depression, for example, the physiological measures (and treatment) appear to be largely insensitive to whether the depression is reactive or endogenous (Holden, 1991). All mental processes, normal or abnormal, have their physiological representations, which can be appealed to with operant conditioning. And most mental processes can be described in terms of several languages, one being that of psychology, another that of neurophysiology. A choice between them is one of convenience and purpose, not one of exclusionary validity. Historically, however, it is clear that the language chosen in a particular case could significantly constrain the evidence that would be admitted to the discussion.

III. STRUCTURE VERSUS FUNCTION

Because the issue of a structural or functional basis for psychopathology is so central to gaining a hearing for the claims of EEG biofeedback, it is important to review some history. The issue is beautifully framed in the following vignette, taken from David Comings' *Tourette Syndrome and Human Behavior* (Comings, 1990, p. 78):

> . . . In one case, a woman was operated on who had intractable headaches, an irritable bowel, and emotional instability. A wire was introduced into the anterior thalamus and showed a 14-Hz positive spike which spread to the frontal and temporal lobes. Destruction of this part of the thalamus resulted in the complete alleviation of her complaints.

It is interesting to note that in this case there was only functional evidence for a problem, namely, EEG activity. However, there was no difficulty making a leap to the conclusion that the EEG had revealed a structural flaw in the thalamus that mandated resection. It is also noteworthy that the disappearance of three totally disparate symptom types was all ascribed to this one intervention.

With our modern perspective of EEG biofeedback, we might respond as follows: It is likely that the abnormal 14-Hz activity could be observed at cortex. However, regardless of whether it could be discerned or not, *some* 14-Hz EEG activity could be detected there and subjected to the challenge of operant conditioning. The subject would be given information about the magnitude of the 14-Hz component of the EEG from moment to moment, and rewarded for changing it with respect to a threshold. Our own clinical experience is very favorable for headaches, and good outcomes have also been achieved with irritable bowel syndrome and with emotional instabilities. This experience permits us to hazard the prediction that such a challenge could also have resolved all three symptom categories in this person, as well as normalized the EEG in terms of its 14-Hz activity. In other words, it is possible that the deficit could be seen from the perspective of brain function. The brain may have somehow "learned" this inappropriate activity, which ultimately became firmly entrenched, almost as if a lesion had given rise to it.

It has been an abiding assumption of neuroscientists that at the basis of most neuropathology lies the lesion (Sohmer & Student, 1978). However, as far back as the work of Hughlings Jackson more than 100 years ago, it has been found that even seizures could arise out of apparently healthy brain tissue. Lesions were not always identified at the seizure focus on autopsy. Nevertheless, such disorders as dyslexia and even ADHD were thought to be grounded in lesions. Autopsies of dyslexics of course often yielded the finding of microlesions, and these were then assigned the burden of the dyslexia, even though nothing could be proved in that regard (Rumsey, 1996). Wender ascribed ADHD potentially to a "biochemical lesion," which term carries with it a certain ambiguity (Wender, 1974). It retained the concept of a structural lesion (the problem was assumed to be metabolic), but implicitly held out the hope of functional remediation. David Comings used the above citation to make the case that ADHD might be a "biochemical abnormality in the thalamic-frontal lobe structures." This terminology likewise retains ambiguity as to whether the abnormality is structural in character, or, being merely biochemical, could be remediable through behavioral or other functionally based approaches.

Pharmacological efficacy was also adduced as an argument for a physical basis of the disorders at issue. If drugs could remediate a problem, then that argued for a "biological basis" of the problem. Peter Kramer reviewed this thesis beautifully in his book, *Listening to Prozac* (Kramer, 1993). However, this argument cuts both ways. The transient effect of drugs such as stimulants can be used to argue that the brain is merely changing in

functional state, and that the stimulant is not addressing a hardware problem. That is, the states to which stimulants give access are already within
the functional inventory of that particular brain; and in some manner the
drugs shift the balance of neuromodulator systems to promote a different
behavioral state. If this is the case, then it is only a small step to argue that
such a change in behavioral state could (in principle at this point) also
be achieved with operant conditioning, if the operant is the bioelectrical
manifestation of these same neuromodulator systems, namely, the EEG.

Stimulants act quickly on the brain, and the brain's response can therefore be considered of the first order. However, the clinical effects of most
psychotherapeutic drugs, including antidepressants and neuroleptics, typically are slow in onset. Here the mechanism of action appears to be via
long-term brain adaptations in response to the medication challenge, and
can therefore be considered to be of second order. This again implies a
degree of plasticity within the brain. It is also a better analog for what
happens with EEG biofeedback. The operant conditioning of the EEG
promotes a particular shift in states. However, no single such state character-
izes a functional organism. Significantly constraining the brain to a particular
state (as reflected in the EEG) should be expected to constrain the organism
in the functional realm as well! Improvement in neuromodulator function
therefore arises, it is assumed, not only from the first-order reaction of the
brain to the challenge of the conditioning (which could in principle even
be dysfunctional), but also from the second-order response of the brain
to this challenge: more robust neuroregulatory functioning. Whereas it is
possible for the brainwave training to constrain the system and lead to
temporary dysfunction (that can be readily observed clinically), the effect
is *generally* to increase the envelope of function, and to increase behavioral
flexibility. That is, the diversity of accessible brain states usually increases
rather than diminishes in response to the operant conditioning challenge.

Thus, from the perspective of EEG biofeedback a very different interpretation is made of the data from pharmacology. Psychopharmacology, in
our view, has already implicitly made the case for a considerable functional
plasticity of the neuromodulator systems that govern activation, arousal,
sympathetic/parasympathetic balance, etc. (e.g., Katz *et al.,* 1996; Oken *et
al.,* 1995; Scheife & Graziano, 1991; Klein, 1997). EEG biofeedback does
not require anymore brain plasticity than has already been demonstrated
to exist by the effects of drugs impinging on neuromodulator function. By
continuing administration of the EEG biofeedback challenge, the brain can
be induced to make long-term adaptations similar to those induced by the
drugs. However, because the brain will have achieved these changes entirely
autonomously, there may be no continuing need for drug administration
to sustain them. In fact, clinical experience with thousands of cases demonstrates that the dosage of most psychoactive drugs will most likely have to
be titrated down during the course of training, perhaps even to zero dose.

If this is not done, then symptoms of drug overdose and drug-induced toxicity may manifest. In many cases, therefore, optimum functioning of the client will require a combination of medical management and EEG training. This interaction of EEG training with medication management supports the view that both influence common neuromodulatory systems. Because the EEG training is nonspecific with respect to individual neuro-modulator systems, in contrast to most medications, we may conjecture *a priori* that EEG training could in principle be helpful for almost any mental condition for which psychotropic medication has been demonstrably helpful.

Perhaps the best illustration of the historical contention between structural and functional models of psychopathology is given by obsessive-compulsive disorder (OCD) and Tourette's syndrome. Richard Restak (1995) recalls his early training in his book *Brainscapes:*

> Tourette believed the symptoms of the [Tourette's syndrome] disorder occurred involuntarily, and thus exactly opposite of the way that obsessive-compulsive disorders were thought to happen. For this reason the two disorders were "adopted" by different specialties of the human mind: OCD was appropriated by the psychiatrists who remained convinced of its psychological origins and spun elaborate theories to account for it; Tourette's remained under the banner of the neurologists who emphasized the motor tics and inquired little about their patients' inner experiences.
>
> During my own training I don't recall any reference to OCD by my neurologists, nor anything said about Tourette's by my psychiatric instructors. (p. 105)

The two disorders, Tourette's syndrome and OCD, are so strongly comorbid that they have been referred to as a dual diagnosis (Rapoport, 1986). That is, if you have the one, you most likely have the other. More recent neurophysiological models show that both disorders involve the same neuronal circuitry (Stein, 1996). In fact, both motor and vocal tics and obsessions and compulsions can be thought of in terms of a feedback loop involving the orbitofrontal and cingulate cortex, the caudate nucleus and ventral striatum, the globus pallidus, and the thalamus (see also Modell *et al.,* 1989). With high loop gain in this system, one may observe perseverative activity, narrow attentive focus, motor and vocal tics, and obsessive thoughts or compulsive behaviors.

In his recent review of the neurobiology of OCD, Stein (1996) submits that

> although OCD may be a disorder of the brain, a comprehensive understanding of the condition also requires attention to brain-based emergent cognitive-affective structures and processes. It seems clear that effective intervention can take place at the level of such structures and processes and that this intervention, in turn, results in changes in the brain. Thus, in both the clinic and the laboratory, OCD must be considered both in terms of the brain and the mind. In this way, it provides an outstanding exemplar of complex neuropsychiatric disorders.

This frames the issue beautifully, and undermines the separability of the realms of structure and function. We can understand neither OCD nor Tourette's with an exclusive focus on either the neurological or the psychiatric/psychological realm. Moreover, these two domains act on one another. We must therefore also allow into our neurophysiological models the possibility of interaction with higher functions, which are more parsimoniously treated in terms of the familiar psychological categories. Another implication is that we must be permitted to talk about "mind" without being accused of a mentalist perspective or a throwback to dualism.

It is likely that Stein's statement of the problem got a push from the work of Lewis Baxter *et al.* (1992), who demonstrated that both cognitive-behavioral intervention and drug intervention with OCD led to a decrease (normalization) in glucose uptake in the caudate, as demonstrated with PET scans. As remarkable as the result itself was the stir that it caused in the popular scientific consciousness by having documented this nexus between the functional and the structural domains.

In any case, here is a demonstration that talk therapy can have the effect of normalizing neurophysiological functioning, which also proves that the normal range of functioning was already within the inventory of the brains involved. We now assert (and will hope to illustrate) that EEG biofeedback can similarly appeal directly to the feedback loops involved in these disorders through bioelectrical manifestations as seen in the EEG, with the effect that through them the neuromodulatory systems can be restored to more normal levels of function.

IV. THE KINDLING MODEL OF PSYCHOPATHOLOGY

Having argued in the preceding sections that the functional and structural models of brain activity are in some sense two sides of the same coin, and that we must be conversant with both kinds of models for a complete description, there are instances where one model must dominate our considerations. This is obviously the case for epilepsies resulting from trauma, and for genetically based disorders such as Huntington's chorea. However, the success of psychopharmacology has made physiology the primary consideration for mental disorders in considerable generality. Is there then a way one can obtain some insight into the relative roles of the psychodynamic causation and the physiological dimension of mental disorders? Perhaps the most relevant case for a primary and distinct role for a disordered physiology (vis-à-vis the psychodynamic perspective) can be made by looking at the time course of disorders in people's lives. For this we look to a generalization of the kindling model, which was originally applied to epilepsy, and subsequently to bipolar disorder (Bolwig, 1989; Post, *et al.,* 1986; Post & Weiss, 1989).

The kindling model suggests that there are practice effects, if you will, as the brain successively experiences dysfunctions. The brain can learn misbehavior as well as appropriate behavior. With respect to kindled epilepsy, the model predicts that precursor phenomena can often be identified in the epileptic child, and these manifest a progressive vulnerability of the brain to seizures. With respect to bipolar disorder, it is clear that the disorder never starts there, but rather that bipolar disorder is a kind of end stage of a more fundamental brain instability which has identifiable precursors perhaps going back to dysphoria in childhood (cf. Post & Weiss, 1989; Post et al., 1986). This is not to say that every case of dysphoria in childhood ends up in end-stage bipolar disorder in adulthood. However, there may be an equivalent here to Malthusian pessimism regarding populations, and Galbraithian pessimism regarding our economic institutions, which is the principle that if left to themselves, vulnerable brains will tend to get worse, not better.

The kindling model for bipolar disorder was first proposed by Post et al. (1986). It has been revisited by Goodwin and Jamison (1990) in their work, *Manic-Depressive Illness.* There the evidence is recounted that depressive cycles tend to get shorter over time, which suggests that the experience of a depressive event prepares the stage for its recurrence. However, matters are even worse than that, for if one looks at the recurrence interval for late-onset depressive episodes, one finds that interval to decline with age as well. This means that the nervous system that is vulnerable to depressive episodes has a tendency to get more unstable with age even without the experience of a major depressive event.

In addition to its role in the epilepsies and in bipolar disorder, the kindling model may play a role in unipolar depression, in Tourette's syndrome, in migraines, and in the anxiety disorders (Adamec, 1990; Wada, 1990). In Tourette's, for example, children never start out with very complex tics, nor do they start out with complicated compulsive behaviors. Such only emerge over the years or decades (Carter et al., 1994; Park et al., 1993). In the case of depression, a history of dysthymia may precede the first incident of a major depressive episode. And whereas the first episode of major depression is likely to have a traumatic antecedent in the majority of cases, that is true in only a third of the cases of a (first) recurrence. An unstable physiology becomes progressively unmoored from life events. A similar progressive trajectory can be traced for some anxiety disorders, ending possibly in full-blown panic disorder.

If we regard this phenomenology from the standpoint of the brain as a servosystem, one would say that the brain in these instances has simply become ever more unstable. In most of these brains, a more or less normal level of function does lie within the inventory of accessible states. Even the most intractable cases of bipolar disorder often experience extended periods of their lives in which they are in neither a manic or a depressive state (though one might hesitate to call that state normal) (Pardoen *et al.*, 1996; Stefos *et al.*, 1996). Even the medically intractable epileptic usually spends most of his time not in seizure. The person susceptible to panic disorder is not usually in panic, and suicidality in the depressive is usually an episodic phenomenon, not a steady-state condition.

Thus, the distinction between the psychodynamic and the physiological realm comes into clearest relief when this is a function of time within a single individual, thus avoiding the additional complexities of between-subject comparisons. The kindling model also enhances the case for a physiologically based intervention. In all of these instances of kindling, a disregulated physiology is progressively the issue to be addressed therapeutically, quite irrespective of any psychodynamic causation. In attempting to fill this role, however, psychopharmacology has shown itself to be less effective in dealing with severe instability conditions than with those conditions (generalized anxiety or dysthymia, for example) that are much more stable over time. Medical management of the severe instabilities (epilepsies, migraines, rapid cycling bipolar disorder) generally entails some compromise to the general functioning of the nervous system. A more suitable approach would be one that addresses the instability itself and that is not limited to one neuromodulator system. Such a technique is EEG biofeedback. By rewarding the brain for maintaining a particular state over a period of time, the technique seems to enhance the internal stability of the nervous system against inappropriate excursions. Significantly, the training that enhances stability in the brain also augments behavioral flexibility. This can only be the case if the training impinges on the regulatory mechanisms themselves, as opposed to promoting a particular state. That is, only if network stability is assured can the brain take advantage in terms of extending its envelope of function.

The preceding discussion has been with respect to the more common instabilities in the realm of mental disorders. However, the model is deemed to apply to other conditions as well, such as to reactive psychosis, schizophrenia, post-traumatic stress disorder (PTSD), and dissociative disorders. Each of these is characterized by sudden discontinuities and shifts in mental state, so that an instability model can be applied. The case can be made that both PTSD and dissociative identity disorder (DID) manifest in vulnerable brains and are progressive in their clinical development. Recently, it has been proposed that schizophrenia is also progressive in character. According to Judith Rapoport, ". . . adolescents who received a diagnosis of schizophrenia as children display a progressive loss of brain tissue and quirks in physiological activity that resemble patterns seen in later-onset schizophrenia. . . . It seems most economical to assume that a single, continuous process [of brain changes] exists from fetal through adult life" (Rapoport *et al.*, 1997).

Despite the reference to loss of brain tissue in this quotation, it is likely that much of the pathology of schizophrenia is more functional than structural in nature (Chua & McKenna, 1995). Even drugs cannot work on brain tissue that has been "lost." There is some clinical evidence that EEG training can be helpful in restoring function to the schizophrenic, and this also argues for a functional deficit model. However that may be, there is now clear evidence that EEG biofeedback can also be helpful in cases of manifest organic injury or organically based disorder, such as stroke, cerebral palsy, autism, multiple sclerosis, major traumatic brain injury, and progressive dementia in the aging. One must suppose that even if there are true structural injuries (hardware problems) in these conditions, the effect of these may spread to healthy brain tissue, affecting its function as well, and that this is recoverable with training. Efficacy for focal epilepsy may be regarded in the same manner. The training does not expunge any structurally based seizure focus. Rather, it enhances general cortical stability so that any inappropriate activity at the focus does not recruit larger regions. In conclusion, the presence of organic injury does not preclude efficacy of EEG training.

In the above, the case has been made for a progression throughout life of psychopathology from more psychogenic or psychosomatic origins to more intractable physiologically driven, or somatopsychic, phenomenology. This is probably a general truth, beyond the conditions mentioned, and is suggestive of a learning model for psychopathology in which the vulnerability is increasingly encoded physiologically. The fact that significant recovery of function is possible anywhere along the time line with EEG biofeedback suggests further that the pathology is encoded largely in the domain of functional patterns of neuromodulation, and is not necessarily to be looked for in neuronal attrition or other gross organic malfunction.

V. THE DISREGULATION MODEL
OF PSYCHOPATHOLOGY

The kindling model of functional disorders lays the basis for the formulation of a model of psychopathology in terms of the dysfunction of the brain's neuromodulatory machinery. In this model, the very essence of the problem is disregulation, a malfunction of the brain in its essential regulatory capacities. This is easy to demonstrate for the "intractable" end stage of the disorders already mentioned, but is also true to a lesser degree in the earlier stages, which may be at the root of the developing pathology.

This model implies certain characteristics about mental disorders that can be verified. Also, one can make certain predictions from this model, which can serve to test it. The primary and central distinguishing feature of the model is that the disregulation is likely to be associated with certain central regulatory functions, and therefore is not restricted to specific clinical categories. *The central prediction is that if disregulation is the problem, then a modality to achieve re-regulation must constitute a remedy.* Hence, to the extent that the disregulation model is valid—and to the extent that rhythmicity is involved in neuroregulation—EEG biofeedback training or a similar intervention must in principle be effective in remediation. Such efficacy must address the specific regulatory systems involved, and therefore again cut across clinical diagnostic categories.

It may seem that this model is at its core in conflict with the mainstream view as embodied in the DSM-IV. This is not entirely the case. There is no claim that the DSM-IV is driven by neurophysiological models. Clearly it is a phenomenological construct, and certainly it has managed to achieve a reasonable internal consistency. It is not so much a mistaken view as it is unhelpful when we are looking for underlying neurophysiological drivers. A different intervention such as EEG biofeedback, operating on different principles, may simply need a different organization of the same material. The practical difficulty has been that adherence to the rigid classifications of the DSM-IV can interfere with openness to other formulations.

In fact, there has been mainstream support already for a disregulation model of certain disorders. We cite evidence for both ADHD and for depression. With regard to ADHD, it is ironic that as one of the persons most responsible for focusing on attention as the fundamental issue in ADHD (as opposed to hyperkinesis), the Canadian psychologist Virginia Douglas now speaks in terms of a disregulation model. This model is reviewed in Pennington (*Diagnosing Learning Disorders*): ". . . ADHD children have a generalized self-regulatory deficit that affects organization of information processing, the mobilization of attention throughout information processing, and the inhibition of inappropriate responding, and . . . this self-regulatory deficit is present across visual, auditory, and perceptual motor modalities" (Pennington, 1991; Douglas, 1988).

In Douglas's formulation, organization of information processing encompasses planning, executive function, metacognition, optimum set maintenance, regulation of arousal and alertness, and self-monitoring. This framing of the issue is remarkable for its breadth of coverage, and for the key role assigned to "self-regulatory deficit." However, this is still just a perspective on ADHD limited to the concerns of a cognitive psychologist. It is not nearly inclusive enough for all of the phenomenology encompassed by ADHD. For example, it ignores the affective dimension of behavior, which clearly plays an important role.

Rothschild (1988) makes the case for the disregulation model of depressive disorders:

> While there is sufficient evidence to support the notion that abnormalities in monoamine systems are an important component of depression, the data currently available do not provide consistent evidence either for altered neurotransmitter function or for disruption of normal receptor activity.

This has led to a dysregulation hypothesis, which states that there is a more general perturbation in the mechanisms that regulate the activity of the monoamine neurotransmitters and that the clinically effective drugs restore efficient regulation.

More recently, Harro and Oreland (1996) have taken this further, seeing depression as a spreading neuronal adjustment disorder with a brain stem origin, which only secondarily leads to the serotonergic disregulation presumptively addressed by the selective serotonin reuptake inhibitors (SSRIs).

Both of these perspectives (Douglas's and Rothschild's) would appear to provide room for a modality that addresses itself to the re-regulation of attentional and arousal functions, and normalization in the affective domain. Such a modality would be likely to address the whole spectrum of attentional and depressive disorders, respectively. It is helpful to observe, in that regard, that numerous researchers are projecting a return to the spectrum theory of mental disorders, which will require a reclassification of disorders, presumably along lines more driven by neurophysiological function. This thrust is very congenital to the emerging perspective.

VI. RETURN TO THE SPECTRUM THEORY OF MENTAL DISORDERS

Joseph Biederman has made a careful study of ADHD and its comorbidities (Biederman *et al.*, 1991, 1996). Taking only the most important ones (conduct disorder, anxiety, and depression), fewer than 50% of ADHD cases are found to be uncomplicated by these conditions. Oppositional-defiant disorder is found to have a 60% overlap with ADD. If one also considers the tic disorders, as well as mania and bipolar disorder, sleep disorders, chronic head and stomach pain syndromes, immune function disorders, elimination disorders (enuresis and encopresis), disregulation in blood glucose level, and specific learning disabilities, then only a small percentage of ADHD subjects will fall into the bin of pure ADHD. If one further admits into consideration all of the above issues where they are qualitatively and significantly present, but do not necessarily meet clinical diagnostic criteria, then the pure ADHD subject represents a small subset of all ADHD children.

It takes only a small shift in perspective to regard many of the comorbidities as helping to define the condition of ADHD and as being part and parcel of it. ADHD is then a composite disorder, in which symptoms are highly variable among individuals, depending on their genetic endowment and the insults their nervous system has suffered. Very little homogeneity would be expected. Weinberg has taken this perspective, and suggested that ADHD is intrinsically a composite disorder, with contributions from an anxiety dimension, from a primary disorder of vigilance, and from learning disabilities (Weinberg & Harper, 1993; Weinberg & Brumback, 1992). Weinberg's position was not generally accepted, but it has appeal, and may simply have been before its time. Perhaps all that will survive of the model is the concept of ADHD as a composite or spectrum disorder.

Goodwin and Jamison (1990) make the case for a spectrum theory of depressive illness: "The debate about whether depressive disorders should be divided into categories or arrayed along a continuum has gone on for decades, without resolution. In our view, there is more evidence consistent with the spectrum concept than there is with the idea that depressive disorders constitute discrete clusters marked by relatively discontinuous boundaries" (p. 75).

Comings (1990) makes the case for Tourette's syndrome (TS) as a spectrum disorder. Although his interest has been in teasing out the genetics of TS, his extensive clinical engagement has allowed him to uncover numerous comorbidities in TS with good statistics. Some key comorbidities and their prevalence in TS, if known, are the following:

OCD	68%
Coprolalia	58%
Sleep disorders	48%
Self-destructive behaviors	48%
Learning disorders	40%
Panic attacks	33%
Schizoid behaviors	33%
Speech problems	32%
Hypersexuality	32%
Phobias	30%
Migraines	27%
Enuresis, encopresis	20%

These symptoms are of startling variety, and appear to have little in common. What does it mean if many, if not most, of these conditions are responsive to one or two medications, or to one or two protocols of EEG biofeedback training, in a person with Tourette's syndrome?

Peter Kramer (1993) also contributes to the debate in his popular book, *Listening to Prozac:*

> Within a couple of years of its introduction, Prozac was shown to be useful in depression, OCD, panic anxiety, eating disorders, PMS, substance abuse, ADD, etc. . . . What does it mean when the same medication can treat depression and anxiety? . . . drug response can emphasize commonality, and the futility of attempts at mechanistic categorization.
>
> A virtue of the functional theory of illness and cure is that it explains an apparent paradox of Prozac, a medication that is at once specific in its biochemical action and useful in a variety of disorders. The functional theory predicts precisely this relationship: "The greater the biochemical specificity of the drug, the greater is the chance that it will be nosologically (i.e., diagnostically) nonspecific."

Medications, it is increasingly understood, alter neurochemical systems. They do not treat specific illnesses. (pp. 45–46).

This discussion prepares the ground well for the claims of EEG biofeedback. EEG biofeedback addresses regulatory function directly, through its manifestation in the EEG, and as such is expected to be diagnostically nonspecific. Biofeedback alters bioelectrical networks. It does not treat specific disorders.

Over the years, anticonvulsant medications have broadened in application to include not only seizure disorders but end-stage bipolar disorder, mania, schizophrenia, and even conduct disorder, some autism, some cerebral palsy, and some types of ADHD (e.g., Sporn & Sachs, 1997; Kanba *et al.,* 1994; Suffin & Emory, 1995). This breadth of coverage, over conditions that have been viewed as having no clinical kinship, argues for a different conceptualization of these disorders as being fundamentally characterized by instabilities and discontinuities in mental functioning. Just as with Prozac, the anticonvulsants are lumpers, not splitters, of diagnostic categories. A neurological model for this will similarly tend toward a lumped perspective. Suffin and Emory showed that certain neurometric subgroups could be identified which correlated with medication response, but cut across the diagnostic categories of affective and attentional disorders. Thus, one neurometric subgroup responds to stimulants, irrespective of whether they were diagnosed with depression or ADD; another subgroup responds to antidepressants; and a third to anticonvulsants. Just as with the antidepressants and anticonvulsants, EEG biofeedback is deemed to address brain-based instabilities and discontinuities generally and not address itself to any specific disorder.

In summary, an easy unification between the prevailing models of mental disorders and the proposed spectrum model can be achieved by simply reframing the current emphasis on specific disorders and their comorbidities in terms of more inclusive spectrum disorders. The spectrum concept, then, focuses attention on teasing out a hopefully modest set of principal or characteristic failure modes of neurophysiological systems which underpin these various spectrum disorders. An analogy can be drawn here with the plate tectonics theory of continental drift. The diversity of geology over all the continents does not gainsay the existence of a single mechanism governing the process of crustal formation and continental drift over the globe.

Similarly, the great variety of clinical manifestations of disorders does not invalidate the expectation of a smaller set of causal chains of failure in the neurological domain. The spectrum concept is compatible with the disregulation model, and both jointly support the case for a general efficacy of EEG biofeedback in neuroregulation of central nervous system functions. Since the recent revival of the spectrum concept arose out of observations relating to pharmacology, it is clearly compatible with pharmacology as well. Just as Prozac may be seen as an intervention for any serotonin-mediated processes (as opposed to being labeled an antidepressant), EEG biofeedback may be seen as impinging on all those neuroregulatory mechanisms that have their key frequencies within the operative training bands.

VII. A BIOELECTRICAL MODEL OF NEUROREGULATION: BASIS FOR THE FUNCTIONAL THEORY

The cerebrum has perhaps 30 billion neurons, each with hundreds to as many as 100,000 synaptic connections per neuron. Moreover, each of the resulting 10^{13} synaptic connections does not play a unique, dedicated role as does a memory location in a computer, but plays many different roles in different contexts. The potential for signal overload exists, and an enormous organizational challenge confronts the brain. An apparent bias for excitation in the circuitry must also be matched by resources of an inhibitory character.

The most obvious manifestations of a compensatory inhibition bias are as follows: (1) The inhibitory postsynaptic potential excursions (IPSPs) typically last some 10 times as long as the excitatory ones (EPSPs), and (2) the vast majority of synaptic connections are inhibitory in character. Additionally, the brevity of the EPSP defines the narrow window over which the signal can be efficacious, and in this sense the neuron can be regarded as a kind of coincidence detector with a very narrow time window (on the order of 20 msec). This temporal selectivity also serves to protect the network from signal overload. There remains the problem of how the brain organizes the signal streams into meaningful entities. This challenge is greatest when the brain does parallel processing, as it must in the management of visual imagery, for example.

When a monkey is given a brief visual discrimination task, followed immediately by a bright blanking pulse that obscures the image, it is found that the monkey can perform well as long as the presentation time is 40 msec before the blanking pulse is applied. The performance decays toward chance levels with a presentation time of 15–25 msec. In this image recognition process, all the necessary information for subsequent higher level processing must therefore already be available with a mere 40-msec presentation (Adkins *et al.*, 1969). Given the finite firing rate, the burden of visual discrimination must therefore be managed largely by parallel processing networks.

A key organizing principle appears to be that coincidence in the time domain defines units of cortical activity that belong together. As Wolf Singer puts it colloquially, "what fires together wires together." The wiring together here may refer to a transient, functional connection or integration, as well as to a permanent hard-wired connection. The principle of integration by means of time is called *time binding,* and the potential significance of this mechanism is perhaps just beginning to be appreciated. Christoph von der Malsburg (1995) suggests that "We are in the middle of a scientific revolution, the result of which will be the establishment of binding as a fundamental aspect of the neural code." Scientists do not use the words scientific revolution lightly. From our perspective, time binding may not only be the key to the neural code, but also provide the theoretical underpinnings for EEG biofeedback.

According to von der Malsburg (1995), time binding may subserve such functions as figure-ground separation, storage and retrieval, generalization of patterns, rapid (e.g., single-shot) learning, scene representation, logical reasoning, language processing, and ultimately even consciousness. ". . . Even if only a tiny fraction of all bindings in the nervous system are handled by temporal signal synchrony, it may still play a central role in brain function, forming the basis for its tremendous flexibility that is one of its most puzzling aspects" (p. 523). In other words, time binding may constitute an ubiquitous, central organizing principle for the transmittal of information within the central nervous system (CNS). The same mechanism could possibly hold for the maintenance of states as well.

According to Peter Koenig and Andreas Engel (1995), ". . . synchronous firing is not restricted to the visual system, but may be the ubiquitous property of cortical networks" (p. 514). Many examples exist of a kind of parsimony of mechanisms in nature, and it may be that synchrony in fact subserves many more functions than are easily demonstrable on first encounter. Whereas the preceding discussion has focused on the higher frequency domain, where specific cognitive function must be organized, there may be an extension to the lower frequencies for those functions that have greater persistence (a longer time constant). These include the sleep–wake cycle, pvigilance, and the general tone of the nervous system with respect to attentional functions, the emotions, etc. These functions have both a global, whole-brain, aspect (which probably goes together with long time constants of change), as well as implications for specific brain regions that may be more transient in their effect. The burden of orchestration and organization is similar to that for sensory processing, and could well be served by the same mechanisms of rhythmic organization, operating at lower octaves. Whether the term *time binding* will be applied to this mechanism, or reserved for its higher frequency role, is not yet clear. In the following, the term *time binding* will be used for all frequency domains.

It is also enticing to speculate that the low-frequency rhythmic activity may serve as a kind of metronome for the high-frequency bursts that organize "units" of cognitive processing. It is known, for example, that distant pyramidal cells can fire within 3 msec of one another. Perhaps this is somewhat like the wind over a field of grain, where the wind initiates certain characteristic wave patterns over the field. The wave pattern is dominated by the characteristics of the grain. It was not to be found in the wind, but rather is in turn impressed on the wind. The individual grains are "loosely coupled" to each other, and entrain each other. The result is a considerable long-range order in the waves over the field, and the rhythmic swaying of one head of grain is correlated with that of grains many near-neighbor distances away. One can imagine that if an explicit coupling between grains were to be introduced, the degree of long-range order could be increased arbitrarily. Tight temporal coincidence over large regions is not beyond the reach of such networks. Even if such a "central" mechanism is operative, however, we might not find very clear evidence for it in such a gross measure as the EEG. After all, the brain must process many things contemporaneously, each of them requiring maintenance of its own internal coherence.

Time binding may provide the key to understanding the mystery that so many severe mental disorders have apparently little morphological or histological evidence to support them. This has been a particular problem with traumatic brain injury (TBI), where tests of morphology such as CAT scans and conventional MRI scans may show nothing, yet the victim may complain of the standard litany of TBI symptoms. Antonio Damasio (1994) has suggested that "Any malfunction of the timing mechanism would be likely to create spurious integration and disintegration. This may indeed be what happens in states of confusion caused by head injury, or in some symptoms of schizophrenia and other diseases" (p. 95). In this conjecture, the structural or functional deficit in the head injury need merely be sufficient to disrupt the mechanisms by which timing is organized. It need not account for all the observed deficits in their painfully enumerated detail. By the same token, a technique like EEG biofeedback then is merely required to restore the timing mechanisms by operant conditioning, and it is not necessary to address explicitly all the specific deficits. This global reach of EEG biofeedback has up to now been difficult to understand and to embrace.

Results of an experiment were recently published that provide evidence for some of the above propositions, and shed light on brain stem activation mechanisms as well (Munk et al., 1996). Neural spike trains were monitored in both the left and right hemispheres of the visual cortex of a cat, while a colored square was moved across the visual field. The correlations in firing events between the hemispheres was observed. In one experimental condition, an electrical stimulus was given to the mesencephalic reticular formation (MRF), thus alerting the cat to the importance of the information. The response was to increase the temporal coherence of firing events across the hemispheric fissure, among those neurons which were "illuminated" by the square. That is, the alerting signal produced an increased local binding of the neuronal populations, even between the hemispheres. No difference in the absolute firing rate was observed when the stimulus was applied versus the stimulus-neutral condition. In earlier work, the absence of an obvious influence on the firing rate made for an ambiguity in the role of attentional mechanisms. Now the answer appears to have been found in the relative timing (coincidence) of individual constituents of the pulse train.

In a further experiment, the colored square was divided in two, and the two were sent across the visual field in opposite directions. With the electrical stimulation, the neuronal ensembles organized themselves again into subpopulations by time, with the coherence extending across the hemispheric fissure, but restricted each to its own square. This implies the existence of a local mechanism to organize the timing, in addition to the governing subcortical mechanism. It is presumed that the subcortical process establishes the basic rhythm (the conductor or metronome model), and the local cortical influences determine the spatial extent over which coherent firing prevails.

The experiment was revealing in another sense. When the power spectral density of the EEG was plotted over a range of frequencies extending from 0 to 100 Hz for both experimental conditions, it was found that the electrical stimulation led to a decrease in spectral power at frequencies below about 32 Hz, and an increase in the range of 32–50 Hz. (A further suppression was noted around 60 Hz, but that was not consistently observed.) A congenital interpretation of these results is that the frequency range below 30 Hz is involved in the governance of activation and arousal. The decline in power here reflects partial desynchronization of the EEG when an activating pulse is delivered to the MRF, which is in accord with expectations. The increase in spectral power around 40 Hz is likely to be related to the time binding of a specific cognitive event, in this case the organization of figure/ground differentiation of the colored square.

In this elegant and straightforward experiment, we can find considerable support for the emerging model of EEG biofeedback. First of all, it must be apparent that the key to the management of arousal and attention lies in the timing and electrical realm, which is not readily accessible to interpretation strictly in terms of the biochemistry of neuromodulator function. Whereas neurochemistry can help to explain how the nervous system "tone" is set at any given time, a crucial role is also played by timing, and the organization thereof, in the process of neuromodulation. This is really an argument for economy in model building: Ultimately, the timing relationships are of course also mediated by neuromodulator chemistry. But the description is cumbersome. The point is that the hierarchy of control places timing relationships near the top, and these in turn impress their own demands on the neurochemistry. A second key observation from this experiment is that different levels of activation are reflected in alterations in synchrony at the lower frequencies (<30 Hz). Third, operant conditioning in this frequency regime could potentially have effects similar to that of the electrical stimulation pulse, namely, to engage the mechanisms by which activation is managed.

Once the key role of rhythmic mechanisms has been established in neuromodulation, possible failure modes suggest themselves. Given the central role of the functions of activation and arousal, failures in the proper governance of rhythmicity can in principle lead to significant dysfunction. It is in this light that photic epilepsy may be understood. A periodic optical signal can lead to slight changes in periodicity over the cortex, which may be sufficient to lead to oscillatory behavior and seizures in vulnerable brains. The phenomenon of photic epilepsy can be taken as an indicator of how sensitive the brain is to the state of its own rhythmicity. By extension, disturbances at lower levels in the regulation of rhythmicity can lead to other types of dysfunction.

It is also likely that rhythmic activity is the key to understanding working memory. Repetitive oscillations may serve the purpose of refreshing information and allowing us to "hold a thought" until we are finished processing the material. Many of the shortcomings in cognitive functions such as short-term memory could be traceable to an inability to maintain the integrity of this rhythmic activity for a sufficient length of time. It may be helpful to generalize the concept of working memory to other functions in which the brain must maintain continuity, but where conscious awareness is not involved. Thus one can speak about maintenance of states in general, including here not only the general state of arousal of the organism but also microstates in various parts of the brain (Stevens *et al.,* 1997; MacCormac, 1996; Wright & Liley, 1996). Much of psychopathology can be traced to more or less obvious discontinuities in mental function. This is most apparent in multiple personality disorder and schizophrenia, but could likely be discerned in a wide variety of conditions if it is explicitly tested for.

The nexus between the bioelectrical world of information and the chemical encoding of information is most readily seen in the transition between short-term and long-term memory (Izquierdo & Medina, 1997). This transition takes from minutes to hours, and therefore requires the integrity of the bioelectrical "storage" of the information to be maintained over some considerable period of time. Rhythmic activity may well be required to "refresh" this information until it is more permanently encoded, and rhythmic activity may be required to reaccess the information as well. The quality of memory function may conceivably be one of the most sensitive tests of the integrity of the rhythmic generator mechanisms. Conversely, the catastrophic disruption of memory mechanisms even in people who have suffered apparently minor brain injuries can be rendered understandable. On the basis of this treatment, it becomes reasonable to suggest that remedies addressed specifically to management of rhythmic activity in the brain could in principle result in substantial remediation of even severe deficits, including memory loss. The mechanism of generation of brain rhythms remains to be discussed.

VIII. THE THALAMUS: GENERATOR OF BRAIN RHYTHMS

All sensory information comes to cortex via the thalamus, with the exception of smell and some pain pathways. The thalamus is the central gating mechanism by which the brain modulates its own sensitivity to the incoming information. A circuit has been identified that can initiate rhythmic activity through its mutual interaction, or operate in a desynchronized manner, depending on both sensory inputs and inputs from the brain stem reticular formation. The very first EEG rhythm identified by Hans Berger in the late 1920s and early 1930s was the alpha rhythm, in the range of 8–13 Hz, which predominates in visual cortex, particularly in the eyes-closed condition. It can be thought of as the idle rhythm of the visual system. It was subsequently demonstrated to be thalamically generated (Anderson & Anderssen, 1968).

A similar mechanism was identified by M. Barry Sterman in his work during the 1960s with cats using operant conditioning of the EEG (Wyrwicka & Sterman, 1968; Sterman et al., 1972). In the work, which ultimately led to the emergence of this discipline of EEG training, Sterman observed that the motorically idle cat often exhibited rhythmic bursts at sensorimotor cortex (Roth et al., 1967; Sterman et al., 1969). Because of spatial localization, it was referred to as the *sensorimotor rhythm*. The center frequency of this rhythm was in the range of 12–15 Hz. This could be considered the idle rhythm of the sensorimotor cortex by analogy to the alpha rhythm for the visual system (Chase & Harper, 1971). Both rhythms manifest the apparent paradox of the EEG, namely, that large-amplitude rhythmicity is concomitant with idleness, low amplitude with activation. In subsequent experiments, Sterman (1977) trained the EEG explicitly to increase the incidence of rhythmic bursting, and found it to be easier to train behavior by this route than training behavior directly.

A representative sample of EEG is shown in Fig. 11.1 (Howe & Sterman, 1972) from the sensorimotor cortex of the cat. The first trace shows the raw signal in a broad bandpass extending from nominally 0.5 to 30 Hz. The second trace shows the same signal when passed through a narrowband filter centered on 13 Hz and having a nominal 2-Hz bandwidth. It is observed that the filtered signal is much easier to discriminate from the ambient background. The third trace is a relay output from a burst detection circuit, which signal is used as feedback to the cat through a feeder mechanism. The fourth trace shows a concurrent change in firing pattern at a corresponding neuron in the ventralis-postero-lateralis (VPL) nucleus of the thalamus,

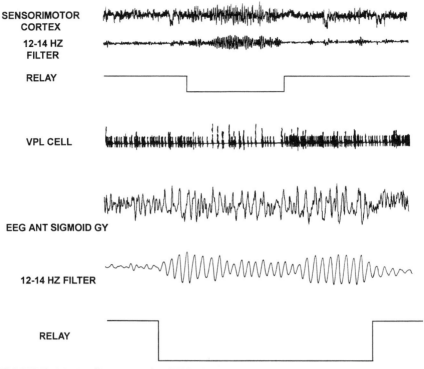

FIGURE 11.1   Representative EEG signals from the sensorimotor cortex of the cat, with simultaneous recording from the VPL nucleus of thalamus. See text for description.

through which proprioception and other body sensations are passed to cortex. The fifth trace shows the raw EEG signal on a more expanded timescale, followed in trace 6 by the narrowband filtered version. The correlation of cortical and VPL signals supports the model of their mutual interaction.

As a totally unexpected, serendipitous fallout from this work, it was found that those cats which had been trained to produce more rhythmic activity also exhibited higher thresholds to the onset of chemically induced seizures (Sterman *et al.,* 1969, 1977; Sterman, 1976, 1977). This striking finding was later replicated with primates (Wyler, 1977; Sterman *et al.,* 1978) and with human subjects (Sterman & Friar, 1972; Sterman *et al.,* 1974; Sterman & MacDonald, 1978; Sterman & Shouse, 1982). This initial epoch-making research was followed by a number of confirming studies in other centers (Seifert & Lubar, 1975; Finley *et al.,* 1975; Lubar *et al.,* 1981; Kaplan, 1975; Ellertson & Klove, 1976; Kuhlman & Allison, 1977; Tozzo *et al.,* 1988). And it was later followed up by a fully controlled, blinded study of EEG biofeedback with complex partial seizures (Lantz & Sterman,

1988). Unfortunately, this transpired at a time when the neurosciences were moving from the realm of behavior to studying subcellular mechanisms, and this work was not generally recognized for its significance.

In this extension to human subjects, it had to be recognized that the human waking EEG did not exhibit the striking rhythmic bursts that could so easily be discerned in the cat. In humans, such obvious rhythms are observable only during Stage II sleep, when activating input from the reticular formation is withdrawn from thalamus (and when it is fruitless to do EEG biofeedback) (Sterman and Shouse, 1980). In the waking EEG, the sensorimotor rhythm shows a lower amplitude. Nevertheless, the work with human subjects was successful. To understand this, it is assumed that the training merely challenges the brain in terms of the degree of rhythmicity. This still exercises all the relevant mechanisms by which rhythmicity is managed (the regulatory challenge model).

The relevant thalamocortical circuit has been subjected to extensive study over the years (cf. Steriade & Deschenes, 1984; for a review, see Sterman, 1976). The transmission of sensory information to the cortex involves three-neuron networks, the second stage of which is the thalamo-cortical junction, the source of the thalamically generated rhythm. The regulatory network involves the thalamus, the cortex, and the reticular nucleus of the thalamus (which encases most of the thalamus like an egg-shell) through which nearly all of the sensory pathways must pass to reach the cortex. The principal elements of the circuit are shown schematically in Fig. 11.2. Thalamic cells project to cortex and also send collaterals to the reticular nucleus. Cortical cells project back to the thalamus and also send collaterals to the reticular nucleus. The reticular neurons, on the other hand, only project back to thalamus.

The circuit is more completely laid out in Fig. 11.3. It is best analyzed in the extremes of its range of function. In the aroused and waking state (shown as W in Fig. 11.3), the thalamic relay cell is provided with sensory input from prethalamic afferents (perhaps originating in the dorsal spinal column nuclei) accompanied by neuromodulatory input from acetylcholine (Ach) modulated terminals, as well as from norepinephrine (NE), histamine (HA), and serotonin (5-HT) modulated terminals, which have not been shown. These inputs maintain the network in a tonic firing mode, which relays the incoming signal to cortex. In this figure, the circuit has been driven into this tonic firing mode by supplying the relay cell with an applied current until a certain degree of cell depolarization is reached.

If input is now withdrawn from the relay cell, it does not go entirely quiet but rather enters a bursting mode with a fundamental frequency in the delta range of 0.5–4 Hz. The cell is capable of sustaining that mode of oscillation on its own. As the cell moves toward hyperpolarization, a voltage-dependent discharge current is activated that moves the cell back toward depolarization, until a burst firing occurs that restarts the cycle

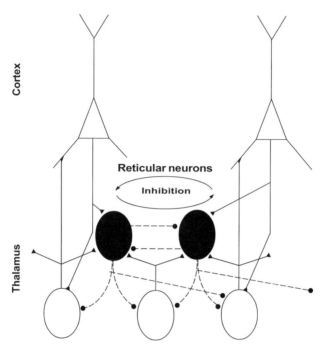

FIGURE 11.2   Simplified schematic diagram of the basic thalamocortical regulatory circuit. See text for details. (Reprinted with permission from Steriade, M., McCormick, D. A., & Sejnowski, T. J. (1993). Thalamocortical oscillations in the sleeping and aroused brain. *Science* **262,** 679–685. Copyright 1993 American Association for the Advancement of Science.)

toward hyperpolarization. The circuit shown in fact abets this process. The burst firing of the relay cell causes the reticular cell to fire as well. Projections from the reticular cell terminate exclusively back on the relay cells. Thus, the reticular cell returns fire to the relay cell by means of an inhibitory GABA projection, which drives the relay cell actively toward hyperpolarization, causing the cycle to start all over again. When the relay cell is embedded in this circuit, the cyclic operating frequency of the thalamic rhythm can vary widely, depending in detail on the various inputs. During deep sleep, one may see something closer to the free-running intrinsic delta rhythm of the thalamic cell, as most modulatory and sensory signal inputs are withdrawn. As incoming signals from the reticular formation begin to wake up the thalamus in the morning, the dominant frequencies become much higher, covering the range of theta, alpha, and beta bands. Thus, the circuit is able to express the full continuum of function between the slow-wave bursting mode of deep sleep and the tonic firing mode of a highly alert organism. Also, it is likely that the continuum in behavioral responsiveness, and the variability thereof, is traceable to a dynamic distribution in thresholds at which different thalamic cells move from the bursting domain to the signal processing mode.

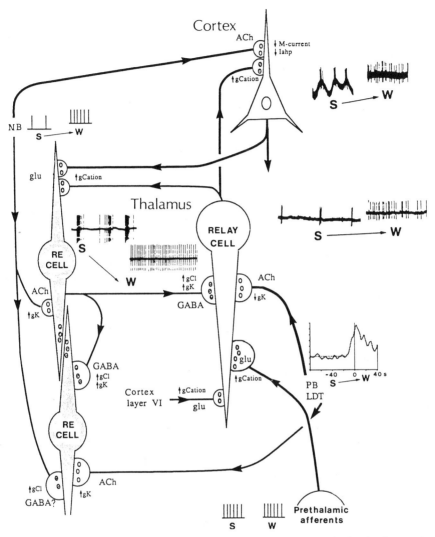

FIGURE 11.3   Detailed schematic of thalamocortical relay network, showing key modulatory inputs. See text for discussion.

In addition to this explicit thalamic generator of rhythmicity, there are probably numerous other mechanisms by which cortical rhythmicity can be kindled. Modeling has shown that suitably interconnected networks have a tendency to fall into rhythmic firing modes. Explaining the existence of rhythmic activity may therefore turn out to be less of a challenge than understanding how it is managed. The thalamocortical circuit may be the closest approximation in our brain to our mythical conductor, and one of its primary roles may be to orchestrate the degree of rhythmicity on a broad range of spatial scales over the cortex, as well as over a broad range of frequencies.

One obvious puzzle must be addressed. Why is it that an increase in activation is accompanied by a decrease in amplitude of the relevant low-frequency rhythms (2–30 Hz)? It is assumed that at low amplitudes the rhythm imposes a modulation of the membrane potential that is much less than the firing threshold in magnitude. It then simply affects the probability modestly of whether threshold criterion is met for a particular distribution of EPSPs. At low modulation levels, the effect is likely to be linear (du Lac & Lisberger, 1995). At much higher amplitudes, the modulation of membrane potential could be such that the modulating signal comes to dominate the output. The modulation becomes the signal! However, the modulation waveform is not itself the bearer of relevant information. By completely dominating the firing patterns, rhythmicity in fact diminishes the utility of the neuron as a linearly responsive information transfer medium. Thus, as the amplitude of the driving rhythm increases, the neuronal output becomes increasingly predictable, and predictability reduces the information content. The state of high-amplitude rhythmicity seems to be in some sense a readiness state, rather than a processing state.

In what sense might this state represent readiness? First of all, it must be noted that the relay cells, even in their burst mode, are still responsive to inputs. (We can still hear, even when we are in deep sleep.) But the response is highly nonlinear, as the cell network is driven between hyperpolarization and depolarization. This makes the circuit sensitive to sudden changes and therefore suitable for the detection of novelty, as opposed to signal processing, which is more representational of the inputs. Perhaps another way in which the bursting circuit represents readiness, therefore, lies in the very essential role of maintaining timing relationships, or coherence, across the network. As information must be processed, the transition from high-amplitude bursting to low, or an increase in bursting frequency, can perhaps be accomplished with maintenance of temporal coherence across the network (see Sherman & Guillery, 1996, and references therein; Munglani & Jones, 1992). Thus the entire range of circuit operation, from phasic bursting mode to tonic signal processing mode, may be behaviorally relevant and in need of management.

The case can be made that the frequency of the oscillation is correlated with the timescale of the phenomenon subserved by the particular rhythm. In this view, the lower frequencies manage those states which are maintained over longer periods of time, and the higher frequencies organize transient phenomena (Spitzer & Sejnowski, 1997). What then is the role of rhythmicity when tonic organismic activation is punctuated by sudden phasic arousal? To this topic we now turn our attention.

IX. THE ROLE OF RHYTHMICITY IN
TRANSIENT PHENOMENA

It has been of interest during the last few years to determine the EEG concomitants of various levels of task engagement. In this endeavor the EEG has been particularly useful, since it is essentially the only "imaging" technique which affords the time resolution necessary to dissect the cognitive processes of task recognition, decision making, and responding. The various components of the evoked potential have been studied for decades, and the entirety of the evoked response occurs in a time frame smaller than the time resolution of such imaging techniques as PET or even functional MRI. By looking at elicited responses in the frequency domain, it is now possible to extract additional information relative to cortical–cortical communication pathways, with a view toward understanding their role in coordinating distributed cortical activity.

Results have been reported by Sterman *et al.* (1996) for the frequency-domain analysis of event-related EEG changes associated with a continuous performance challenge of high-functioning adults. Results are shown in Fig. 11.4 for one individual undergoing a challenge of responding to certain letters and ignoring others. The challenge was presented every 2 sec. The response time in milliseconds is indicated at the bottom. A zero response time indicates that a nonresponse was appropriate. The most prominent feature of the EEG is a parietal and occipital synchronization with a dominant frequency near 10 Hz. This has been referred to as postreinforcement synchronization (PRS). The interpretation is that after the successful completion of a challenge, the brain enters a kind of self-soothing, resting, or preparedness state. The presentation of another challenge leads to an immediate desynchronization of this rhythm, until the new challenge has been met. Figure 11.4 shows one event with slow reaction time and one with fast. The slow reaction time event is preceded by greater levels of synchronization and a delay in time to desynchronize. The latter can be used to discriminate good from poor performers. (Poor here is relative, because the entire test population consisted of highly selected individuals, namely Air Force pilots.) This dependence is illustrated in Fig. 11.5. In this figure, it is also apparent that good performers desynchronize their EEGs more completely, and recover to a higher level of synchronization more quickly.

We see in Fig. 11.4 that the features of good performance and bad performance are replicated in a given individual during good and bad epochs. It has recently been suggested that there may be some intrinsic limit to how low variability in response time can go, due to intrinsic brain mechanisms (Barinaga, 1996). There may be some supportive evidence for this proposition in Fig. 11.5. Poor reaction time performance is observed when the alpha spindle is progressing toward its highest amplitude just as

C:\PROCESS\sc11r1.raw

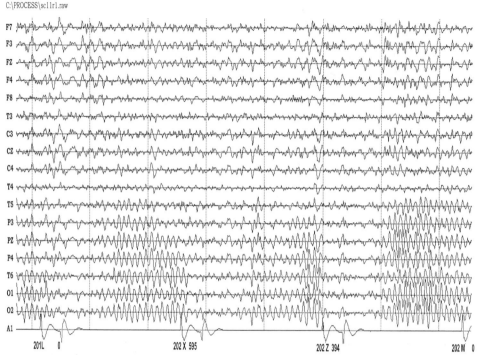

FIGURE 11.4 Standard EEG tracings under continuous performance test challenge. The challenge was to acknowledge certain letters with a motor response. Response time is shown at the bottom in milliseconds. The implications of parietal/occipital synchronization and desynchronization for performance are discussed in the text.

the challenge is presented. Good reaction time may correlate with those instances in which the alpha spindle is already being deconstructed. There may be an internal dynamic in the alpha spindle, by which it maintains itself and is resistant to disruption. Indeed, the original papers by Andersen and Sears (1964) on the alpha spindle already surfaced evidence that it is under active management. That is, precursor excitatory excursions of the local field potential are seen to build up gradually until spindle formation is elicited, and near the end of the spindle inhibitory excursions are seen to dominate, implying that the spindle was actively quenched. Thus, operant conditioning of EEG amplitudes may be seen as addressing itself to the mechanisms that govern the waxing and waning of that amplitude. The spindle amplitude and duration are not merely an incidental or artifactual reflection or concomitant of a certain physiological state, but rather appear to be the purposeful result of regulatory activity by which activation and arousal are managed. This appears to be true not only in the steady state, but in the management of transients as well.

It appears, then, that a measure is available in the EEG that correlates

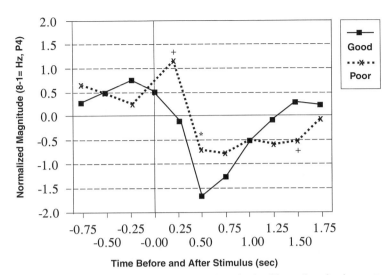

FIGURE 11.5   Differences in transient synchronization/desynchronization pattern between good and poor performers on a letter recognition continuous performance task (25%).

with performance both microscopically and on average. It is also closely related to the remediation at hand, since the rhythmic component of the EEG is our operant. In the following, results will be shown to prove that response time such as this can be successfully trained by operant conditioning of the degree of rhythmicity. Paradoxically, rhythmicity is typically trained to increase, yet reaction time decreases, and maintenance of vigilance improves. This is consistent with the view of EEG training as an exercise of brain regulatory mechanisms, rather than primarily a matter of moving the brain to a different state. The training may indeed move the brain to a different operational state in the moment, but that is believed to be largely incidental to the process.

The transient EEG behavior illustrated in Fig. 11.4 and 11.5 is referred to as event-related desynchronization (ERD), and has been studied extensively by Pfurtscheller (1977, 1992). In one such study (Rappelsberger *et al.*, 1994), the ERD was studied in connection with finger movements. The changes in synchronization accompanying finger movement are shown in Fig. 11.6. Cortical sites near where the left finger is represented on the homunculus at sensorimotor cortex (C4) are subject to the greatest degree of transient desynchronization. At the same time, the coherence between certain distant sites is found to increase. Thus, in particular, the sites C4 and F4 are more closely correlated in their activities, most likely because of the role of frontal sites in motor planning. Similarly, there is increased correlation between the contralateral sites of C3 and C4, probably because of the way movement is organized: The movement of a left finger also means directing the right finger not to move. In any event, frequency

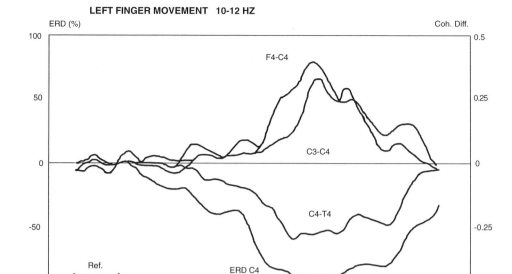

FIGURE 11.6 Synchronization/desynchronization in the EEG observed in the local and nonlocal environment upon execution of a finger movement. While transient desynchronization is observed locally at sensorimotor cortex, communication with certain other cortical regions is reflected in increased synchronization. (Reproduced from Rappelsberger *et al.,* 1994, with permission.).

dissection of the EEG in this manner gives direct evidence of changes in communication relationships between sites that are just beginning to be explored. These can then give guidance on training communication pathways directly with EEG biofeedback. Evidence has already emerged that training such pathways can have specific benefits relating to the functions being subserved by those pathways. This is once again paradoxical, because the role of the long cortical–cortical loops is quite transient in nature, yet the EEG training sets a steady-state goal. The resolution of this paradox lies, once again, in postulating that the EEG training challenges a control mechanism, as opposed to trying to achieve any particular state.

In Fig. 11.7, results are shown (cf. Mann *et al.,* 1996) that illustrate the relative degrees of desynchronization at central and parietal sites when the challenge is one of (1) a passive eyes-open condition (EO), (2) visual tracking, and (3) managing a motor challenge, combined with visual tracking (DM). Of greatest significance for our purposes is the fact that the EEG desynchronizes much more at C3 and C4 than at Cz for a motoric challenge. This suggests that if the synchronization/desynchronization cycle is being

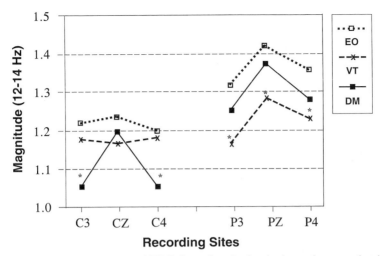

FIGURE 11.7   The amount of EEG desynchronization is shown for central strip and parietal sites under conditions of passive eyes-open condition (EO), visual tracking (VT), and motoric response (DM). A significant desynchronization is seen at C3, C4 with the motor task. (Reproduced from Mann *et al.*, 1996, with permission.)

trained with the EEG biofeedback, then the sites C3 and C4 might have advantages over Cz placement. This has turned out to be the case.

X. PARTITIONING OF BRAIN FUNCTION

Whereas the partitioning of brain function in the time or frequency domain is a relatively recent notion, it has been known for a long time that brain function is to a certain extent spatially partitioned. Of course, function cannot be completely localized. There must be integration with other functions, so there are uncertain boundaries between the domains of local and global functioning. EEG biofeedback requires a choice to be made in electrode placement, so the tool can both take advantage of what is known in terms of localization of function and further illuminate the question of localization. In any event, it is necessary to address the topic in order to learn how to apply the EEG biofeedback technique. The findings indicate that EEG biofeedback elicits both localized and global effects.

It is fruitful to consider brain function partitioning along three axes. The first is the lateral axis of hemispheric specialization. The second is that of front–back partitioning in terms of output and input related functions, respectively. The third is the vertical axis of the relationship between cortical and subcortical functioning. It has become axiomatic in our view of EEG biofeedback that the training impinges directly on the thalamocortical network already discussed, thus involving the cortical–subcortical axis. It is assumed that this is the case regardless of electrode placement. Further, even if cortical–cortical communication loops are also being explicitly trained, it is assumed that this occurs via modulation of the thalamacortical networks as well. After all, there are intrathalamic networks effectively coupling different cortical regions as well as direct cortical–cortical loops (Sherman & Guillery, 1996). The assumption of the primacy of thalamocortical networks in EEG training is not, however, universally agreed to among practitioners in the field and deserves more explicit confirmation.

Historically, the electrode sites that have been used for training most commonly consist of those which monitor the primary sensory modalities: the visual cortex at O1, O2; the sensorimotor cortex at C3, C4, and Cz; and the primary auditory cortex near T3, T4. The apparent survival of these principal training sites in clinical practice suggests they may offer unique efficacy. It may be conjectured that training at such primary sensory sites takes advantage of the most direct coupling to the thalamocortical circuit of interest, with the least ambiguity in outcomes.

Training at C3 and C4 places the electrodes near the Rolandic fissure, which separates the somatosensory and somatomotor cortices. This would appear to make for some confusion as to whether input- or output-related functions are being trained. In fact, the spatial segregation into input and output areas is not as rigorous as first thought. There is some 30% admixture of primary motor neurons located in the somatosensory area and vice versa. In any case, little evidence has surfaced to date as to whether the input- or output-related loops are being selectively trained. On the contrary, it appears that heightened vigilance, alertness, and arousal has implications for both input processing and for motor system readiness on the output side; that heightened sensitivity to somatosensory input goes along with increasing motoric tone. Thus, training of arousal and attentional control does not require selective focus on either input- or output-related functions.

That having been said, it is also true that as one progresses backward from the sensorimotor strip (say, from C3 toward P3) one is increasingly involved with sensory processing functions in the association areas of the parietal lobe. These sites are found to be preferable for addressing certain reading and spatial visualization problems, for example. As one moves forward from the sensorimotor strip (say, from C3 toward F3), one encounters first the premotor area, involved in motor planning, training of which can be helpful in articulation disorders, for example. As one moves further forward to prefrontal placements, one can address some of the more basic regulatory issues involving executive function. These may include such issues as working memory, motivation, and other aspects of emotional control. Such functions as appetite regulation have also been successfully addressed with frontal training.

Evidence such as that mentioned earlier can be used to support models of localized function. However, the evidence is often more ambiguous. Output functions, after all, generally involve a regulatory loop that also depends on monitoring by input functions. Stuttering is a case in point. Other problems may involve a failure of functional integration of several subunits of activity. Dyslexia may be a good example. The fact that one may successfully remediate both of these conditions by training at a single placement cannot by itself prove that the deficit is localized. Rather, it can be understood in the regulatory challenge model; namely, that if even one part of the regulatory loop is challenged, all of it may reorganize.

XI. HEMISPHERIC ORGANIZATION

The third axis is the left-right organization of brain function. The existence of left-right cortical symmetry gives the central nervous system the opportunity for specialization, which it has taken advantage of to a remarkable degree—surprising, given the histological homogeneity of the entire cortex which has persisted throughout mammalian evolution. The two hemispheres have adopted two different processing styles, and these are so incompatible in terms of their processing demands that they must have dedicated cortical real estate. This subject has been much discussed (cf. Bradshaw & Nettleton, 1981, for an extensive review). In the following, primary reference is made to the model of hemispheric specialization of Tucker and Williamson (1984). Their formulation is summarized in Table 11.1. The left hemisphere is fundamentally oriented toward sequential activity and, hence, has not only a special role for language, but is bound up with all planning of activity. Its orientation is prospective. Because planning is also the province of the frontal lobe, an intimate relationships exists between frontal and left hemisphere function. The right hemisphere is oriented toward parallel processing and simultaneity. As such, it manages the response to novelty, and in this connection maintains an intimate relationship with the association areas of parietal cortex.

The division of roles also means that the hemispheres exhibit their own characteristic failure modes. The left hemisphere is responsible for maintenance of vigilance and, hence, is to be addressed for the failure mode we term inattention. The right hemisphere owns the orientation to novelty and habituation to new inputs. Hence, it is more responsible for distractibility, impulsivity, and stimulus-seeking behavior.

A model of ADHD based on these considerations has been promulgated by Malone *et al.* (1994). It postulates that ADHD involves a functional deficit in both dopamine and norepinephrine systems of neuroregulation. The dopaminergic pathways link the frontal lobe to left hemisphere processing, and the noradrenergic pathways of the right hemisphere link to parietal processing. ADHD is deemed to involve "a bi-hemispheric dysfunction

TABLE 11.1   Characterization of Left and Right Hemisphere Function according to Tucker and Williamson (1984)

Left Hemisphere	Right Hemisphere
(Ventral/anterior)	(Dorsal/posterior)
Sequential processing	Parallel processing
Analytic specialization	Synthetic specialization
Anterior motor control	Posterior perceptual processing
Expressive hemisphere	Receptive hemisphere
Tonic activation (maintains motor readiness)	Phasic arousal (regulates sensory responsiveness to perceptual input)
Routinization (activation system is biased for constancy, maintenance of goal-directed behavior)	Novelty (arousal system is biased for novelty and change)
Redundancy bias	Novelty bias
Effortful processing (slow and serial)	Automatic processing (fast and simultaneous)
Constriction	Expansiveness
Emotionally unexpressive	Emotionally expressive
Introverted/internal focus	Extraverted/external focus
Anticipatory of the event	Responsive to the event
Internal locus of control	External locus of control
Persistent	Fast habituation
Depressed	Manic
Anxious	Hysteric
Stereotypic motor behavior tics, OCD	Impulsive
Perseveration	Distractibility
Rumination	Stimulus-seeking behavior
Dopamine-dominated (slow) + acetylcholine (fast)	Norepinephrine-dominated (fast) + serotonin (slow)
Localized function	Distributed function
Vigilance	Alertness

characterized by reduced dopaminergic and excessive noradrenergic functioning" (p. 181).

This model has considerable appeal and can be partially confirmed with EEG biofeedback. The standard protocol in our clinic for ADHD for many years consisted of training at C3 and C4. It was found that inattention responded preferentially, though by no means exclusively, to left-side training, and that impulsivity and distractibility responded primarily, though not at all exclusively, to right-side training. After some years of working with these standard placements, it was found empirically that involving the frontal lobe in left-side training often gave additional benefit in training. Similarly, involving the parietal lobe in training the right hemisphere was also found to be beneficial in many cases. The simultaneous training of two sites was accomplished with bipolar placement at C3–Fpz, and C4–Pz, respectively. One virtue of the model is that it can also explain the "paradoxical" efficacy of Ritalin for ADD, in addition to providing a basis for understanding the EEG biofeedback protocols. It is postulated that Ritalin boosts dopamine function on the one hand, while down-regulating norepinephrine function on the other. In our emerging model, we would prefer to generalize to disregulation of the dopamine and norepinephrine systems, rather than speaking in terms of underactivation and overarousal, respectively.

It is noteworthy that the DSM-IV has likewise acknowledged that the primary discriminants in ADHD are inattention and impulsivity, not hyperactivity. This is in line with the preceding observations, and begins to align the diagnostic categories with neurophysiological underpinnings. Thus, the predominantly inattentive subtype is deemed to be left-hemisphere related, and the predominantly impulsive subtype right-hemisphere dominated.

A division of clinical categories into their hemispheric constituents has since occurred in a number of other areas. This development has been somewhat driven by PET scan studies. Thus, in the case of the affective disorders of depression and anxiety, it has been found that each hemisphere has its characteristic failure modes, just as in ADHD. Thus, the left hemisphere mediates depression in the "helpless and hopeless" sense (Beck, 1976). Awareness of how one feels and the ability to talk about it is dependent on the left hemisphere. The right hemisphere, on the other hand, harbors the vulnerability of anger, of agitated depression, and of suicidality. Such symptoms need not bear any relation to existential circumstances and may not even be comprehensible to the more left-hemisphere consciousness of the sufferer. With regard to anxiety, it is the left hemisphere that manages worries and is in a position to articulate them. The right hemisphere, on the other hand, bears responsibility for fear and dread. It is also the one that panics, and the person may not know why. These findings have found support from—if they did not in fact originate with—PET scan studies. Thus we have from Heller *et al.* (1997): "Most of the [PET] studies that found right-hemisphere activity were looking at panic or some kind of stressful state . . . . Most of the studies that found more left-hemisphere activity were looking at worry" (p. 377).

This model also applies to bipolar disorder. As stated succinctly in their text, *Manic-Depressive Illness,* Goodwin and Jamison (1990) state: "Depression tends to be associated with damage to the left side of the brain, and mania with damage to the right" (p. 507). In each of these instances, our own findings of hemispheric specificity of the EEG training are consistent

with the distinctions mentioned earlier. Thus, unipolar depression is generally addressed with left-hemisphere training, whereas manic states and
suicidal depression are addressed with right-side training. Confirmation of
this model is further advanced when it is noted that training of the wrong
hemisphere in these instances can increase symptom severity on a transient
basis. Thus, hemispheric specificity of the training is one of the most important organizing principles for EEG training protocols, and this turns out
to be true in general, not just for attentional and affective disorders. Fortu-
itously, this differential response as a function of electrode placement allows
each patient to serve as his or her own control in the EEG training. The
fact that each patient can serve as his or her own control moreover makes
for a very rapid learning curve for the therapist, leading to optimization
of training parameters within the adopted paradigm. Such a learning curve
cannot of course give assurance that a global optimum has been reached
in terms of training strategies. As a side benefit, the existence of such
dramatic differential sensitivity disposes of the argument that we may be
dealing with placebo factors.

XII. PARTITIONING IN THE
FREQUENCY DOMAIN

Having reviewed the partitioning in the spatial domain, it is of interest
to return to the partitioning of this technique in the frequency domain.
Historically, the early researchers using this technique, M. Barry Sterman,
Joel Lubar, and others, employed training at the dominant frequency of
the sensorimotor rhythm, as manifested in the sleep spindle. Most commonly, the training band was 12–15 Hz. Since the SMR rhythm in fact
extended out to about 19 Hz, early work was also done at a higher frequency
band, 15–18 Hz for exploratory purposes (Sterman et al., 1974). The focus
on the sensorimotor rhythm followed first of all on the work with cats, and
followed secondarily on the assumption that the technique was primarily
applicable to motor seizures. In its application to ADD, it was thought to
calm hyperactivity directly by influence on the poise of the motor system,
as set by the gamma motor neuron system. Lubar subsequently added
training at 15–18 Hz as well for ADD (Lubar & Lubar, 1984).

As the work with EEG biofeedback was extended (by our group and
others) to other conditions such as affective disorders, sleep disorders,
chronic pain, etc., a pattern emerged in which both the higher frequency
band of 15–18 Hz and the lower band of 12–15 Hz appeared to play specific
roles in the remediation. Whereas the higher frequency training tended to
move a person toward greater sympathetic arousal, the lower frequency
training tended to promote parasympathetic arousal. The shifts were global,
in that when sympathetic arousal was elicited with the training, parasympa-

thetic arousal would be suppressed, and vice versa. These reciprocal relations have been appreciated for a long time. W. R. Hess (1954) originally elicited similar global shift with electrical stimulation of the diencephalon of the cat, and he referred to these as ergotroptic (sympathetic) and trophotropic (parasympathetic shifts). The most elegant explanation, then, is that the EEG characteristic training frequency is monotonically related to physiological arousal, and that a crucial fulcrum point appears to exist in the vicinity of 15 Hz, above which the subject will be moved toward sympathetic arousal, and below which parasympathetic dominance will be promoted.

If this is the case, then one might expect an exercise of the brain in terms of these mechanisms to be helpful in stabilizing disorders of arousal on the one hand, and those disorders which primarily manifest themselves in parasympathetic/sympathetic disregulation on the other. Relevant to the first category mentioned, the training has indeed been found to be very helpful in remediating depression and anxiety disorders, both in their arousal and affective dimension. With respect to disregulation of sympathetic/parasympathetic arousal, migraine headaches are the most obvious case in point, and PMS may also be relevant. It is found that migraine susceptibility responds almost universally to this intervention, both in terms of acute and chronic manifestations. That is, the EEG training technique can frequently be used to abort an ongoing migraine. In the majority of cases, the severity of an ongoing migraine will be reduced in-session. Longer term training of about 20–30 sessions will ordinarily raise the threshold of onset of migraines so that they are no longer an issue. The second relevant condition is that of PMS, where central arousal disregulation is primary, but which also features some symptoms of autonomic nervous system disregulation. Again, the technique is almost universally successful in relieving the immediate symptoms in-session to a certain degree, as well as in reducing or eliminating symptomatology over the longer term (on the order of 20–30 sessions). As befits the circumstances, both the higher and lower frequency training (called *beta* training and *SMR* training, respectively) may be required to achieve remediation for both migraines and PMS. This further supports the exercise or regulatory challenge model of EEG biofeedback, in that both hemispheres—and both frequency bands—need to be trained to effect the remediation.

The frequency specificity of the training is such that if the higher frequency band is appropriate in a particular circumstances, then the lower frequency band may at the same time exacerbate symptoms temporarily. On another occasion, and under different circumstances, but with the same individual, the opposite will be the case. In the case of the more severe instabilities, such as bipolar, the person may experience a dramatic change in state in-session, requiring a prompt adjustment in protocol. Thus, the training must address itself to the state in which the person finds himself at that moment. However, this is not all. It would be surprising indeed if human physiology were so uniform that each of us would exhibit the same "fulcrum frequency" of 15 Hz. In fact, there is individual variation in this regard, and individuals have been found differentially responsive to the training when frequencies of training bands have been shifted by as little as 0.5 Hz. Thus, a person in training may reproducibly report that a particular shift in training band is perceived to be either better or worse. These reports are single blind, in that the client is not aware of the direction or even the specific timing of the shift in training frequencies. This kind of specificity in training is a powerful argument against placebo factors being significant in outcomes.

Appropriate utilization of the EEG training technique therefore requires an understanding of the partitioning in both the frequency and the spatial domains. In this regard, it must be mentioned that the two are not uncorrelated. Thus, it is found empirically that left hemisphere training tends to require the higher frequency, or beta, training, and the right hemisphere generally requires the lower frequency, or SMR, training. This correlation has emerged as a general rule for application of this technique and, hence, demands explanation. The skeptical view is that this pattern simply emerged out of the history of this technique, in which these standard training bands were initially adopted following Sterman. However, the cumulative clinical evidence is becoming compelling. Beta training on the left side can often help depression, whereas SMR training on the left side would make it worse. Similarly, SMR training on the right side may help anxiety, but beta training on the right side may lead to agitation or mania. SMR training on the left side can lead to transient loss in cognitive function, just as beta training improves it. If beta training on the left side is found to help with a migraine, then SMR training is likely to make it worse. And if SMR training on the right side is found to help nocturnal myoclonus, then beta training there may make it worse. The effects are strong enough that a clinician would not utilize the wrong protocol for very long and still retain the clients. Such negative experiences in the dynamics of the training serve to shape the behavior of the sensitive clinician adroitly. Now that the technique is being refined by permitting minor shifts in training band (in 0.5-Hz steps) for optimization, it is found that this pattern of correlation survives.

The pattern may be understandable on several grounds. First of all, the left hemisphere tends to organize localized functions. This is deemed to occur at higher frequencies than the more distributed functions organized by the right hemisphere. Since the difference in training frequency between left and right is small in percentage terms, however, this is unlikely to be the explanation. A second and more important observation is that the left hemisphere failure modes tend toward underactivation, underarousal, and failure by behavioral "implosion" or collapse, which is remedied with the "spine-stiffening" higher frequency training. The right hemisphere failure modes, on the other hand, tend toward overarousal and overactivation, and are likely to involve behavioral "explosion" and outward eruptions. These require the calming and stabilizing effects of the lower frequency training. It must be acknowledged at this point that this argument is largely circular and self-referential. It is because mania, anger, dread, panic, suicidality, and explosive behavior respond to the calming right-hemisphere training that they are assigned to the right hemisphere in our model. We are also aware of cases in which a left-temporal seizure focus can give rise to behavioral disruptions we have just attributed to the right hemisphere! Is the right hemisphere in this case destabilized by the left? These questions remain for further evaluation.

Thus, a kind of skeletal framework has emerged to which new clinical findings are accreted. The new data serve to modify and refine the framework over time, while reinforcing the original conception.

XIII. THE EEG BIOFEEDBACK METHOD

The clinical approach used in the training consists of rewarding the patient for a transient increase over threshold of EEG activity in either the (nominally) 15–18 Hz or the 12–15 Hz spectral bands, with concurrent inhibition of activity over threshold in the frequency regimes of 22–30 Hz and 4–7 Hz (alternatively 2–7 Hz). Filter roll-off characteristics were soft, at 24 dB/octave. Typically, 15–18 Hz training would be employed at C3, and 12–15 Hz training would be employed at Cz or C4. Inhibition of the low-frequency activity was intended in the first instance to avoid any inappropriate rewards in the training band. Elevated low-frequency activity, such as interictal or other paroxysmal activity, is typically so irregular that it is has higher frequency (Fourier) components, which could yield false rewards in the reward band. Elevated low-frequency activity could also accompany low arousal conditions and may also be associated with trauma histories and dissociative states. Training to inhibit the excessive low-frequency activity has also been shown to be helpful all by itself in teaching control of state. Hence, it can be seen as an important part of the feedback signal in its own right.

Inhibition of the high-frequency band can also be seen in the first instance as a way of preserving the integrity of the reward signal. This is because elevated activity at the higher frequencies can also spill over into the training band by virtue of the overlapping filter skirts. Secondly, the high-frequency inhibit also has value in its own right, because it may reflect anxiety states, as well as states of high scalp muscle tension. Thus, inhibiting the high frequencies can also be seen in terms of inducing appropriate state change, and teaching control of state.

The feedback signal is derived from the bandpass filtered EEG signals by means of rectification and smoothing. A 0.5-sec integration time constant is employed for a smoothly iterated visual display. The resulting feedback signal is made available to the client by means of visual, auditory, and sometimes tactile feedback. The visual feedback consists of either a set of colored squares, the dimensions of which reflect the instantaneous amplitudes in the three bands, or of a Pacman-like game, in which the object speed and brightness reflect the reward and inhibit signal levels. Auditory feedback is a beep, which is issued after reward conditions have been met for at least 0.5 sec, and are repeated at a maximum rate of 2/sec.

The raw EEG signal and the three training band signals are displayed to the therapist continuously on a separate monitor. The therapist uses these signals to set reward contingencies. An artifact inhibit threshold is used on the raw signal, to discriminate against gross movement and eye blink or heartbeat artifacts. Thresholds on the other bands are set dynamically for maximum training effectiveness. The criteria are based on learning models. The challenge must be such that the client feels motivated and rewarded, which lies somewhere between boredom and frustration. The challenge must also be adjusted so that the information content is relatively high. It is highest when the reward criterion is met some 50% of the time. In practice, thresholds are set to reward the client approximately 60% of the time in the reward band, subject to the effect of the inhibit bands, which are set to inhibit the reward some 20 or 10% in the case of the low- and high-frequency inhibits, respectively. This yields a net reward incidence of about 50%.

XIV. CLINICAL VALIDATION

One of the first—and currently the most prominent—applications of EEG biofeedback has been to attention deficit hyperactivity disorder. This is largely attributable to the early work of Joel Lubar and associates in applying Sterman's methodology to what was then seen mainly as a problem of hyperactivity (Lubar & Shouse, 1976; Lubar & Lubar, 1984). More data have been accumulated relative to ADHD than for any other indication. As was explained earlier, ADHD has also become a paradigm for the disregulation model. It is therefore appropriate to focus on this condition for present purposes.

It has been customary to evaluate ADHD with behavioral rating scales. However, the EEG technique requires an additional assessment more attuned to neurophysiological mechanisms. To this end, the continuous performance test (CPT) is appropriate. It is important to note at this point that the function of the CPT in this connection is not to corroborate a diagnosis of ADHD, but rather to tease out the style of functioning of a particular nervous system. Hence, discussions of false positives and false negatives in CPT measures are not at issue. For the sake of uniformity, our efforts were concentrated on the TOVA (test of variables of attention) (Greenberg, 1987). The test uses a nonletter symbol that requires only up–down discrimination between target and nontarget conditions. The test is 22 min long, so that maintenance of vigilance can be assessed. Halfway through the test, the conditions change from a target-infrequent condition to the opposite. The interstimulus interval is held constant throughout so as not to induce a novelty response. The test primarily assesses inattention (in terms of missed targets), impulsivity (in terms of hits on nontargets), reaction time, and variability of the reaction time. Pre- and post-training results for these four categories are shown for children and adolescents with attentional difficulties in Fig. 11.8. The children had gone through the standard assessment and EEG training for 20 sessions. The feedback protocols were deemed appropriate to the particular client in each case on the basis of assessment data and were not necessarily invariant over the 20 sessions. Results are shown in terms of standard score, where a score

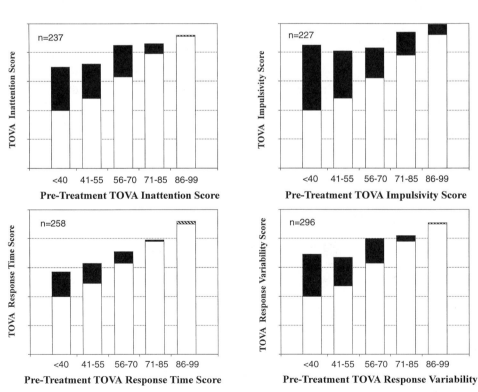

FIGURE 11.8   Results of pre- and post-testing with the TOVA, a continuous performance test. Results are shown for the four subtests of the TOVA. Results are highly significant, and exhibit substantial effect size for those in significant deficit in any area.

of 100 is average for the reference population, and the standard deviation is 15. All data were truncated at no more than four standard deviations from the norm (standard score of 40). Some 342 subjects were included. However, each graph displays only those with standard scores below 100 on the particular measure.

The data demonstrate statistically significant improvement ($p = 0.001$). The effect size is also substantial. It is observed that the average change for those in significant deficit may be larger than a standard deviation. In the case of impulsivity, and a starting standard score of 40, the average change is three standard deviations. This is clearly sufficient to be of clinical interest. There is considerable individual variation in response to the training, and this is illustrated for impulsivity in Fig. 11.9, where every subject is shown as a separate line, ranked in the order of starting value of standard score.

In Fig. 11.9, data are shown irrespective of the starting point in terms of standard score (that is, even starting scores larger than 100 are included). Notably, subjects still have a significant tendency to improve their scores, even if they are above norms. Hence, the training is not a matter of restoring persons to some norm. Rather, it is a means of potentially improving function regardless of starting point. Note that some small fraction of clients worsened their scores in pre- and post-testing. Understandably, some of this relates to the circumstances of the retesting. However, some of the declines in scores are believed to be "real." This could be attributable to the fact that impulsivity may not have been of primary concern in the

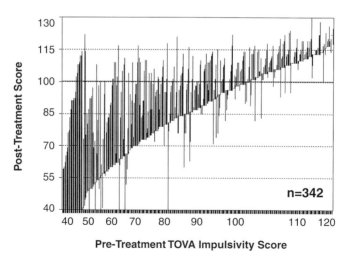

FIGURE 11.9 Individual results in terms of TOVA impulsivity are shown as standard scores. Every subject is shown as a separate line on the graph, ordered by starting value of impulsivity. The graph demonstrates the individual variation in response to the training.

training, which may have been directed toward some of the comorbidities of ADHD.

In the normal course of events, training would not necessarily stop at 20 sessions, particularly if some of the variables were still in deficit; it would continue with an emphasis on remediating the residual issues. When comparison is made to the post-training TOVA scores obtained in our clinic over several years, certain trends are identified. Data obtained most recently are tending to be better than those obtained previously. This suggests that refinements of the training protocol selection schemes are reaping rewards in terms of improved training outcome. It is also important to observe that if one combines both significantly positive and also negative outcomes, then nearly all nervous systems appear to respond to this training to some significant degree. This is counter to the placebo hypothesis.

The benefit of adding additional training sessions is shown in Table 11.2. The subject pool is of course dominated by those who did not normalize their scores in the first 20 sessions and were motivated to continue training. Significant further improvements are noted for this population, amounting to more than half a standard deviation in all categories except reaction time. This continued progression toward normalcy is also counter to expectations for placebos.

Results for adults are similar to those for children and adolescents. The individual scores for impulsivity are shown in Fig. 11.10. The results for all four subtests are shown in Table 11.3. These results indicate that the adult brain retains the needed functional plasticity to benefit from the intervention.

In addition to evaluation with a continuous performance test, a number of ADHD children ranging in age from 6 to 14 were given pre- and postevaluations with cognitive skills tests. The results are shown in Fig. 11.11 for 64 subjects undergoing the normal EEG training. The population as a whole was in deficit only for Word Fluency and Digit Span. For these tests, a significant improvement was noted (about 1.5 standard deviations in each case). The subject population as a whole was not in deficit with respect to the Grooved Pegboard and Symbol-Digit Modalities Test (SDMT). Never-

TABLE 11.2   TOVA Results in Standard Score for an Additional 20 Sessions of Training

	20 Sessions	40 Sessions	Change
Inattention	80.5	89.3	+ 8.8
Impulsivity	91.9	101.3	+ 9.3
Response time	81.5	82.8	+ 1.3
Variability	74.0	83.0	+ 9.0

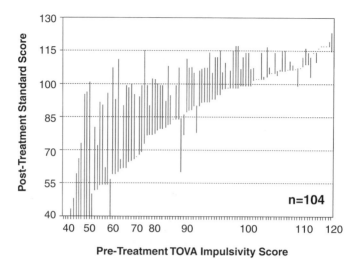

FIGURE 11.10   Individual results in terms of TOVA impulsivity scores are shown for adults. It is evident that adults can respond to the training and substantially normalize their function with respect to the TOVA measures.

theless, significant improvements ($p < 0.01$) were observed, so that in fact the post-training mean was above a standard score of 100. In the case of the Benton Visual Retention Test (BVRT), the population was near normal; hence, the overall population change was slight (though significant). In looking over the individual case results composing this sample, it is clear that the training can be helpful with visual retention where it is in deficit. The fact that population means can be systematically moved above naïve population means is counter to expectations for placebo models.

Some years ago, we conducted a clinical study of our ADHD protocols that included Wechsler IQ tests. The results were revealing. They were never submitted for publication because the changes in IQ were so large

TABLE 11.3   Results of TOVA Testing in Standard Score on Adults[a]

	Pretraining	Post-training	Change
Inattention	82.9	95.5	+12.5
Impulsivity	82.7	96.3	+13.7
Response time	100.5	99.1	− 1.4
Variability	86.6	94.0	+ 7.4

[a] Significant gains are seen in all areas in which a functional deficit is observed.

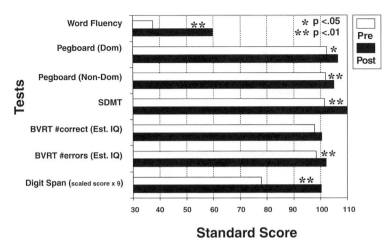

Standard Score

FIGURE 11.11   Effect of EEG biofeedback on seven cognitive tests for 64 children and adolescents. Pre- and post-treatment standard scores are presented (except for the Digit Span, where a scaled score is used). The two categories in deficit show improvement of more than one standard deviation. Three of the tests show improvement beyond naïve norms (Grooved Pegboard and Symbol-Digit Modalities Tests).

that they would be more likely to evoke skepticism than belief and, hence, would not be accepted unless they were replicated in a controlled design. However, it is useful to review them here. The tests were done by an independent clinical psychologist who had no stake in the outcome, and indeed had no intimate acquaintance with what was involved in the intervention. The population consisted of 15 subjects with primary issues of attention and behavior. Initially 18 were entered into the study; 3 dropped out early in training. Retesting took place some 6–12 months after the initial test.

Results of the Wechsler Intelligence Scale for Children–Revised (WISC-R) are shown in Fig. 11.12. The pretest average subtest scores reflect the expected ADHD pattern, with ACID subtest categories low (Arithmetic, Coding, Information, and Digit Span). The average IQ, however, was 107, slightly above normal. After the training, average IQ was 130, for a gain of 23 points. The curve reflects the same character as before. In first approximation, it is simply elevated. Every subtest (with exception of Block Design) improved by at least 2 units, a substantial and worthwhile change. This suggests that function has been improved globally, that the technique does not simply remediate manifest deficits. This is consistent with our emerging sense of this technique: It addresses the neurological machinery at such a basic level that essentially nothing in the realm of cognitive function remains entirely untouched. It is helpful to go into some additional detail.

It is remarkable for example that the average change in Arithmetic score is 5 units on the WISC-R. (This cannot be explained in terms of test–retest

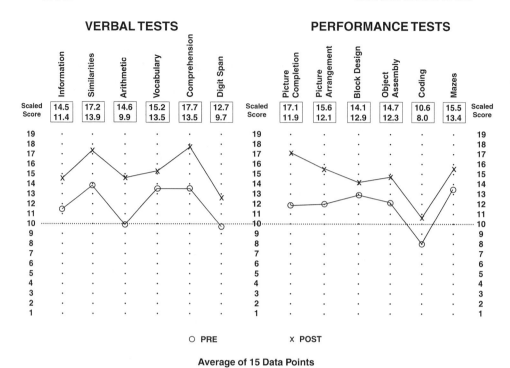

O PRE   x POST

Average of 15 Data Points

FIGURE 11.12   Results of pre–post Wechsler IQ testing for a cohort of 15 children and adolescents. Pretest data show the expected ADHD pattern. Post-testing shows function to be globally elevated. Average IQ score improvement was 23 points, from 107 to 130.

error, because the arithmetic test is stopped after three errors. Thus, on retest, the now well-performing child is seeing new problems.) Manifestly, the children already had the knowledge to perform the arithmetic challenges. The problem lay in the execution. It is most reasonable to assume that the training gave them better working memory, a greater continuity in mental state so that problems could be taken to a successful conclusion. This may also underlie the huge changes in Picture Arrangement and Picture Completion as well. The two subtests which are most revealing of neurological deficits are Block Design and Coding. Curiously, Block Design was not in deficit, in contrast to Coding. It also showed the least amount of favorable change. The average change in the Coding subtest was 2.6 units, which is substantial. The subject population divides, however, between those who changed significantly on Coding and those who did not change at all. A number of children made improvements of four units or more on this subtest, which is quite remarkable. At the time this testing was done, EEG training was predominantly with a single protocol on the left side. It is possible that this protocol was selectively effective with one particular neurophysiological subtype or with one type of deficit.

The data allow comparison of changes in the Verbal and Performance categories. Results for all subjects are shown individually in Fig. 11.13. Note that most of the children changed comparably in both verbal and performance area, despite the fact that the training was predominantly on left hemisphere. This is an indication that in first order the training is nonspecific with respect to lateralized function. A challenge to the left hemisphere is also a challenge to the right. However that may be, this is not to be taken to mean that it does not matter where the electrode is placed or that little is to be gained by contralateral training!

The IQ changes are plotted in Fig. 11.14, rank-ordered in terms of starting value of IQ. The most obvious feature of the data is that the largest improvements are observed for the lowest starting values of IQ. In this regard, the data may be somewhat influenced by the "headroom" limit of 165 IQ of the WISC-R. Children at the right-hand part of the graph still report favorable change, however it may not register very well on the WISC-R. Second, it is apparent that the low starting values of IQ do not

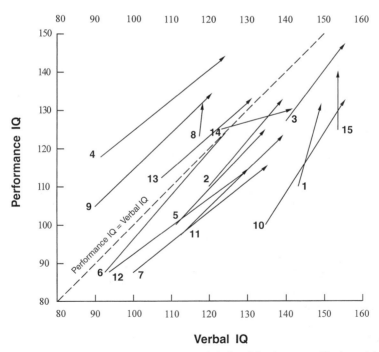

FIGURE 11.13 Comparison of Wechsler Verbal and Performance IQs in training cohort. Generally comparable changes were observed in both, although the training was predominantly done on the left hemisphere.

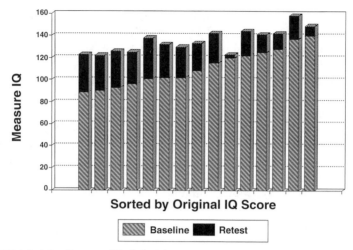

Sorted by Original IQ Score

FIGURE 11.14   Pre–post Wechsler IQ scores shown rank-ordered according to starting value. The largest changes, on the order of 30 points or more, are seen at the lowest starting values.

prevent children from benefiting from the training. In fact, anecdotal reports from other therapists indicate that IQ's of 70 and below have also been worked with successfully. This suggests that the issue of mild retardation may also need to be revisited. It is possible that some of the deficits here may also lie in the functional realm and thus be amenable to at least partial remediation. It is apparent that the task places a very modest "cognitive demand" on the child. In fact, the training has been used successfully with severely compromised nervous systems (traumatic brain injury) and even with preverbal children.

The IQ data give evidence for the broad reach of the EEG training in terms of the functional capacities affected, irrespective of whether they relate to left or right hemisphere function. It is therefore necessary to inquire whether other factors may be partly responsible for these results. It is possible that the training has impacted factors not directly involved with cognitive function, but which are expected to have a more global effect. One such factor is sleep. Intake data on the children in this study showed that two-thirds of them had disregulated sleep patterns (e.g., sleep onset problems, inability to fall asleep in one's own bed, frequent waking, night terrors, nightmares, bedwetting, sleep walking, sleep talking, nocturnal bruxism). Most of these problems resolved themselves during the course of the training. Hence, it is possible to trace some functional improvement simply to the fact that the children were no longer in chronic sleep debt. (One could of course regard sleep disorders as simply another manifestation of one underlying pattern of disregulation.) Another such factor is pain. Significantly, one-third of the study population indicated a history of chronic head or stomach pain. These pain syndromes also generally resolved themselves with the training, and could explain some of the improvement in level of function.

A third and perhaps most intriguing factor was a general improvement in motivation. This was not explicitly evaluated before and after, but revealed itself in a later review of the client notes from the testing. A profound change in motivation and level of engagement was observed in a number of the children, particularly those who came with concomitant behavioral complaints (oppositional-defiant disorder and conduct disorder). The data themselves cannot settle the issue of whether motivation simply followed from a greater level of manifest competence, or whether the demonstrated higher competence was mediated by greater motivation—or both.

From the remediation of oppositional-defiant disorder and conduct disorder that is also observed, it follows that the technique appears to impinge on mechanisms underlying motivation, emotionality, and attachment. The core issue in much of ADD may not be merely at the surface level of attention and distractibility, but rather also in the limbic, emotional realm, which determines what is valued and what is worth attending to. Given that there is a comorbidity of 60% of ODD with ADHD, then it is possible that a "subclinical" level of motivational and emotional disregulation extends over much of the remaining ADHD population as well. It is found that items relating to socially unacceptable conduct discriminate between ADHD/non-ADHD much more cleanly than other behavioral litmus tests such as hyperactivity (Stewart *et al.*, 1966). If a core issue of ADHD in fact lies in the affective domain, as Weinberg suggested early on, then this may also help to explain the apparent increase in the occurrence of ADHD in our society. It could be attributable to a more impoverished early emotional life of many of our children. By contrast, in the cognitive realm, children have by and large experienced a life of attentional and cognitive challenge, one that would be expected normally to lead to increased mastery. Moreover, it must be explained why much ADHD symptomatology is so situational. The child who tests poorly in the classroom environment may yet do well on the basketball court. Some do very poorly at home and well at school, or vice versa. Much of ADHD and some of its comorbidities may be one of the observables of emotional disorders in their subclinical manifestations. Work in this realm has been summarized in a text titled *Affect Regulation and the Origin of the Self,* by Alan Schore (1994).

Two additional tests performed with this study population may shed additional light on these issues. Results for the Benton Visual Retention Test are shown in Fig. 11.15. It is observed that this group was characterized by very poor initial performance on the BVRT, in contrast to the average IQ, which was normal. The scores improved significantly with the training. (Test–retest error cannot be an explanation, since A and B versions were used. Moreover, if the child cannot recall a figure over a time frame of

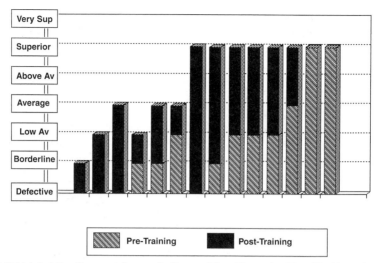

FIGURE 11.15   Pre–post data on the Benton Visual Retention Test. Significant improvements are shown for many of those in deficit.

seconds, he is not going to remember it for 9 months.) The Benton test may have exposed a specific deficit that could help to account for the attentional and other academic problems of many of the children in the study. The benefit from the training can be explained in terms of improved working memory or in terms of improved short-term memory. In either event, improved continuity in mental processing is indicated.

The second test was the Tapping Subtest of the Harris Tests of Lateral Dominance. Results are shown in Figs. 11.16 and 11.17. The first figure shows the changes in tapping score, plotted to compare right- and left-hand performance. The test is deemed to indicate lateralization of function if one hand is 20% better than the other. The average improvement in tapping score was 20%; the median change, however, was 40%, and three subjects improved their score by more than 100%. These data suggest that fine motor control or eye–hand coordination was also suboptimal in this population. Even more striking are the findings when plotted in terms of the ratio of right–left performance. Prior to the training, a broad distribution of ratios is observed. After the training, a narrow distribution is observed for ostensible right-handers, and a small peak for presumptive left-handers. Intriguingly, laterality as measured by this test was found to change in some instances. Some children even strengthened in their left-handedness, despite the use of predominantly left-hemisphere training. The most appealing explanation of these results is that the training restored native laterality, one that may have been compromised with birth injury or subsequent minor traumatic brain injury. Sonogram studies of fetal thumb-sucking have shown

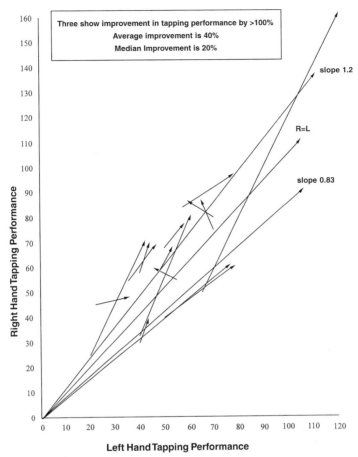

FIGURE 11.16   Pre–post data on the Tapping Subtest of the Harris Tests of Lateral Dominance. Significant improvement in tapping performance is shown by a number of subjects, as well as changes in measured laterality.

that some 95% of fetuses prefer their right thumb. This ratio changes to 85% after birth (Hepper *et al.,* 1990, 1991). The change in this early indication of prospective handedness may be seen as the brain's accommodation to the trauma of birth. Such trauma may affect one hemisphere more than another, leading to compromised laterality. It is more probable for the brain to move from right dominance to mixed or left than the reverse.

The tapping test is in some sense the most robust measure of neurophysiological change as a result of the training. After all, the training does not involve use of the hands at all. Insofar as the training involves the sensorimotor cortex directly, it trains the brain toward a lowered setpoint of activation of the motor pathway. More particularly, however, the change

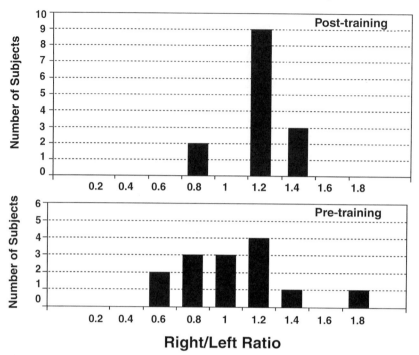

FIGURE 11.17   Pre–post data for the ratio of right-hand to left-hand tapping performance. Prior to training, a broad distribution in ratios is observed. After training, the distribution has normalized, with depletion of outliers and those of mixed dominance.

was totally unexpected. It was not looked to as a measure reflecting remediation of ADD, for example. This test was included for completeness of the
evaluation. The test is therefore free of some of the usual experimental
biases. The test supports the view that the EEG training promotes control
in general as opposed to a particular state. It supports the existence of
global as well as local training effects. Most significantly, however, it is
difficult to invoke placebo factors to explain these results. It is even possible
to rule out extraneous factors such as motivation. It would be difficult,
after all, to argue that motivation had much to do with the differential
performance of the two hands.

Thus, the extensive testing performed on this group makes the case both
for the existence of specific deficits and for more global dysfunctions in
the constellation of ADHD. Looked at from the perspective of clinical
phenomenology, then, ADHD appears as a highly heterogeneous condition
with many contributing factors. It appears as a composite, as in the view
of Weinberg, or as a spectrum disorder, similar to the manner in which
Comings views Tourette's syndrome. This view would not be far removed
from the conventional one described by Biederman if one simply reframed

comorbidities as part of the spectrum. Looked at from the perspective of the remediation, however, it must be recognized that all of these symptoms, in all of their marvelous variety of expression, responded to a single intervention, with a single training frequency band (in nearly all cases), and with a single training site (again, in nearly all cases). This too must be explained.

The simplest explanation, we believe, is that the core issue of ADHD and its comorbidities is disregulation, a disruption or discontinuity in the processes by which different brain regions maintain communication and continuity of mental processing. Further, this disruption is not limited to any one brain region or to any one functional area, or to any one neuromodulator system, but rather extends broadly to the domains of cognitive function, motor coordination, emotional regulation, pain threshold, sleep regulation, and appetite—as well as to those specific faculties that allocate attentional resources and maintain vigilance.

The emphasis we have placed on our early data was intended to make the point that much could be accomplished with a single training protocol. This tends to support the spectrum disorder concept, and the supposition that there are a limited number of failure modes underlying much of the phenomenology of ADHD. There has been a proliferation of protocols in recent years to address other specific concerns, so the perspective of the broad reach of a single protocol tends to get lost. The early work can therefore be considered another serendipitous experiment, if you will, because it would not be ethical to replicate it, now that more is known.

The pervasive deficits in motor function and laterality that were revealed in this population also draw attention to the matter of brain injury, which takes us back to the earlier formulation of this syndrome as "minimal brain dysfunction" subsequent to brain injury. The fact that the deficits were largely remediable means that they were in the functional realm, even though a physical injury (anoxia, forceps delivery) may have occurred. In the course of taking thousands of histories prior to EEG training, it emerges that similar deficit profiles can arise subsequent to an emotionally traumatic event, or even under conditions of persistent psychic stress. This supports the model in which trauma and severe stress may be encoded physiologically in terms of functionally disregulated neuromodulator systems, manifesting in poorer regulation of arousal, attentive functions, affect, sympathetic/parasympathetic balance, pain, sleep, endocrine function, and immune system function. As with our ADHD population, if we test relevant subjects with other diagnoses in terms of cognitive function and vigilance, deficits will often be found that are indicative of the same failure modes that we see in the ADD population. We interpret these in the same way as a lack of continuity in mental processing and a breakdown in communication pathways.

The burden of treatment then becomes a matter of assessing the quality of functioning of a particular nervous system and devising a strategy toward normalization. The renormalization of function then prepares the ground for psychological resolution of any residual issues. This is the reverse of the usual pattern of psychotherapeutic intervention and is appropriate whenever disregulation has become the primary issue, such as when the somatization of psychological symptoms has taken on a life of its own. This schema is made possible by the emerging realization that much of psychopathology can be characterized by a relatively modest set of primary failure modes, and that these can be appealed to by a likewise parsimonious set of training protocols.

Whereas our understanding of the "disregulation model" arose largely out of our work with ADHD, it can in fact be applied to many of the conditions that are now separately treated in the DSM-IV as distinct disorders. This includes first of all the disruptive behavioral disorders (conduct disorder and oppositional defiant disorder), which we prefer to view as part of the ADHD "spectrum," the various learning disorders, communication disorders (articulation problems, stuttering), and the affective disorders in childhood. It includes the elimination disorders (enuresis and encopresis), the tic disorders, and childhood sleep disorders (sleep onset anxiety, nightmares, night terrors, and nocturnal bruxism). The disregulation model may also apply to a degree for conditions with a more obvious organic or structural component, where the training has nevertheless been found helpful in the general case. This includes even the more severe developmental disorders of pervasive developmental delay, Asperger's syndrome, and autism. It also includes cerebral palsy, fetal alcohol syndrome, petit mal seizures, complex partial seizures, traumatic brain injury, and anoxia. Despite the existence of organic injury, there appears to be considerable recovery capacity available, presumably because the compass of functional disturbance extends beyond the region of organic injury.

Outcomes for the conditions mentioned can be highly variable, however. The above is not intended to suggest that EEG biofeedback constitutes a comprehensive remedy for cerebral palsy, for example, or for autism. Rather, it is to suggest that the application of EEG training is generally found to be worthwhile, and may lead to some useful increase in function in such cases. In cases where the organic injury is either diffuse or not discernible at all, as in cases of anoxia and many cases of traumatic brain injury, self-report often indicates recovery of 70–90% of premorbid function. This can be achieved even years post-trauma, by which time all other interventions will have been terminated and no further recovery is to be expected.

Work with ADHD and its comorbidities, mainly in children, led to successful training of adults. Thus, the responsivity of children with dysthymia, depression, and anxiety in the context of primary ADHD caused the work to be extended to adults, and then to individuals for whom the affective disorders were the primary issue. In this manner, the scope of clinical practice was gradually enlarged. Success with anxiety and depression led in turn to success with other conditions of depressive character, PMS foremost among them. Few disorders respond as well as PMS, and few fit the "disregulation model" better. PMS encompasses a wide variety of symptoms, including those of physical, behavioral, cognitive, and emotional character. Significantly, all of such symptom types that we have seen, without any exception to date, have been observed to respond favorably to only one or two protocols of EEG training. This is seen as a significant confirmation of the disregulation model.

Significantly, this success includes PMS-related migraines, which have resisted conventional medical management. This work generalized to other kinds of migraines. (We had already mastered regular "tension" headaches.) Over time, a training strategy emerged that was consistently successful with migraines and tension headache syndromes, with only rare treatment failures. Since migraines were often immediately responsive to the training in-session, they were a very useful probe for the continued evolution of the EEG training technique. That is, the migraine quickly "trained" the therapist to do the right thing. (Preferably, of course, training is conducted while the person is not having a migraine.) In this manner, the left-hemisphere and right-hemisphere contributions to headache management were teased out, and the frequency dependences for each were determined. As it turns out, the same patterns of left- and right-side training were found to be appropriate to a variety of other conditions. This tended to support the theory that we were looking at a limited set of characteristic failure modes, and that most of these could be managed with a limited set of protocols. Additionally, since most migraines have significant brain stem involvement, it is likely that the training affects brain function even at the brain stem level.

In the spirit of an attempt to model much of psychopathology in terms of the principal failure modes of control systems, we found useful a classification of conditions into either setpoint errors or instabilities of various kinds. Along with seizures, both migraines and PMS were classic cases of brain instabilities. Another obvious case was bipolar disorder. Early work with depression led to acquaintance with mania, which then had to be managed as well. A protocol emerged in which the depressive excursions were addressed with left-hemisphere beta training, and mania with right-hemisphere SMR training. Then we took on some medically refractory cases of bipolar disorder who were in crisis and without other recourse. It was found that the training could stabilize these people over time against excursions into mania and major depression. Moreover, it was found that the condition itself "guided the therapist" into adopting the appropriate protocol. Just as with seizures, however, a large number of training sessions might be required (60 or more).

In surveying this history, it becomes clear that whereas pharmacotherapy can often deal successfully with setpoint errors (dysthymia, unipolar depression), it actually does a poor job with instabilities. By contrast, instabilities are the forte of the EEG biofeedback technique, by virtue of the fact that it promotes brain stability. (It is the very startling efficacy with such intractable conditions as end-stage bipolar disorder and migraines that invites skepticism. And it is for this reason that we chose to prepare the ground with our theoretical discussion.) Other instabilities that were found to respond to the training were panic disorder, agitated depression, suicidality, episodic rage, irritable bowel, Crohn's disease, and vertigo.

The increasing scope of our work and that of others also leads us to believe that the "disregulation model" and the "regulatory challenge" model of EEG biofeedback will find applicability to dissociative disorders, to post-traumatic stress disorder, to obsessive-compulsive disorder, to substance-related disorders, and perhaps also to schizophrenia. (For each of these categories, our own clinical experience is limited to a small number of cases.) Even in those conditions where disregulation does not appear to be the core issue, EEG biofeedback may be a very useful initial intervention. Personality disorders may be a case in point. Even if the condition is seen as primarily—and appropriately—in the psychological or psychiatric realm, it is still possible to appeal to the physiological concomitant and aid the person to a more stable physiology so that psychotherapy can proceed more productively.

XV. SUMMARY

A model has been presented in which ADHD and its comorbidities can be seen as a composite or spectrum disorder grounded in the disregulation of basic neurophysiological mechanisms underlying attentional, cognitive, and affective function. This model has been extended so that much of psychopathology can be seen in neurophysiological terms as "disorders of disregulation," traceable to a relatively small number of characteristic failure modes of the brain acting as a control system. These failure modes fall into two classes: setpoint errors and instabilities. Both types of failures can be modeled in terms of long-term functional disregulation of neuromodulation networks, or breakdowns of continuity of function, as well as disruptions of cortical and subcortical communication. These deficits are best understood in terms of the brain's necessity to organize itself in the bioelectrical or time domain. It is argued that the functional organization relies centrally on rhythmic mechanisms, which appear to be ubiquitous in cortex, to organize localized function as well as to bring distributed processes into coordination. The functional deficits underlying much psychopathology are often largely remediable by means of operant conditioning of the EEG to exercise the mechanisms by which these rhythmic processes are established and maintained. This is referred to as the "regulatory challenge" model of

EEG biofeedback. Good evidence exists that the key rhythmic processes at issue are governed by thalamocortical feedback loops.

The EEG biofeedback training for a large variety of conditions has been accomplished to date with a parsimonious set of protocols. Such protocols had their origins in basic research, but have since been evolved and refined empirically. These protocols can be motivated by a straightforward partitioning of brain function in the spatial and frequency domains. Such remediation may result in the essentially complete amelioration of symptoms attendant to various disorders, many of which have been refractory to standard medical interventions. Data supportive of this proposition are most robust for the attentional, behavioral, cognitive, and affective domains. Whereas data have been presented herein only for the remediation of cognitive deficits and attentional deficits, the clinical evidence is compelling also for the disruptive behavior disorders, anxiety disorders, depression, PMS, sleep disorders, and pain syndromes, including migraines. Considerable data have been accumulated indicating that the training is worthwhile even for the more severe developmental disorders, such as autism, and in cases of cerebral palsy and birth-related or other physical trauma.

Further, clinical data indicate that broad generalization of these principles may be possible to the domain of psychopathology at large, including among others the dissociative disorders, addictions, eating disorders, and even personality disorders. In the realm of neurology, neurofeedback efficacy for epilepsy has a long, favorable (but unfortunately neglected) research history. Data on these conditions can be efficiently gathered because the training involves subject-specific choices of protocol that effectively make the subject his or her own control in this intervention. Moreover, all of the data are mutually supportive of the disregulation model, and hence need not be fragmented into discrete disorders.

Research into this technique should be a high priority for the mental health disciplines. The availability of the tool of operant conditioning of the EEG will not only be clinically useful but also helpful to the neurosciences in furthering the understanding of cerebral control mechanisms. Discovery and validation through research of the practical implications of brain regulation in the bioelectrical domain could potentially lead to a scientific revolution comparable to the development of pharmacotherapy in both the therapeutic and the scientific realm.

XVI. ADDENDUM

In the treatment of many mental disorders, one is not done even when normalization of physiological function has been achieved with EEG biofeedback. The work of psychological reintegration remains. EEG training in the low-frequency regime of 4–12 Hz has been found to be helpful here.

This is known as *alpha–theta training*. The person is taken to a state of low arousal, one that apparently facilitates the recovery of memories and the resolution of traumatic issues. This is a discipline for which entirely different considerations apply and it is not discussed further here. No devaluation of this technique is implied by our neglect to cover it in detail. On the contrary, the work to be done in the alpha–theta domain is often crucial for ultimate resolution of the issues. The changes induced in the individual may be even more profound. And the experience of the training draws more fully on our human capacities than is the case for the higher frequency training discussed here. It is simply more appropriate to leave that discussion to those more expert in that discipline.

From the physiological perspective, however, and for completeness, it can be said that alpha–theta training seems to expand the horizon for whole-brain integration, for the training of whole-brain communication, and for hemispheric balancing. The case can be made that trauma may be more selectively encoded in the right hemisphere. However, the right hemisphere cannot "make itself heard" without passing through the censorship of the verbal left. Alpha–theta training is believed to quiet the left hemisphere, tame hypervigilance, and suppress sympathetic overarousal. It allows right-hemisphere content to be seen through imagery, and the self can process this material efficiently and nontraumatically. In this capacity, the technique has inherent advantages over conventional talk therapy and hypnotherapy.

Whereas the present treatise has concerned itself largely with normalization of neurophysiological functioning, the related discipline of alpha–theta training addresses psychological reintegration in a manner that is complementary to the higher frequency training, and we commend the attention of the reader to this discipline as well.

REFERENCES

Adamec, R. E. (1990). Kindling, anxiety and limbic epilepsy: Human and animal perspectives. *In* "Kindling 4. Advances in Behavioral Biology" (J. A. Wada, ed.), Vol. 37, pp. 329–341. Plenum Press, New York.

Adkins, J. W., Fehmi, L. G., & Lindsley, D. B. (1969). Perceptual discrimination in monkeys: Retroactive visual masking. *Physiol. Behav.* **4,** 255–259.

Anderson, P., & Anderssen, S. A. (1968). "Physiological Basis of the Alpha Rhythm." Appleton Century Crofts, New York.

Andersen, P., & Sears, P. A. (1964). *J. Physiol.* **173,** 469.

Andersen, P., Andersson, S. A., & Lomo, T. (1967). Some factors involved in the thalamic control of spontaneous barbiturate spindles. *J. Physiol.* **192,** 257–281.

Barinaga, M. (1996). Neurons put the uncertainty into reaction times. *Science* **274,** 344.

Baxter, L. R., Schwartz, J. M., Bergman, K. S., Szuba, M. P., Guze, B. H., Mazziotta, J. C., Alazraki, A., Selin, C. E., Ferng, H-K., Munford, P., & Phelps, M. E. (1992). Caudate glucose metabolic rate changes with both drug and behavior therapy for obsessive-compulsive disorder. *Arch. Gen. Psychiat.* **49,** 681–689.

Beck, A. T. (1976). "Cognitive Therapy and the Emotional Disorders." New American Library, New York.

Bennett, E. L., Diamond, M. C., Krech, D., & Rosenzweig, M. R. (1996). Chemical and anatomical plasticity of brain. *J. Neuropsychiat. Clin. Neurosci.* **8,** 459–470.

Biederman, J., Newcorn, J., & Sprich, S. (1991). Comorbidity of attention deficit hyperactivity disorder with conduct, depressive, anxiety, and other disorders. *Am. J. Psychiat.* **148,** 564–577.

Biederman, J., Faraone, S., Mick, E., Wozniak, J., Chen, L., Ouellette, C., Marrs, A., Moore, P., Garcia, J., Mennin, D., & Lelon, E. (1996). Attention-deficit hyperactivity disorder and juvenile mania: An overlooked comorbidity? *J. Am. Acad. Child Adolesc. Psychiat.* **35,** 997–1008.

Bolwig, T. G. (1989). Do kindling-like phenomena unify hypotheses of psychopathology? *In* "The Clinical Relevance of Kindling" (T. G. Bolwig & M. R. Trimble, eds.), pp. 1–13. John Wiley & Sons, Chichester, England.

Bradshaw, J. L., & Nettleton, N. C. (1981). The nature of hemispheric specialization in man. *Behav. Brain Sci.* **4,** 51–92.

Carter, A. S., Pauls, D. L., Leckman, J. F., & Cohen, D. J. (1994). A prospective longitudinal study of Gilles de la Tourette's syndrome. *J. Am. Acad. Child Adolesc. Psychiat.* **33,** 377–385.

Chase, M. H., & Harper, R. M. (1971). Somatomotor and visceromotor correlates of operantly conditioned 12–14c/sec sensorimotor cortical activity. *EEG Clin. Neurophysiol.* **31,** 85–92.

Chua, S. E., & McKenna, P. J. (1995). Schizophrenia: A brain disease? A critical review of structural and functional cerebral abnormality in the disorder. *Br. J. Psychiat.* **166,** 563–582.

Comings, D. E. (1990). "Tourette Syndrome and Human Behavior." Hope Press, Duarte, CA.

Connor, C. E., & Johnson, K. O. (1992). Neural coding of tactile texture: Comparison of spatial and temporal mechanisms for roughness perception. *J. Neurosci.* **12,** 3414–3426.

Damasio, A. R. (1994). "Descartes' Error." G. P. Putnam, New York.

Douglas, V. I. (1988). Cognitive deficits in children with attention deficit disorder with hyperactivity. *In* "Attention Deficit Disorder: Criteria, Cognition, Intervention" (L. M. Bloomingdale & J. Sergeant, eds.). Pergamon Press, New York.

du Lac, S., & Lisberger, S. G. (1995). Cellular processing of temporal information in medial vestibular nucleus neurons. *J. Neurosci.* **15**(12), 8000–8010.

El-Hilu, S. M., Abdel-Dayem, H. M., Sehweil, A., Almokhtar, N., & Higazi, E. (1997). Cerebral perfusion changes in newly diagnosed acute and never treated schizophrenic patients pre and post psychopharmacotherapy using Tc-99m HMPAO SPECT. *Eur. J. Psychiat.* **11,** 81–89.

Ellertson, B., & Klove, H. (1976). Clinical application of EEG biofeedback training in epilepsy. *Scand. J. Behav. Ther.* **5,** 133–144.

Ferster, D., & Spruston, N. (1995). Cracking the neuronal code. *Science* **270,** 756–757.

Finley, W. W., Smith, H. A., & Etherton, M. D. (1975). Reduction of seizures and normalization of the EEG in a severe epileptic following sensorimotor biofeedback training: Preliminary study. *Biolog. Psychol.* **2,** 189–203.

Gabbiani, F., & Koch, C. (1996). Coding of time-varying signals in spike trains of integrate-and-fire neurons with random threshold. *Neural Comput.* **8,** 44–66.

George M. S., Ketter T. A., & Post R. M. (1993). SPECT and PET imaging in mood disorders. *J. Clin. Psychiat.* **54,** 6–13.

Goodwin, F. K., & Jamison, K. R. (1990). "Manic-Depressive Illness." Oxford University Press, New York.

Greenberg, L. M. (1987). An objective measure of methylphenidate response. Clinical use of the MCA. *Psychopharmacol. Bull.* **23,** 279–282.

Grotstein, J. S. (1986). The psychology of powerlessness. Disorders of self-regulation and interactional regulation as a new paradigm for psychopathology. *Psychoanalytic Inquiry* **6**, 93–118.

Hamilton, J. C., Greenberg, J., Pyszczynski, T., & Cather, C. (1993). A self-regulatory perspective on psychopathology and psychotherapy. *J. Psychother. Integration* **3**, 205–248.

Hardcastle, V. G. (1996). The binding problem and neurobiological oscillations. *In* "Toward a Science of Consciousness: The First Tucson Discussions and Debates, Complex Adaptive Systems" S. R. Hameroff, A. W. Kaszniak, & A. C. Scott, eds.), pp. 51–65. The MIT Press, Cambridge, MA.

Harro, J., & Oreland, L. (1996). Depression as a spreading neuronal adjustment disorder. *Eur. Neuropsychopharm.* **6**, 207–223.

Heller, W., Nitschke, J. B., Etienne, M. A., & Miller, G. A. (1997). Patterns of regional brain activity differentiate types of anxiety. *J. Abnormal Psychol.* **106**, 376–385.

Hepper, P. G., Shahidullah, S., & White, R. (1990). Origins of fetal handedness. *Nature* **347**, 431.

Hepper, P. G., Shahidullah, S., White, R. (1991). Handedness in the human fetus. *Neuropsychologia* **29**, 1107–1111.

Hess, W. R. (1954). "Diencephalon: Autonomic and Extrapyramidal Functions." Grune & Stratton, New York.

Holden, C. (1991). Depression: The news isn't depressing. *Science* **254**, 1450–1452.

Howe, R. C., & Sterman, M. B. (1972). Cortical-subcortical EEG correlates of suppressed motor behavior during sleep and waking in the cat. *EEG Clin. Neurophysiol.* **32**, 681–695.

Izquierdo, I., & Medina, J. H. (1997). The biochemistry of memory formation and its regulation by hormones and neuromodulators. *Psychobiology* **25**, 1–9.

Judd, K. T., & Aihara, K. (1993). Pulse propagation networks: A neural network model that uses temporal coding by trials. *Neural Net.* **6**, 203–215.

Kanba, S., Yagi, G., Kamijima, K., Suzuki, T., Tajima, O., Otaki, J., Arata, E., Koshikawa, H., Nibuya, M., & Kinoshita, N. (1996). The first open study of zonisamide, a novel anticonvulsant, shows efficacy in mania. *Prog. Neuropsychopharm. Biolog. Psychiat.* **18**, 707–715.

Kaplan, B. J. (1975). Biofeedback in epileptics: Equivocal relationship of reinforced EEG frequency to seizure reduction. *Epilepsia* **16**, 477–485.

Katz, L., Fleisher, W., Kjernisted, K., & Milanese, P. (1996). A review of the psychobiology and pharmacotherapy of posttraumatic stress disorder. *Can. J. Psychiat.* **41**, 233–238.

Klein, D. F. (1997). Initiation and adaptation: A paradigm for understanding psychotropic drug action: Comment. *Am. J. Psychiat.* **154**, 440.

Klemm, E., Danos, P., Grunwald, F., Kasper, S., Moller, H. J., & Biersack, H. J. (1996). Temporal lobe dysfunction and correlation of regional cerebral blood flow abnormalities with psychopathology in schizophrenia and major depression—a study with single photon emission computed tomography. *Psychiatry Res.* **68**, 1–10.

Koenig, P., & Engel, A. (1995). Correlated firing in sensory-motor systems. *Curr. Opin. Neurobiol.* **5**, 511–519.

Kramer, P. D. (1993). "Listening to Prozac." Penguin, New York.

Kuhlman, W. N., & Allison, T. (1977). EEG feedback training in the treatment of epilepsy: Some questions and some answers. *Pavlovian J. Biolog. Sci.* **12**, 112–122.

Lantz, D., & Sterman, M. Barry, (1988). Neuropsychological assessment of subjects with uncontrolled epilepsy: Effects of EEG feedback training. *Epilepsia* **29**, 163–171.

Lubar, J. F., & Bahler, W. W. (1976). Behavioral management of epileptic seizures following EEG biofeedback training of the sensorimotor rhythm. *Biofeedback Self-Regul.* **1**, 77–104.

Lubar, J. F., & Shouse, M. N. (1976). EEG and behavioral changes in a hyperkinetic child concurrent with training of the sensorimotor rhythm (SMR): A preliminary report. *Biofeedback and Self Regulation* **1**, 293–306.

Lubar, J. O., & Lubar, J. F. (1984). Electroencephalographic biofeedback of SMR and beta for treatment of attention deficit disorders in a clinical setting. *Biofeedback Self-Regul.* **9,** 1–23.

Lubar, J. F., Shabsin, H. S., Natelsen, S. E., Holder, G. S., Whitsett, S. F., Pamplin, W. E., & Krulikowski, D. I. (1981). EEG operant conditioning in intractable epileptics. *Arch. Neurol.* **38,** 70–74.

Lubar J. F., Swartwood M. O., Swartwood J. N., & O'Donnell P. H. (1995). Evaluation of the effectiveness of EEG neurofeedback training for ADHD in a clinical setting as measured by changes in T.O.V.A. scores, behavioral ratings, and WISC-R performance. *Biofeedback Self-Regul.* **20,** 83–99.

MacCormac, E. R. (1996). Fractal thinking: Self-organizing brain processing. *In* "Fractals of Brain, Fractals of Mind: In Search of a Symmetry Bond. Advances in Consciousness Research, Vol. 7" E. R. MacCormac, M. I. Stamenov, eds. pp. 127–154). John Benjamin Publishing Co., Philadelphia, PA.

Malone, M. A., Kershner, J. R., & Swanson, J. M. (1994). Hemispheric processing and methylphenidate effects in attention-deficit hyperactivity disorder. *J. Child Neurol.* **9,** 181–189.

Mann, C. A., Sterman, M. B., & Kaiser, D. A. (1996). Suppression of EEG rhythmic frequencies during somato-motor and visuo-motor behavior. *Int. J. Psychophysiol.* **23,** 1–7.

McCormick, D. A., & Pape, H. C. (1990). Properties of a hyperpolarization-activated cation current and its role in rhythmic oscillation in thalamic relay neurones. *J. Physiol.* **431,** 291–338.

McGaugh, J. L., Weinberger, N. M., & Lynch, G. (1995). "Brain and Memory: Modulation and Mediation of Neuroplasticity." Oxford University Press, New York.

Modell, J. G., Mountz, James M., Curtis, George C., & Greden, J. F. (1989). Neurophysiologic dysfunction in basal ganglia/limbic striatal and thalamocortical circuits as a pathogenetic mechanism of obsessive-compulsive disorder. *J. Neuropsychiat. Clin. Neurosci.* **1,** 27–36.

Munglani, R., & Jones, J. G. (1992). Sleep and general anaesthesia as altered states of consciousness. *J. Psychopharmacol.* **6,** 399–409.

Munk, M. H. J., Roelfsema, P. R., Koenig, P., Engel, A. K., & Singer, W. (1996). Role of reticular activation in the modulation of intracortical synchronization. *Science* **272,** 271–274.

Newman, J. P., & Wallace, J. F. (1993). Diverse pathways to deficient self-regulation: Implications for disinhibitory psychopathology in children. *Clin. Psychol. Rev.* **13,** 699–720.

Oken, B. S., Kishiyama, S. S., & Salinsky, M. C. (1995). Pharmacologically induced changes in arousal: Effects on behavioral and electrophysiologic measures of alertness and attention. *EEG Clin. Neurophysiol.* **95,** 359.

Pardoen, D., Bauwens, F., Dramaix, M., & Tracy, A. (1996). Life events and primary affective disorders: A one year prospective study. *Br. J. Psychiat.* **169,** 160–166.

Park, S., Como, P. G., Cui, L., & Kurlan, R. (1993). The early course of the Tourette's syndrome clinical spectrum. *Neurology* **43,** 1712–1715.

Pennington, B. F. (1991). "Diagnosing Learning Disorders: A Neuropsychological Framework," p. 93. The Guilford Press, New York.

Pfurtscheller, G. (1977). Graphical display and statistical evaluation of event-related desynchronization (ERD). *EEG Clin. Neurophysiol.* **43,** 757–760.

Pfurtscheller, G. (1992). Event-related synchronization (ERS). An electrophysiological correlate of cortical areas at rest. *EEG Clin. Neurophysiol.* **83,** 62–69.

Post, R. M., & Weiss, S. R. B. (1989). Kindling and manic-depressive illness. *In* "The Clinical Relevance of Kindling" (T. G. Bolwig & M. R. Trimble, eds.), pp. 209–230. John Wiley & Sons, Chichester, England.

Post, R. M., Rubinow, D. R., & Ballenger, J. C. (1986). Conditioning and sensitization in the longitudinal course of affective illness. *Br. J. Psychiat.* **149,** 191–201.

Rapoport, J. L. (1986). Childhood obsessive-compulsive disorder. *J. Child Psychol. Psychiat.* **27,** 289–295.

Rapoport, J. L. (1990). Obsessive compulsive disorder and basal ganglia dysfunction. *Psycholog. Med.* **20,** 465–469.

Rapoport, J. L., Giedd, J., Kumra, S., Jacobsen, L., Smith, A., Lee, P., Nelson, J., & Hamburger, S. (1997). Childhood-onset schizophrenia: Progressive ventricular change during adolescence. *Arch. Gen. Psychiat.* **54,** 897–903.

Rappelsberger, P., & Pfurtscheller, G., Filz, O. (1994). Calculation of event-related coherence—a new method to study short-lasting coupling between brain areas. *Brain Topog.* **7,** 121–127.

Restak, R. (1995). "Brainscapes." Hyperion, New York.

Rieke, F., Warland, D., de Ruyter, R. van Steveninck, & Bialek, W. (1996). "Spikes: Exploring the Neural Code." The MIT Press, Cambridge, MA.

Roth, S. R., Sterman, M. B., & Clemente, C. D. (1967). Comparison of EEG correlates of reinforcement, internal inhibition and sleep. *EEG Clin. Neurophysiol.* **23,** 509–520.

Rothschild, A. J. (1988). Biology of depression. *Med. Clin. North Am.* **72,** 765–790.

Rumsey, J. M. (1996). Neuroimaging in developmental dyslexia: A review and conceptualization. *In* "Neuroimaging: A Window to the Neurological Foundations of Learning and Behavior in Children" (G. Reid Lyon, Judith M. Rumsey, eds.), pp. 57–77. Paul H. Brookes Publishing Co., Baltimore, MD.

Sakurai, Yoshio (1996). Hippocampal and neocortical cell assemblies encode memory processes for different types of stimuli in the rat. *J. Neurosci.* **16,** 2809–2819.

Saugstad, L. F. (1994). The maturational theory of brain development and cerebral excitability in the multifactorially inherited manic-depressive psychosis and schizophrenia. *Int. J. Psychophysiol.* **18,** 189–203.

Scheife, R. T., & Graziano, P. J. (1991). Principles of neuropharmacology. *In* "Neurology in Clinical Practice, Vol. 1, Principles of Diagnosis and Management" (Walter G. Bradley, Robert B. Daroff, Gerald M. Fenichel, & C. David Marsden, eds.), pp. 687–712. Butterworth Heinemann Publishers, Boston, MA.

Schore, A. N. (1994). "Affect Regulation and the Origin of the Self. The Neurobiology of Emotional Development." Lawrence Erlbaum Associates, Hillsdale, NJ.

Schwartz, G. (1979). Biofeedback and the behavioral treatment of disorders of disregulation. *Yale J. Biolog. Med.* **52,** 581–596.

Schwartz, G. E. (1989). Disregulation theory and disease: Toward a general model for psychosomatic medicine. *In* "Psychosomatic Medicine: Theory, Physiology, and Practice" (Stanley Cheren, ed.). International Universities Press, Madison, CT.

Seifert, A. R., & Lubar, J. F. (1975). Reduction of epileptic seizures through EEG biofeedback training. *Biolog. Psychol.* **3,** 157–184.

Sherman, S. M., & Guillery, R. W. (1996). Functional organization of thalamocortical relays. *J. Neurophysiol.* **76,** 1367–1395.

Sillito, A. M., Jones, H. E., Gerstein, G. L., & West, D. C. (1994). Feature-linked synchronization of thalamic relay cell firing induced by feedback from the visual cortex. *Nature* **369,** 479–482.

Sohmer, H., & Student, M. (1978). Auditory nerve and brain-stem evoked responses in normal, autistic, minimal brain dysfunction and psychomotor retarded children. *EEG Clin. Neurophysiol.* **44,** 380–388.

Spitzer, N. C., & Sejnowski, Terrence J. (1997). Biological information processing: Bits of progress. *Science* **277,** 1060–1061.

Sporn, J., & Sachs, G. (1997). The anticonvulsant lamotrigine in treatment-resistant manic-depressive illness. *J. Clin. Psychopharmacol.* **17,** 185–189.

Stefos, G., Bauwens, F., Staner, L., Pardoen, D., & Mendlewicz, J. (1996). Psychosocial predictors of major affective recurrences in bipolar disorder: A 4-year longitudinal study of patients on prophylactic treatment. *Acta Psychiat. Scand.* **93,** 420–426.

Stein, D. J. (1996). The neurobiology of obsessive-compulsive disorder. *The Neuroscientist* **2,** 300.

Steriade, M., & Deschenes, M. (1984). The thalamus as a neuronal oscillator. *Brain Res. Rev.* **8,** 1–63.

Steriade, M., McCormick, D. A., & Sejnowski, T. J. (1993). Thalamocortical oscillations in the sleeping and aroused brain. *Science* **262**, 679–685.

Sterman, M. B. (1976). Effects of brain surgery and EEG operant conditioning on seizure latency following monomethylhydrazine intoxication in the cat. *Exp. Neurol.* **50**, 757–765.

Sterman, M. B. (1977). Sensorimotor EEG operant conditioning: Experimental and clinical effects. *Pavlovian J. Biolog. Sci.* **12**, 63–92.

Sterman, M. B., & Friar, L. (1972). Suppression of seizures in epileptic following sensorimotor EEG feedback training. *EEG Clin. Neurophysiol.* **33**, 89–95.

Sterman, M. B., & MacDonald, L. R. (1978). Effects of central cortical EEG feedback training on incidence of poorly controlled seizures. *Epilepsia* **19**, 207–222.

Sterman, M. B., & Shouse, M. N. (1980). Quantitative analysis of training, sleep EEG and clinical response to EEG operant conditioning in epileptics. *EEG Clin. Neurophysiol.* **49**, 558–576.

Sterman, M. B., & Shouse, M. N. (1982). Sensorimotor mechanisms underlying a possible common pathology in epilepsy and associated sleep disturbances. *In* "Sleep and Epilepsy" (M. B. Sterman, M. N. Shouse, & P. Passouant, eds.), Academic Press, New York.

Sterman, M. B., Wyrwicka, W., & Roth, S. R. (1969). Electrophysiological correlates and neural substrates of alimentary behavior in the cat. *Ann. NY Acad. Sci.* **157**, 723–739.

Sterman, M. B., Lucas, E. A., & MacDonald, L. R. (1972). Periodicity within sleep and operant performance in the cat. *Brain Res.* **38**, 327–341.

Sterman, M. B., MacDonald, L. R., & Stone, R. K. (1974). Biofeedback training of the sensorimotor electroencephalogram rhythm in man: Effects on epilepsy. *Epilepsia* **15**, 395–416.

Sterman, M. B., Shouse, M. N., Lucia, M. B., Heinrich, R. L., & Sarnoff, S. K. (1977). Effects of anesthesia and cranial electrode implantation on seizure susceptibility of the cat. *Exp. Neurol.* **57**, 158–166.

Sterman, M. B., Goodman, S. J., & Kovalesky, R. A. (1978). Effects of sensorimotor EEG feedback training on seizure susceptibility in the rhesus monkey. *Exp. Neurol.* **62**, 735–747.

Sterman, M. B., Kaiser, D. A., & Veigel, B. (1996). Spectral analysis of event-related EEG responses during short-term memory performance. *Brain Topog.* **9**, 21–30.

Stevens, A., Lutzenberger, W., Bartels, D. M., Strik, W., & Lindner, K. (1997). Increased duration and altered topography of EEG microstates during cognitive tasks in chronic schizophrenia. *Psychiat. Res.* **66**, 45–57.

Stewart, M. A., Pitts, F., Craig, A., & Dieruf, W. (1966). The hyperkinetic child syndrome. *Am. J. Orthopsychiat.* **36**, 861–867.

Suffin, S. C., & Emory, W. H. (1995). Neurometric subgroups in attentional and affective disorders and the association with pharmacologic outcome. *Clin. Encephalog.* **26**, 76–83.

Tozzo, C. A., Elfner, L. F., & May, Jr., J. G. (1988). EEG biofeedback and relaxation training in the control of epileptic seizures. *Int. J. Psychophysiol.* **6**, 185–194.

Tucker, D. M., & Williamson, P. A. (1984). Asymmetric neural control system in human self-regulation. *Psycholog. Rev.* **91**, 185–215.

von der Malsburg, C. (1991). Self-organization of orientation sensitive cells in the striate cortex. *In* "Pattern Recognition by Self-Organizing Neural Networks" (Gail A. Carpenter & Stephen Grossberg, eds.), The MIT Press, Cambridge, MA.

von der Malsburg, C. (1995). Binding in models of perception and brain function. *Curr. Opin. Neurobiol.* **5**, 520–526.

von der Malsburg, C. (1990). A neural architecture for the representation of scenes. *In* "Brain Organization and Memory: Cells, Systems, and Circuits. (J. L. McGaugh, N. M. Weinberger, & G. Lynch, eds.), pp. 356–372. Oxford University Press, New York.

Wada, J. A. (1990). "Kindling 4." Plenum Press, New York.

Weinberg, W. A., & Brumback, Roger A. (1992). The myth of attention deficit-hyperactivity disorder: Symptoms resulting from multiple causes. *J. Child Neurol.* **7**, 431–445.

Weinberg, W. A., & Harper, Caryn R. (1993). Vigilance and its disorders. *Neurolog. Clin.* **11,** 59–78.

Weinberger, D. R. (1997). The biological basis of schizophrenia. *J. Clin. Psychiat. Mono. Ser.* **15,** 4–6.

Wender, P. H. (1974). Some speculations concerning a possible biochemical basis for minimal brain dysfunction. *Life Sci.* **14,** 1605.

Whittington, M. A., Traub, R. D., & Jeffreys, J. G. R. (1995). Synchronized oscillations in interneuron networks driven by metabotropic glutamage receptor activation. *Nature* **373,** 612.

Wright, J. J., & Liley, D. T. J. (1996). Dynamics of the brain at global and microscopic scales: Neural networks and the EEG. *Behav. Brain Sci.* **19,** 285–320.

Wyler, A. R., Lockard, J. S., DuCharme, L. L., & Perkins, M. G. (1977). EEG operant conditioning in a monkey model: II. EEG spectral analysis. *Epilepsia* **18,** 481–488.

Wyrwicka, W., & Sterman, M. B. (1968). Instrumental conditioning of sensorimotor cortex EEG spindles in the waking cat. *Physiol. Behav.* **3,** 703–707.

12

THE NEURAL UNDERPINNINGS
OF NEUROFEEDBACK TRAINING

ANDREW ABARBANEL

Aptos, California

I. INTRODUCTION

This chapter presents a set of electro- and neurophysiological processes as a basis for the efficacy of neurofeedback training (NT), particularly for attention deficit hyperactivity disorder (usually referred to as AD/HD or ADHD), depression, and obsessive-compulsive disorder (OCD). It then suggests neurophysiological commonalities among these disorders and suggests the possibility of adapting it to treat schizophrenia and other serious clinical syndromes.

There are a number of compelling reasons to work toward a neurophysiologically sound understanding of neurofeedback training. The primary reason, of course, is to guide us toward optimal treatment techniques. We also need to understand why NT seems to simulate the results (and sometimes even the side effects) of the more traditional and far more extensively researched treatment modality for mental disorders: psychopharmacology. Unfortunately, this is not only an intellectual, but also a practical and political, imperative; the use of neurofeedback training continues to be devalued or neglected by the mainstream medical community (and by insurance carriers). Therefore, emphasis here will be on understanding commonalities in the physiological mechanisms subserving pharmacological and neurofeedback phenomena—commonalities underemphasized both in practice and in the literature. This approach will demonstrate that the different treatment modalities can be utilized, not to force a choice, but rather to suggest useful ways to understand the neurophysiological aspects of a range of psychiatric disorders and of the mechanisms underlying their successful treatment. Ideally, this understanding can also suggest, for example, how the modalities can be optimally combined. Neural mechanisms will be suggested to account for the long-term efficacy of neurofeedback for ADHD. Because the mechanisms generating field potentials (that is, the electromagnetic fields measured as "brain waves"), on the other hand, are themselves still incompletely understood, any discussion about procedures utilizing them must involve significant uncertainty, especially in the anatomical and physiological details involved. Nonetheless, discussion can transcend the uncertainties in the details involved and focus on the general principles and conclusions reached. In this way, it can stimulate research both to explicate the details, and to help unravel aspects of brain function and dysfunction.

For several reasons, this chapter focuses on ADHD. For one thing, some of the mechanisms proposed here regarding ADHD suggest parallels to current neurophysiological ideas generally and also to recent ideas about schizophrenia (Carlsson & Carlsson, 1990a, b) specifically. It will be suggested throughout that for ADHD, operant conditioning by neurofeedback rests on the same well-established neurophysiological principles that mediate the effects of psychotropic medication. In Section IV the emphasis on the mechanisms and treatment of ADD is generalized to a range of psychiatric conditions that NT clinicians find amenable to treatment. In Section IV we suggest that these disorders (including post-traumatic stress disorder, OCD, mood disorders, and possibly schizophrenia) all exhibit deficiencies in attentional mechanisms, and that this circumstance explains why they, too, respond to NT.

II. NEUROPHYSIOLOGICAL PROCESSES RELEVANT TO NEUROFEEDBACK TREATMENT

It is not logical to assume that normalizing a patient's EEG power spectrum, within a single session or over time, will automatically normalize his or her symptoms. Nonetheless, it may be true. This section attempts to explicate several extensively researched neural mechanisms that will help explain how NT works.

For clarity and simplicity, our discussion is restricted to theta–beta ratio training (e.g., training for decreases in ratio of 4 to 8 Hz EEG amplitude to 13–20 Hz). Justification for the efficacy of NT for ADHD is offered here at three levels. The first, and simplest, is empirical: (1) an elevated theta–beta (or theta–SMR) ratio correlates empirically with the presence of ADD symptoms, and a reduced theta–beta (or theta–SMR) ratio correlates empirically with the resolution of these symptoms. (In the following, SMR refers to 12–14 Hz, the "sensorimotor" rhythm.)

On a second, more general (and theoretical) level, it can be suggested that in NT, the patient learns to exert neuromodulatory control over the circuitry system mediating the attentional process. Over time, long-term potentiation (see Section II,D) in the circuitry involved consolidates an optimization of attentional processes. In terms of network theory it can be said that during NT the system is neuromodulated into an *attractor state,* a stable point of equilibrium for the system; other states functioning close to these will settle into their configuration (Cohen & Servan-Schreiber, 1992). At this level of explanation, one can analogize what happens in NT to learning a motor task like typing or riding a bicycle. As a person practices the skill, sensory and proprioceptive input initiates feedback regulation of the motor circuits involved (in sensorimotor cortex, basal ganglia, etc.); over time practice automatizes the skill. The parallel to NT can be visualized by imagining a child working with a specific NT paradigm (like the raising of a balloon on a computerized visual display as an index of a decreasing theta–beta ratio. As the balloon rises, the child watches and "feels" himself moving it; he feeds these perceptions and "feelings" back to whatever neural circuitry decreases theta–beta ratios (and which therefore increases attentional competence). Over time, practice automatizes the improved attentional capacity.

A third level of explanation involves details of physiological processes that are disordered in ADD. Its aim is to relate theta–beta ratios and attentional competence through discovery of exactly what neural processes mediate them. As noted earlier, physiological or anatomical explanations at this level must involve a degree of uncertainty because of uncertainties about the processes generating field potentials and regulating the attentional process.

Despite formidable difficulties in reaching precise formulations for the relationships of EEG rhythms, neural mechanisms, and attentional competencies, recent advances in neurophysiology and electrophysiology are beginning to allow more direct access to the processes mediating attentional phenomena. These include improved understanding of oscillatory modes, event-related potentials, long-term potentiation (LTP), and neuromodulation. It is hoped that what is learned about the anatomy, physiology, and treatment of attentional processes and their treatment by NT can also help clarify the even thornier issues of the neurophysiology and treatment of mood and thought disorders (see Section IV).

A. GENERATION OF CORTICAL POTENTIALS

Despite a good deal of recent progress (Steriade *et al.,* 1990; Lopes da Silva, 1991), the neural mechanisms generating theta, SMR, and beta range scalp potentials remain controversial. Some of the details, however, are being clarified. Oscillatory activity is best understood in the brain stem–thalamus–cortex axis, especially in the case of alpha spindles (9–12 Hz), though even here there is some controversy (Vanderwolf, 1992; Vander-wolf & Stewart, 1988).

In both the thalamus and the limbic system, certain neurons display oscillatory behavior; this intrinsic activity is significantly affected by inputs from other neurons. Because the thalamic neurons and processes are the best understood of the centers considered here, the discussion in this section is limited to that center. As justified later, it is assumed that the fundamental process here generalizes to pacemaker centers in the limbic regions involved in attentional process.

In vitro, thalamic neurons oscillate in the 6–10 Hz range. There are three types of neurons in the thalamic relay system: (1) thalamocortical neurons (TCR), (2) reticular nucleus neurons (RE) that provide inhibitory (hyper-polarizing) feedback control to the TCR neurons, and (3) local interneurons that help coordinate the interactions between the first two (see Fig. 12.1). The TCR neurons function in two distinct modes: (1) as relay cells that depolarize in response to input volleys, thereby transmitting (and to some extent integrating) ascending sensory input, and (2) as oscillatory cells that fire in a collective rhythm, thereby blocking input to the cortex. Which

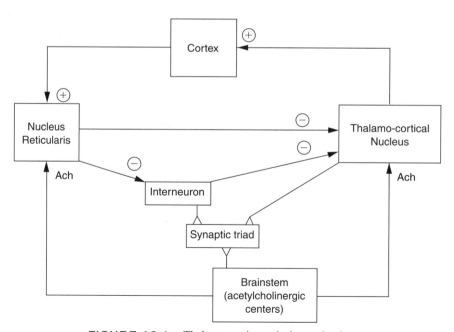

FIGURE 12.1   Thalamo-cortico-reticular nucleo loop.

modality appears depends on how close the RE and TCR resting membrane potentials are to their firing thresholds. The resting potentials in turn are determined by neuromodulation from brain stem centers. Neuromodulation provides either depolarizing or hyperpolarizing influences to thalamic neurons by adjusting thalamic membrane permeabilities to ion flow. This process adjusts the firing characteristics of the TCR and RE cells, therefore establishing either the relay or oscillatory state.

Alpha spindle generation is the best understood example of brain stem neuromodulatory control (Lopes da Silva, 1991). If brain stem cholinergic modulation is withdrawn from RE and TCR neurons, the oscillatory mode appears. If cholinergic modulation is increased, the relay mode appears. About 1 sec before the onset of sleep, there is a decrease in the firing rate of the cholinergic input to the thalamus. This establishes the oscillatory mode in the TRC neurons, which shields the cortex from sensory input as sleep ensues. The TCR cells transfer the alpha rhythm to the cortex, which in turn generates the potentials measured on the scalp EEG as alpha spindles.

For frequencies out of the alpha range, understanding is less complete. In a recent review and synthesis of neural mechanisms underlying NT, Sterman (1994) proposes that three systems of (integrative) brain activity influence the thalamic generation of field potentials at scalp level. He calls these (1) vigilance, (2) sensorimotor integration, and (3) cognitive integration. The *vigilance* system involves diffuse neural networks and specific centers in the brain stem and their ascending influence on thalamic, subcortical, and cortical centers. The *sensorimotor* system involves the ascending touch and proprioceptive pathways and their projections to thalamus and on to sensorimotor cortex, along with afferents from this cortical area. This system generates the sensorimotor rhythm (SMR), the 12–14 Hz rhythm over the sensorimotor strip. *Cognitive integration* involves a wide range of neural centers that process and integrate sensory inputs and motor responses.

Sterman suggests that SMR, alpha, and theta rhythms appear when inputs from the three systems are withdrawn from thalamus. As noted earlier, the prototypic example is that of the generation of alpha rhythms from the thalamus by brain stem cholinergic activity. If sensorimotor inputs are withdrawn, the SMR appears. Further, if cognitive processing is withdrawn (as in relaxed states without cognitive activity), alpha appears. Finally, if vigilance is withdrawn (as in states of inattentive drowsiness), theta appears. Thus the presence of these rhythms on the EEG indicates the influence on the thalamus of underlying brain states related to vigilance, cognitive processing, and sensorimotor integration. If it is assumed that attentiveness intrinsically accompanies states of SMR-associated stillness (including frequencies between 15 and 20 Hz), the connection between Sterman's scheme and what is observed in NT for ADHD becomes more clear. Specifically, the combination of higher activity in the beta or SMR range and lower activity in the theta range associates directly with states of increased stillness and attentiveness and with decreased drowsiness (and other cognitive disturbances associated with theta activity). Section III elaborates on these arguments.

Sterman's synthesis does not discuss how intrinsic oscillatory activity in the limbic system contributes to the generation of cortical field potentials. Though there is some evidence that hippocampocortical circuitry can generate scalp-measured field potentials (see, for example, Miller, 1991), there is little support for this in the literature. We assume in the following discussion, therefore, that the thalamus is the main generator of scalp-level field potentials. We also assume that the effect of other centers on scalp potentials is through their influence on the thalamus. These assumptions, however, do not affect the major premises of this paper. Because a good deal of work implicates the limbic centers in attentional processes (see reviews by Sieb, 1990, and Pribram & McGuinness, 1992), however, it is reassuring that Sterman's scheme is consistent with a number of observations on limbic contributions to attentional capacity (see Section III).

Before we can pursue matters beyond the (relatively) familiar confines of the thalamus, further details about neuromodulation and the gating function of oscillatory states are needed.

B. NEUROMODULATOR CONTROL

If NT is to make effective and lasting changes in the neural circuitry mediating attentional functions, those circuits must be adjustable by feedback control as well as able to maintain those adjustments over time. In neurological terms: The systems involved must be sufficiently *plastic*. Two mechanisms subserving such neuronal plasticity are *neuromodulation* and *long-term potentiation*. Though historically these processes were introduced in different contexts (LTP in hippocampal circuitry, neuromodulation in ascending brain stem systems), their actions are not altogether independent. For convenience, however, they are first presented separately (here and in Section II). Then Section III will discuss how they combine to mediate the effect of NT on the attentional circuitry.

Neurotransmission, the process by which the electrical properties of a neuron change as a result of synaptic stimulation, can be separated into two subtypes: fast-acting *neurotransmission* proper (usually involving fast Na^+ and Cl^- channels) and *neuromodulation* (usually involving slower K^+ and Ca^{2+} channels). In neuromodulation, the adjusted ionic flows act to change the membrane potential on the postsynaptic neuron such that firing characteristics are changed. Acetylcholine or noradrenergic alpha type 1 receptors, for example, act by closing K+ channels, thereby raising membrane potentials. In this way, the firing rates of individual neurons can be adjusted, and the group characteristics of neuronal circuits can be changed (state changes). Another mechanism of neuromodulation is the flow of Ca^{2+} into cells; this influx can change membrane potentials directly as well as precipitate intracellular chemical and structural changes so that the firing characteristics of the postsynaptic neurons are changed.

Neuromodulation is best understood in the ascending modulator control from the brain stem. There are four major brain stem systems: the locus coeruleus (noradrenergic), the nucleus basalis and surrounding areas (cholinergic), the raphe nuclei (serotonergic), and the central tegmental area and substantia nigra (dopaminergic). These centers respond to incoming stimuli and discharge to higher centers; they react to global aspects of incoming stimuli, like novelty or intensity (Derryberry & Tucker, 1990). Noradrenergic discharge from the locus coeruleus, for example, follows the perception of unexpected, intense, or aversive stimuli–situations requiring rapid attention and response. Higher centers are thereby adjusted to suppress extraneous activity and to attend to the aversive stimuli while ignoring others. The dopaminergic system responds to a range of cues, which arouses fear and then facilitates activity in higher centers during stressful encounters. It facilitates a number of prepackaged motoric responses that are useful in situations requiring a "flight or fight" response. Thus the dopaminergic and noradrenergic centers respond to cues relevant to functions impaired in ADHD—perceptual, evaluative, motoric, etc. These factors are very likely to account for the effectiveness of noradrenergic and dopaminergic agents for ADHD.

Neuromodulation appears to be central to the mechanisms subserving NT in the following ways. Ascending brain stem modulation of thalamic and limbic centers affect switches between states, rates of group oscillations, and other changes in (mainly thalamic and limbic) circuitry necessary to optimize attentional capacity. At the same time, limbic centers exert neuromodulatory control over several centers (Derryberry & Tucker, 1990; Isaacson, 1980). The same neural network, for example, with two different degrees (or types) of neuromodulation can carry out two entirely different motor functions. Therefore, changes in neuromodulation can effect switches between brain states and, therefore, brain functions. A pre-hatchling chick, for example, uses the same neural networks to control pecking through its shell, and then, with a change of neuromodulation, controls its movements as it begins to walk. Another example is the human sleep regulating system: Different neuromodulatory input maintains the cortex at different levels of consciousness (from wakefulness through the different levels of sleep).

Our rapidly growing understanding of so-called deterministic chaotic systems may provide the best explanation of how (and how rapidly) neuromodulation causes changes between brain states. Chaos theory involves a study of systems controlled by nonlinear dynamics. Technically speaking, its variables may be described by a set of nonlinear differential equations. The nonlinearity allows small changes in initial conditions to cause very large changes in the state of a system over time. Small changes in neuro-modulation, for example, can cause significant changes over time in the functioning of the system modulated. Thus only a few sessions of NT might have major behavioral effects. Elbert *et al.* (1994) and Stam *et al.* (1996) provide summaries of nonlinear phenomena in physiological processes.

C. RHYTHMIC OSCILLATIONS, BRAIN STATES, AND INFORMATION FLOW

Sections A and B introduced the ideas of relay and oscillatory *states* of the thalamic centers, and of changes between them. The change between states can also be conceptualized by a circuitry metaphor: as either the opening or closing of a *gate* that blocks information flow or as a switch regulating changes between different states of a brain center. Such switching of brain centers between different *states,* and *gating* of the information flow are two important functions of oscillatory activity (a third, *resonance,* is discussed in Section III).

A similar, if more complex, set of circumstances appears in the limbic centers. As detailed in Section III, these centers contribute significantly to attentional processes; thus, details of the gatings and state changes effected by oscillators in the limbic system are discussed here in some detail. Figure 12.2 shows the main limbic oscillatory generators and pathways. The septal nuclei and hippocampus comprise the main pacemakers of the system, though cells in the dentate and entorhinal cortices also generate oscillatory modes (Bland & Colom, 1993). Ascending brain stem modulation projects to pacemakers in the septal nuclei and, to a lesser extent, to those in the hippocampus directly. The major circuitry in this area involves the septal–hippocampal–septal loops and the trisynaptic circuit from entorhinal cortex to dentate through the hippocampus, and back to the entorhinal cortex (see Fig. 12.2).

Similarities between this combination of pacemaker centers modulated by feedback circuitry (autonomous oscillation with surrounding feedback centers) and those in the thalamocortical system can be seen in a comparison of Figs. 12.1 and 12.2. This analogy is pursued in Section III,B in the service of suggesting cooperation between the analogous thalamic and limbic sys-tems in the control (and dyscontrol) of attentional processes. Therefore, the remainder of this section summarizes some details in the functioning of these limbic centers.

Three main patterns of field potentials are measured in the hippocampus: (1) *theta* or *RSA* (rhythmic slow activity), between 3 and 11 Hz (depending on species), (2) *LIA* (large-amplitude irregular activity) in a broad range between 0.5 and 25 Hz, and (3) *beta,* fast waves between 20 and 60 Hz. There are (at least) two neurotransmitter systems in the septal innervation of the hippocampus: cholinergic and GABAergic. The balance between

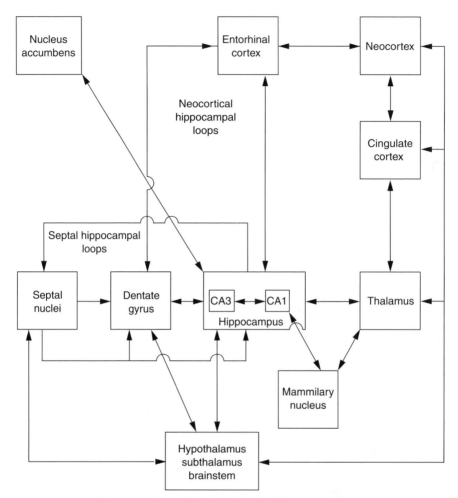

FIGURE 12.2   Septal and cortical hippocampal loops

these inputs, themselves under brain stem modulation, determines whether LIA or RSA dominates in the hippocampal field potentials (Bland & Colom, 1993). The frequency of rhythmic input signals also affects hippocampal rhythms by entraining its oscillations across a range of frequencies.

A study of these rhythms across a range of animal species shows that each rhythm can be correlated with particular behavioral states, each of which relates to attentional processes. Cross-species studies (including with man) can help clarify the correlations in relation to attentional process. In a number of species RSA appears during activities of particular survival value for (and therefore characteristic of) each species and in the memory storage of what was learned during those activities (Winson, 1972, 1990;

Miller, 1991). In the rat, for example, RSA occurs with exploratory behavior; in the rabbit, in active scanning of the environment; and in the cat, in stalking behavior. The behavioral correlates across species of LIA are less well documented, though for a range of species, studies have connected it to the maintenance of immobile posture (Vanderwolf, 1992); this finding is reminiscent of Sterman's finding that a 12–14 Hz rhythm over the sensorimotor cortex of the cat was correlated with immobile vigilance. The higher frequency beta components have been correlated with focussed attention in a number of species. These findings reinforce the suggestion of limbic–thalamic cooperation, including frequency entrainment between rhythms of these structures.

In addition to survival-related activity, animal studies have defined broad classes of behavior that correlate to RSA and LIA. For example, in the rat so-called type 1 behavior (motor acts like walking, jumping, swimming) is correlated to RSA; type 2 behavior (waking immobility along with patterns of licking, chattering the teeth, grooming) is correlated with LIA (Vanderwolf, 1992). Experimental limitations make the extrapolation of animal studies to man difficult. Extension of animal results to man must be done cautiously (for some time even the existence of human hippocampal theta was questioned). A few studies, however, are available; these have taken advantage of unusual surgical opportunities to study human hippocampal EEG directly. They do seem to establish both the existence of hippocampal theta as well as the correlation of specific behavioral states with specific rhythms–thereby suggesting that the relationship in lower animals between specific rhythms, behavioral patterns, and gatings of information flow also apply to man (Meador et al., 1991; Arnolds et al., 1980). The behaviors involved, however, are more subtle than those with other animals; changes in rhythm relate less to motor activity and more to verbal behavior.

It appears, then, that frequencies in both theta and beta ranges exist in human hippocampal circuitry, and they relate to state changes and gatings of information in the same way as does the thalamic circuitry in animals. Further, they follow the same general patterns of correlation to behavioral states as with the lower animals. The interrelation of thalamic to hippocampal function and frequency ranges, therefore, is more likely. As noted earlier, this circumstance will be useful to a discussion of human attentional capacity in section III.

D. LONG-TERM POTENTIATION

One of the central reasons to pursue both the implementation and understanding of NT is the now commonplace finding of ongoing remission of ADD symptoms long after discontinuation of neurofeedback treatment. It is likely that the high degree of plasticity of neurons in the limbic system contributes to this circumstance. Specifically, the neurons respond to repetitive afferent signals by increasing the efficacy of their receptors in a way that persists after the trains of repetitive signals cease. This process is called *long-term potentiation* (LTP), and has been studied intensively during the last two decades (see reviews by Bliss & Lynch, 1988; Lynch *et al.*,1990; Doyere *et al.*, 1993; Massicotte & Baudry, 1991; Teyler & DiScenna, 1987). LTP is defined formally in terms of laboratory measurements; it is a stable and relatively long-lasting increase of synaptic response to a constant afferent volley following brief high-frequency stimulation of the same afferents (Teyler, 1989). There is a corresponding process of long-term depression (LTD), in which synaptic strengths are diminished by repetitive afferent stimulation (Tsumoto, 1990); presumably LTD complements LTP in the development of plasticity in neuronal circuitry.

The relationships between very high frequency (tetanic) stimulation by implanted electrodes, LTP, and conditioning have been established as follows. LTP is observed in conjunction with behavioral conditioning in the *absence* of tetanic stimulation by implanted electrodes (Thompson, 1983; Weisz *et al.*, 1984; Bloch & Laroche, 1981, 1985; Ruthrich *et al.*, 1982). The reverse is also true; that is, hippocampal LTP, induced by high-frequency stimulation of the perforant pathway (that is, without behavioral conditioning), can lead to an increased rate at which animals learn in subsequent classical conditioning experiments (Berger, 1984). Further, electrical stimulation of the midbrain reticular formation enhances LTP at perforant path synapses, prolongs its duration (Bloch & Laroche, 1985), *and* facilitates behavioral conditioning (Bergis *et al.*, 1990; Bloch & Laroche, 1981; Laroche *et al.*, 1983).

LTP was first studied in the trisynaptic circuit of the hippocampus (Bliss & Lomo, 1973; Bliss & Gardner-Medina, 1973). Within the limbic system, the effect of LTP is optimized when the frequency of incoming volleys is within the RSA range (Larson & Lynch, 1986; Larson *et al.*, 1986)–a reassuring result in light of the central role of RSA in limbic processing. Since these early studies in the limbic system, LTP has been studied extensively in the neocortex (Tsumoto, 1990). A comparison of hippocampal and neocortical LTP (Teyler, 1989) shows differing magnitudes, temporal and developmental aspects, numbers of afferent pathways required, and possibly receptor types; nonetheless, the process is basically the same in all areas–increased synaptic efficacy by repeated afferent stimulation, whether by electrode or rehearsal. It is found in the cat, for example, that for motor cortex LTP to occur, afferent stimulation from both the ventrolateral (VL) thalamus and the sensory cortex is required (Iriki *et al.*, 1989). In these processes, LTP does not occur in the thalamus itself (Lee & Ebner, 1992); presumably, this fact leads to a stability that preserves the thalamus's stability as an unchanging relay and gating station. For each area (neocortical or limbic), LTP has a characteristic time course during development. In the auditory and visual cortex, for example, there are early *critical periods* during which LTP is at a maximum (Tsumoto, 1990); following this, there is a significant diminution of potentiation throughout life.

Recent reviews of neuronal plasticity and LTP suggest a number of component processes (Wolff *et al.*, 1995; Weiler *et al.*, 1995; Voronin *et al.*, 1995). These include changes in the arrangement of synapses, in the size of synapses, in the numbers of so-called *concave* and *spinule* synapses (which increase synaptic efficiency), and in synapse formation and elimination. Work has shown (summarized in Wolff *et al.*, 1995) that there is continuous turnover of synapses throughout life. This turnover includes changes in the number of synaptic junctions per axon terminal, and in the branching patterns of dendrites and terminal axons. The changes occur on the order of days to weeks. In some cases, the remodeling and elimination of synapses can lead to *irreversible* modification of networks (this corresponds to the concept of attractor states mentioned earlier).

LTP in the *prefrontal cortex* is of particular relevance to ADHD and its treatment. A number of studies (reviewed in Doyere *et al.*, 1993) find that in active animals, electrical stimulation mimicking short bursts of action potentials at hippocampal sites induces LTP in the prefrontal cortex. In one study (Laroche *et al.*, 1990), facilitation by paired pulses to the CA1/subicular hippocampal field induced LTP in the prefrontal cortex. Interpulse intervals between 40 and 200 msec (corresponding to 5–25 HZ) were effective; the range from 80 to 200 msec (5–12.5 Hz) was optimal. Thus, hippocampal stimulation in the range of both RSA and LIA induced LTP changes in the prefrontal cortex. Later, Doyere's group (1993) found that short high-frequency bursts at 7.7 Hz induced LTP in prefrontal cortex, though only for 1 day. The same group measured the prefrontal cortex response in rats to assess effects of stimulation of the CA1/subicular area before and after a classical conditioning experiment. Rats subjected to a paired conditioning paradigm showed a LTP response in prefrontal cortex to the stimulation, whereas pseudoconditioned rats showed a depression of postsynaptic potentiation of prefrontal responses.

The role of LTP in NT assumes added clinical relevance in light of recent work (Wilson & McNaughton, 1994) showing that networks of hippocampal cells, correlated in their firing patterns during the learning of spatiobehavioral tasks, are reactivated during slow-wave sleep (SWS) with the same correlation patterns. Further, the hippocampal activity during SWS has been found to activate areas in the entorhinal cortex (Chrobak & Buzsaki, in press); presumably the hippocampus is programming into cortical circuitry what was learned during the day. It has also been reported recently that learning perceptual tasks similar to those used to measure attentional capacity (and to diagnose ADHD) is found to be consolidated during REM sleep (Karni *et al.*, 1994); hippocampal or cortical field potentials were not measured in this study, but the parallels to the Wilson and McNaughton study are compelling.

These findings add support to the suggestion that the hippocampus can induce LTP in networks of cortical neurons in such a way that the cortical networks code information already processed in the hippocampus; in the example of Wilson and McNaughton, this involves learned motor behavior (cf. Miller, 1991). As detailed by Winson (1972, 1990), this process is mediated by the theta rhythm. Miller (1991) has calculated that this process involves transit times from hippocampus to neocortex to hippocampus on the order of 200 msec (corresponding to 5 Hz), thereby supporting a resonance at the theta frequency between the two sets of networks. This process, *resonance,* the facilitation of information exchange between brain centers resonating at the same frequency, is the third physiological function mediated by group oscillations that is relevant to the present work (Lopes da Silva, 1991, 1992).

Neuromodulation and LTP are clearly related both biochemically and functionally. Each process represents the influence of one neurotransmitter system on another, thereby allowing increased flexibility of synaptic activity. In the Schaffer/commissural synapses in CA1/subicular hippocampal areas (Lynch *et al.,* 1990), for example, LTP involves two types of glutamate receptor (NMDA and AMPA); the NMDA receptor induces LTP by activating an inward Ca^{2+} current, thereby precipitating a number of chemical changes that modify the activity of AMPA receptors. These express the LTP effect. This can be compared to the neuromodulatory effect in the rat CA1 region (Brinton, 1990), for example, in which vasopressin acts as a neuromodulator for the noradrenergic receptor by effecting a Ca^{2+} flow into the cell; the NE induced level cAMP (the second messenger in the NE system) is thus enhanced. In the hippocampal mossy fiber-to-CA3 neurons in the guinea pig, Fisher and Johnston (1990) found that norepinephrine and acetylcholine affect LTP differently: Norepinephrine increases it and acetylcholine decreases it. Thus, changes in a range of neuromodulators from any one center can make a number of adjustments in a range of synaptic activity in other centers, thereby adding flexibility to the systems involved.

III. NEURAL MECHANISMS UNDERLYING ATTENTION AND NT

In Chapter 11, Othmer, Othmer, and Kaiser emphasize that neurofeedback augments the brain's capacity to regulate itself, and that this self-regulation lies at the heart of its clinical efficacy. The question of which factor (the brain's capacity to self-regulate, or the particular states into which it regulates itself) or, better, what combination of these factors contributes to NT's therapeutic effects remains unclear. Recent work, however, suggests that at least temporary clinical improvement can occur without training self-regulation. Mental conditions including depression, for example, respond positively to entrainment by externally applied oscillating magnetic fields in the beta range (Kircaldie *et al.*, 1997). Consistent with electrodynamic theory, these fields will induce electric fields at the same frequencies.

For these reasons, the following subsections emphasize the specific states and frequencies (and of balances between them) and how certain processes generate and maintain them.

A. ANATOMICAL ASPECTS

As noted earlier, Sterman's synthesis of the centers and processes subserving the generation of field potentials emphasizes the centrality of the brain stem–thalamic–cortical system. His conceptualization of the influence of the systems of vigilance, sensorimotor integration, and cognitive processing on the thalamus provides a framework for filling in the details in his system.

However, a good deal of research suggests that centers in the prefrontal cortex, the limbic system, and surrounding areas should be included in any outline of attentional processes. As already noted, like the thalamus, the limbic and surrounding areas contain their own autonomous pacemaker centers (in the septal nuclei, hippocampus, dentate, and entorhinal cortex) that oscillate autonomously (Lopes da Silva *et al.*, 1990). This suggests parallels between the brain stem–thalamic–cortical system and that of a set of limbic–brain stem–thalamic–cortical systems. In addition, clinical experience shows that the mood disorders (clearly mediated by limbic centers) typically involve disturbances in limbic functioning and disturbances of attention and concentration. Correspondingly, attentional disorders often involve depressed mood. Also, both mood and attentional disorders involve difficulties with memory, a function mediated through limbic centers.

In addition, animal studies of both prefrontal and hippocampal lesions reveal symptoms reminiscent of ADHD in humans (Pribram & McGuinness, 1992; Crowne & Riddell, 1969; Douglas & Pribram, 1969; Lopes da Silva *et al.*, 1990): hyperactivity, distractibility, and a tendency toward preoccupation with certain activities that verges on pathological undistractibility (reminiscent of some ADHD children's tendency to become mesmerized by television or video games). Recent reviews (Sprict, 1995, for example) emphasize the role of the hippocampus in terms of its widespread input for all sensory modalities, its reciprocal connections with the entire association cortex, its role as an integration center for sensory fields, as a center for comparing input with stored data, and, as such, a center to filter out irrelevant (that is, distracting) stimuli that might lead to maladaptive arousal responses.

An especially important reason to expand Sterman's focus to regions anterior to the thalamus is the efficacy of psychotropic medications in treating the same conditions as NT. Specifically, the antidepressants (affecting the serotonin and norepinephrine systems) and the stimulants (affecting primarily the dopamine system) have effects at limbic and anterior sites. These chemicals would not be expected to affect the thalamic GABA or acetylcholine systems as much as the limbic and prefrontal areas. Further, limbic sites are most likely relevant to admixing a motivational aspect to attentional processes–clearly a significant component.

The interactions among these subsystems is complex, and must be both reliable and adaptive. Early on, Mesulam (1981) presented a network theory of these interactions. Relying on physiological, anatomical, and behavioral studies of the macaque monkey, he suggested that an area (referred to as area PG in the monkey brain) in the dorsal portion of the inferior parietal lobule integrates four categories of inputs during attentional process: (1) sensory association, (2) limbic, (3) reticular, and (4) motor. In this way, area PG coordinates motivational clues in sensory events, modulates the level of arousal, and guides the motor functions of exploratory and orienting behavior necessary for scanning the environment. Mesulam is careful to note that the extrapolation from monkeys to humans is incompletely understood, but nonetheless suggests that it is likely that a cerebral network with similar organization is present in humans. Mesulam's system is represented in Fig. 12.3.

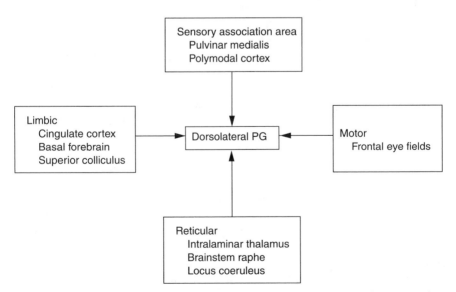

FIGURE 12.3   Mesulam's model of inputs to dorsolateral pg during attentional processing.

In 1990, Sieb presented a framework in which to understand the integration of attentional processes. His paper presented a system similar to that of Mesulam but, because it included ideas relevant to EEG measurements, is more relevant to an understanding of the relationship of NT. Sieb suggests that as sensory input reaches the brain stem, it processes and transmits these signals to the thalamus, and activates other centers, particularly septal nuclei, hippocampus, and frontal cortex. The hippocampus then orchestrates several components of the attentional process by selectively inhibiting a number of functions at a number of centers; these include orientation, alertness, awareness, and arousal. This orchestration facilitates the focusing of attention on only one set of environmental signals. By 300 msec after the initial stimulus, inputs from brain stem, mediodorsal thalamus, and several cortical centers converge on the prefrontal cortex. This area, in turn, processes the input and organizes a response to it. The response includes a major signal to the septal nuclei (which Sieb relates to the P300 evoked potential wave). The septal nuclei in turn signal the hippocampus to release its inhibition of the functions mentioned above. Thus for Sieb, the prefrontal–septal–hippocampal axis is a major lynchpin of the attentional process.

Further, Sieb suggests that the initial inhibitory action of the hippocampus is mediated by an oscillation in the theta range, and that the prefrontal signal to the septal nuclei induces a hippocampal beta rhythm that blocks the theta inhibiting signal. Thus, the suggestion that the hippocampus and prefrontal cortex exert selective inhibitory actions on a number of centers corresponds to the withdrawal of combinations of cognitive processing and vigilance functions in Sterman's scheme (in which these withdrawals generate oscillatory modes in the thalamus). However accurate in its details, Sieb's concept of pairs of balanced processes (theta versus beta oscillations, hippocampal inhibition versus activation) introduces an important conceptual leitmotif about attentional processes that will appear repeatedly below.

Figure 12.4 represents a skeletal outline of the processes suggested by Sterman, Mesulam, and Sieb. The characteristics of the circuitry shown that are most relevant to NT are its degree of (1)adjustability and of (2) stability. The *adjustability* is provided by the flexibility of and collaboration of LTP neuromodulation. LTP operates throughout the network discussed previously. It is well known, for example, that brain stem centers neuromodulate thalamic centers (Lopes da Silva, 1990; Sterman, 1994) and can induce LTP in the hippocampus (Doyere *et al.*, 1993). Stimulation in hippocampal centers, for example, has been shown to induce LTP in prefrontal cortex (Laroche *et al.*, 1990; Doyere *et al.*, 1993). Further, hippocampal and other limbic centers can neuromodulate centers in the brain stem (Derryberry & Tucker, 1990). LTP has been shown in motor neurons stimulated simultaneously by thalamic and sensory cortical neurons (Iriki *et al.*, 1989), in motor cortex stimulated by polysynaptic cortical stimulation

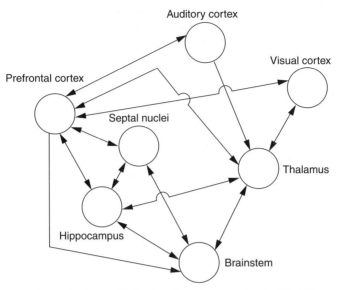

FIGURE 12.4   Skeletal outline of centers involved in NT.

(Sutor & Hablitz, 1989), and in sensory cortex stimulated by VM thalamus (Lee & Ebner, 1992). Finally, stimulation in basal forebrain can induce cortical LTP (Lee & Ebner, 1992).

The *stability* of the attentional system adjusted by neurofeedback is of central importance clinically, but a thorny problem theoretically. If the system is in a stable attractor state, small imbalances at any point in the system will tend to be damped out by the functioning of the system as a whole. If it is not in such a state, small imbalances at any juncture will be maintained or amplified. Specifically, the fact that NT involves self-regulation suggests that brain states can be "moved" closer to attractor states than they can by more globally applied exogenous influences–like medication. This last concept is revisited later in this chapter.

B. BALANCES IN THE ATTENTIONAL SYSTEM: AN EXAMPLE

As noted earlier, it is not clear whether the ability to entrain particular brain centers and frequencies of brain circuits into specific configurations (of brain states and scalp potential frequencies) represents a major component of NT efficacy. Because we know a good deal about the neuromodulation, circuitry, neurotransmitters, and frequencies involved in the attentional system, this system can help organize an answer to this question by providing a useful area of exploration.

As also noted previously, the motif of pairs of balanced functions recurs repeatedly in observations and conceptualizations of the attentional system, particularly in limbic and prefrontal centers. Studies in the rabbit (Krnjevic *et al.*, 1988; Brazhnik *et al.*, 1993; Vinogradova *et al.*, 1993a, 1993b, 1993c), for example, suggest a balance between the GABAergic and cholinergic septal–hippocampal signals. The GABAergic signal is more immediate, and seems to "reset" the hippocampal circuitry before processing a new set of inputs. The cholinergic signal is slower in onset, and serves to filter out cortical input of information coded during earlier signals. When performing correctly, these operations appear to lock the hippocampal circuitry onto only one set of inputs at a time, thereby facilitating selective attention to that set.

In a similar manner, a number of anatomical and functional balances have been suggested for the prefrontal cortex (reviewed in Fuster, 1989). In primates this area is composed of two general regions: dorsolateral and ventromedial. The areas differ phylogenetically and ontogenetically, in their pattern of connections with other brain centers, and in their roles in attentional processes. In man, for example, dorsolateral lesions lead to a decreased awareness of the environment, whereas ventromedial lesions lead to hyperactivity and distractibility (that is, increased and indiscriminate attention to the environment).

Pribram and McGuinness (1992) discuss a pair of attention-related functions (and centers that subserve them) that will help us to understand the relationship between hippocampal and cortical field potentials. Their discussion is based on earlier work in the cat (Macadar *et al.*, 1974; Lindsley & Wilson, 1976) that identified two systems of neurons affecting theta synchronization and desynchronization in the hippocampus. Madacar *et al.* locate these systems in the brain stem. The first is medial, producing desynchronization of hippocampal theta (leaving scalp-level LIA and beta range frequencies synchronized). The other is lateral and produces synchronized hippocampal theta. These authors associate the first system (which desynchronizes theta) with exploration of more or less familiar territory, and the second (which synchronizes theta) with generalized orienting with immobility when food is encountered. These observations correspond to the behavioral correlates of hippocampal RSA, and LIA presented in Section II. These studies found that, to a good approximation, when the first system synchronizes theta in the hippocampus, it desynchronizes theta in the cortex, and vice versa for the second system. This circumstance will be useful later for interpreting theta–beta ratios in scalp-level field potentials.

This extended dialectic of paired functions and processes leads to an integrative hypothesis: That imbalances in one or more of these pairs can lead to deficits in attentional capacity (as in ADD). The imbalances can be in the timing of signals, intensity of potentials, amplitude of frequency components, balances between neuromodulator inputs, and so on. The suggestion is that in attention-disordered patients there are a number of possible imbalances between the myriad signals and countersignals, processes and counterprocesses, that amount to a coarseness or imbalance in the "tuning" of the circuitry. The coarseness of control causes an attentional disorder marked by excessive attention to either external or internal stimuli, or both. This hypothesis can be correlated with clinical experience with mental disorders in several ways. In Section IV,B, for example, we discuss a similar set of balanced neural processes in the case of schizophrenia.

Because the centers shown in Fig. 12.4 are so densely interconnected, any imbalance at any one center or connection can lead to imbalances in the system as a whole. Because of the central role of the septal–hippocampal inputs, however, a consideration of imbalances in that system, whether primary or as a result of its connections to other centers, is particularly useful in extending the above hypothesis to clinical experience. Specifically, the septal–to–hippocampal input determines the RSA/LIA balance of hippocampal rhythms; it, in turn, is regulated by brain stem, prefrontal, and hippocampal afferents. Consequently, imbalances in any of these centers can lead to imbalances in the septal signal. The suggestions of Vinogradova's group (that the cholinergic/GABAergic balance determines the balance between hippocampal resetting and cortical input blocking) lead to the following idea: An imbalance in the septo–hippocampal system can be correlated directly with one of the seminal characteristics of ADHD in the following way. A too early cutoff of the hippocampus from cortical input (the cholinergic function) makes it lock onto subsequent inputs without connecting them to prior input and trains of thought. This corresponds to a *too selective attention* to each input without adequate integration into the background context of observation and thought; in other words, it leads to *distractibility*. On the other hand, the reverse circumstance, too much blocking of inputs with respect to blocking of prior contexts (the GABAergic function) leads to a general inattention to inputs–clinically represented by the *daydreaming* or generally *inattentive behavior* characteristic of ADHD children. This includes becoming "lost" to the environment when watching television or playing computer games. Figure 12.5 schematizes the two clinical patterns. [Incidentally, this model also raises the possibility that psychotic or autistic states may represent an especially exaggerated instance of an (input)/(internal context) imbalance. It is of interest, therefore, that during acute psychotic episodes, patients *do* show ADHD-like profiles in the power spectral analyses of their evoked potential signals. This pattern resolves with the resolution of the psychosis (Koukkou, 1980).]

C. SYNTHESIS OF NEURAL PROCESSES IN NT

Earlier an analogy was suggested between a child learning to ride a bicycle and learning to move an object on a computer display screen that

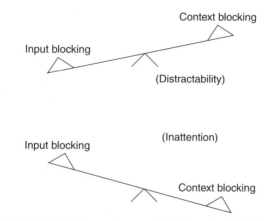

FIGURE 12.5   Two extremes of imbalance in limbic circuitry.

indexes his theta–beta ratio. When the child is given an instruction, for example, to "lower the balloon" in the display, he experiences a period of internal experimentation during which signalings along various internal paths are tried until the right combinations are found to lower the balloon. During this process the prefrontal cortex monitors the level of the balloon through afferents from the visual cortex and signals the septal–hippocampal system (and possibly the brain stem and/or the thalamus directly). From the pathways shown in Fig. 12.4, there are feedback loops (from brain stem, thalamus, and hippocampus back to the prefrontal cortex, from the hippocampus back to the septum, from brain stem and thalamus back to the hippocampus, from hippocampus, thalamus, and prefrontal cortex back to brain stem, and so on), available to neuromodulate the prefrontal activity. Directly, through the hippocampus, the brain stem, or the cortex, or perhaps through all three, it can therefore regulate the frequency distribution of the thalamus and other sites) to produce a decreasing theta–SMR (or beta) ratio. Rehearsal of these activities during ongoing NT sessions (and possibly during SWS) can then stabilize the system through LTP.

The preceding discussion assumes that cortical (and therefore scalp) frequencies correlate with those generated in the limbic and thalamic centers. As discussed by Lubar and Lubar in Chapter 5, the cortical frequencies appear to be determined by cortical neuronal characteristics and by local and global interneuronal transit times. It is possible that these cortical frequencies significantly change the frequency of afferents from thalamocortical cells to the cortex.

Nunez (1995), however, points out that the thalamocortical circuits can be set in resonance such that cortical frequencies are locked into the frequencies of the thalamic neurons that drive them.

IV. RELEVANCE TO MENTAL DISORDERS

A. CLINICAL FINDINGS

The stimulus for this work was the observed efficacy of both NT and medication for both mood and attentional disorders, as well as the observation that NT often lowers the dose of medication needed to treat ADD and depression. A number of published objective findings support the relevance of the mechanisms suggested earlier to those disorders. Recent electroencephalographic research on these and other psychiatric disorders suggests that a range of psychiatric disorders should respond to some form of NT, and in fact clinical experience confirms this. This work includes power spectral analysis (PSA) patterns reported for ADHD (Mann *et al.*, 1992), alcoholism (Peninston & Kulkosky, 1989), and PTSD (Peninston *et al.*, 1993). Other work suggests its use with schizophrenia (Schneider & Pope, 1992). It also includes experiments with depressives who demonstrated specific patterns in cortical slow potentials (CSPs). The latter are slowly changing negative dc changes in scalp field potentials with anticipation of motor or cognitive tasks. Normal controls, as well as depressed and schizophrenic patients appear to regulate their PSAs and CSP patterns differently (Schneider, 1992a, 1992b). Both normal controls and schizophrenics can change their PSAs, but controls can maintain the changes between NT sessions, whereas schizophrenics cannot (Schneider & Pope, 1992). Changes from controls in these parameters are also seen in alcoholics (Schneider *et al.*, 1993).

In addition, a number of subjective experiences support the relevance of the mechanisms proposed to ADD and depression. The case is strongest with the mood disorders. Patients who respond to antidepressant medication, for example, often report feeling more "bulletproof"; that is, after recovery, they feel emotional pain from losses, reproaches, or humiliations much less intensely. Their descriptions are reminiscent of patients treated with opiates: they still perceive the pain, but do not seem to care about it anymore. One can imagine that with recovery from depression, information flow in limbic circuitry is rerouted such that input to certain "psychic pain" centers (analogous to thalamic and cortical centers for the experience of physical pain) is rerouted by oscillatory gating. Alternatively, the states of such centers may be adjusted to be less receptive or less fragile. One can also imagine frequency changes such that resonances between areas are facilitated or suppressed. Further, the mysterious switches between manic and depressed states may involve switchings controlled by ascending or descending neuromodulation that initiates switches or gatings that cause state changes in relevant brain centers.

One must wonder, too, whether the antimanic effects of anticonvulsants like carbamazepine, valproic acid, and clonazepam (Kaplan & Boggiano,

1989) are related to these neurophysiological processes. Electroconvulsive treatment (ECT), for example, does rely on the induction of seizure activity for a brief period (Weiner, 1989). It may be that, in the same way that theta frequency optimizes LTP in limbic circuits, the seizure oscillations affect limbic pathology in such a way as to change states, reroute information, and so on. The new psychotherapy technique of eye movement desensitization training (Shapiro, 1991), in which rapidly alternating lateral gaze changes seem to mobilize affect-laden memories, may involve similar mechanisms. Because the pontine gaze centers project strongly to the septal nuclei, it may be that the oscillatory signals from the repetitive gaze alternation induces changes in septal–hippocampal activity, thereby bringing to awareness memories previously phase or frequency locked out of consciousness.

B. MAJOR PSYCHIATRIC DISORDERS AS GENERALIZED ATTENTIONAL DISORDERS: CIRCUIT THEORIES

A number of recent studies and corresponding theoretical constructions based on them are beginning to support the preceding speculation. Regional blood flow studies of depression (Drevets *et al.,* 1992; Drevets & Raichle, 1992), OCD (Baxter, 1994), and schizophrenia (Carlsson & Carlsson, 1990a, 1990b), when combined with several decades of neurophysiological study, suggest the existence of sets of balanced circuits (themselves regulated by balances of neuromodulators) in similar fashion as those suggested here for ADD.

Work as early as 1937 (Papez, 1937) proposed that reverberations through the limbic system were responsible for generating emotional activity. Much more recently, Drevets and colleagues proposed, based on PET scan regional blood flow studies with depressed patients, that abnormal activity in a pair of circuits was responsible for the symptoms of depression. The blood flow studies found that *actively depressed* patients (not depression-prone individuals not currently depressed), had increased blood flow in the left prefrontal cortical areas (specifically, an area extending from the left ventrolateral prefrontal cortex onto the medial prefrontal cortical surface). This suggests that increased prefrontal blood flow is a state marker–present, that is, only with active depression. The left amygdala had increased blood flow in depressives whether or not they were actively depressed (though the differences from control were significant only in the actively depressed group). The data suggest, then, that the increased left amygdala blood flow was a *trait* marker–its presence indicating a depressive disorder, whether or not it is active. In addition, there is increased blood flow in the mediodorsal thalamus, decreased flow in the left medial caudate nucleus, and other changes in a number of related areas.

Combining these findings with other neurophysiological data, Drevets and coworkers suggest abnormal functioning in a pair of interacting circuits. Specifically, they suggest that the functioning of a prefrontal–amygdala–medial dorsal thalamic (PAM) circuitry in depressed patients is overactive, and that this generates a number of symptoms of depression. These would include the perseverative negative ruminations, the ongoing and repetitive negative self-evaluations, and so on. They suggest that an amygdala–striatal–pallidal–medial dorsal thalamic circuitry, normally inhibitory to the PAM circuit, is underactive in depressives, and that therefore the first circuit is disinhibited in depression. They suggest that neuromodulation with dopamine, norepinephrine, and serotonin adjusts these circuits and that antidepressant medication, by normalizing these systems, can restore normal function to the interlocking systems.

Recent regional blood flow studies produce similar findings for obsessive-compulsive disorder (OCD). In this case the changes are mainly in the orbital prefrontal cortex and the caudate nucleus (Baxter, 1994). Baxter suggests that in OCD inadequate sensory information gating allows self-sustaining loops, and that overactivity in the loop drives prepackaged behavioral routines result.

In 1990 Maria and Arvid Carlsson proposed that two circuits function abnormally in schizophrenia, and that this is the result of an imbalance of dopamine, glutamate, and GABA, which regulate these circuits. The relevance of these circuits to schizophrenia, they suggest, is that they modulate thalamocortical signaling; with inadequate modulation of these pathways, the schizophrenic is flooded with incoming information. This process has been associated for many years with the cognitive experience of the schizophrenic. The Carlssons offer it as an explanation of the activity of dopaminergic antagonist medication. Specifically, they suggest that it is the cortical–striatal–thalamocortical feedback loop that protects the cortex from the overload of thalamic input. In this circuit glutamatergic corticostriatal neurons are excitatory, GABA striatothalamic neurons are inhibitory, and glutamate/aspartate thalamocortical neurons are excitatory. Conversely, they suggest that the mesostriatal dopaminergic pathways act in the opposite direction, widening the thalamocortical filter and increasing information flow to the cortex. Based on these considerations, the Carlssons suggest that glutaminergic agonists might be useful supplements for treating schizophrenia, and that glutaminergic antagonists might be useful for treating Parkinson's disease.

For each of these disorders, then, this chapter suggests that imbalances in sets of circuits result in psychopathology. In each case one can suggest intuitive connections between the malfunctioning of the circuits and the clinical symptoms. In schizophrenia the patient's experience of overwhelming sensorial flooding is the result of an inadequate modulation by the basal ganglia centers of the thalamocortical signals. For depression and OCD, the overactive circuits represent autonomous and exaggerated activity of prefrontal or basal ganglia circuits that code for negative imagery of self and the world (for depression), or of fixed behavioral or ideational circuitry (OCD).

One can also visualize these circuits as mediating abstract mental operations that have developed by modeling on concrete motor functions (in the Piagetian sense that increasingly abstract mental functions develop by modeling on more concrete ones). In a related sense, because mental functions in neurological disorders tend to parallel the neurological symptoms (for example, mental perseveration in Parkinson's disease as a parallel to bradykinesia), the symptoms of depression or OCD can be seen as the parallels of certain childhood motoric activities. Specifically, one can suggest that in depression the sense of badness and the generalized inhibition are abstract parallels of the childhood motor functions that are disinhibited during the experience of depression. Turning the head away from the breast, for example–an action that involves both inhibition (of sucking) and the judgment that it is bad (more milk causes pain)–forms the basis for subsequent (depressive) experiences that self and the world are bad, the impulse to withdraw, the experience of psychological pain, and so on. Normally, these experiences are suppressed, but not in depression. Psychiatric symptoms result from an overactivity (disinhibition) of the circuits mediating the more abstract (further evolved) experiences of badness, inhibition, and so on.

Another way to understand how a number of disorders all respond to NT is to consider them as members of a class of generalized attention disorders. That is, they involve a person's (relative) inability to attend appropriately to the mix of inner and outer sources. As illustrated in Fig. 12.5, ADD involves dysfunction in the ability to balance attention on inner versus outer inputs (and vice versa). Post-traumatic stress disorder, on the other hand, involves a dysfunction in the screening of inputs from the environment: Inputs that represent memories from the original trauma are preferentially attended to and acted on. In depression and OCD, fixed internal ideas occupy attention out of proportion to perceptions from the outer world (and others from the inside) that might influence or temper them. With depression, for example, convictions of low self-value, a sense of being overwhelmed, hopelessness, and helplessness preoccupy the person despite whatever external actuality that might counter. It is the same with OCD.

V. SUMMARY AND CONCLUSIONS

This chapter suggests that the effects of neurofeedback techniques can be understood in terms of well-known neurophysiological mechanisms. It is suggested that neural networks mediating attentional processes can be adjusted through neuromodulation and stabilized through long-term potentiation into stable (attractor) states. It is suggested further that during NT for ADHD, the patient consolidates an enhanced capacity to regulate state changes and gatings of signals between brain centers such that attentional capacity is enhanced. It is argued that this process yields long-lasting results compared to stimulant medication treatment of ADHD because it employs the same sort of neuromodulatory control and LTP that with practice indelibilizes such sensorimotor skills as riding a bicycle.

Further suggestions were offered to elaborate the details of this process for those unfamiliar with the details of electrophysiology and the neurophysiology of attentional processes. A review of some neural underpinnings of the attentional process was presented in order to identify connections between the theta, SMR, and beta field potentials employed in neurofeedback for ADD and specific neural processes in a number of brain centers. Several schemes were offered, but it is suggested that the most likely process involves thalamic generation of theta, SMR, and beta waves under modulation from a number of cortical, limbic, and brain stem centers that regulate various checks and balances in the component functions of the attentional process; LTP then makes these changes persistent during practice NT sessions. It is suggested further that the attentional disorders represent coarseness in the limbic control of attentional processes; neuromodulation during neurofeedback can fine-tune this control, and long-term potentiation over the course of treatment can make the changes permanent. Conceptually parallel suggestions are offered for OCD, PTSD, and other psychiatric disorders.

It is suggested that neurofeedback results are more persistent than those with stimulant medication because neurofeedback and stimulants may operate at different locations with different receptivity to long-term potentiation by neuromodulation. Finally, it is suggested that there is a commonality of mechanisms in ADD, OCD, depression, and schizophrenia that can (1) let us conceptualize each of these as variants of a generalized attention disorder and (2) suggest a basis for the positive neurofeedback effects with ADD, OCD, and depression (and perhaps someday schizophrenia).

It is very important to emphasize that the details of the schemata presented here can be imprecise, or simply incorrect, without affecting the validity of more general ideas offered. It is also important to emphasize that this chapter does not resolve the question of whether an increased capacity for self-regulation into nonpathological (perhaps stable attractor) states, or simply the entrainment of brain centers into those states, is more central to the efficacy of NT. Rather, what is presented is intended to be consistent with either viewpoint—or a combination. However, a valuable hint about this question can be inferred from the work on LTP in hippocampal (and surrounding) centers. There, two observations were made: (1) that inducing LTP externally, independent of practicing, led to improved motor learning, and (2) that practice led, through LTP, to more efficacious circuitry with which to carry out the practiced motoric activity. Fortunately, clinical success does not force us to decide between viewpoints.

REFERENCES

American Psychiatric Association. (1994). "Diagnostic and Statistical Manual," 4th Ed. American Psychiatric Association, Washington, DC.

Arnolds, D. E. A. T., Lopes da Silva, F. H., Aitink, J. W., Kamp, A., & Boeijinga, P. (1980). The spectral properties of hippocampal EEG related to behavior in man. *EEG Clin. Neurophysiol.* **50,** 324–328.

Baxter, L. R., Jr. (1994). Positron emission tomography studies of cerebral glucose metabolism obsessive compulsive disorder, *J. Clin. Psychiat.* **55**(10, Suppl.), 54–59.

Berger, T. W. (1984). Long-term potentiation of hippocampal synaptic transmission affects rate of behavioral learning, *Science,* **224,** 627–30.

Bergis, O. E., Bloch, V., & Laroche, S. (1990). Enhancement of long-term potentiation in the dentate gyrus two days after associative learning in the rat. *Neurosci. Res. Commun.* **6,** 119–128.

Bland, B. H., & Colom, L. V. (1993). Extrinsic and intrinsic properties underlying oscillation and synchrony in limbic cortex. *Prog. Neurobiol.* **41,** 157–208.

Bliss, T. V. P., & Gardner-Medwin, A. R. (1973). Long-lasting potentiation of synaptic transmission in the dentate gyrus of unanaesthetized rabbit following stimulation of the perforant path, *J. Physiol. (Lond.)* **232,** 356–374.

Bliss, T. V. P., and Lomo, T. (1973). Long-lasting potentiation of synaptic transmission in the dentate area of the anaesthetized rabbit following stimulation of the perforant path. *J. Physiol. (Lond.)* **232,** 331–356.

Bliss, T. V. P., & Lynch, M. A. (1988). Long-term potentiation of synaptic transmission in the hippocampus: Properties and mechanisms. *In* "Long-Term Potentiation: From Biophysics to Behavior" (P. W. Landfield & S. A. Deadwyler, eds.), pp. 3–72. Alan R. Liss, New York.

Bloch, V., & Laroche, S., (1981). Conditioning of hippocampal cells: Its acceleration and long-term facilitation by post-trial stimulation. *Behav. Brain Res.* **3,** 23–42.

Bloch, V., & Laroche, S. (1985). Enhancement of long-term potentiation in the rat dentate gyrus by post-trial stimulation of the reticular formation., *J. Physiol. (Lond.)* **360,** 215–231.

Brazhnik, E. S., Vinogradova, O. S., Stafekhina, V. S., & Kitchigina, V. F. (1993). Acetylcholine, theta-rhythm and activity of hippocampal neurons in the rabbit–I. Spontaneous activity. *Neuroscience* **53**(4), 961–970.

Brinton, R. E. (1990). Neuromodulation: Associative and nonlinear adaptation. *Brain Res. Bull.* **24,** 651–658.

Carlsson, M., and Carlsson, A. (1990a). Interactions between glutamatergic and monoaminergic systems within the basal ganglia–implications for schizophrenia and Parkinson's disease. *Trends Neurosci.* **13**(7), 272–276.

Carlsson, M., & Carlsson, A. (1990b). Schizophrenia: A subcortical neurotransmitter imbalance syndrome? *Schizophrenia Bull.* **16**(3), 425–432.

Chrobak, J. J., & Buzsaki, G. (1996). High-frequency oscillations in the output networks of the hippocampal-entorhinal axis of the freely-behaving rat. *J. Neurosci.* **126,** 3056.

Cohen, J. D., & Servan-Schreiber, D. (1992). Introduction to neural network models in psychiatry. *Psychiatric Annals* **22**(3), 113–118.

Crowne, D. P., & Riddell, W. I. (1969). Hippocampal lesions and the cardiac component of the orienting response in the rat. *J. Compar. Physiolog. Psychol.* **69**(4), 748–755.

Derryberry, D., & Tucker, D. M. (1990). The adaptive base of the neural hierarchy: Elementary motivational controls on network function. *Nebraska Symp. Motivation,* pp. 289–342.

Douglas, R. J., & Pribram, K. H. (1969). Distraction and habituation in monkeys with limbic lesions. *J. Compar. Physiolog. Psychol.* **69**(3), 473–480.

Doyere, V., Burette, F., Redini-Del Negro, C., & Laroche, S. (1993). Long-term potentiation of hippocampal afferents and efferents to prefrontal cortex: implications for associative learning. *Neurophychologia* **31**(10), 1031–1053.

Drevets, W. C., & Raichle, M. E. (1992). Neuroanatomical circuits in depression: Implications for treatment mechanisms, *Psychopharmacol. Bull.* **28**(3), 261–274.

Drevets, W. C., Videen, T. O., Price, J. L., Preskorn, S. H., Carmichael, S. T., & Raichle, M. E. (1992). A functional anatomical study of unipolar depression. *J. Neurosci.* **12**(9), 3628–3641.

Elbert, T., Ray, W. J., Kowalik, Z. J., Skinner, J. E., Graf, K. E., & Birbaumer, N. (1994). Chaos and physiology: Deterministic chaos in excitable cell assemblies. *Physiolog. Rev.* **74** (1), 1–47.

Fisher, R., & Johnston, D. (1990). Differential modulation of single voltage-gated calcium channels by cholinergic and adrenergic agonists in adult hippocampal neurons. *J. Neurophysiol.* **64**(4), 1291–1302.

Fuster, J. M. (1989). "The Prefrontal Cortex: Anatomy, Physiology, and Neurophysiology of the Frontal Lobe," 2nd Ed. Raven Press, New York. Gerbrandt, L. K., Lawrence, J. C., Eckardt, J. J., & Lloyd, R. L. (1978). Origin of the neocortically monitored theta rhythm in the curarized rat. *EEG Clin. Neurophysiol.* **45**, 454–467.

Iriki, A., Pavlides, C., Keller, A., & Asanuma, H. (1989) Long-term potentiation in the motor cortex. *Science* **245**, 1385–1387.

Isaacson, R. L. (1980). A perspective for the interpretation of limbic system function. *Physiolog. Psychol.* **8**(2), 183–188.

Kaplan, P. M., & Boggiano, W. E. (1989). Anticonvulsants, noradrenergic drugs, and other organic therapies. *In* "Comprehensive Textbook of Psychiatry" (H. I. Kaplan & B. J. Sadock, eds.), 5th Ed., pp. 1681–1688. Williams and Wilkins, Baltimore, MD.

Karni, A., Tanne, D., Rubenstein, B. S., Askenasy, J. J. M., & Sagi, D. (1994). Dependence on REM sleep of overnight improvement of a perceptual skill. *Science* **263**, 679–682.

Kircaldie, M. T., Pridmore, S. A., & Pascal-Leone, A. (1997). Transcranial magnetic stimulation as therapy for depression and other disorders. *Australian NZJ Psychiatry* **31**(2), 264–272.

Koukkou, M. (1980). EEG reactivity in acute schizophrenics reflects deviant (ectropic) state changes during information processing. *In* "Functional States of the Brain: Their Determinants" (M. Koukkou-Lehman & Lehman, eds.), pp. 265–290. Oxford, England.

Krnjevic, K., & Ropert, N. (1982). Electrophysiological and pharmacological characteristics of facilitation of hippocampal population spikes by stimulation of the medial septum. *Neuroscience* **7**(9), 2165–2183.

Krnjevic, K., Ropert, N., & Casullo, J. (1988). Septohippocampal disinhibition. *Brain Res.* **438**, 182–192.

Laroche, S., Falcou, R., & Bloch, V. (1983). Post-trial reticular facilitation of associative changes in multiunit activity: Comparison between dentate gyrus and entorhinal cortex. *Behav. Brain Res.* **9**, 381–387.

Laroche, S., Jay, T. M, & Thierry, A.-M. (1990). Long-term potentiation in the prefrontal cortex following stimulation of the hippocampal CA1/subicular region. *Neurosci. Lett.* **114**, 184–190.

Larson, J., & Lynch., G. (1986). Induction of synaptic potentiation in hippocampus by patterned stimulation involves two events. *Science* **232**, 985–988.

Larson, J., Wong, D., & Lynch, G. (1986). Patterned stimulation at the theta frequency is optimal for the induction of hippocampal long-term potentiation. *Brain Res.* **368**, 347–350.

Lee, S. M., & Ebner, F. F. (1992). Induction of high frequency activity in the somatosensory thalamus of rats *in vivo* results in long-term potentiation of response in SI cortex. *Exp. Brain Res.* **90**, 253–261.

Lindsley, D. B., & Wilson, C. L. (1976). Brain stem-hypothalamic systems influencing hippo-campal activity and behavior. *In* "The Hippocampus" (R. L. Isaacson & K. H. Pribram, eds.), Vol. 2, pp. 247–274. Plenum Press, New York.

Lopes da Silva, F. (1991). Neural mechanisms underlying brain waves: From neural membranes to networks. *EEG Clin. Neurophysiol.* **79**(2), 81–93.

Lopes da Silva, F. (1992). The rhythmic slow activity (theta) of the limbic cortex: An oscillation in search of a function. *In* "Induced Rhythms in the Brain" (E. Basar & T. H. Bullock, eds.). pp. 83–102. Birkhaüser, Boston.

Lopes da Silva, F. H., Witter, M. P., Boeijinga, P. H., & Lohman, A. H. M. N. (1990). Anatomic organization and physiology of the limbic cortex. *Physiolog. Rev.* **70**(2), 453–511.

Lynch, G., Kessler, M., Arai, A., & Larson, J. (1990). The nature and causes of hippocampal long-term potentiation. *Prog. Brain Res.* **83**, 233–250.

Macadar, A. W., Chalupa, L. M., & Lindsley, D. B. (1974). Differentiation of brain stem loci which affect hippocampal and neocortical electrical activity. *Exp. Neurol.* **43**, 499–514.

Macrides, F., Eichenbaum, H. B., & Forbes, W. B. (1982). Temporal relationship between sniffing and the limbic theta rhythm during odor discrimination reversal learning. *J. Neurosci.* **2**(12), 1705–1717.

Mann, C. A., Lubar, J. R., Zimmerman, A. W., Miller, C. A., & Muenchen, R. A. (1992). Quantitative analysis of EEG in boys with attention-deficit-hyperactivity disorder: Con-trolled study with clinical implications. *Ped. Neurol.* **8**(1), 30–36.

Massicotte, G., & Baudry, M. (1991). Triggers and substrates of hippocampal synaptic plasticity. *Neurosci. Biobehav. Rev.* **15**, 415–423.

Meador, K. J., Thompson, M. S., Loring, D. W., Murro, A. M., King, D. W., Gallagher, B. B., Lee, G. P., Smith, J. R., & Flanigin, H. F. (1991). Behavioral state-specific changes in human hippocampal theta activity. *Neurology* **41**, 869–872.

Mesulam, M.-M. (1981). A cortical network for directed attention and unilateral neglect. *Ann. Neurol.* **10**, 309–325.

Miller, R. (1991). "Cortico-Hipocampal Interplay and the Representation of Contexts in the Brain." Springer-Verlag, Berlin.

Nunez, P. L. (1995). Toward a physics of neocortex. *In* "Neocortical Dynamics and Human EEG Rhythms" (P. L. Nunez, ed.), pp. 68–132. Oxford University Press, New York.

Papez, J. W. (1937). A proposed mechanism of emotion. *Arch. Neural Psychiat.* **79**, 217–224.

Peninston, E. G., & Kulkosky, P. J. (1989). Alpha–theta brainwave training and beta endorphin levels in alcoholics. *Alcohol. Clin. Exp. Res.* **13**(2), 271–279.

Peninston, E. G., Marrinan, D. A., Deming, W. A., & Kulkosky, P. J. (1993). EEG alpha–theta brainwave synchronization in Vietnam theater veterans with combat-related post-traumatic stress disorder and alcohol abuse. *Adv. Med. Psychother.* **6**, 37–50.

Piaget, J., & Inhelder, B. (1969). *The Psychology of the Child.*

Pribram, K. H., & McGuinness, D. (1992). Attention and para-attentional processing: Event-related brain potentials as tests of a model. *Ann. NY Acad. Sci.* **678**, 65–92.

Raskin, L. A., Shaywitz, S. E., Shaywitz, B. A., Anderson, G. M., & Cohen, D. J. (1984). Neurochemical correlates of attention deficit disorder. *Ped. Clin. North Am.* **31**(2), 387–396.

Rie, H. E., & Rie, D. D. (1980). "Handbook of Minimal Brain Dysfunction: A Critical Review." Wiley and Sons, New York.

Ruthrich, H., Matthies, H., & Ott, T. (1982). Long-term changes in synaptic excitability of hippocampal cell populations as a result of training. *In* "Neuronal Plasticity and Memory Formation" (C. A. Marsan & H. Matthies, eds.), IBRO Monograph Series, Vol. 9, pp. 589–594. Raven Press, New York.

Schneider, F., Heimann, H., Mattes, R., Lutzenberger, W., & Birbaumer, N. (1992a). Self-regulation of slow cortical potentials in psychiatric patients: Depression. *Biofeedback Self-Regul.* **17**(3), 203–214.

Schneider, F., Rockstroh, B., Heimann, H., Lutzenberger, W., Mattes, R., Elbert, T., Birbaumer, N., & Bartels, M. (1992b). Self-regulation of slow cortical potentials in psychiatric patients: Schizophrenia. *Biofeedback Self-Regul.* **17**(4), 277–292.

Schneider, F., Elbert, T., Heimann, H., Welker, A., Stetter, F., Mattes, R., Birbaumer, N., & Mann, K. (1993). Self-regulation of slow cortical potentials in psychiatric patients: Alcohol dependency. *Biofeedback Self-Regul.* **18**(1), 23–33.

Schneider, S. J., & Pope, A. T. (1992). Neuroleptic-like electroencephalographic changes in schizophrenics through biofeedback. *Biofeedback Self-Regul.* **7**(4), 479–490.

Shapiro, F. (1991). Eye movement desensitization: A new psychotherapy treatment. *California Psychol.* **18**, 19–20.

Sieb, R. A. (1990). A brain mechanism for attention, *Med. Hypotheses* **33**, 145–153.

Sprick, U. (1995). Functional aspects of the involvement of the hippocampus in behavior and memory functions. *Behav. Brain Res.* **66**, 61–64.

Stam, C. J., van Woerkom, T. C. A. M., & Pritchard, W. S. (1996). Use of non-linear EEG measures to characterize EEG changes during mental activity. *EEG Clin. Neurophysiol.* **99**, 214–224.

Steriade, M., P. Gloor, R. R., Llinas, F. H., Lopes da Silva, & Mesulam, M.-M. (1990). Basic mechanisms of cerebral rhythmic activities. *EEG Clin. Neurophysiol.* **76**, 481–508.

Steriade, M., Dossi, R. C., & Pare, D. (1992). Mesopontine cholinergic systems suppress slow rhythms and induce fast oscillations in thalamocortical circuits. *In* "Induced Rhythms in the Brain" (E. Basar & T. H. Bullock, eds.). Birhauser, Boston, Basel, Berlin.

Sterman, M. B. (1994). Physiological origins and functional correlates of EEG rhythmic activities: implications for self-regulation. Unpublished work.

Sterman, M. B., Wyrwicka, W., & Roth, S. R. (1969). Electrophysiological correlates and neural substrates of alimentary behavior in the cat. *Ann. NY Acad. Sci.* **157**, 723–739.

Sutor, B., & Hablitz, J. J. (1989). Long term potentiation in frontal cortex: Role of NMDA-modulated polysynaptic excitatory pathways. *Neurosci. Lett.* **97**(1–2), 111–117.

Teyler, T. J. (1989). Comparative aspects of hippocampal and neocortical long-term potentiation, *J. Neurosci. Meth.* **28**, 101–108.

Teyler, T. J., & DiScenna, P. (1987). Long-term potentiation. *Annu. Rev. Neurosci.* **10**, 131–161.

Thompson, F. F. (1983). Neuronal substrates of simple associative learning: Classical conditioning. *Trends Neurosci.* **6**, 270–75.

Tsumoto, T. (1990). Long-term potentiation and depression in the cerebral neocortex. *Jpn. J. Physiol.* **40**, 573–593.

Vanderwolf, C. H. (1992). The electrocorticogram in relation to physiology and behavior: A new analysis. *EEG Clin. Neurophysiol.* **82**, 165–175.

Vanderwolf, C. H., & Stewart, D. J. (1988). Thalamic control of neocortical activation: A critical re-evaluation. *Brain Res. Bull.* **20**, 539–538.

Vinogradova, O. S., Brazhnik, E. S., Stafekhina, V. S., & Kitchigina, V. F. (1993a). Acetylcholine, theta-rhythm and activity of hippocampal neurons in the rabbit–II. Septal input. *Neuroscience* **53**(4), 971–979.

Vinogradova, O. S., Brazhnik, E. S., Stafekhina, V. S., & Kitchigina, V. F. (1993b). Acetylcholine, theta-rhythm and activity of hippocampal neurons in the rabbit–III. Cortical input. *Neuroscience* **43**(4), 981–991.

Vinogradova, O. S., Brazhnik, E. S., Kitchigina, V. F., & Stafekhina V. S. (1993c). Acetylcholine, theta-rhythm and activity of hippocampal neurons in the rabbit–IV. Sensory stimulation. *Neuroscience* **53**(4), 993–1007.

Voronin, L., Byzov, A., Kleschevnikov, A., Kozhemyakin, M., Kuhnt, U., & Volgushev, M. (1995). Neurophysiological analysis of long-term potentiation in mammalian brain. *Behav. Brain Res.* **66**, 45–52.

Weiler, I. J., Hawrylak, N., & Greenough, W. T. (1995). Morphogenesis in memory formation: Synaptic and cellular mechanisms. *Behav. Brain Res.* **66,** 1–6.

Weiner, R. D. (1989). Electroconvulsive therapy. *In* "Comprehensive Textbook of Psychiatry" (H. I. Kaplan & B. J. Sadock, eds.), 5th Ed., 1670–1678. Williams and Wilkins, Baltimore, MD.

Weisz, D. J., Clark, G. A., & Thompson, R. F. (1984). Increased responsivity of dentate granule cells during nictitating membrane response conditioning in rabbit. *Behav. Brain Res.* **12,** 145–154.

Wilson, M. A., & McNaughton, B. L. (1994). Reactivation of hippocampal ensemble memories during sleep. *Science* **265,** 676–679.

Winson, J. (1972). Interspecies differences in the occurrence of theta. *Behav. Biol.* **7,** 479–487.

Winson, J. (1990). The meaning of dreams. *Sci. Am.* **262,** 86–96.

Winson J., & Abzug, C. (1977). Gating of neuronal transmission in the hippocampus: Efficacy of transmission varies with behavioral state. *Science* **196,** 1223–1225.

Wolff, J. R., Laskawi, R., Spatz, W. B., & Missler, M. (1995). Structural dynamics of synapses and synaptic components. *Behav. Brain Res.* **66,** 13–20.

Wyrwicka, W., & Sterman, M. B. (1968). Instrumental conditioning of sensorimotor cortex EEG spindles in the waking cat. *Physiol. Behav.* **3,** 703–907.

13

THEORIES OF THE EFFECTIVENESS OF ALPHA–THETA TRAINING FOR MULTIPLE DISORDERS

NANCY E. WHITE

The Neurotherapy Center, Houston, Texas

I. INTRODUCTION

Twenty-five years ago EEG feedback was of major significance in the field of biofeedback. Elmer and Alyce Green at The Menninger Institute were experimenting with theta training and creativity, Thomas Budzynski with twilight learning, Lester Fehmi with open focus, Barry Sterman with epilepsy, Joel Lubar with attention deficit hyperactivity disorder (ADHD), and Joe Kamiya with alpha training. Others also were focusing on the training of the brain and central nervous system, but, because the technology was crude, promises of the value of brain wave training seemed to evaporate. EEG feedback became an almost forgotten stepchild.

With the publication of the research of Peniston and Kulkosky (1989), the "child" returned from exile and is growing and developing and expressing its original, almost forgotten, promise. Peniston's focus was a population of alcoholics, all of whom had been difficult alcoholics for more than 20 years and had been in rehabilitation unsuccessfully four to five times. Using his protocol of alpha–theta brain wave training combined with imagery of desired outcome, he was able to show reduction to elimination of craving for alcohol. To my knowledge this original research population is still showing better than 80% success rate some 9 years later.

Peniston and Kulkosky (1991) then expanded their research to a population of Vietnam veterans who were hospitalized for post-traumatic stress disorders and were having nightmares, flashbacks, and many other problems, dysfunctions, and diagnoses. By the end of the research protocol, the symptoms of this population also appeared to have resolved. They were no longer having nightmares and flashbacks. Whereas all subjects were on medications at the beginning of the study, only one was on medication by the end of the study and his dosage had been reduced by one-half. Perhaps the most remarkable outcomes of both of these studies were the major personality shifts that were recorded in their pre- and post-Minnesota Multiphasic Personality Inventory (MMPI-2) and Millon Clinical Multiaxial Inventory (Millon II) scores. Most of the pathology of these personalities had normalized (Peniston & Kulkosky, 1990).

A. THE PENISTON PROTOCOL

To summarize briefly the protocol originally used by Dr. Peniston in his research, the training began with several sessions of thermal biofeedback and autogenic training as an entrée into EEG feedback. In the original research the protocol involved fifteen 30-min sessions, typically performed twice a day, 5 days a week, on Veterans Administration Hospital in-patients. In the field today there are many versions of this original protocol, with the most common employing the original thermal and autogenic training followed by approximately 30 EEG feedback sessions, including an imagined scene of the rejection of the undesired behavior and imagery of desired outcome, which are introduced at the beginning of each EEG session and repeated in each session throughout the treatment.

The electrode placement typically is O1, monopolar, referenced to linked ears and a forehead ground with feedback tones of the computer rewarding attainment of clinician-set thresholds of increasing alpha and theta brain wave amplitudes. Other placements might be CZ, PZ, or O2. Each clinician seems to have his or her own variations on the theme. Despite the differences in placement, results seem to be consistently positive in treatment of addictions and other symptomology.

In the initial stage of this protocol, a layman's explanation of the brain, the limbic area, the neurochemistry, and its process to effect change is believed to offer the patient both a conscious and an unconscious program to follow and, along with the clarification of goals, to create a clear intention for the desired outcome. The subsequent development of imagery of the desired outcome apparently enhances the result.

Handwarming with autogenic training and temperature biofeedback follow as the next step of this protocol. Handwarming has been used in the field of biofeedback for many years as an effective tool to correct hypertension and other symptoms of sympathetic overarousal. It is helpful in teaching one to relax and be calm in any situation. Handwarming involves the circulatory aspect of the sympathetic branch of the autonomic nervous system involved in the "fight or flight" response. In the fight or flight response, the body is alerted and blood flow is increased to the major organs. This can become a chronic stress response. To counter this state, as the peripheral circulation is increased with training, the body relaxes. Handwarming also is a way of teaching the body to respond to cues from a tangible feedback to which the patient can easily relate and acts as a bridge to lower arousal states as a pretraining to eventual achievement of alpha and theta EEG frequencies. Autogenic training exercises (Green & Green, 1977) are used in combination with the temperature biofeedback training to achieve further relaxation of the body and a quiet, inward turned state of mind. In addition, rhythmic diaphragmatic breathing is taught to still body functions and focus attention.

During his or her initial sessions of thermal feedback and autogenic training exercises, the patient and his or her therapist develop a graphic, detailed visualization of the desired outcome, including a scene rejecting undesired behavior or a "clearing" of the condition to be altered. This final state visualization also involves the image of being already healed, which is believed to skirt the problems of potential harm that might result from imaging the healing process incorrectly, and is designed to reprogram the "unconscious" in a desired direction. "Programming the unconscious" with mental rehearsal of new images and intentions of desired change seems to effect healing and change both physiologically and psychologically (Green & Green, 1977; Achterberg, 1985; Simonton & Simonton, 1978). Imagery is one of the earliest forms of healing. There is archaeological evidence suggesting that the techniques of the shaman using imagination for healing are at least 20,000 years old, with vivid evidence of their antiquity in the cave paintings in the south of France. Asclepius, Aristotle, Galen, and Hippocrates, often regarded as the fathers of medicine, used imagery for diagnosis and therapy (Achterberg, 1985). At the present time Drs. Dean Ornish, Bernard Siegel, Norman Shealy, Carl Simonton, Larry Dossey, and others collectively (and courageously) are reinstating the role of the imagination in healing. Imagination is said to act on one's physical being. Images may communicate with tissues and organs, even cells, to effect change (Simonton & Simonton, 1978; Achterberg, 1985; Rossi, 1986; Siegel, 1986).

Many theories for the apparently remarkable success of alpha–theta brain wave training have been proposed by researchers and clinicians in the field of neurotherapy. Is it practical to take this protocol apart in its different aspects to find its power, or would this be reductionistic thinking akin to examining the vocal cords to see how one is a talented singer and another is not? The power of this protocol seems to lie in its generalized interaction with many aspects, and it may be of greater value to examine how its impact in specific areas contributes to a whole that creates a positive outcome for most patients treated.

Empirical science, as we know it, seeks to understand reality from the point of view of the five senses. However, this protocol seems to represent a technology designed for the induction of higher states of consciousness and insight, and one's relationship to the world is altered by these insights. It is a therapy that contains elements of the five senses, but its very nature takes one beyond the five senses to abilities that may lie latent within us all. It is a transpersonal therapy. Toward the end of his life, Abraham Maslow, one of the major pioneers in humanistic psychology, called attention to possibilities beyond self-actualization in which the individual transcended the customary limits of identity and experience. In 1968 he concluded, "I consider Humanistic, Third Force Psychology, to be transitional, a preparation for a still 'higher' Fourth psychology, transpersonal, transhuman, centered in the cosmos, rather than in human needs and interest, going beyond humanness, identity, self-actualization, and the like" (Maslow, 1968; Walsh & Vaughan, 1980). This protocol seems to follow his prediction. In this chapter I propose to show that within the protocol itself rational explanations of its generalized effectiveness may be found.

II. THEORIES OF THE PROTOCOL'S EFFECTIVENESS

To begin, the seemingly remarkable workings of the alpha–theta protocol tend to fit well within the framework of generally accepted psychological contexts, among them the functions of various states of consciousness, state-dependent learning and retrieval of memories, the relatedness of multiple diagnoses in patients with major dysfunction and addictions, the effects of childhood trauma, mind–body connections, and patient–therapist relations. Each of these is discussed in the following sections.

A. STATES OF CONSCIOUSNESS AND THE CONTINUUM OF AROUSAL

Brain wave frequencies are correlated with various states of consciousness/arousal. With a predominance of beta waves (approximately 13 Hz and higher), arousal occurs and the thinking process with its accompanying ego reactions is engaged. There is a focus on the external world. With a predominance of delta waves (0–4 Hz), a sleep state, the brain is at the opposite end of the arousal spectrum, and one basically is disassociated from the external world. With a predominance of theta waves (4–8 Hz) focus is on the internal world, a world of hypnogogic imagery where an "inner healer" is often said to be encountered. Alpha brain waves (8–13 Hz) may be considered a bridge from the external world to the internal world and vice versa. With some addicts and patients previously exposed to major trauma, alpha amplitudes can be low, thereby creating an inflexibility that keeps one from shifting readily between inward and outward states (M. Sams, personal communication, May 1996). Generally with such patients there is an avoidance of internal states where one may find awareness of self.

In everyday existence, the ideal state of the ego may well be a state of poise between the inner world of self and the outer world of objects. As one increases alpha amplitudes via neurotherapy, he or she gains the ability to shift with ease and appropriateness. Any overintense concern with the outer world is tempered and the individual may gain detachment with a sense of humor and loss of ego-centeredness. As one turns inward and attains deeper states, sensorimotor awareness tends to decrease and consciousness centers on questions concerning the meaning of life. Patients exposed to these states usually describe the latter experience as serene and peaceful, providing them with new abilities and possibilities. They seem to develop a powerful coping skill and may have access to such inner calm no matter what is occurring in their environment (Wuttke, 1992).

Another related notion is suggested by the work of Thom Hartmann (1997), who states: "Everybody is familiar with the edge between normal waking consciousness and sleep: it's often a time of extraordinary feelings, sensations, and insights, particularly as we move from sleep into wakefulness. . . . When the brain is brought to the edge of the world of God, the place of 'true' consciousness, a fractal intersection occurs. An unstable and dynamic system is created, and, like the rainbow colors of water and oil, new energies and visions are created." The Peniston alpha–theta protocol seems to enhance this ability to shift states, to move to this edge. In such states many aspects of the self involving wisdom and insight may be encountered, and awareness of earlier traumas (or "woundings") occurs, thus making them more accessible for healing.

B. STATE-CONTEXT DEPENDENT LEARNING AND RETRIEVAL

An aspect of the power of this protocol might be found in the realm of state-dependent learning and memory, or state-context dependent learning and retrieval as Jon Cowan (1993) has noted. The predominant waking brain wave frequency of children under the age of 6 is in the 4–8 Hz range associated with the "theta" frequency band in adults. As we mature, our average brain wave frequencies get faster, and in adulthood these lower frequency waves are usually associated with reverie and hypnogogic imagery, occurring largely in the transitions from wakefulness to sleep.

The surfacing of memories from early childhood during the alpha–theta brain wave training fits observations of "state-dependent memory." Because information learned while in one state of consciousness may be more difficult to access when in another state of consciousness, the natural shift in dominant brain wave frequencies during maturation could result in dysfunctional childhood learnings being preserved in the unconscious as an adult. To gain access to most of these "state-bound" memories, one may have to return to the state in which they were created, in other words, a predominantly "theta state." In utilizing the Peniston protocol of alpha–theta therapy, there is often a profound alteration in the state of consciousness of the patient. As the "subconscious" appears to become more accessible to consciousness in this deeply altered state, traumatic memories of the past are often released and appear as flashbacks from the past. As these flashbacks are relived with current adult resources and perceptions available, the contents of the "subconscious" seem more readily available for healing and alteration.

Dr. Tom Budzynski (1971, 1997) reported that a predominance of theta in the EEG was the ideal state for "rescripting" or "reimprinting" the brain, eliminating destructive behaviors or attitudes that are a result of "scripts" laid down in childhood (during times when the child is naturally in a theta state) and replacing them with more suitable and more positive scripts for a mature adult. Rossi (1986) states that each time we access the state-dependent memory, learning, and behavior processes that encode a problem, we have an opportunity to "reassociate and reorganize" or reframe that problem in a manner that resolves it. This reliving, releasing, and rescripting may be one of the few ways in which an adult can modify old scripts and store new information in the subconscious.

Robert Boustany (personal communication, 1998), a biophysicist involved in neurofeedback research, also alludes to phenomena related to state-dependent learning. He suggests that NMDA receptors act as a double lock and key to encoded patterns of behavior in the individual, and that ability to "broadly" activate the NMDA receptors is essential to personal transformation. As proposed, this activation must occur in the hippocampus of the brain, but also may occur in the amygdala and a few other areas. The use of the term *encoded patterns* indicates that children will learn certain survival response patterns while they are very young and the brain is still forming. These patterns are reflected in the subtle structure of the brain and are correlated with behavior. They may be considered as electronic circuits, which respond in specific ways. The response patterns encoded in the brain of the young child create unconscious responses later in life, some of which may be maladaptive. As an older child or an adult, a cognitive awareness that a certain behavior causes problems will not change the behavior until the "emotional pliability" to handle that insight is developed. Neurofeedback may be one means of creating more adaptive behavior by facilitating change in these encoded patterns. While neurofeedback has been used successfully in the treatment of a variety of problems, the NMDA receptors hypothesis seems particularly well demonstrated in the treatment of alcoholism as explained later in this chapter.

Boustany proposes the following mechanisms and reasoning with respect to neurofeedback's effectiveness with alcoholism. The neurotransmitter glutamine has a protective effect against alcohol, and can be used to prevent an individual from becoming inebriated. Glutamine in the brain also relates to function of the NMDA receptors. Glutamine is required at the first stage of the two-stage process of reaching long-term potentiation (LTP) in NMDA receptors. (LTP refers to a process in which cell response to a given stimulus becomes increasingly frequent and of increasingly greater amplitude than usual.) Without LPT in certain brain regions individuals show rigid aversion to change. Although adequate levels of glutamine normally are required for LTP, certain types of repeated stimulation and theta wave production also are reported to facilitate LPT, which persists for hours or even days. Thus, in the absence of sufficient glutamine, training for high-amplitude theta waves (relative to other frequencies) with neurofeedback is believed to facilitate LTP in certain hippocampal cells, with resulting decreases in rigidity and an increasing ability to access and change encoded patterns of maladaptive behaviors. In the alcoholic, glutamine is present in reduced quantities, and hence LTP is reduced. Such persons tend to be tense and rigid and have great difficulty spontaneously producing high-amplitude theta waves. Nevertheless, with sufficient numbers of sessions, they often learn to produce such waves. In treating alcoholism, the production of high-amplitude theta waves, as learned through neurofeedback, results in a more adaptive individual, as indicated by pre–post MMPI 2 testing. Individuals with proper neurofeedback training recognize both cognitively and emotionally the nature of their behavior and seem more readily able to walk away from addictive behaviors. It also is common for the individual who has undergone proper neurofeedback protocols to have remarkable insights into the reason for the addiction, which is a strong indication that learning, flexibility, and adaptability have increased. Typically, the individual can no longer tolerate even small amounts of alcohol, and seems readily able to end addictive behavior. In summary, Boustany's theory asserts that NMDA receptors act as a double lock and key on encoded patterns of behavior, and when LTP is reached in certain NMDA receptors, the individual can gain conscious access to these patterns, and thus become more adaptive, physically predisposed to stop alcohol use, mentally perceptive relative to the addiction, and emotionally able to relate to the need for change.

C. TRAUMA AND MIND–BODY INTERACTION

In the following section I discuss the notion that childhood traumas or "woundings" are the basic source of many different psychiatric disorders, several of which may exist simultaneously. Next, I discuss evidence for mind–body interactions in the manifestations of effects of early trauma, and speculate on how various alpha–theta related changes in higher conscious processes may relate to the many positive results so commonly observed during and following neurotherapy.

In surveying the field of neurotherapy we are finding that many seemingly disparate diagnoses are being treated successfully. In addition to Peniston and Kulkosky's (1989, 1990, 1991) published research on populations presenting with alcohol addiction and post-traumatic stress disorder (Vietnam veterans), Dr. Carol Manchester (1995, 1997; Manchester et al., 1998) reports achieving integration of dissociative identity disorder in 30–60 sessions, a disorder usually requiring years of therapy and even then with inconsistent results. Brownback and Mason (1998) have reported similar results. Psychological disorders, including affective disorders, personality disorders, "rage-aholism," eating disorders, addictions, and relational dysfunctions (including marital conflict and codependency) presumably are being successfully treated (White, 1994). Somatic complaints including hypertension, cardiovascular problems, chronic fatigue, and immune dysfunction (Schummer, 1995) were reported to be improved with this unusual approach. Several clinicians offer peak performance training. One has even worked with Olympic athletes (R. Patton, personal communication, April 1991).

Addictions, along with multiple personality disorders (MPDs), or dissociative identity disorder (DID) as it is now frequently called, usually present with a multiplicity of diagnoses. MPD patients frequently meet the diagnostic criteria for many psychiatric disorders, including depression, borderline personality disorder, somatization disorder, substance abuse, bulimia and anorexia nervosa, panic disorder, and others. There also has been much written recently about dual diagnosis (usually multiple diagnoses) in the addict and the negative effect on recidivism (Wolpe et al., 1993; Continuum, 1993) and yet these patients are reported to be good candidates for this protocol of an altered state therapy.

In our work at the Neurotherapy Center in Houston, multiple diagnoses are being addressed and showing positive outcomes as measured by the MMPI and the Millon administered both pre- and post-treatment. For example, our center did an outcome analysis focusing on the five scales of depression found in these two personality tests. The population was 44 heterogeneous patients taken in order of presentation. In four of the five scales we found a statistically significant reduction ($p > 0.001$) in depression (White, 1995, 1996).

With the appearance of both research and clinical reports describing the multiplicity of disorders being addressed, most of them quite successfully, skeptics have been aroused. One of the major critics of EEG feedback (at least in the field of attention deficit disorder) speaks for many of them. Russell Barkley publicly stated during an interview by Russ Mitchell for the *Eye to Eye with Connie Chung* television show (Mitchell, 1994): "We have a rule of thumb in this business. The more things you claim you can cure, the less effective your treatment is likely to be. It's a good rule of thumb to keep in mind." In spite of the skeptics, we see remarkable positive shifts in people presenting with multiple diagnoses when using the Peniston protocol.

What accounts for the far-reaching effects of this protocol on so many disorders, including both physical, mental, and emotional diagnoses? Perhaps it is that, since we are working with the brain and central nervous system regulation with all its manifestations, we are going to the source of the problem. With the feedback tones of a computer set to reward the production of alpha and theta brain waves, the slowed cortical activity may set the stage for generalized healing and the emergence of higher states of consciousness (Wuttke, 1992).

1. Childhood Trauma and Stress

One might consider the work of Dr. Bruce Perry (1992, 1997) who states that prolonged "alarm reactions" induced by traumatic events during infancy and childhood can result in altered development of the central nervous system (CNS). He hypothesizes that with this altered development one would predict a host of abnormalities related to catecholamine regulation of affect including anxiety, arousal/concentration, impulse control, sleep, startle, and autonomic nervous system regulation. He further states that it is likely that the functional capabilities of the CNS system mediating stress in the adult are determined by the nature of the stress experiences during the development of these systems *in utero* and during infancy and childhood. When the stressful event is of a sufficient duration, intensity, or frequency, stress-induced "sensitization" occurs–the neurochemical systems mediating the stress response change, becoming more sensitive to future stressful events. Many factors appear to be important in the lasting impact of the trauma, for example, the nature of the trauma, the degree to which body integrity is threatened, the family support system following the trauma, whether the trauma is acute or chronic or both, and whether the pattern of the trauma and/or abuse is continued into adulthood.

A child who is reared in an unpredictable, abusive, or neglectful environment may have evoked, in his or her developing CNS, a milieu that will result in a poorly organized, "dysregulated" CNS catecholamine system. Early life trauma may play an important role as a facilitator of genetically determined vulnerabilities to a variety of neuropsychiatric disorders and medical conditions. That is, it could be hypothesized that such an individual would be susceptible to the development of more severe signs and symptoms when exposed to psychosocial stressors through the course of his or her life. For instance, Schneider (1998) states that a child, particularly in the first year, who lives in a constant state of fear from abuse will often exhibit an overdevelopment of the sympathetic pathways that may lead to post-traumatic stress disorder (PTSD). With the brain bathed in dopamine and acetylcholine, the amygdala is overstimulated, with lasting and permanent effect in the orbital frontal area of the cortex. Ventral tegmental dopamine is accelerated and the sympathetic system is overstimulated. The child is potentiated to develop PTSD later in life. When trauma is experienced, the vulnerable system from childhood may elicit PTSD symptoms. PTSD involves a heightened excitation of both sympathetic and parasympathetic systems as defense against trauma. Even if the brain itself is not injured, the old PTSD-eliciting circuits apparently remain.

From the field of genetics, Blum (Miller & Blum, 1996) has offered further information on the handling of stress. His research proposes a reward deficiency syndrome (RDS), which involves imbalance of neuro-transmitters in the brain related to the A1 allele of the dopamine receptor gene (DRD2). Originally called "the alcohol gene" it is now recognized that it is not limited to an alcoholism marker, but may be a gene involving pleasure states. To feel pleasure or relief from pain, the brain's receptors must be stimulated with large amounts of dopamine, particularly in times of high stress. When there is an imbalance or shortage of dopamine and other pleasure-related chemicals, the addict will ingest mood-altering substances to control stress and restore a sense of well-being, a desire for euphoria. (These substances imitate and fit into the brain's receptors for natural brain chemicals and prevent the reuptake of these naturally occurring "feel good" chemicals, creating a flood of such chemicals and resulting in feelings of euphoria.) A traumatized person with this gene variant could illustrate this inability to manage stress. In fact, there is one report that 59% of Vietnam veterans diagnosed with PTSD showed this DR2 gene variant (Miller & Blum, 1996).

In a recent issue of *Science News,* two brain-imaging studies, conducted independently, were reported which indicated that severe, repeated sexual abuse in childhood may result in damage to the hippocampus, a structure in the brain that helps orchestrate memory. Significant reductions in the size of the hippocampus were found both in a study of Vietnam veterans and in a population of women who had suffered severe sexual abuse during childhood. The severe trauma reportedly had unleashed a cascade of stress hormones that harmed the hippocampus and related areas over time (Bower, 1996). Such cerebral injury may predispose people to experience an altered state of consciousness known as dissociation, which involves an alteration in consciousness induced by terror, including absorption in one's thoughts to the exclusion of the external world, feelings of detachment from one's body or self, and/or memory lapses. Such injury often leads to the development of other symptoms of PTSD, perhaps exacerbated if the genetic marker for RDS occurs as mentioned earlier.

As the studies mentioned suggest, there is much evidence that trauma, especially childhood trauma, can have negative effects on brain development and function and later resistance to stress.

2. Mind–Body Relationships

The work of Candace Pert (1993, 1997) illustrates that emotion and body chemistry are inseparable, "mind is body and body is mind." It is known that stress elicits neuropeptides and that the whole body undergoes physical changes when it is under stress. Years of research from scientists such as Walter Cannon and Hans Selye have shown the potential for stress to hamper the immune system. Furthermore, it has been shown that feelings of helplessness and powerlessness can suppress immune response (Schummer, 1995). However, it also has been reported that a variety of techniques, such as eliciting specific images or positive feelings, giving certain suggestions, and learning to respond to stressors in more relaxed ways, all have the potential for increasing the ability of the immune system to counter disease (Achterberg, 1985). Further studies have shown that the immune system itself is under direct control of the central nervous system, perhaps especially those areas of the brain implicated in the relating of imagery to body processes (Achterberg, 1985; Rossi, 1986). Thus, something as intangible as one's perception of an event alters the chemistry of the body (Pert, 1997). It follows from this that the imagined rejection of unwanted behavior and the image of desired outcome involved in the alpha–theta protocol have potent roles to play.

On this mind–body point, Steve Fahrion (1995), quoting Henry (1992), stated, "Activities that are usually unconscious in the early stages of life must be allowed to arise in the form of symbols (in other words, hypnogogic imagery) that have both emotional and informational value that themselves serve to integrate the activities of the limbic system and the neocortex." Perhaps this is the condition produced when one enters the "theta state" and is held there by the feedback loop. In this state one experiences awareness without active thought (process without content), a sort of void in which unconscious material is accessible apart from the surveillance of the waking ego and in which only "potential" exists. As the void is extended in this state (as with Dr. Deepak Chopra's "silent space between the thoughts"), elements of the "hidden blueprint of intelligence" (Chopra, 1989) may be unmasked and altered by the patient's current intent, earlier made real to him or her through active visualization.

It is known that emotions alter neurochemistry and vice versa, and that neurochemistry alters brain waves. Could it not happen the other way around? Could not the altering of brain waves alter neurochemistry? The brain's cortex interacts with the limbic system, often referred to as the emotional brain, by means of its cortical–subcortical connections. These cortical–subcortical connections process elements of emotional memory orchestrated by the limbic system, perhaps from "banks" of the unconscious and perhaps mediated by the hippocampus (Winson, 1990). By consciously and deliberately increasing amplitude of theta during neurofeedback, a specific state of consciousness may be created into which one can "drop" imagery of desired outcome, providing intent to this goal-directed system as an agent of change.

It has been stated that we have no voluntary control over production of theta brain waves (Sterman, 1995). If so, we must question whether or not, during neurotherapy, one is simply learning the ability to let go of the "thinking" mind and enter a state where theta waves are dominant. With the feedback tones of neurofeedback equipment, one learns to enter this state with some degree of reliable consistency. It would seem that this essentially constitutes the equivalent of deliberate control of the theta rhythm. In any event, from the research mentioned earlier, one can readily hypothesize that the changes which occur during neurotherapy are reflected not only in the brain wave patterns, but in the underlying neurochemistry as well.

To summarize this section on trauma and mind–body interaction, the view was presented that traumas, especially early childhood "woundings," adversely affect brain structure, neurochemistry, and the immune system, giving rise to multiple symptoms and diverse psychiatric diagnoses. It was suggested that the altered state associated with production of theta frequency EEG (perhaps in conjunction with specific visual imagery) alters neurochemistry in positive directions, thus accounting for its reported effectiveness with diverse disorders.

D. PATIENT–THERAPIST RELATIONSHIP

In examining possible reasons for effectiveness of the alpha–theta protocol, it would be inappropriate to overlook the importance of the therapeutic alliance. Brugental (1987) states, "The art of psychotherapy . . . insists that what goes on inside the therapist, the artist, is crucial to the whole enterprise." Relatedly, others such as Dr. Edgar Wilson have reported brain wave synchrony between healer and patient at the time of peak effectiveness (Cowan, 1993). Fahrion et al. (1993) found that this interpersonal EEG synchrony was highest during times of apparent healing, especially in the alpha frequencies between left occipital areas of the practitioner and the patient. Several instances have been reported by clinicians in which even the thoughts of the therapist in another room simultaneously seemed to influence the subject matter of spontaneous imagery of the patient.

White and Martin (1998) state that the quality of the patient relationship with the therapist seems to be a significant component, especially during the abreaction/catharsis. The therapist's empathy and sensitivity to the patient's emotional healing experience during the highly charged, vulnerable experience of the theta state is important to create the atmosphere of trust needed for the patient's willingness to "let go." The seasoning of the therapist, not so much by the years lived, but by life traumas the therapist has experienced and from which he or she has healed, may create the power and compassion of the therapist's "inner healer" that connects with the inner healer of the patient and offers hope. While the exact nature of any such connection may be unmeasurable at present, neurotherapists generally agree that trust of the therapist and rapport between therapist and client are crucial to successful treatment. As in Bell's theorem (Herbert, 1988), the therapist and patient can no longer be considered as separate and independent units, because both are changed in the process of healing.

III. TOWARD A SYNTHESIS

Section II of this chapter covered views of the effectiveness of neurotherapy from the viewpoint of generally accepted constructs in psychology, that is, varying states of arousal associated with different EEG frequencies, state- and context-dependent learning and memory, and effects of early stress and trauma on subsequent development and behavior. These perspectives on the effectiveness of the alpha–theta protocol seem to have common threads which lead to the possibility of a synthesis. To get to that point it is important to view these seemingly disparate approaches not as isolated viewpoints, but as parts of a system. In this section I attempt to do this by first discussing the concept of chronic trauma disorder.

Colin Ross (1989), an authority on multiple personality disorder (MPD), writes that the *Diagnostic and Statistical Manual* (American Psychiatric Association, 1994) should have a category for chronic trauma disorder, of childhood or adult onset, with and without MPD. This would be a hierarchical diagnosis of which currently disparate diagnoses are a part, with persons who had been most severely abused earlier in life and who developed dissociation as a defense becoming MPD. Those who were less severely traumatized (or less "gifted" at dissociation) might develop somatic symptoms, personality disorders, panic disorders, depression, and/or addiction, all probably exacerbated by genetic predispositions.

Ross (1989) analogized that chronic trauma disorder is a single field, with distinct regions. These different regions are called affective disorder, eating disorder, substance abuse, and so on. Numerous regions of the field can be activated simultaneously in a given patient. These subregions can occur in different combinations in different patients. From this point of view, chronic trauma disorder could be seen as a single diagnostic entity.

Following such reasoning, the core issue (the chronic trauma) may be hidden in one's unconscious, and may be viewed as permeating all levels of the self: physical, mental, emotional, and spiritual. Thus, childhood trauma would become the source out of which multiple symptoms and disorders flow. Relatedly, results of acute trauma in adulthood would correspond to PTSD. Severity and chronicity of previous trauma could account for the varying severity and multiplicity of diagnoses seen in clients. Perhaps a core diagnosis of trauma disorder would be most appropriate, with modifiers of acute versus chronic, childhood versus adult onset, and with or without dissociative features.

We all have experienced some degree of trauma or "wounding." That is, we all were born small, helpless, and dependent in a world of giants who controlled our lives and abused some of us. How could we escape some trauma at an age where we may not have been permitted, or had the opportunity, to process events of emotions and, in most cases, were not capable of processing them had we been allowed to? So, in this view, each of us carries with us core issues based on earlier trauma that helped form the foundation of present and future patterns of beliefs, reactions, and emotions. The more deeply wounded carry with them repressions that manifest themselves as symptoms leading to multiple psychiatric diagnoses.

In the following paragraphs I attempt to explain how the alpha–theta neurofeedback protocol may be effective in overcoming or ameliorating trauma disorder. In doing this, there will be some reiteration and elaboration of ideas presented in Section II, along with introduction of some additional ideas mainly from the field of transpersonal psychology.

A. A MULTILEVEL MATRIX

The Peniston protocol (Peniston & Kulkosky, 1989), initially focusing on the reduction to elimination of addiction, has, in my opinion, created a multilevel matrix approach that can simultaneously treat multiple diagnoses such as affective disorders, anxiety, post-traumatic stress disorders, personality disorders, and some somatic complaints along with addiction. As shown in graphic form in Fig. 13.1, I perceive these disorders as ranging along a horizontal continuum. Juxtaposing certain aspects of self–the unconscious, physical, emotional, mental, spiritual, and transpersonal aspects in this case–along a vertical axis creates a multilevel matrix describing the potential reach of this protocol. Computerized EEG feedback, a therapeutic relationship between patient and clinician and the imagery of desired outcome, succeeds in interfacing technology with compassionate personal contact. I believe this protocol concurrently affects the physical addictions, the underlying neurological conditions, psychological states, *and* the client's spiritual nature.

Major details of the dynamics of this matrix of intervention may be further understood by considering concepts such as COEX systems, and various concepts from the transpersonal domain.

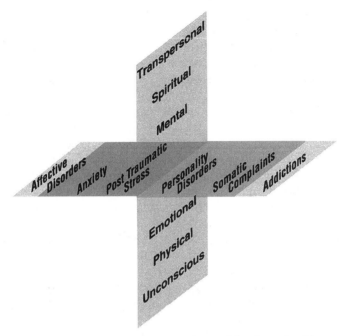

FIGURE 13.1   The Peniston protocol creates a multilevel matrix of intervention with its horizontal axis of diagnoses and presenting problems and its vertical axis of levels of the Self and Self connected to All That Is.

B. COEX SYSTEM

In deeply altered states, when people experience abreactions and flashbacks, they are encountering what some refer to as the *psychodynamic realm.* These experiences are associated with and derived from material from the subject's life, particularly from emotionally highly relevant events, situations, and circumstances. They seem related consistently to important memories, problems, and unresolved conflicts from various periods of the individual's life since early childhood. These flashbacks can take the form of reliving memories of traumas not accessible in normal states of consciousness. The memories may take the form of a variety of experiences that reflect unconscious material in the form of symbolic disguises, distortions, and metaphorical allusions, often presenting as hypnogogic imagery that seems to spring into consciousness from unconscious sources. This concept relates to the writings of Stanislav Grof (1976, 1980, 1985) and his work at the National Institute of Mental Health with LSD psychotherapy, another consciousness-altering type of therapy used in the 1950s and 1960s until the drug was scheduled by the federal government. Grof offers the principle of specific memory constellations, for which he has used the name COEX systems (systems of condensed experience). A COEX system can be defined as a specific constellation of memories from different life periods of the individual. The memories belonging to a particular COEX system have a similar basic theme or contain similar elements, and are accompanied by a strong emotional charge of related quality. The deepest layers of this system are believed to be represented by vivid memories of experiences from the period of birth, infancy, and early childhood, and seem to represent a summation of the emotions belonging to all the constituent memories of a particular kind. A given individual can have several COEX systems. Entering the deeper state evoked by alpha–theta neurofeedback training, with its apparent access to deeper layers of repressed emotion, perhaps affords one the opportunity to confront certain COEX systems containing unprocessed energies related to past trauma (state-dependent retrieval).

In "normal" or waking consciousness, in both our internal and external perceptions, we experience ourselves as existing within the boundaries of our physical body and are confined by the usual spatial and temporal boundaries. We vividly experience our present situation and our immediate environment. We recall past events and anticipate the future. We live in our "life drama." In the training with feedback tones of a computerized EEG, as the patient obtains deep alpha and theta states, there appears to be a disidentification with the "ego self." It is within this state that many of our clients spontaneously report experiences of flashbacks of earlier forgotten and traumatic times, events that may have been etched in memory systems because of their perceived survival value. From this detached state, the intensity of the emotional reaction is greatly lessened. "Ego bracing" is lessened to eliminated. In this state, which I call "suspended animation," with the encounter with suppressed material facilitating inner resolution of the earlier trauma, the personality system seems to move to a higher order of functioning (White & Martin, 1998).

As noted earlier, COEX systems are said to be specific constellations of memory accompanied by strong emotional charges of related quality. When consciously accessed, affect related to traumatic memories may be discharged (catharsis) and neurochemistry modified in a positive manner. When trauma is "released" in this manner, it may make it possible for new, more desirous "programs" to be entered into the "unconscious" by way of the prescribed, intentional imagery involved in the alpha–theta protocol.

If one ascribes to the theory of chronic trauma disorder and to the idea that, as children and perhaps as adults, all of us have lived on a continuum of actual or perceived abuse, we all may have a need to explore related COEX systems. What causes one to experience test anxiety or fear of talking before groups? What causes the athlete to clutch in that moment when ultimate performance is needed? Could it be anxiety of many possible etiologies, most of which involve childhood adaptations? Many peoples' lives show evidence of excessive fear of not being good enough, an obsessive need to prove oneself, extreme need for approval, a perceived need to perform extremely well, a need to be loved and accepted at any cost, or a need to be number one, all possibly growing out of some early trauma-related sense of inadequacy and low self-confidence. While there could be as many degrees and specific causes of these as there are people and childhoods, alpha–theta neurofeedback may, for the reasons suggested earlier, have value in most such cases.

To summarize Section III thus far, alpha–theta neurotherapy seems to enhance the ability of the brain to shift state. By encouraging the brain to move toward the lower end of the arousal continuum, the protocol may access theta state-dependent memories of early traumas, which when retrieved, can be altered in a positive way, with accompanying positive changes in neurochemistry.

C. THE TRANSPERSONAL DOMAIN

While the preceding paragraphs are an attempt to synthesize several views on dynamics of neurofeedback, no examination of the effectiveness of the alpha–theta protocol would be complete without commenting on the transpersonal realm reportedly often encountered using this protocol. Observations of the transpersonal realm are beginning to suggest that consciousness is involved in the so-called material world in ways previously unimagined (Grof, 1993). Amit Goswami (1993), professor of physics at the University of Oregon, even offers the premise that consciousness creates the material world. In any event, the material world and the world of consciousness and creative intelligence, rather than being from two distinctly different realms with discrete boundaries, appear to be engaged in a constant dance, their interplay forming the entire fabric of existence. This is echoed by physicist Nick Herbert, in his book *Quantum Reality* (1985), and is a notion that is being confirmed in research by others in modern physics, biology, thermodynamics, information and systems theory, and other branches of science (Grof, 1993). Out of his government research with 4,000 patients in LSD psychotherapy in controlled settings and a further 20,000 "Holotropic Breathwork" sessions with people from all walks of life, Stanislav Grof, M.D., formerly a professor at Johns Hopkins School of Medicine, offers a cartography of inner space that transcends linear space and time and includes, but goes beyond, one's individual biographical domain to the transpersonal such as out-of-body experiences, spirit guides, visions of light, sense of being pure energy in the cosmos, and so on. In general, this realm moves beyond the Newtonian cause-and-effect world and parallels ancient views of human consciousness that have existed for millennia. Philosopher and writer Aldous Huxley called this the "perennial philosophy." There are parallels with shamanism, the great spiritual philosophies of the East (such as different systems of yoga), various schools of Buddhism or Taoism, the mystical branches of Judaism, Christianity, and Islam, and with many other esoteric traditions of all ages. This mystical reality is said to bring knowledge and insight from sources beyond, and can happen in an altered state if the barriers separating self from nonself become fluid, and the imagination reaches beyond the intellect (Achterberg, 1985). Related to this, it is not unusual for some neurotherapy patients to report experiencing an "inner guidance." This takes many forms, on a continuum from deep insight to the sense of another being or animal appearing to them.

Among the transpersonal experiences reported by many alpha–theta neurofeedback patients, three concepts seem to be especially common and facilitative of major positive change. The first of these is what some have called the "witness consciousness." In this phenomenon the client appears to be transported into a suspended, objective state wherein he or she experiences an observing self. Deepak Chopra (1989, 1993) offered a metaphor for this type of process with a verse from an ancient Indian Upanishad: "A man is like two doves sitting in a cherry tree. One bird is eating of the fruit while the other silently looks on." This dimension of self seemingly is able to experience and perceive a "bigger picture" of any original trauma, enabling the patient to perceive from a broader domain and experience less judgment and more acceptance. This capacity to go beyond the pain of the original trauma seems to allow one to release and discharge prior unexpressed emotional pain. There seems to be a carryover when the patient returns to what one might call "normal" waking consciousness, with one then living more in a state of acceptance of "what is" rather than how one wishes it to be, and more able to "let go" of unwanted thoughts and feelings.

A second concept is the "resource self." This seems to be an aspect of the witness consciousness although there is a different quality to the experience. Whereas the witness consciousness could be defined more as an "observing self" that watches with interest and without judgment, the resource self is experienced as the personal adult self available to the child being abused in the abreactive flashback situation and becomes "his" or "her" champion and rescuer. In essence, it seems the individual incorporates the protective and nurturing "inner parent" for representing/rescripting his life. A part of self thus is reclaimed that is not the victim and can take care of and care for oneself.

The third concept is that of the "inner healer." The deeply altered state of consciousness that some neurotherapy practitioners term the "theta" state may also produce this inner healer that "targets" somatic issues, strengthens the immune system, and, otherwise, physically energizes the subject (Schummer, 1995).

One middle-aged professional man, who had no prior experience of the transpersonal realm, reported during treatment that he had experienced a guide that he referred to as his "higher power," which appeared in different guises. Initially his guide appeared as a hawk. Frequently, the guide appeared as a Native American who told him he was his great, great, great grandfather (who was known to have been an American Indian). In one alpha–theta session, the hawk reportedly appeared to him and took him on its wings and soared out into the cosmos. From there, the hawk pointed out the earth to him and then the pinpoint that was his home. He explained to him the insignificance of his local reality in comparison to the vastness of the cosmos. No sooner had he absorbed this idea, than he claimed he was quickly propelled to earth where he was taken to the microcosm world of the earthworm. It was then explained to him the significance and importance of all things. Truth is often found in paradox (White & Martin, 1998). This same man had had a difficult relationship with his father for most of his life. They were not close and he did not understand his father and his coldness. During one session, he was "taken back" in time to where he reported experiencing that he was his father as a child. He returned to normal waking consciousness with a new understanding and compassion for his father (White & Martin, 1998). Again Grof (1993) confirms this: ". . . people in non-ordinary states have reported that they experienced episodes occurring long before their own conceptions. For example, many report being able to enter the consciousness of their parents during their mother's and father's childhoods and to experience through their parent's consciousness events from that time."

To help understand these transpersonal experiences that seem to positively alter attitudes and create healings, one might turn to quantum physics, which claims reality is an undivided wholeness and that, in spite of its obvious partitions and boundaries, the world in actuality is a seamless and inseparable whole (Herbert, 1985; Capra, 1975). Similarly, the English physicist David Bohm states that one is led to a new notion of unbroken wholeness, which denies the classical analyzability of the world into separately and independently existing parts. The inseparable quantum interconnectedness of the whole universe is the fundamental reality (Bohm, 1983). On the other hand, one might consider such experiences simply as akin to dreams experienced in the altered state of sleep that, nevertheless, appear to facilitate positive behavioral change. Perhaps these phenomena also could be conceived of as resulting from neurofeedback-induced changes in neurochemistry. In any event, they often are reported and seem to be important correlates of successful healing experiences.

The alpha–theta neurotherapy protocol may recapitulate the Hero's journey (Campbell, 1988) where life sends us on our odyssey from the warmth of the oneness and safety of the womb (naiveté) to experience the "sacred wounding" of the young child, to the adult's healing of the wounds and the insightfulness that follows that healing, to the return to more conscious oneness with conscious knowing (maturity). This is a cycle in which the external journey becomes the journey inside the self, spiritually and psychologically, perhaps returning to the center of our own existence.

IV. A CASE STUDY

The case study of B.K. offers a means to further illustrate various points made earlier in this chapter. B.K. was the first patient our clinic trained with the alpha–theta protocol several years ago and, though we have trained many since, she still remains a very clear example of the healing process that can occur.

A. BACKGROUND AND TREATMENT EXPERIENCE

B.K. was referred to us by her Alcoholics Anonymous sponsor who called to say that B.K. had been sober for 3 years, but had begun drinking about 3 months prior and was craving alcohol. Her sponsor knew of nothing more to do with her and asked if we could help.

B.K. made an appointment and appeared at our office in what seemed to be a somewhat anxious and skeptical state, but stating that she wanted help with her dilemma. Typical of most of our patients who are treatment resistant and/or high risk, she presented with multiple diagnoses. She was obese and reported that she had frequent panic attacks, was a binge eater, was depressed and had suicidal ideation, though she had no plan and said she really did want to live. She was a self-mutilator and had migraine headaches. Perhaps the most difficult aspect of her case was that she was "emotionally phobic"–unable to express any feelings and would panic, become immobilized, dissociate, binge eat, or leave and get drunk when pressed to face any emotion-arousing situation.

B.K. came from an alcoholic family. Her sister is an alcoholic; her mother, a nurse, died of alcoholism; her father, a doctor, senile before his death, also was alcoholic. Her mother's brother froze to death on a porch at age 19 when he came home drunk and his family would not let him in the house. She said she knew that her paternal grandfather was alcoholic, and believed that some of her mother's family members also may have been.

Her initial testing with the MMPI-2 revealed an anxiety disorder or dysthymic disorder superimposed on a schizoid personality disorder. Both of the diagnoses fit our clinical impression of her. Her testing also showed a possible schizophrenic disorder. Results of Millon II testing revealed some elevation on borderline personality and on the compulsive and dependent scales, all of which also fit our impression of her.

She agreed to treatment using neurotherapy. At the sixth session, she experienced abreactions during the session and was having auditory hallucinations, but desired to continue with sessions. She began having flashbacks and during the fifteenth session experienced a flashback and perceived that she had been sexually abused in the crib, presumably by her father. She recognized this as the probable core of her lifelong problems. She had lived her life as a victim (her own and others'), yet when she had the flashback of crib abuse, she claimed her adult self appeared to her in the room and said in a booming voice, "How dare you!" and took the baby from the abuser. This apparently was what some call the "resource self" that had not appeared in her life before. Using neurotherapy, we have found that this phenomenon occurs with many female clients who have reportedly experienced sexual abuse. The adult self will enter the flashback and say "How dare you!" or "Don't you ever do that again!" and rescue the child. An inner resource seemingly is reclaimed, and the patient never is fully the victim again. This has been a spontaneous occurrence, apparently emerging from some part of the self and not programmed by us.

B.K. completed the treatment with a total of 30 sessions and was retested. The MMPI-2 (see Fig. 13.2) showed no clinical diagnosis on Axis I and personality disorder NOS on Axis II. There was a major drop in the Depression scale from 81 to 53. She was no longer suicidal. She showed the same shifts on the Millon II with the Dysthymia scale dropping from 102 to 34, and Borderline dropping from 86 to 70. These scores also fit our impressions of her. Perhaps most noteworthy was her pretreatment Millon II score of 71 on the Schizoid scale reflecting her unwillingness to process any emotional content. Her post score of 00 on this scale suggested that she now could be "emotionally available" for further therapeutic treatment. Her elevation

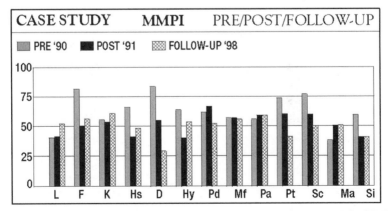

FIGURE 13.2   Pre-, post-, and follow-up testing graph of the MMPI-2 of B.K.

on the Histrionic scale on the post-treatment Millon II (see Fig. 13.3) may be perceived as a positive developmental step, suggesting she was now not blocking her emotions. She was still slightly high on Psychopathic Deviate on the MMPI-2 scale. We often see this scale remaining slightly high after EEG feedback training, and this could be related to a developmental stage of owning one's own creativity and independence. She came in for five "booster" sessions during the next year when she felt stressed and sensed that she was losing some of her inner peace and connection to herself.

After the completion of the neurotherapy program, B.K. reported no

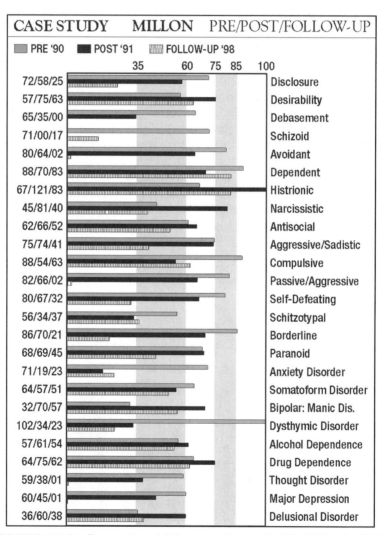

FIGURE 13.3   Pre-, post-, and follow-up testing graph of the Millon II of B.K.

craving for alcohol and said she was able to face her emotions. She then went through our center's PAIRS program, which is an intense 120-hour group program extending over 4–5 months, attended by couples and singles. The focus is predominantly on the relationship with one's self. It is usually a very emotional experience, and our belief is that she could not have gone through this if she had not completed the EEG feedback training. During this extensive period of time, she only left the room and the group one time. She was gone for about an hour and returned. She shared with the group that she had left, and told them that she knew why she had left–it was the weekend on sexuality. She reported, quite proudly, that she knew why she had left and that, though she had left, she never left the building and had returned.

B. FOLLOW-UP

Several years later I saw B.K. at a lecture and she came up to speak. She appeared healthy and well groomed. She was still overweight, but said she was no longer bingeing on food and had remained sober. She said she was in an incest survival group and that memories were still surfacing, but when they did she would feel sad and grieve for a few days and then be able to let the associated negative feelings go and move on with her life. She reported a good relationship with her husband and claimed to be doing well on her job.

At the time of this writing she agreed to do an almost 8-year follow-up on her MMPI-2 and Millon II personality inventories (see Figs. 13.2 and 13.3). All scales of the MMPI-2 now are fully within normal limits. The computerized printout stated that this clinical profile is within normal limits, with no clinical diagnosis provided on either Axis I or Axis II. The Psychopathic Deviant score had dropped to within normal limits, and the Depression scale had dropped from its original T score of 81 to 30. The Millon II follow-up showed that the Borderline scale (originally scored 86) now is 21; Dysthymia (originally 102) now is 23; Debasement is 0; Avoidant and Passive-Aggressive scores are 2, with Thought Disorder and Major Depression scores of 1. B.K. has continued her sobriety and her path to health.

B.K.'s case involves many aspects of the healing commonly seen using this protocol and illustrates many points, including what have been called the "witness consciousness" and the "resource self," which were described in the preceding section.

V. SUMMARY AND CONCLUSIONS

Alpha–theta neurotherapy has demonstrated what the research team of Elmer and Alyce Green and Dale Walters at The Menninger Foundation said in the 1970s: Causing the brain to generate theta activity daily over a period of time seems to have enormous benefits, including boosting the immune system, enhancing creativity, and triggering or facilitating "integrative experiences leading to feelings of psychological well-being." The protocol seems to transcend the patient's lack of motivation to change, initial incapacity to create internal visual imagery, and/or disbelief in the effectiveness of the treatment. Frequently a patient's experience and results far exceed the goals targeted (in the visual imagery).

Entering a deeply altered alpha–theta EEG state of arousal seems to create a link to a subconscious realm where a wider vision of the self without its ego adaptations is contacted. This link may be associated with concepts of context and state-dependent learning and memory. Beyond overcoming the presenting problem, the treatment appears to evoke in the patient more general, adaptive shifts in behaviors, attitudes, relationships, health, mental processing, job performance, and creativity. A large number of psychiatric diagnoses appear to respond to this treatment. In this chapter, it was suggested that this may be due in large part to neurofeedback enabling conscious access to repressed memories and related to affect concerning earlier trauma, especially childhood trauma. With this access may come cathartic reactions, positive changes in neurochemistry, and an "opening" of formerly unconscious realms to the effects of positive imagery and suggestions. Furthermore, it was speculated that when the conscious mind enters the EEG range of theta and "surrenders" to what some call the "mind field" the brain/mind system is enabled to go through a dramatic and profound reordering process much like that described by Illya Prigogine (Capra, 1996) as "escape to a higher order." Such transcendent experiences may involve transpersonal realms that some have attempted to explain through concepts of quantum physics. These transpersonal phenomena include frequent experiences during neurofeedback of a witness consciousness, a resource self, and an inner healer. Whether one ascribes these phenomena to explanations from quantum physics or to dreams or hallucinations, they appear to be important factors in many of the major personality changes seen following neurofeedback.

In the alpha–theta protocol the raising of amplitude of alpha and theta EEG is seen as a precursor to the process of healing. The possibility exists that if one could create a structured meditation program for a patient, over a period of time there would be similar deep shifts in personality and behavior. However, as Walsh *et al.* (1980) state, meditation training is usually extraordinarily intense and arduous, often demanding decades if not a major portion of life to reach complete fruition. I suspect that with neurotherapy we are compressing time, and, in less than 2 months, achieving results that adepts such as yogis experience only after many years of meditating. Achterberg (1985) states, "Electronic technology used as biofeedback has taught us to enter an altered state of consciousness at will. Shamanism, as it has been practiced in the traditional manner of healing, may become obsolete after 20,000 years."

The broad range of effectiveness of this therapy might lack credibility if it were not for the fact that early childhood trauma has such a wide range of psychological and physiological effects. It is sometimes proposed that addiction is the behavioral expression of an emptiness the addict finds within and the attempt to find a spiritual connection to fill this void. The same might be said for most of those who carry residue of childhood trauma expressed in some complex interaction with the central nervous system. Perhaps, in addition to the theories of the effectiveness of alpha–theta training discussed in this chapter, it is the experience of such a spiritual connection that is a major healing force behind the extraordinary healing so often seen with this training. In other words, one connects with the God within, in whatever terms one wishes to express that, and opens one's heart to love–love of oneself and love of the other.

REFERENCES

Achterberg, J. (1985). "Imagery in Healing." New Science Library, Boston.

American Psychiatric Association (1994). "Diagnostic and Statistical Manual of Mental Disorders," 4th Ed. American Psychiatric Association, Washington, DC.

Bohm, D. (1983). "Wholeness and the Implicate Order." Routledge & Kegan Paul, London.

Bower, B. (1996). Child sex abuse leaves mark on brain. *Science News* **147,** 340.

Brownback, T., & Mason, L. (1998). Brownback-Mason protocol utilizing neurotherapy with dissociation/addiction. Presented at the Futurehealth Conference, Palm Springs, CA.

Brugental, J. F. T. (1987). "The Art of Psychotherapy." W. W. Norton, New York.

Budzynski, T. (1971). Some applications of biofeedback-produced twilight states. Presented at the Annual Meeting of the American Psychological Association, Washington, DC.

Budzynski, T. (1997). The case for alpha–theta: A dynamic hemispheric asymmetry model. Presented at the Annual Conference of the Society for the Study of Neuronal Regulation, Aspen, CO.

Campbell, J. (1988). "The Power of Myth with Bill Moyers." Doubleday, New York.

Capra, F. (1975). "The Tao of Physics." Shambhala, Boulder, CO.

Capra, F. (1996). "The Web of Life." Doubleday, New York.

Chopra, D. (1989). "Quantum Healing." Bantam Books, New York.

Chopra, D. (1993). "Ageless Body, Timeless Mind." Harmony Books, New York.

Continuum. (1993). Dual disorders: High recidivism presents challenge to professionals. *Hazelton Educational Materials,* October–November.

Cowan, J. (1993). Alpha–theta brain wave biofeedback: The many possible theoretical reasons for its success. *Biofeedback* **21**(2), 11–16.

Fahrion, S. (1995). Observations of the psychophysiology of personality transformation. Presented at the Futurehealth Conference, Key West, FL.

Fahrion, S., Wirkus, M., & Pooley, P. (1993). EEG amplitude, brain mapping, and synchrony in and between a bioenergy practitioner and client during healing. *Subtle Energies* **3**(1), 19–51.

Goswami, A. (1993). "The Self Aware Universe. New Instincts, Archetypes and Symbols." J. P. Tarcher, Los Angeles.

Green, F., & Green, A. (1977). "Beyond Biofeedback." Knoll Publishing, New York.

Grof, S. (1976). "Realms of Human Unconscious." B. P. Dutton, New York.

Grof, S. (1980). "LSD Psychotherapy." Hunter House, Pomona, CA.

Grof, S. (1985). "Beyond the Brain." State University of New York Press, New York.

Grof, S. (1993). "The Holotropic Mind." HarperCollins, San Francisco.

Hartmann, T. (1997). "The Prophet's Way." Mythical Books, Northfield, VT.

Henry, J. P. (1992). "Instincts, Archetypes and Symbols: An Approach to the Physiology of Religious Experience." College Press, Dayton, OH.

Herbert, N. (1985). "Quantum Reality." Doubleday, New York.

Herbert, N. (1988). How Bell proved reality cannot be local. *Psycholog. Perspect.* **20**(2), 313–319.

Manchester, C. (1995). Application of neurofeedback in the treatment of dissociative disorders. Presented at the Mid-Atlantic Regional Biofeedback Conference, Atlantic City, NJ.

Manchester, C. (1997). Treating high risk patients with neurofeedback under managed care. Presented at the Futurehealth Conference, Palm Springs, CA.

Manchester, C., Allen, T., & Tachiki, K. (1998). Treatment of dissociative identity disorder with neurotherapy and group self-exploration. *J. Neurother.* 40–53.

Maslow, A. (1968). "Toward a Psychology of Being," 2nd Ed. Van Nostrand Reinhold, New York.

Mitchell, R. (1994). "Eye to Eye with Connie Chung." CBS, June 30, 1994.

Miller, D., & Blum, K. (1996). "Overload: Attention Deficit Disorder and the Addictive Brain." Andrews and McMeel, Kansas City.

Peniston, E. G., & Kulkosky, P. J. (1989). Alpha–theta brain wave training and beta-endorphin levels in alcoholics. *Alcohol. Clin. Exp. Res.* **13**, 271–279.

Peniston, B. G., & Kulkosky, P. J. (1990). Alcoholic personality and alpha–theta brain wave training. *Med. Psychother.* **3**, 37–55.

Peniston, E. G., & Kulkosky, P. J. (1991). Alpha–theta brain wave neuro-feedback for Vietnam veterans with combat-related post-traumatic stress disorder. *Med. Psychother.* **4**, 47–60.

Perry, B. (1992). Neurobiological sequelae of childhood trauma. *In* "Catecholamine Function in Post-traumatic Stress Disorder: Emerging Concepts" (M. Murberg, ed.). American Psychiatric Press, Washington, DC.

Perry, B. (1997). Incubated in terror. *In* "Children in a Violent Society." Guilford Press, New York.

Pert, C. (1993). *In* "Healing and the Mind" (B. Moyers, ed.). Doubleday, New York.

Pert, C. (1997). "Molecules of Emotion." Scribner, New York.

Ross, C. (1989). "Multiple Personality Disorder." John Wiley & Sons, New York.

Rossi, E. (1986). "The Psychobiology of Mind–Body Healing." W. W. Norton, New York.

Schneider, C. (1998). Considerations of right frontal lobe damage and the Phineas Gage phenomenon. Presented at the Futurehealth Conference, Palm Springs, CA.

Schummer, G. (1995). Self-regulation of the immune system. *J. Mind Technol. Optimal Performance. Megabrain Report* **III**(1), 30–39.

Siegel, B. (1986). "Love, Medicine & Miracles." Harper & Row, New York.

Simonton, C., & Simonton, S. (1978). "Getting Well Again." J. P. Tarcher, Los Angeles.

Sterman, M. B. (1995). How does the brain make waves, what do they mean and where should I place my electrodes? Presented at the Futurehealth Conference, Key West, FL.

Walsh, R., & Vaughan, F. (1980). The emergence of the transpersonal perspective. *In* "Beyond Ego" (R. Walsh & F. Vaughan, eds.). J. P. Tarcher, Los Angeles.

Walsh, R., Elgin D., Vaughn, F., & Wilber, K. (1980). Paradigms in collision. *In* "Beyond Ego" (R. Walsh & F. Vaughan, eds.). J. P. Tarcher, Los Angeles.

White, N. (1994). Alpha–theta brain wave biofeedback: The multiple explanations for its clinical effectiveness. Presented at the Annual Meeting of the Association for Applied Psychophysiology and Biofeedback, Atlanta, GA.

White, N. (1995). Alpha–theta training for chronic trauma disorder. *J. Mind Technol. Optimal Performance. Megabrain Report* **II**(4), 44–50.

White, N. (1996). Alpha/theta feedback in the treatment of alcoholism. Presented at the Annual Meeting of the Association for Applied Psychophysiology and Biofeedback, Albuquerque, NM.

White, N., & Martin, K. (1998). Alpha–theta neurotherapy as a multi-level matrix of intervention. *In* "Applied Neurophysiology & Brainwave Biofeedback" (R. Kall, J. Kamiya, & G. Schwartz, eds.). Futurehealth, Bensalem, PA.

Winson, J. (1990). The meaning of dreams. *Sci. Am.* November, 86–96.

Wolpe, P. R., Gorton, G., Serota, R., & Stanford, B. (1993). Prediction compliance of dual diagnosis inpatients with aftercare treatment. *Hosp. Community Psychiat.* **44** (1) 45–49.

Wuttke, M. (1992). Addiction, awakening, and EEG biofeedback. *Biofeedback* **20**(2), 18–22.

LEGAL AND
ETHICAL ISSUES

14

ETHICAL, LEGAL, AND PROFESSIONAL PITFALLS ASSOCIATED WITH NEUROFEEDBACK SERVICES

SEBASTIAN STRIEFEL

Psychology Department, Utah State University, Logan, Utah

Is EEG biofeedback or neurofeedback different from other forms of biofeedback in terms of promises, pitfalls, and concerns? What are the special ethical, legal, and professional concerns associated with EEG uses, including quantitative EEG, about which practitioners should be aware? Neurofeedback has great potential for helping many different types of clients with many different types of problems. The technology available today is providing opportunities that could only be dreamed about as recently as 5 years ago. The number of practitioners now wanting to provide neurofeedback services is increasing very rapidly and poses a potentially serious problem for the future credibility of neurofeedback. Exaggerated claims like those made in the 1970s about alpha training, the provision of incompetent services that result in harm to clients, and the lack of a good, solid research base can all seriously hinder the growth of this very useful technology and both its acceptance and its use. We need to be truthful in what we say and print. We need to work hard to ensure that those who are providing neurofeedback services are competent in what they do and we need to increase the amount and quality of research available to support what practitioners do.

I. PURPOSE

The purpose of this chapter is to discuss the ethical, legal, and professional pitfalls associated with neurofeedback services. The intent of the information is to help practitioners provide services that meet the expected practice standards (duty of care) that clients and third-party payors expect, while simultaneously helping practitioners avoid unnecessary risks. At the outset it must be stated, that from an ethical, legal, and professional viewpoint, *neurofeedback is more similar to, rather than different from, other biofeedback applications.* For example, the ethical issues encountered by neurofeedback practitioners are the same as those encountered by practitioners using other biofeedback modalities. In addition, many, if not all, neurofeedback applications are considered to be experimental or nontraditional interventions by conservative groups like state licensing boards. As with all nontraditional, experimental biofeedback procedures, there are potential special pitfalls that must be addressed by practitioners if they are to avoid necessary risks and maintain good working relationships with their clients. A variety of potential pitfalls of doing neurofeedback are discussed in the sections that follow. It is assumed that readers are familiar with the standards of practice and ethical principles for their own discipline, if they have one, or with those of the Association of Applied Psychophysiology and Biofeedback (AAPB) if they are not licensed in any specific discipline. For more information on professional ethical behavior in applied psychophysiology and biofeedback the reader is referred to Striefel (1995c), and for more information on risk management and ethical applications in neurofeedback the reader is referred to Striefel (in press).

II. DEFINITIONS

Neurotherapy and *neurofeedback* are terms that are often used synonymously with electroencephalographic (EEG) biofeedback, yet each term has somewhat different connotations and there are advantages and disadvantages to the use of each term. The term *neurotherapy* implies therapy of some kind, which for most people means some process engaged in by a professional with a patient rather than with a client. As such, the term implies licensure or supervision by someone who is licensed and it includes all of the privileges and restrictions that go with licensure. The term even implies the use of the "medical model." *Neuro* for most people means "having to do with the nervous system and/or the brain." Therefore, the term neurotherapy means therapy on or with the brain and nervous system. Some providers prefer to use a new term like neurotherapy to avoid any negative implications associated with the term EEG biofeedback. Doing so can also mean losing any positive connotations associated with the term EEG biofeedback.

The use of the term *EEG biofeedback* allows one to take advantage of the long history of successful uses of all types of biofeedback when working with third-party payors. Strosahl (1995) pointed out that "the 23rd rule of insurance acquisition states that a service gains status through public exposure" and that the likelihood of acceptance increases regardless of the data support that exists (p. 133). In essence, many third-party payors have been paying for biofeedback services in general and some have been paying for EEG biofeedback specifically, presumably because they know what biofeedback is. There are reimbursement codes for biofeedback, but not for neurotherapy or neurofeedback. It could take a long time to educate third-party payors using a new term. The term EEG biofeedback, however, is probably confusing to much of the general public. The term does not clearly communicate who does what with whom; but it sounds like a medical term and so gets placed within the "medical model" and the "mystique" that goes with it. The managed care movement is pushing for accountability and for the demystification of professional practice (Hayes, 1995).

The term *neurofeedback* on the other hand seems more general and does not seem to imply a medical model, that is, a doctor-patient relationship. Its connotations are more broadly based, allowing for "feedback about the brain and/or nervous system," to anyone by any type of practitioner (e.g., licensed, unlicensed, certified, uncertified). The term is more "user friendly" and thus is more easily understood by the public and allows for many different types of relationships between clients and practitioners, for example, peak performance training with a nonpatient, education, etc. However, this term is new enough that it may be unfamiliar to others such as third-party payors. In addition, as stated before, there is no reimbursement code for neurofeedback; thus, it may be more difficult to get them to pay for any services that are provided and billed under this term.

Suffice it to say that the use of each term has advantages and disadvantages and that great care should be taken when deciding what term to use for general purposes and for very specific purposes. Some of these terms may have more prestige and a higher probability of acceptance by different stakeholders, that is, individuals with a vested interest such as consumers, medical doctors, insurance company representatives, etc. Perhaps it is easier to educate managed care and other third-party payors by using the term *biofeedback* when discussing EEG treatment applications with them and to use the term *neurofeedback* when communicating with the clients served. This chapter uses the term neurofeedback because it is more representative of the broader implications of using EEG technology to train or treat individuals.

III. COMPETENCE

A. TRAINING

Neurofeedback deals with the most complex aspects of human physiology, the human brain and its functioning. Because the brain and nervous system are the major control centers for all human physiology, the implications for practitioner competence are many. The major implication is that perhaps practitioners need to have a broader base of competence when providing neurofeedback services than when providing biofeedback services using other modalities. Clearly, a weekend or even week-long workshop on neurofeedback is not sufficient in and of itself for making a practitioner competent to do neurofeedback. So what type of training is sufficient?

B. SUPERVISION

The answer is that training by itself is probably never sufficient for making someone competent to provide neurofeedback services. Competence also requires one to have supervised experience. Niedermeyer (1993) for example, points out that EEG interpretation cannot adequately be taught from a textbook; but rather, requires the eye to be trained to recognize patterns that may be normal or abnormal. Such training of the eye takes time and requires supervision from one with the skill already established. How much supervision is needed depends on a number of factors, including, but not limited to: a) how much published information exists on the specific EEG application, and whether the practitioner has read and understands the information; b) whether the practitioner has had a recent course on the functioning of the human brain, nervous system and other human physiology and how much recent reading on these topics the practitioner has done; c) whether the practitioner is competent in other biofeedback applications (the less experience and competence the practitioner has with other biofeedback applications, the more supervised experience that will be necessary for the practitioner to become competent to provide neurofeedback services); d) the complexity of the EEG application; and e) the amount of knowledge and experience the practitioner has with medical, and especially with the DSM IV diagnostic categories, and the behaviors and symptoms of individuals who meet the criteria for such a diagnosis (American Psychiatric Association, 1994). Sterman (1996) argues rather convincingly that practitioners must know the neurophysiological and functional bases of EEG characteristics if they are to avoid serious errors in conceptualizing appropriate treatments. In fact, at a minimum, practitioners should be knowledgeable and competent in all of the areas listed in the *Blueprint of Knowledge: Certification in EEG Biofeedback* developed by the Academy of Certified Neurotherapists (ACN) and the Biofeedback Certification Institute of America (BCIA). It may well be that all neurofeedback practitioners should be certified by BCIA before practicing independently.

It is best for practitioners who are new to neurofeedback applications to obtain ongoing supervision for at least 1 year and such additional time as the supervisor believes is necessary for the trainee to become and remain competent. Why 1 year? One year is the typical length of an internship for an individual who has completed the course work and some practical experience placements (practica) needed to receive a college degree in a professional discipline such as social work, psychology, etc. Why additional supervision? Additional supervised experience is usually necessary to take the licensing examinations and is usually required on the assumption that such additional supervision is necessary to get a sufficient amount of appropriate experience so as to become competent in at least some areas of service provision. Lubar (1995) recommended a supervised internship lasting 1–2 years to become competent to provide neurofeedback services. It is also a good idea for all practitioners to have periodic or ongoing consultation and/or supervision to ensure that they are and remain competent (Clayton & Bongar, 1994; Striefel, in press).

It has been common practice for practitioners to attend a weekend of training and then to assume that they can begin to treat clients using neurofeedback. The risk when using this approach with neurofeedback is probably relatively small overall, but may be higher than for other areas of biofeedback because many of the conditions treated with neurofeedback have medical and psychological implications and could result in some practitioner not being competent or even legally allowed to provide the needed services. It is best to arrange for training and supervised practice that is extended over some months, to ensure competence. There are some reports of potential harm to clients or negative side effects that might occur if appropriate precautions are not taken. Fried (1993) reported that there is more than one type of theta and that care should be taken before training someone to increase their theta output. Fried also cited several studies that indicate that some theta is associated with reduced brain blood flow (ischemic hypoxia) and metabolism and numerous types of brain pathology. Sterman and others questioned Fried and his conclusions at the Society for the Study of Neuronal Regulation (SSNR) conference in Austin, Texas (S. Striefel, personal communciation, September 1998). Byers (1995) and others report that excess theta is found in clients with head injuries, attention deficit hyperactivity disorder (ADHD), attention deficit disorder (ADD), and epilepsy. What is not clear, is how long theta must be present or at what magnitude or frequencies, before damage starts to occur. When is theta excessive? Clearly this is an area needing more research to clarify the relationship between different frequencies and amplitudes of theta and whether and to what extent neurological damage occurs.

What are the implications of doing the alpha-theta protocol reported to be so effective in dealing with alcohol abuse (Peniston & Kulkosky, 1989)? The effectiveness of the Peniston protocol seems to occur at a point when the amplitude of theta is greater than that of alpha, often called the "crossover." Perhaps the term *theta* needs to be refined, as several researchers have suggested, by using narrower frequency bands or differentiating changes in blood flow associated with different amplitudes of theta. Perhaps there are negative impacts associated with the lower frequencies of what is typically considered to be theta and positive outcomes with the higher frequencies of theta. Does the site at which theta is recorded have any implications on whether neurological damage is likely to occur? Is the process that produces the theta frequency pattern in the EEG related to whether the impact of theta is positive or negative? Sterman (1996) identified at least three separate processes for producing theta, and Fried (1993) identified others. Budzynski (1994) reported that certain repressed traumatic memories are likely to come to conscious awareness when certain clients are producing predominately brain waves in the alpha-theta crossover range.

Unless the practitioner uses physiological markers as guides to become aware of when this repressed material is likely to surface, too much material may surface too quickly and the client may be flooded by intolerable feelings and memories. Practitioners need to be prepared to deal with such memories if they do surface and should be aware of how to control the amount of information that is allowed to surface at any one time. Rescripting of traumatic information that surfaces has been shown by Peniston to be part of the successful treatment of post-traumatic stress clients and of alcoholics. Many practitioners discuss clinical issues at conferences; but not many of the issues have made it into the published literature. For example, Nancy White (personal communication, December 1994) discussed a situation in which training of a child with ADHD resulted in coherence shifting in a negative direction. She was able to correct the coherence problem through a small number of additional training sessions because she had collected a pre- and post-Quantitative EEG (QEEG). What the likely repercussions would have been if she had not had a pre- and post-QEEG are unknown. Such situations make clear the importance of having sufficient training, supervision, and/or consultation to be aware of potential problems. Competence and awareness are the keys to the development of good clinical judgment skills. Supervision allows one to determine the level of clinical judgment skills a practitioner has developed and areas in need of further refinement. In the previous example, the issue of whether or not all neurofeedback practitioners should be collecting pre- and post-QEEGs is raised. A later section in this chapter discusses this issue further.

C. ETHICAL PRINCIPLES

The *Ethical Principles of Applied Psychophysiology and Biofeedback* [Association of Applied Psychophysiology and Biofeedback (AAPB), 1995], hereafter called the *Ethical Principles,* were developed to provide guidance and education to practitioners, administrators, researchers, educators, and students engaged in psychophysiological self-regulation activities, including all forms of biofeedback. Members of AAPB are required as a condition of membership to adhere to these principles. Nonmembers are also encouraged to adhere to the *Ethical Principles* for at least two reasons. First, by doing so, the reputation of biofeedback and other psychophysiological services will be enhanced. Perhaps even the quality of services will be enhanced. In either case, it is more likely that consumers will seek services, other practitioners will make referrals and maybe third-party payors will consider paying for services. Second, in litigation, courts have the option of evaluating a practitioner's behavior against any existing local or national guidelines (e.g. the *Ethical Principles*) and they often do so (Corey, Corey and Callanan, 1998).

D. THE BOUNDARIES OF COMPETENCE

The *Ethical Principles* state that "members recognize the boundaries of their competence and operate within their level of competence using only those biofeedback and other psychophysiological self-regulation techniques in which they are competent by training and experience," (AAPB, 1995, p. 2). Thus each neurofeedback provider must be prepared to demonstrate that he or she is competent by training and experience to provide neurofeedback and related services in general and also any specific neurofeedback and related services that are or have been provided by that practitioner.

E. DETERMINING COMPETENCE

There are several ways to determine and/or verify that a practitioner is competent to provide general or specific neurofeedback and related services. None of the methods for verifying competence is without problems. As such, it is recommended that practitioners be conservative in evaluating the boundaries of their areas of competence to avoid being accused of misrepresenting their qualifications, which is also an ethical violation (AAPB, 1995). A conservative approach would be to ask oneself, "What would a court, a licensing board, an ethics committee and my biggest professional competitor accept as an adequate verification of competence?" Some useful guidance for deciding one's levels of competence for providing neurofeedback and related services will be discussed in the sections that follows.

1. Course Work and Other Training

One should have documentation of completion of several university degrees, courses and/or workshops and other forms of continuing education over time on all topics relevant to the types of services that one provides, e.g., topics such as: a) the brain and nervous system and how they function;

b) the particular symptoms and diagnostic categories being treated, e.g., Depression, Attention-Deficit/Hyperactivity Disorder (ADHD), and Alcohol Abuse as defined in a diagnostic manual such as the DSM-IV (American Psychiatric Association, 1994); c) all applicable state and federal laws; d) all applicable ethical principles and standards of practice, including those of AAPB and of one's professional discipline if one has one; e) EEG applications, protocols, use of equipment, QEEG, etc.; and f) other areas covered by the EEG Blueprint developed by the BCIA. One can also gain a knowledge base by reading books and appropriate journals but it is more difficult to document for others that one has actually engaged in such activities. Documentation of course work alone is not equivalent to being competent. *Being competent means that one must know what to do, when and if to do it, how to do it and why you are doing it* (Striefel, 1995a). The "bottom line" is that the practitioner be able to demonstrate that he or she has both the knowledge base and experience for providing the neurofeedback and related services being provided to the type of clientele being served. The services that are provided must be safe for the client, clinically appropriate and clinically effective in producing positive outcomes for those served (Pallak, 1995). A practitioner should be able to cite the scientific basis for any treatment provided (Pallak, 1995; Sterman, 1996). If one has no training in working with children or with a particular diagnostic problem, e.g., ADHD, it will be difficult to convince a licensing board that one is competent by training and experience to provide neurofeedback and related services to children with a a diagnosis of ADHD. A similar relationship between training and experience must be verifiable for other problems, diagnoses, and client services.

2. Entry Level Skills

One "should have at least entry level competence," before providing services without supervision (AAPB, 1995, p. 2). Entry level has in the past been defined as: a) being licensed or certified in a relevant health care discipline by the state in which one practices; b) being certified by a relevant professional certification association, e.g., being certified in EEG biofeedback through the certification available from the BCIA; or c) being both licensed or certified by the state and certified by BCIA (AAPB, 1995). Being licensed or certified in some discipline by a state or being certified by BCIA means only that at one point in time some group believed that an individual was competent enough to be licensed or certified by that group. It is not an endorsement to engage in treatment activities in which one cannot demonstrate competence by training and experience. Nevertheless, licensing is often inappropriately interpreted by practitioners as an endorsement to do whatever they like (Hayes, 1995), which becomes problematic if they get in difficulty with a licensing board or ethics committee. To be licensed typically means that one has had certain training, passed an exam and has had at least one year of supervised practice. To be certified by BCIA means that one has had some training and some number of hours of supervised practice. After the "grand fathering" period is over, it will also mean having passed some examination. Practitioners who are licensed and/or certified must still restrict their activities to those areas in which they are competent, unless appropriately supervised. Licensing and certification are not a guarantee that a practitioner will restrict their activities to those areas in which they are competent; however it does provide a basis for others to determine that the practitioner has been recognized by some group as having at least some level of entry skills for providing some services. Licensing and certification are also not a guarantee that the services provided will be empirically based or of high quality (Hayes, 1995).

Professional certification without state licensure or certification may be insufficient for engaging in independent (unsupervised) neurofeedback practice activities. The independent practice of biofeedback, including neurofeedback, in some states, by law, requires a practitioner to be licensed by the state. There will be more discussion of this topic in the section later in this chapter entitled "Neurofeedback and the Law." Some individuals obtain certification from a professional certification organization via a process of "grand fathering" (i.e., without taking a test to demonstrate competence). Often clear standards for deciding competence are not yet available during this "grand fathering" period; thus it is in the best interest of those being certified via "grand fathering" to be sure that they can in fact demonstrate competence. If advertisements include indications of specialty certification, the courts have ruled that the practitioner is holding her or himself out to the public as being an expert. In court proceedings, experts are held to a higher standard of competence than are those who do not hold themselves out to the public as experts. Experts may well need to demonstrate a higher level of competence and should, in fact, be able to demonstrate to a court that they do have the training and experience expected of an expert providing particular services. Being competent in one area of neurofeedback, e.g., treating ADHD, does not necessarily mean one is competent to provide neurofeedback services in another area, e.g., treating substance abusers. Competence must be demonstratable in each area of service.

Licensing by itself may soon no longer be sufficient for demonstrating professional competence (Favell, 1997; Hayes, 1995). Professional groups and managed care, for different reasons, are both pressing for verification of skills, especially speicalized skills, and neurofeedback would well fit a category of what would be considered by many to be a specialized skill. Professional groups are increasingly recognizing that licensing requirements and examinations have little direct relevance for determining competence in specialized areas (Favell, 1997). Managed care organizations are increasingly becoming concerned with determining who has the specialized skills they are seeking to provide specific services to clients as part of their provider panels. The American Psychological Association (APA) has established a system for specialty and proficiency recognition (Favell, 1997). "Biofeedback: Applied psychophysiology" was given proficiency recognition by APA in August of 1997. Only one area had previously been approved by APA for proficiency certification. That area was the *Treatment of Alcohol and Other Psychoactive Substance Use Disorders.* Neurofeedback practitioners who are psychologists may soon find that they also need to have this proficiency certification in order to be included on managed care panels. It may soon be that to practice independently, practitioners will need to both be licensed by the state to practice and certified in a variety of specialties related to the services that they provide.

3. Supervisor Verification

One should have received sufficient supervision consultation in a particular service area to be able to demonstrate competence. Written statements by competent supervisors attesting to one's level of competence to provide specific services can be a very useful way for a practitioner to determine the boundaries of his or her levels of competence. In some areas of neurofeedback it may be difficult to obtain sufficient face-to-face supervision from a competent supervisor because one is the only practitioner in a particular geographic area, or because the application is very new and/or experimental and thus competence has not yet been defined or few people are available nationwide who have demonstrated competence in that application. In such cases, a practitioner may have to rely on consultation services from other practitioners via telephone or e-mail. It is in the best interests of neurofeedback practitioners faced with such situations to proceed cautiously, to obtain honest and complete, signed informed consent from clients, and to continue to work on becoming competent via training, supervision (yes, supervision should be pursued over time and distance), and experience. Periodic live or videotaped observations of treatment sessions by a competent supervisor or consultant can help verify one's level of competence. It is also important to document all consultation and supervisory sessions and their content.

4. Client by Client and Problem by Problem

One must continue to be sensitive to the issue of competence every time a practitioner considers accepting a client into treatment. A practitioner should evaluate his or her level of competence on a client-by-client and problem-by-problem basis (Striefel, 1995a). This can be accomplished informally and rather quickly by answering questions such as the following:

- Am I competent to treat the problem that this client or potential client has?

- Do I have the psychotherapy skills that might be needed to work with this client or does this client need to be in simultaneous treatment with a mental health practitioner?
- What kind of medical consultation or support, if any, is needed for treating this client?
- Do I need supervision in order to provide competent treatment to this client?
- Should this client be referred elsewhere for treatment?
- Do I need to receive additional training for dealing with such problems or clients in the future?

Practitioners can add to this list of questions, as needed, to determine their level of competence for dealing with specific clients and/or problems. Ongoing monitoring and awareness of the boundaries of a practitioner's own level of competence are very good ways of reducing the risk of injuring a client or of having someone file an ethical complaint or lawsuit against the practitioner.

5. Self-Assessment/Self-Disclosure

One should conduct a self-assessment of one's level of competence for dealing with specific types of clients and presenting problems. Such a self-assessment includes all of the factors specified in the previous four sections: course work and other training, entry level skills, supervisor verification, and client-by-client and problem-by-problem determinations of competence. All of the factors related to training, experience, and supervision can be summarized in a written self-disclosure statement that has as an end goal the clarification of what types of clients and problems one is competent to treat and what kinds of intervention approaches a particular practitioner is competent to use (Striefel, 1995a). A self-disclosure statement can be shared with current and former supervisors for accuracy and with managed care organizations when one is vying for inclusion on provider panels. Feedback from peers, referral sources, and clients, along with client outcome data can be used to evaluate and update a practitioner's awareness of his or her levels of competence.

F. QUESTIONING A PRACTITIONER'S COMPETENCE

Questions concerning a practitioner's level of competence are likely to arise whenever a client is injured; a new or experimental application is used; someone considers the claims made by a practitioner to be exaggerations; a practitioner is accused of unethical, illegal, or unprofessional behavior; or a practitioner's activities begin to impact negatively the income of other practitioners in the area served. In any and all unusual situations, practitioners should access supervision and/or consultation to ensure that the services they provide are competent, that the claims they make are accurate, and that other practitioners agree that the practitioner's approach to neurofeedback and related services meets at least the minimal standards of care expected of human services providers.

One problem in demonstrating competence in neurofeedback is that a validated and reliable examination is not yet readily available (although ACN and BCIA are working on developing one) nor has a set of practice standards for the many different neurofeedback applications been developed. The availability of such examinations and standards will ultimately provide practitioners with additional guidance on what is expected of them and another way of assessing competence and for gaining credibility with managed care oreganizations, other third-party payors, and consumers.

IV. NEUROFEEDBACK AND THE LAW

State laws govern who can and who cannot provide neurofeedback services in a particular state. AAPB recognized the importance of state laws in determining who can be independent practitioners and published a policy statement that defers to state law on who can and who cannot practice independently without supervision (Striefel, 1995b).

A. TITLE VERSUS PRACTICE ACTS

More and more state licensing laws are shifting from what were called Professional Title Acts to what are now often called Professional Practice Acts. A *Professional Title Act* is simply a law that protects the use of a specific title, for example, psychologist. Under such a law, a practitioner can do everything that a licensed professional protected by such a title can do (unless of course prohibited by some other part of the law), as long as the practitioner does not use the protected title (label) to refer to him- or herself. If the protected title is "psychologist," the practitioner cannot call him or herself a "psychologist" unless he or she is licensed as such. This means that the practitioner cannot advertise or otherwise lead the public to believe that she or he is a licensed member of the specified profession unless, of course, the practitioner is in fact licensed as such.

Professional Practice Acts have gone further and include a definition of what is specified in the law as being included in the practice of a specific discipline, e.g., psychology. Unless exempted by that specific law or some law that takes precedent over that law, one cannot legally engage in those professional activities. It is becoming common for Professional Practice Acts in many discipline to define biofeedback (regardless of whether one prefers the name neurotherapy, neurofeedback, or EEG biofeedback) as *an activity that can only be performed by professionals licensed in specific disciplines or supervised by such licensed professionals* (e.g., Utah and Texas). Someone who is not licensed in an appropriate discipline in such a state cannot legally practice neurofeedback independently.

Professional Practice Acts are legalized in order to achieve several goals, such as making it easier for members of that specific discipline to obtain reimbursement for a specific service, such as EEG biofeedback, by defining the activity as something members of that discipline do legitimately, and second, to protect the public by keeping presumably unqualified (i.e., incompetent) practitioners from practicing independently. The assumption is that if a practitioner is not eligible for a license, then he or she is not competent to practice independently. Interestingly, there is no published literature to show that licensed individuals do a better job of serving clients then do those who are not licensed (Hayes, 1995). In fact, several studies show that paraprofessional helpers generally are as effective as professionals in achieving psychotherapeutic outcomes for most common mental health problems treated (Christensen & Jacobson, 1994; Tan, 1997). Is there any reason to believe that the results would be any different in neurofeedback or in biofeedback per se? This author does not think so. Licensing laws all have the side effect of, to some degree, protecting the incomes of those who are licensed in a specific discipline by restricting legal practice to those who have "jumped the hoops" necessary to become licensed.

B. DETERMINING WHO CAN PROVIDE NEUROFEEDBACK

Those wishing to provide neurofeedback services in a particular state must check with the various licensing boards, read the licensing laws, consult with appropriate attorneys, or otherwise find out whether or not they can legally provide neurofeedback services in that state. It is important not to mislead an attorney if one is going to get an accurate legal opinion. Asking an attorney whether one can provide neurofeedback services independently without informing him or her that neurofeedback is another term for EEG biofeedback could result in a legal opinion that erroneously states that it is legal for one to provide neurofeedback services because that term does not appear in any law. In fact, if the state law regulates biofeedback, it also regulates neurofeedback and neurotherapy, that is, a rose is a rose no matter what you choose to call it.

C. PENALTIES AND CHANGING THE LAW

The penalties for providing services like neurofeedback, if not legally allowed to do so, can be severe. For example, in Texas it can result in fines of $1000 per day per violation. As such, it is best for potential and actual practitioners to know and abide by state practice laws. The author learned that in early 1997 a practitioner in Texas who was not licensed to provide biofeedback services was contacted by a state licensing board and told to "cease and desist" in terms of providing biofeedback services or show that he or she was in compliance with the Texas Practice Act for Psychologists. The provider was also informed that it was a Class A misdemeanor to be in violation of the licensing law in that particular state.

Yearly monitoring of state laws is necessary, because what was legal during one year may no longer be legal the next year. If a law seems unfair, practitioners could organize to change that law. Changing laws that could negatively impact the incomes of professionals licensed in some specific discipline is likely to be strongly opposed by members of the discipline(s) whose income is likely to be negatively impacted. Therefore, getting a law changed, unless supported or at least not actively opposed by members of many disciplines, can be both time consuming and expensive in terms of dollars. Changing an unfair law probably will require the involvement of a group of practitioners from several disciplines.

D. EDUCATION VERSUS TREATMENT

Some practitioners would like to define neurofeedback as an educational rather than treatment approach. There are at least three potential problems with such a redefinition of neurofeedback. First, it has been a rare exception for third-party payors to pay for educational services. In fact, the probability of payment for such services is probably even lower than before because of the cost containment procedures associated with managed care. Second, and more important, is the fact that many state laws have already defined biofeedback, and therefore neurofeedback, as a professional practice activity restricted for use, to members of certain licensed disciplines or those supervised by such licensed professionals. Third, in working with any of the clients who are candidates for neurofeedback services there is often an overlap with other professional activities that are restricted (e.g., diagnosis, therapy, etc.) for use by members of certain licensed disciplines. For example, the Utah Psychologists' Licensing Act (Title 58, Chapter 25a, 1989) defines the practice of psychology not only as including biofeedback, but also as including the "diagnosis and treatment of mental and emotional disorder or disability; alcoholism and substance abuse disorder or habit or conduct; as well as the psychological aspects of physical illness, accident, injury or disability and psychoeducation evaluation, therapy, remediation and consultation" (p. 632). This law defines rather broadly the practice of psychology as including many of the activities in which a neurofeedback practitioner might engage, such as providing supportive services to a client with a diagnosis of ADHD or substance abuse. Other similar laws define certain activities as the practice of medicine, or social work, etc.

E. OTHER RELEVANT LAWS

Practitioners need to know and adhere to all federal and/or state laws that are relevant to their practice activities. The laws may vary from state to state, but generally include:

- State licensing laws (title or practice acts)
- Child abuse and neglect reporting laws
- Records retention laws
- Privileged communications laws (often included in licensing or mental health laws)
- Billing and fee collection laws
- OHSA regulations concerning prevention of diseases (e.g., in disinfecting electrodes)
- Infectious diseases reporting laws
- Duty to warn and/or protect laws

Each of these laws, as relevant to a particular state, can be obtained by contacting several sources. Good places to start are with the state office of licensing and the state department of mental health. They often are familiar with the relevant state laws and can provide access to other relevant laws. Computer searches and library visits are also good ways to access relevant information.

V. PROFESSIONAL DECISION MAKING

A. INTERVENTION VERSUS REFERRAL

Neurofeedback practitioners make decisions on a daily basis about whether or not to accept a particular client for treatment. A number of variables are considered in making such decisions, including but not limited to, the symptoms the client has, any diagnosis that has been used to label the client's problem, the duration of the symptoms, previous treatments tried and how well they worked, existing laws, and the practitioner's areas of competence. Practitioners should determine whether or not they are competent to treat the client and his or her problems, with or without supervision; whether or not they can legally do so; and if they should refer a client elsewhere.

B. DECISION-MAKING FLOWCHART

Making such decisions about treatment can be complex; however, the flowchart in Fig. 14.1 provides one way of conceptualizing such decisions. By sequentially answering the question in each of the diamonds in Fig. 14.1 and following the appropriate route based on the directional arrows,

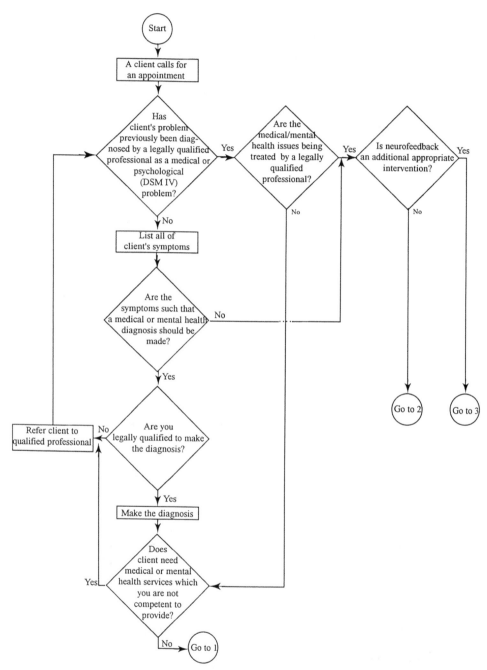

FIGURE 14.1   Flowchart for deciding if you can provide services to a client.

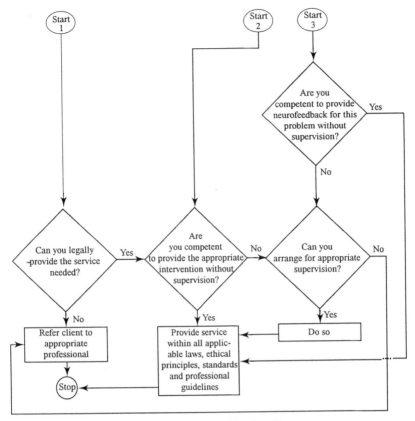

FIGURE 14.1 (*Continued*)

the reader should be able to determine what action to take concerning treatment for any potential client and presenting problem.

VI. CAUTIONS AND CONTRAINDICATIONS IN USING NEUROFEEDBACK

A. CAUTIONS

Practitioners should be aware of those areas in which other practitioners providing neurofeedback services have had difficulties with licensing boards. In general, licensing boards because of their gatekeeping functions tend to be conservative, thus practitioners should be proactive in terms of how they engage in the practice of neurofeedback. Planning ahead can help avoid problems later; "an ounce of prevention is worth a pound of cure." Some of the areas in which practitioners have been questioned by licensing boards or professional colleagues follow.

1. Experimental versus Traditional Approaches

Practitioners are advised to be cautious in terms of how they explain neurofeedback interventions to clients when getting informed consent. According to Beutler and Davidson (1995) there is no one agreed-on standard for when a treatment approach is considered to be valid and reliable and thus no longer experimental. A standard proposed by the American Psychological Association Task Force on Promotion and Dissemination of Psychological Procedures (1993) is that there be at least two published, controlled studies conducted by different researchers in different locations that attest to the validity and reliability of an intervention or assessment approach in comparison to a control or established comparison treatment.[1] Most neurofeedback interventions do not yet meet this standard and those that do may in fact not be accepted by conservative groups that use a different standard (Barkley, 1992). For example, Blue Cross-Blue Shield's Technology Evaluation Center has for 2 years ruled that biofeedback does not have sufficient research support to be considered efficacious in the treatment of hypertension (TEC, 1997). Yet they found and reviewed 11 published controlled studies.

The preceding example points out that there is no one agreed-on standard for making decisions about when a procedure or approach is no longer experimental. One new standard that may well be used by managed care organizations in the future are outcomes based on large, national, multisite databases (Pallak, 1995). The use of such databases could shift the standard from reliance on randomized controlled studies to what is reported as being effective in these large databases. At present, many biofeedback practitioners do *not* consider neurofeedback to have enough documented research support to be considered a traditional, valid, and reliable treatment approach. If other biofeedback practitioners still consider neurofeedback to be a promising but experimental intervention, how can neurofeedback practitioners expect the public, other professionals not involved in biofeedback, or third-party payors to accept neurofeedback as an accepted, verified intervention?

Striefel (1998) stated that EEG biofeedback per se is no longer experimental. This conclusion was based on the availability of many published studies attesting to the efficaciousness of EEG biofeedback. However, EEG interventions for specific client problems can be readily placed on a continuum that ranges from those interventions that are well validated to those that are totally experimental (Striefel, 1998). Neurofeedback interventions

---

[1] In the fall of 1997, the Association of Applied Psychophysiology and Biofeedback adopted this criterion as a beginning standard for determining clinical efficacy.

for each different problem may well need to be dealt with individually as either validated, promising or as an experimental procedure until the following occur:

1. Sufficient published research is available to convince most practitioners that the specific neurofeedback intervention is no longer an experimental treatment approach.
2. Neurofeedback becomes one of the predominant treatment approaches for a particular problem or diagnosis.
3. Third-party payors regularly pay for the specific neurofeedback intervention.
4. Neurofeedback is accepted by licensing boards and is written into their state licensing laws and administrative regulations.
5. Neurofeedback is regularly requested by consumers as the treatment they prefer for dealing with one or more of their problems.

As such, for all practical purposes, neurofeedback interventions should probably be explained to potential clients as an intervention that some or many practitioners are likely to consider experimental. This does not preclude a practitioner from explaining to a client why he or she does not consider it to be an experimental approach for the particular client's problem if he or she believes that neurofeedback is not experimental for that problem. However, to protect the practitioner, the informed consent obtained should be in written form, and in addition to explaining the support that exists for using neurofeedback to treat the client's problem, the form should include a statement that neurofeedback is considered to be experimental by some or many practitioners.

Written informed consent is important for several reasons, including (1) the ethical principles of AAPB require that informed consent be obtained for all experimental procedures and that it be obtained in written form; and (2) written informed consent provides documentation of what a client was or was not told and to what they agreed, should later questions be raised by the client, a competitor, or a licensing board. Such information has been very useful for several neurofeedback practitioners in dealing with situations that arose after the fact (Striefel, 1997a). The informed consent process should meet the requirement for informed consent of providing the client with the information needed to make a decision, that the client has the capacity to give consent, and that the consent be given voluntarily (Striefel, 1990, 1997b). As a general rule of thumb, the less published literature that exists to support a specific neurofeedback intervention, the more cautious a neurofeedback practitioner should be in his or her explanation to the client and the more documentation, supervision, and/or consultation a practitioner should seek.

2. Advertising

The ethical principles for several professional disciplines require members to report actual or suspected ethical violations. Advertisements that members of such disciplines consider to be dishonest or exaggerations can result in a complaint being filed by a well-meaning professional who is trying to protect the public and the reputation of a particular discipline or treatment approach (Striefel, 1997b). Several neurofeedback practitioners have been questioned by colleagues and/or licensing boards on the basis of what they put in their brochures or other advertisements (Striefel, 1997a). Claims that are considered to be exaggerations by others, especially those whose incomes are being impacted because clients are going to a neurofeedback practitioner, have in the past resulted in formal or informal complaints being filed.

Licensing laws often contain statements about dishonest and/or misleading advertisements. Thus, licensing boards have in the past become concerned about neurofeedback advertisements that they considered to be exaggerations or untrue. The actions of such licensing boards have resulted in practitioners being required to "tone down" or reword advertisements to fit what the board considered to be realistic and honest statements. Clear, honest, and truthful ads that can be supported by the existing published literature can help a practitioner avoid problems, clarify the situation if questions arise, and enhance the credibility of neurofeedback. One deceptive or exaggerated claim can negatively impact the reputation of neurofeedback per se and of those who provide such services. It is best to be conservative in what is included in a practitioner's advertisements and to have ads reviewed by a colleague who has a reputation for being honest in terms of the feedback he or she gives. It is also a good idea to keep on file a copy of all advertisements, brochures, and even radio or television ads in case questions arise.

3. Boundary Issues

Practitioner's need to be aware of the practice boundaries for different groups of licensed professionals. Care should be taken to avoid practicing in an area reserved for practice by those licensed in another professional discipline. Making a medical diagnosis or discussing with a client changes in medication if one is not a licensed medical practitioner are examples of areas in which a practitioner can easily cross the boundary into practicing medicine without a license. Neurofeedback practitioners need to know not only the boundaries for their own discipline but also those for other professional disciplines. There is nothing wrong with suggesting to a client that he or she ask his or her physician if a medication adjustment might be appropriate. If one is not a physician it is not appropriate and is, in fact, illegal to suggest to a client that he or she stop taking a medication. Caution in selecting the words used will help protect one from practicing beyond the boundaries of one's discipline and area of competence.

At least one psychologist was required by a state licensing board to restrict practice activities related to QEEG to those areas that the board narrowly defined as being within the defined areas of practice for psychology and to not engage in those activities that the board interpreted to be the practice of medicine. Several neurofeedback practitioner's (including this author) wrote to the licensing board to get them to more broadly interpret the practice of QEEG uses in psychology. The board chose to ignore the input that did not support their position. Litigation to override a licensing board could be extremely expensive.

B. CONTRAINDICATIONS

Contraindications to providing neurofeedback depend in part on the skill and experience level of the particular practitioner, supports he or she has available in terms of supervision and/or consultation, the likelihood that other practitioners in the specific geographic area will file a complaint, risk-taking level of the practitioner, etc. Some of the contraindications have been discusssed previously in this chapter and others have not. Some contraindications to consider in deciding whether or not to provide neurofeedback and related services, include:

- Theta training could trigger seizures for clients with a history of seizures (Sterman, 1996). A good medical history should be collected on all clients being considered for neurofeedback services. Clients with a history of seizures are not good candidates for any type of neurofeedback that includes theta training.
- Unstressing, decompensation and flashbacks (often called abreactions) could be triggered by neurofeedback training, especially theta training, for clients with a history of post-traumatic stress disorder, multiple personalities, or schizophrenia (Budzynski, 1994). A good psychological history should be collected on all potential neurofeedback treatment clients to determine the probability of encountering abreactions. Byers (1995) stated that ethical considerations in dealing with post-traumatic stress disorders dictates that the neurotherapist should first be a psychotherapist. A practitioner must understand the disorder that produces such abreactions and must know how to deal with them and with other manifestations of unconscious processes (Byers, 1995). If psychotherapy is a part of the treatment protocol, the practitioner may by state law, need to be licensed in an appropriate mental health discipline or supervised by someone who is because psychotherapy is often governed by state licensing laws.

- Some organic medical disorders can masquerade as psychological or functional problems, e.g., hyperthyroidism disorders may look like anxiety, depression, hyperactivity or mania; and lupus crythematosis may look like anxiety, depression, or multiple bodily symptoms (Small, 1993). A good medical work up can be a great asset to the neurofeedback practitioner in helping clients get the correct treatment for their problem.
- The lack of a rationale or published literature supporting a specific neurofeedback application places the practitioner at greater risk. In such situations, the practitioner should carefully assess his or her motivation for proposing neurofeedback as an appropriate intervention and should consult with an appropriate expert to be sure he or she is aware of any potential risks to the client before proceeding.

VII. RESPONSIBLE PRACTICE

Neurofeedback practitioners are held to many standards of accountability, some of which overlap and some of which depend on individual practitioner variables, such as professional discipline, professional memberships, licensure, and/or certification status. All neurofeedback practitioners are expected to behave in the ways specified in the ethical principles and standards of practice for one's discipline and of AAPB, if one is a member; the licensing laws of the state in which one practices, if licensed, and those of one's supervisor if one has one; BCIA certification requirements, if certified; and other rules and regulations that get applied to service providers. All neurofeedback practitioners are responsible for (Corey *et al.,* 1998; Striefel, 1995a) the following:

- What they do and what they fail to do. Excuses for failing to be competent (and remaining competent) or for not being current on what is expected of neurofeedback practitioners are not a protection if an ethics complaint or lawsuit is filed against a practitioner. Be prepared to do it right!
- What those they supervise (students, trainees, employees, etc.) do or fail to do. Practitioners should supervise others only in those areas in which they themselves are competent as demonstrable by training and experience, unless of course also supervised by someone who is competent.
- Being and remaining competent and knowledgeable about neurofeedback and other services provided. Yearly, continuing education is important for remaining current.
- Operating only in those areas in which one is competent, unless appropriately supervised by someone who is.

- Being in compliance with the laws of the state that pertain to neurofeedback and the related activities which one provides (e.g., licensing law, child abuse and neglect, duty to warn and protect, records retention, billing and collections).
- Obtaining appropriate, written informed consent.
- Maintaining good professional relationships with other professionals, including those from whom one's clients are receiving other services.
- Respecting clients and their rights (e.g., confidentiality, privileged communication, decision making).
- Addressing the misconduct of other neurofeedback practitioners.
- Obtaining medical consultation if not a physician, when (1) a client has serious physical symptoms that have not been diagnosed or which are not being treated by a physician (e.g., a headache can have many causes including a brain tumor); (2) a client is on medications, the need for which may change over the course of treatment (e.g., the need for Ritalin if receiving neurofeedback for ADHD); or (3) a client's condition raises questions that seem to be medically related.

Behaving responsibly requires an ongoing process of education, planning, self-assessment, feedback from others, and sensitivity to what is happening with the clients served.

VIII. QEEG CONSIDERATIONS

Should practitioners have available a pre- and post-QEEG or clinical EEG for every client treated with neurofeedback? If a practitioner does not have available a pre- and post-QEEG or clinical EEG, how would he or she defend him- or herself if a client filed a lawsuit claiming that the practitioner caused shifts in the EEG other than what was being trained and thus caused harm to the client? If a practitioner is going to collect routine QEEGs, should he or she interpret them or should they be interpreted by someone who specializes in QEEGs? Who is competent to administer and to interpret a QEEG? To what uses can the QEEG be put? These and numerous other questions arise when one looks at the potential role of the QEEG.

A. PRE- AND POST-QEEGS

The example discussed earlier that dealt with a practitioner detecting a potential coherence problem because she had available a pre- and post-QEEG might well indicate that practitioners who do not collect such data might be at a slightly greater risk of having a problem occur with a client without even being aware of it.

B. INTERPRETATIONS

The issue of who is competent to interpret QEEGs is a complex one. Duffy *et al.* (1994) suggest restricting the use of QEEGs to *physicians* who:

- Possess EEG board certification from a group such as the American Board of Electroencephalography
- Possess additional documented training in the type of statistics used with QEEGs; artifact recognition, detection, and control; recognition of the signatures of relevant diseases and discriminant functions; and the use of specific software and equipment
- Have had supervised experience.

Some of these guidelines are useful; but restricting use only to physicians can easily be seen as an attempt to protect "turf" and the income that might go with it. Because of the complexity of QEEGs, some sort of certification is probably going to become essential. For example, if a practitioner who does not meet the Duffy *et al.* (1994) criteria were to become involved in a lawsuit over some interpretation he or she made of a QEEG, he or she could be faced with an expert witness for the other side who does meet the criteria. Some sort of national certification with credibility would be extremely useful in establishing that one has the relevant training and experience to be doing QEEG interpretations. Establishing credibility for a QEEG certification will require a serious evaluation of the type of skills, training, and experience one should have in order to be certified. The certification must be one that is acceptable to national and international professional groups.

Another part of this turf issue is for professionals to begin now to get QEEGs written into state licensing laws for those disciplines where that is appropriate. If QEEG gets defined narrowly as a practice activity for use only by physicians, its potential usefulness to those doing neurofeedback could be severely restricted.

C. FDA ISSUES

In the past practitioners and vendors alike have had trouble with the Food and Drug Administration (FDA) for using biofeedback equipment for purposes for which the specific piece of equipment was not FDA approved. EEG and QEEG equipment is generally classified by the FDA as medical equipment (Class 2 prescriptive device), which is to be sold only to professionals licensed in a health care field. As such, EEG equipment is subject to specific FDA rules, including that each piece of equipment can legally be used only for the specific purposes for which it was approved by the FDA or for purposes accepted by the FDA as a "nontherapy use" (whatever that is). The assumption by the FDA is that unapproved uses could result in harm to clients or patients.

Practitioners should be sure that they get in writing, before they purchase a piece of equipment, the list of purposes for which that equipment has FDA approval. Failure to do so could be costly. Practitioners should also restrict the use of equipment to those purposes for which it was approved by the FDA or should go through the process of filing the paperwork necessary for getting FDA approval for using the equipment for specific experimental purposes. Information about the FDA process can be obtained from the FDA or from an attorney who specializes in such matters.

Most, if not all, QEEG equipment currently on the market has not been approved for purposes of making diagnoses. The information disseminated by vendors of QEEG equipment should make a clear statement about approved and nonapproved functions. For example, the user's manual for Lexicor's NeuroSearch-24 states "The NeuroSearch-24 is not intended for use in the evaluation of cerebral death or diagnosis of tumors, multiple sclerosis, epilepsy or any other disorders of the brain or nervous system" (Lexicor, 1993, p. 2). In working with neurofeedback clients where a QEEG will be collected, it is recommended that the informed consent form include some statement that clarifies that the QEEG is not being collected for purposes of making a diagnosis, but rather for purposes of identifying specific EEG features that will help the practitioner understand the client's unique EEG characteristics so that he or she can provide the most appropriate neurofeedback services.

In essence, the practitioner should tell the client how he or she will use the QEEG within the legally approved purposes. Some practitioners use the QEEG before training as a baseline against which to compare later QEEGs to see if brain function appears more normalized. Others use it to compare the QEEG against normative databases (care needs to be taken here not to use it alone to make a diagnosis) to help support the direction training takes, etc. Practitioners should know and adhere to the FDA rules or organize to get them changed.

IX. STANDARD OF CARE

Standards of care are guidelines developed by some professional association or organization to help guide the practice activities of its members, to inform third-party payors and consumers of what acceptable practice behavior is, and to preclude unnecessary regulation by other groups such as state legislators. Neurofeedback practitioners must render services at least as competently and skillfully as they would be by the ordinary practitioner. The intent of standards of care is to prevent injury to clients and thus also to reduce the risk of the practitioner. Failure to meet the relevant standard of care expected of a practitioner can result in a malpractice lawsuit, filing of an ethics complaint, or both. For more information on malpractice issues the reader is referred to Bennett *et al.* (1990) and Striefel (1995c; in press).

At present no published set of practice standards exists for neurofeedback or for biofeedback in general. An AAPB committee is in the process of developing a set of practice standards and guidelines for use by its member and others. Practitioners should adhere to the practice guidelines for their professional discipline, those of their supervisor, or those used by some closely related discipline. When AAPB standards become a available, practitioners should also adhere to those standards. Some common standards for practitioners to consider follow:

- Adhere to all relevant state and federal laws, guidelines, and regulations.
- Adhere to all relevant ethical principles and standards of practice.
- Protect the rights and welfare of those you serve by doing no harm through acts of omission or commission.
- Make no exaggerated claims for neurofeedback in either verbal or written form. Be honest in all of your dealings with clients, with those you supervise, and with other professionals.
- Do not exaggerate your qualifications.
- Obtain written informed consent for all neurofeedback applications. Be cautious in what you tell clients in terms of which treatments are experimental and/or verified.
- Engage in no sexual activity with current or former clients and avoid other problematic dual relationships with clients, supervisees, students, and research subjects.
- Know the boundaries of your areas of competence and practice only within them. Refer clients for treatment to another practitioner if you are not competent to provide quality services even if supervised.
- When a type of client, presenting problem, or treatment approach is new for you or when in doubt about how to proceed, seek competent supervision and/or consultation.
- Supervise only in those areas in which you are competent unless you are also appropriately supervised.
- Delegate to supervisees only those responsibilities that they are competent to perform.
- Do not try to treat every problem that comes into your office with neurofeedback. Be sure the treatments you recommend and/or provide are appropriate for the client in terms of efficacy and cost.
- Continue to maintain and enhance your skills through continuing education and supervision.

- Monitor your own mental state, physical health and behavior for signs of fatigue, burnout, and personal and emotional problems that could negatively impact client services.
- Know and abide by state laws concerning billing, insurance, and fee collections and do the same for the rules and regulations of third-party payors. Obtain informed consent from clients on your fees before or during the first treatment session whenever possible or as soon thereafter as is reasonable.
- Accept your responsibilities for what you do and fail to do.
- Do not abandon a client in need. When and if appropriate, help clients access needed services from other providers.
- Maintain a backup system for dealing with after-hour emergencies and your absence.
- Keep good clinical records that adhere to state law. The more experimental the treatment approach used, the better your records should be in terms of detail.
- Inform clients of the limits of confidentiality as soon as possible (preferably in the first session) and do not violate confidentiality without a reason recognized by other professionals as acceptable. Obtain a signed release of information before releasing confidential information in all nonemergency situations.
- Do not falsify any diagnostic or procedural codes in an effort to collect from third-party payors.
- Do not discriminate against any client on the basis or age, race, gender, nationality, sexual preference, religion, disability, or socioeconomic status.
- Do not engage in sexual harassment.
- Inform all parties concerned of any conflict of interest. Do not exploit clients, supervisees, students, or research subjects.
- Address any potential ethical violation by another by trying to resolve it with the person involved where possible or by reporting it to the appropriate ethics committee or licensing board if it does not seem appropriate for informal resolution.
- Do not make false statements or complaints about other practitioners.
- Do not intentionally or unintentionally influence a client inappropriately, for example, by imposing your belief system on the client.
- Know and adhere to the laws of your state concerning duty to warn and protect, reporting child abuse and neglect, reporting infectious diseases, involuntary commitment, etc.

Practitioners should review this list and add to it in light of their own training and experience.

X. SUMMARY

This chapter has reviewed some of the issues dealing with competence, the law, decision making, responsibility, QEEGs, and standards of care. Practitioners are encouraged to continue their education so as to maintain and enhance their areas of competence. It is also recommended that they be cautious in terms of the claims they make concerning neurofeedback. A claim made can readily be used by a client as a promise or contract and can result in problems for the practitioner if the claim is not fulfilled. Ongoing supervision and consultation are also recommended as ways of avoiding or minimizing some of the pitfalls and concerns that were discussed.

REFERENCES

American Psychiatric Association (1994). "Diagnostic and Statistical Manual of Mental Disorders," 4th Ed. American Psychiatric Association, Washington, DC.

American Psychological Association (1993). Promotion and dissemination of psychological procedures. An unpublished task force report for Division 12. American Psychological Association, Washington, DC.

Association of Applied Psychophysiology and Biofeedback (1995). "Ethical Principles of Applied Psychophysiology and Biofeedback." Association for Applied Psychophysiology and Biofeedback, Wheat Ridge, CO.

Barkley, R. A. (1992). Is EEG biofeedback treatment effective for ADHD children? *Cha-ADDer Box*, pp. 5–11.

Bennett, B. E., Bryant, B. K., VandenBos, G. R., & Greenwood, A. (1990). "Professional Liability and Risk Management." American Psychological Association, Washington, DC.

Beutler, L. E., & Davidson, E. H. (1995). What standard should we use? *In* "Scientific Standards of Psychological Practice: Issues and Recommendations" (S. C. Hayes, V. M. Follette, R. M. Dawes, & K. E. Grady, eds.), pp. 11–24. Context Press, Reno, NV.

Budzynski, T. (1994). The new frontier. *Megabrain Report* **3**(2), 58–65.

Byers, A. P. (1995). "The Byers Neurotherapy Reference Library." Association for Applied Psychophysiology and Biofeedback, Wheat Ridge, CO.

Christensen, A., & Jacobson, N. S. (1994). Who (or what) can do psychotherapy: The status and challenge of nonprofessional therapies. *Psycholog. Sci.* **5**, 8–14.

Clayton, S., & Bongar, B. (1994). The use of consultation in psychological practice: Ethical, legal and clinical considerations. *Ethics Behav.* **4**(1), 43–57.

Corey, G., Corey, M. S., & Callanan, P. (1998). "Issues and Ethics in the Helping Professions." Brooks/Cole Publishing Company, Pacific Grove, CA.

Duffy, F. H., Hughes, J. R., Miranda, F., Bernard, P., & Cook, P. (1994). Status of quantitative EEG (QEEG) in clinical practice: 1994. *Clin. EEG* **25**(4), VI–XXII.

Favell, J. E. (1997). Practice standards and credentialing: New choruses for old melodies. *Psychol. Mental Retardation Develop. Disabil.* **23**(1), 1–4.

Fried, R. (1993). What is theta? *Biofeedback Self-Regul.* **18**(1), 53–58.

Hayes, S. C. (1995). What do we want from scientific standards of psychological pratice? *In* "Scientific Standards of Psychological Practice: Issues and Recommendations" (S. C. Hayes, V. M. Follette, R. M. Dawes, & K. E. Grady, eds.), pp. 49–66. Context Press, Reno, NV.

Lexicor (1993). NeuroSearch-24: Software manual. Lexicor Medical Technology, Boulder, CO.

Lubar, J. (1995). Neurotherapy for the management of attention deficit/hyperactivity disorders. *In* "Biofeedback: A Practitioner's Guide" (M. S. Schwartz, ed.), pp. 493–522. Guilford Press, New York.

Niedermeyer, E. (1993). The normal EEG of the waking adult. *In* "Electroencephalography: Basic Principles, Clinical Applications, and Related Fields" (E. Niedermeyer & F. L. Da Silva, eds.), pp. 131–152. Williams & Wilkins, Baltimore, MD.

Pallak, M. S. (1995). Managed care and outcomes-based standards in the health care revolution. *In* "Scientific Standards of Psychological Practice: Issues and Recommendations" (S. C. Hayes, V. M. Follette, R. M. Dawes, & K. E. Grady, eds.), pp. 73–77. Context Press, Reno, NV.

Peniston, E. G., & Kulkosky, P. J. (1989). Alpha-theta brainwave training and beta-endorphin levels in alcoholics. *Alcohol. Clin. Exp. Res.* **13**(2), 271–279.

Small, J. G. (1993). Psychiatric disorders and the EEG. *In* "Electroencephalography: Basic Principles, Clinical Applications, and Related Fields" (E. Niedermeyer & F. L. Da Silva, eds.), pp. 581–596. Williams & Wilkins, Baltimore, MD.

Sterman, M. B. (1996). Physiological origins and functional correlates of EEG rhythmic activities: Implications for self-regulation. *Biofeedback Self-Regul.* **21**(1), 3–33.

Striefel, S. (1990, Winter). The informed consent process. *Biofeedback* **18**(1), 51–55.

Striefel, S. (1995a). Ethical areas of confusion: Part 2—Professional competence. *Biofeedback* **23**(1), 13–14.

Striefel, S. (1995b). Policy statement on licensing and supervision and guidance on interpreting the policy on licensing and supervision. *Biofeedback* **23**(1), 20–21.

Striefel, S. (1995c). Professional ethical behavior for providers of biofeedback. *In* "Biofeedback: A Practitioner's Guide" (M. S. Schwartz, ed.), pp. 685–705. Guilford Press, New York.

Striefel, S. (1997a). Response to Fahrion *et al. Biofeedback* **25**(2), 16–17.

Striefel, S. (1997b). Ethical issues in EEG biofeedback. *Biofeedback* **25**(1), 6–7.

Striefel, S. (1998, Summer). Is EEG biofeedback per se experimental? *Newslett. Soc. Study Neuronal Regul.* pp. 5–8.

Striefel, S. (in press). Ethics and risk management. *In* "Applied Psychophysiology, Biofeedback & Behavior Medicine: Theory, Application & Practice" (R. Kall, M. Shtark, & E. Sokhardze, eds). Futurehealth, Trevose, PA.

Strosahl, K. (1995). Behavior therapy 2000: A perilous journey. *Behavior Therapist* **18**(7), 130–133.

Tan, S.-Y. (1997). The role of the psychologist in professional helping. *Prof. Psychol. Res. Pract.* **28**(4), 368–372.

TEC (1997). "Biofeedback for the Treatment of Hypertension." Blue Cross and Blue Shield Association, Chicago, IL.

Utah Psychologists' Licensing Act, Title 58, Chapter 25a (1989).

INDEX